The Harlem Renaissance in
Black and White

The Harlem Renaissance in Black and White

George Hutchinson

The Belknap Press of
Harvard University Press
Cambridge, Massachusetts
London, England

Copyright © 1995 by the President and Fellows of Harvard College
Printed in the United States of America

Page xii constitutes a continuation of the copyright page.

Library of Congress Cataloging-in-Publication Data

Hutchinson, George.
    The Harlem renaissance in black and white / George Hutchinson.
        p.   cm.
    Includes bibliographical references (p.   ) and index.
    ISBN 0-674-37262-X (cloth : alk. paper)
    1. American literature—Afro-American authors—History and criticism.   2. Literature
and anthropology—United States—History—20th century.   3. Afro-Americans—Intellectual life—20th century.   4. Modernism (Literature)—United States.   5. Afro-Americans
in literature.   6. United States—Race relations.   7. Harlem Renaissance.   I. Title.
PS153.N5H86   1995
810.9′896073—dc20   95-21826

Second printing, 1996

To Portia, Spencer, and Geoffrey

Let the cripple who climbs a palm tree thank the one who holds him up.

—Mossi proverb

Contents

Acknowledgments

For two years, from 1975 to 1977, I was a well-digger in the village of Zéguedéguin, Burkina Faso (then Upper Volta), and lived with the family of Benewendé, Bangba, Pesgo, Félix, and Amei Dabilgou and their children, Tenère, Hadowé, Pascal—a farming family, Mossi, in the dry savannah that borders the Sahel. I would like to believe that this book is true to the sensibility and the perspective on my country, on "race," on our time, and on the meaning of gratitude I learned with them, that it is a book adequate to our friendship.

John McCluskey first introduced me to the Harlem Renaissance only a few months after I came back from Africa—a strange student, I'm sure, and often inconsiderate of his time. I also studied Wright, Ellison, and Baldwin under him. It is not difficult to see that aspects of his thinking inform this book. A poetry course taught by Michael Harper years ago introduced me to the poetry of Robert Hayden and Sterling Brown and opened new vistas on the United States I have not ceased exploring.

Although I take issue with them, I would like to acknowledge here my indebtedness to the pathbreaking scholarship of the late Nathan Huggins and of David Levering Lewis on the Harlem Renaissance. In its early stages, my research also benefited enormously from the scholarship of Daniel Aaron, who, through the intervention of my friend Christoph Irmscher, and in a spirit of generosity I have since learned is typical of him, read the manuscript as I was completing it and bolstered my sorely taxed faith in what I was attempting. Subsequently, Werner Sollors also gave encouragement and suggestions for which I am very grateful.

Several colleagues at the University of Tennessee and the University of Bonn have taken the time to read portions or all of the manuscript and to comment on or otherwise support it: Allen Dunn, Christoph

Irmscher, R. Baxter Miller, Bob Leggett, John Hodges, Stan Garner, and Charlie Biggs. I especially want to thank Allen Dunn for his comradeship and intellectual sustenance on our long hikes and rows together. The readers for Harvard University Press responded quickly and encouragingly with valuable comments. I would like to express thanks to the students in my recent graduate seminars at the University of Tennessee and the University of Bonn for thinking with me about the issues addressed in this book. One of them, Claudia Milstead, undertook the immense task of checking the references and quotations very conscientiously. I have also benefited greatly from the understanding, interest, and expert assistance of Lindsay Waters, Katarina Rice, Donna Bouvier, and Alison Kent at Harvard University Press.

A 1988 summer stipend and a 1989–90 fellowship from the National Endowment for the Humanities were helpful, as were grants from the Graduate School and the John C. Hodges Fund of the English Department at the University of Tennessee, Knoxville. My friend and former colleague Chris Wheatley of Catholic University kindly put me up when I was doing research in Washington. Allen Carroll, my department head, has been very supportive.

Among librarians, I would like to thank the administrators and staffs of the Beinecke Rare Book and Manuscript Library, Yale University; the Moorland-Spingarn Research Center, Howard University (in particular, Esme Bhan); the Lilly Library, Indiana University; the Fisk University Library (Ann Allen Shockley); the Houghton Library, Harvard University; the Amistad Research Center (Rebecca Hankins); the Syracuse University Library; and the John C. Hodges Library of the University of Tennessee. Thanks to Harold Ober Associates for permission to quote from Langston Hughes manuscripts and to Valena M. Williams (Waits) for permission to quote from manuscripts of Aaron Douglas. Manuscripts and poems of Claude McKay are used by permission of The Archives of Claude McKay, Carl Cowl, Administrator.

A version of Chapter 10 has appeared in *African American Review* (Winter 1994), and brief fragments of other chapters have appeared in essays published in *Texas Studies in Literature and Language* (University of Texas Press); *American Literature* (Duke University Press); and *The Continuing Presence of Walt Whitman,* ed. Robert K. Martin (University of Iowa Press, 1992). I am grateful to the publishers for permission to reprint.

This book owes most to those named in the dedication, my wife and sons, in thought of whom I wrote it out of my whole heart.

The Harlem Renaissance in
Black and White

Introduction

In his preface to the 1968 Atheneum edition of *The New Negro,* Robert Hayden contrasted the Harlem Renaissance with Garveyism and late-1960s black nationalism, pointing out that New Negro writers wanted to stress both their blackness and their "Americanism." While acknowledging charges that the authors at times played to the fascination of jaded whites with the primitive and exotic, Hayden stressed, almost alone among commentators, that this more spectacular side was counterbalanced by an interest in American cultural nationalism, among both black and white intellectuals.[1] He lamented that this aspect of the movement had been largely suppressed or, at least, had escaped serious notice. *The Harlem Renaissance in Black and White* was conceived to address this deficiency, which remains a serious problem in understanding not only the Harlem Renaissance but American modernism and indeed the interracial history of American culture.

Interpretations of the Harlem Renaissance have been shaped predominantly by powerful patternings of the history of interracial relations in the United States, by traditional conceptions of American modernism, by the elision of African American intellectuals from discussions of American cultural nationalist movements, and by the marginalization of American cultural nationalism in studies of African American modernism. To read the Harlem Renaissance in relation to American cultural nationalism, and to read American cultural nation-

1

alism in the light of the Harlem Renaissance, has the effect of putting governing assumptions within each of these "fields" in question. This study therefore challenges received notions of American modernism and complicates the story of American nationalism; it challenges, as well, the assumed oppositions between American and African American cultural nationalisms, and between assimilationism and multiculturalism. It looks upon American racial discourse with a skepticism that opens it to satire and transformation. As opposed to the method of the theorist who looks for purity of origins and the continuity of a tradition identified with a given stock, my method will be that of the satirical genealogist tracing the illegitimacy of origins, the cobbling together of traditions out of heterogeneous elements and a babel of tongues. More specifically, I will argue that in the second and third decades of the twentieth century the struggle between different ideas of American culture fundamentally shaped the "cultural racialism," as Alain Locke called it, of the Harlem Renaissance; and that the meeting of black and white intellectuals on the grounds of American cultural nationalism was a development with long-lasting and generally positive results. In making this point I tell a new story of the contexts, crosscurrents, and effectiveness of the Harlem Renaissance.

This book was originally to be devoted mainly to readings of major texts, but as I pursued the topic in relation to the intellectual preoccupations and cultural positions of various African American authors, I found myself repeatedly at odds with previous interpretations of the background and cultural history of the movement—particularly in its interracial dimensions. My work became entangled, almost inevitably, with the history of cultural institutions as they shaped the literary field and the imagining of American/African American (and by extension African) culture. This has been an area of no little concern to prior accounts of the Harlem Renaissance, and so I have been confronted with the necessity of recovering contextual details and intellectual crosscurrents that were repressed, distorted (from my perspective), or ignored in prior accounts. The webs of relation, details of cultural border-crossings, intellectual threads that have been, in some cases, discussed singly or by fragment but never in their complicated and fascinating interweavings, captivated me and convinced me that before I could progress with my readings of the texts I must map the contours of the literary field in which those texts had emerged. What I at first intended as a long introductory section of a book, then, has itself become a book, though still a prologue to a more extensive project of rereading the Harlem Renaissance and the problematics of American cultural nationalism. But even that project is only a prologue to something more, for what has come to be at issue is the problem of rethinking American cultural history from a position of interracial marginality, a position that sees—if I may here revert to the vernacular—"white" and "black" American cultures as intimately intertwined, mutually constitutive.

The Harlem Renaissance and the American Cultural Field

In his study of ideology and social structure during the Reformation, the Enlightenment, and the rise of European socialism, Robert Wuthnow has asked how it is possible for a cultural movement to develop and successfully challenge the status quo. He identifies what he calls the "problem of articulation": a cultural movement, even a single work of art or literature that affects the social order, must relate closely enough to its social environment to be recognizable, yet maintain relative autonomy from it. His approach, which has much in common with Pierre Bourdieu's sociology of literature, shows how "ideas are shaped by their social situations and yet manage to disengage from these situations," helping set the terms for their own debates and thus creating the conditions for their own perpetuation.[2] While such issues have been addressed, in a sense, by such earlier cultural historians of the Harlem Renaissance as Nathan Huggins and David Levering Lewis, they have been framed within limited parameters, with too exclusive a focus upon issues of race, inadequate notions of American modernism, insufficiently particularized narratives of the intellectual and institutional mediations between black and white agents of the renaissance, and curiously narrow conceptions of the larger "environmental conditions" (Wuthnow's term) in which those agents acted.

What were the general social, cultural, political, and economic contours of the period in which the Harlem Renaissance came into being? It is important, but not sufficient, to point to the migration from the South, black participation in World War I and the militancy following it, the black nationalism of Marcus Garvey, disaffection with "Western civilization," white intellectuals' supposed fascination with the primitive and exotic, and the social power of racist science and "plantation school" literary stereotypes (which actually were being powerfully chal-

lenged and displaced throughout the 1920s). As a matter of fact, as in
the cases of the Enlightenment and the rise of socialism, the cultural
movement known at the time as the "Negro renaissance" depended on
a general "conjuncture of economic expansion and realignment among
ruling elites"—which in turn encouraged transformations in the fields
of art, literature, and cultural critique.[3] Economic expansion and massive shifts of population interacted with institutional arrangements both
to restructure the contexts in which black and white authors and audiences interacted and to shape the forms of American "modernism."

Much of this book concerns the development of new institutions associated with American modernism, institutions that shaped the specific
contexts in which new ideologies—and new concepts of the "literary"—
were created and disseminated. While previous studies of the Harlem
Renaissance have attempted to speak to issues of its institutional structure, it is my contention that these attempts have failed because of an
inattention to the general cultural politics in which particular organizations were engaged, the problematics that oriented their various positions, and the specific details of their engagement.

As Pierre Bourdieu has argued, the structure of the cultural field
takes shape and offers a space of possibilities, "a problematic (objectively in the form of an ensemble of real or possible positions)" that
tends to orient intellectual and artistic projects "by defining the universe of possible questions. . . . Product of the history of the field itself,
this space is marked by the ensemble of intellectual bench marks, often
incarnated in intellectual 'stars' or various 'isms.' These must be mastered, at least in practice, in order to participate in the game." The field
is not some sort of direct reflection or embodiment of the ideology of a
dominant class, as orthodox Marxists would hold; but neither is it totally
independent of "the actors and institutions that put it into practice and
bring it into existence," as followers of Foucault would suggest.[4] One
cannot explain processes of cultural change by considering only relationships between texts; but neither is a strictly external approach adequate.

The notion of the "field" as a relatively autonomous space structuring
cultural contests allows for an articulation between "external" and
"intertextual" approaches, recognizing that even our identification of
the texts that define the intertextual dimension depends upon external
considerations. Thus Henry Louis Gates and Houston Baker, for
example, both define an "autonomous" African American literary tradition in ways most Harlem Renaissance authors explicitly rejected, even

as they contributed to the tradition(s) Gates and Baker seek to expli-
cate—or, more accurately, invent. I am not arguing against the value of
such invention, but I do want to argue *for* the value of more carefully
nuanced historical investigations of the field in which Harlem Renaissance authors operated. If we should not, as Gates and Baker have
argued, assimilate the culture of the "other" to some ethnocentric
(though supposedly universal) standard of our own, neither, as Hazel
Carby has insisted, should we assimilate the world of those we choose to
acknowledge as ancestors to a deceptively transhistorical, *intræ*ethnically
"universal" problematic we identify with mythic origins and ourselves.[5]
The social formation in which the writing of the Harlem Renaissance
was produced is identical neither with that of the present nor with that
of the nineteenth-century slave. To quote Bourdieu again: "One cannot
understand what is going on without reconstructing the laws specific to
this particular universe, which, with its lines of force tied to a particular
distribution of specific kinds of capital (economic, symbolic, cultural,
and so on), provides the principle for the strategies adopted by different producers, the alliances they make, the schools they found, and
the art they defend."[6] The field functions "as a sort of common reference system that situates contemporaries . . . by virtue of their common
situation within the same intellectual system."[7]

Institutions bring people together in particular configurations, but
their meeting can also prove a catalyst for the formation of new ideas
and programs that, in turn, transform those institutions and give rise to
new organizations solidifying positions in the battleground of cultural
politics. This is particularly true when persons otherwise inhabiting
vastly different social spheres come in contact and exchange ideas, creating the sort of "liminal" conjunctions that foment cultural change. In
fact, one of the most fascinating aspects of the Harlem Renaissance is
the extent to which direct interpersonal relationships and intellectual
networks that crossed many traditional boundaries led to the creation
of the institutions that supported the literary movement.

Hence the significance of Manhattan. Some critics, beginning with
Sterling Brown, have objected to the identification of the "Negro renaissance" as the "Harlem Renaissance." But while it is certainly true that
much of the literature of the movement was not produced in or about
Harlem and that in limited respects it was prefigured elsewhere, one
must acknowledge that without the particular conditions existing in
Harlem, and Manhattan generally, the "Negro renaissance" would have

been vastly different. For one thing, the significant new publishers and magazines were virtually all in New York, along with a mix of pragmatist philosophers, Boasian anthropologists, socialist theorists, and new journalists. The print culture of New York, moreover, created new social groups, communities of face-to-face interaction, that in turn fostered new developments in the print culture—journals, publishing houses, theaters, forms of graphic design and political cartooning, and so forth—as people congregated among like-minded culture-workers for intellectual exchange, training, or even intimate relationships. That the publishing industry had come overwhelmingly to concentrate in New York, where American cultural diversity was also greatest, meant that this was where new institutions to complement and compete with traditional ones would arise. The location was also significant because of the relative weakness of traditional elites compared with those of, say, Boston, Washington, and Philadelphia—a point as true of white society as of black. As Paul DiMaggio has pointed out, the white elite of New York "was too large and too poorly integrated to monopolize cultural authority" in the early twentieth century.[8] Similarly, in New York black authors found release from the restrictive intraracial atmosphere typical of Philadelphia or Washington. And most of the significant artists working in Manhattan were from someplace else.

New York provided a freer atmosphere for the black artist both because of the concentration, dynamism, and diversity of racial consciousness in Harlem *and* because of the greater freedom and variety of *inter*racial and *inter*ethnic relationships, which only intensified the experimental development of new forms of "racial" expression. Jean Toomer's dramatic development as a writer came not only as a result of his brief months in rural Georgia but also because of his relationship with writers like Waldo Frank in New York. His work reflects his belief that black Washington society, which he knew only too well, was too staid and "Puritan" to nourish a modernist movement of cultural self-invention—in part because it lacked the kind of interethnic and interracial exchange that New York, filled with people adrift from their old moorings, offered.[9] The biographies of other authors—notably Claude McKay, Zora Neale Hurston, Nella Larsen, George Schuyler, and Langston Hughes—bear out the same point.

Literary change cannot be explained entirely by factors internal to the textual system; the direction of change depends not only on the available stylistic and formal possibilities but also, as Bourdieu insists, on the social interests of the artists and their actual positions in the field.[10] In the case of the Harlem Renaissance, the notion of the field is complicated by the duality of its dimensions. On the one hand, African American modernists, occupying a subordinate racialized position, share a desire to transform the structure of the literary field so they will not be dependent on white power in their artistic agency. Yet the only way to accomplish or even envision the shape of such a transformation is in the context of disputes between positions in the general, white-dominated cultural field—between those that seek to preserve or to transform the field, and between those envisioning different ends or methodologies of transformation. The African American modernists thus take up positions relative to the problematics structuring the literary field as a whole, problematics (American nationality, for example) in which "racial" issues are thoroughly implicated. The fissures within African American modernism tended to correspond with fissures in American modernism generally, even when these fissures opened over conceptions of the race and its proper "representation." Indeed, many of the arguments between the major players of the Harlem Renaissance cannot be adequately understood without a far broader and, at the same time, more detailed understanding of its intercultural matrix than has so far been attempted.

The problematic of American cultural nationality, which I take to be of preeminent significance to the era, concerned not literature alone; in American modernism, it concerned particularly philosophy and anthropology as well as democratic cultural theory. The state of the accepted problematic—inherited from previous struggles—oriented the questions different writers argued over and their respective proposals for cultural work. The problematic, I would argue, can be reduced to neither cultural nor economic determinations; rather, it informs both of these dimensions, which in turn influence its development. Without presuming to reduce the structure of the debate over American nationality and the place of race within that debate to socioeconomic factors, then, I will here briefly outline such factors that ought to be taken into account.

Nationalization and the Structure of the Field

The Harlem Renaissance came on the heels of what Martin J. Sklar has called the "birth time" of "basic institutions and social relations of twentieth-century U.S. society."[11] The years from 1890 to 1916 witnessed the transformation of the American economy from the dominance of proprietary capitalism to the dominance of corporate capitalism, and from a phase of capital accumulation to a phase of "disaccumulation"— defined by Sklar as the "increasing release of labor from engagement in the immediate production and reproduction of the material means of life."[12] The economic shift had dramatic implications for cultural development. It was, to begin with, because of national economic development that the United States had a surplus of educated young people freed of the necessity to engage directly in production of basic goods, and therefore in a position to function as "intellectuals" outside traditional social institutions.[13] Economic "disaccumulation" also accounts for the fact that their audience was immensely larger than any preceding one in U.S. history. Between 1900 and 1930, the college student population multiplied by a factor of five, graduate student and high school enrollment by eight. The number of teachers and professors increased at two and a half times the rate of the general population. All of this, as Sklar has pointed out, made the "little magazines" possible, which in turn made new publishing ventures possible.[14]

The 1920s, in fact, witnessed an explosion of literary output in the United States—a crucial point to keep in mind when noting the "explosion" of black literature often attributed to the "vogue" of the New Negro. Writers and artists generally were in vogue, especially young ones. The publishing industry expanded and diversified, nourished by a rapidly growing market, the recent, massive waves of immigration, and a stimulating clash of ideologies.[15] Black writers found their various niches within the diversifying publishing system; they were not all of one mind, nor did they all publish in the same places. However, the places in which they did publish were interconnected, making up a varied, dynamic network that challenged the cultural status quo. The circumstances out of which the new generation emerged, related to capitalist disaccumulation, the "incorporation of America" (as Alan Trachtenberg has called it),[16] and the immense migration of peoples to cities—above all, New York—made for new ways of thinking, associated in literature with naturalism (particularly that of Dreiser), "vernacular" poetics, and regionalist and ethnic social realism.[17] Such developments go a long way toward explaining why the literary culture at home seemed so different from that of the European metropoles.

Among the general trends associated with the shift to corporate capitalism from the 1890s to the 1920s, nationalization appears again and again in intimate relation with modernization. With the establishment of the large corporation's dominance in the field of business came the creation of the Federal Reserve System and the constitution of the "basic structural framework of the economy in its subsequent development"—a framework specifically national in form. Sklar finds, at the same time, a "trend away from localism in markets, political power, and social identities"; quickly growing federal regulation of markets; a spread of bureaucratic standards and forms of organization; the beginning of mechanisms for administering agricultural market structures and the accommodation of farmers to a corporate-capitalist economic order; the "definitive adaptation of work to mass production and mass distribution technique, and a corresponding adaptation of the labor movement to an ascendant collective-bargaining outlook"; the emergence of modern, nationally based, feminist, labor, and civil rights movements; the emergence of the modern university; and "the assumption by the U.S. government of new roles and alignments in the international economy and world politics."[18] In short, during the two to three decades leading up to the 1920s, the basic social relations and institutions of the United States were being nationalized as never before.

It should not be surprising that the issue of American *cultural* nationalism would, in these circumstances, achieve a dynamic significance unmatched since the years of the "American Renaissance" just preceding the Civil War. At the same time, the entire development must be situated within an understanding of the *international* dominance of the concept of nationality. The cultural imagination—most particularly the literary imagination—would be faced with the challenge of "representing" and interpreting the meanings of these social developments and the lives people lived amidst them.

Contributing to this development were the massive, indeed historically unparalleled, migrations of peoples to and within the nation, a development also linked to the expansion of corporate capitalism. These movements were significantly different from what was going on in Europe connected with metropolitan "modernism," in both scale and cultural effect. The immigrations from Europe and the Caribbean were practically as important to the form of the "Negro renaissance" as was the migration of rural blacks from the South, for the concepts of cultural pluralism and the debates over the nature of the nation that shaped the literary movement developed as often as not in conjunction with debates about the Americanization of immigrants, just as many of the black social "uplift" organizations in the urban North (such as settlement houses) formed along lines paralleling the organizations created to help immigrants adapt to American society. Moreover, immigration helped restructure the literary field in two interconnected ways: immigrants composed new audiences for writing that was not being published by the established houses and magazines before 1915; and many of the new publishers and editors were themselves immigrants or second-generation Americans—the houses they founded spearheaded one of the greatest transformations in all of American publishing history, beginning in the second decade of the century. They were also the publishers of the Harlem Renaissance.

A sort of "nationalization" of the "Negro race" accelerated at this time, aided by the expanding technologies of communication and transportation. This was also the birth time of the "New Negro" as originally defined.[19] Increasingly, African Americans came to feel a common identity regardless of region or social status. The "mulatto elite" identified its interests more and more with those of the black masses, in part because of the intensification of racism and the firmer drawing of the color line in every region of the nation. Southern and Northern blacks, rural and urban, came to feel more commonality, not only because so many Northern blacks had recently moved from the South, but also because the migration had provoked white Northerners to institute or firm up policies of racial segregation. Antimiscegenation laws spread. After 1910 the "mulatto" designation disappeared from the census. And of course there were race riots in the North as well as the South, atrocities quickly reported in national news media and thus vital catalysts for racial unity. Meanwhile the rate of literacy was rising dramatically among the African American populace. The growing sense of "Negro" national consciousness cannot be divorced from the expanding articulations and permutations of American nationality.

Just as capitalist development, in shifting to a corporate structure and mass distribution, and the labor movement, in response to this development, were becoming increasingly national (and nationalized, in the sense of being regulated by the federal government), so were such intellectual fields as ethnography, sociology, and literature. Similarly, of course, institutions of reform were also becoming national—as in the cases of the National Association for the Advancement of Colored

People and the National Urban League, which gained in importance while Booker T. Washington's more regionally circumscribed Tuskegee machine lost power and prestige. Even the institutions of literature and cultural critique with which African American modernism most closely affiliated centered their attention upon the forms and meanings of American nationality, and in many cases conceived of themselves in chiefly national terms. Because of the importance of nationhood to social and institutional structures, then, it is foolish to ignore the importance of American nationalism to literary culture in the early twentieth century. If all the vectors of social power were being organized increasingly along national lines, the cultural responses were bound to focus upon struggles for the "national soul."

Yet, in attending to the issues of nationalization and nationalism as contexts of American modernism, we must think of American nationalism as a realm of conflict rather than a unitary ideology; there were many nationalisms, many conflicts over the definition of U.S. national culture, often homologous to conflicts over the nature of the national economic policies, social controls, and educational policies, which were typically branded "un-American" or "American" by warring parties. The myth of American national identity as a unitary, self-contained sphere was never so open to question, which in itself helps explain the intensity of concern over what American national consciousness should be. Moreover, the ideas of American cultural nationality were not simply homegrown; they depended upon international intellectual currents. A certain ambivalence and contradiction was thus inherent in the idea of national cultural identity. American cultural nationalism, particularly in its left-wing cultural pluralist or "transnationalist" form, was part of a global movement to which the Harlem Renaissance contributed importantly.

What makes the case of the Harlem Renaissance all the more significant is the complicated relationship that has always held between the concept of race and that of nation, a relationship whose greatest intensity in the United States has centered around the relationship of peoples of Native American and African descent to the national identity. As Tzvetan Todorov and Werner Sollors have stressed, the idea of nation has been constructed on two models, that of "race" ("descent," a community of blood) and that of "contract" (a community of "consent").[20] The nation as race conceives of national identity as predetermined, a pure projection of a racial past (though this is never the historical case). Even when, as in recent incarnations, the concept of genetic purity is eschewed for cultural continuity along strictly "racial" lines, the essential determinism of this racial conception of the nation remains intact, predisposed to virulent chauvinisms.[21] The nation as a contractual entity, on the other hand, stresses individual choice, freedom over determinism. As Todorov writes, "To belong to a nation is above all to accomplish an act of will, to make a commitment to live together by adopting common rules, thus by envisioning a common future."[22]

The two concepts, Todorov and Sollors both suggest, oppose each other point for point. Todorov believes we can "overcome" the antinomy by adopting the notion of nations as *cultures:* "Just as 'race' does, culture exists prior to the individual. . . . But culture also has features in common with the contract model: it is not innate but acquired."[23] It so happens that the notion of culture Todorov adopts here first gained currency precisely among left-wing intellectuals in New York in the second and third decades of the twentieth century, in close connection with attacks on the concept of race and with the development of the theory of cultural pluralism as the "true" form of American cultural nationalism—with significant effects that I will discuss in Part I. The Harlem Renaissance was deeply involved in battles over the relationship between race, nation, and culture that were pivotal in American intellectual history. The African American writers and intellectuals recognized that nationalism, as Benedict Anderson has pointed out, is "the most universally legitimate value in the political life of our time."[24] And they also recognized that they had a particularly strategic relationship to American nationhood.

The literary renaissance was in part an attempt to augment the value of black culture within the national cultural field—to accrue what Bourdieu terms "cultural capital" as *one* aspect of the struggle for social power and justice. It appealed to the symbolics of American national identity even as it strove for a reappraisal and reconnection to "African" identity (which, at the time, barely existed as such). To attempt to define the "spirit" of the nation, to control its public meanings, is to fight for the cultural talisman that will, presumably, help confer social power, self-survival, the ability to shape the future for one's kin. This, at least, was its significance in the "New Negro" renaissance, as it had been in the 1840s and 1850s (during the first American Renaissance), and would be again during at least the first decade of the civil rights movement. It remains a primary concern among all parties to the debate over multiculturalism in the United States today.

There are those who will object that the appeal to American nationalism is precisely what compromised the movement, what helps expose its "bourgeois" weakness. Indeed, the Harlem Renaissance can be regarded as an example of the workings of hegemony, in particular of what Sacvan Bercovitch calls "the American ideology."[25] But hegemony is never total or completely "centered"; and, as Bercovitch himself has emphasized, national symbolism evokes complex struggles between different oppositional as well as hegemonic groups. Moreover, those who disdain the "bourgeois" nature of the Harlem Renaissance blind themselves to the strategic importance of middle-class contests for cultural power in the United States. The issue of American national identity was, in any case, the dominant *problematic* structuring the literary field relevant to the Harlem Renaissance. Appeals to national identity could challenge the dominant, racist consensus, encouraging diversity, reform, subversion on some levels while ultimately assenting to a very "American" utopian vision, however different from earlier such visions. The attempt, overall, came down to an effort to expand the notion of "the people" who compose the American national community, and thus who, in a liberal democratic state, have an acknowledged, socially *legitimated* right to help set the general direction and specific policies of that community—have a moral claim, according to that community's self-understanding, upon the common conscience and the structuring of the social order.

That the movement for social justice should place such emphasis on culture—and, relative to the masses of African Americans, *elite* culture at that—should not be surprising. The explosion of the market for art and literature, as I have pointed out, characterized the 1920s. Furthermore, it seemed to many that aesthetic experience could be a powerful impetus to the destruction of social convention, the awakening of new types of consciousness, and the creation of new forms of solidarity across traditional boundaries.[26] One need not accept blindly the optimism of such beliefs to recognize that alliances and understandings formed during the Harlem Renaissance by chiefly cultural exchanges were critical to advances made during the 1930s—through inclusion in the Federal Writers' Project, the Federal Theatre Project, and the Federal Arts Project, for example—and a modicum of social inclusion that, though savagely short of equity, could scarcely have been imagined twenty years earlier.

Interracial Dynamics and the Harlem Renaissance

The limitations and exclusions built into traditional views of modernism have much to do with the problems afflicting understandings of the institutional contexts and intellectual trajectories of the Harlem Renaissance. Thus, although judgments and interpretations of the movement are wildly discordant, most of them share similar assumptions about the white modernists associated with the movement, and base their readings of the movement itself in part upon extrapolations from these assumptions. Hence, Houston Baker's response to the exclusion of African American writers from modernism, for example, has been to polemically position African American modernism as the subversive "other" to a white modernism conceived along very traditional lines. Indeed, it is still the case that discussions of modernism and the Harlem Renaissance often pit black writers against white writers like Eliot, Pound, and Stein, who inhabited a very different space (literally!) in the modernist landscape, while ignoring or giving little careful attention to the forms of uncanonical, "native" (white) modernism with which the African American renaissance was intimately related. We thus end up with a binary model of racial literatures reinforcing the dominant structure of American racial discourse and repressing the various forces at work during the Harlem Renaissance to assail and dismantle that structure.[27]

Yet if criticism of the Harlem Renaissance can be faulted for misleading dualisms, and if the importance of American cultural nationalism to the movement has been ignored or repressed, studies of the (white) American cultural nationalists and pragmatists of the early twentieth century have almost entirely ignored African American writing, thus comporting with the conventional differentiation of American from African American culture, the exclusion of blackness from definitions of Americanness.[28] African American modernists themselves were only too aware of this phenomenon, which has been fundamental to most (white) constructions of American cultural nationalist ideology, constructions challenged by writers such as Frederick Douglass and Harriet Jacobs in the midst of the American Renaissance of the nineteenth century. African American culture has existed until very recently as a kind of "black hole" in Americanist discourse, invisibly shaping the field and challenging its legitimacy, as Ralph Ellison has brilliantly demonstrated in novel and essay. Yet, arguably, the African American modernists provided the most probing questions about and the most challenging articulations of American cultural nationalism we have prior to Ellison, beginning with W. E. B. Du Bois's *The Souls of Black Folk*. Their repeated references to "unknown soldiers" who turned out to be black, to "brotherhood" of black and white recognized only in the face of death on European battlefields, to the betrayal of kin by white men with "mulatto" sons, and to lynching not only as a crime but as a peculiarly *American* crime, all reflect the extent to which the Harlem Renaissance (and not just in its canonical texts) was caught up in a struggle over the meaning and possession of "America."

A study of the Harlem Renaissance inevitably must deal with the issue of its interracial dynamics. Indeed, virtually every critique of the movement has hinged upon an interpretation of this issue. Broadly speaking, one finds that whether the critic speaks for or against the movement's effectiveness, the argument pivots upon widely accepted beliefs about the nature of white modernism and, by extension, the motivations for white involvement with black culture and black involvement with white intellectuals, beliefs based on a stray quotation or two confirming prior assumptions and deployed to preclude more careful investigation. Historical dramas have been interpreted in such a way as to fit relatively fixed ideas about interracial relations, and the complexity of these dramas is lost. Those elements in a given scene that match conventional expectations and understandings—elements resembling the trappings of the minstrel show, for example, or elements of "primitivism"—are promptly seized upon as essential to the scene, while the rest of the scene is interpreted to revolve around this central cluster. The historical drama is leached of its unique qualities, its dynamism and uncertainties; cultural complexity is reduced to easily grasped terms that obscure as much as they signify.

Additionally, and related to these reductive readings of interracial dynamics in the 1920s, several of the more ambitious interpretations of the Harlem Renaissance turn upon a critique of opposing views whose shortcomings are attributed to white influence—mirroring the tendency to measure the "failure" of the movement itself according to its relative tendencies to co-optation by whites. I am not speaking here simply about disagreements over the issue of white hegemony but rather about the rhetorical use of whiteness as a sort of trump card played from almost every conceivable position in the critical game.

The interpretations tend to divide up like this: If the renaissance failed (the most common view in the major scholarly studies), it did so because white influence steered it in the direction of the "primitive and exotic," and/or it was motivated by bourgeois assimilationist desires to minimize cultural differences between blacks and whites, to win acceptance according to white cultural norms. If it succeeded, it did so to the extent that it cannily took advantage of neurotic (and racist) white patrons and audiences to promote an independent cultural movement without their realizing how radical it was, and/or it succeeded in overtly detaching black from American or Western literary tradition, anticipating later black nationalist and Afrocentric cultural movements. I contend that each of these positions is partly right but mainly wrong. The Harlem Renaissance succeeded in different ways and to an extent greater than is generally recognized—but its accomplishments owe much to both its interracial character and its related intraracial diversity. Moreover, two bedrock assumptions of virtually all commentary on the Harlem Renaissance can no longer be sustained: support for black writing from white institutions was not overwhelmingly motivated by a sudden fascination for the primitive and exotic, nor did that support end when the Depression began. Black writers, by and large, were not tricksters, guerrilla warriors, assimilationists, or dupes in their dealings with white intellectuals. It is time to recognize that a deeply institutionalized, and very American, cynicism about interracial relationships has obscured our understanding of the nature and achievements of the Harlem Renaissance.

To Harold Cruse, for example, the interracial, integrationist character of the Harlem Renaissance emasculated and inhibited the emergence of an independent ethnic cultural movement, and therefore is principally responsible for its failure. Assumptions about the taint of the white modernists inform his entire judgment of the movement: "The Harlem Renaissance became partially smothered in the guilty, idealistic, or egotistical interventions of cultural paternalism. But this was typical NAACP 'interracialism,' extended by [James Weldon] Johnson from the politics of civil rights to the politics of culture."[29] To Cruse, in fact, integrationism created barriers to the emergence of black creative writers, most dramatically when it became evident that white writers could outsell black writers on "Negro themes." Cruse's oversimplification of the literary scene extends even to his strange charge that the Harlem Renaissance lacked "critical standards," by which he apparently means a unified prescriptive criticism, for "if the Negro creative intellectuals had taken a strong position on critical standards during the 1920's, there could have been a lot more constructive criticism within the Harlem Renaissance, which would have benefited the development of the movement."[30] As a matter of fact, African American intellectuals took a number of strong positions on critical standards; but they did not agree on what those standards should be. The result was the encouragement of a range of possibilities, from "vernacular" poetry and fiction, to "propaganda" fiction, to "folk" drama, to novels of upper-class manners and mores, to new developments of the "mulatto" theme. Never before had there been such variety or productivity, or so much critical dissensus—a point that holds as well for the white literary world as for the black.

Nathan Huggins views the "failure" of the Harlem Renaissance in terms related to Cruse's, although more carefully nuanced. Lacking full confidence in their own experience and cultural authority—specifically their *American* experience and authority—black writers, Huggins charges, followed false leads; in particular, "white guidance and encouragement probably prevented those few men and women of real talent from wrestling with their senses and plodding through to those statements which the thrust of their lives and experiences would force them to make."[31] Oddly, Huggins' point of view about what African American authors ought to have done, and about the perils of white patronage, is virtually identical to that of the most respected white critics who followed the movement and commented on it in *The Nation, The New Republic, American Mercury, The Crisis, Opportunity,* and other magazines most closely allied to or identified with the "Negro renaissance." Thus Eugene O'Neill, for example, wrote to A. Philip Randolph in a letter reprinted in *The Messenger:*

> If I have one thing to say—(and I grant that "I" is a presumption)— to Negroes who work, or have the ambition to work, in any field of artistic expression, it is this: Be yourselves! Don't reach out for *our* stuff which *we* call good! Make *your stuff* and *your good!* You have within your race an opportunity—and a shining goal!—for new forms, new significance. . . . There ought to be a Negro play written by a Negro that no white could ever have conceived or executed. By this I don't mean greater—because all art is equally great—but *yours, your own,* an expression of what is deep in you, *is* you, *by* you![32]

O'Neill's comment is hardly unique.

Similarly, Huggins' thesis that the Harlem Renaissance writers should have claimed their "American nativity," should have had greater faith

in their "native culture" and not had their heads turned by whites' longings for an updated minstrel show à la "primitivism and exoticism"
echoes the strongest and most consistent critical assumptions that
informed the various wings of the movement. Black writers were by and
large most certainly striving to work out from their "American" nativity
and inheritance, and both white and black editors and critics were
encouraging them in this; the problem is that they could not agree on
what the implications of "American" nativity and inheritance should be
for authors of (at least partially) African descent.

If Huggins feels that black writers failed because white friends
encouraged them to forfeit their American birthright, George Kent
instead identifies Americanness with whiteness and measures the
Harlem Renaissance's relative "success" according to the extent to
which it achieved "a dissociation of sensibility from that enforced by
American culture and its institutions."[33] "American culture and its institutions" form a rather coherent category of analysis for Kent, and yet
some of the institutions of American culture were encouraging precisely the sort of vernacular cultural experimentation that Kent feels
such institutions could only compromise or oppose. Even more to the
point, it was precisely institutions insistently calling for an "American"
culture with a sensibility dissociated from European culture that promoted the tendencies Kent values. But Kent can hardly be faulted, for
no study of the Harlem Renaissance has carefully examined the overall
cultural politics of the institutions connected with the movement; nor
have studies of those institutions that were white paid significant attention to their treatment of the Harlem Renaissance.

By scholarly consensus, easily the most pervasive motive of white
interest in African American culture during the twenties was a craving
for the primitive and exotic, which has developed into a shibboleth
impeding careful analysis. The emphasis upon this factor is linked to an
uncritical acceptance of traditional ideas of something called "Anglo-
American modernism" that has seemingly swallowed all nonblack modernist American authors whole. Thus, for Chidi Ikonné, "the emergence of Negro self-confidence in literature and art in the 1920s took
place mainly because of the crisis in confidence regarding European
and American 'civilization.' The white man, dissatisfied with his own
baby (his un-primitive civilization which could save him neither from
emotional desiccation nor from wars and rumors of wars), had, in a
desperate volte-face, discovered in the Negro what he thought was the

opposite of the product of his own civilization—the 'primitive' being, charmingly clothed with unbridled instincts."[34] As I hope to demonstrate, careful analysis of the institutions associated with the Harlem Renaissance and of the critical approaches adopted toward African American modernism supports such contentions very equivocally, to say the least. Nonetheless, these contentions are foundational in the scholarly literature. My point here is not simply to complicate the story of what Langston Hughes called, in a book satirizing white primitivism but dedicated to a white friend, "the ways of white folks—I mean *some* white folks" during the Harlem Renaissance;[35] what is more important is to recognize how the story told about white folks' ways has structured the narrative about the spiritual strivings and aesthetic manifestations of the souls of black folk.

Ikonné treats only of what he considers the "early new Negro literature" appearing from 1903 to 1926, or from the appearance of Du Bois's *The Souls of Black Folk* to that of Van Vechten's *Nigger Heaven*. For this critic, the movement, before 1926, was largely free of corrupting white influences, and the range of subjects open to black writers was "almost limitless." After 1926, the range of subjects was "compelled by mercenary considerations (of publishers mainly) to be limited to those aspects of Negro life which had proved financially successful"—what was successful being, as the story would have it, the primitive and exotic.[36] Although Ikonné intends to downplay the significance of white influence, then, it ends up playing the pivotal role in his history of the movement and his critical approach. Yet Ikonné's contentions are not even supported by the evidence of what was published after 1926. Langston Hughes, for example, *after* meeting Carl Van Vechten and especially after connecting with the *New Masses* radicals, moved *away* from the kind of primitivism and exoticism that had marred *The Weary Blues*.

Wilson Moses, too, in his admirable project of opposing the Harlem-dominated image of the "New Negro" movement with a more varied understanding of the black cultural tradition, connects the valorization of the black "bohemian" writers of the twenties with the dominance of white modernist criteria: "Judged by these criteria, black literature is interesting for its exotic quality rather than its more tough-minded traditions." For Moses (echoing an important point of Huggins' book, which also correlates with several remarks by Du Bois), the left wing of the Negro renaissance abandoned its cultural bearings to put on an updated version of the minstrel show, and the effects have yet to be overcome.[37] The now-conventional critical identification of the New Negro with the Harlem Renaissance, to Moses, derives from the influence of white culture-brokers, who, "with their erotic/exotic predilections, were interested in advancing only those authors who would nourish their perceptions of Negroes as frightening, or picturesque, or titillating."[38] Moses' perception of the predilections of the culture-brokers, virtually an article of faith in American literary study today, cannot possibly accommodate the most serious criticism African American authors were attending to in the 1920s. Nor can it acknowledge the diversity of American modernisms. But what I also want to emphasize here is that, to push his own version of the New Negro, Moses feels the need to charge other African-Americanists with playing into the white man's hands. This is a pervasive rhetorical ploy in African American criticism since the 1960s.

Leaving entirely to the side the issue of what influence white interlopers may have had, there is far more value to be found in the left wing of the movement than Moses allows; but to find it, while *also* appreciating the many other positive and often conflicting contributions of the movement, one must give up the strategy of playing each side off against the stereotypical "white cultural imperialist" or a monolithic white "literary establishment"; one must give up the practice of scapegoating interracial dynamics that challenge the color line.

As I hope to show, there were many different white positions (as well as black positions) on African American literature, and these positions tended to correlate with positions on the nature of American culture and the meaning of culture in the modern age. Moreover, while many of the participants in the Harlem Renaissance complained about white exploitation of the movement, they often did not agree on *which* whites were exploiters. Conversely, virtually all of them thought of certain white authors as models for Negro writing, but they disagreed on who these models should be—John Millington Synge, John Keats, Edna St. Vincent Millay, Walt Whitman, Edgar Lee Masters, Zona Gale, Henry James, Julia Peterkin, DuBose Heyward, Jane Austen, or Eugene O'Neill, to mention a few. Different white authors stood in for different positions on the literary field.

As just one example of how we tend to play fast and loose with historical particulars by invoking reductive racialist categorizations of cultural difference, one might notice how many critics have rung changes on Du Bois's pettish comment that the writing of the Harlem Renaissance was "written for the benefit of white people and at the behest of white readers," but have failed to notice that he himself heartily praised and encouraged some of the same white readers and authors whom some critics would now make prime exhibits of his point (for instance, Eugene O'Neill and Ridgely Torrence).[39] He and Jessie Fauset even asked them to be judges of *Crisis* literary contests. Neither is it mentioned, in the context of such arguments, that Du Bois made equivalent comments about jazz, on the basis of the same cultural assumptions! Let me emphasize that I am not suggesting the white allies of the movement were *above* American racial ideology; Du Bois's judgments are not always wrong or right. My point has to do instead with the use of "whiteness" as a ubiquitous cultural signifier whose specific historical referents have become less important than the use of the signifier itself to represent a vast array of shifting negative positions in relation to which a positive black presence is constructed.

Like recent critics, New Negroes tended to accuse their antagonists of being enthralled to white values and predilections. In fact, *white* critics criticized black writers for being enthralled to white values—usually some *other* white person's white values. (The tendency continues today.) This charge of enthrallment to the cultural imperialists could work from a variety of positions. If the black writer emphasized black difference, he might be accused of playing to white stereotypes of the exotic primitive; if she emphasized cultural Americanness or wrote a novel of black bourgeois manners, she might be criticized for failing to see that the "Negro experience" requires a transformation of novelistic form. When white critics adopted these techniques of criticism, they were expressing, of course, their own sense of what black literature should or at least should not be (thus extending their hegemony?); but they were also, consciously or not, adopting a chief rhetorical tool of African American literary criticism, the tool that continues to function crucially in all studies of the Harlem Renaissance.

If the Harlem Renaissance is often faulted for stressing black "exoticism," it has also been attacked from the opposite angle—as an essentially assimilationist movement. David Levering Lewis plausibly faults the New Negro movement for the naïve idea that bringing the educated classes of both races together for cultural exchange would lead to the dismantling of racism. The leaders of the New Negro era, faced with a choice between direct action leading to possible genocide or some less heroic, more accommodating tactic for racial advancement, "deceived themselves into thinking that race relations in the United States were amenable to the assimilationist patterns of a Latin country."[40] The extent to which such "assimilationism" is an adequate label to put on the cultural politics of the Harlem Renaissance needs to be rigorously questioned, particularly considering what this term stands for in the minds of most readers. One needs to take a careful look at the different positions staked out on the cultural battlefield, in the form of editorial tendencies at specific magazines and related publishers that nourished the movement and offered diverse points of attack on the citadels of the "dominant culture." This has never been adequately done.[41] But (as Houston Baker has suggested) one also ought to ask about the standards for success implied in the common view that the Harlem Renaissance failed. Is its inadequacy to the task of achieving social equality for the black masses by the 1930s an appropriate measure of its achievement? For Lewis, the failure of the movement is signified by the eruption of the Harlem race riot of 1935—which ignores the fact that much of the movement's cultural legacy was amplified throughout the late 1930s and institutionalized in programs such as the Federal Writers', Arts, and Theatre Projects, which incubated the next generation of African American artists.

It is hard to know how to respond to a critique for which the standard of success of an artistic movement is its effectiveness in ending centuries of oppression. This standard, however, seems to be in the background of many disappointed interpretations of the Harlem Renaissance, including, admittedly, those of some participants themselves—such as Langston Hughes, from whose autobiography Lewis takes the title for his book, *When Harlem Was in Vogue*. It is important to notice the genealogy of this lament, for its locus is the 1930s, when great numbers of American writers turned against the culture of the twenties, considering it escapist and blind to the need for social revolution. Many misleading impressions of the decade date from the shift to more politically hard-headed and occasionally "vulgar Marxist" criticism in the thirties, obscuring the important role that left-wing cultural politics played throughout the Jazz Age. Roderick Nash has pointed out the inadequacy of the stereotype of the twenties as "an unreal world of nonsense that died in the stock-market crash of 1929."[42] This sort of characterization is as insufficient for the Harlem Renaissance as it is for the white Roaring Twenties, but it is largely responsible for the idea that the Depression killed the "Negro renaissance" because patronizing whites suddenly lost all interest in the "vogue." As a matter of fact, and as I will partially demonstrate, many whites interested in the movement continued to support black cultural advancement and civil rights throughout the Depression and beyond—a point perhaps less significant than the fact that continuity of effort can also be found in the development of black arts from the mid-1920s to the emergence of Richard Wright.

Lewis' accusations of "assimilationism" have been seconded from another angle by Henry Louis Gates's charge that the Harlem Renaissance writers, by and large, attempted to transmute the true aesthetic richness of the black oral tradition into bourgeois Standard English forms, primarily for white audiences. For Gates, the general failure of the movement derives from its turn away from the vernacular African American tradition in the belief that proving black talent in standard literary forms would do more than anything else to end racism. He comes to this conclusion because of his commitment to a view of the uses of "literacy" and "signifyin(g)" in the diasporic African tradition, combined with a conviction about the continuity of white American cultural traditions with the European Enlightenment tradition of equating human equality with sameness and full "humanity" with the ability to write.[43] Thus specifically North American cultural history is consumed by culturally African and European frames of reference. In Gates's assimilationist version of the Harlem Renaissance, even the cultural pluralist Alain Locke is accused of promoting an image of a New Negro "who was 'just like' every other American": "If the New Negroes of the Harlem Renaissance sought to erase their received racist image in the Western imagination, they also erased their racial selves, imitating those they least resembled in demonstrating the full intellectual potential of the black mind."[44] This is a far cry from Houston Baker's view of the publication of *The New Negro* as an act of "radical marronage" and racial nationalism, which I will come to soon, and yet it depends upon the same white/black binary opposition. Exaggerating the extent to which Harlem Renaissance writers "diluted" the vernacular, stressing their supposed desire to be like those they *"least* resembled" (whoever this diametrically opposed other might be, particularly for the likes of Jean Toomer, Langston Hughes, Sterling Brown, Walter White, Nella Larsen, and so on), Gates wants to avoid racial essentialism and yet to distinguish definitively between black and white cultural traditions. He can do this only by relying upon Eurocentric notions of American identity and American literature.

As Barbara E. Johnson has astutely commented in response to a paper by Gates,

> The terms "black" and "white" often imply a relation of mutual exclusion. This binary model is based on two fallacies: the fallacy of positing the existence of pure, unified, and separate traditions, and the fallacy of spatialization . . . , as if there could really remain such a thing as *cultural* apartheid, once cultures enter into dialogue, or conflict. . . . Cultures are not containable within boundaries. Rhetorical figures are not Euclidean. New logical models are needed for describing the task of finding a "vernacular" theory, models that acknowledge the ineradicable trace of Western culture within Afro-American culture (and vice versa) *without* losing the "signifying black difference."[45]

Johnson's critique is remarkable for a number of reasons, but one of them is its kinship with positions taken during the Harlem Renaissance itself (by Alain Locke, among others) and indebted to philosophical pragmatism. Indeed, Johnson's point takes on a decidedly pragmatist cast, one with which several writers, both black and white, during the Harlem Renaissance would have concurred: "To be a subject means to activate the network of discourse from *where one stands*. Discourse is not a circle with one center, but more like a mycelium with many mushrooms. To be a subject also means to take nourishment from more than one source, to construct a new synthesis, a new discursive ragout."[46] Not only does this formulation fit the forms of cultural pluralism adopted by figures as diverse as Du Bois, Locke, Dewey, Hurston, and Charles S. Johnson, but it also allows for a return to the category of "experience" that the pragmatists stressed and that Gates has striven to displace from theories of African American literary production in favor of "textuality."

Houston Baker's *Modernism and the Harlem Renaissance* presents a fascinating counterpoint to Gates's point of view. Where Gates (like Lewis) sees "assimilation," Baker sees "mastery of form." Countee Cullen and Claude McKay, for example, were "forced" to adopt traditional Western poetic forms as "masks" to get a hearing; and then, presumably unbeknownst to the "master," they deformed and remade the white conventions with a difference, exemplifying one of the classic strategies of the black vernacular trickster-hero. One gets no historical sense of the actual institutional context in which Cullen and McKay operated. Baker braces his argument with a set of simplistic assumptions about "British,

Anglo-American, and Irish modernism"—identified with a limited range of authors and completely ignoring African American writers' own testimony about their relationship to other modernisms. For Baker, the twenties was an era "populated by Tom Buchanans in the upper echelon, Theodore Bilbo and Woodrow Wilson in local and national politics, Lothrop Stoddard and William Graham Sumner in scholarship, Octavus Roy Cohen in popular media, and Snopeses everywhere."[47] One would not know that such magazines as *The Liberator, American Mercury, The Nation, The Seven Arts, The Freeman,* or *The New Republic* had ever existed—which is not to say that these journals are free of "Western ideology" or ethnocentrism, but merely to insist that the Harlem Renaissance was part of a much more complicated cultural drama than Baker's reading can possibly accommodate. Baker is thus able to set up a series of binary oppositions, collectively turning around the master/slave dichotomy that he regards as paradigmatic for all intertextual relations between African American and so-called European American cultural expression. This allows him to come up with a reading of *The New Negro* as an act of "extreme deformation" of mastery, of "radical marronage," while he largely elides or sublimates the diverse interracial and interethnic cultural resources brought to bear on the production of that volume.[48]

To help enforce the authority of his interpretation, Baker also adopts the typical rhetorical method of charging that the critics he hopes to supersede (particularly Lewis) have been conned into adopting a "white" or "Western" value system. Indeed, what Baker's strategies reveal throughout is a deep need to defend, preemptively, against any blurring of the color line—a need white literary scholars themselves are only too willing to indulge.[49] If you can't argue that the Harlem Renaissance failed because of its uncritical "NAACP interracialism," Baker seems to have concluded, you can argue that its marginal interracialism was just a minstrel show masterfully performed to con the white cultural establishment. In either case, interracialism is decidedly a bad thing. And yet the most important African American literary modernists were those who were *both* most prone to interracial intimacy (despite its frequent cost) and most secure in their convictions about the cultural wealth of black America. These two intertwined and mutually reinforcing aspects of their personalities were integral to their modernism.

What all of this suggests is that every interpretation of the movement turns upon an attempt to either suppress or scapegoat its interracial qualities. I understand that this problematic is in part a response to the brute facts of white supremacist practice, yet I am equally convinced that it is part and parcel of a destructive social drama, for it must perpetually reproduce the symbolic victimization of interracial communion as a necessary and enabling condition for black critical discourse.

"Race" remains a powerful social determinant; it is useless to speak of "transcending" it or to wish it away, however fictional it may be. What, then, to do? A place to begin is with a recovery of historical complexity, particularly at those moments when and places where the intertwined discourses of race, culture, and nation were exposed to questioning, to skepticism, to transformation, however small and localized, and when possibilities for coalitions of cultural reformers were envisioned and exploited. This act of recovery also requires a recognition of the national (and therefore hybrid) character of our racial identities as well as the racial character of our American identities, for the national subconscious affects our feelings of "race" as surely as the "racial" subconscious affects our ideas of the American nation. While sensitive to difference, one must avoid the reification of otherness. One must, in William E. Connolly's words, learn to cultivate care for "the ambiguous relations of identity/difference"; one must go in fear of abstractions, particularly those "monsters of abstractions" that "police and threaten us," to quote Robert Hayden's "Words in the Mourning Time."[50] The stance requires one to interrogate exclusions built into the politics of identity, to pursue an "agonistic ethic of care" that accepts self-contingency.[51] Buried relations emerge.

This book begins with an investigation of intellectual formations—pragmatism, Boasian anthropology, and cultural pluralism—that deeply influenced many important figures associated with the Harlem Renaissance and that shaped the institutions that subsequently supported the movement. I also show how each of these intellectual formations was influenced by the African American presence. I thus outline in Part I the development of new intellectual frameworks affecting a left-wing, pluralistic notion of American culture before, in Part II, showing how various positions deriving from these frameworks became institutionalized, bringing together cultural agents to form the complex networks that eventually produced the literary Harlem Renaissance and subsequently institutionalized black literary modernism. I make no attempt at comprehensive treatment but have focused upon the most relevant magazines and publishers. However, I repeatedly diverge to interpolate organizational histories and brief biographies of editors, publishers, or magazine contributors in order to flesh out both the cultural politics of the relevant institutions and the interrelations between them. Finally, I examine how the vectors of force examined in Parts I and II came together in dynamic relation to produce a key text, *The New Negro*. I leave it to my readers to determine how the historical excavation, the point of view, and the method of this study might alter understandings of other expressions of American modernism, cultural nationalism, and interracial relations in the United States. The method, of course, is partial, focused upon the thread of American cultural nationalism as it relates, directly or indirectly, to African American modernism and as African American modernists challenge and transform concepts of American culture.

The method is also partial in that, while acknowledging stereotypical views of African Americans as pervasive in even the most "progressive" writing of the period (often by blacks as well as whites), it necessarily shifts the focus of attention from these factors—which have received voluminous treatment in other important studies—in order to allow different, previously marginalized factors to emerge, factors that were of the first importance to everyone involved in the cultural drama being played out and that remain, I believe, of the first importance to understanding the politics of American cultural identity today. My partiality to intentionally egalitarian interracial efforts, intimacies, and commitments in the United States, my belief in their efficacy and necessity, will be obvious to all and will be shared, perhaps, by only a few. That such relationships usually (and predictably) fall short of ideological purity, "true" equality, and complete dialogue seems to me less significant than that they work at all in a culture so patently hostile to their existence. I do not, in any case, see any viable alternative to nourishing them. We must go beyond abstract judgment to validate *and* critique those active crossings that, however imperfect, open a path and create new conditions for principled action. Undoubtedly, my position on this issue, which derives from specific, existential commitments, has effected certain blindnesses. Nonetheless, as Franz Rosenzweig wrote, "The thinker must proceed boldly from his own subjective situation. The single condition imposed upon us by objectivity is that we survey the entire horizon; but we are not obliged to make this survey from any position other than the one in which we are, nor are we obliged to make it from no position at all. Our eyes are, indeed, only our own eyes; yet it would

be folly to imagine that we must pluck them out in order to see."[52] The
vision affirmed here is limited yet actual, experimental and contingent.
It guides action (and looks out from the place of action) with the knowledge that it is not transcendentally true but, one hopes, locally effective,
the thing needed in a current predicament as best one can tell. It braces
itself against other visions in the known field. It is suited to a culture of
creative democracy.

I

American Modernism, Race, and National Culture

DISCUSSIONS OF MODERNISM AND THE HARLEM RENAISSANCE NORMALLY assume a configuration of "high modernism" dominated on the "American" side by such expatriate authors as Eliot, Pound, Hemingway, Stein, and Fitzgerald. Against this panoply of modernists—indeed, according to the conventional understanding of literary modernism—the Harlem Renaissance hardly seems modernist at all, or it seems modernist in such a radically different way that it directly contradicts and subverts the tenets of canonical modernism. Thus Houston Baker characterizes Anglo-American, Irish, and British modernism as driven by threats against "an assumed supremacy of boorishly racist, indisputably sexist, and unbelievably wealthy Anglo-Saxon males."[1] The white modernists, identifying with the civilization that was apparently breaking up, by various methods sought to check "the precipitous toppling of man and his towers." Fitzgerald's Tom Buchanan is their fictive representative. Yet the very fragmentation of the Victorian certainties that supported European domination could be seen as providing the break within which a very different, African American modernism would emerge. Moreover, far from lamenting the degeneration of a "botched civilization," it sought renewed continuity with treasured Old World traditions in Africa, which it occasionally offered as resources for the regeneration not only of African American culture but of the African diaspora and even global civilization. Between black and white modernisms there

29

would seem to be little common ground. Black modernism, one might conclude, is the inverse of white modernism, its exuberantly subversive "other," or perhaps the revolting Caliban to Europe's and white America's debunked Prospero.

And yet the writers of the Harlem Renaissance, if we are to believe their testimony, did not see things this way. They considered themselves participants in, and the potential vanguard of, an American modernist movement—a movement that, to borrow from Cornel West, fell in with the American "evasion of philosophy," embracing Jamesian pluralism, Deweyan attacks on traditional Western dualisms and social barriers, and Boasian transformations of the meanings of "race" and "culture."[2] They were inspired by white playwrights' groundbreaking treatments of "Negro themes" in "serious drama" (however flawed), by Chicago Renaissance authors' experiments in vernacular poetry and regionalist fiction, by the adaptation of African technique in modernist pictorial and sculptural art, by the folk drama and poetry of the New Ireland and the New Russia, and by the attack of American cultural nationalists upon the more hypocritical excrescences of the "American creed." At the same time, they believed that their specific contributions would be essential to the development of a modern, "native" American literature.

One reason for the superficial appeal of assertions of a radical disjunction between black and white modernisms is that traditional definitions of modernism that have excluded African American artists have also excluded the white artists with whom they associated. By and large, African-Americanists have taken Eurocentric conceptions of modernism as representative for so-called Anglo-American modernists generally (frequently using the latter term to include even U.S. writers of Jewish and German descent). In their typically reductive views of a monolithic white Western modernism, borrowed rather unquestioningly from the standard critical repertoire, students of the Harlem Renaissance underestimate the "native" forms of modernism with which the black writers and artists affiliated. In this, Houston Baker and other scholars of African American culture are not alone, for the strains of European and American modernism with which the Harlem Renaissance was most closely associated were not those most often taught in universities today. Indeed, since the late 1930s the institutionalization of "high" and "lost generation" brands of literary modernism has done much to obscure the affiliations between white American modernism and the Harlem Renaissance.

In saying this, I am not ignoring previous scholars' frequent allusions
to the white patronage that black writers enjoyed and often chafed
under, nor the various references to white literary exploitation of
African American subject matter. The links between modernist American cultural nationalism, cultural pluralism, and the Harlem Renaissance were more deeply rooted, more personal, more political, more
enabling, and more pervasive than anyone has so far suggested. At the
same time, the Harlem Renaissance provided a challenge to and extension of American cultural nationalist traditions of signal importance,
one that can potentially alter typical ideas of what American modernism
is all about. Claiming American cultural nationalism was more than a
rhetorical move toward the mainstream for black writers, and more
than a sly manipulation of white liberals for a black nationalist project. It was a claim, akin to that of Martin Luther King, Jr., in a later
era, to disfigure and refigure what "American culture" meant. But it
was not in simple opposition to some monolithic white concept; it was
part of a broad movement of imaginative transformation we have little
acknowledged, precipitated in part by the dramatic changes in material relations that brought members of formerly segregated groups
together in liminal spaces of relative speculative freedom, transracial
commerce and conflict, and intellectual experimentation. To enter the
history of American modernism by way of an interracial perspective, I
believe, can offer a new vision of the period. To fully appreciate the
links between ostensibly opposite racial traditions—to appreciate a
once-acknowledged but long-forgotten and repressed *kinship*—we must
first look back to the years before World War I and a series of intellectual movements as well as institutional transformations that helped
foster the new movement in black arts.

1

Pragmatism and Americanism

It has been argued that American modernism begins with pragmatism, and particularly with William James and John Dewey—"surely the two key figures in the process of importing the new culture to this country and giving it American roots."[1] But modernism was not entirely imported; as Cornel West has argued, pragmatism itself can be traced back to Emerson in part, and certainly Whitman and Poe must be counted among the inspirers of European modernism from the symbolists forward. A good deal of James's and Dewey's work could be glossed productively as meditations on the implications of Emerson's essays and Whitman's poetry for the era of American "incorporation." Pragmatism's emphasis upon process, its embrace of pluralism, its insistence that truths and morals are produced through historically specific practices, its liberating acceptance of epistemological uncertainty, helped undermine Victorian beliefs that supported, among other things, "scientific" racism, imperialism, and Anglo-American ethnocentrism. Pragmatism also produced a new conception of the relationship between aesthetics and social change, particularly for a multiracial democracy.

The two major components of pragmatism are its critique of realist and idealist conceptions of truth and its method. Pragmatists regard the traditional centrality of epistemology to philosophy as a cul-de-sac in its reliance upon the hope for some ultimate, absolute basis for knowledge. Idealists look for this basis in the correspondence between our ideas and some final Truth, the Unity of all things in a realm transcending phenomenal reality. Realists look for Truth's basis in the match between ideas and a "real," empirically known world. What neither position, idealist or realist, will acknowledge is the indubitable situation of all knowledge as a product of *experience*. But experience is not merely a mental phenomenon occurring within a subject; it is the product of an interaction between the self and the world, pertaining to both. For the pragmatist, no truth exists independent of this interaction—truth is a product of experience and not a reflection of some preexistent reality.

The pragmatic method, then, roughly modeled on a conception of the scientific method, stresses judging ideas by their consequences. It attempts, as William James wrote, "to interpret each notion by tracing its respective practical consequences. What difference would it practically make to anyone if this notion rather than that notion were true?"[2] If the truth of a statement resides in the consequences of believing and acting upon it, then it is not the end of a quest for the real, not a solution, but merely "a program for more work, and more particularly . . . an indication of the ways in which existing realities may be *changed.*"[3] "Truth" is creative. Thus, if our aim is human community, then we will achieve it not by finding hidden common denominators of human essence but by acts of making—especially acts of aesthetic making. As Richard Rorty writes, "In the process of playing vocabularies and cultures off against each other, we produce new and better ways of talking and acting—not better by reference to a previously known standard, but just better in the sense that they come to *seem* clearly better than their predecessors."[4] They create conditions for further "good works." Judged by such standards, one must say that pragmatism itself comes out rather well in relation to African American modernism.

The interdisciplinary pragmatist movement accorded a central importance to aesthetic experience and production even while attacking the fetishizing of "high Art," its removal from the realm of everyday experience and social reconstruction.[5] In contrast with tendencies in post–World War I Europe "to focus on apocalyptic experience and a concomitant cult of the irrational," the American modernists, as Joseph Singal points out, were preoccupied with "pragmatic empiricism and democratic pluralism."[6] They also connected pragmatist philosophy with a concept of a "new" American cultural nationalism explicitly opposed to "old" European nationalisms and American imperialism (both external and internal). William James can serve as an example here. "What ran deep in James," Frank Lentricchia has written, "is a sense of American history and society as severely ruptured from its European origins and from European institutions synonymous with oppression. . . . Especially after 1900, James conceived the role of the intellectual in specific American terms as one of guarding our freedom from those European institutionalizing impulses which might and *did* rebirth themselves here from the ('theoretical') 'passion of mastery' and in the form of 'national destiny.'"[7] The consequences of American Eurocentrism, in James's view, were truly catastrophic for the development of a democratic culture along the American lines envisioned by such prophets as Emerson and Whitman. The philosophical issues for James, vice president of the New England Anti-Imperialist League, were not simply academic. Moreover, as Cornel West has claimed, pragmatism exemplified a determined intervention in actual social practices, with the aim of expanding the meanings of democracy.[8]

Philosophy with a Democratic Face

West's argument is that the American pragmatists conceived of philosophy "as a form of cultural criticism in which the meaning of America is put forward by intellectuals in response to distinct social and cultural crises. In this sense, American pragmatism is less a philosophical tradition putting forward solutions to perennial problems in the Western philosophical conversation initiated by Plato and more a continuous cultural commentary or set of interpretations that attempt to explain America to itself at a particular historical moment."[9] While West can be faulted for his attempt to demonstrate an "organic" growth of pragmatism from a single origin and according to a singular line of descent,[10] his more important point about the role of pragmatism in joining disparate forces for progressive change can be supported by careful investigation of the cultural politics of the twenties and their legacy. The aim that united the New Negroes of the twenties, and indeed their white allies, was in fact an "attempt to explain America to itself" in a very new way, centering upon the perspectives and experiences and expressive traditions of African Americans, preeminently through the arts.

Nonetheless, Houston Baker has intimated that "it is difficult . . . for an Afro-American student of literature like me—one unconceived in the philosophies of Anglo-American, British, and Irish moderns—to find intimacy either in the moderns' hostility to *civilization* or in their fawning reliance on an array of images and assumptions bequeathed by a *civilization* that, in its prototypical form, is exclusively Western, preeminently bourgeois, and optically white."[11] Leaving aside, for the moment, the fact that some American modernists were engaged precisely in attacking traditional definitions of "civilization," one cannot help but note that Baker's difficulty in finding intimacy in the philosophies of white moderns did not afflict the two chief philosophers of the Harlem Renaissance—W. E. B. Du Bois and Alain Locke.

Du Bois had concentrated in the study of philosophy at Fisk University before matriculating as a junior at Harvard, where he "landed . . . squarely in the arms of William James . . ., for which God be praised."[12] He was, as he wrote in two autobiographies, "repeatedly a guest in the house of William James; he was my friend and guide to clear thinking."[13] Wanting initially "to get hold of the basis of knowledge," to "explore foundations and beginnings," he instead abandoned scholastic philosophy for "realist pragmatism," becoming "a devoted follower of James at the time he was developing his pragmatic philosophy."[14] Du Bois, in turn, seems to have had a strong impact on James; the latter, in 1903, would send a copy of the just-published *Souls of Black Folk* to his brother Henry, recommending he read it in preparation for his trip to America.[15] It was James the pragmatist who steered Du Bois away from philosophy: "The turning was due to William James. He said to me, 'If you must study philosophy you will; but if you can turn aside into something else, do so. It is hard to earn a living with philosophy.' So I turned toward history and social science."[16] Taking his "first steps toward sociology as the science of human action," Du Bois decided to apply philosophy "to an historical interpretation of race relations."[17] This direction led him to write *The Suppression of the African Slave Trade*, which would be the first of a series called Harvard Historical Studies.

Du Bois's writings from this first book to *The Souls of Black Folk*, as Arnold Rampersad has pointed out, reflect his acceptance of certain basic tenets of pragmatism as a philosophic method, striving "to serve science, art, and the need for political action" simultaneously.[18] In *Souls* the pragmatic method was explicitly enunciated in the final paragraph of the first chapter, when the author stated that the "Negro Problem" was "merely a concrete test of the underlying principles of the great republic."[19] Taking the pragmatic method out of the white middle-class context in which it had developed as a philosophy, Du Bois saw black culture, black labor, and racist oppression as far more central to American civilization than could the dominant pragmatists of the early twentieth century. He thus pointed up, as Cornel West argues, "the blindnesses and silences in American pragmatist reflections on individuality and democracy."[20] One might wonder how much the issues Du Bois raised, particularly in *Souls*, affected James's own philosophizing; for, as Frank Lentricchia has pointed out, in his later work,

> the isolated self becomes a political entity endowed with its own vital national secret and its indigenous story. So James's pluralism and his antinomianism become in his later writings more a pluralism of social narratives, an antinomianism of nations, cultures, and subcultures, and not so much of persons, though the antinomianism of persons remains his point of departure. Because in the United States we are something of an incoherent anthology of cultures, the human costs of imperial stupidity and injustice, of imperialist imposition within our borders run very high.[21]

Whether James came to such modifications of the social implications of his thought as a direct result of his friendship with Du Bois (and perhaps Horace Kallen) may be impossible to determine; he is clearly responding to a growing consciousness of American group differences and the modern conception of "culture," which was just developing, especially in the United States. In any case, this development of James's theory had further ramifications in the interracial development of the theory of cultural pluralism as an anti-imperialist and democratic form of American cultural nationalism.

Du Bois over time followed a sequence enunciated by James himself in *Pragmatism*, away "from verbal solutions . . . towards concreteness and adequacy, towards facts, towards action and towards power."[22] It is altogether fitting that this journey brought him to the NAACP, an organization with close ties to philosophical pragmatism via William English Walling (a co-founder), Moorfield Storey (its first president), Jane Addams (a board member), and John Dewey (a board member). The ubiquity of pragmatists among such organizations and on the editorial boards of magazines that advanced cultural pluralism and social democracy may help answer the criticism of Cornel West's genealogy of pragmatism which charges that his entire argument for the beneficent consequences of pragmatism rests upon the belief that Du Bois was, strictly speaking, a pragmatist.[23] As later chapters in this book will show, a large proportion of the people and institutions, black and white, that were fighting for black liberation (as well as those fighting for feminism and against imperialism) in the first three decades of the twentieth century had been molded by pragmatism and considered themselves pragmatists.

This is not to say they were pragmatist in the strict philosophical sense; and the individuals connected to the Harlem Renaissance cannot be identified solely with this philosophical movement. Rather, pragmatism became a constellation in the intellectual field to which virtually everyone responded. Mencken, for example, attacked it on Nietzschean grounds for excessive "sobriety"; others identified with it wholly or in part. And there were different kinds of pragmatism. Overall, however, it pervaded the intellectual networks that were important to black writers. (Langston Hughes may not have read pragmatist philosophy, but his short stories in *The Ways of White Folks* are like examples and arguments for pragmatist aesthetics.) Du Bois himself may not have been, in the final analysis, a pragmatist.[24] He often implies the existence of an absolute Truth, an ungraspable ideal existing "above the veil," which should spur human beings to action—an idea with closer affinities to Josiah Royce's "absolute pragmatism" than to James's "pragmatism"; but all parties would agree that the "truths" by which we live are tested and transformed by experience, whether they have ultimate reference to a monistic, transcendent Truth (as Royce would hold) or not (as James would argue). The truths we know bear reference to the "good," as achieved only through temporal struggle. In any case, Du Bois's career is a tremendously inspiring example of how the quest for effective truth has productive consequences and leads to social action.

Du Bois's aesthetic preferences, though commonly (and, to a great extent, correctly) characterized as elitist and "genteel," are not unrelated to Santayana's belief that the aesthetic function cannot be divorced from the "practical and moral," or from James's idea that "truth is *one species of good* and not, as is usually supposed, a category distinct from the good, and coordinate with it. *The true is the name of whatever proves itself to be good in the way of belief, and good, too, for definite, assignable reasons.*"[25] Hence Du Bois's insistence that all art is propaganda, and that he did not "care a damn for any art that is not used for propaganda"—a position that only hardened in the late twenties with the rise of the more "bohemian" realism and what he regarded as an "art for art's sake" mentality.[26] Earlier the editor of *The Crisis* had himself criticized black audiences for insisting upon one-sided racial propaganda in art, an insistence that inhibited artistic integrity and aesthetic freedom, discouraging the experimentation from which great achievement and "racial" truth might come.[27]

Du Bois's chief antagonist as a philosopher and aesthetician was to be Alain Locke, another Harvard graduate, who had majored in philosophy and, like Du Bois, had been most deeply influenced by the thought of James, Royce, and Santayana. The differences between Locke and Du Bois surfaced in the intense and thinly veiled competition in the mid-1920s between *Crisis* and *Opportunity* magazines for leadership of what they would come to call the "Negro renaissance." Overall, Locke was a more thoroughgoing cultural pluralist than Du Bois, and the reason may lie partly in their childhood training. Whereas Du Bois gained his early education in a still-"puritan" corner of New England in awe of God's "Truth" and never fully shook off the values there instilled in him, Locke was sent by his mother, a teacher and "disciple of Felix Adler," to one of the pioneering Ethical Culture schools in Philadelphia.[28] Adler, believing that all religions had a common ethical basis, advocated a "social religion" that placed a heavy emphasis upon ethics, which, indeed, dominated the curriculum of the Ethical Culture schools in grades one through five.[29] In particular, Adler sought to awaken in children a sense of "humanity" and sympathy, stressing both the unity and variety of human beings. Points of likeness, Adler emphasized, help create sympathy between people, while points of difference help them overcome provincialism and widen their horizons; all types make their contributions to human civilization.

He proposed, in other words, an intercultural ethic that, while broadly assimilationist (Waldo Frank, also educated in Ethical Culture schools, later disdained Adler's watered-down Judaism), looked gingerly forward to something like Horace Kallen's "cultural pluralism." Adler believed, as would Locke throughout life, that "this is not an English but an American country with the American type still in the process of making."[30] In a period of massive immigration and rising nativism, he viewed "Americanization" as a process of harmonizing, not "melting" differences, with each group having much to offer from its own tradition. Adler's general orientation was moralistic and paternalistic, though it was, for the time, notably liberal on racial matters. He invited Booker T. Washington and W. E. B. Du Bois to lecture at the Ethical Culture Society, and specifically wanted black students in his own school. An advocate of workers' education as well as "liberal arts," moreover, he was "a rather regular visiting lecturer at both Hampton and Tuskegee."[31] Several of Adler's followers were instrumental in founding both the NAACP and the National Urban League.[32]

In 1911, he and Du Bois were elected co-secretaries of the American section of the First Universal Races Congress, which was first proposed by Adler and organized by the International Ethical Union, bringing together over fifty "races." At the opening session, Adler addressed the congress with a speech entitled "The Modern Conscience in Relation to Racial Questions."[33] Du Bois later wrote that the meeting "would have marked an epoch in the racial history of the world if it had not been for the World War."[34] According to Arnold Rampersad, it "marked an epoch in his personal understanding of race and of the possibilities for world cooperation."[35]

Adler gave the issue of racism an important place in his model school curriculum; the freshman year of high school included teaching on slavery and poverty, "the negro problem," and "the inalienable worth of every human being."[36] By the time he would have taken this curriculum Locke had moved on to Central High School, but Ethical Culture helped form at an early age Locke's approach to ethics, aesthetics, "race adjustment," and pedagogy—interests that would remain intertwined as the central concerns of his career. Significantly, Locke joined the Ethical Society in Boston soon after matriculating at Harvard. Moreover, the Ethical Society in Philadelphia was intimately connected with "Whitmanism" and the iconoclastic interrelation of "native" socialism, unchurched spirituality, and vernacular aesthetics that this term signified at the turn of the century. From early on, Locke viewed Whitman as the prophet of a new world and the father of American modernism, as his first critical essay (on Whitman's Belgian disciple Emile Verhaeren) shows.[37]

An honor student at Harvard with particular interests in philosophy and literature, Locke became involved with the Philosophical Club. Unlike Du Bois, he resisted being drawn into exclusively black social circles and embraced the friendship of white fellow students, including some from his alma mater, Philadelphia's Central High School. With a select few of these intimates, for many years following graduation from Harvard he exchanged ideas about modern art, philosophy, and the burgeoning literature of sexuality, particularly relating to homosexuality—another field in which Whitman had a quasi-apostolic following with which Locke was well acquainted. His correspondence reveals an astonishing breadth of reading in both the classics and contemporary literature from the pre-Raphaelites on.

After a Rhodes Scholarship at Oxford, Locke eventually returned to Harvard with hopes of studying under Josiah Royce, James's favorite philosophical sparring partner. Despite their metaphysical differences, James and Royce had in common a commitment to tolerance of cultural differences, which Royce called "wholesome provincialism" or "loyalty to loyalty," a social ethic that Locke was well prepared to embrace and extend. Unfortunately, Royce had died by the time Locke returned to Harvard, so he chose as his mentor and dissertation director Ralph Barton Perry, author of a two-volume study of William James. As a graduate student, according to Jeffrey C. Stewart, Locke "immersed himself" in James's writings,[38] and although he remained for many years a philosophical idealist, pragmatism profoundly influenced his ideas about ethics, aesthetics, and cultural pluralism. Like a good pragmatist, in his post-renaissance essay "Cultural Relativism and Ideological Peace" he would argue that "value disciplines [should] take on the tentative and revisionist procedure of natural science."[39]

Despite recent suggestions that Locke was less of an empiricist than the pragmatists, his theory of value was remarkably close to that of Dewey, whose stress on an experimental attitude too often has been misinterpreted as a faith in the objectivity of science. What Dewey emphasized, in his *Theory of Valuation,* for example, was "the experimental attitude which recognizes that while ideas are necessary to deal with facts, yet they are working hypotheses to be tested by the consequences they produce."[40] Indeed, far from privileging scientific knowledge as objective, Dewey regarded true science as a form of *art,* a "handmaiden" to the consummatory experience of nature, which culminates in artistic creation.[41] Like Dewey, Locke rejected value absolutes. In trying to resolve the problem of how we should decide between conflicting claims to value, he held that we should give "positive value to any effort aimed at overcoming conflicts in human relations due to opposing values" while giving negative value "to any effort aimed at erecting stronger barriers between people of different interests and desires." This was a view strongly advocated by Adler and generally shared by James, Royce, and Dewey. According to Ernest D. Mason, "The measure in which an effort approaches the aim of removing such barriers between human beings determines for Locke the *degree* of its positive or negative value."[42]

Like Josiah Royce, Locke prized mediators and cross-cultural "interpreters"; and he sought, despite his residual idealism (in fact, his apparently intense religiosity), to further "human solidarity" not through abstract identification with humanity as such—as something existing prior to our acts of recognition—but rather through specific acts of recognition and identification with particular realms of otherness.[43] Many writers associated with the Harlem Renaissance, both black and white, believed that realistic fiction, poetry, and drama would bring greater interracial understanding by exploring the psychology of racism as well as opening a space for the re-creation and expression of diversely "American" selves. This is one reason that the NAACP and the Urban League supported the literary movement so visibly during a period of crushing racial oppression.

Ernest D. Mason has argued that what is unusual in Locke's idea of assessing values according to whether they remove barriers between human beings is the role *feeling* plays: "It is not a deficiency of thought or knowledge that prevents people from living together, but a deficiency of *feeling*"; hence we must attend to our feelings—our motives and attitudes—in order to understand both ourselves and others better.[44] Mason's point helps us see why artistic creation and appreciation of the art of all peoples take on crucial significance to Locke, the philosopher of values in quest of intercultural harmony. He believed that art educates feeling, thus fundamentally affecting our ability to live together in peace. This helps explain what Henry Louis Gates and others have reductively characterized as his belief that art would prove the "humanity" of black people to whites. Proving one's humanity was not the chief issue; achieving dialogue and community was, for this was the means of realizing liberty and democracy.[45] Furthermore, as I will show in later chapters, the Harlem Renaissance writers were less concerned with proving their humanity than with demonstrating their Americanness, in the process challenging their white kinfolk to remake themselves and their concepts of America.

Pragmatist Aesthetics

Recent criticism of Alain Locke, and of the Harlem Renaissance in general, has failed to appreciate the force and importance of the aesthetic aspect of experience. For pragmatists, as for Locke, the inherent aesthetic quality of experience is crucial. From their point of view, the culture of an ideal society would be "no longer dominated by the ideal of objective cognition but by that of aesthetic enhancement."[46] Charles Sanders Peirce himself, the "founder" of pragmatism, held that even logic was dependent on ethics, and ethics dependent on *aesthetics.*[47] Thus Charles W. Morris, commenting on "the high place accorded to aesthetic experience (and hence to art and artists) by the American pragmatists," declares, "Indeed, there is a sense in which emphasis upon the aesthetic aspect of experience is the culmination of this philosophic movement."[48] Certainly John Dewey came, almost inevitably, to view aesthetic experience as "the primary instance of meaning," in relation to which "affairs of knowing and action" are determined.[49] Moreover, his focus on the role of art developed in the *very years* that black civil and economic rights advocates began focusing on the arts. The chapter called "Experience, Nature, and Art" is the climax of his most important philosophical work, *Experience and Nature* (1925). Only by means of freedom and development in the aesthetic realm, Dewey felt (like Whitman), through the growth of a truly democratic *culture,* would political freedom finally be begotten.[50] The relation of aesthetic experience to social reconstruction was crucial for Dewey, who (echoing Whitman's "Democratic Vistas") wrote that the purpose and the very meaning of all social institutions "is to set free and to develop the capacities of human individuals without respect to race, sex, class or economic status. And this is all one with saying that the test of their value is the extent to which they educate every individual into the full stature of his possibility."[51] The most encompassing form of such education was the development of the aesthetic powers—meaning not those powers that are divorced from practical action and immediate feelings, but one's receptivity to the full range of sensuous experience in the common world.[52]

W. E. B. Du Bois's important and often misunderstood essay of a year later, "Criteria of Negro Art," can be read productively with Dewey in mind. Here Du Bois responded to the question "How is it that an organization like this [the NAACP] . . . can turn aside to talk about art?" He argued that in the development of a vision of "Beauty" and the desire to express it lay a fundamental social imperative. Indeed, conversely, in the search for social justice lay a profoundly *aesthetic* motive, the desire for a truly "beautiful world." Du Bois speaks of social reconstruction in terms of artistic creation, realizing the vision of a world that could be, "if we had the true spirit; if we had the Seeing Eye, the Cunning Hand, the Feeling Heart; if we had, to be sure, not perfect happiness, but plenty of good hard work, the inevitable suffering that comes with life; sacrifice and waiting and all that—but, nevertheless, lived in a world where men know, where men create, where they realize themselves and where they enjoy life. It is that sort of a world we want to create for ourselves and for all America."[53] Dewey could have expressed his own vision in nearly identical terms.

Dewey's most extended discourse on aesthetics, *Art as Experience* (delivered in 1931, published in 1934), appeared in print well after the onset of the Harlem Renaissance, yet it merely formalizes the ramifications of pragmatism in the realm of aesthetic theory which had been evident all along and which he had begun to enunciate in the 1920s, specifically in conjunction with the Harlem Renaissance. Actually, his argument in *Art as Experience* owes a great deal to the earlier arguments of students and friends (Albert C. Barnes and Max Eastman) who were applying Deweyan pragmatism to aesthetic theory in the teens. In his "Dedication Address of the Barnes Foundation" (March 1925), Dewey noted the importance of the foundation's famous African art collection, the first to display African art works permanently not as ethnographic specimens but as "aesthetic" masterpieces. Dewey pointed out that the collection demonstrated the contribution by people of African descent to the global development of art, and suggested the potential of artistic enterprises to critique racial domination. Echoing a thought that was pervasive among "New Negroes," Dewey optimistically proposed that "it is the demonstration of this capacity for doing beautiful and significant work which gives the best proof of the fundamental quality, and equality, of all people."[54] Great art is not something apart from or "above" the common life of a people, "but something which should give the final touch of meaning, of consummation, to all the activities of life."[55] It therefore reveals the particular *quality* of a "people" and in the process proves to doubting, ethnocentric "others" their equality—but it also offers the most effective possibilities for intercultural understanding.

Locke and Dewey developed their aesthetics from similar philosophical bases (both citing James, Royce, and Santayana as the strongest influences upon them), even though Locke was ultimately an idealist (or "absolute pragmatist" like Royce) while Dewey was a thoroughgoing antifoundational pluralist. Even more significantly, Dewey's *Art as Experience* is dedicated to his close friend Albert C. Barnes—the owner of the Barnes Foundation and the person upon whom Locke and *Opportunity* relied as their house expert on African aesthetics and its relation to European modernism. Locke even called upon Barnes to contribute to *The New Negro,* and he borrowed his views of African art wholesale from the irascible manufacturer (who later tried to get Aaron Douglas and Gwendolyn Bennett to accuse Locke of plagiarism).[56]

Barnes graduated in 1889 from Philadelphia's Central High School (Locke's alma mater) along with his friends John Sloan and William Glackens, who became prominent as members of the "Ash Can School" and the left-wing community of *The Masses* and *The Liberator.* Barnes was the first person ever to buy one of John Sloan's paintings; to Glackens' children he was "Uncle Albert."[57] Legend has it that he partially supported himself as a student in Heidelberg by singing Negro spirituals, of which he was a lifelong admirer.[58] In fact, Barnes traced his interest in both art and "the Negro" to the inspiration of African American music at a camp meeting he attended when he was eight years old: "The impression was so vivid and so deep that it has influenced my whole life, not only in learning much about the Negro, but in extending the aesthetic phase of that experience to an extensive study of art in all its phases, and particularly the art of painting."[59] Barnes did not come to black art as a result of European-inspired exotic primitivism; he came to European modernism by way of the aesthetic inspiration of black gospel singing, which melded with philosophical pragmatism.

Raised in poverty, Barnes helped invent a chemical to treat urogenital diseases, became a multimillionaire, and located his factory in a poor black Philadelphia neighborhood where he employed an interracial work force. A committed pragmatist, he used William James's psychology as a basis for his marketing techniques and reorganized the company on a cooperative basis in 1908. Within the next decade his employees began spending two hours every afternoon in seminars discussing Dewey's philosophy of education, H. G. Wells's *Outline of History,* and Bertrand Russell's *Why Men Fight,* as well as the fine arts.[60] At the same time he was becoming known as a voracious buyer of modernist art. Having taken Dewey's seminar at Columbia in 1917–1918, Barnes applied Dewey's principles to the criticism of art and dedicated his most important book, *The Art in Painting* (1925), to Dewey, "whose conceptions of experience, of method, of education, inspired the work of

which this book is a part."[61] The educational foundation itself was instigated when one of Barnes's black employees began making copies of
some of the paintings and showed his work to Barnes, who suggested
he should try something of his own. From that point the employees
became interested in studying art more systematically; as their studies
became known outside the factory, others asked to see the collection.
According to Gilbert Cantor, "This experiment with the Negro
employees of the Argyrol factory was the real beginning of the Barnes
Foundation."[62] Barnes consulted with John and Alice Dewey, who
encouraged his plans for an educational foundation, finally chartered
in 1922. He often spoke on African and African American art, early and
late in his period of prominence, from the twenties through the thirties;
and by "art" he meant a broad range of aesthetic activities (in the pragmatists' sense), from the creation of spirituals to the managing of base-
ball teams.[63]

Aaron Douglas, the most famous of the African American painters
of the Harlem Renaissance, later attested to the impression Barnes's
criticism made upon him, judging him a "terrific critic" whose books
on painting had never been surpassed.[64] Dewey acknowledges that his
conversations with Barnes over "a period of years" and Barnes's own
books had shaped Dewey's thinking about the "philosophy of esthetics."
Indeed, Barnes went over every chapter of *Art as Experience* with Dewey.
It is not unreasonable, then, to suggest that Dewey's own theory is at
least partly indebted to African and African American aesthetics as filtered through Barnes.[65] In other words, not only did pragmatism influence African American aesthetics, but African aesthetics itself (whether
"correctly" understood or not) corroborated and influenced pragmatist
aesthetics. At the same time, the fit between pragmatism and African
art—as much as a rage for the exotic—helps explain the growing
enthusiasm for both African and African American art. Barnes would
ultimately donate his entire collection to Lincoln University, Langston
Hughes's alma mater—after consulting frequently with Dewey about
what to do with his legacy.[66]

In *Art as Experience*, Dewey argues that the aesthetic object is anything
that intensifies the sensation of living. Formerly, and even now in many
non-Western cultures, it had not been set off in another realm but
rather had been part of ongoing life—as in the decoration of the body,
utensils, and weapons, or in the pantomime and dancing attendant on
religious rituals. Artistic objects in such cultures are "enhancements of

the processes of everyday life," not "elevated to a niche apart." The rise of "the compartmental conception of fine art" can be attributed to historical developments, including European nationalism and imperialism. Each nation has come to believe it must have a museum as a memorial to the rise of national identity and imperial power—the Louvre, for example, which contains the spoils of Napoleon's conquests.

The growth of capitalism was another powerful influence. Being rare, works of fine art can become very costly; the wealthy amass them to achieve standing in society. (Here Dewey follows Thorstein Veblen, who, in turn, had borrowed concepts from Franz Boas' studies of the Kwakiutl potlatch ceremony.) Communities and nations, moreover, follow the same logic in building their museums and opera houses. Thus, argues Dewey, art comes to "reflect and establish superior cultural status," no longer functioning as a "*part* of a native and spontaneous culture."[67] Anticipated point for point by Alain Locke in his essay "Art Lessons from the Congo" (which owed much to Barnes's ideas), Dewey's meditations also closely resemble those of the prewar American cultural nationalists Van Wyck Brooks, Waldo Frank, and Randolph Bourne.[68] Dewey laments, "As works of art have lost their indigenous status, they have acquired a new one—that of being specimens of fine art and nothing else." Set off from common experience, they no longer gain validity and significance "because of their place in the life of a community." This is hurtful both to art and to the common life. Thus Dewey wants to recover "the continuity of esthetic experience with normal processes of living."[69]

Dewey's ideas did not preclude what today might be mistaken for formalist ideas about the nature of the consummate work of art. The whole point of aesthetic creation, according to Dewey, is to intensify living; its function is to bring both artist and audience through conflict and tension to a new harmony.[70] This, for Dewey, is what we mean when we speak of "*an* experience," one which conveys the impression of culmination, completeness in itself. In distinctively aesthetic experience such characteristics are controlling; in the dominantly aesthetic object, "the factors that determine which can be called *an* experience are lifted high above the threshold of perception and are made manifest for their own sake."[71] These thoughts also pervade the literary theory of Max Eastman (Claude McKay's protégé and champion) and inform Alain Locke's critique of "propaganda" (which is not to say Locke got his critique from Dewey).[72]

One does not set artistic values "with primary regard for moral effect," but to the pragmatist all aesthetic experience ends up *having* a moral effect.[73] Indeed, it is the most effective means of achieving moral development because it trains the sensibilities upon which ethical consciousness depends. As Dewey wrote in 1925:

> While poetry is not a criticism of life in intent, it is in effect, and so is all art. For art fixes those standards of enjoyment and appreciation with which other things are compared; it selects the objects of future desires; it stimulates effort. . . . The level and style of the arts of literature, poetry, ceremony, amusement, and recreation which obtain in a community, furnishing the staple objects of enjoyment in that community, do more than all else to determine the current direction of ideas and endeavors in the community. They supply the meanings in terms of which life is judged, esteemed, and criticized.[74]

Similarly, in "The Ethics of Culture" (1923), Locke had argued for the necessity of re-instantiating beauty as a motive of morality. While rejecting Matthew Arnold's concept of culture for its tendency to cut culture and the arts off from daily living, Locke nonetheless asserted the crucial importance of art as culture—that is, "the proper training of the sensibilities": "Without a refinement of the channels through which our experience reaches us, the mind cannot reach its highest development."[75] Locke's ideas were less "democratic" and egalitarian than Dewey's but nonetheless proceeded from similar bases. Like Dewey, he regarded life itself as an art, and lamented that the arts and culture in the United States, thanks to the influences of Puritanism and materialism, were considered "artificial, superficial, useless, selfish, over-refined, and exclusive." Nonetheless, like Santayana he insisted that "culture must develop an elite," must have rigorous "standards." The problem in black America was that the creative talent did not yet have an adequate "cultured" black audience that could appreciate what it produced—a discouraging predicament for the artist. Moreover, Locke believed, the good effects of culture did not get a chance to enrich the "mass." Self-culture, he concluded, was a duty to the Negro group, because it is through culture, largely, that the group might win its "just reward and recognition."[76]

Locke's emphasis upon aesthetics, upon the importance of art being developed free of the prescriptions of propagandists, contributed to a major rift with Du Bois and *Crisis* magazine, as a result of which *Opportunity* came to be the more influential vehicle of the Harlem Renaissance—but Locke's aestheticism carries a subtle social and political charge that has escaped many critics of the Harlem Renaissance, beginning with Du Bois. Aesthetic judgment becomes itself a form of social participation, essential to the building of community and the interactive orientation of diverse individuals and social groups to a common world. Alain Locke, along with the editors of such journals as *Opportunity, The Liberator, The New Republic,* and *The Nation,* I am suggesting, followed an essentially pragmatic aesthetic theory (not necessarily derived from Dewey but developed from similar bases). Du Bois, in his greater insistence upon art as a directly "pragmatic" weapon and his more genteel aesthetic preferences, misinterpreted the goals of Locke and the "realists." These goals were not the same as those of the canonical expatriate modernists.

Experimentation with "form" by the high modernists, Dewey felt, often produced "sterile" products. At its best, however, modernist formal experimentation helped educate the organs of perception in "new modes of consummatory experience," thus enriching the range of human sensibility. Dewey thus came to a surprising conclusion somewhere between (and connecting) the aesthetics of Locke and those of Du Bois: "Fine art *consciously* undertaken as such is peculiarly instrumental in quality. It is a device in experimentation carried on for the sake of education. It exists for the sake of a specialized use, use being a new training of modes of perception. . . . [I]n the end, [creators of works of art] open new objects to be observed and enjoyed. This is a genuine service; but only an age of combined confusion and conceit will arrogate to works that perform this special utility the exclusive name of fine art."[77] Denigrating neither social realism nor formal experimentation, Dewey could find no use for an "art for art's sake" doctrine, regarding it as a logical consequence of the unfortunate division that had developed in the West between "the consummatory" and "the instrumental," or "culture" and labor. In striving to distinguish the aesthetic qualities of capital-*A* "Art" from "every thing that is existential in nature" and from "all other forms of good," high modernist critics and artists had carried to conclusion "the isolation of fine art from the useful, of the final from the efficacious. They thus prove that the separation of the consummatory from the instrumental makes art wholly esoteric."[78]

It is fitting that Claude McKay would ask Dewey to write the introduction to his *Selected Poems*. In that introduction, Dewey would single out
McKay's ability to evoke the wonder that clings "to life's commonplaces"
as well as his genius at using poetry as a vehicle of protest in which
the protest is integral with the aesthetics of experience. For Dewey, no
distinction could be made between "useful" and "fine" art, only between
"good" and "bad"—good art being that which most fully conjoins creative "process" and "product," that which, indeed, unites the recurrent
and ordered with the incomplete, uncertain, spontaneous, and novel.
These are qualities as inherent in McKay's sonnets as in Hughes's free
verse and blues. It is almost as if Dewey was attempting to articulate a
blues or jazz aesthetic as a basis for American artistic practice.

"Publicity" and Pragmatic Sociology

The editor of *Opportunity*, Charles S. Johnson, who turned to Alain
Locke as the magazine's chief aesthetician, was also a philosophical
pragmatist.[79] At the University of Chicago, where Dewey had taught
from 1894 to 1904, a true school of interdisciplinary thought had
emerged as nowhere else in the United States since Concord's transcen-
dentalism. It continued to develop long after Dewey left for Columbia,
affecting the fields of philosophy, psychology, education, religious
studies, sociology, economics, and political science. Within such an
environment Johnson developed his own orientation to African American social and cultural development.[80] Specifically, Johnson had
studied under Robert E. Park, the influential sociologist and disciple of
William James, John Dewey, and Booker T. Washington.

Johnson's interests in the arts and journalism directly related to his
training under Park, with whom he was very close, being the favorite of
all Park's students; at the end of his life, Park moved to Fisk at Johnson's
invitation and died there, attended by his younger friend. Johnson did
a number of long obituary notices on Park, not only for black publications but for mainstream sociological journals as well, for his relationship to Park was well known. In his memorial to Park at Fisk, Johnson
attested, "There has never been a time since [my first semester at Chi-
cago] that I have not been his student, down to the last great and brilliant lectures from his sick bed."[81] Since Park's views have been carica-
tured in the criticism of the Harlem Renaissance even more egregiously
than Johnson's, and since what evidence we have of Johnson's intellec-

tual framework suggests a strong kinship to Park's, reconstructing Park's intellectual history can help us understand Johnson's; more important, it illustrates the web of interrelations between pragmatist philosophy, the social sciences, literature, black culture, and American cultural nationalism in the early twentieth century that set the stage for the Harlem Renaissance.

Park had been an avid student of John Dewey's at the University of Michigan, taking no less than six philosophy courses under him as an undergraduate. Dewey deeply influenced Park's whole intellectual framework—particularly regarding the relationship between the individual and society, the idea that personalities are fully realized only in cooperation with others to achieve collective ethical ends.[82] Undoubtedly, Dewey's emphasis on communication and communities of interpretation influenced Park's decision to become a journalist at the height of the muckraking period, in the late 1880s. Indeed, Park later attested: "It was from Dewey that I got, to use a newspaper phrase, my first great 'assignment,' the assignment to investigate the nature and social function of the newspaper. I have been working on that assignment ever since."[83] Furthermore, the two became involved in an abortive journalistic experiment that, despite its failure, had a profound impact upon both of them.

In 1889 (after a period at the University of Minnesota and Park's graduation), Dewey returned to the University of Michigan, just as the focus of his interest was shifting from metaphysics to ethics. Here he specialized in ethics and political philosophy, developing his early democratic theory. In the process he came to the conviction that democracy depended upon the egalitarian distribution of knowledge and that a major obstacle to democracy in the United States was the control of that distribution by class interests. He therefore joined a journalist named Franklin Ford in an experiment in mass communications, coinciding with Dewey's ideas, to be entitled *Thought News;* Robert Park was the third man in this project. Ford, Dewey, and Park conceived that social practice depends upon broad consent to ideas that express the interests of the dominant class of society, consent won by various forms of "publicity" in the broad sense (newspapers, research reports, advertising, literature); their position resembles what later gave rise to the concept of hegemony in Marxist thought. Hence their aim: to instigate a radical reorganization of the production and distribution of knowledge in order to aid the empowerment of each individual, to free people from the domination of the class interests that controlled the spread of information. According to Robert B. Westbrook, the *Thought News* experiment, Dewey's first effort to unite theory and practice, was crucial in his growth as a social theorist and directed him toward "radical democracy,"[84] even though he withdrew from the project for complex reasons. It was also Robert Park's initiation into the calling he would pursue for many years; it "shaped his mind more than any experience until he met Booker T. Washington in 1904."[85]

From 1889 to 1897 Park worked as a journalist. But in 1898 he went to Harvard to study philosophy and psychology, coming under the spell of William James. Park later credited James with disabusing him of the common reverence for "progress" as well as scholastic "theory"; like Du Bois, Park subsequently abandoned philosophy for sociology and "praxis." In class one day, James read his just-completed essay "On a Certain Blindness in Human Beings," an essay Park quoted repeatedly in his own work and teaching and considered, "in preference to anything else that James or anyone else has written, . . . required reading for sociologists and for teachers."[86] As Johnson wrote in an obituary for Park, this lecture stamped all of Park's later work, "as he strove to remove from his own eyes that blindness to the meaning of other peoples' lives to which James referred."[87] "On a Certain Blindness" profoundly shaped Park's idea of journalism, in that he considered the essay "the most radical statement of the difficulty and necessity . . . of communication in a society composed of individuals as egocentric as most of us naturally are."[88] The role of mutual "recognition" in democratic culture and in the pursuit of social justice became the most fundamental assumption in Park's entire subsequent career. Concerned about the difficulty of achieving such recognition in a complex, modern, industrial society, Park meditated all the more intensely on the importance of mass communication.

Cutting short his education at Harvard, Park moved on to the universities of Berlin, Strassburg, and Heidelberg, single-mindedly preparing himself for a career as a radical journalist. He returned to Harvard in 1903 for a one-year assistantship under William James, then took a position as secretary of the Congo Reform Association (helping found its American chapter) in hopes of bringing media attention to the horrific practices of the Belgian regime in central Africa. (Ever after, Park would express deep disdain for the condescension of reformers with a "missionary" attitude and paternalistic philanthropy.) As Stanford Lyman points out, Park's early essays on the Congo atrocities partake of the literary gothic, while locating the "heart of darkness" not in Africa but in a Europe whose dehumanizing representations of cultural others work to justify colonization. The essays on the Congo, according to Lyman, express in embryo a critique of capitalist imperialism as a sort of preternatural vampire that "must roam the earth in search of its source of life-giving sustenance, human blood, and in the process turn its victims into its soulless followers."[89] Park provides, Lyman adds, an intriguing alternative to Marx's sociology of modernity and values. An integral aspect of that alternative is the interpretation of the place of race and racism in modernity, a recalcitrant phenomenon that has proven to be spectacularly impervious to Marxist theory. In fact, Park was "one of the few post-bellum sociologists to take up the race question in the United States and Africa and to treat it as both a national and a world problem."[90]

Just as Park was about to leave for a reporting trip to Africa, he met Booker T. Washington, who suggested that he might find a visit to Alabama as edifying as one to the Congo. Thus, in 1904, he went to Tuskegee for a brief visit and ended up staying ten years, acting as Washington's chief assistant, ghostwriter, and publicity agent. With Monroe Work and Emmett Scott, he also co-founded the *Negro Yearbook* Publishing Company in 1910, which combated racist propaganda by publishing facts and statistics about African Americans. The *Yearbook* became a basic resource for the research departments of the NAACP and the National Urban League.[91]

Park later remarked that Washington had been his most influential teacher. Park's enthusiasm for Washington, which seems directly contradictory to his supposed democratic radicalism, followed in part from Dewey's educational philosophy. That philosophy stressed vocational education as a means of preparing students not to take subordinate roles within an accepted structure but rather to enter the industrial regime as active, intelligent agents, creative individuals who would transform it to serve their own self-realization and that of their community, the exercise of all their powers. To Dewey, all education was vocational. Rejecting the oppositions between "manual training" and "liberal arts," "labor" and "culture," he taught that schools should be engines for social transformation. Such thinking may, in fact, throw needed light upon Booker T. Washington's educational strategy as well as Robert Park's lifelong commitments.

Park considered the methods of education at Tuskegee the most inspiring examples of pragmatist educational philosophy he ever encountered: "They seemed to me to illustrate what every form of education might well strive to be, namely, at once a voyage of discovery, and a means and medium for an intelligent participation in the life of the community. . . . [It] would not relegate technical education to the status of a means or instrument of a successful career, but make it rather a method of participation in a way of life."[92] In the annual Negro Farmers Conference, for example, Washington had farmers report on their own observations, experiences, and achievements, thus exchanging "information" and "news" as the group worked collectively to educate itself. Nearly all the farmers' learning derived from work experience. Eventually, Park claimed, the conferences "brought into existence a form of oral or folk news, which, like the traditional folk ballads, tended as it circulated to assume the form of a folk literature."[93]

Park felt especially drawn to the news element of the process—viewing news as "a form of knowledge" that "presupposes the existence of a common interest or a common enterprise in which the community and the public to which the news is addressed participates."[94] He marveled at the fact that a former slave, largely self-educated, "should conceive and establish, not a school merely, but an industrial school, which put into operation methods of teaching, designed to educate men and women, less for any one specific occupation than for the actual business of life, that is to say, participation not merely in the economic life of the community but in all the varied interests that constitute the conscious life of a race or a people."[95] Independently, Washington had effectively developed an educational method *and community* consonant with Dewey's ideas but surpassing anything Dewey achieved in actual practice, a point Charles S. Johnson made himself in an article on Washington for *Opportunity*.[96] Responding to Dewey's and James's philosophical pragmatism and Washington's pedagogy, Park developed his notion of sociology: "Sociology must be empirical and experimental. It must, to use Booker Washington's expression, 'learn by doing'; it must explore, invent, discover, and try things out."[97]

During his Tuskegee period, Park accepted Washington's strategy as a practical means of coping with racial oppression in the South while building a foundation for black advancement, self-direction, and eventual equality through the accommodation of African Americans to the capitalistic, white Protestant ethic of American society. It was a stage in the history of civilization as modernity created a new, all-encompassing moral universe superseding traditional folk cultures and eventually "drawing the peoples of the earth into new non-ascriptive forms of association."[98]

After leaving Tuskegee, however, and particularly during the twenties as a result of the Harlem Renaissance, Park came to a new conception of racial history in which African Americans would not eventually assimilate entirely with European Americans but rather continue to develop their own social history and cultural traditions.[99] Horace Kallen's cultural pluralist thesis also affected Park's thinking on the issue:

> The Negro race, as Booker Washington used to say, is a nation within a nation. For somewhat different reasons the Jews in this country are in a similar situation. The Jews are seeking to preserve their culture while accommodating themselves in other respects to the conditions of American life. Different as they are in other respects, the Negro and the Jew are alike in this. . . . The Jew and the Negro are . . . the two outstanding illustrations of the impending cultural pluralism so interestingly advocated by Horace Kallen. What Mr. [W. D.] Weatherford proposes for the Negro, Mr. Kallen proposes for all the races and language groups in America. He would add to the federation of states the federation of races. The American people have not fairly faced this issue. But the Ku Klux Klan and the Nordic propaganda are unquestionably preparing the way for such a new constellation of the forces in the cultural life of America.[100]

This development had, in Park's view, world-historical and global implications for the reconceptualizaton of how democracy might develop and international, interracial peace eventually be secured.

Not sanguine about white Americans' ability to overcome their racism in the near future, Park expected racial nationalism to continue to retard the process of both democratization and eventual assimilation of the races even as he refused to abandon his belief that the direction of history was toward a global culture incorporating all the world's peoples into a single system impelled by economic relations. Eventually, however, Park adopted the position that race relations would assume different configurations in different parts of the world, varying from caste systems to cultural pluralism to complete assimilation.

Professors at the University of Chicago became so impressed with the quality of the work Park was producing at Tuskegee that they recruited him for their own school, from which his influence as a pioneer of urban ecology would spread far and wide, in part through the great African American sociologists he trained. Charles S. Johnson entered graduate school at Chicago in 1917, shortly after Park had arrived, and signed up for a course with Park in his first quarter. Without taking anything away from Johnson's own creativity and intellectual accomplishments, it is easy to show that much of what Johnson later undertook as editor of *Opportunity* adheres remarkably to Park's principles. In his course on the social survey, for example (which he taught from 1916 to 1926), Park emphasized "the function of publicity as a means of social reform and social control."[101] In place of pushing a dogma or doctrine, he insisted upon carefully investigating facts and then publicizing them, "matter-of-factly," to shape public opinion. This was precisely the method of *Opportunity* magazine, differentiating it from the more polemical *Crisis*.

In his seminal essay "The City" (1915), Park stated that surveys are really a form of journalism, "dealing with existing conditions critically and seeking through the agency of publicity to bring about radical reforms. Their object is to shape public opinion."[102] In societies based on secondary relationships, public opinion becomes the most important source of social control, and therefore students of society must attend closely to the chief instruments for shaping, instructing, and exploiting public opinion—particularly newspapers, but also the new research agencies that disseminate the fruits of their work through the press, the pulpit, and popular entertainment. Hence journalism and publicity were crucial elements of Park's sociology, which he considered uniquely American and inherently the servant of democratic activism.

In European nations, the government administered sociological surveys to be read only by administrators; but in the United States, Park insisted, surveys should instruct and inform the broader public through the general media. This aspect of Park's teaching derives not only from his desire for democratization and his interest in national-popular criticism but from his pragmatist notion of the social fact: "Facts are, so to speak, only facts in a universe of discourse. A universe of discourse, I might add, is something which has come into existence to enable individuals associated in any one of the several sciences, or associated for any other common purpose, to think consistently and to act understandingly, and in some sort of concert."[103] A fact, moreover, "only becomes a fact in the fullest sense of the term when it is delivered and delivered to the person to whom it makes a difference. This is what the survey seeks to do."[104] This, indeed, is also what Washington's farmers' conferences had exemplified for Park; it is what such magazines as *Survey Graphic* and *Opportunity* would set out to do; and it is what *The Negro in Chicago,* largely the achievement of Charles S. Johnson while he was Park's student, sought to do.[105]

Fully one-fourth of *The Negro in Chicago* concerns public opinion— the opinions black and white Chicagoans have of each other, and the opinion-making agencies of the press. Much of the material for these sections of the book was gathered by students in Park's course "The Crowd and the Public," which Johnson himself had taken. The opinion surveys were conducted mainly by racially matched interviewers and the results presented in virtually raw form, with little interpretation. The point was to learn what went on "behind the faces" of people, on the premise that their sentiments shaped their actions. Above all, what were the reactions of particular Negroes to their daily problems, reactions and problems to which whites were largely oblivious? The pragmatist emphasis upon particularity rather than generalization and "theory," and the obvious attempt to counteract the "certain blindness in human beings," were fundamental to the Chicago Race Commission's historic report. Black and white newspapers were also analyzed for their content concerning a range of social issues and found to be important factors in creating racial tensions in Chicago, especially because of their biased reporting of issues concerning blacks, including the particular *language* used in that reporting, which fostered distorting images and feelings. *Opportunity* would similarly publish critiques of white journalism and social-scientific reports to uncover bias, even as it presented survey data collected by its own research committee (headed by Johnson). Johnson's editing of *Opportunity* (the readership of which was at one point 40 percent white)[106] was clearly aimed to publicize (in "objective" fashion, shorn of indignant rhetoric) the results of sociological research and to reduce racial prejudice both through such publicity and through the dissemination of imaginative literature that helped reveal the mind, emotions, and imagination of the New Negro as he or she "bid for par" in the American democracy.

Significantly, all of Park's education and experience up to the time that Charles S. Johnson met him had impressed upon him the conviction that an understanding of the subjective life of the "other" was crucial to a valid sociology—and that imaginative literature was an important vehicle of such understanding. He would stress the uniqueness of the individual's response to social forces, would resist categorization and reduction. Hence Park stressed the value of literature—particularly realistic fiction—to foster understanding between peoples, to counteract inevitable "ethnocentrism" (a term he picked up from William Graham Sumner) by dramatizing subjective experience and provoking efforts to empathize with others. Indeed, the role of literature could go beyond empathy by instigating aesthetic attachment—a practical rather than theoretical appreciation of otherness that Park considered indispensable to a truly democratic culture.

Park recognized literature as one of the best expressions of a people's sense of significance in their lives, and thus an important tool for both producing solidarity in a people and enabling communication and cooperation with others. In Park's eyes, according to Martin Bulmer, "literature and sociology . . . were not very far removed from each other," and realistic fiction could provide important sociological insights. Thus Park encouraged his students to read novels and autobiographies. Bulmer has suggested that realistic and naturalistic fiction may have influenced Chicago sociology as much as Chicago sociology influenced fiction writers like James T. Farrell (and, I would add, Richard Wright).[107] An obvious relationship exists, then, between Charles S. Johnson's sociological training and *Opportunity*'s support of the realistic fiction of the New Negro, which often modeled itself on the fiction of Sherwood Anderson, Theodore Dreiser, and Sinclair Lewis.

Although an important aspect of Park's legacy (to his student E. Franklin Frazier, for example) was the strain of African American sociology that regarded much of black lower-class culture as pathological, Johnson developed a positive view of African American folk culture in the South, differentiating himself strongly from earlier black nationalists who denigrated "lower-class" black culture. Johnson's view of black culture was, moreover, thoroughly integrated with a pragmatist orientation to social action and interpretation. Citing Dewey extensively in his "Notes on a Personal Philosophy of Life," Johnson argued that meaning must come, values must be forged, out of experience, not derived from abstract beliefs in a "group mind" or "racial spirit," as older black nationalists (including Marcus Garvey and, briefly, Du Bois) had argued. This was indeed one of the important philosophical differences between the black cultural nationalism of the Harlem Renaissance and the largely anti-egalitarian black nationalism of the nineteenth and early twentieth centuries, which also adhered to extremely elitist, "genteel"—and Anglophile—aesthetic preferences.[108]

It follows from Charles S. Johnson's overall stance toward culture (and particularly black culture) that *Opportunity*, unlike *The Crisis*, strongly encouraged "folk realism" in the arts as well as fiction focusing on the urban lower classes. "I am convinced," Johnson wrote in his "Notes on a Personal Philosophy," "that the road to new freedom for us lies in the discovery of the surrounding beauty of our lives, and in recognition that beauty itself is a mark of the highest expression of the human spirit."[109]

Johnson embraced the pragmatist aesthetic theory that the arts are the most effective instruments for training people to cultural pluralism, creative democracy, achieving the widest possible range of human sympathy and understanding (although this effectiveness, of course, depends upon how works are *used,* in every sense). The democratic ethos depends primarily not on a governmental form, as important as that is, but upon ideas and beliefs "spontaneously fed by emotion and translated into imaginative vision and fine art."[110] The pragmatist would view the democratic ethos as something to be carried by people in the very structure of their imaginations and feelings, taking on a religious value in harmony with scientific beliefs and day-by-day activities.[111] As Johnson wrote, "Dewey redefines faith in terms of attitudes, as 'tendency toward action.' . . . Adherence to any body of doctrines and dogmas, based upon a specific authority, as adherence to any set of beliefs, signifies distrust in the power of experience to provide, in its own on-going movement, the needed principles of belief and action. He challenges to a new faith in experience itself as the sole ultimate authority."[112] Dewey's philosophy, while avoiding essentialist assumptions, affirms the commonsense belief that only one who has "experienced" the world as I have can write my story, can adequately communicate the intimate meanings of my existence—which is not to say that these meanings are *opaque* to cultural others. Dewey, Johnson adds, feels that the future of religion itself lies "in the development of faith in the possibilities of human experience and human relationships that will create a vital sense of the solidarity of human interests, and inspire action to make this sense a reality."[113] As editor of *Opportunity* and, later, president of Fisk University, Johnson put such a faith to the test. The development of a "New Negro aesthetic" for the arts was a vital part of his vision for achieving, on the one hand, an "art of life" adequate to the needs of black Americans and, on the other, the integration and spiritual invigoration of a pluralistic and truly American civilization.

A Philosophy of Decolonization

Johnson read Dewey well. Indeed, in *Reconstruction in Philosophy* (1920), for example, Dewey contrasts his emphasis on process with the traditional European philosophical emphasis on the permanent and the fixed as the only source of absolute value; moreover, his stress on process necessarily entails value pluralism: "Where there is change, there is of necessity numerical plurality, multiplicity, and from variety comes opposition, strife. Change is alteration, or 'othering' and this means diversity."[114] Against these threats, Western philosophers from Plato forward have favored the rule of unity, permanence, and theoretical, contemplative knowledge over practical knowledge. Dewey opposes his own method to this tradition and identifies pragmatism specifically with democracy and with the meaning and direction of American culture:

> It is easy to be foolish about the connexion of thought with national life. But I do not see how any one can question the distinctively national color of English, or French, or German philosophies. . . . I believe that philosophy in America will be lost between chewing a historic cud long since reduced to woody fibre, or an apologetics for lost causes (lost to natural science), or a scholastic, schematic formalism, unless it can somehow bring to consciousness America's own needs and its own implicit principle of successful action.[115]

Moreover, this cultural nationalism would be pluralist, poised against the belief in "the single, final and ultimate" which was an intellectual product of a feudal social organization.[116] American pragmatism, then, is not only an "American" philosophy in the sense that it *arose in* the United States; it is also a philosophy *of* the United States, interculturally developed, and is intimately connected with American cultural nationalism from Ralph Waldo Emerson (and, arguably, Frederick Douglass) to Richard Rorty and Cornel West. Abandoning, on the one hand, the kind of idealism that measures current thought against an absolute standard (of metaphysical or ideological perfection, for example) outside of history, and, on the other, the a priorism of British empiricism's appeal to the "factuality" of what has existed in the past, Dewey embraces the necessity of thinking creatively within the moving and unfinished present toward ends that cannot be fully envisioned but only projected out of the best one currently (and ethnocentrically) knows: "Faith in the power of intelligence to imagine a future which is the projection of the desirable in the present, and to invent the instrumentalities of its realization, is our salvation."[117] To understand the kinds of cultural nationalism the pragmatists or their fellow travelers envisioned and distinguished from European nationalisms, however, one must take account of the transformation of the meaning of "culture" in left-wing American intellectual circles, particularly in New York, coinciding with the rise of pragmatism and cultural pluralist theory. In this development, Dewey's colleague Franz Boas is the pivotal figure.

2

The Americanization of "Race" and "Culture"

The connections between Boasian anthropology, pragmatism, and the Harlem Renaissance have never been carefully explored, despite the fact that the confluence of these "communities of interpretation" offers a model of the sort of effective interdisciplinary and intercultural exchange to which many academic intellectuals today aspire. Among other things, it again exemplifies the crosscurrents of thinking about race, culture, and nation that had such a profound impact upon American modernism. Boasian concepts became bedrock assumptions among "New Negro" authors of virtually every persuasion and are among the factors differentiating *both* the assimilationist and black cultural nationalist aspects of the movement from the assimilationism and black nationalism of the late nineteenth century. Boasian ideas also conditioned the reception of African American modernism in contemporary white magazines and publishing houses. Furthermore, the Boasian transformation of thinking about race and culture derived its basic shape from the American context and its situated response to debates over the future of American culture.

Franz Boas and his students not only led a devastating assault upon "scientific" racism in the realm of physical anthropology; they also redefined the concept of culture and, in doing so, contributed to the ideology of cultural pluralism (despite Boas' own "assimilationism"). Years before Zora Neale Hurston became his student at Barnard, Boas' ideas

62

were closely followed by the "New Negro" intellectual community. In 1906, for example, W. E. B. Du Bois had invited him to deliver the commencement address at Atlanta University. Boas used the occasion to speak on the greatness of African cultures and urge the students to reclaim their African heritage: "Say that you have set out to recover for the colored people the strength that was their own before they set foot on the shores of this continent."[1] Du Bois later recalled the incident in *Black Folk Then and Now.* "Franz Boas came to Atlanta University where I was teaching history in 1906 and said to a graduating class: You need not be ashamed of your African past; and then he recounted the history of black kingdoms south of the Sahara for a thousand years. I was too astonished to speak. All of this I had never heard and I came then and afterwards to realize how the silence and neglect of science can let truth utterly disappear or even be unconsciously distorted."[2] In the same year, Boas wrote to his Columbia colleague Felix Adler of his attempt to establish an African museum in the United States to help combat racism and raise the self-esteem of African Americans by featuring the past achievements of African civilizations.[3] His focus on sub-Saharan as opposed to ancient Egyptian and Ethiopian cultures presaged the focus of the Harlem Renaissance upon revitalizing the West African cultural heritage. Boas also spoke at the first Pan-African Congress. He was virtually the house anthropologist for *Crisis* magazine subsequent to the paper he delivered at the Second National Negro Conference of May 1910, through which the NAACP was founded. From 1906 onward, both Du Bois and Alain Locke based their ideas of race upon his and his students' findings.

Here again we find an important line of difference between the "New World" modernism of the Harlem Renaissance and the "high" modernism of Europe and the expatriates. Francesco Loriggio has recently written that "the anthropology the American writers and critics who were contemporaries of Dewey looked up to was penned not by Boas or Sapir or Ruth Benedict but, essentially, by Frazer and the Cambridge School. With the Eliots, the Pounds, the American interdisciplinary mixture is actually an Anglo-American one."[4] The other, "native" American modernists, however, rarely mention Frazer and the Cambridge School. In these circles and the magazines they wrote for— *The Crisis, Opportunity, The Nation, The Liberator, The New Republic*—the Boas school dominated the anthropological side of the intersection between literature, philosophy, anthropology, and cultural critique. Indeed, Edward

Sapir and Ruth Benedict were both well-published "native" American poets themselves. In 1930 Sapir even participated in Jean Toomer's writers' workshop in Chicago![5] On the other hand, American expatriates knew little or nothing of the crucial developments in American anthropology that were coming out of Columbia University.

In the context of massive immigration and reactionary Anglo-Saxonism, virulent antiblack racism, and beliefs that Native Americans were doomed to extinction because of their lack of biological "fitness," Boas mounted a relentless assault upon racist intellectual paradigms and social policies, often paying dearly for his efforts. His wide-ranging work deserves recognition as one of the most important contributions to American modernism.[6] In physical anthropology, he undermined racial formalism by discrediting what had seemed unquestionable assumptions about the stability of human "types." Whereas other scientists had used anthropometry (particularly the measuring of heads) to show racial differences and inequalities, assuming the stability of head shape and size in each race, Boas did virtually the opposite: he used anthropometry to show how the social and natural environment affected physical characteristics that were thought to be strictly hereditary. At a time when powerful forces were seeking "scientific" evidence of the inferiority of new immigrant groups (which would support new immigration restrictions), Boas showed that the children of immigrants could have very different head shapes from their parents. These findings had obvious ramifications for antiblack racism, which sought support in anthropometric measurements. Boas and his students first proved the instability of head shape and cranial capacity and then went on to argue that cranial capacity did not necessarily correlate with intelligence anyway.[7]

In *Anthropology and Modern Life* (1928), a book he wrote for a broad audience in part to combat racism, Boas contended that there was no persuasive evidence of racial differences in intelligence and that there is no definite connection between the size of the brain and its functioning. Moreover, environment, culture, and language affect mental functioning with respect to the performance of specific tasks. Hence, "intelligence" tests are culturally specific; they do not really measure intelligence but rather the ability to think in certain ways, perform certain functions thought of as important in a particular cultural environment.[8] In earlier years Boas had not claimed that the racial types were absolutely equal in intelligence—he did not have sufficient "evidence" to make such a claim—yet he severely criticized those who thought they could prove hereditary biological inferiority. Beyond that, his later arguments about cultural conditioning undercut the idea that intelligence itself was something that could be objectively measured.[9]

One reason that Boas' findings were so important—and so fiercely resisted—is that they directly contradicted the argument that different racial types (particularly Southern European, but African and African American as well) were suited to different types of civilization—an argument that was used to impose immigration restrictions, since only Northern Europeans were thought to have the proper racial characteristics for assimilation to "the American way of life." Boas' antagonists assumed a close and even determining relationship between race and culture. Cultural differences, in other words, could be largely attributed to genetic racial differences. Furthermore, many people believed that racial hatred was a natural *instinct*. The savagery of lynching and white race riots could be blamed on the whites' supposedly instinctive desire to protect their "racial integrity." Such beliefs supported arguments that the United States was and must remain an essentially Anglo-Saxon nation. Boas' arguments also opposed what Marvin Harris calls "Neo-Hegelian racist visions of national souls working their way toward ineffable glories"[10]—visions popular in proto-fascist European intellectual circles in the late nineteenth century and informing the rhetoric of elitist black nationalists as well as white racists in the United States a generation before the Harlem Renaissance.

Against such deeply entrenched beliefs Boas developed his revolutionary contention that race and culture are independent of each other. This, according to George Stocking, initiated a "paradigmatic shift" in the social sciences, which gradually came to explain human behavior in mainly cultural rather than biological terms.[11] Boasian views are partly responsible for the dramatic change from the racialist concept of black nationality held by Alexander Crummell and the early Du Bois to the "culturalist" concepts usually informing the Harlem Renaissance. Du Bois and Crummell had shared the dominant nineteenth-century view of the nation as a "natural" unity expressing a racial "spirit," above all through literature. (Du Bois's concept changed by 1911 directly because of Boas' arguments.)[12] The formation of racial groups, Boas argued, is a social rather than a biological phenomenon.[13] People invent racial classifications and see individuals as representatives of such classifications for social reasons.

Going further yet, Boas and his students attacked the almost universally accepted concept that cultures could be "rated" on an evolutionary scale, with white, Northern European culture, of course, at the apex. They were the first anthropologists to regularly use the term "cultures," in the plural, departing from the essentially monistic view of "Culture," according to which different groups had achieved different "stages" of it.[14] Boas graphically initiated this revolution in anthropological thinking by arranging museum exhibits according to "culture area" rather than according to the unitary plot of "civilization's" evolution, at a time when even black nationalists still thoroughly agreed with the evolutionist viewpoint.[15] Insisting that cultures should be understood on their own terms, as having developed within particular circumstances, with their own specific histories and standards of judgment, he developed a new historical method of carefully collecting the folklore and material culture of an area and arranging it according to the canons of interpretation used by the culture itself.

These ideas and techniques obviously reinforced cultural pluralism as it was developing out of pragmatist philosophy, and indeed some of Boas' students, notably Ruth Benedict and Alexander Goldenweiser, were also followers of John Dewey. (Boas even co-taught a seminar with Dewey in 1914–1915 on "evolutionary and historical methods in the study of intellect.")[16] Moreover, Boasians were particularly attentive to aesthetic production. Boas actually developed a pluralistic aesthetic theory in which he noted that one's creativity is always limited by culturally specific concepts of beauty. If artistic enjoyment derives from the mind's reaction to form, then as we are taught to react to different forms in different cultures we develop differing aesthetic preferences.[17] If this is so, then "the art and characteristic style of a people can be understood only by studying its productions as a whole,"[18] and according to its own aesthetic standards. Boas' paper "The Decorative Art of the Indians of the North Pacific Coast," Melville Herskovits has written, "represents a pioneer analysis of the symbolisms of a nonrepresentational art-form in terms of its own canons of interpretation."[19]

Understanding peoples of other cultures on their own terms—impossible as this might be in the ultimate sense—was important not only because of the ethical imperative to respect their individuality. It could also, in Boas' opinion, help one understand one's own culture better and thereby free one of unconscious shackles of custom and prejudice.

(In fact, one of the most serious charges that can be leveled against Boas is that he saw the uses of ethnography mainly in terms of helping "white" societies become more free and democratic—a typical problem of liberal anthropology.) Moreover, contact between cultures had always been a source of creative growth. Boas, then (unlike some of his followers), partially avoided the romanticization of the "primitive," the "folk," as the source of authenticity.[20] He recognized that all cultures are, in the final analysis, mixed. The modernism of Boas' ideas shows particularly in his validation of the profound and constant effects of culture contact and transformation, as opposed to the "organic" development of civilization according to a unitary plan. His student Alexander Goldenweiser would call culture contact "the veritable yeast of history,"[21] and the "civilizational role of borrowing" fundamental, directly opposing his ideas to the evolutionary theories deriving from Herbert Spencer.

Boas was early in recognizing the importance of language to culture and society, and insisted on the significance of its varied structures and functions, rejecting the idea that one language may be considered superior to another.[22] Just as he had argued that material artifacts and folklore must be interpreted in relation to the culture from which they come, he insisted that a language must be analyzed in terms of its own inherent structure, not by comparison with a European standard. He used Native American languages (which he called "American" languages) as the basis for this observation.[23] As early as 1888, against Daniel G. Brinton's idea that Native Americans had a vague, "tentative language," Boas argued that that apparent vagueness was caused by the ethnologist's culturally derived linguistic limitations. In recording an informant's words, the listener tends to assimilate the sounds to those he or she is accustomed to hearing and using.[24] This was an insight with tremendous ramifications for anthropology (and, for that matter, literary criticism), but it also had implications for the literary use of "dialect" that surely were not lost on Zora Neale Hurston.[25] In letters to Boas during one of her "collecting" trips to the South, Hurston berated earlier (white) collectors of black folklore for confusing stories, words, and pronunciations because of their sloppy methods and their inability to hear what informants were saying.[26]

Boas insisted on preserving a speaker's diction and style, encouraging his students to develop methods for retaining the "spoken form" of a language.[27] Notably, his method of translation of Native American "oral texts" remains a subject of debate among people striving to recover such texts for the American multicultural canon, if only because so much of the available recorded Native American oral literature was collected by Boas and his students.[28] From 1908 to 1923 he edited the *Journal of American Folklore* and the *Memoirs* of the American Folklore Society (which he had helped found), publishing enormous quantities of this material. This work—which included African American folklore as well—contributed greatly to the general movement toward a reevaluation of black folk culture, a movement of critical importance for the Harlem Renaissance and that continued with historic results through the 1930s by way of the Federal Writers' Project. Like Robert E. Park, Boas was also an associate of Carter G. Woodson in the founding of the Association for the Study of Negro Life and History in 1915. The work of Boas and his students paralleled and to some extent anticipated the growing literary interest in American folk cultures that we find in Mary Austin, Carl Sandburg, Langston Hughes, Paul Green, Zora Neale Hurston, Julia Peterkin, and others. These writers would attempt a far more "realistic," quasi-ethnographic approach to folk experience and expression than had their regionalist literary precursors.

Because of his anthropological approach, indeed his basic orientation toward cultural reality, Boas largely escaped the primitivist and exoticist proclivities of many Western students of African and Native American arts. According to Herskovits, he rejected, on the one hand, the equation of "primitive" people with children, and, on the other, "the ecstatic phrasings of the art critics, especially those dealing with the graphic and plastic arts, who saw in the art of 'primitive' man exotic, mystical manifestations of some deep instinctual urge, to be regarded with awe, and understood but dimly by 'civilized' man as he responds from his deepest being to this thing he can never intellectually comprehend."[29] Boas' view of so-called primitive art—the symbolic and aesthetic complexity of which he was quick to recognize—was more pragmatic; it also eschewed the still pervasive tendency to view traditional non-Western peoples as living in some "other time" prior to "our own."

To Boas, mythology and literature indicated through formal properties as well as content what was considered important to a particular people, providing "an autobiography of the tribe."[30] Folklore, he believed, reveals a people's world view as well as their ethical and aesthetic values. Thus, in classifying texts, he attempted to follow the generic rules of the group he was studying rather than Western ideas of genre. Moreover, he liked to trace the filiations of myths, tales, and lyrics, which partly explains his enthusiasm for Zora Neale Hurston's discovery of connections between African American, Afro-Caribbean, and African cultural practices. (His student Melville Herskovits would be the most influential social scientist to prove extensive African retentions in the New World.) Suspicious of "universals," he consistently rejected archetypal interpretation.

Recently Boas has been accused of standing up against antiblack racism merely as a way of camouflaging his more genuine interest in attacking anti-Semitism, and also of failing to devote much energy to attacking discrimination against blacks.[31] Yet in the early twentieth century Boas specifically wrote against antiblack racism; his antiracist work and that of his students was repeatedly published in *The Crisis* and *Opportunity* as well as left-wing white magazines. Nor was this a cover for attacking anti-Semitism. Actually, Boas did attack anti-Semitism, but as an American citizen he seems to have been more concerned about anti-Negro racism. Moreover, believing that culture, not race, was the operative category of group identity, Boas did not consider himself Jewish, for he did not practice the Jewish religion and did not feel himself to have been raised in a Jewish culture. His identification of himself as American—or, when pushed, German-American—was consistent with his attack on racialist thinking.[32]

A formidable opponent of such powerful racists as Madison Grant, Boas paid for his conviction (and his Germanness) by being excluded from the National Research Council's Committee on Anthropology in 1916, when the scientific community was being mobilized to aid national military preparedness—an example of the relationship between the war and the politics of American modernism. Later, Boas' opponents in the field of psychology played an important role in administering intelligence tests to American soldiers in World War I—tests that became "the most important single scientific buttress for the racism of the 1920s." As George Stocking has pointed out, "Much of the work of the Boas group was specifically focused on a critique of intelligence testing."[33] This is one reason that Boas and his students became so closely associated with the movement against white racism in the years of the Harlem Renaissance. By 1926—after having suffered terrible setbacks because of xenophobia, anti-Semitism, eugenics, racist psychology, and the popularity of such works as Madison Grant's *The Passing of the Great Race* (1916)—Boasian cultural anthropology was reasserting its power, and its connections with the Harlem Renaissance should not be underestimated. Echoes and paraphrases of his work reverberate through novels as diverse as Jessie Fauset's, Wallace Thurman's, and George Schuyler's. Both Schuyler's "The Negro-Art Hokum" and its rebuttal, Langston Hughes's "The Negro Artist and the Racial Mountain," base their arguments on the Boasian tenet that culture is shaped by experience and historical conditions rather than organic or spiritual "racial" inheritance; where they differ is on the issue of how deep the differences are between the socioeconomic conditions of and the cultural influences upon black American and white American experiences of modernity.[34]

Neither is it true that Boas failed to encourage blacks to become anthropologists; his encouragement of Zora Neale Hurston, despite the almost insuperable obstacles to a career for a black (and female) scholar in the fledgling field of anthropology at the time, is well known.[35] Yet Boas' very encouragement of Hurston as an anthropologist has, in recent years, been used against him in arguments (long on innuendo, short on evidence) about how she had to fight for creative independence![36] Boas also encouraged Arthur Huff Fauset (Jessie's half-brother) and pushed for a fellowship at Columbia for a Howard graduate, James F. King, to study anthropology and psychology, which would have made King, Melville Herskovits wrote to Alain Locke, "practically invincible as far as getting a position is concerned."[37] Moreover, the reason even more studies of black Americans were not undertaken is not due to lack of interest on Boas' part; for years he tried to stimulate interest in universities for such research but was stymied by their fears of antagonizing benefactors.[38] Certainly Boas had his failings, but much of the case brought by a few recent scholars against him can be attributed to his choosing to attack the color line without being black himself.

In "The Eleventh Hour of Nordicism" Alain Locke would attest to the importance of Boas' efforts. Noting first the timidity with which both black and white sociologists had addressed "the race question," he wrote:

> That this situation is finally changing after nearly two decades dominated by such attitudes is due to the influence of just a few strong dissenting influences,—the most important of which has come from the militant but unquestionably scientific school of anthropologists

captained by Professor Boas. They have dared, in season and out, to challenge false doctrine and conventional myths, and were the first to bring the citadel of Nordicism into range of scientific encirclement and bombardment. An essay in itself could be written on the slow but effective pressure that now has ringed the Nordic doctrines and their advocates round with an ever-tightening scientific blockade.[39]

By 1930 Boas' theories of race and culture, which had almost no credibility before 1910, had become institutionalized throughout the cultural and political left in the United States.

Of course, anthropology's involvement in racism and imperialism is more complicated than the use of anthropological research for patently racist purposes, and can even inform antiracist work like that of the Boasians.[40] Recently anthropologists have come to recognize their complicity in ethnocentric practices and imperialist ideology, which are inherent in the processes of observing and writing about an "other" who is in a less powerful position within the global system.[41] To write about people of an "other" culture is necessarily to translate them into one's own discourse, to superimpose one's own ideological map upon their lives, no matter how noble one's intentions. This important understanding of the textuality of anthropological knowledge, however, is actually an extension of some of Boas' own more skeptical meditations. Indeed, in 1887 Boas quite explicitly argued: "It cannot be said too frequently that our reasoning is not an absolutely logical one, but that it is influenced by the reasoning of our predecessors and by our historical environment; therefore our conclusions and theories, particularly when referring to our own mind, which itself is affected by the same influences to which our reasoning is subject, cannot but be fallacious."[42] Boas extended this epistemological problem to the study of other peoples, recognizing that all of us are trapped by the customs and habits (including mental ones) of our cultural environment. Science itself is always prone to entrapment by convention.

Such philosophical recognitions led Boas to his most important innovations in anthropological method. The fieldworker, he argued, must try to set aside all a priori assumptions, try to adapt herself as much as possible to the way of thinking and feeling of the people she was studying, try to divest herself of the opinions and feelings determined by her own culture. This could never be accomplished fully, as one cannot speak from any position other than one's own. However, that position is revisable, so long as one attends carefully to the lives and speech of the other and opens a space in which the other can tell her own story in her own way. The aesthetic experience of such an exchange revises the self and its negotiations with the world. Empirical findings must remain similarly tentative and revisable. Indeed, Boas was famously resistant to theory and generalization, preferring practice and empirical investigation. Much of his "theory" is extrapolated from his essentially pragmatic method. Like William James, in his mature years he seems to have rejected epistemological foundations while preserving a realist ontology—that is, there is *something* out there, but we know it only through our operations and actions, which of course are shaped by our cultures and disciplines, our "communities of interpretation." Like James as well, Boas emphasized the importance of rigorous self-critique and introspection, which he regarded in some respects as the most important result of anthropological fieldwork. To borrow Cornel West's description of James's theory of truth, Boas' *anti-scientistic* idea of scientific truth "locates truth at the end of a verifying process, though it remains contingent and revisable. To be in time means to be in pursuit of new and basic truths; any truth is subject to change though the best available truths are warranted and acceptable." Both men stressed "the distinctively concrete, particular, and effective—as opposed to the abstract, general, and vague."[43]

Even while Boas strives toward the goal of positing laws of human culture, as Arnold Krupat has written, he insists "again and again on impossible conditions for such generalization, noting that laws will legitimately be discovered only when all the facts are in."[44] Moreover, his recognition that the "facts" depend upon culturally shaped perceptions "undermines the foundations for any claims to scienticity."[45] Hence, in a passage John Dewey would quote at length from *The Mind of Primitive Man* (1911), Boas points out that scientists necessarily begin their work from received assumptions and attempt to "amalgamate" new "facts" to "other previously known facts"; there is no help for this. "We are only too apt, however, to forget the entirely general, and for most of us purely traditional, theoretical basis which is the foundation of our reasoning, and to assume that the result of our reasoning is absolute truth."[46]

Boas is traditionally characterized as a cultural relativist, but this characterization is not quite accurate. His quest to understand diverse cultures on their own terms did not entail the abandonment of critical reflection and ethical or political judgment. Certainly it required sustained critical *self*-reflection and doubt of one's ability to feel what is most meaningful and valuable—or most painful and humiliating—in the life experience of the cultural "other." Such a point of view, as William James wrote in "On a Certain Blindness in Human Beings," "absolutely forbids us to be forward in pronouncing on the meaninglessness of forms of existence other than our own; . . . neither the whole of truth nor the whole of good is revealed to any single observer, although each observer gains a partial superiority of insight from the peculiar position in which he stands."[47] But like James, Boas was no thoroughgoing relativist; behind his enormous anthropological accomplishments lay a fervent political commitment. He claimed that the most important factor in his life was having grown up in a household in which the memories of the 1848 revolutions in Europe were living realities, and to serve the spread of democratic equality was the fundamental impetus of his work.[48] Indeed, he became an American precisely for this reason, writing to his future wife during his first fieldwork in Baffinland: "I do *not* want a German professorship because I know I would be restricted to my science and to teaching. . . . I should much prefer to live in America in order to be able to further those ideas for which I live. . . . What I want to live and die for, is equal rights for all, equal possibilities to learn and work for poor and rich alike! Don't you believe that to have done even the smallest bit for this, is more than all science taken together?"[49] This is not relativism but the sort of democratic socialism that informed Deweyan pragmatism. Boas prized equality and free communication between diverse communities; he firmly believed, like Dewey, that modern cultures could be judged according to their tendencies to promote or inhibit such communion. Alain Locke and W. E. B. Du Bois would not have disagreed, although they placed greater emphasis than Boas upon the necessity of building self-conscious racial traditions, given the importance of race, nationality, and hierarchies of power in the modern world.

In "The Real Race Problem," published in the second issue of *The Crisis,* Boas presented his arguments against the supposed superiority of whites; yet he projected a gradual assimilation of Negroes to whites, physically as well as culturally, which would level distinctions between the races and result in more cooperation: "The less Negro society represents a party with its own aims and its own interest distinct from those of the members of the white race, the more satisfactory will be the relation between the races."[50] Boas reasoned that whites were dominant and would not accept black self-assertion (he may also have been thinking of the experience of German-Jewish Americans). However, he did not conceive that black culture would simply disappear; he foresaw instead an assimilation of each type toward the other (a view that later appears repeatedly in *The Messenger* magazine and in Schuyler's and Toomer's work, and that apparently was held by a number of NAACP officers, black and white). Indeed, Boas went so far as to suggest that ultimately the "race problem" in the United States could be solved only through interracial marriage, which would reduce racial differences and the social divisions based upon them.[51] Unfortunately, by the 1920s Boas saw few signs that the United States was moving in this direction; he noted that all groups seemed, on the contrary, to be insisting on and even "exaggerating" their differences.[52]

The effect of Boas' views in the second and third decades of the century was to suggest that black American culture was not—and should not become—distinctly different from white American culture; and yet those views could, and did, equally well support an opposite conclusion. Until the middle to late 1920s, Boas believed (like most of the "New Negroes") that African culture had been forcibly stamped out in the United States under slavery. Indeed, he believed early in the century that what was widely regarded as the "degraded" situation of contemporary African American culture could be attributed to the loss of cultural foundations that came with removal from Africa and enslavement. Melville Herskovits' early work, including the piece of his that appeared in *The New Negro* ("The Negro's Americanism"), followed these ideas and stressed similarities between white and black Americans. Similarly, his book *The American Negro: A Study in Racial Crossing* stated that "Harlem . . . is to all intents and purposes an American community peopled by individuals who have an additional amount of pigmentation in their skins"[53]—an idea Jessie Fauset and George Schuyler, among others, were also trying to push. Herskovits noted that many of the African Americans he interviewed shared the nativist views of most whites and resented suggestions of cultural differences between themselves and white Americans.

At the same time, the main point of Herskovits' first book was that the American Negro was a new racial type, "distinctive among human beings."[54] In a period of declining interracial sexual relations combined with social isolation and "race consciousness" enforced from both within and without, the "American Negro" was stabilizing into a physical type distinct from both Caucasian and Negro races.[55] Herskovits sees an interesting coincidence with the New Negro "literary and artistic naissance." "The movement has been of no little social significance, for it means that the American Negroes—or, in any event, a small group of them—are claiming a portion of their heritage as Americans, and are identifying themselves more and more closely with the culture of this country which is theirs by birth."[56] The cultural "naissance" happens to match the current process of formation of "a veritable New Negro, the American Negro" as an indigenous physical type. Herskovits' work connects the New Negro movement, American cultural nationalism, and Boasian anthropology. Not coincidentally, he was a favorite reviewer and commentator with editors of *The Crisis* and *Opportunity* as well as *The Nation* and *The New Republic.*

While arguing for the existence of the American Negro as a new "homogeneous population group, more or less consciously consolidating and stabilizing the type of which he [*sic*] has commenced the formation," Herskovits does not call this type a new race.[57] Indeed, following Boas he finds the term "race" exceedingly unscientific, and states that he has adopted the term "Negro" only for sociological reasons, because of the way people in the United States define races. In other words, he comes out distinctly against essentializing tendencies. But if the term "race" makes no scientific sense, it has nonetheless played an important role "in our political and social life." A distinctively American racism fostered the creation of a distinctively American "type," which in turn adhered to the dominant U.S. attitudes toward "miscegenation" and thus protected its "racial" integrity. A related equation shows up repeatedly in the Harlem Renaissance: both racism and black American culture (the latter profoundly shaped in relation with the former) are closely identified with what makes American culture distinct from any other. If lynching is the national crime, black music is the national music, and the spirit of America is carried most authentically in the souls of black folk. Charles S. Johnson, for example, believed that the meaning of liberal social justice and democratic community could be known fully only by those who had been denied both in a nation purporting to provide "liberty and justice for all." The "original sin" of racism peculiarly identified American culture and ironically conferred indigenous American cultural authority upon the African American community.

Before long, Herskovits found himself abandoning the idea that white and black Americans were culturally indistinguishable, and by the early 1930s, perhaps nudged by the work of Zora Neale Hurston and Arthur Huff Fauset, he was discovering the connections between African and African American culture that would go into his influential book *The Myth of the Negro Past*. However, in the 1920s, few informed people, white or black—except the racists!—were arguing that the differences between black and white American culture were caused primarily by African *cultural* (as opposed to temperamental or spiritual) survivals, even if, like Alain Locke, W. E. B. Du Bois, Franz Boas, and Albert Barnes, for example, they wanted African Americans to develop pride in the African tradition and to reconnect with it culturally.[58] Minimizing the Africanness of the "American Negro" was not simply an example of the hold of racist ideology but was the result of a specific rhetorical situation. (One might add that black Americans' own views on the subject apparently influenced Melville Herskovits, who did research in Harlem and at Howard University, and whose early conceptions of African American culture were directly affected by college-educated black Americans' resistance to the idea that their culture differed significantly from white Americans'.) Arguments for black cultural distinctiveness, in the racist milieu of the 1920s, could be used to justify segregation and immigration restrictions, as Herskovits himself worried when he started publishing his path-breaking work on continuities between African American and African cultures in the mid-1930s. More important than the idea of the traditional Africanness of African American culture to the Harlem Renaissance was the idea that black Americans, unlike any other group, had been almost completely stripped of their ancestral cultural identity, and precisely because of this had developed the most authentically *American* folk culture. The "Africanist" wing of the New Negro movement was mainly an attempt to reconnect with Africa, a spiritual homeland that, after three centuries, seemed so far away and yet, like a lost mother, so deeply desired.

In the final analysis, it is apparent that Franz Boas bequeathed a dual, even contradictory, legacy to the 1920s. On the one hand, his research and teaching provided invaluable ammunition for the attack on Anglo-Saxon hegemony and had a deep influence on the rise of theories of cultural pluralism. His advocacy of the greatness of West African civilizations (joining earlier black Egyptianism and Ethiopianism) enhanced racial pride and countered ideas of African primitivism; his attack on

Spencerian evolutionist theories of civilization, his critique of the equation of culture and race, his insistence upon the integrity of diverse cultural traditions, and his resistance to the assumption of universal standards for the judgment of cultural expressions, supported value relativism and thus movements to revitalize distinctive ethnic and racial identities. On the other hand, taking account of the deeply rooted nature of American racism, and probably influenced by his own ethnic background, he explicitly advocated assimilationism—even "racial intermixture"—and felt that the drive toward cultural pluralism would only exacerbate the difficulties of achieving a truly democratic and egalitarian society.[59] Both of these tendencies of his thought can be found interwoven throughout the writing of the Harlem Renaissance, even uneasily coexisting in the pages of *The New Negro* itself. Moreover, both coincided with and supported the movement in literature and cultural criticism to divorce American literature from English tradition, to redefine the nature of culture in the United States.

3

Cultural Pluralism and National Identity

In contrast to the assimilationist bent Boas proposed, while nonetheless profiting enormously from his work, one of the most significant spinoffs of James's (and, less directly, Dewey's) pragmatism was the theory of cultural pluralism, of which Locke's *The New Negro* is a dramatic demonstration. As John Higham once pointed out, W. E. B. Du Bois was enunciating concepts similar to cultural pluralism well before Horace Kallen coined the term. In "Strivings of the Negro People" (1897), Du Bois insisted that the African American would not "bleach his Negro soul in a flood of white Americanism, for he believes—foolishly, perhaps, but fervently—that Negro blood has yet a message for the world. He simply wishes to make it possible for a man to be both a Negro and an American without being cursed and spit upon by his fellows, without losing the opportunity of development."[1] Couched similarly in essentialist terms of racial "blood" messages and "spirit," Kallen's work of the teens also projected a vision of a "federated" field of American culture, one composed of "harmonious" co-workers. (By the end of the 1920s, partly because of Boas' influence, "culture" would replace blood and spirit as the effective category of group identity for both Kallen and Du Bois.)

Kallen approached his social ethic from the standpoint of a Jewish immigrant, and his discussions of cultural pluralism focused on the new "hyphenate" citizens who were flooding Manhattan from Eastern

Europe during the same period that the black migration from the South took place (a migration Kallen totally ignored). Moreover, the thrust of his argument is such as to position Jewish Americans in a central role vis-à-vis "true Americanism." Du Bois approached the problem of American cultural pluralism from the standpoint of the native American of African (as well as European) descent whose culture had been systematically abused, repressed, and/or plundered for generations but upon whose condition the history of America had centered "for thrice a hundred years."[2] Partly because of this history, perhaps, Du Bois's concepts were finally more assimilationist than Kallen's—seeking the moral reformation of white America toward its own professed "universal" values and African American spirituality, as well as African American assimilation of European culture. The concept of cultural pluralism, then, had different existential groundings and visionary endings for each man, yet both came at their theories with similar academic training and philosophical bases—specifically, the influential concepts of William James and Josiah Royce. Yet even more important for the "black aesthetic" theory of the Harlem Renaissance than Du Bois was Alain Locke, whose cultural pluralism is even more closely tied to Kallen's, and who also derived it in part from the writings of James and Royce.[3] Locke's intellectual pilgrimage to "cultural racialism" exemplifies the dependence of cultural pluralist ideology upon interracial, intercultural processes as well as the centrality of American nationalism to the theorizing of a New Negro cultural renaissance and black modernist aesthetics.

James's attacks on absolutes and on all appeals to solutions dependent on "transcendental" truths not experienced by human beings had two consequences of particular importance for cultural pluralists, Zionists (including Kallen), and black aestheticians of the early twentieth century. First was James's emphasis upon the temporality of truth, which entailed pluralism. Truth, in James's view, is not something fixed, timeless, independent of our subjective experience, but rather is relational and humanly constructed. As he wrote in *Talks to Teachers*, "There is no point of view absolutely public and universal."[4] Hence, we cannot talk about the world independent of its experienceability. Moreover, we know the world as relational; it comes to us not as a series of objects or "facts" but already structured by relations that the mind uses to order the flow of perceptions. Under the influence of the Boasians, Dewey would come to call these relations "cultural."

Obviously, many of the relations we automatically assume as we interpret reality are governed by our personal, social, and historical circumstances. No knowledge is independent of these circumstances. People in any given cultural and historical setting will emphasize certain relations and repress or fail to perceive those that seem important to other people. Aesthetic judgments are a particularly acute example of this insight; for, if the rich subtleties of each culture are to be found in the ordering of relations between known things, then aesthetic choices— dependent as they are upon relations between immediate objects of sense such as sounds, colors, and shapes, and upon habitual uses of organs of the body like the tongue, larynx, and lips—express the most intimately distinctive relations any culture or community can "know." Emphasizing, and indeed celebrating, the *process* of experience and the openness of the universe, James argued that the pluralism of experiences, interpretations, and perspectives is not a temporary condition en route to some all-inclusive view, some Absolute; it is inherent in the way we know the world. Each truth will be tested by further experience, be revised, and have an effect in action, which in turn helps constitute the future course of experience—and the future "truths" we construct.

James's pluralism, while placing heavy emphasis on individual experience, does not atomize communities. Nor does it support a conception of plural individuals or communities wholly divorced from one another as if each has a separate history and is maintained by impermeable boundaries. As John J. McDermott has written, "The perspective of other persons is partially constitutive of their reality and, therefore, by shared custom, partially constitutive of ours as well. If there is no single vantage point from which the world can be seen or interpreted or experientially had as whole, then every person makes his or her contribution to the ongoing statement as to how it is with the world, and how the world comes to be for me is in some way due to how the world has come to be for the other, for you."[5] Thus the various subcultures within the American field help determine the forms of one another's discourse, not only because of directly political and economic relations, but particularly insofar as each subculture orients its discourse in relation to the "meaning" of a shared if multivalent symbol—"America"—that is politically as well as culturally constitutive. Ironically, and perhaps inevitably, as John Higham has noted, American cultural pluralism itself is one of the hardier products of the "melting pot."[6]

In addition to the pragmatists, the philosopher whom Locke had originally wanted to direct his graduate studies (and one whom Du Bois had also known and admired) was an important intellectual ancestor of the cultural pluralists. In the context of rising nativism and fear of both immigrants from Southern Europe and migrating African Americans, Josiah Royce argued, like Franz Boas, that so-called scientific concepts of race and "innate" racial prejudice were really rationalizations for Anglo-Saxon self-regard and domination. Against the popular notions of his day, he argued that race prejudice is a socially determined phenomenon.[7]

More centrally, Royce developed a "philosophy of loyalty" and a theory of "wholesome provincialism" that attracted both Du Bois and Locke, along with such white cultural pluralists as Horace Kallen. Arguing that "the tendency toward national unity and that toward local independence of spirit, must henceforth grow together,"[8] Royce extolled provincial idealism. Indeed, each province should *be* an ideal— rather than "a mere boast"—so that its members would maintain a constant desire for achievement of their shared dream of being-together.[9] If James emphasized pluralism and individualism, Josiah Royce's main contribution to the theory of cultural pluralism, and surely to Du Bois's and Locke's thinking, was his theorizing about community.[10]

Though Royce's work on "provincialism" was implicitly and pervasively blind to the significance of racial and ethnic realities of American life, though he spoke of "provinces" rather than racial communities, and though he actually encouraged immigrants to new communities to assimilate to the culture of their adopted place, his work had obvious ramifications for ethnic and racial groups in the United States that were not lost on his students Du Bois and Locke. Upon hearing of Royce's death, Du Bois published an obituary in *The Crisis* and urged all African Americans to read his work.[11] Royce's ideas undoubtedly had a great deal to do with Locke's transformation from intensely assimilationist Anglophilia to "cultural racialism." The problem of achieving "universalism" without denying group differences, ambitions, and interests, Locke regarded as one of the most important in all social theory; and he considered Royce his guide on this subject: "Josiah Royce, one of the greatest of the American philosophers, saw this problem more clearly than any other Western thinker, and worked out his admirable principle of loyalty, which is nothing less than a vindication of the principle of unity in diversity carried out to a practical degree of spiritual reciprocity."[12] Indeed, Locke had wanted to do his graduate work under Royce but was unable to because Royce died before Locke returned to Harvard for his Ph.D.

Like many other intellectuals at the turn of the century, Royce was concerned about the leveling and homogenizing tendencies of modern civilization. But he also worried that Americans felt no deep identification with the nation that had come into being through the Civil War; the "nation" remained an abstract political entity, associated with centralized power—a *civic* rather than *cultural* reality. His answer to this problem was that a deeper cultural nationalism should be developed by way of provincialism and "loyalty to loyalty." Provincial loyalties would mediate between the individual and the nation, while the ethic of being loyal to the loyalties of others would bind the different provinces to one another. Hence, for Royce the issue of national cohesion and common identity called for essentially cultural solutions at the local level, such as communal rituals and public "adornments."

The province would act as a counterforce against the worst features of modern nationalism. It would foster critical intelligence; loyalty to it would guard against national hysteria by emphasizing that the province's duty to the nation entailed "its right to attain and to cultivate its own unique wisdom."[13] Moreover, the higher provincialism was cosmopolitan; the province would learn freely from abroad but insist on its own local interpretation of the common good. It would appropriate all "borrowings" for its own ideal purposes while respecting the desire of other provinces to do the same. Finally, it would express itself in art and adornment, thus rendering its ideals and sensibilities in forms that would evoke communal identity and pride as well as the recognition and appreciation of others. The various communities would be bound to one another through the dialogical processes of aesthetic creation and reception.

Royce, in fact, thought of members of a true community as "artists in some form of cooperation, . . . whose art constitutes, for each artist, his own ideally extended life." To be such an artist in the complex orders of the modern world required love, because mere intelligence could no longer furnish consciousness of the entire community's operations, the contributions of each of its members. As an epitome of the love he has in mind, Royce uses the model of the artist's love for a collective art project, something very close to religious love; it "depends . . . upon seeing in the successful cooperation of all the members precisely that

event which the individual member most eagerly loves as his own fulfillment."[14] Nourished by common memories and a common hope, this
love finds expression in devoted individual lives.

Royce argued that a "wise provincialism" insists that others should be
able to "possess such ideal values in their own equally unique fashion."
Indeed, each province, like each individual in a "realm of genuinely
spiritual individuality," is irreplaceable by virtue of its uniqueness. "But
for just that very reason all the unique individuals of the truly spiritual
order stand in relation to the same universal light, to the same divine
whole in relation to which they win their individuality."[15] This is the
main point on which Royce's "absolute pragmatism," as he eventually
called it, diverged from the Jamesian pragmatist's cultural pluralism.
Locke, too, at least during the Harlem Renaissance, held to the idealist
belief in a "universal light" or "spiritual order" in relation to which the
various distinct cultures gained meaning. To Locke, different cultures
should form complementary elements of a universal whole. This basic
aspect of his thought remained constant through his successive affiliations with Ethical Culture, Royce's philosophy of loyalty, cultural pluralism, and Baha'ism, perhaps only toward the end of his life changing
into a full-blown acceptance of a "pluriverse" that humans *make* into a
"universe." Horace Kallen was right, however, in pointing out that *The
New Negro* suggests the sort of primary pluralism Locke had not yet
accepted philosophically.[16] In the 1920s, his residual idealism under-
pinned his belief that black artists, by attending to the particularity of
their own cultural visions and transcending the prescriptions of the propagandists of race, would ultimately develop a universal art. Ralph
Waldo Emerson, one of Locke's intellectual heroes from his pre-college
days, would have concurred.

While Royce advocated loyalty to one's "provincial" ideals, he also
argued that one must learn freely from abroad, adapting the lessons of
others to one's own belief system. Significantly, he held up the Japanese—a "race" that many Europeans and white Americans considered,
like the "Negro race," apelike because of its alleged imitativeness—as
an example. To many whites the Japanese individual seems "submissive"
and "docile," but "he" adapts all imported concepts and techniques to
his own ideals: "With a curious and on the whole not unjust spiritual
wiliness, he has learned indeed our lesson, but he has given it his own
interpretation. . . . [H]e remains absolutely his own master with regard
to the interpretation, the use, the possession of all spiritual gifts, as if

he were the master and you the learner." The Japanese could well give Europeans a lesson in "the spirit of true provincialism," Royce argued.[17] Locke adopted a similar approach to the relation between black and white American cultures; accepting pervasive ideas that blacks, like the Japanese, were expert at mimicry, he denied the further assertion that this proved their docility and lack of intellectual originality.[18] It proved, instead, their greater inherited openness and essentially cosmopolitan spirit.

Despite his admiration for the Japanese (whose immigration to Royce's own California had aroused intense nativism from the turn of the century), by using the geographical province as the essential unit for his theory, Royce left ethnic and racial differences invisible in relation to American nationality. Thus his pluralistic model of American cultural nationalism was weakened by ethnocentrism and a fundamental blindness to American cultural reality. This blindness can be attributed largely to Royce's own ethnic and regional backgrounds as well as his historical moment—he was, after all, an Anglo-Saxon of California birth transplanted to New England. And his concern about newcomers to a province "assimilating" to the ways of their adopted home, while expressed in relation to migrants like himself, surely had an even more telling reference to the thousands of immigrants from Asia and Southern and Eastern Europe.

The chief thinker with whom Locke personally debated the issue of cultural pluralism during his formative years as a philosopher was Horace Kallen, a lifelong friend who had helped guide him as an undergraduate at Harvard and who also attended Oxford in 1907, when Locke was there on his Rhodes scholarship. Having immigrated from Silesia as a child and been raised in a strict Jewish home dominated by his father, a rabbi, Kallen rebelled as he approached adulthood and "intentionally separated himself from his Jewish background and heritage"—until, ironically, the notoriously Anglocentric professor of American literature at Harvard, Barret Wendell, convinced him of the "Hebraic elements in American political and literary thought and institutions." At this point, according to Milton Konvitz, he "began consciously and conscientiously to reclaim, and to identify himself with, his Jewish inheritance, Jewish culture, and the Jewish community."[19] Thus, discovering the Jewishness of the American Way helped lead Kallen to Zionism. The other crucial influence was William James, whom Kallen considered his "master." As he later wrote:

The commingling of James's lectures and Wendell's [literary history] crystallized in my mind into a new outlook, the results of which were: first, *discovery of the meaning of "equal" as used in the Declaration* [of Independence]; second, recognition of the social role of freedom and of individual and group differences, later to be expounded at length in my own philosophy, and finally, such a reappraisal of my Jewish affiliations as required an acquiescence in my Jewish inheritance and heritage, an expanding exploration into the content and history of both, and a progressively greater participation in Jewish communal enterprises.[20]

American cultural nationalism, then, was an important impetus to his Jewish cultural nationalism. The irony matches that of Alain Locke's development.

But, as Sara L. Schmidt and Werner Sollors have shown, the biographical convergences between Kallen's and Locke's adoption of cultural pluralism are more intimate than mere parallels suggest. Kallen's recounting of the development of his concept bears quoting here:

It was in 1905 that I began to formulate the notion of cultural pluralism and I had to do that in connection with my teaching. I was assisting both Mr. James and Mr. Santayana at the time and I had a Negro student named Alain Locke, a very remarkable young man— very sensitive, very easily hurt—who insisted that he was a human being and that his color ought not to make any difference. And of course, it was a mistaken insistence. It *had* to make a difference and it *had* to be accepted and respected and enjoyed for what it was.

Two years later when I went to Oxford on a fellowship he was there as a Rhodes scholar, and we had a race problem because the Rhodes scholars from the South were bastards. So they had a Thanksgiving dinner which I refused to attend because they refused to have Locke.

And he said, "I am a human being," just as I had said it earlier. What difference does the difference make? We are all alike Americans. And we had to argue out the question of how the differences made differences, and in arguing out those questions the formulae, then phrases, developed—"cultural pluralism," "the right to be different."[21]

That this founding drama centered around the ritual of Thanksgiving dinner—a commemoration of originary Anglo Americanization in mythic relation to the indigenous "other"—is as richly significant as it is disturbing and ironic, setting the stage for Locke's and Kallen's challenge to the very meaning of Americanness embodied in the Thanks-giving legend.

In his own gloss on this episode, Werner Sollors has shown how con-flicted Kallen's attitude to Locke's race seems to have been and has asked whether Locke's correspondence might reveal another dimen-sion of the story.[22] As it turns out, Locke's correspondence with Kallen reveals little, but his correspondence with his mother and the black historian William C. Bolivar reveals what an unlikely candidate he would be, at the time he came to know Kallen, to advance black aes-thetics, and particularly to champion the "folk school" of the Harlem Renaissance. It reveals instead Locke's Anglophile, assimilationist stance (which his mother and Bolivar encouraged), his attempts to escape the "clutches" of a group of fellow black students who repeatedly sought his company, his disdain for black "self-segregation," and his feeling of repugnance toward what he called, in a letter to his mother, "typical southern niggers."[23] For both Locke and Kallen, the turn to cultural pluralism and affirmation of a distinctive "racial" heritage came not as a *continuation* of an ancestral orientation, but through a break with an ancestral identity, followed by an "Anglo-conformist" phase, a deepened exploration of the "American idea," and then an emphatic modernist ethnic reconstruction—not simply a return. Cultural pluralism, for Kallen and Locke after their "conversions," was the true mode of American cultural nationalism, whereas Anglo-conformity (their earlier orientation) was fundamentally "un-American."[24]

Kallen, at least in his initial formulations, did not clearly distinguish between biological and cultural aspects of race or nationality. Like Du Bois, he tended toward romantic racialism, blurring the boundary between genetic and culturally determined characteristics, and he spoke in terms of "realization of the race-self."[25] As Sollors shows, two serious difficulties show up in Kallen's theorizing of American cultural pluralism. First, his pluralism breeds a kind of intolerance: it necessarily represses and even attacks melting-pot identities. Intercultural or inter-ethnic subjectivity must be excluded from his pluralistic embrace, since it threatens the purity of the ethnic spirit of each group. Secondly, he envisions the orchestration only of "European harmonies."[26] Hence, as John Higham observed, "the pluralist thesis from the outset was encap-sulated in white ethnocentrism"—a fact that is extraordinarily ironic in view of Kallen's own narrative of how he developed his concept.[27] Alain

Locke evaded both of these weaknesses in Kallen's theory; and on the first score he was anticipated by John Dewey.

Dewey, who had by now become acquainted with Boas' ethnography and even co-taught a seminar with him, cringed at Kallen's tendency to reify ethnic identity, emphasizing each group's unitary "origins," "spiritual" continuity, and "psycho-physical inheritance" while neglecting the profound and complex interrelations between different cultural groups. This way of thinking about cultural pluralism left little room for peoples to form mutual commitments to each other in their particularity, commitments that require forms of aesthetic attention and notions of self and "culture" more fluid than Kallen initially assumed. So long as the abstract, transcendental existence of the ethnic group as such—rather than ongoing "experience," in the Deweyan sense—is the primary basis of communal identity, the goals and ideals of the group will be historically predetermined and tragically self-limited.[28] In a letter responding to "Democracy versus the Melting-Pot," Dewey wrote to Kallen that he agreed with the basic point of the essay but lamented Kallen's inattention to the need for interaction between groups in a democratic society and the implications of this necessity for the pluralistic vision.[29]

Notably, Dewey argued that such terms as "Irish-American" falsely assume the existence of something called "American" already in existence, to which the other factor is "hitched on." Dewey countered that the American is himself or herself always already a hyphenated character—international and interracial in his or her makeup. We must ensure that the hyphen connects instead of separates. "And this means at least that our public schools shall teach each factor to respect every other, and shall take pains to enlighten all as to the great past contributions of every strain in our composite make-up." Dewey believed that "the dangerous thing is for each factor to isolate itself, to try to live off its past, and then to attempt to impose itself upon other elements, or, at least, to keep itself intact and thus refuse to accept what other cultures have to offer."[30] Each group, moreover, should give its best to the "common fund of wisdom and experience." Americanization is not a process by which "foreign" elements fit themselves into an established structure but rather an endless process of interacting cultural reinventions, with no transcendental, "unified" end in sight. But if "unity" is a cultural as well as philosophical chimera, so is pure "plurality," the idea of organically unified cultures developing side by side according to singular lines of descent.

Like the self, the existent "culture" is always at risk when one is engaged in the creative use of intelligence, the aim of which is to liberate action for ends determined in the process of experience, not preformulated by the social order. "Action restricted to given and fixed ends may attain great technical efficiency," Dewey wrote, "but efficiency is the only quality to which it can lay claim. Such action is mechanical (or becomes so), no matter what the scope of the pre-formed end, be it the Will of God or *Kultur.*" Indeed, such use of intelligence, to Dewey "*is* servile, even when the end is labeled moral, religious, or esthetic." In contrast, the "pragmatic lesson" is that the creative intelligence develops "within the sphere of action for the sake of possibilities not yet given."[31] Hence the exemplary role of artistic creation in cultural development, poised against the specter of metaphysical *Kultur* and its corollary, enslavement.

Aesthetics acquired a particular importance in cultural pluralism in part because of the view of art as "consummatory" of experience, in the sense Dewey proposed (that is, experience as "involved, meaningful, and shared response to the world"),[32] not because of an elitist divorcing of "art" from material production and everyday experience, or a belief that art revealed eternal truth and beauty. Similarly, the interest of Boasians like Ruth Benedict and Edward Sapir in patterns of aesthetic "intuition" built up over time within each cultural group surely owed something to their admiration for Dewey.[33] Indeed, recognition of the relative, historically contingent nature of aesthetic value and the view of art as active, patterned "consummation" of experience is another link between the Boasians and the pragmatists.[34] Remarkably, even Boas' own turn (in the 1920s) from historical reconstructionist studies to interest in the relationship of individual invention to cultural change followed upon his acquaintance with Dewey and was carried on most notably by Benedict—who was Dewey's student before becoming Boas'.[35]

Dewey's ideas also fit the Boasian anthropologists' resistance to all forms of determinism and their historicist interest in cultural patterns or complexes built up out of fragments acquired in accidental contacts, as opposed to the British functionalist emphasis upon unified and internally consistent or "organic" cultural systems. As a matter of fact, in *Experience and Nature* Dewey quotes a passage from Alexander Goldenweiser that undoubtedly had been produced out of Goldenweiser's own assimilation of both Dewey and Boas: "Cultural reality is never

wholly deterministic nor yet wholly accidental, never wholly psychological nor yet wholly objective, never wholly of yesterday nor yet wholly of
today, but combines all of these in its existential reality. . . . A recon-
structive synthesis re-establishes the synthetic unity necessarily lost in
the process of analytic dismemberment." Dewey writes that these words
"fairly define the problem of philosophy, although intended for
another purpose."[36] Years later he lamented that his book *Experience and
Nature* should have been entitled *Culture and Nature,* because of the
common misunderstanding of his use of the term "experience." Culture, Dewey came to believe, is the very form of human experience.

Clearly the interethnic and interdisciplinary traffic between pragmatism, ethnography, and cultural pluralism was fruitful in each direction.
Cultural anthropology was a crucial factor in making Dewey understand
that a philosophy of experience must take "cultural" factors into
account.[37] And, much like Dewey, Kallen sought a solution to the
problem of the Western divorce between "vocation" and "culture" in
the idea that the human vocation *is* culture, the "art" of being human
(also Ruth Benedict's position). Hence "the segregation of the codes of
the consumption of products from the arts of producing the products
consumed" results in a "cut-flower culture" and strictly utilitarian labor,
a divorce between work and consummatory experience—the unifica-
tion of which was Dewey's idea of "art as experience."[38] As Kallen would
later tell the story, the Germans had begun the practice of identifying
Kultur with "an exclusive racism of attitudes, thought and things," identifying "culture" with a master race and servile labor with all those inherently lacking it. The divorce of labor from culture was intertwined with
the development of racist science. (It should be pointed out here that
a strong countertradition, from which Boas emerged, also existed in
Germany in the late nineteenth century.)[39] Kallen pointedly credited
anthropologists for "the notion that the vocations of a community were
the nucleus of its culture; that their relations were reciprocal and com-
penetrative" and if you divorced them from each other you menaced
both culture and "supporting vocations."[40]

By the mid-twenties Kallen also apparently turned away from his earlier racial essentialism as he began emphasizing the importance of
being free to join and leave different communities. This changing conception of the full implications of pluralism went together with a new
concept of "culture." Any living "culture," as Kallen now thought of it,
is inherently "plural," a function of the diversity of actions of the indi-

viduals that "belong" to it. Moreover, "cultural growth is founded upon Cultural Pluralism. Cultural Pluralism is possible only in a democratic society whose institutions encourage individuality in groups, in persons, in temperaments, whose program liberates these individualities and guides them into a fellowship of freedom and cooperation." Kallen left Americans with a stark choice between "Kultur Klux Klan or Cultural Pluralism."[41] A live culture must continually change to accommodate the unexpected, that which will not "fit" inherited paradigms—and the "temperament" most susceptible to such alteration is "democratic." The great artists and revitalizers of democratic culture would be those who cross thresholds of social difference and who cultivate an intercultural expansion of sensibilities, a tremendous receptivity to otherness at constant risk to the coherence of the self, of "the culture."

One form of the "other" that challenged Kallen's theorizing was African American culture. In 1924, in a footnote to his essay "'Americanization' and the Cultural Prospect," he wrote: "I do not discuss the influence of the negro upon the esthetic material and cultural character of the South and the rest of the United States. This is at once too considerable and too recondite in its processes for casual mention. It requires a separate analysis."[42] Even for Kallen, the relationship of African Americans to the American polity was too complex, too "different" from that of the "European strains," to be easily integrated into his discussion. The vital role of African Americans in the actual production of the so-called American Idea (including his own reformulation of it!) presented contradictions to his concept of America—invariably Eurocentric—that he never addressed.[43] The same could be said of John Dewey and Randolph Bourne. But at the very moment that Kallen penned his footnote, a movement was being announced that performed a transformation of his concepts as it staged the importance of African American experiences and aesthetics to U.S. culture. For 1924 was also the year of the coming-out of the "New Negro."

The Harlem Renaissance program of using the arts to advance freedom and equality derived not from a desire to prove that blacks could reason and write, as has often been charged, but from a belief in the central role of aesthetic experience in the achievement of new forms of solidarity and understanding, and thus in the transformation and national integration of cultures. The Harlem Renaissance was in fact a striking experiment in cultural pluralism, with pervasive connections to philosophical pragmatism and Boasian anthropology. As one of the chief aesthetic theorists of the New Negro, Alain Locke is a particularly significant figure in this regard.

Locke, with most other participants in the movement, objected to thinking of the African American literary tradition as a cultural "bulkhead" rigidly separated from the so-called Anglo-American tradition, or even as a linear development of black writers influenced chiefly by each other. Nonetheless, he believed in the continuing importance of race to the understanding of culture and affirmed the "cultural racialism," as he called it, of the Harlem Renaissance.

Throughout his important article of 1924, "The Concept of Race as Applied to Social Culture," Locke relied upon—and responded to—the works of Boas and his students.[44] He noted the importance of their point that there is no organic or causal connection between race and culture, yet he differed with the denial of Robert Lowie, in particular, of "all significant connection between racial and cultural factors."[45] To Locke this contention was premature; he believed that eventually race would be necessary in a restricted form to explain cultural differences.

Although race may not be inherently connected with culture, one does find factors integrally related that cannot be explained as mere historical coincidences; one finds "combinations of group traits" that resist change. (An equivalent point is actually made by Boas himself in *Anthropology and Modern Life,* although not with specific reference to race.) Adopting Alexander Goldenweiser's startling contention that race is culturally determined, not the other way around, Locke contends that the term "race" can be retained as an explanatory tool without reliance on racial essentialism.[46] However fortuitously a "racial type" may have come into existence, once in place, the race concept reinforces a culture complex, enhances loyalty to it, makes it highly resistant and self-perpetuating.

Indeed, Locke makes a point later developed by George Devereux and Fredrik Barth: that ethnicization and assimilation often go on simultaneously. That is, a group with a weak sense of racial or ethnic identity becomes increasingly race-conscious as its contacts with another group increase. Contact leads to heightened boundary construction and racial stress, even as acculturation goes on.[47] Indeed, each group affects the other in many and complex ways so that all are "composite" rather than "pure" or traceable to a single ancestral source (Dewey's point about "American" cultures). Nonetheless, they choose (or are forced) to maintain their "racial" identities. The culture as a whole, then, embracing these group identities that insist on difference even while bound together by certain shared values, domains of conflict, and discursive formations (including shared concepts of race), can "only . . . be explained as the resultant of the meeting and reciprocal influence of several culture strains, several ethnic contributions."[48] Locke's theory addresses two of the central issues of American cultural studies today: In what way can we speak of "American culture," given the diverse traditions it must include? And how can we adopt an ironic attitude toward the concept of race without effacing the real consequences of racialism and racism in U.S. history?

Locke's very focus upon the relationship between race and culture points to the specific North American racialist heritage; the form cultural pluralism has taken in the United States has been powerfully shaped by American constructions of race—which have, it should be added, changed over time. Yet cultural pluralism clearly *need not* proceed along racial vectors in the way it has in the United States, a fact Locke does not seem to have considered. His is a distinctively (North) "American" racialization of cultural pluralist ideology.

Beyond suggesting that there is indeed an "American" cultural field—a scene of conflict and commerce—that diverse cultural groups share (unequally) in antagonistic as well as cooperative relations shaped by the distribution of social and economic power, Locke jettisons the assumption that the shared "culture" of a nation is best represented by that of the politically dominant group. Attention must be paid to "fusion values" of the various constituent elements. "Especially does this newer view insist upon the disassociation of the claims of political dominance and cultural productivity, and combat the traditional view that all or even the best elements of a culture are the contribution of the ethnic group which in a mixed culture has political dominance and is in dynastic control."[49] Extrapolating from Boasian anthropology and cultural pluralism, and affirming the value of cosmopolitanism as opposed to racial exclusivism, Locke developed his theory that African American culture would not only build upon its unique values, but as the most "mixed" of American cultures was best endowed to advance American aesthetics and thus to play the dominant role in the Americanization of culture in the United States—a position toward which the ideas of both Locke and Du Bois, as well as a host of younger artists, converge. This Americanization would be at the same time a "neo-Africanization," deeply affected by the work of Boasians and Dewey's friend Albert Barnes in developing appreciation of African cultures and arts, combating (unevenly) the cult of the African as "primitive and exotic."

The cultural pluralist movement—which was also emphatically an *American cultural nationalist* movement—included a heterogeneous group, but the lines most germane to the Harlem Renaissance ran from James and Royce through Du Bois, Dewey, Kallen, Locke, and Charles S. Johnson, along with the *Seven Arts* group and members of the *Nation, New Republic, Masses,* and *Liberator* editorial staffs. The intellectual connections between these individuals were important, but so were the effects of their combined influence upon the institutions of elite culture. Their ideas helped spawn—and create audiences for—new magazines and publishers that transformed the cultural landscape and opened spaces for the emergence of African American literary modernism. Thus the argument for the crucial significance of connections between the Harlem Renaissance and pragmatism, Boasian anthropology, and cultural pluralism does not depend simply on individual "influences," such as the relationships between James, Du Bois, Fauset, Dewey, Park, Washington, Charles Johnson, Royce, Locke, Kallen, Boas, Herskovits, Hurston, and so forth. It does not even depend on an argument for the centrality of particular persons to the Harlem Renaissance as elder philosophers or deans of the movement. It depends at least as much upon the way the American intellectual terrain was transformed through the circulation of pragmatist, Boasian, and cultural pluralist theories, setting up a new field of forces, a new web of positions that became institutionalized on the left wing of U.S. literary culture, precisely by the 1920s.

4

Cultural Nationalism and the Lyrical Left

The relationship of New Negro cultural politics to the most vocal white literary nationalists of the teens and twenties must also attract attention in any attempt to situate the Harlem Renaissance vis-à-vis American modernism. In recent years the importance of the prewar "rebellion" centered in New York (though incubated in Chicago from as early as Dewey's and Van Vechten's years there) has received increasing recognition, but its close relationship with the Harlem Renaissance remains obscure. While treatments of the cultural nationalist "lyrical left" (John P. Diggins' apt phrase)[1] have paid scant attention to the relationship between the white intellectuals and African American culture, treatments of the Harlem Renaissance in turn make only passing allusions to the ways in which the spirit of the *Seven Arts* group, for example, intertwined with the African American intellectual tradition. Scholars frequently mention Madison Grant's *The Passing of the Great Race* as defining the context of the Harlem Renaissance; they rarely stress Randolph Bourne's "Trans-national America," which was published in the same year and directly opposed Grant's point of view.[2] Nor have they attended very closely to Van Wyck Brooks's version of American cultural nationalism in *Letters and Leadership*. Yet these essays precisely define the reference points to which Alain Locke alludes in *The New Negro* when he aligns his project with the search for a new America.

Toward the Americanization of American Literature

As Marcus Klein has said, "When Ezra Pound greeted the American *Risorgimento* of the years following 1912, he was in fact recognizing an effect largely created by the Young Americans."[3] Though later overshadowed by the expatriate modernists whose status Pound would do so much to institutionalize, the Young Americans actually found, or perhaps created, the audience for the new magazines and publishers that Pound and company initially relied upon. The young rebels, in Klein's words, "would acknowledge the cultural possibilities of all of that America which was most foreign to New England"—contributing in the process to New York's decisive triumph over Boston as the publishing capital of the nation, led by new firms founded by Jews.

Too often these literary journalists and culture critics are assimilated by opponents of the "canon" with academic critics who established the professional field of American literature in universities. As Gerald Graff has pointed out, although the left-wing culture critics of the teens and twenties helped shape the academic study of American literature (and perhaps gave it crucial impetus), by the time the absorption of some of their ideas had taken place in the universities a reaction against them had already set in; even their cultural nationalist and "transnationalist" views were co-opted and transformed. Ironically, for example, American literature as an academic discipline got a crucial boost from the patriotic hysteria during and after World War I—the same hysteria that killed *The Masses* and *The Seven Arts*.[4] Current emphasis upon an almost predestined opposition between "canonical" texts (usually by white male authors) and "oppositional" writers on the margin of the "dominant culture" as it is now constituted results from the specific history of academic cultural politics since the 1930s and obscures significant interrelations predating World War II.

Interest in black writing and in revising the American literary canon were parts of the turn toward a pluralistic conception of American society, stimulated greatly by the massive immigration of polyglot peoples which began some years before the black migration from the South. Van Wyck Brooks himself had grown up in an almost purely Anglo-Saxon world, but the world he found himself inhabiting as an adult—specifically, New York—was different and required a change in cultural perspective. His second book, *America's Coming-of-Age*, he had planned to entitle *A Fable for Yankees* until his Jewish publisher, Ben Huebsch, pointed out that not all Americans were Yankees: "They were as multi-racial as the crew of the 'Pequod' in *Moby-Dick.*" The perspective represented by Melville, Whitman, Jefferson, Paine, and Lincoln attracted him, for "*this* line had no parallel in Europe or elsewhere. . . . It expressed a country that was settled 'by the people of all nations,' as Melville said, and that 'all nations' might therefore 'claim for their own'—in short, the cradle or germ of the world state of the future in which all men were [as Whitman had written] 'children of an equal brood.'" The Midwest, which had preceded Greenwich Village in spawning a native literary movement and had then lost its bright young writers (Dreiser, Van Vechten, Floyd Dell, Francis Hackett, Marianne Moore, and Sherwood Anderson, for example) to New York, seemed to Brooks the answer to Oswald Spengler. *The Decline of the West,* Brooks felt, certainly did not refer to Whitman's West, "the predestined home of this country's distinctive realities and ideas." Brooks connected his hopes for a new (North) American culture with liberation movements and new cultural nationalisms in India, China, and South America, on which *The Seven Arts* glowingly reported.[5]

The Seven Arts viewed the supposed exhaustion of European civilization positively, for it gave the colonized peoples of Asia and Africa, as well as North and South America, an opportunity to achieve cultural "self-possession" while promising a new and freer development of global cultures out of the toils of feudalism and empire. Late in life Brooks still held to this faith, arguing that "Europe's extremity had been the opportunity of Asia and Africa, and a limitless horizon opened out before the peoples there. . . . How could Americans feel that the 'decline of the West,' certainly true for Europe, was true for them? And yet our literary life was still under the European spell and reflected its apprehension of the end of all things."[6]

The villain in the wings here is, of course, T. S. Eliot. In stark contrast to Brooks's idea of a "native" modernism that identified American transnationalism with global anti-imperialism, Eliot sought to "recover a past ritualistic [European] civilization," in Stephen Spender's words. "The young Eliot seemed to visualize politics as the war of the traditional forces in the society against the liberal and progressive, cosmopolitan ones," and he was overtly anti-Semitic.[7] Eliot's Anglophilia, moreover, went together with a horror of "paganism" and, specifically, Africa. Eliot's attitude toward Africa, Neo-African religious ritual, and pre-Christian Greece were interconnected, identified with the Conradian horror of the geographical "heart of darkness": "The Africa of 'cactus land,' impenetrably black nights, suffocating heat, scrub deserts, ticking insects, and throbbing tom-toms means in his poetry the horror that will finally engulf the Dantesque light 'lume' of the European civilization."[8] For Eliot, Africa was *the* representation of "the horror" on the cosmographic map, the place from which the Carthaginian St. Augustine had been plucked, "burning," by God. As Spender further informs us, "Toward the end of his life, when his health required it, he had to spend winters in North Africa and Barbados. He dreaded this."[9] If Greenwich Village cultural nationalists shared certain stereotypical images of Africa with Eliot, they evaluated them in a radically opposed manner, one that affiliated them with the African American writers of Harlem more than with their white compatriots in London. Moreover, Eliot's dread of Africa and Barbados cannot, in the final analysis, be entirely separated from his dread of Mark Twain's and Langston Hughes's Missouri.

The connection between blackness and Americanism did not escape the white critics of the left, although they did not give it nearly the importance it deserved in their most influential essays and books. This connection exists, moreover, in uncertain relation to "exoticism" and "primitivism," which by definition stress radical difference rather than transracial identity. Rosalie M. Jonas, for example, wrote in an article for *Art World,* excerpted by *The Crisis* in 1917, that black Southern culture had yet to receive the treatment it deserved in literature, and that without such treatment there could be no genuine Southern literature of distinction. Whites, Jonas argued, had done little to develop a native folk culture in the South; even Joel Chandler Harris had been able to give only "artificial reflections" of the South's only folk tradition: "For none of these have gone—perhaps none of our 'superior' race can ever go—as simply, as directly, so with 'the heart of a little child' to Nature. And of all the aliens grafted on the South from France, Spain and Ireland, everywhere, the Negro is the one exotic whose roots, so fiercely wrenched from their native soil, have taken firmest hold."

Jonas' comments ring with the romantic and even Emersonian glorification of the "primitive" and "childlike" as she argues for the artistic advantages of the once-enslaved: "Enslaved by man, the Southern land adopted him with tenderness and warmth. And he grew so close to her that he became her spokesman, her interpreter"; now whites of the

South can only produce art by borrowing from him. But even in borrowing, they have seen only the "funny side" or doted on the Negro's "affection," "fidelity," and "humility," while coon songs and minstrel shows have obscenely debased "the only real Minstrel this noise-deafened country has ever known!" Yet white exploiters will be duly repaid, for "Art herself, now, to shame us, is holding out her hand to him and thrusting us aside." For all its primitivism, Jonas' critique is both political and aesthetic. The revival of the South's most dramatic and "picturesque" material awaits only the "spirit of intellectual democracy" and will come from Negroes above all. Moreover, Jonas suggests the necessity of a "Negro Poetic" that elitist "free versifiers" will likely reject as too tuneful to be "modern."[10]

Jonas' remarks indicate that an audience was awaiting work like that of Hughes. Yet the primitivism she espouses, which was hardly unique, stresses an "organic" connection between black folk and the American soil typical of romantic nationalism going back to Herder; this primitivism actually conflicts with exoticism except to the extent that "America" remains exotic to white Southerners—conversely, to the extent that they remain "exotics" in America. Jonas' thesis, then, inverts the assumptions of such earlier abolitionists and colonizationists as Harriet Beecher Stowe, who portrayed African Americans as exotics in an essentially white nation (a motif carried on even in some early Hughes poems). Nonetheless, her argument fortifies romantic racialist notions that affected the cultural field in which the Harlem Renaissance emerged. Notably, one of Jonas' "race" poems published in *The Crisis* has recently been included in an anthology of black women's poetry from the Harlem Renaissance.[11]

The best-known white romantic nationalists did not pick up on the point Jonas had made, one that had been made for years in relation to spirituals. Despite their cultural nationalist and cultural pluralist positions, and despite their sympathy for and occasional participation in the movement for black civil rights, authors such as Brooks, Randolph Bourne, Lewis Mumford, and even Waldo Frank repeatedly failed to appreciate the significance of African American culture. This is particularly striking in Brooks's case, for his best friend and Harvard roommate, Edward Sheldon, had anticipated the movement for a "Negro drama" with his controversial work of 1909, *The Nigger,* provocatively subtitled *An American Play.*[12] Black writers would take it upon themselves to reconceptualize what American cultural nationalism might mean—

sometimes, like Jonas, by emphasizing their "organic" relation to the soil, but more significantly by demonstrating the centrality of race and the power of blackness in American civilization.

One can easily imagine Alain Locke's thought process as he read such works of Van Wyck Brooks, his Harvard classmate, as *America's Coming-of-Age* (Locke would later speak of the Negro's coming of age) or the *Seven Arts* essays that became *Letters and Leadership*. Indeed, S. P. Fullinwider has referred to Locke as "the Van Wyck Brooks of the black Americans," and briefly compared the Harlem Renaissance with the "Little Renaissance" of New York in which Brooks figured so prominently.[13] Supporting Fullinwider, Charles C. Alexander suggests that Carl Van Vechten, for one, "grasped the basic fact that what was commonly called either the Harlem Renaissance or the Negro Renaissance was a reenactment in microcosm of the insurgent movement within white thought and culture in the prewar period."[14] Significantly, some of Van Vechten's pioneering criticism on black popular music was published in *The Seven Arts;* Van Vechten was also instrumental in reviving Melville's reputation in this period.[15]

Brooks and the *Seven Arts* critics probably did not so much "influence" Locke in the traditional sense as confirm positions he had developed or was in the process of developing, while giving him hope for a break in the Anglo-American tradition that would benefit African American letters. Like Locke, Brooks had been intellectually shaped by the arguments of Santayana against the "genteel tradition," and some of his positions had been anticipated by Locke's essay "The American Temperament," which had appeared in the *North American Review* in 1911.[16] Even Randolph Bourne's celebrated essay, "Trans-national America," would not have struck Locke as entirely new, since he had been intimately involved in Horace Kallen's conceptualization of cultural pluralism. Yet it is clear that Locke picked up new ammunition, particularly from Brooks, for his critical program; furthermore, Locke's incorporation of the *Seven Arts* critics' ideas foreshadowed the development of related positions by younger authors such as Langston Hughes and Jean Toomer.[17]

Brooks, of course, is famous for the influence of his argument in *America's Coming-of-Age* that the weakness of American literature and art derived from the hegemonic "Puritan" and "pioneer" traditions, which had fostered a commercial civilization and prevented the emergence of a native literature true to the vulgate realities of American life. In his works of the teens, Brooks and his cohorts at *The Seven Arts* provided a cluster of terms that helped shape the discourse not only of the "Little Renaissance" but of the New Negro movement. In the process they also, as Gorham Munson would point out, "found the audience that would grow and support the younger publishing houses of the Twenties— firms like Boni & Liveright and Alfred A. Knopf and B. W. Huebsch."[18] These were the firms that published the cultural pluralists and left-wing cultural nationalists and subsequently the New Negroes. Moreover, in addition to publishing Claude McKay for the first time in the United States, *The Seven Arts* printed Eugene O'Neill's first story, criticism by Joel Spingarn, and work by Sherwood Anderson (whose wife founded the Ethiopian Art Players), Carl Van Vechten, and Robert Edmond Jones (set designer for the Provincetown and, on occasion, the Hapgood Colored Players). The magazine also published Hiram Moderwell's and Van Vechten's pieces arguing for ragtime as the basis of American vernacular music.[19] Thus the connection of *The Seven Arts* with the Harlem Renaissance is closer than one would guess based upon its general neglect of African American culture. Arna Bontemps regarded the appearance of "The Harlem Dancer" in the magazine as a herald of what was to come: "Now this I submit was the anticipation and the theme of an early outburst of creativity later described as the Negro or Harlem Renaissance."[20]

The *Seven Arts* (and *Masses*) group's orientation was greatly affected by John Butler Yeats, William's father, who frequently talked about the Irish Renaissance writers, "so many of whom had grown up in his studio and presence." Only a year after the elder Yeats had immigrated to New York in 1908, Brooks and Sheldon fell in with him (about the time Sheldon's *The Nigger* opened); before long he found himself surrounded by Robert Henri, John Sloan, and George Bellows—artists connected with the "Ash Can School" and *The Masses,* and among the first American artists to portray African Americans "realistically." Yeats had been an early Irish admirer of Whitman and Thoreau; now, holding forth in the restaurant of Petitpas' rooming house on West Twenty-ninth Street, he served as a conduit of Celtic Revival concepts to Manhattan. As Brooks would write, "We felt we were on the verge of a not dissimilar movement of our own, the first phase of another revival that expressed an American coming-of-age, an escape from our old colonial dependence on England."[21] Other figures of the Irish movement were also in New York by then, attending the Petitpas' gatherings, notably Mary (Mollie) and

Padraic Colum. Padraic had been the first of the new Irish dramatists to have his work produced, and had inaugurated, with John Millington Synge, the Irish peasant drama. It was such Irish writers, in fact, who helped Brooks come to appreciate Emerson, Thoreau, and Whitman as creators of an "indigenous" literature of "spirit."[22] Mary Colum found the modern extensions of this literature in the "new regionalism" of Dreiser and Sherwood Anderson, in which an "American" people, unlike any to be found in England, struggled toward conscious expression.

Brooks and his associates looked to the arts—especially poetry—to provoke a revolution in consciousness and, by extension, the social order. Attacking the Anglocentric literary nationalism of the genteel tradition and contemporary humanist criticism, which dominated the literary marketplace until the mid-teens, Brooks found little upon which to found a new, genuinely "American" literary and intellectual tradition. The America he saw lacked the peasantry and folk traditions of European cultures, from which great culture was supposed ordinarily to develop. The "pioneers" had been a restless, mobile, materialistic people, always seeking out the "better chance." And, perfectly suited to the imperatives of a pioneering people, the Puritan ethic had driven a wedge between the spiritual and the material realms, making the life of the soul and the feelings intensely private and otherworldly, "effeminate," repressed. In the place of a native tradition expressing the spirit of the (male?) people as it had been shaped by daily realities, the United States had, on the one hand, an imported culture, "highbrow" and unassimilable except as a false gauge of status; and, on the other hand, a thoroughly degraded and commercialized popular culture.

The point of Brooks's criticism, then, was to precipitate a cultural movement that could provide the American people with a "collective spiritual life," and in this he considered himself to be going beyond the pragmatists. His critique of "pragmatic sociology" is telling. While James and Dewey personally had seen the necessity for faith in something more than intelligence and the efficient pursuit of already chosen objects, they had not, according to Brooks, passed this critical perspective on to their followers, in whom their philosophy was used to justify a "complacent, mechanistic view of life." As a result, the reformers, muckrakers, and social workers of the settlement houses could not see beyond the idea of "raising" the downtrodden to the mediocre level of the average American community. The people they wanted to "lift," charged Brooks, were already "immeasurably above [that level] in the scale of the spirit."[23] Brooks was speaking particularly of immigrants, but the application to African Americans must have been obvious to black readers, as it was to Locke and, later, to Jean Toomer. Brooks felt that the immigrants, detached from the nourishing cultures they had left, needed not to be simply assimilated into a spiritually bankrupt society. Instead, he said, "we" must show them a culture worth "grafting onto," and this could be achieved only through visionary art.

Ultimately, Brooks envisioned a "newly-found center" around which currently disorganized elements would eagerly order themselves, each contributing its unique attributes. Yet one cannot help suspecting an assumption on Brooks's part that the "center" would be defined by white male intellectuals of more than one generation's residence in North America, and his references to the "racial" inheritance of the United States have clear ethnocentric overtones. Black writers, on the other hand, would point out that the United States *did* have a native folk culture, born of suffering and intimate with the soil, emotionally expressive, and above all rich in spirit as only the culture of an oppressed people could be. "There are today," W. E. B. Du Bois had written more than a decade before Brooks's *America's Coming-of-Age,* "no truer exponents of the pure human spirit of the Declaration of Independence than the American Negroes; there is no true American music but the wild sweet melodies of the Negro slave; the American fairy tales and folklore are Indian and African; and, all in all, we black men seem the sole oasis of simple faith and reverence in a dusty desert of dollars and smartness."[24] Nonetheless, Brooks's views helped shape the institutional context in which the Harlem Renaissance would develop. As V. F. Calverton correctly pointed out in *The Liberation of American Literature,* "It was not until the development of a national consciousness, and the consequent interest in things native, that the Negro's contributions to art were taken with any seriousness."[25] The interest in black writing was intimately connected with the beginning of the extra-academic canonization of such white authors as Whitman, Thoreau, Melville, Dickinson, and Mark Twain.

Brooks's friend Randolph Bourne wrote much closer to the spirit of Horace Kallen, whose work—like that of Josiah Royce and William James—he greatly admired.[26] With Brooks, Bourne helped define the combined aesthetic and political agenda of the prewar "Rebellion." A former student and disciple of John Dewey's—as well as Joel Spingarn's—at Columbia, he died before fulfilling his intention of addressing the "Negro problem," but his work is worth reading in relation to the Harlem Renaissance, which blossomed after his death. In his important essay, "Trans-national America," Bourne attacked ethnocentrism and racist ethnology (praising Boas) and called for a higher ideal than the "melting-pot," which equated "Americanizing" with "Anglo-Saxonizing." Moreover, he commented on the irony that, of all the ethnic groups in the United States, Anglo-Americans were the most firmly bound to their Old World culture and yet the quickest to complain that more recent immigrants did not sufficiently embrace "Americanism." Amplifying the views of Kallen that people should retain their cultural distinctiveness, he charged: "Just so surely as we tend to disintegrate these nuclei of nationalistic culture do we tend to create hordes of men and women without a spiritual country, cultural outlaws, without taste, without standards but those of the mob."[27] To Bourne, the "assimilated" citizen was a *marginal* one, at the fringe of a cultural community; outside the centripetal force of a cultural "nucleus," he or she became a "detached fragment," the vacuous member of the American crowd, whose only culture was consumer culture.

Bourne stood for a sort of pluralist-"integrationist" position like Kallen's in which different ethnic identities would be joined in a cosmopolitan federation. The war in Europe itself proved the necessity for such federalism, not to mention the folly of identifying the United States with European civilization. Opposing American nationalism to the "weary old nationalism" of Europe—"belligerent, exclusive, inbreeding"—he envisioned the United States as the first "international nation." Its citizens would "demand for integration a genuine integrity, a wholeness and soundness of enthusiasm and purpose which can only come when no national colony within our America feels that it is being discriminated against or that its cultural case is being prejudged." Incredibly, Bourne never explicitly applied his theory to the situation of African American culture, even as he lamented the lack of any "tenacious folk-tradition and folk-style" in the United States.[28]

Bourne found tremendous significance in the opening of Ridgely Torrence's *Three Plays for a Negro Theatre* on the verge of American entry into World War I. "The incredible stupidity of the plays' press representative seems to have kept both the colored and the white public from being prepared for the enormous significance and impressiveness of this production," he wrote. Torrence's folk plays, reminiscent of

Synge's, represented the sort of direction that Bourne felt the United States should be exploring rather than entangling itself in a capitalist, Anglocentric war effort. Particularly ironic was the closing play, *Simon the Cyrenian* (probably the inspiration of a later Countee Cullen poem of that title), as produced on Good Friday, the very day the United States declared war: "You could hear the audience catch its breath as it realized the piercing meaning of this heroic little drama of non-resistance played before a Christian nation that was going into a world war on the very day that its churches celebrated devoutly the anniversary of this very warning."[29] The same war that would end the brief life of *The Seven Arts* (directly because of Bourne's vocal pacifism) closed the production of Torrence's plays after only a week's run, a poignant indication of the politics of culture at the turning point of American modernism. Unfortunately, however, Bourne left little evidence of interest in black culture beyond his response to Torrence's "Negro drama"; he died young in December 1918. One can only speculate about what effect the Harlem Renaissance might have had on his thinking.

Bourne's view of the war deserves mention here because it suggests the effect of the war upon the ethno-cultural politics of American modernism. From Bourne one begins to sense how profoundly American entry into the war affected the direction of American literary culture vis-à-vis the prewar cultural nationalist movement. Led by the least democratic, most Anglocentric elements of American life and by big business, the war effort, charged Bourne, linked American fortunes to English and French problems and dampened the movement within the United States toward an integration of disparate ethnic groups as well as toward an "indigenous" social-democratic ethos. Moreover, after it, many of the most gifted American writers would be caught up in the escapist dramas of expatriation and the postwar pessimism of Europe. "Our intellectual class might have been occupied, during the last two years of war," he wrote in 1917, "in studying and clarifying the ideals and aspirations of the American democracy, in discovering a true Americanism which would not have been merely nebulous but might have federated the different ethnic groups and traditions. . . . They might have turned their intellectual energy not to the problem of jockeying the nation into war, but to the problem of using our vast neutral power to attain democratic ends for the rest of the world and ourselves."[30] Bourne astutely critiqued the liberal idealism that led the likes of

Dewey, Du Bois, and Spingarn to "close ranks" with Wilson's armies. The "nebulous ideals of democracy and liberalism and civilization," he charged, "had never meant anything fruitful to those ruling classes who now so glibly used them," yet intellectuals fell into the trap of accepting such rationalizations. "The whole era has been spiritually wasted. The outstanding feature has been not its Americanism but its intense colonialism. . . . The official, reputable expression of the intellectual class has been that of the English colonial. . . . The great masses, the other ethnic groups [except German apologists], were inarticulate."[31]

Far from supporting the war for rational reasons, to make the world more democratic, liberal intellectuals had succumbed to the age-old colonial mentality of their class: "Never having felt responsibility for labor wars and oppressed masses and excluded races at home, they had a large fund of idle emotional capital to invest in the oppressed nationalities and ravaged villages of Europe."[32] Such charges hit John Dewey hard; he apparently never forgave his former student, even though, as Robert B. Westbrook has pointed out, Bourne's ideas are more faithful to Dewey's philosophy than his own position on the war.[33] One reason for Bourne's virulent opposition was his conviction that even the hoped-for "League to Enforce Peace" would merely solidify international relations in their current imperialistic form.[34] To Bourne, then, the threat American entry into the world war posed to American cultural nationalism cum cultural pluralism was integral with the threat to genuine international peace and justice. Surely Dewey himself eventually recognized the force of Bourne's argument, even if he could never admit it. His disillusionment with Wilson and the League of Nations marked a turning point in his career. Significantly, he found rejuvenation of his hopes in China, where he spent most of 1919–1921 lecturing and observing the New Culture movement, which adopted him as an intellectual celebrity.

Prewar to Postwar

The basic thrust of the "transnational" cultural nationalist movement continued through the twenties, notably in regionalist and ethnic fiction; indeed, one could argue that it expressed itself most forcefully through the Harlem Renaissance. Most students of the twenties, following Henry May, have accepted too easily the idea that all the intellectuals were disillusioned after the war. On the contrary, even John Dewey had written, "The war has shown that we are a new body and a new spirit in the world."[35] Van Wyck Brooks and Waldo Frank took heart in the knowledge that even as Eliot achieved preeminence among poets in the English tradition, writers in India, Ireland, Russia, and South America still revered the tradition of Paine, Jefferson, Emerson, Whitman, and Lincoln. Neither in America nor in Russia had the war destroyed the sense of "a world beginning again."[36] Anatole France himself had told Waldo Frank, "Make no mistake. Europe is a tale that has been told. Our long twilight is before us. But I believe in your American dream."[37]

The twilight of Europe and the rise of a new order connected with hopes for the rise of dominated people of color around the globe. Romain Rolland, the prewar prophet whose *Jean-Christophe* electrified Frank, Locke, and Toomer among others, and who became Europe's chief proselytizer for Gandhi in the 1920s, wrote in a letter excerpted for *The Crisis* on October 26, 1923, "I believe that we are but at the beginning of a great catastrophic era in which shall disappear a great part of our old 'white' civilization, with its virtues, its vices, its beauty, its ugliness. Another again shall flourish, a new order shall take birth."[38] As Charles C. Alexander has argued, interpreters have been so preoccupied with a *portion* of the period's literature—neatly identified as that of a "lost generation"—that they have missed important continuities with the idealistic prewar rebellion.[39]

One of the crucial links between the prewar and postwar periods was Waldo Frank's *Our America,* a book that Brooks called "the Bible of our generation."[40] With Brooks and Randolph Bourne, Frank had been one of the leaders of *The Seven Arts* and among the first critics to welcome Sherwood Anderson. His encouragement of and intimate friendship with Jean Toomer during the composition of *Cane* is well known. Indeed, Toomer had been greatly impressed by *Our America* even before meeting Frank at a New York party, when he still aspired to become a musician à la Jean-Christophe. Gorham Munson's reflections provide a fitting testimony to *Our America*'s influence upon a type of postwar youth that has been largely forgotten: "The book dazzled my immediate generation. We were then two or three years out of college and more recently out of military service. . . . We had begun to read Whitman . . . the *Little Review,* . . . the *Nation,* and the *New Republic.* . . . We were ready for eloquence on the promise and the dream of America. Waldo Frank came swiftly to proclaim that promise and dream; and his was the voice that spoke thrillingly of a conception of America to be created by the young writers and artists."[41] To Munson, Frank's clarion call of a *religious* awakening to the meaning of America heralded the spirit of the twenties, a movement beyond muckraking, critical realism, and naturalism. As Munson's remarks reveal, at least one wing of the prewar rebellion kept faith in the "promise" of the nation even while castigating the culture they saw about them.

Our America built on some of Van Wyck Brooks's most important ideas. Anglo-Saxons, extroverted and culture-denying, had thrown off a rich culture to be shaped by harsh new conditions. Ascetic about sensuous living, Puritan and Pioneer had come together in their goal of acquisition and accumulation. Religion as a "mystical consciousness" did not survive the trans-Atlantic voyage of immigration. The subjective life shrank as the "boundless outer world" absorbed all attention and energy.[42] As a result, Frank charged, Anglo-Americans had never put down roots in the continent, while the cultures of the Indian and Mexican had succumbed to the white, industrial civilization. Those "earlier" groups had once had highly developed *cultures* with distinct and important spiritual relations to the world, much like the cultures indigenous to Europe and other continents. Yet the native American cultures were not superseded by ethnic cultures from Europe; the latter surrendered to forces of American materialism and Puritanism. Industrialism and materialism took over as gods, leaving the nation a cultural and spiritual wasteland. Yet Frank believed the "American chaos" would finally give birth to the living culture prophesied by Whitman and given heroic human form in the person of Lincoln.

The "spiritual pioneers" of the rising generation were answering the call of *Democratic Vistas,* he believed, moving beyond the sheer critical realism of the early Dreiser and the bleak though accurate poetry of Edgar Lee Masters. Frank's vision offered a direct counterpoint to the "lost generation" scenario. He conjured up the image of a sensitive soldier returned from the war with the awareness of society's rottenness, of its imminent breakup. Like a Hemingway character, the veteran sees the old promises and myths for the lies they are, yet "he slaps his thigh and finds that only he is sound. And who is he? That also he begins to understand. He is what America has immemorially denied: the dreamer, the lover. He is the failure. And he alone stands healthy above the crumble of worlds. . . . Give him time. He is the bringer of a new religion, he is the maker of multitudes." The voices of the revolutionist and the artist have yet to be fully integrated and widely heard, so "the impulse of New America is still unfused."[43]

If Waldo Frank's hopeful and mystical "religious" program looks rather ridiculous today, it did not lack followers in the 1920s, the age of A. R. Orage and G. I. Gurdjieff, who attracted black converts of the Harlem Renaissance among others. Yet one is struck by Frank's utter silence on the subject of African American culture, which would seem to offer much of what the other groups he mentions lack. In fact, his "veteran" could be one of the black veterans populating countless poems, sketches, and novels by African American authors after the war. Jean Toomer was quick to notice this in the book that had first drawn him to Frank; when they became close friends, he brought it up with his mentor, who subsequently planned a new edition including a section on black America.

As African American modernists read the laments about America's lack of a genuine folk tradition, lack of a peasantry out of which indigenous art could arise, lack of an adequately indigenous literary language, the implications were obvious. If the Anglo-American was a mobile pioneer bent on subduing the wilderness, aided by a Puritanism that banished spirituality to a private or otherworldly sphere, spiritually and emotionally repressed and denying himself the joy of sheer living, then African American culture seemed to provide everything the Anglo-American could not for a great artistic renaissance. In 1928 Alain Locke would write, "The Negro's predisposition toward the artistic, promising to culminate in a control and mastery of the spiritual and mystic as contrasted with the mechanical and practical aspects of life, makes him a spiritually needed and culturally desirable factor in American life."[44] Confined to plantations to work the land, denied opportunity for material wealth, denied even the *ambition* to be rich and "successful" in the conventional sense, thrown back upon the development of a rich spirituality as the only "freedom" achievable and the most impregnable defense against self-abasement in an oppressive, caste-based society, Southern black folks, ironically, had everything white folks most needed.

There were times, indeed, when thinkers like Du Bois and Locke wishfully worked the rigid dualism of American racial ideology into a vision of complementarity. The United States was destined to be the place where each race would give to the other what it lacked (a point that would also be a central theme of Waldo Frank's *Holiday* and an article of faith to Jean Toomer). In *The Souls of Black Folk,* for example, Du Bois stresses "the ideal of fostering and developing the traits and talents of the Negro, not in opposition to or contempt for other races, but rather in large conformity to the greater ideals of the American Republic, in order that some day on American soil two world-races may give each to each those characteristics both so sadly lack."[45] Part of the difficulty was proving to white people that blacks had anything of importance to offer. To prove this would require nothing less than a radical transformation in the consciousness of most whites. And art—such as *The Souls of Black Folk* itself—was one means of accomplishing such a transformation.

It should be obvious from this discussion of the prologue to the twenties that there were more complex and various ideological bases for the interest in black literature than a fascination for the primitive and exotic. That such a fascination did exist is undeniable, but it coexisted with very different, even contradictory, interests and beliefs, even in the same people. Moreover, the stereotypical images of blacks were not simply carryovers from the minstrel show tradition. They were, in many cases, deformations of that tradition and were often set out explicitly to undermine it. The uses of sexuality/sensuality and vernacular language are particularly important examples of how modernist American cultural nationalism "transvalues" the values of previously denigrated realms of expression.

Reclaiming the Vernacular and Emancipating the Body

The association between liberation of the body and American cultural nationalism was typically derived from Whitman, who was as much an ancestor of Hughes and Toomer as of Carl Sandburg and Waldo Frank. Moreover, for Whitman the liberation of the body carried political meanings associated with the liberation of women and of slaves. The banning of *Leaves of Grass* as an obscene book, the firing of "the good gray poet" from his job in the federal government for his poems of the body, made him an obvious ancestor to the new prophets of sexual freedom. And his underground reputation among homosexuals made him a particularly attractive model to the many New Negro writers who were bisexual or gay, such as McKay, Locke, Cullen, Wallace Thurman, Bruce Nugent, and possibly Hughes.[46]

From Whitman through the early "bohemian" American cultural nationalists to the "bohemian" wing of the New Negro movement, the liberation of sexual expression from Victorian prudery was regarded as one aspect of the liberation of U.S. culture from Anglophilia, Puritanism, and the "respectability" of the dominant classes. The "culture" of those classes confirmed their own alienation from the vital sources of whatever authentic culture the United States might develop. And whatever the new culture might be, it must acknowledge the repressed "reality" at the root of actual living—not only the sexual instincts but the intimate, sensuous response to the world, to other people, to one's own body, which was the fundamental prerequisite to any indigenous culture, to all art. The theme of bodily liberation, moreover, Whitman inevitably linked with a political as well as religious assault on American slavery, in passages famous to Harlem Renaissance authors. These were connections to which Langston Hughes, in particular, intensely responded.[47]

It is too easy, then, to lump all interest in the presumed "sensuality" and "sexual uninhibitedness" of poor black folks of the South and the Harlem nightlife under the single heading of white folks' sexual and racial neuroses. To be sure, there were plenty of such neuroses to go around, but they are far from the whole story. To Toomer, Hughes, and McKay—the first black writers to assault Victorian prudery in African American literature directly—the example of Whitman was far more important than the precepts of Freud, and the same can be said of many of the white people who took a serious interest in African American culture during the twenties. This is to take nothing away, incidentally, from the even more radical examples of female blues singers that Hazel Carby has discussed.[48] However, for a poet of Hughes's background, the blues singers fit into a discourse of the body related to Whitman's, and vice versa—as one of Hughes's letters to Carl Van Vechten, merging Whitman's rhythms and very phrasing for sexual desire with that of women's blues, pointedly exemplifies: "In the Gulf Coast Blues one can feel the cold northern snows, the memory of the melancholy mists of the Louisianna [sic] low-lands, the shack that is home, the worthless lovers with hands full of gimme, mouths full of much oblige, the eternal unsatisfied longings."[49]

Clearly the liberation of the body had its corollary in the liberation of the "many uttering tongues" of the people, the breaking of the bonds of literary language; and a crucial area of concern in the Harlem

Renaissance was the representation of African American speech. The great challenge was to do justice to the rich, poetic qualities of what linguists now term Black English Vernacular without falling into the conventions of the earlier plantation school "dialect" tradition. And here again, the experiments of African American writers—notably James Weldon Johnson, Hughes, Toomer, Sterling Brown, and Hurston—did not emerge within a strictly black context. By the 1920s the issue of vernacular language had long been important to the American cultural nationalist movement. Van Wyck Brooks, influenced no doubt by the Irish Renaissance, had attacked the problem in *America's Coming-of-Age,* pointing out that the gap between "Highbrow" and "Lowbrow" was particularly evident (and devastating to a native literature) in the domain of language. "Literary English" in *England,* he argued, was living speech, occupying the "middle of the field" and expressing "the flesh and blood of an evolving race." But in the United States, literary English, like Anglo-Saxon law, was simply a tradition: "They persist not as the normal expressions of a race, the essential fibre of which is permanently Anglo-Saxon, but through prestige and precedent and the will and habit of a dominating class largely out of touch with a national fabric unconsciously taking form 'out of school.'"[50] By the time he wrote these meditations, distinguishing American speech from English had already become an obsession to many as they strove to convey the "raciness" of the vernacular without conjuring up the stereotyped lower-class comic foils of the traditional novel. (It is no coincidence that this was the era in which H. L. Mencken wrote *The American Language,* a pioneering study.) The great precursors, of course, were Whitman and Mark Twain. But the more contemporary models were the Irish dramatists, particularly John Millington Synge.

The challenge of escaping the minstrel show tradition was a parallel, if more dramatic and momentous, task for the African American writer. And, in fact, Whitman and Synge show up repeatedly in discussions of how to treat black "dialect" in the teens and twenties. In a review of James Weldon Johnson's poetry volume *Fifty Years and Other Poems,* Floyd Dell had criticized Johnson's use of "literary English" and standard poetic techniques, stating that the most important task of the Negro poet—the task no white poet could perform—was to create poetry true to the temperament, sensibility, and tongue of the racial tradition. He was not calling for "darky" poems or even the formula to which Paul Laurence Dunbar had often been forced to adhere, but for something analogous to what Synge had done for the Irish.[51] Whether Dell's review influenced Johnson or not, in the preface to his next volume of poetry, *God's Trombones*, Johnson would state that Synge had been a model for him in striving for idiomatic expression, advancing from his earlier Dunbar-like division of "literary" from "dialect" verse. Sterling Brown, Alain Locke, and Willis Richardson, too, subsequently referred to Synge as a model; and Hughes had first come to enjoy poetry as a schoolboy reading Sandburg, Masters, and other vernacular poets of the Midwest.[52] Locke seems to have been thinking along these lines from his student years at Harvard, where he spent afternoons in the library reading the Irish playwrights and dreaming of a parallel Negro drama.[53]

My point here is not to trace influence, however, and to debate temporal priority is to miss the more important issue entirely—that contradictions and boundaries inherent in the literary discourse of the late nineteenth century had come in question transracially and even transnationally. African American writers did not approach the problems within their racial tradition separately from those within American literature generally. And, as Alain Locke's comments for William Stanley Braithwaite's 1926 yearbook of American poetry suggest, neither did white writers approach the boundary between "literary" and "vernacular" language without a strong interest in black vernacular:

> Negro genius has shared liberally in the renaissance of American poetry and made a substantial and distinctive contribution to it. Indeed, contemporary American poets, engaged in spite of all their diversities of outlook and technique in a fundamentally common effort to discover and release the national spirit in poetry, have sensed a kindred aim and motive in Negro poetry, and have turned with deep and unbiassed interest to Negro materials as themes and Negro idioms of speech and emotion as artistic inspiration.[54]

This project of transracial experimentation with vernacular traversed every genre and even helped soften boundaries between genres. It is no coincidence that fiction writers particularly meditated on the lessons of *The Adventures of Huckleberry Finn,* a work with complex relations to black oral tradition.[55]

The approach to vernacular in the early twentieth century was not simply a refinement or extension of the dialect tradition. On the contrary, it was part of the cultural nationalist revolt against the "genteel" tradition which had fostered and applauded "dialect" poetry in the first place and which, according to Van Wyck Brooks, had finally spoiled Mark Twain. As Henry May has pointed out, James Whitcomb Riley, although famous for his Hoosier dialect poetry, "swore whenever he even thought of Whitman"; like his friend Dunbar (who also heard no music in Whitman), he wrote a good deal of genteel poetry in conventional meter and diction as well as the dialect verse that was his bread and butter. And William Dean Howells, who had praised Dunbar for his dialect poetry, likewise—and for similar reasons—declared Riley one of America's greatest poets. Riley was admired and befriended by "proper people" like Robert Underwood Johnson, "the archfoe of slang."[56] This Johnson, editor of that bastion of cultural conservatism, *The Century,* had helped found the American Academy of Arts and Letters (to which Riley belonged) in an inane attempt to preserve Anglo-Saxon cultural hegemony and the purity of the English language against the twin threats of immigration and modernism.[57]

Dialect poetry, in other words, was quite cozy with the genteels. It posed no threat to the literary hierarchy because, unlike Whitman's poetry, it made no claims to compete with the language of the classics. Hence the strict differentiation between the two-thirds of Dunbar's poems in "literary English"—for which he wanted to be known primarily—and the one-third in "dialect" (both black *and* white dialect!), which Dunbar once termed "a broken tongue." Furthermore, the distinction between the educated poet and the uneducated dialect speaker is implicitly insisted upon in poems fitting, say, an antebellum sermon into conventional meters and rhymes of the English tradition. Despite their interest, ingenious theories of Dunbar's use of "double-voiced discourse" minimize the historical matrix of his work to idealize a transhistorical racial tradition and ignore its specific transracial American coordinates.[58] For all his empathy for the black masses and the depth of his racial feeling, Dunbar was caught in a theory of literature and an institutional matrix tragically inadequate to his poetic resources. Refracting, in a sense, Jim Crow practices, the sharp division between "dialect" and "literary language" in the work of Riley and Dunbar preserved the linguistic hierarchy that the cultural nationalists assailed. Langston Hughes and Sterling Brown may have learned a lot from Dunbar, but on the whole their work derives from a different orientation to the poetic—one that, like Jean Toomer, they specifically connected with Whitman and the development of a new American literature.[59] They were important contributors to and beneficiaries of a broad redefinition of the "literary" in the United States, a redefinition that increasingly took hold in the major journals of cultural criticism between 1910 and 1920.

Vernacular Realism and Social Consciousness

With the demise of *The Seven Arts*, the spirit of that magazine was carried into two magazines— *The Freeman* and *The Dial*—originating in Chicago. It was *The Freeman* that originally published James Weldon Johnson's poem "The Creation" in 1920, a significant precursor to the transformation of vernacular poetics in the Harlem Renaissance. Albert J. Nock and Francis Neilson used *The Freeman* (whose title, signaling their belief in "economic emancipation," they bought from a black newspaper of that name in Indianapolis) as a platform for pressing socialist and anti-imperialist views, bringing on Van Wyck Brooks and John Macy to treat "cultural" issues.[60] A notable essay is Brooks's ambivalent piece on Ezra Pound:

> It is really Mr. Pound's loss that he hasn't been able to ally himself with the most vigorous creative forces of our day, on the side, I mean, of the intellectual-proletarian movement. For the first time in generations the aristocrat of the spirit has an opportunity to share, without abating a whit of his artistic conscience, in a great constructive effort of humanity. Because Mr. Pound does not feel this and is consequently obliged to regard humanity as inimical, he expends a good deal of spleen in a manner that strikes us as rather tiresomely out-of-date.[61]

Modernist indeed! However, *The Freeman* was almost exclusively a magazine of political and social criticism. More important for carrying the cultural criticism of *The Seven Arts* into the postwar period was *The Dial*, which initially combined an openness to various forms of modernist writing with social criticism.[62]

The Dial had been started in Chicago in 1880 and by the beginning of World War I had degenerated into moribund gentility—although its owner, A. C. McClurg, had been the one to ask W. E. B. Du Bois to collect several of his essays for a volume that became *The Souls of Black Folk*, published by McClurg in 1903.[63] In 1916 Martyn Johnson bought *The Dial*, intending to turn it into a voice of literary modernism and polit-

ical progressivism, as the magazine's manifesto proclaimed: "It will try
to meet the challenge of the new time by reflecting and interpreting its
spirit—a spirit freely experimental, skeptical of inherited values, ready
to examine old dogmas and to submit afresh its sanctions to the test
of experience."[64] With help from Scofield Thayer, Johnson moved the
magazine to New York to advance his design. He appointed Bourne
and Brooks contributing editors in 1917, then invited Dewey to become
associate editor (along with Thorstein Veblen) in 1918, the year Bourne
died. Initially, then, *The Dial* carried on the *Seven Arts* style of cultural
criticism, with contributors like Van Wyck Brooks, Paul Rosenfeld, Sherwood Anderson, and Franz Boas' student Edward Sapir. It attacked the
Treaty of Versailles in terms *The Seven Arts* might have used, as a betrayal
of the ideals for which Dewey and others had supported American entry
into the war. (Dewey had hoped for a settlement involving thoroughgoing anti-imperialism, antiracism, and the economic equalization of
all nations to ensure democratic development globally.)[65] This point of
view on international politics initially bore a revealing relationship to
the magazine's national cultural criticism.

Dewey's own "Americanism and Localism," written from China
during the "New Culture" movement, remarked on the significance of
local, regional, and ethnic cultures to the possible emergence of an
American literature. Significantly, the New Culture movement, as
Dewey explained in an article for *The New Republic* at about the same
time, had developed in response to the intransigence of the political
establishment. Turning to "culture" as a means of transforming society
(like much of the U.S. political left in the 1920s), the young intellectuals aimed "to make the spoken language the standard language for
print," replacing classical Chinese (which few people understood) with
the vernacular—in journalism, education, and literature. Literary clas-
sicists reacted with the argument that the movement threatened the
moral and cultural unity of the nation, whereas "Young China"
regarded the turn to the vernacular as critical to grappling with the
problems of contemporary society and to developing democratic institutions.[66] Dewey's articulation of the message of Chinese literature,
need I say, was different from that of Ezra Pound, who was interested
in the "classics." The connection between the literary revolt in China
and that within the United States was clear. Dewey's very distance from
the States—effecting a "transnational" perspective—impressed upon
him the importance of localism and the vernacular in American
culture.

Contrasting the vividness of local reporting in American newspapers with the textbook blandness of "national" and "international" news stories, Dewey noted the lesson for cultural development: American literature must be local first, "for the country is a spread of localities." These localities were not only regional. Ethnic localism, Dewey argued, should be equally important, despite the blindness of Anglo newspaper editors to this fact:

> These same papers that fairly shriek with localisms devote a discreet amount of space to the activities of various Americanization agencies. From time to time, with a marked air of doing their duty, there are earnest editorials on the importance of Americanization and the wickedness of those who decline to be either Americanized or to go back where they came from. . . . One vaguely wonders whether perhaps the recalcitrants who are denounced may not also be infected by the pervading spirit of localism. . . . One gathers of course that Americanization consists in learning a language strangely known as English. But perhaps they are too busy making the American language to devote much time to studying the English.[67]

The creation of "American" language and culture, as Dewey would have it, is an ongoing project of interconnected "localisms." Apparently borrowing from Josiah Royce and reflecting upon parallels with China, he suggested that the wider the formal unity of a country, the more intense and important is its local life.

His point, however, was not primarily to advance a political argument; rather, "the bearing of these remarks is upon the literary career of our country." American authors must learn from such late-nineteenth-century regionalists as Mary Wilkins Freeman but add to their faithful limning of local custom and character a greater critical consciousness of "social environment," tradition and "descent." Beginning with an abstract understanding that "the locality is the only universal," American writers had begun to create a new vernacular poetry. "When the discovery sinks a little deeper, the novelist and dramatist will discover the localities of America as they are, and no one will need to worry about the future of American art. We have been too anxious to get away from home. Naturally that took us to Europe even though we fancied we were going around America. When we explore our neighborhood, its forces and not just its characters and color, we shall find what we sought."

In his brief essay Dewey exemplified the linkage between philosophical pragmatism, internationalism, American literary nationalism, and regionalist critical realism of the sort advanced by such poets as Masters, Vachel Lindsay, and Sandburg, and such novelists as Theodore Dreiser, Floyd Dell, Carl Van Vechten, Sherwood Anderson, Zona Gale, and Willa Cather. This type of fiction, moreover, Dewey explicitly aligned with that of "ethnic" writers beginning to appear on the scene—an alignment that appeared throughout the twenties and that was embodied in institutional networks involving magazine editors, publishers, and authors crucial to, among other things, the literary Harlem Renaissance. However, *The Dial* would not be an important part of that network by the time the most important work of the Harlem Renaissance began coming out—for revealing reasons.

The magazine began shifting direction after Thayer and James Sibley Watson bought it from Johnson in late 1919.[68] The *Seven Arts* style of cultural criticism quickly vanished from the journal as Ezra Pound, in particular, increasingly shaped its editorial direction. Pound reported on the Paris arts scene, Eliot on London, while the cultural nationalists were pushed out. This particular episode may have something to do with the bitterness of Van Wyck Brooks's later complaints about Eliot. It wasn't, Brooks claimed, that he could not forgive Eliot for becoming a British citizen but that "he made a popular intellectual cause of attacking what gave America its uniqueness and distinction."[69] In the 1920s, *The Dial* became unabashedly highbrow and emphasized that American writers worked "in the same *milieu* and in the same tradition of letters as the Europeans," that "we are all in the Western-civilized-Christian-European-American tradition."[70] This is a far cry from the old *Seven Arts* and from the traditions upon which New Negro authors would draw. The cultural nationalist and transnationalist critics would have to turn to other outlets. But by this time the American publishing scene had been vastly transformed, and the outlets existed in a diverse array of magazines and publishing houses, emerging from the ferment of the teens, that would welcome—and to some extent shape—the writing of New Negroes.

In using whatever cultural resources were at hand, black authors were intervening in the debates over American culture. Adopting and adapting the tools that were most available, appropriate, and powerful in the context of the cultural fray, they affiliated primarily with a type of literature that critiqued, in a "realistic" mode, the forms of American social hierarchy. The writers with whom they affiliated, generally speaking, were those connected not with avant-garde magazines of the twenties emphasizing the separation of the artistic from other institutions of society but rather with magazines in which cultural criticism connected closely with ethnography and with economic and political critique. Given all the factors in the dialectical construction of canonical "modernism" and "modernist" literary criticism within the academy (overwhelmingly in contradistinction to "realism" and other qualities embodied in New Negro writing), it should not be surprising that the Harlem Renaissance writers have only recently begun to be considered modernists. This reconsideration, indeed, fits Raymond Williams' insistence on recognizing early twentieth-century naturalism as crucial to modernism rather than its "other."[71] At modernist naturalism's center was "the humanist and secular—and, in political terms, liberal and later socialist—proposition that human nature was not, or at least not decisively, unchanging and timeless, but was socially and culturally specific." Moreover, "what is most clear in modernist Naturalism . . . is its challenging selection of the crises, the contradictions, the unexplored dark areas, of the bourgeois human order of its time."[72]

Because realism and naturalism together have served as the straw man designating whatever modernism *is not* in Europe and the United States since the 1930s, the modernism of the Harlem Renaissance has been difficult enough to detect *irrespective* of the grip of racism on the academy. Typically, modernism is regarded precisely as the sort of literary practice that is anti-"realistic" in the sense that it refuses "to communicate according to established socio-semiotic contracts."[73] Astradur Eysteinsson has shown how this contrast opened up in Edmund Wilson's *Axel's Castle*. Wilson contrasts Shaw with Yeats, Anatole France with Valery, and so forth to show the split between two different responses to the "modern" condition. One is immersed in the affairs of the social world, "highlighting its objective reality as his *content*, while the other, directing his creativity into aesthetized *form*, ultimately opts for a subjective and solipsistic retreat from the world into 'Axel's castle.'"[74] Wilson, by then a regular contributor to *The New Republic*, did not *endorse* the "high modernist" project. Moving to the socialist left, he was actually ambivalent about it; but this ambivalence was not transported into the academy.

Harlem Renaissance authors for the most part chose not to follow the high Modernists into Axel's castle. Perhaps they felt that many of the qualities high modernists rejected were precisely the qualities one must use to acquire public power. The drifting apart of social and personal spheres typical of high modernism is not typical of New Negro writing; nor is it typical of the writing of the socialists, cultural nationalists, and regional realists who responded to their work and with whom they affiliated.[75] Even the formal experiments of Harlem Renaissance authors are most often attempts to incorporate folk forms into poetry or fiction, or to bend generic conventions from Western literary tradition to their own uses, while the so-called bourgeois writers such as Larsen and Fauset were unabashedly "realistic," in an almost old-fashioned sense, except for the nature of their subject matter and the people to whom they gave voice. Collectively, the African American modernists looked more to Shaw, Synge, Stanislavsky, Tolstoy, Sinclair Lewis, Whitman, and Sandburg than to Yeats, Joyce, Meyerhold, Kafka, Stein, or Pound.

Harlem Renaissance writers depended far more than the high modernists upon realist discourse because their objective social position vis-à-vis the dominant language differed from the modernists'. The very voicing of formerly suppressed speech could be an intervention in the settled language of literature no less "new" and disruptive than the experiments of the avant-garde. Raymond Williams makes this point: "There was then a now familiar polarization, of an ideological kind: between on the one hand the 'old, settled' language and its literary forms and on the other hand the 'new, dynamic' language and its necessarily new forms." Yet the concept of the "old, settled" language (that of "commonsense" realism) being the imposed form of the dominant class was true only on one level. "Uses of a language of connection and of forms of intended communication remained an emphasis and an intention of other social groups, in both class and gender [and, in the United States, in ethnicity and race], whose specific existence had been blurred or contained within the imposed 'national' forms."[76] The selective academic definition of modernism, then, ignores the asymmetries of power that effected different modes of expressive modernity. Modernism should not be identified with a single position on language in the avant-garde. "On the contrary, we need to identify a range of distinct and in many cases actually opposed formations, as these have materialized in language."[77]

The Harlem Renaissance brand of modernism is actually closer to Latin American *modernismo* than to high modernism, which ought to remind us of the close relationship authors like Langston Hughes and Waldo Frank sought with Latin American authors, as well as the fact that Alfred A. Knopf (Hughes's publisher) was the first U.S. publisher to travel to South America seeking manuscripts. In its later phase (on the verge of World War I), *modernismo* sought a genuinely "American" expression—"to capture the life and atmosphere of the peoples of America, to translate their fears, ideals, and hopes."[78] Reacting against the influence of French symbolism, with its interest in the exotic, in decadence, in precious language and imagery, *modernismo* turned to indigenous themes and was linked to left-wing politics as well as the idolization of Whitman. A gap therefore widened between Spanish and Latin American modernism. Both rebelled against the excesses of romanticism and worn-out forms, clichéd ideas and phrases; but "over and over one encounters references to the tyranny of Spanish literary precepts and the stultifying clichés of the times. When the Spaniard reacts to this environment, he reacts to his own tradition and society. When the American rebels, he is reacting to a culture that he no longer considers wholly his own."[79] *Modernismo* was the movement through which Latin American writers in Spanish broke from the Spanish literary tradition and established the basic vectors of their own indigenous bearings. To North American academic eyes, their "modernism" looks much like realist localism.

The "realist" novels and "vernacular" poetry praised in *American Mercury, The New Republic,* and *The Nation* emphasized the workings of various social institutions in the "common world"—the family, the corporation, the political machine, and so forth. This literature, moreover, to borrow from David Lodge, seeks to depict a shared reality by using a broadly shared language—"realism" in literature being "the representation of experience in a manner which approximates closely to descriptions of similar experience in nonliterary texts of the same culture."[80] Such realism need not presume a positivist claim to "objectivity," as is commonly assumed in studies defining "modernism" against a preceding nineteenth-century "realism." Critical "realism" can be compatible with pragmatism's denial of epistemological foundations and its emphasis upon the "flux" of experience, upon the necessarily partial, ethnocentric, and contingent nature of any act of writing.[81]

Close to the Ground: "Low" Modernism and the Common World

When Richard Rorty writes that "pragmatism is the philosophical counterpart of literary modernism, the kind of literature which prides itself on its autonomy and novelty rather than its truthfulness to experience or its discovery of pre-existing significance," he departs from his hero John Dewey's concept of the fit between pragmatism and the various forms of modernism.[82] Dewey and his followers, such as Max Eastman, insisted on continuity between art and experience and objected to the concept of artistic autonomy. To say a fiction was "true to experience" was not necessarily to say it discovered with "absolute truth" either some "objective" or "subjective" reality (in the conventional sense), for "experience" to the pragmatist signified something other than the objectively knowable or the privately felt; it took for granted the *enculturation* of all human experience and regarded experience not as something residing within the autonomous human subject but as an aspect of nature in common with the subject.

Max Eastman expressed a pragmatist position when he accused both the high modernists (whom he termed "Neo-Classics") and "Humanists" of basing their literary positions upon misunderstandings of modern science. For Eastman, what was important about the new science was its method—a skeptical method rather than a method of arriving at absolute truth. "Knowing is not a state-of-being in which 'the mind' becomes a copy or reflection of 'things.' Knowing is an act of comprehending the elements of experience in their relations to each other and to our human interests and modes of behavior."[83] Both the "Neo-Classics" (Tate, Pound, Eliot, Winters, and company) and the "Humanists" misunderstood the challenges posed by science; though they fought each other, "the battle although loud is not very interesting, because the hostility is not deep." Trying to hold the castle against a common enemy, they argued that literature required "another order of intelligence." But this was merely a flimsy rationale for their real object—to maintain the prestige of humane letters. "They are defending the last relics of that nobler status which was accorded in the feudal society to the study of 'polite literature,' to an impeccable acquaintance with 'the classics,' to a mastery of 'the humanities,' as opposed to the rather low social rating of the vulgar pursuit of useful knowledge."[84] Applying Veblen's theory of the leisure class, Eastman charged: "Experimental knowledge is plebeian, not only because being useful it carries a flavor of work rather than of sport. It is plebeian also because it develops in close association with productive work, and looks mainly to successful working for the test of its validity. It is plebeian because it continually suggests the possibility of changing things, and the patrician, being well placed in the *status quo*, is disinclined toward any too wonderful generalization of this idea."[85] For Eastman, then, the modern critical "realist" program, in opposition to that of both the humanists and "Modernists," joined with modern experimental method in pledging its labors to the project of democracy and the sort of social transformations necessary to make democracy more than an empty slogan.

Eastman continued: "The opposition of our literature professors to extreme and bitter realism [such as Dreiser's] is not due to the suggestion of fatality or hopelessness of action which it conveys to weak and enervated minds. It is due to the suggestion it conveys to strong minds that action is necessary."[86] This was even more true of the "neo-classical" critics, whose leanings toward fascism Eastman recognized early. Gesturing their superiority to the problems of industrial civilization rather than dedicating themselves to its intelligent control, they claimed a "Higher Intelligence" and were homesick for feudalism. Against the resistance of both the "Humanists" and the "Modernists" to communication with the larger society, against their flight from the common world, Eastman stressed that the purpose of art is to intensify experience, to make us aware of its range and qualities; artistic creation is above all an act of communication.

Thus, Harlem Renaissance and pragmatist critics privileged regional and ethnic realism not on the basis of a positivist faith in a transcendentally "objective" perspective, but took perspective to be essential to the fiction and its form. But neither did they espouse a view of "modernism" as pure foregrounding of "subjective experience," for they regarded the opposition between subjective and objective realities as false, like the opposition between nature and culture (or nature and experience, if experience is taken in Dewey's sense, meaning "involved, meaningful, and shared response to the world"). For this reason they encouraged Harlem Renaissance authors to develop a distinctively "Negro" aesthetics—which frequently shaded into the privileging of a kind of primitivism. However, as I will demonstrate in the chapters to follow, the best of the critics resisted primitivist proclivities and argued for the significance of black vernacular traditions not only as the bases of a distinctively African American literature but as crucial to the rethinking of an American cultural nationalism in service of democratic community.

Thus recent arguments for the fit between high modernist literature and pragmatism—however valid they may be—obscure the perhaps closer relationship between critical realism, multiethnic literature, and pragmatism. Certainly this is the story the journals of the era tell—the story, in fact, that John Dewey and his closest associates tell (as in the introduction Claude McKay asked Dewey to write for his *Selected Poems*).[87] Ironically, Richard Rorty's controversial renewal of Deweyan pragmatism is instructive here; for Rorty argues that solidarity is achieved not by philosophical argument or by reflection but by imaginative creations that allow people to see each other as "fellow sufferers":

> It is created by increasing our sensitivity to the particular details of the pain and humiliation of other, unfamiliar sorts of people. Such increased sensitivity makes it more difficult to marginalize people different from ourselves by thinking, "They do not feel it as *we* would," or "There must always be suffering, so why not let *them* suffer?"
>
> This process of coming to see other human beings as "one of us" rather than as "them" is a matter of detailed description of what unfamiliar people are like and of redescription of what we ourselves are like. This is a task not for theory but for genres such as ethnography, the journalist's report, the comic book, the docudrama, and, especially, the novel.[88]

Whether or not Rorty's point holds true, it certainly represents a cardinal belief of diverse contributors to African American modernism in the first third of the twentieth century.

The emphasis upon the relationship between lived experience and literary art remains instructive at a time when much advanced African American literary theory has attempted to divorce the rhetorical or "textual" tradition from earlier notions of its grounding in the "black experience," connected with beliefs in racial essences. I agree with bell hooks that some concept of the importance of "black experience" in the development of African American culture must be recuperated, though without the essentialist baggage often attached to it and without the sort of racial exclusivism that denies the possibility of interracial dialogue and community, that denies the effort to subvert racialist thinking in pursuit of alternative futures. By recuperating the significance of conscious experience, and of cultural production and reception as the consummate practical issues of experience as well as powerful forms of social participation,[89] we can understand why promoters of the Harlem Renaissance saw literature and art as crucial to the achievement of democracy, not merely as a means of "proving" the humanity of African

Americans. The point was not to appeal to abstract human nature but to win solidarity through "detailed empirical descriptions" such as those provided by ethnologists, journalists, and novelists; and, in the manner of "strong poets," to redescribe the world in new vocabularies, thereby both exposing the cruelty of the powerful and bringing excluded persons into positions from which they could contribute powerfully to the definition of what it meant to be American. Zora Neale Hurston expressed the point well in "What White Publishers Won't Print," arguing that novels on the order of Sinclair Lewis' *Main Street* were needed concerning the lives of "average" Negroes: "Argue all you will or may about injustice, but as long as the majority cannot conceive of a Negro or a Jew feeling and reacting inside just as they do, the majority will keep right on believing that people who do not feel like them cannot possibly feel as they do, and conform to the established pattern. It is well known that there must be a body of waived matter, let us say, things accepted and taken for granted by all in a community before there can be that commonality of feeling. The usual phrase is having things in common."[90] Ethnographic realism, to Hurston, was a method of attacking conventional social formations by transforming racial structures of feeling to create interracial, national solidarity—as well as black self-affirmation. She explicitly connects her program with the principles of what she calls American national art.

Similar convictions can be found in the work of other writers of the time, even those who wrote quite differently from Hurston. Black writers were engaged in a larger movement to make aesthetic experience and capacities more central to social reconstruction and democratic politics in the United States.[91] They appealed, over and over again, not to an abstract human essence but to "Americanism" and the need for a reconceptualization of the meaning of "American" national culture that took seriously the significance of racism in American history—as well as African Americans' creative response to the cruel conditions of their New World existence.

II

The Transformation of Literary Institutions

To DIVIDE LITERATURE FROM OTHER MODES OF CULTURAL expression may seem arbitrary from a certain theoretical standpoint—the standpoint, for example, of those tracing pure racial traditions across the boundaries of different media and art forms—but from a practical standpoint it is obvious that what we call "literature" depends upon unique processes of production, distribution, and reception. Reading a literary text is not only a different type of experience from listening to a blues singer; it is also the final stage in a unique series of productive processes. These processes, indeed, shape the form of literature itself in myriad ways. Institutions grow up to nourish, transform, exploit, control, and disseminate literary forms. The most important of these institutions in the early twentieth century—when universities had not yet come to dominate our literary culture—were magazines and publishers.

To understand the institutional contexts of the New Negro movement requires a careful examination of the *overall* cultural politics of the journals and publishing houses that promoted it and of the conditions that gave rise to these journals and houses in the first place, rather than a single-minded focus upon their treatment of racial issues. Such issues cannot be walled off from the complex negotiations of cultural power within the American field as a whole. Neither can the mere interrogation of the racial attitudes of various individuals and gossip about the parties they went to get one very far in understanding how American literary traditions interacted and changed through the mediation of institutional settings.

The Harlem Renaissance followed not only (as is often stressed) the black migration and World War I but also the emergence of a whole new matrix of magazines centered in New York City. As V. F. Calverton would later recall, "The day when *The Atlantic Monthly* was the final authority for American intellectuals was dead. . . . New magazines had arisen and the old magazines had to change their character, that is become more American, in order to survive. Publishing houses also had to give audience to the new tendency."[1] Indeed, to a great extent the magazines found and created the audience that would support the new publishers. Significantly, before the teens, these magazines either did not exist or were under the control of more conservative editors, a fact that has a lot to do with the timing of the Harlem Renaissance. Combined with magazines created by organizations of African American "uplift" and reform, such journals governed the literary field inhabited by Harlem Renaissance writers. Attention has focused in the past on literary discussion groups and social gatherings, and these did play a role in the emergence of black modernist networks. But what was discussed in these meetings, as far as we can tell, had to do with what was being published, and what resulted from the meetings in turn found its most reliable expression in published form.

The "white" magazines—particularly *The Nation, The New Republic, The Liberator,* and *The Seven Arts*—and the writers and editors associated with them first shaped and promoted what is now thought of as the American literary "canon," before authors such as Whitman, Poe, Thoreau, Melville, Dickinson, and Mark Twain had been accepted in the universities. Indeed, contrary to current assumptions, the formation of the now-"traditional" American Renaissance canon and the blossoming of the Harlem Renaissance were parallel and complementary, not antagonistic, developments. They not only happened at the same time but were promoted by the *same people*, magazines, and publishing houses (including African American writers, magazines, and publishing houses). Black writing fit into the basic social and cultural reforming program of these magazines that wanted to distinguish American from English aesthetics, often on grounds of cultural pluralism, vernacular experimentation, and social egalitarianism. Primitivism, for the most part, was a later and always subordinate concern, although it too fit the broad front of attack against the "genteel" tradition.[2]

The magazines that allied with the New Negro were by and large "highbrow" or "intellectual" general-interest journals.[3] "White" mass-circulation magazines like the *Saturday Evening Post* had virtually nothing to do with the movement besides providing grist for the mill of critique and satire (to which the editors of these popular magazines apparently paid little attention). On the other hand, the strictly "literary" magazines such as *Palms, Poetry,* and *The Little Review* published some black writing, even an occasional special issue focusing on the New Negro, and the *Saturday Review, Vanity Fair,* and *The Bookman* published some criticism; but the main support and publicity for the movement came from *The Nation, The New Republic, American Mercury, The Liberator, Modern Quarterly,* and the like. Among black publications, the strictly "literary" organs such as *Harlem* and *Fire!!,* although of great interest, for the most part died too quickly to have a sustained impact, and so *The Crisis* and *Opportunity* became the chief journals of African American literature and criticism.

These factors in the institutionalization of the movement are especially interesting because of the way the clustering of audiences and contributors linked people across boundaries of genre as well as of race. The new writing appeared in a broadly interdisciplinary context—concerned with new developments in anthropology, social theory, literary criticism, and political commentary. Thus, although a book review or poetry editor might have a slightly different political and social orientation from that of the chief editorial writers, the mutual attractions were stronger than the repulsions, and often quite strong indeed. Furthermore, the general social and cultural orientation of the magazines shaped the production *and* the reading of all that appeared within each issue as well as largely determining the likely audience.

The different magazines (like the different publishers) institutionalized, to a certain extent, different approaches to American cultural reality. I do not mean to insist that they were internally consistent and thoroughly discrete units, but rather that they provided relatively distinct points of view and contexts of discussion; and they talked back and forth to each other. They even shared and swapped subscribers. Advertisements appeared in *The New Republic,* for example, offering readers reduced-rate joint subscriptions to *The New Republic* (a weekly) and *The Atlantic* and *American Mercury* (two monthlies); and in *The*

Nation offering joint subscriptions with *The Liberator, The Survey, The Century,* or *The New Republic.*[4] Advertisements for *The Crisis* and *Opportunity* appeared in *Modern Quarterly, The Nation,* and *The New Masses,* and vice versa.[5] Magazines also offered special rates on books they felt their readers would like, often in connection with reduced-rate subscriptions. Thus *The New Masses* offered readers a subscription to the magazine and a copy of V. F. Calverton's *Anthology of Negro Poetry* at a combined cost of two dollars, fifty cents off the normal price.[6] Similarly, contributors traveled freely between magazines; George Schuyler published regularly in *The Messenger* and *American Mercury* and contributed an iconoclastic piece to *The Nation* that caused an editor there to solicit a response from Langston Hughes.

The magazines represented different positions in the cultural debates, albeit all were more or less on the same "side" vis-à-vis the dominant culture. They were contentious allies on a discursive field in which cultural disputes took place, with individual participants inhabiting different positions relative to the perspectives dominant in each magazine. Within the pages of *The Nation,* Schuyler was a voice of dissent toward the notions of black cultural distinctiveness; in *American Mercury* he was a black Mencken satirizing the carnival of American race relations, in tune with the magazine's general tone and perspective; in *The Messenger* he was the authoritative New Negro critic and editor, a guiding force, and an antagonist of *The Crisis* and *Opportunity.* Similar examples could be multiplied: Eric Walrond worked for *Opportunity* and wrote reviews for *The New Republic;* Du Bois contributed important pieces to most of the white magazines publicizing the New Negro while editing *The Crisis* and writing his books; Hughes contributed chiefly to the more left-wing and explicitly socialist magazines; and so forth. One important point that bears upon issues of canonization and gender is that by and large the black women writers were *not* called upon by white editors for contributions or reviews—nor did they have much to do with *The Messenger*—although they were an important presence in *The Crisis* and *Opportunity.*

As a literary movement, the Harlem Renaissance was peculiar for its close identification with two specific reform organizations. The NAACP and the National Urban League, both founded shortly before the movement began, played crucial roles in its success. They publicized it, hired its writers, established magazines that published its products, and helped connect it with white publishing outlets. Du Bois's trenchant writing and inspiring leadership, in particular, had an immense impact on virtually all the New Negro authors in their early years. The importance of the work of Jessie Fauset at *The Crisis* and Charles S. Johnson and Alain Locke at the Urban League's *Opportunity* should never be underestimated. And yet many of the younger writers resented the control the older black leaders attempted to exert over their work. They were caught between competing demands and allegiances. Under the circumstances, however, the competition was not entirely unhealthy. Obviously, the black magazines offered concentrated treatment of issues concerning African Americans; there was no fear of appearing to give "too much" attention to "the race problem." White magazines, on the other hand, gave only limited attention to African American culture in the context of other dominating concerns. (In an average issue of *The Nation,* the only item concerning African American culture might be a report of a lynching or a book review on a sociological treatise or novel. To put it another way, in the language of the index to each volume, perhaps twenty items concerning "Negroes" would appear in an entire year. Black culture was hardly as voguish as we have been led to believe.) Thus Claude McKay fought to get *The Liberator* to pay more attention to racial issues—even as he fought to get *The Crisis* to attend more to class issues—but Max Eastman worried that if "race problems" took up too much space the small readership of the magazine would shrink further, costing the magazine its survival.

Despite the drawbacks of turning to white magazines, however, black writers found these journals to be crucial, not only because they reached a larger white audience than black magazines but also because they encouraged types of ideological and artistic freedom and experimentation the African American editors either shied away from or did not appreciate. Such, at least, was the belief of several of the authors, including McKay, Toomer, Thurman, and Hughes. The short-lived *Fire!!* and *Harlem* were declarations of independence from the established black periodicals as much as from the white magazines, which came in a wider variety. In his introductory Editorial in *Harlem,* Wallace Thurman wrote that the problem with white magazines was not any resistance to black art, but rather the fact that few black people would consistently *buy* a white magazine just for the black contributions, and hence one could not reach one's primary audience through such publications. It was the black editors that, in Thurman's view, hampered artistic freedom. The New Negro artist "revolted against shoddy and sloppy publication methods, revolted against the patronizing attitudes his elders assumed toward him, revolted against their editorial astigmatism and their intolerance of new points of view."[7]

Claude McKay made similar complaints, more vehemently, on more than one occasion. He read mostly "the less conservative literary organs" (such as *The Masses*) because he wanted to emulate those who wrote with utter "conviction."[8] His early poem "The White Fiends" was rejected by *The Crisis* before he sent it to Frank Harris' *Pearson's,* which published it. And his first poems to appear in the United States would be published by *The Seven Arts.* At a time when *The Crisis* would not accept his poetry, he turned to the radical white magazines and fell in with the *Liberator* crowd. Hubert Harrison, the brilliant socialist who started the tradition of street-corner political speechifying in Harlem, wrote in 1920 apropos McKay's experience: "Without any aid from Negro editors or publications, he made his way because white people who noted his gifts were eager to give him a chance while Negro editors, as usual, were either too blind to see or too mean-spirited to proclaim them to the world."[9] More often, they may have been simply too worried about the response of their black bourgeois and white liberal readership to the radical poetry and fiction that could be published more readily in the socialist and "bohemian" magazines.[10]

McKay feared the influence of the "Afro-American" judges of the *Opportunity* prize contest and refused to enter it in 1926. "I must write what I feel what I know what I think what I have seen what is true and your Afro-American intelligentsia won't like it. I know that."[11] On editorial matters, McKay wrote, "I am always forced into the unpleasant position of making comparisons between white gentleman [*sic*] and black gentleman to the disadvantage of the black ones."[12] Black editors, McKay felt, were both too bourgeois in outlook and too worried about what white people would think of their magazines. "I don't want my name nor my work to be deliberately massacred because of the exigencies of false, momentary racial aspirations," he wrote Alain Locke on one occasion.[13] McKay felt the black editors' timidity was, in any case, misplaced because of a misreading of their particular white audience. Whereas the leaders of the "Negro Renaissance" thought they were breaking into the mainstream, gaining entrance to elite white culture, the whites who were genuinely interested in black art were not mainstream at all but rather at odds with the mainstream, frequently kicked out of it when not in flight from it, sometimes fired from their jobs, subject to all forms of intimidation for their beliefs. "The radical nature and subject of their interest," wrote Mckay, "operated against the possibility of their introducing Negroes further than their own particular homes into coveted white society."[14] The statement is only a slight exaggeration.

Jean Toomer's view was similar to McKay's, broadly speaking. He believed that African American intellectuals were more enslaved to bourgeois "Anglo-Saxon" conventions than were intellectuals of the predominantly white left because of their reaction against racial stereotypes. Indeed, he believed that the "radical" whites associated with such magazines as *The Liberator* and formerly *The Seven Arts* had transcended the "Anglo-Saxon ideal," achieving a kind of liberation not yet attained by the black bourgeoisie. Writing his friend Mae Wright in August 1922, as he worked on *Cane,* he implied that his relationship with white cultural critics had helped free him into a new appreciation of the Negro:

> They are receptive of what the English, the Irish, the Teuton, the Latin, the Slav, the Chinese, the Japanese, the Indian, the Jew, the Negro, have to give. This means that they have successfully transcended the narrow implications of the entire Anglo-Saxon ideal. Can we say the same for yourselves [*sic!*], we of the darker skins, of a somewhat different heritage? We cannot. Paradoxical as it may seem, we who have Negro blood in our veins, who are culturally and emotionally the most removed from Puritan tradition, are its most tenacious supporters.[15]

Toomer goes on to suggest the need to liberate (bourgeois) African Americans into an appreciation of their own beauty and of "the abundance and power of Negro-derived emotions. . . . To do these things is to create a living ideal of one's own."[16] Toomer regarded it as his own duty "to aid, perhaps in a large measure, to crystallize this ideal"; but he expected literate Negroes initially to reject his efforts, "(so hidebound are they by Anglomania), but the time will come when the truth of what I have to say will seep in."[17] In Toomer's case, it is clear that close relationships with writers of the white left—specifically, writers of *The Seven Arts, The Nation, The New Republic,* and *The Liberator*—were crucial to his attempts to aesthetically revitalize Negro identity. His brief months in Georgia were artistically productive because he was prepared for them by New York.

Although he published some of his early work in *The Crisis* and passed his manuscripts along to Alain Locke before publication, Toomer turned first to *The Liberator* and similar magazines, magazines he had been assiduously reading in the period he began his "apprenticeship" as a writer. It is worth noting that Arna Bontemps, himself a renaissance writer, viewed Toomer, after Claude McKay, as "the second, and in some ways the most inspiring, of the writers who made the Harlem Renaissance significant in the long-range development of the Negro writer in the United States."[18] It was precisely because, like most innovative artists, these men straddled the threshold of social difference and journeyed *between* white and black intellectual communities that they were of signal importance to the Harlem Renaissance. They were able to straddle this threshold—indeed, virtually required to straddle it—because of their educational backgrounds and devotion to literature.

Another factor that caused some African American modernists to distrust the black magazines from an artistic point of view was their sense that the editors and reviewers were too willing to publish and praise mediocre writing. McKay, for example, wrote Walter White that black writers needed good, honest criticism, not patronizing indulgence or "indiscriminating praise from Negro journals."[19] Langston Hughes had to write to W. E. B. Du Bois more than once to ask him to return or destroy old poems of his, for work that Hughes considered weak continued to appear in *The Crisis* without his prior knowledge. McKay had a similar experience.[20] Regardless of such problems, however, the enthusiastic encouragement and prolific publication of African American writing in *The Crisis* and *Opportunity* was indispensable to African American modernism.

On the other hand, the importance of such magazines as *The Nation, The New Republic, The Masses, The Liberator, The Seven Arts, The Freeman, American Mercury,* and *The New Masses* to the Harlem Renaissance does not lie only—or even chiefly—in their publication of writing by black authors. Going through these magazines issue by issue, one finds that not much writing by African Americans appeared in them, although there was a great deal more than in other white journals, and although the work they *did* publish was often of striking significance to African American literary tradition. (Indeed, if there is as great a difference between "white aesthetics" and "black aesthetics" as we are often told, one has to wonder why such a high proportion of what the white magazines first published is generally agreed to be the best work of African

American literary modernism.) But what is at least as important is that, in addition to *The Crisis* (*Opportunity* not having existed before 1923), these were the magazines the most innovative of the young black authors followed carefully even before they began publishing. They eagerly appropriated the aesthetic and cultural concepts advanced in these magazines, adapting them to their own needs. Thus, under "Suggestions for Good Reading," in 1919 the black editors of *The Messenger* recommended *The Liberator, The Nation, The Dial, The New Republic,* and *Pearson's*.[21] In 1926 W. E. B. Du Bois editorialized: "The suspension of *The World Tomorrow* [a Christian socialist magazine] is a public calamity. A nation that cannot support *The Freeman* and *The World Tomorrow;* that persecutes *The American Mercury* and gives but half-hearted support to *The New Republic* and *The Nation,* is not thoroughly civilized."[22] George Schuyler remembered that when he lived in Harlem in 1919 he followed closely *The Nation, The New Republic,* and *The Call* (a socialist publication), and in the early twenties attended meetings at the Cooper Union (site of the first NAACP conference) and the Rand School, where he would have heard the socialists and other radicals associated with such magazines as *The Nation, The Freeman,* and *The Liberator.* At about this time Toomer and Hughes were attending lectures at the Rand School as well—an institution frequently mentioned or advertised in *The Messenger* and *The Crisis.*

Toomer would later regret that he had not encountered such institutions earlier, remembering how an English professor had placed before him *The New Republic* and *The Nation* and recommended that he become familiar with the ideas he could find therein:

> Suppose I had! Suppose I had followed this good man's advice. . . . In 1914 I would have stepped directly into the one current of American life in which I was fitted eventually to participate. The ideas then being expressed in those magazines would have helped me emerge from confusion and find myself and find my direction. I would have been guided to Walt Whitman and Emerson, to Bernard Shaw and H. G. Wells. I would have been introduced to the writings of Dreiser, Van Wyck Brooks, Waldo Frank, Herbert Croly, Villard, Randolph Bourne, Carl Sandburg, and many others.[23]

Although he did not take advantage of the opportunity when first offered, he reported that when his most intense intellectual development did begin, "I began reading these magazines: *The Dial, Poetry, The Liberator, The Nation, The New Republic,* etc."[24] The people associated with these publications were precisely the company in which he would later find himself. About the time that Toomer's professor was making his recommendation, Langston Hughes was exposed to the same magazines and authors by his Jewish schoolmates and a high school English teacher in the Midwest; he claimed that it was this exposure that first interested him in writing poetry.[25] Claude McKay's position as editor on *The Liberator* staff inspired him; later Hughes served as an editor of its successor, *The New Masses.* In the late 1920s, Richard Wright was inspired by old copies of *The Masses* and current issues of *American Mercury.*[26]

It is not surprising, then, that the chief white allies of the Harlem Renaissance would prove to be the editors of and contributors to these periodicals. It was these editors and contributors (except for the *Masses-Liberator* crowd, the "radicals") who were invited to the famous Civic Club dinner of 1924 that led to the publication of *The New Negro.* It was they who were drawn upon to serve as judges in the *Opportunity* literary contests. It was they, among many other hangers-on, who attended the parties at Carl Van Vechten's, James Weldon Johnson's, and Walter White's. They were also frequently solicited to contribute to *Opportunity* or *The Crisis* and to review books for those magazines. Conversely, they frequently solicited reviews, articles, poems, and stories from Harlem Renaissance authors, when they did not review those works themselves.

Any reasonably open-minded analysis of the cultural politics of these journals (not to mention the biographies and correspondence of the black intellectuals) reveals a scenario of productive intercultural dialogue that is almost impossible to square with the view that Urban League and NAACP officials were cunningly taking advantage of "white disunity" and fascination with the exoticism of Negroes. "Not being taken seriously," David Levering Lewis claims, "—or [being] taken seriously for the wrong reason—had advantages, so long as leaders like Charles Johnson, James Weldon Johnson, and Du Bois knew what they were doing, were cautious about it, and adroitly manipulated their white patrons and allies."[27] For better or worse (and mostly for better), many of the interracial relationships that helped shape African American literary modernism were not nearly as cynical as many people today might like to believe.

Despite the interconnections between the various magazines I have mentioned, they can be divided roughly into four groups according to the main imperatives of their cultural politics: instruments of African American uplift and reform organizations (*The Crisis* and *Opportunity*), mainstream weeklies of the moderate left (*The Nation* and *The New Republic*), quarterlies of the bohemian and radical left (*Masses-Liberator-New Masses* and *Modern Quarterly*), and quarterlies of iconoclastic satire (*The Messenger* and *American Mercury*). Such is the order in which I will be discussing the magazines in the chapters ahead, followed by a discussion of the publishers of the Harlem Renaissance.

5

The Crisis and the Nation's Conscience

After his conversion in Mecca, Malcolm X used to say that sincere whites who wanted to help black people should organize among themselves to attack racism among white people, rather than attempting to join black organizations—which, in his view, were inevitably compromised and made ineffective by white influence. This kind of initiative, he charged, had never been attempted.[1] Actually, however, the most venerable of today's African American civil rights institutions originated in precisely such an effort. The founding of the NAACP exemplified in many crucial respects the intersections between American cultural nationalism, transnationalism, radical journalism, socialism, literature, and the black liberation movement in the creation of institutions that would support the Harlem Renaissance. And since the NAACP "began," according to those who were there, in response to an article by William English Walling published in *The Independent* and entitled "The Race War in the North," Walling's personal history is worth sketching briefly.[2]

From Native Socialism to the NAACP

A graduate of the University of Chicago, in the late 1890s Walling was a factory inspector living in a tenement district near Hull House. Here he met labor leaders, settlement workers, and the radical journalists and aspiring writers of the new urban realism who were to invigorate

137

American fiction. He moved to New York in 1902 and became a resident at the University Settlement in the largely Jewish Lower East Side, joining an energetic community of young writers and reformers, the forerunners of New York's "Little Renaissance." In 1905 he visited Russia to cover the abortive revolution there, writing pieces in which he idealized the oppressed Jews of czarist Russia as symbolic of oppressed people everywhere. Walling emphasized the importance of the peasants in the Russian Revolution, considering them true democrats, and opposed the bolsheviks because of their antidemocratic leanings. Lenin's revolution, Walling felt, was German-inspired rather than indigenously and democratically based, as any "true" socialism must be. Hence Walling's internationalism and socialism were wedded to a radical democratic, cultural nationalist and transnationalist ideology that he derived from Whitman and Dewey.

"Authentic" American socialism, Walling believed, was a product of American democracy, the outgrowth of specifically American experiences, institutions, and cultural traditions, with a heritage antedating Marxism.[3] One of Walling's unique divergences from canonical Marxism involved his definition of "class." Rather than dividing people into classes according to their relationship to the means of production (capitalists and workers), he based class divisions on access to wealth and power (the privileged and the nonprivileged). Walling's American socialism was thus inherently more attentive to the significance of racism (and sexism) in society than was the communism taking shape in Moscow. Moreover, Walling identified true socialism with radical democracy and pragmatism, attacking state socialism as a new form of class rule. As Robert B. Westbrook points out, Walling's approach is "a remarkable anticipation of the reasoning that would lead Dewey himself to an unorthodox democratic socialism some years later."[4]

Walling even tried to steer American socialists away from dependence on Marx and Engels, in great part by emphasizing the importance of Dewey. If all knowledge is a product of interaction with the social environment at a particular time and place, Walling believed, the mere application of "theories" is reactionary and dogmatic. All social truth is born in social struggle; Marx and Engels, although anticipating pragmatism in certain respects, had been too bent on using Hegel for socialist purposes and devoted vain efforts to the concept of materialist dialectics. *True* socialism must grow from different roots, responsive to particular cultural-historical realities.

Overall, Walling tried to reconcile modern socialism with democratic individuality. Yet he understood the development of the self as inherently social, always occurring in relation to other people, in distinct communities.[5] An early adherent to the idea of cultural pluralism, Walling thus believed that immigrant cultures should be free to develop in their own directions. In fact, he would attribute this position to Whitman in his book *Whitman and Traubel* (1916), which sought to discover the traditions of a socialist radical individualism in American poetry—indeed, to demonstrate "the socialist potential in the American character."[6]

Walling's cultural nationalism connected with a cosmopolitan sensibility, evidenced by his marriage to the radical journalist Anna Strunsky, who had been imprisoned in Russia for her revolutionary activities. In the months after their arrival in the United States, Walling and Strunsky wrote and lectured often on the Russian Revolution. In fact, they were in Chicago to lecture in late 1908 when the Springfield race riots broke out, and they decided to drop what they were doing to observe it. They were horrified by what they saw, a racist orgy of destruction and murder in Abraham Lincoln's home town on the ninety-ninth anniversary of his birth. Anna immediately sent reports to a black newspaper in Boston, while William wrote "The Race War in the North" and fired it off to *The Independent*. "Either the spirit of the abolitionists," he wrote, "of Lincoln and of Lovejoy must be revived and we must come to treat the Negro on a plane of absolute political and social equality, or Vardaman and Tillman will soon have transferred the race war to the North."[7]

After the publication of his article, Walling continued lecturing on Russia but found himself increasingly absorbed by the "Negro problem" in the United States and began featuring it in his lectures, noting that the Negro suffered more in the United States than did the Jew in czarist Russia. After one such lecture at the Cooper Union in December 1908, Mary White Ovington, already a W. E. B. Du Bois admirer, approached him and asked what he intended to *do* about the "race war." At the time, she was living in a "Negro tenement" and finishing her book *Half a Man,* on the plight of urban blacks. The two determined to take the responsibility of "doing something" upon themselves. For their initial conversations on the project they invited the socialist and muckraking journalist Charles Edward Russell to join them. Since he could not make the appointment, they called on Henry Moskowitz, a social worker and Jewish immigrant from Russia who was head resident of the Madison House social settlement on the Lower East Side. Meeting at Walling's apartment, the three drew up their initial plans for an organization to combat racism and decided to put out a national call for action on Lincoln's birthday in 1909.

Initially the three organizers were concerned that their project would fail for being perceived as too radical because of their own affiliations, so they recruited Oswald Garrison Villard to join them, a man perfectly positioned both to publicize the movement and to counteract the impression among potential allies that they were a bunch of far-left crackpots. Villard (grandson of William Lloyd Garrison) was publisher of the *New York Evening Post* and later *The Nation,* which he re-infused with the old abolitionist spirit of its founders and made into one of the mainstream forums of the Harlem Renaissance—as well as American literary nationalism. Indeed, the NAACP first operated rent-free out of the offices of Villard's *Evening Post.*

When the call for a national meeting to address the expanding racist activism went out on Lincoln's birthday in 1909, it was signed by sixty men and women, including John Dewey, W. E. B. Du Bois, Jane Addams, William Dean Howells, and Lincoln Steffens—the preeminent pragmatist, black activist intellectual, settlement house organizer, turn-of-the-century literary nationalist, and muckraker. The conference opened on May 30, 1909, with a reception given by Lillian Wald at the Henry Street Settlement, one of the few New York establishments that would serve a mixed group (and later the home of the Neighborhood Playhouse, one of the most important institutions of the little theater movement).[8] William Hayes Ward, editor of *The Independent,* delivered the opening address, blasting racist views about the inferiority of people of African descent, and was supported by the lecture of Livingston Farrand, professor of anthropology at Columbia, who outlined the Boasian argument against "scientific" racism. John Dewey pointed out that American society was defeating itself if it did not provide an environment in which all individuals could fully develop their powers.[9]

Walling himself believed that the real founding of the NAACP dated from Du Bois's arrival as an officer; in fact he originally proposed Du Bois for chairman of the Executive Committee, Walling's own position at the time, but the proposal failed, and Du Bois became director of publications and research. By attracting Du Bois, the NAACP connected up with the Niagara Movement, on which Mary White Ovington had reported at the time of its founding. This movement's "Address to the Country" of 1906, from John Brown's grave at Harper's Ferry, demanded complete social and political equality, in the name of the True "American Creed": "The battle we wage is not for ourselves alone but for all true Americans. It is a fight for ideals, lest this, our common fatherland, false to its founding, become in truth the land of the Thief and the home of the Slave—a by-word and a hissing among the nations for its sounding pretensions and pitiful accomplishment."[10] The manifesto strikes what would be the dominant chord of *Crisis* magazine, a magazine that sought to be not only a beacon to black folk but the conscience of the nation. Indeed, *The Crisis* got its name from a poem written by James Russell Lowell in the heat of the war to save the nation and, in the event, to free the slaves.[11] The name also echoes that of Tom Paine's fiery pamphlet series of the American Revolution.

In a rhetorical strategy often employed in *The Crisis* and going back to the slave narratives, the Harper's Ferry statement parodies the American national anthem to give an inverted image of the national ideal; yet it implicitly embraces the terms it replaces—"the land of the free and the home of the brave"—as it claims intimacy with the "fatherland" and the nation's founding. Indeed the very name of the movement, Niagara, recalls a symbol internationally identified at that time with the United States; it also recalls Thomas Carlyle's famous essay "Shooting Niagara," which had featured the granting of social and political rights to African Americans after the Civil War as the perfect proof of democracy's absurdity, provoking Whitman's ringing response and classic critique of American culture, *Democratic Vistas*.

The Niagara Movement's positions were largely identical to those of the NAACP, but the organization lacked the funding and influence that would have given it a greater base of power. It also explicitly prohibited full membership by whites. The NAACP seemed to promise greater effectiveness for the campaign against institutionalized racism. Du Bois himself wrote Joel Spingarn in 1914 about the usual failures of race reform efforts: "No organization like ours ever succeeded in America; either it became a group of white philanthropists helping the Negro like the Anti-Slavery societies; or it became a group of colored folk freezing out their white co-workers by insolence and distrust."[12] Never (to say the least) free of these problems itself, the NAACP nonetheless managed to accomplish a great deal, considering the odds. Among its most important accomplishments in the early years was the publication of *The Crisis* magazine, which surely ranks as one of the great journalistic enterprises in American history.

The Crisis and American Ideals

The Crisis fulfilled a longstanding dream of Du Bois to edit a "high class of journal" circulating among "the intelligent Negroes" and binding them together in pursuit of "definite ideals."[13] Although Du Bois was not always in direct control of the day-to-day operation and literary aspects of *The Crisis,* the magazine unmistakably expressed his point of view.[14] In its cultural criticism, it continually hammered home the point that whatever was most American, culturally speaking, had an African American origin. This idea goes back to the abolitionist period, and was shared, incidentally, by such transcendentalists as Theodore Parker and Margaret Fuller.

The point—a cardinal theme of *The Souls of Black Folk*—went hand in hand with the overriding equation that officers of the NAACP repeatedly made between "emancipation of the Negro race in America and the emancipation of America itself," as they stated in their "Resolutions at the Cooper Union on Lincoln's Birthday." If America could not yield equality to her black citizens, "then America herself is impossible and the vast dreams of Washington, Jefferson and Lincoln are vain."[15] Quoting Thoreau on the cover of the February 1915 issue, *The Crisis* asked: "Do you call this the land of the free? What is it to be free from King George and continue the slaves of King Prejudice? What is it to be born free and not to live free?"—this at a time well before Thoreau entered the American canon. Just as the movement for racial equality was a "concrete test" of American ideals, so were American ideals thought to be most profoundly exemplified in African American culture. Contrastingly, to judge from *Crisis* editorials and cartoons, the most distinctively American cultural practice of white citizens was the ritual of lynching.

In the role of scapegoat, the Negro, according to James Weldon Johnson, had helped shape the white American ethos and psyche: "Estimate, if you can," he would write in his autobiography, "the effect upon the making of the character of the American people caused by the opportunity which the Negro has involuntarily given the dominant majority to practice injustice, wrong, and brutality for three hundred years with impunity upon a practically defenseless minority."[16] Johnson hinted at the pervasive importance to white American development of its own "racialization" and the rituals by which it sought to preserve its presumed "racial purity." This point formed a sort of leitmotif in issues of *The Crisis* throughout the 1910s and 1920s. For Johnson and the *Crisis* staff, the lynching victim became a kind of national icon, and one mission of the magazine was to expose the moral bankruptcy and hypocrisy of "nigger-hating America."

A parallel and complementary perspective upon the nightmare of racism was that the suffering of the black American, however connected to the fate of the "darker races" everywhere, was a peculiarly *American* suffering. Thus the cultural practices invented to cope with it, challenge it, and transform it into expressive value are deeply and essentially "American," in a way that opens upon fundamental existential questions and religious form. In the souls of black folk alone, *The Crisis* often stated or implied, is the spiritual foundation of "America"—according to the black transvaluation of that term. Du Bois, of course, explicitly connected the suffering of the American Negro with that of the "darker races" globally but viewed the United States as the most racist of all nations; and the contradiction between her racism and her egalitarian pretensions made the United States distinctive even among white-dominated countries. Moreover, the placement of the American Negro gave "him" a distinctive mission in the world, particularly in the century whose chief problem, as Du Bois then saw it, was "the problem of the color line." Black Americans were the vanguard of all "the darker races," uniquely situated to play the role of the "chosen people" in a messianic drama infused with the ideology of American exceptionalism.

The argument for the "indigenous" quality of African American culture found a particularly receptive audience in 1917 when James Weldon Johnson attended a three-day conference of the Intercollegiate Socialist Society (notable members of which included Charles Beard, John Dewey, Franz Boas, Randolph Bourne, Clarence Darrow, and William English Walling) and read a paper on the contribution of the Negro to American culture. The paper had a widespread effect, in part because of its impact on a young reporter in the audience. Herbert J. Seligmann, who had served on the editorial staffs of the *New York Evening Post* (Villard's paper) and *The New Republic,* reported enthusiastically on the speech for the *New York Times;* paragraphs of his summary went around the globe and were reprinted by periodicals abroad.

According to Johnson himself, "The statement that evoked the greatest interest—and some controversy—was that the only things artistic in America that have sprung from American soil, permeated American life, and been universally acknowledged as distinctively American, had been the creations of the American Negro."[17] Soon Seligmann was hired by the NAACP to be its director of publicity, establishing a news service that helped relieve *The Crisis* of the responsibility to publicize NAACP affairs, allowing it to become more exclusively a cultural and political journal in the 1920s.[18]

The incident illustrates once again the crosscurrents of American cultural nationalism and the New Negro movement, for Seligmann was also a poet and follower of Alfred Stieglitz (who, as Seligmann liked to point out, put on the first show anywhere in which African sculpture was displayed as art rather than ethnographic specimen).[19] Indeed, between 1922 and 1923 Seligmann helped edit the Stieglitz-instigated magazine, *MSS,* which published work by such artists as Sherwood Anderson, Ernest Bloch, Charlie Chaplin, Charles Demuth, Arthur Dove, Waldo Frank, Georgia O'Keeffe, Carl Sandburg, and William Carlos Williams.[20] Seligmann was a good friend of Stieglitz in the period when Jean Toomer joined the group, as he was completing *Cane*. Both viewed Stieglitz in heroic terms, "fighting for the very existence of the living spirit in America"; through his early lonely efforts, Seligmann wrote, Stieglitz had cultivated "something distinctly national, a potential flowering akin to those utterances in which nations of the past had come to their own timeless and essential character."[21] In the mid-1930s, Toomer similarly called Stieglitz "the man who has *done* more for modern art in America than any other single person, who has established a standard of truth."[22] After the photographer's death, Georgia O'Keeffe (at Carl Van Vechten's urging) donated a large and stunning portion of his private art collection to Fisk University. Seligmann's interest in Stieglitz developed *at the same time* as his involvement with the NAACP, and his views of American modernism informed his work in both areas. Hence *The Negro Faces America* (1920) addresses the emergence of a "new Negro" with a militant political awareness joined to a consciousness of cultural power; the book concludes with the statement that "the American Negro, disillusioned, newly emancipated from reliance upon any white savior, stands ready to make his unique contribution to what may some time become American civilization."[23] Implicit in Seligmann's argument is once again the general NAACP argument that the condition of the American Negro is a test of the emancipation of American culture itself from a colonial mentality.

The aspects of black cultural nationalism that Du Bois and others associated with *The Crisis* embraced were wedded to a militantly integrationist vision founded in what they perceived as American ideals. On this point even the most embittered antagonists in the ongoing power struggles within the NAACP could agree. When Du Bois fought for total control over *The Crisis,* with resistance coming particularly from Villard (who saw it as an organ of the NAACP), he rhetorically buttressed his argument with a reminder of the fundamental purpose of the magazine, as agreed to by all: "the great ideal of establishing in the United States a dignified and authoritative organ of public opinion which should stand for the fundamental principles of American democracy."[24] This aim had not yet been achieved, and could not be without total editorial freedom. Villard stepped down from the chairmanship of the NAACP in 1914, to be replaced by the celebrated literary critic of "Young America," Joel Spingarn. Given Spingarn's reputation as a champion of intellectual independence, it was an inspired choice. Du Bois called the event "the first real although tacit decision as to my power over the policy of the *Crisis.*"[25]

From the early teens into the twenties, *The Crisis* emphasized the American Negro's desire to share in a common American civilization, with racial distinctions subordinated to common aspirations and common values. This did not mean accepting the contemporary civilization of the United States as the "American" norm. To the extent that *The Crisis* could be characterized as "assimilationist" at times in its ultimate vision of the United States, its idea of assimilation entailed the "blackening" of the national culture, a process it recognized as having begun before the founding of the nation itself and apparently accelerating in the early twentieth century, despite a simultaneous intensification of racism. At the same time, the magazine consistently argued that the American Negro was thoroughly a product of American experience and institutions.

While *The Crisis* promoted pan-Africanism, the liberation of Africa, and the solidarity of "the darker races" against worldwide white domination, it was anything but Afrocentric—hence its well-known, impassioned opposition to Marcus Garvey. As James Weldon Johnson would point out, the main reason for Garvey's failure to win broad support among what Johnson termed "thoughtful American Negroes" was his

"African scheme," which evoked memories of the Colonization Society of a century earlier. According to Johnson, the first national convention of Negroes in America was called by people opposing a return to Africa, and the NAACP was not about to buckle under to the concept that America could not be "home" to African Americans: "The central idea of Garvey's scheme was absolute abdication and the recognition as facts of the assertions that this is a white man's country, a country in which the Negro has no place, no right, no chance, no future." To Johnson, the "overwhelming majority of thoughtful American Negroes will not subscribe" to such an idea.[26]

Even when *The Crisis* pushed pan-Africanist ideas in the years of the New Negro, it did not conceive of this thrust as antithetical to the Americanness of the American Negro, any more than Horace Kallen, for example, conceived of Zionism as antithetical to the Americanness of the American Jew. In one of his most forceful editorials after the close of World War I, "Africa for Africans," Du Bois carefully differentiated his position from Garvey's, in phrases that Jessie Fauset would put in the mouth of one of the heroes of *There Is Confusion:* "Once for all, let us realize that we are Americans, that we were brought here with the earliest settlers, and that the very sort of civilization from which we came made the complete adoption of western modes and customs imperative if we were to survive at all. In brief, there is nothing so indigenous, so completely 'made in America' as we."[27] Amelioration of conditions in Africa would aid the amelioration of conditions for people of African descent everywhere; the movement for the liberation of Africa paralleled the Zionist movement as a "centralization of race effort and the recognition of a racial front." It was part of a worldwide tactical movement against white supremacy but not necessarily against the western cultural inheritance of African Americans, let alone their identification with the civilization of the United States.

Instead of supporting Garvey's insistence on separation from American culture and society, *The Crisis* challenged the equation of American culture with *white* American culture and promoted a variant of American civil religion, basing its critiques of American society on the society's betrayal of the sacred vision for which the likes of Crispus Attucks, Lincoln, Lovejoy, and John Brown had died—along with black soldiers of the Revolution, the Civil War, and World War I. While Lincoln was a figure revered in the nation as a whole, publications in *The Crisis* emphasized that the real meaning of his life had been lost to most white Americans, as exemplified in the race riots in Springfield that prompted the formation of the NAACP. Lincoln belonged first of all to black America, as James Weldon Johnson suggested in his featured birthday invocation of the martyred ancestor, "Father, Father Abraham":

> Father, Father Abraham,
>   To-day look on us from above;
> On us, the offspring of thy faith,
>   The children of thy Christlike love.[28]

That black intellectuals' enthusiasm for Lincoln has considerably cooled since Johnson's generation should not prevent us from appreciating the importance many African Americans of the early twentieth century placed upon claiming him as one of their own. Many felt a deep identification with the American icon, as with the heroes of the Old Testament—an identification that helped reinforce the powerful, unkillable belief in their American birthright. As Johnson wrote again: "We've bought a rightful sonship here, / And we have more than paid the price":

> Think you that John Brown's spirit stops?
>   That Lovejoy was but idly slain?
> Or do you think those precious drops
>   From Lincoln's heart were shed in vain?[29]

Even "Lift Every Voice and Sing," popularly known as the black national anthem, was written in celebration of Lincoln's birthday by James Weldon and Rosamond Johnson.[30]

The point that Lincoln's martyrdom was being betrayed by white America was also made in Vachel Lindsay's short story contribution of 1914, "The Golden-Faced People: A Story of the Conquest of America." In this story, a recently "emancipated" people, white and indigenous to the continent, are oppressed by a Chinese people who once invaded and enslaved them. The Chinese hypocritically observe the birthday of a Chinese emancipator of the whites, "Lin-Kon," with racist ceremonies, including one in which the story's cowardly white narrator gives an accommodationist, Booker T. Washington–style speech to the Chinese overlords and thus betrays the fight for full equality.[31] What is striking here is not merely the relativizing of racial identities or the identification of "Lin-Kon" with the racial "other," but also the identification of that "other" as indigenously American, in contrast to the oppressors. Lindsay's story—an early one in his career—fits in well with Du Bois's vision.

The Crisis valued "The Golden-Faced People" highly, only to criticize its author later for his poem "The Congo" for its presentation of American Negroes as exotic "Africans." Obtuse to the criticism, Lindsay wrote asking for an explanation, and Du Bois published a response from Joel Spingarn: "You look about you and see a black world full of a strange beauty different from that of the white world; they look about them and see other men with exactly the same feelings and desires who refuse to recognize the resemblance. You look forward to a colored Utopia separate and different from the hope of the white man; they have only one overwhelming desire, and that is to share in a common civilization in which all distinctions of race are blurred (or forgotten) by common aspiration and common labors."[32] Even for Spingarn, this was an unusually assimilationist point of view, provoked by the rhetorical situation of countering Lindsay's caricatures, but it was pretty much of a piece with the cultural orientation of *The Crisis.*

In general, Spingarn was a "soft" cultural pluralist (or "cosmopolitan"), believing in the importance of black culture to American culture as a whole and combining support for black cultural distinctiveness with a militant integrationism.[33] But Spingarn apparently had very little to do with the critical stance of *The Crisis;* on this score, he was more involved with *The Seven Arts* in the late teens. He was a close friend of Van Wyck Brooks and Lewis Mumford, who occasionally stayed at his estate in Amenia. "Troutbeck"—formerly the home of Walt Whitman's great friend and champion John Burroughs—would also serve as a retreat for important NAACP functionaries and as the setting for two of the organization's important conferences.

Spingarn's own preferences in critical theory and literature had little to do with his functions at the NAACP; but these two aspects of his life join in his commitment to intellectual freedom and American idealism, and there is no question about his admiration for Du Bois's prose. Du Bois later attested that of all the judgments on him, he cherished most the verdicts of John Hope and Joel Spingarn, who had written him in 1918: "I know that some people think that an artist is a man who has nothing to say and who writes in order to prove it. The great writers of the world have not so conceived their task, and neither have you.

Though your service has been for the most part the noble one of teacher and prophet (not merely to one race or nation but to the world), I challenge the artists of America to show more beautiful passages than some of those in *Darkwater* and *The Souls of Black Folk*."[34] Above all, Spingarn regarded Du Bois as a great American hero battling the main threat to what he called "the whole American tradition of toleration and human equality."[35] Despite his heated confrontations with Du Bois over what he considered the latter's insubordination, Spingarn appears always to have recognized Du Bois's importance to American literature and society; Du Bois, in turn, held Spingarn's literary judgment in high regard.[36]

Arbiters of Literary Americanism: Braithwaite and Fauset

Generally speaking, those men and women of letters whose judgment Du Bois trusted and featured in *The Crisis* based their literary criticism on an assumption of the Americanness of "the American Negro," and did not see important distinctions between black and white aesthetics. In the years leading up to the Harlem Renaissance, for example, Du Bois featured William Stanley Braithwaite as black America's premier literary critic and the chief authority on poetry for *Crisis* magazine, calling him in 1915 "the foremost critic and expositor of American poetry," and querying, "Curious, is it not, that this defense of poetry among white folk should come and come so naturally from colored lips?"[37] Braithwaite, who in early issues was listed on the cover of *The Crisis* with Carter G. Woodson as one of Du Bois's two editorial consultants, won the NAACP's prestigious Spingarn Medal in 1918 for the highest achievement by an American of African descent "in any field of human endeavor." To Du Bois, Braithwaite's position in the American literary world (as critic for the Boston *Transcript* and yearly anthologist of American poetry from 1913 to 1929) promised the fulfillment of his own prophecy that "the great gift of Negro blood to America" would be in art and "realization of beauty."[38] Braithwaite regarded the development of African American poetry in the early years of the century as part of the general American poetic "renascence" he himself was promoting with all his energy.

Braithwaite believed that American poetry from the turn of the century, belatedly catching on to Whitman's example, had begun to "disengage" from English and European poetry. The chief duty of the American critic, he felt, was to encourage this development. He noted that by 1917 American poetry still had a need for criticism answering the challenge issued ten years earlier by Joel Spingarn that America had failed to develop a "creative criticism." In its place, what Braithwaite found was a "disintegrating" criticism, developed along "alien lines": "It clings to the tradition that artistic standards must be imported, and in applying those standards compares American poetry to its disadvantage with English and European poetry, forgetting that in all essentials of life, experience, and culture America is fundamentally and superficially different from Europe."[39] This criticism, moreover, stressed "styles and form," "rules and tradition," above matters of "substance," intellectual and emotional content, and "spiritual qualities" specific to the American situation. Hence, in Braithwaite's view, "the influence of this kind of criticism can do more harm to American poetry at present than any other influence whatever." It would inhibit public appreciation and depress the market for American poetry, which, in a democratic nation without a tradition of patronage, would discourage further poetic production.[40]

The reign of British ideals over American art was "exhausted" by the end of the century, Braithwaite believed, while Whitman's challenge was finally finding its first timid answerers. Interestingly, Braithwaite would include Longfellow, Poe, and Lowell in the British line of descent, with Whitman at the head of an alternative tradition.[41]

Yet despite his admiration for Whitman, Braithwaite's criticism was far from radical by contemporary standards; in fact, in his reading, Whitman was important above all as "a spiritual artist and mystic."[42] To Braithwaite the great poet was an ecstatic, able to plumb spiritual mysteries and express them lyrically. On the subject of formal experimentation, Braithwaite believed that new techniques should "communicate adequately and appealingly the substance dealt with."[43] No poetry could aspire to a higher function than to express "truth and beauty" in accessible forms. Braithwaite's (and *Crisis* magazine's) hope for African American poetry cannot be understood in isolation from such aesthetic values, nor in isolation from the conviction that it must be understood as *American* poetry, in a broadly assimilationist sense. Little of the poetry published in *The Crisis* used dialect or vernacular forms; in fact, most of it did not address racial issues at all.

In his important essay for *The Crisis* of 1919, "Some Contemporary Poets of the Negro Race," Braithwaite began by noting that "the present revival of poetry in America could scarcely advance without carrying in its wake the impulse and practice of a poetic consciousness in the Negro race."[44] This introductory statement implies not only the identity of the budding New Negro poetry with the American cultural nationalist revival, but also the importance of that poetry *to* the revival. Yet it is interesting to see who he thought were important figures of the time. Countee Cullen and James Weldon Johnson he considered poets carrying on an American tradition with E. Merrill Root, Scudder Middleton, John Hall Wheelock, Sara Bard Field, Rosa Zagnoni Marinoni, Glenn Ward Dresbach, and Lizette Woodworth Reese.[45]

To Braithwaite, who was repeatedly a judge for *Crisis* poetry contests and later the Harmon Award, the Negro was not a "bi-national" artist. The folk tradition, for example, he did not consider the beginning of a separate black American tradition in poetry, albeit he acknowledged a beauty in black folk expression akin to that of folk expression the world over. He considered "dialect" merely an attempt to imitate the speech of a dominant class; he did not look for an African American literary tradition developing out of folk speech and folk rhetoric.[46] Thus the poetry of the spirituals, for example, was "the poetry of an ancient race passing through the throes of an enforced re-birth into the epoch of an alien and dominating civilization."[47] As the last gasp of the spirit that moved the spirituals, the dialect tradition had decidedly run its course, finding its culminating expression in Dunbar—"it was the finale, in a rather conscious manner, of centuries of spiritual isolation."[48] Dunbar had voiced the "end of a regime, and not the beginning of a tradition."

Behind the fading echoes of that regime could be heard the new sounds of an "awakening impulse" that finally broke out in W. E. B. Du Bois's lyrically impassioned prose. In *The Souls of Black Folk*, Braithwaite boldly contended, Du Bois "began a poetic tradition," profoundly redirecting the "spiritual nature of the race" and revealing to all the world the high idealism and aspiration of the American Negro. With a fulsome statement of faith in Du Bois's contribution and the direction of African American poetry, Braithwaite prophesied that "it is only through the intense, passionate, spiritual idealism of such substance as makes 'The Souls of Black Folk' such a quivering rhapsody of wrongs endured and hopes to be fulfilled that the poets of the race with compelling artistry can lift the Negro into the only full and complete nationalism he knows—that of the American democracy."[49]

Braithwaite's favorite novels of the Harlem Renaissance period, not surprisingly, were Jessie Fauset's and Nella Larsen's—Fauset he considered one of the best American novelists, in the tradition of Sarah Orne Jewett, Mary Wilkins Freeman, Edith Wharton, Dorothy Canfield Fisher, Willa Cather, Julia Peterkin, and Zona Gale. She was "the potential Jane Austen of Negro literature."[50] This is another indication of the continuity of critical positions taken toward literature in *The Crisis* through the mid-1920s, as Fauset would become literary editor on the verge of the Harlem Renaissance decade.

Braithwaite did not, as Claude McKay once charged, counsel black poets to avoid "racial themes"; he believed that poets could express racial aspirations and write on "racial material" in ways that expressed the "fundamental passions and primary instincts of humanity"—that is, in ways he would call universal. And he found such poetry in James Weldon Johnson's *Fifty Years* (calling Johnson the "foremost poet of the race" in 1919) as well as Claude McKay's early sonnets for *The Seven Arts*. Criticizing the treatment of blacks in American literary works by white authors, he expected black writers to contribute an important dimension to, and an implicit critique of, the "native" tradition even while he emphasized that, by and large, the "advanced class" of black Americans had absorbed essentially the same cultural traditions as their white American cohorts, producing a "standard of form in written and oral speech" that was characteristic of a "class co-racial consciousness."[51] Did not the very critique of racism voiced by such authors as Johnson, Du Bois, and Fauset bespeak their cultural "Americanness"? While such a point of view has inherent limitations, all too apparent today, we need to resist caricature in order to understand it.

The *Crisis* editors, in common with Braithwaite, would decry an over-emphasis on the ways in which black Americans departed from white middle-class norms for two main reasons. As is well known, the "exaggeration" of difference tended to play into white stereotypes about blacks and the fiercely resented white tendency to identify all black people with the behavior of the "worst" of their "group" while ignoring the fact that middle-class African Americans had achieved the same levels of education and "refinement" as their white cohorts. But even more important, much of the literature on "Negro themes" of the late 1920s implicitly accepted white middle-class behavior as normative, playing off the behavior of both lower-class and middle-class blacks against its "mainstream" stability, supposed ordinariness, and false con-

fidence. The fiction of the "black bourgeoisie" that *The Crisis* wanted to
see would take the black middle-class point of view as normative,
judging the white upper and middle classes from the vantage point of
the highly educated American of African descent, a person who took
pride in defining *herself* as American, and taking the measure of white
America's failure to become either thoroughly "civilized" *or* "Americanized." Thus Du Bois and Fauset found the American white upper classes
morally inferior and vulgar, and the middle and lower classes often
"savage." The bumptious, parochial nationalism, insensitivity, and
downright cruelty that they depicted as standard aspects of the white
American character were played off against the civility, cosmopolitanism, and committed democratic idealism—in short, cultured Americanism—of their black heroines and heroes.

Du Bois's "Criteria of Negro Art" provides a good example of this
strategy. "We want to be Americans," he writes, "full-fledged Americans,
with all the rights of other American citizens. But is that all?" After a
description of American tourists loudly interrupting his meditations at
the shore of the lake Walter Scott had immortalized in "The Lady of
the Lake," he notes that "their hearts had no conception of the beauty
which pervaded this holy place"—in short, they lacked "culture," aesthetic refinement, which is continuous with "good manners," and
simple consideration for others. Black Americans, Du Bois argues,
realize the shallowness of materialistic and selfish ideals "sooner than
the average American because, pushed aside as we have been in
America, there has come to us not only a certain distaste for the tawdry
and flamboyant but a vision of what the world could be if it were really
a beautiful world," if we "lived in a world where men know, where men
create, where they realize themselves and where they enjoy life. It is that
sort of a world we want to create for ourselves and for all America."[52] Du
Bois's utopia here, dependent as it is on the development of specifically
aesthetic powers, shares central features with those of Max Eastman and
John Dewey even as he turns his redefinition of Americanism against
what he regards as "white" Americanism.

A similar theme plays an important part in Jessie Fauset's short story
"There Was One Time!," published in *The Crisis* in the April and May
issues of 1917. Director of the magazine's "What to Read" department
since 1912, Fauset would serve as literary editor from 1919 until 1926
and produce four novels between 1924 and 1934. Langston Hughes
later stated that she, together with Charles S. Johnson and Alain Locke,

"midwifed the so-called New Negro literature into being."[53] Throughout her fiction as well as her criticism and correspondence one finds a tension, as Arnold Rampersad has pointed out, between an emphasis on the distinctive experience of African Americans and Fauset's conviction of basic cultural similarities between bourgeois blacks and whites.[54] This tension, indeed, pervaded the cultural criticism of *The Crisis* generally. The Americanness of the American Negro—as much as the ingrained racism of the white American—was one of Fauset's principal themes, embodying this very tension within itself.

"There Was One Time!" is a prime exhibit of what *The Crisis* looked for in fiction. A love story, it focuses on the relationship between the teacher Anna Ritter, a "typical American girl done over in brown" who had grown up in a white neighborhood with little experience of racism, and Richard Winter, a well-educated and idealistic young man whose goal is to be a settlement house worker and eventually preach a gospel of black American pride. He aspires "to tell our folks that there is nothing more supremely American than the colored American, nothing more made-in-America, so to speak."[55]

At twenty-six, Anna has only recently become fully aware of the many ways in which racism will always affect her life—from restricting job opportunities to making her the object of white men's vulgar sexual advances. One manner of escaping these pressures momentarily is to fantasize; at the moment she meets the hero, she has been strolling in a park, imagining herself as a French shepherdess, only to be rudely brought back to reality by the sexual solicitation of a white tramp whom the courteous and calmly courageous Dick Winter frightens away. For Fauset, the answer to racism in American life is not alienation from one's race *or* country, but rather a reenvisioning of that race and that country, a pride precisely in the Americanness of the American Negro and the blackness of the "true" America. The point is brought home with a special intensity because Winter, though born and raised to age ten in America, has spent most of his life in British Guiana and France; this experience has caused him to identify all the more fiercely with his native land and people. He was born in the town identified with Walt Whitman, Fauset's own home town—Camden, New Jersey—"and if that doesn't make me American I don't know what does."[56] On his homecoming, he wanted to wave his hat and shout, "I'm an American and I've come home. Aren't you glad to see me? If you only knew how proud

I am to be here."[57] Yet to get a room at a decent New York hotel he had claimed to be British. (Subtly, this incident suggests the cultural insecurity of white America, the obeisance to Europe that, ironically, is part and parcel of its uniquely American racism.)

Fighting the implication that a black man must sacrifice his Americanness to save his pride, Winter repudiates white definitions of what is American. Harlem, the most interesting place in the nation, is "America done over in color"—and truer than downtown New York to the national principles.[58] Yet Winter finds little of the self-confidence in black Americans that a consciousness of their cultural importance should bring: "It struck me there was a lack of self-esteem, a lack of self-appreciation, and a tendency to measure ourselves by false ideals."[59] His cultural nationalism asserts itself in an insistence upon the recognition that there is no sweeter fat than sticks to one's own bones. Moreover, a double alienation is hinted at; if American Negroes measure themselves by false white American ideals, those ideals themselves are not even American, as the incident in the hotel, as well as Anna's fantasy of herself as a French maiden, indicate. Winter had been watching Anna from a distance, "thinking how very American you were and all that sort of thing," when the tramp had intruded upon her French fantasy.[60] Self-awareness and confidence would come "if we could just realize the warmth and background which we supply to America, the mellowness, the rhythm, the music."[61] The background music to Fauset's story, as if to reinforce this point, is provided by the quintessentially American—African American—banjo of Anna's brother, Theo.

At the close of Fauset's tale, Anna and Richard are on the way to becoming engaged, and Richard is about to go to New York to work in a social settlement. He envisions marrying Anna and moving back to Europe after the world war to make a fortune—he building bridges, she drawing the plans—and then returning to America to preach his gospel of black American pride. "Till then," he tells Anna, "you could help me live that wonderful fairy-tale."[62] This is a distinctly *American* fairy-tale, in Fauset's terms, set off against the "false ideals" and foreign models that have kept Americans enthralled. Combining an emphasis on the distinctiveness of black American experience and culture with American cultural nationalism, as well as with the propaganda of racial uplift and the promotion of middle-class values, Fauset's story was in many ways a quintessential expression of the cultural orientation of *The Crisis*. Moreover, despite a tendency toward a conventional ideology of gender, it imagines a relationship between black male and black female based on equal partnership and common goals. Fauset further developed this vision in her novels of the twenties.

As literary editor of *The Crisis*, Fauset gave literature a featured position, thereby promoting the careers of most of the black authors of the era. By and large, her guidance (and attempted guidance) of black writing cohered with Du Bois's tastes. Given his tenacious will to have the magazine express his point of view, this is not surprising; but it may have worked to Fauset's own detriment in the long run, as younger authors frequently carped at what they unsympathetically considered her "prim" and bourgeois preferences. As Carolyn Wedin Sylvander has shown, Fauset was less conventional and Victorian than the image often foisted on her.[63]

Nonetheless, there is no gainsaying the fact that younger authors resisted her critical views—her dislike of vernacular and free verse poetry, for example. This is especially true of Langston Hughes, whom Fauset supposedly "discovered." Far from trusting Fauset's judgment, Hughes repeatedly ignored her advice. On the back of one of the letters she sent him in the mid-1920s, he wrote, in anticipation of her response to *The Weary Blues* and its foreword by Van Vechten: "There will probably be uproar enough that one of their leading (?) poets, and a public representative of the Race allows such a 'delightfully fantastic career' to be exposed to the world. They would have me a 'nice boy' and a college graduate. In other words,—a good example. Middle-class colored people are very conventional."[64] In other letters of the period, Fauset tried to steer Hughes away from free verse and warned him against Van Vechten's baneful influence; in one, for example, she mentioned that, in spite of her distaste for the man, she was inviting him to a party at her place to reciprocate his hospitality to her—this at a time when Hughes was about to come to New York and *stay* with Van Vechten.[65] In general, one gets the impression from Fauset's correspondence with Hughes that any moves he took that conflicted with her advice she attributed to Van Vechten's interference.

Not surprisingly, the publication of *Nigger Heaven* widened the breach between Hughes and Fauset. When she sent him the *Crisis* questionnaire for a series the magazine was to run on how the Negro should be portrayed, she wrote that "the problem as to what is acceptable material in the portrayal of the Negro is creating a pretty serious dilemma for those of us who are either actually creating or who are interested in the development of forms of Negro Art." On the back of this very letter Hughes began immediately to compose his now well-known retort that "the true literary artist is going to write about anything he chooses anyway regardless of outside opinions"—the kernel of his famous argument in "The Negro Artist and the Racial Mountain."[66] Thinking that Van Vechten was trying to dissuade Hughes from going to college, Fauset urged Hughes to apply to Harvard; the contacts and prestige, she pointed out, would help him toward a lucrative career. She explicitly tried to steer him away from Lincoln University.[67]

Claude McKay, on the other hand, hoped that Lincoln would do for Hughes what the University of Michigan had done for Robert Frost— that is, help him develop into a master of vernacular American poetry— adding, "You should [*sic*] be bothered about the whims and prejudices of the Negro intelligentsia. They are death to any wouldbe Negro artist. A plague on them and however hard hit and down I am they won't get their claws on me."[68] Of Van Vechten's *Nigger Heaven*, McKay informed Hughes, "I knew . . . it would be no 'nice' little book to please the exquisite taste of the Negro intelligentsia"; it was just the sort of novel McKay had intended to write. Having been beaten to the idea, he wrote *Home to Harlem*, which, like *Nigger Heaven*, got roasted by Du Bois. However, claimed McKay, he worried more about what his Marxist friends at *The New Masses* would think of his work than about how the Negro "uplifters" responded to it.[69] About this time Hughes himself was becoming increasingly identified with *The New Masses*, and Du Bois's handling of literary affairs at *The Crisis* had alienated virtually all the most promising younger writers. Du Bois apparently never understood precisely how this had come to pass. In *Dusk of Dawn* (1940) he asserted that the drop in circulation of *The Crisis* and in contributions to the NAACP had forced New Negro literature "to place its dependence almost entirely upon a white audience," which drove the young writers into decadence. Nonetheless, he continued,

> we were particularly proud to have had the chance to publish some bits of real literature; like that great poem of the black man's part in the war by Roscoe Jamison:
>
>> These truly are the Brave,
>> These men who cast aside
>> Old memories, to walk the blood-stained pave
>> Of Sacrifice, joining the solemn tide

That moves away, to suffer and to die
For Freedom—when their own is yet denied!
O Pride! O Prejudice! When they pass you by,
Hail them, the Brave, for you now crucified![70]

Fortunately, the young poets heard other drums beating in the wind.

Invoking a "National Negro Theatre"

The continuities as well as shifts in the orientation of cultural criticism
in *The Crisis* can be seen in the magazine's efforts to call a "Negro theatre" into being, encouraged by the general ferment in American
drama of the period, and specifically by the critical acclaim accorded
new (white-authored) "Negro plays." Early on, *The Crisis* featured chiefly
propaganda plays concerning racial oppression in the United States
and the heroic resistance of African Americans. Often the Americanism
of the Negro played an important part in these plays. Thus Alice
Dunbar-Nelson's *Mine Eyes Have Seen,* published in 1918, focuses on the
psychological struggle of a black man drafted to fight in the war. Why,
he wonders, should he enter the ranks of an army to defend democracy
abroad while his own country refuses to treat him as a full citizen? His
family and neighbors, including an Irish and a Russian Jewish immigrant, urge him to enter the lists, citing the parallels between his situation and that of Jews in Russia or the Irish in the United Kingdom.
Stressing the protagonist's American birthright, the heroic contributions of African Americans in the national history, the play reinforces
Du Bois's convictions that the Negro should close ranks with the Allied
forces, the better to fight for democracy after the war; and it ends with
the sounds of a regiment marching to the tune of "The Battle Hymn of
the Republic."[71] A related play, published in 1920, is Joseph Seamon
Cotter's melodramatic *On the Fields of France,* in which a white officer
and a black officer die hand in hand after a battle, together exclaiming
"America!" As they expire, the phantoms of George Washington,
Crispus Attucks, Robert E. Lee, William Carney, and Robert Gould
Shaw summon them to a heaven cum national pantheon.[72]

   This sort of overt appeal to American civil religion increasingly gave
way, after the war, to an interest in more subtle approaches to the
Negro's significance for national identity. *The Crisis,* for example, had
already been calling for a "folk drama" based on the experience of

"Negro American life" when Ridgely Torrence's *Three Plays for a Negro Theatre* reached the stage on the verge of America's entry into World War I.[73] The critic for *The Crisis* (no doubt Du Bois himself) raved over Torrence's effort and quoted him at length concerning the dramatic resources of black America—the "racial coherence" American Negroes had developed as a result of subjugation and segregation, the "epic spirit" of the Negro's longings for liberty, the depth of the black trage-dies unknown to Americans of Anglo-Saxon descent, and the "natural buoyancy of disposition" that had already produced "a wealth of comedy."[74] Here, Torrence prophesied, was the incipient birth of an American dramatic tradition equipped in every respect to rival the modern Irish theater. *The Crisis* seconded Torrence's call for Negro playwrights to take on the task of creating America's first great dramatic movement. It named him one of its "Men of the Month" in September 1917 and attributed "the very fact of [the] existence" of Negro theater to the playwright from Xenia, Ohio.[75] According to another statement in the May issue of the magazine, "The attempt of Mrs. Emilie Hap-good, the promoter; Ridgely Torrence, the playwright, and Robert Edmund Jones, the designer, to start the new Negro drama on Broadway, New York, is nothing less than epoch making."[76]

Such encomiums would continue to appear in *The Crisis* for years after the appearance of Torrence's plays, as the magazine hammered again and again upon the point of the potential and the need for a true "national Negro theatre." Articles along these lines came from the pens of the black playwright Willis Richardson, Alain Locke, Raymond O'Neil, Du Bois, Helen Deutsch, and Stella Hanau (of the Prov-incetown Theatre). In the early 1920s, Du Bois, in particular, regarded the greatest inhibition on black drama to be "the attitude of the Negro world itself" to the representation of black life on stage. The extreme sensitivity aroused by a long history of degrading theatrical caricatures had now become a block to black playwriting, to such an extent that, in Du Bois's estimation, the best contemporary plays of black American life had been written by white men.[77] These men, perhaps, had suc-ceeded in part because they had not known precisely what they were getting into. Du Bois openly sympathized with Ridgely Torrence and Eugene O'Neill over the abuse from black critics they had had to endure. And this coming from the most vehement critic of white exploi-tation of black culture!

One handicap of the Negro playwright was the insistence that "our

Art and Propaganda be one." As a 1921 editorial of Du Bois's pointed out, "This is wrong and in the end it is harmful."[78] Sensitivity to stereotypes had been wrought to such an intensity, particularly among the well educated, that it had become the main inhibition to excellence in black drama. "With a vast wealth of human material about us, our own writers and artists fear to paint the truth lest they criticize their own and be in turn criticized for it. They fail to see the Eternal Beauty that shines through all Truth, and try to portray a world of stilted artificial black folk such as never were on land or sea."[79] The result was shamefully ironic:

> Thus the white artist looking in on the colored world, if he be wise and discerning, may often see the beauty, tragedy and comedy more truly than we dare. Of course if he be simply a shyster like Tom Dixon, he will see only exaggerated evil, and fail as utterly in the other extreme as we in ours. But if, like Sheldon, he writes a fine true work of art like "The Nigger"; or like Ridgely Torrence, a beautiful comedy like "The Rider of Dreams"; or like Eugene O'Neill, a splendid tragedy like "The Emperor Jones"—he finds to his own consternation the Negroes and even educated Negroes, shrinking or openly condemning.[80]

Du Bois closes his panegyric by hailing Sheldon, Torrence, and O'Neill as "forerunners of artists who will yet arise in Ethiopia of the Outstretched Arms."[81]

In the past twenty-five years these men have been routinely excoriated in histories of African American drama as perpetuators of minstrel show and primitivist stereotypes, even presented as the sort of artists black playwrights reacted *against*.[82] Yet black dramatic groups of the 1920s (including those founded *by* blacks) *performed* the very works of white dramatists that recent critics assume black artists considered demeaning. Articles in *The Crisis* actually recommended white-authored plays for production and study. Moreover, *The Crisis* used white dramatists such as O'Neill as judges for its contests, asked for their help in staging plays by black playwrights, and defended the white dramatists against their black and white critics. Finally, the white dramatists themselves made no claims for the "authenticity" of their plays—quite the opposite. DuBose Heyward wrote to *The Crisis:* "I feel convinced that [the Negro] alone will produce the ultimate and authentic record of his own people. What I have done in 'Porgy' owes what social value it has to its revelation of *my* feeling *toward* my subject. A real subjective literature must spring from the race itself."[83] Torrence, O'Neill, and Heyward clearly wanted to help independent black theater groups develop.

The Crisis was not alone in lauding the plays of Torrence and O'Neill. Du Bois's point of view would be echoed in *Opportunity* and *The Messenger* and in the minds of some of the most promising of the New Negro actors and writers. However ideologically flawed we may find these white "Negro plays" today, they were enabling cultural performances for black artists of the time, according to even the often-suspicious Du Bois.

The writers for *The Crisis* had no sense that Torrence's was an attempt to exploit black culture at the expense of black playwrights themselves, for, as they well knew, his whole ambition was to help make an opening for black playwrights as well as actors to develop their own dramatic tradition. It is difficult to understand where Harold Cruse, for example, came up with the idea that white playwrights, with the aid of the NAACP's uncritical "interracialism," effectively squelched a nascent black theater tradition.[84] Like other black magazines of the period, *The Crisis* cried out for new black drama of a high caliber. It repeatedly noted the necessity for black playwrights to mine America's richest store of dramatic materials and bemoaned the feeble response to its encouragement. It offered prizes for scripts; it published one-act plays (fewer than it wanted to); it founded a "little theater" group (the Krigwa Players); it critiqued and applauded "Negro plays" on Broadway and off; it reviewed different "schools" of contemporary and near-contemporary drama to give some sense of the different forms successful theater had taken; it even published an article on how to write a play, with suggested reading attached![85]

The response, however, remained disappointing. (Nor should this be surprising; the United States as a whole had failed to produce a dramatic movement anywhere near proportionate to its size or economic might.) It may well be true that black playwrights would have had a difficult time getting even first-rate plays produced; but those plays had first to be written. *Opportunity* suspended its literary contests in 1927 because of the low quality of submissions. And *The Messenger* continually complained about the mediocrity of black drama, at one point reprinting Eugene O'Neill's comment that the brilliance of black acting contrasted starkly with the quality of black playwriting: "I have read a good number of plays written by Negroes and they were always *bad* plays—badly written, conceived, constructed—without the slightest trace of true feeling for drama—*unoriginal*—and *what revolted me the most, bad imitations in method and thought of conventional white plays!*"[86] The problem was all the more infuriating to these critics because of the tremendous potential they saw for black theater, and the enthusiastic reception they expected it would enjoy.

Willis Richardson's "The Hope of a Negro Drama," written for *The Crisis*, is representative of the optimism about black potentialities in theater on the verge of the twenties: "Is it true that there is coming into existence in America a Negro Drama which at some future day may equal in excellence the American Negro Music? If the signs of the times do not point to such a thing, we must change their direction and make them point the right way; we must have a Negro Drama."[87] Richardson calls for black poets to turn to drama and "lend a hand towards the writing of Negro plays." He praises the efforts of Ridgely Torrence and his backers, as well as Mary Burrill; they had begun the movement in the direction of "the play that shows the soul of a people." And echoing Torrence himself, as well as a host of other writers, he points to the Irish National Theatre as the model for black artists to emulate, noting that "with no richer material, and among a population of less than five millions [half the black American population], the Irish have built a national drama, encouraged and sustained playwrights, who are respected the same as are the other members of their profession in larger countries, and trained a company of actors who have made a decent living by their work on the stage."[88] Not only did black playwrights have a racial experience to draw from at least as rich as that of the Irish; the American Negro had a "natural" gift for the "mimicry" essential to drama, a uniquely rich quality of voice, and a "mellow" dialect beautifully suited to the stage. All "he" lacked was "long and careful training" to make his mark.[89]

Another example of how "Negro drama" articulated with American cultural nationalism is Raymond O'Neil's article in *The Crisis*, "The Negro in Dramatic Art."[90] O'Neil was the director of the Ethiopian Art Players, a so-called Negro theater group whose producer was Sherwood Anderson's wife, Tennessee Anderson.[91] The most artistically creative peoples, O'Neil points out, are those with the most sensuous natures, such as the Negroes of the United States and the Russians (the Moscow Art Players having recently achieved great fame in New York). In contrast, the "non-Negro American" has been, for generations, "the object of a steadily played stream of restrictions and prohibitions which have had as their object the paralyzing and extirpation of his sensuous nature and emotions."[92] The consequences are predictable: "In his own image the good one hundred per cent American has set up his art," guarding against any dormant or unfamiliar emotions. "Thus it comes that in his teeming land of plenty the normal white, Protestant, Nordic American lives without a music of his own, without more than occasional pieces of painting or sculpture, with a literature just emerging from the nursery, and with a stage reflecting a life as hollow and painful as a drilled-out aching tooth."[93] O'Neil uses the stereotypical opposition between the "repressed" Anglo-Saxon and the "spontaneous" Negro temperament to propose a vision of the "Americanization" of culture in the United States.

Anticipating the defense that (white) Americans have been "too busy" building a country to attend to the luxury of developing an artistic tradition, O'Neil counters in a manner that echoes the sentiments of many black writers of the era: the white man has been oblivious to the fact "that another people have been working at his side in the same land, who, though suffering a heavy handicap of political and economic disabilities, have been producing an art as they worked. And here again is a pleasant resemblance between the Russian and the American Negro."[94] The art of the slaves and their descendants (like that of the Russian peasant) has responded to the reality of their daily struggle and toil, providing group "ideals" that answer to their specific needs. Here is no alienation between art and life, culture and labor, no division into highbrow and lowbrow. As the black folk and the Russian peasants have worked in areas only beginning to be developed into new civilizations, they have responded sensuously to the world around them and "created an art, each in his own image."[95]

The romantic ideology infuses O'Neil's comments and indeed invites confusion with racist stereotypes: the Russian and Negro arts are "rich and warm and sensuous. . . . Understanding much, they forgive everything that is human. They spring from the earth. . . . They are wistful, tender, straightforward as a child and they are robust, passionate, sensuous as a youth."[96] If this description encodes both black American and Russian art in inherited racist and classist ideologies, it also specifically encourages self-determination. Just as the Russians guarded their arts as much as possible from Westernization, so the Negro must guard his from "one hundred per cent Americanization. Particularly must he be on his guard against the white friends of his art who will urge its development in the direction of their prejudiced imagination."[97] They must, in short, resist a white aesthetic.

The irony, of course, is that in advising the black dramatist to avoid "Americanization," O'Neil, the "white friend," is himself attempting to steer black art in the direction of *his* "prejudiced imagination." Yet O'Neil, whose company was perhaps best known for its production of works by Shakespeare, Willis Richardson, and Oscar Wilde, sees a threat of "commercial and intellectual exploitation" in the growing white interest in black drama. This "evil white pressure" the Negro must resist, as "he" has other evils from the same source. "For there is nothing more precious in America today than the creative possibilities that the Negro indubitably possesses."[98] O'Neil's very solicitude for the growth of a black aesthetic derives from a cultural nationalist ideology that is by no means of strictly black (or, for that matter, "American") provenance. How could O'Neil be blind to the irony of his own advising? And how could *The Crisis* be blind to it? Clearly, they drew a sharp distinction between the Raymond O'Neils of the world and the white "exploiters."

The *Crisis* crusade for black drama continued throughout the twenties. Despite a rift that had developed between Alain Locke and Washington, D.C.'s NAACP Drama Committee, he published "Steps Toward a Negro Theatre" in *The Crisis* in 1922. Here he credited Du Bois (for *Star of Ethiopia*) and Torrence as the two pioneers of "Negro art Drama," which was one wing of the general "new American drama," including the "community drama" (the pageant movement spearheaded by Percy MacKaye) and "folk-drama" movements. Locke's particular interest, of course, was the "Negro folk drama," which, like so many others, he envisioned in terms colored by the success of modern Irish and Russian theater. This interest of his and Montgomery Gregory's had led to the parting of ways between two groups within the Washington Drama Committee (which had produced Angelina Grimké's *Rachel* in 1917). While the "conservatives" apparently favored propaganda plays of the "best foot forward" protest type, the "radicals" hoped to endow a "national Negro theatre" and develop a distinctive aesthetic out of folk resources. Of "questionable paternity"—apparently because of their "bastard" relationship to the NAACP and connection with white bohemians—the "radicals" were forced to set up a separate enterprise based at Howard University.[99] Despite many black critics and detractors, noted Locke, "it has been amazing . . . the proportion of responsiveness and help that has come, especially from the most prominent proponents of the art drama in this country": Gilpin, O'Neill, Torrence, Percy MacKaye, Du Bois, James Weldon Johnson, "and most especially the valuable technical assistance for three years of Clem Throckmorton, technical director of the Provincetown Players."[100] In its first two years, the Howard Theatre relied upon scripts by white playwrights—Lord Dunsany, Ridgely Torrence, Eugene O'Neill, Percy MacKaye, Matalee Lake, and Edna St. Vincent Millay—apparently as a provocation to students to produce a true Negro drama that would "reveal us beyond all propaganda on the one side, and libel on the other, more subtly and deeply than self-praise and to the confusion of subsidized self-caricature and ridicule."[101]

Du Bois's opinions often matched Locke's on particular white playwrights, despite his conviction that a true "Negro drama" must be written and produced by and for African Americans. To wean black drama from reliance on white audiences, in 1926 Du Bois and the NAACP founded the Krigwa little theater movement, following up, he attested, on an earlier initiative of Ernestine Rose, a white librarian at the Harlem branch of the New York Public Library. His initial announcement of the group suggests a desire to promote "folk drama," perhaps to steer the form of such drama in directions he preferred.[102] According to Eulalie Spence's niece, however, Du Bois mainly wanted propaganda plays. Spence, a regular member of Krigwa throughout its two-year existence, respected Du Bois; but the two "had major disagreements" about what she should write. A "folk dramatist," she felt unqualified to write about lynchings, rapes, and blatant racial cruelties, which had not been part of her experience.[103] Such disagreements exemplify the kind of resistance Du Bois encountered from authors of a new generation.

Although after the publication of *Nigger Heaven* in 1926 Du Bois became increasingly critical of both "sympathetic" white treatments of black subject matter and of what he regarded as the "decadent" school of younger black writers, he continued to distinguish between the dramatic efforts of Sheldon, Torrence, O'Neill, and even Marc Connelly, on the one hand, and the cultural "exploiters" on the other.[104] Even in 1930, for example, Du Bois defended *Green Pastures* against black critics and called it "the beginning of a new era, not simply in Negro art but in the art of America."[105] While he took white audiences to task for desiring plays concerning only a limited portion of African American life—that closest to their stereotypical notions—he would praise plays that, in his opinion, treated that portion of black life truly and beautifully, and he implied that black audiences were often so concerned with what was going on in white playgoers' minds that they failed to appreciate plays that really did justice to their subject matter.[106] As late as 1931 he ran an article by Helen Deutsch and Stella Hanau called "The Provincetown Theatre and the Negro," which described the risks the theater had taken, the threats it had survived, and the successes it had achieved in staging the plays of black American life that writers for *The Crisis* had often praised.

A Parting of Ways

Nonetheless, there is no doubt that *The Crisis* became increasingly suspicious of white authors treating "Negro" subject matter. In this respect, 1926 was a watershed year in the cultural criticism of *The Crisis*. It happened to be the year that Jessie Fauset departed as literary editor of the magazine, which may help explain the new vehemence of the magazine's attacks on the rising appeal to white "decadence" in art concerning the Negro.[107] (Although Fauset partially shared Du Bois's view on this topic, she was more diplomatic and also had closer ties to the younger black writers whom Du Bois criticized.) It was also the year of Josephine Baker's spectacular and immediately famous "banana dance" in Paris, playing directly to the erotics of racialist primitivism. The same year saw the publication of Du Bois's virulent attack on Van Vechten's *Nigger Heaven;* of his NAACP speech, "Criteria of Negro Art"; and of the controversial "symposium" entitled "The Negro in Art: How Shall He Be Portrayed?"[108] Undoubtedly to Du Bois's and Jessie Fauset's chagrin, the response of authors, editors, and publishers to their list of leading questions was overwhelmingly at odds with the position of *The Crisis*. Of the black writers responding, only Jessie Fauset answered all the questions "correctly," although partial support came from Georgia Douglas Johnson and Countee Cullen. By and large, respondents did not even feel that publishers were unwilling to publish novels about the "better sort" of Negro—Du Bois's and Fauset's primary assumption. Du Bois became convinced that white publishers published books on the "sordid" aspects of Negro life because they knew white readers got a thrill from reading "about filth and crime and misfortune. But the victims of these things must not, of course, be themselves or their own people" (ignoring the fact that this was the period in which Dreiser's prestige reached its peak).[109] If *The Crisis* was the nation's conscience, Du Bois could see its waning power over black writing only as an indication of how the barbaric morals of white Americans were once again corrupting the race.

Not surprisingly, then, 1926 also marks the period of *The Crisis*'s relative decline as an influence on the New Negro movement in the arts, as a rift with *Opportunity* opened and the latter magazine grew in influence. In 1926, as Du Bois began attacking the Harlem Renaissance, Countee Cullen (a *Crisis* favorite) became assistant editor of *Opportunity;* even James Weldon Johnson used the pages of *Opportunity* to acclaim *Nigger Heaven* in a featured review essay.[110] The shift in power also followed from the success of *The New Negro* and Alain Locke's alienation from the NAACP. Indeed, in some respects *The New Negro* was a product of the competition between *The Crisis* and *Opportunity*. The dinner of 1924 set up by Charles Johnson (*Opportunity*'s editor) and emceed by Locke, which resulted in the famous Harlem number of the *Survey Graphic*, prophesied a shift that Du Bois deeply resented. While the NAACP staff thought of the dinner as a tribute to Jessie Fauset ("their" literary editor) upon publication of *There Is Confusion,* Johnson and Locke made sure the attendees would think of it as a coming-out party for a younger group of artists writing, for the most part, in a different vein. For this slight Jessie Fauset never forgave Alain Locke.[111]

Within two years she would face further disappointment as a rift developed between her and Du Bois, probably in part over the amount of attention paid to the arts in *The Crisis*. After she left, *The Crisis* became less and less an attractive outlet for African American literary modernists. This was partly, as Carolyn Sylvander points out, because the running of the editorial offices became sloppy without Fauset's management.[112] But undoubtedly the chief problem was Du Bois's overt hostility to what most younger black authors were writing; criticizing Rudolph Fisher for allegedly "pandering" to a white audience rather than writing about people like "his mother, his sister, and his wife" could hardly be expected to win young writers over.[113] Wallace Thurman responded to this criticism of Fisher at length in the new magazine *Harlem,* saying it "set [his] teeth on edge": "I was not so much worried about the effect such a narrow and patronizing criticism would have on Mr. Fisher or on any other of Dr. Du Bois' audience who might take it

seriously, as I was concerned for what it tokened for the reviewer himself. . . . The time has come now when the Negro artist can be his true
self and pander to the stupidities of no one, either white or black."[114]
Even the typeface and design of *The Crisis* looked rather stodgy by the
standards of the late 1920s, a period of tremendous innovation in magazine design.

Allison Davis' article "Our Negro 'Intellectuals,'" following as it did
recent attacks by Du Bois on Julia Peterkin and Claude McKay, did not
help either. Attacking Negro "Menckenites" (Schuyler and Eugene
Gordon) as well as "Van Vechtenites" (Hughes and Fisher), the essay
became an excoriation of modernism generally. Even James Weldon
Johnson, Davis concluded, had yielded to "jazzy primitivism" in enti-
tling his 1927 collection of poems *God's Trombones*. Davis went on to
include Waldo Frank, F. Scott Fitzgerald, Winold Reiss, Aaron Douglas,
Richard Bruce, and even Max Reinhardt and Carl Van Doren in his list
of decadents. It turned out that what all of these people shared was a
desire to distinguish "Negro" from "white" American art; and the
grounds on which they sought the distinction, according to Davis (an
anthropologist), was primitivism. Of course, the charge had an element
of truth in some cases; but for Davis virtually anything distinguishing
Negro from white middle-class culture fell under the same denunciation. Du Bois was also capable of such criticism.

Reviewing Melville Herskovits' *The American Negro* in 1928, Du Bois
found that the book "shows on the one hand the idiocy of talking about
the Negro as an 'unassimilable' and distinct race in the United States,
and of arguing about American Negroes from the same premises as we
argue about the Bantu." Herskovits' book was, "in a real sense, epoch-
making" for it proved that a distinct "American" type—in both physical
and cultural form—had developed in the United States, creating a
homogeneous group that was, at the same time, "mixed" through and
through.[115] In a sense, Herskovits had provided anthropological support for the point of view Du Bois had long been pushing. Significantly,
the review of *The American Negro* immediately followed the review in
which Du Bois had flayed Claude McKay for *Home to Harlem* and praised
Nella Larsen's *Quicksand*, claiming: "Helga is typical of the new, honest,
young fighting Negro woman—the one on whom 'race' sits negligibly
and Life is always first and its wandering path is but darkened, not oblit-
erated by the shadow of the Veil. White folk will not like this book."[116]
Du Bois's curious reading of *Quicksand*, in which a central conflict is

the protagonist's unsuccessful struggle against her entrapment in both black and white discourses of race, reveals once again the hermeneutic that made him obtuse to what younger authors were attempting. To add to the irony, none other than Carl Van Vechten had recommended the manuscript of *Quicksand* to Knopf.

As *The Crisis* became increasingly peripheral to the literary movement it had done more than any other institution to birth, Du Bois became increasingly convinced that white pied pipers were to blame—an ironic situation, since it was precisely black authors' attempts at a more independent African American aesthetic that stirred his wrath. Chief among the influences at work was *Opportunity* magazine, to which Alain Locke had become connected at the urging of Charles S. Johnson, an admirer of both Du Bois and Booker T. Washington.

6

Toward a New Negro Aesthetic

While *Crisis* magazine, driven by Du Bois's disillusionment, faded as the main organ of "New Negro" writing, *Opportunity*'s importance rose. Though its circulation never approached that of *The Crisis,* within a year of its founding it had surpassed the earlier magazine as the premier journal of African American cultural criticism and performance. It provided a legitimizing space for experiments that were losing the confidence of *The Crisis.* The contrasts between the magazines' aesthetic preferences were not unrelated to the contrasts between the organizations to which they "belonged" as well as the differences between their editors. Hence a full understanding of the cultural matrix of the "renaissance" requires a more detailed examination than has previously been offered of the linkage between the institutional and intellectual backgrounds of *Opportunity* and its aesthetic emphases.

"Not Alms but Opportunity"

As Nancy J. Weiss has pointed out, the National Urban League grew out of a "second reform tradition" somewhat different from the "protest tradition" of the NAACP and the Niagara Movement.[1] The Urban League had different methods and a different focus, subordinating the drive for political and civil rights to the need for economic and, to a lesser degree, "moral" progress. Focusing on job opportunities, housing, education, and moral uplift, it also opted for a less militant demeanor. In fact, the Urban Leaguers generally seem to have agreed that the programs of both Du Bois and Washington were crucial to the advancement of blacks in American society and sought to avoid antagonizing either side of the great debate over black social strategy.

The president from the league's beginning in 1911 until 1914 was the Columbia professor E. R. A. Seligman, one of the founders of Greenwich Settlement House and president of Felix Adler's Society for Ethical Culture from 1908 to 1921; Seligman had also participated in the founding of the NAACP and addressed that organization's first conference in 1909. In fact, several people influential in the NAACP, including Mary White Ovington and Oswald Garrison Villard, had been closely involved with organizations that folded into each other to form the Urban League. Moreover, one of the founders of the league, George Edmund Haynes, had studied social and political ethics under Felix Adler on his way to becoming a sociologist. The social philosophies and tactics that coalesced in the Urban League have clear ramifications for cultural politics, as the connections between the organization's founders and Ethical Culture, for example, make clear.

The Urban League would emphasize interracial cooperation in the development of a common civilization and the "moral progress" of the nation. The point was not "charity," but the development of "a sounder national democracy," in the words of Ruth Standish Baldwin, the realization of "sound community living."[2] For years National Urban League stationery carried the motto she had written: "Let us work, not as colored people nor as white people for the narrow benefit of any group alone, but *together*, as American citizens, for the common good of our common city, our common country."[3] This basic point would be reiterated continually in *Opportunity* magazine, side by side with the "literature of the New Negro."

In terms of social activism, the Urban League specifically wanted to avoid duplicating the NAACP's efforts. It would concentrate on opening up employment opportunity and "social services to ease the process of urbanization."[4] Its tactics would also differ. Whereas the NAACP undertook direct action and immediatism, the Urban League tended toward diplomacy and gradualism. As leaders of both organizations agreed, the NAACP would strike and advance the front line, and then the Urban League would hold the ground and solidify positions.

Indeed, this distinction between the organizations is well emblemized in the titles of *The Crisis* and *Opportunity*.[5]

In addition to pushing for greater opportunity for urban blacks, however, the Urban League focused on behavioral reformation of black migrants. Anxious that new arrivals would get into the hands of "the wrong class of people," traveler's aid workers would meet incoming trains and direct people to Urban League offices for help in finding lodging and employment. They sponsored "wholesome" activities to attract their charges away from the tempting brothels and saloons. They taught "modern" hygiene, cleanliness, proper dress, tooth-brushing, good manners, punctuality, efficiency, proper deportment. They discouraged "loud-talking" and "boisterous laughter"—virtually any behavior that caused the new city-dwellers to stand out as "different" and thus arouse antagonism or confirm stereotypes that whites held toward blacks in general. All of these efforts contributed to the overall aim of "race adjustment," economic advancement, and intercultural harmony.

A number of apparent paradoxes become evident when one considers the Urban League's ideological positions and tactics in relation to the aesthetic criticism of *Opportunity*. There is, of course, the obvious question of why a social-work organization would interest itself in artistic affairs at all, which I will address in a moment. Why, moreover, would the magazine of an institution that eschewed "sentimental appeal" and "subjective" rhetoric, that insisted upon the patient collection and "objective" communication of social "facts" to combat American racism, become the defender of what W. E. B. Du Bois considered (wrongly, I believe) an "art for art's sake" aesthetic? Even more to the point, however, how is it that an organization that sought to aid the "adjustment" of rural migrants to Northern cities, that helped them gain "decent" employment and encouraged the acquisition of middle-class manners and morals, that worried about moral degradation hurting the image of the race in the North as Southern peasants settled there—that, indeed, explicitly instructed its members to discourage "shiftless" and "inefficient" blacks from migrating to the North—how is it that the organ of *this* group, rather than that of the NAACP or the socialist *Messenger*, became identified with the bohemian wing of the "Negro renaissance," lauded folk plays set in the black South, promoted the urban realism of fiction and poetry focusing on the urban black masses rather than the "best foot forward" school, and became the champion of what was called, in *Modern Quarterly* advertisements for *Opportunity*, a "New Negro aesthetic"?

Charles S. Johnson and "the Beauty of Familiar Things"

Key to these apparent paradoxes is the intellectual orientation of *Opportunity*'s editor from its inception to 1928, Charles S. Johnson. Several important writers of the Harlem Renaissance later attested to Johnson's importance. Zora Neale Hurston called him "the root of the so-called Negro Renaissance."[6] Langston Hughes said he "did more to encourage and develop Negro writers during the 1920's than anyone else in America"; along with Jessie Fauset at *The Crisis* and Alain Locke in Washington (Johnson's chosen "dean" of the movement), he "midwifed the so-called New Negro literature into being."[7] Echoing Hughes, Arna Bontemps has written that Johnson was a "nursemaid" of the Harlem Renaissance.[8] Johnson gave New Negro literature pride of place in *Opportunity* and acted as the behind-the-scenes manager of the movement. He was primarily responsible for making *Opportunity*, within months of its founding, the most important medium of the Harlem Renaissance, even as he also used it to publicize the results of social research. Far from being unrelated to each other, these two aspects of the magazine together expressed a carefully considered social philosophy that also shaped Johnson's aesthetic preferences.[9]

Typically Johnson's rationale for promoting the arts is attributed either to a belief that artistic achievement would prove the Negro's fitness for full integration into American democracy or to a recognition of the arts as the one area for black advancement that had not been proscribed; providing high visibility and low vulnerability, an artistic movement could provide the entering wedge for black integration. "Through secrecy and manipulation," David Levering Lewis argues, Johnson would try "to redeem, through art, the standing of his people."[10] According to Lewis, it was all part of a confidence game played on unwitting white liberals, who for various self-interested reasons had become fascinated by Negroes. Much as Houston Baker sees Booker T. Washington as "running a game" on myopic white folks who never had any interest in racial equality, Lewis argues that Johnson was applying Washingtonian methods for the Talented Tenth. While there is a partial truth to this characterization, a careful investigation of Johnson's intellectual matrix, revealed by his autobiographical writings, and of *Opportunity*'s cultural criticism forces a more complex and far less cynical interpretation.

Johnson's manuscripts and educational background provide little support for viewing him as a classic trickster using the blindnesses of a supposed racial opponent to "run a game" on him. He was much more interested in achieving dialogue with the "other." Johnson himself mentions that his intellectual development took its first decisive turn when he was an undergraduate working for a charity organization in Virginia. It dawned on him at this time that "no man can be justly judged until you have looked at the world through his eyes," a lesson that became the "core" of his "social philosophy." This conviction, he writes in his "Spiritual Autobiography," led him in 1917 to the University of Chicago and the "great social philosopher and teacher, Robert E. Park. It was he who linked this deep and moving human concern with science and human understanding, and with the great minds that have struggled with these issues—William James, John Dewey, George Santayana, Josiah Royce, all his friends."[11]

As I pointed out in Chapter 1, the most distinctive aspect of Park's sociological approach (both theoretically and methodologically) was his emphasis on the subjectivity of social agents. He quoted James often: "The most real thing is a thing that is most keenly felt rather than the thing that is most clearly conceived."[12] Park encouraged his students to enter into the worlds they studied and to strive to understand the values they found there, for he worried that we "miss the point and mistake the inner significance of the lives of those about us unless we share their experience"—and that "experience" is always connected with a long history we can never fully know.[13] He sought a combination of something akin to the Boasian method of ethnology (which, in fact, he much admired) and the "new" journalist's or novelist's skill at portraying personalities and group life. One of his graduate students remembered his "genuine interests" as being in particulars, and journalistic in nature:

> He was more of a journalist, or artist . . . concerned with individuals, pictures of the life of groups—immigrants, denizens of skid row, hoodlums, etc., much as Dreiser, Gorky, et al., were. . . . I remember well his showing me a doctoral thesis written under his direction. . . . It was an intimate account of a small town in the west. He had everything in it about all the characters, both respectable and otherwise. It was

exactly the sort of thing that Sherwood Anderson and Dreiser wrote. Park was fascinated by it. This is what he was interested in.[14]

It may be worth pointing out that Midwestern realists like Dreiser and Zona Gale were prominent among judges of the *Opportunity* literary contests that Charles S. Johnson organized in the late 1920s.

The more usable aspects of Park's thinking, in terms of Johnson's program at *Opportunity*, come out in Park's own reflections on the emerging "Negro Renaissance" in 1923, in comments that Johnson quoted in an *Opportunity* editorial, "Negro Life and Its Poets."[15] Approving of Robert Kerlin's statement that "a people's poetry . . . affords the most serious subject of study to those who would understand the people—that people's soul, that people's status, that people's potentialities," Park did not note any "primitive and exotic" qualities in the New Negro poetry but rather emphasized its militancy, idealism, black nationalism, and prophetic character:

> In some respects . . . it seems to me the Negro, like all the other disinherited peoples, is more fortunate than the dominant races. He is restless, but he knows what he wants. The issues in his case, at least, are clearly defined. More than that, in this racial struggle, he is daily gaining not merely faith in himself, but new faith in the world. Since he wants nothing except what he is willing to give to every other man on the same terms he feels that the great forces that shape the destinies of peoples are on his side.[16]

Even before Alain Locke's similar observation in *The New Negro*, Park likened the Harlem Renaissance to the nationalist movements of dominated peoples elsewhere in the world, finding the same "natural history" in each, including a linguistic and literary movement, a renaissance—as in Czechoslovakia, Ireland, Finland, Norway, Italy, and the Zionist movement. In Park's view of the cyclical "natural history" of race relations, such nationalistic competition would be followed by accommodation between "national" groups and ultimate integration—first within the United States, and ultimately throughout the world.

Like Park (and Locke), Charles Johnson viewed the "cultural racialism" of the New Negro as integral with the American cultural field as a whole. More than any other group, he insisted, the Negro had been stripped of the ancestral culture upon coming to the "New World";

hence "his" claim to "indigenous" status: "With the exceptions of the Indian and the Appalachian Mountaineer [of Johnson's own natal region], no man in America is so entirely native to the soil. The Negro on the plantation is the only peasant class America has produced, and his is the only native folk culture that America possesses."[17] In fact, as he would state in 1928, the religious expressions of the slave "are no less significant than Puritanism, and the early American farm house, as spiritual and artistic antecedents of contemporary America."[18]

The differences between black and white Americans, Johnson believed, were based not on cultural differences inherited from Africa and Europe but on "physical and racial characteristics" as well as historical experience within the United States—another point on which he was in thorough agreement with Park.[19] In a review of the 1920s he emphasized the rootedness of the new black literature in specifically black historical experience and called the Harlem poets "the legitimate successors of the voices that first sang the Spirituals." He continued: "It is important, therefore, to consider Negro literature, in all its different expressions, as an integral part of a single tradition and as a unique collective experience. Only as these different expressions of the racial life are viewed as parts of a whole is it possible to arrive at any true estimate of the character of the Negro's cultural achievement or his traits."[20] This view differs dramatically from that of, say, William Stanley Braithwaite and the dominant critical stance at *The Crisis*.

One's estimate of the cultural tradition, according to Johnson's formulation, depended upon both the hermeneutic brought to bear on the tradition and the quality of the "expressions of the racial life," and for Johnson this meant a swerve from propaganda and protest. If responsible sociological inquiry required dispassionate methods, so, paradoxically enough, did a truly "self-expressive" fiction. The aesthetic work would not be burdened with "propaganda" of the "best foot forward" sort but instead attempt to exemplify in its very form the cultural meanings (that is, the "experience," in pragmatist terms) of a people. Without giving all the credit (or blame) to Johnson, one can go through virtually all the criticism published in *Opportunity* and find this criterion of judgment to be fundamental.

To look at the cultural orientation of *Opportunity* from this perspective is to see how shallow many critiques of the Harlem Renaissance have been. Shortly after he left New York for Nashville, when the Harlem Renaissance was still (briefly) near its zenith, Johnson quoted

Santayana in a chapel talk to students at Fisk: "Whenever beauty is really seen and loved . . . it has a definite embodiment: The eye has precision, the work has style and the object has perfection."[21] What Du Bois took to be an "art for art's sake" doctrine was really a determination to explore "native values" typical of American writers at the time: "The beginning of the 20th century has been marked in America by a conscious movement 'back to the concrete,' which has yielded the new fascination of watching the strangeness and beauty of familiar things. It is America in revolt against the stiff conventionalism of borrowed patterns. The commentators of the present begin the new era in America with such characters as Sandburg and Robinson, apostles of freedom, who have launched the search for beauty in forgotten lives. It is the spirit of the New America."[22] Could the "New Negro" be far behind? "This compulsion exists now for the new generation of Negroes—the compulsion to find a new beauty in their own lives, ideals, and feelings. The new generation of Negro writers and artists have led the way here. The poetry represents this liberated energy. It is beginning the embodiment of new and beautiful life conceptions. It is revising old patterns, investing Negro life with a new charm and dignity, and power. No life for them is without beauty, no beginning too low."[23] Johnson here expresses the Deweyan point that art and life are inseparable, that art serves the enrichment of everyday experience of the common world, and thus ultimately the improvement of that world for enhanced living—art is, in the widest possible sense, "use-full."

The reformation of art serves the reformation of society. Moreover, discovery of the beauty of one's life is the path to freedom: "I am convinced," Johnson told the Fisk students, "that the road to a new freedom for us lies in the discovery of the surrounding beauties of our lives, and in the recognition that beauty itself is a mark of the highest expression of the human spirit."[24] Johnson suspected that his audience would be wondering, What beauty?—precisely because of their adherence to "alien" concepts of beauty rather than those evoked by common experience in the world.

Just as white American writers needed to become comfortable with "different standards of perfection" from the English—as John Macy, chairman of the second *Opportunity* awards meeting, had argued in *The Spirit of American Literature*—so "American Negroes" needed to become self-assured, with different standards from those of "American Caucasians." "It was the dull lack of some idealism here that held America in a suspended cultural animation until it sought freedom through self-criticism and its own native sources of beauty. In the same manner, American Negroes, born into a culture which they did not wholly share, have responded falsely to the dominant pattern. Their expression has been, to borrow a term which Lewis Mumford employs in referring to Americans in relation to Europe, 'sickly and derivative, a mere echo of old notes.'"[25] This argument is not based on foundationalist premises of unchanging racial "essences" but is instead a corollary to the notion of art as experience: "The cultural difference between an Englishman and an American is not so much in the germ plasm as in the accumulated stores of culture which impose for each different standards of perfection. The same condition applies in the cultural differences between [white] Americans and American Negroes."[26] The New Negro authors provided an aesthetic correlative to Booker T. Washington's statement "You can beat me being a white man but I can beat you being a Negro." "In their new representations of Negro life," wrote Johnson, "the Negro writers and artists ... are doing the same thing for which he found a phrase."[27]

Nonetheless, Johnson contended in the 1930s that there could be no truly separate black culture in the United States: "Those of the younger generation of Negroes, who, by virtue of their competence in the general culture have achieved a measure of cultural emancipation have turned back frankly to discover the beauty and charm of the life of the folk Negro. The result of this emancipation, paradoxically enough, has been to enrich the general culture rather than to develop a distinctive Negro expression."[28] He regarded the aims of the Negro renaissance to be integration, even "assimilation," which would assure the just operation of democratic government. Such assimilation could not occur until the peoples of the United States came to understand their mutual interests and to speak the same language. Johnson argued that people must gradually come to share the same "universe of discourse," for "men must live and work and fight together in order to create that community of interest and sentiment which will enable them to meet the common crises of life with a common will."[29] When cultural differences grow so great that they provoke "racial consciousness" and make full and free discussion of differences impossible, assimilation cannot take place and democracy cannot work. It is crucial to understand that Johnson is talking about an assimilation of separate groups to one another, rather than black culture being "assimilated" to an Anglo norm.

Johnson put this line of reasoning to use by liberally calling upon white writers and critics of the cultural nationalist and regionalist type to review the works of New Negro authors, and by having African Americans review the works of European Americans. Many of the featured critical essays published in *Opportunity* followed this cross-cultural pattern, just as the magazine's literary contests were judged by integrated panels. Was this an example of cynical manipulation on Johnson's part, or a practice in harmony with his expressed convictions?

In an interesting *Opportunity* essay on Booker T. Washington's "social philosophy," Johnson suggests a continuity between the Tuskegee experiment and the "Negro Renaissance." The latter movement would not have been possible, he claims, without Washington's success in precipitating a subjective transformation of a small but important segment of *white* America while simultaneously building up an educational, economic, and social foundation for black self-advancement. "The strategies which he employed consciously or unconsciously, are only now finding their most pronounced effect in the self-concern of Negroes and in the attitudes of white persons with respect to them."[30] Johnson considered Washington's strategy more complex and effective than Du Bois's in bringing about change in the conditions blocking full equality. Furthermore, Washington's "social philosophy" (essentially pragmatist, in Johnson's telling, though developed independently out of the "survival elements" of black culture) was further exemplified in the Negro Renaissance: "The most effective interest of the present is art, and even of this it may be said that it is but an elaboration of Washington's principles of stressing work rather than the rewards of work."[31] Here work is an educative *process* of self-expression, self-development, and social transformation, in which white America "must be untaught the traditions of hundreds of years, and new principles instilled."[32] One sign of Washington's success, Johnson may have believed, was the realistic fiction of the New South by such authors as DuBose Heyward and Julia Peterkin, whose novels were praised extravagantly in the pages of *Opportunity*.[33] American literature of the early twentieth century appeared to be making possible the sort of integrated society Johnson regarded as the nation's only hope.

But Johnson not only recognized the necessity of some sort of national community to help realize the hopes of black Americans; he understood the function of a national press in nourishing the growth of a communal African American consciousness, which was a necessary stage in the development of an integrated America. *Opportunity*, like *The Crisis*, was not only seeking integration through art but also seeking to create a national New Negro community (a process purportedly begun by Booker T. Washington), and Johnson viewed the arts as crucial to that endeavor. A nationally circulated magazine, after all, is a powerful tool for creating a sense of shared life in a world where modernization, migration, and urbanization are shattering older forms of community maintenance (particularly face-to-face interaction) as well as providing opportunities for new types of community. *Opportunity*'s relentless advocacy of a folk drama movement precisely exemplifies its communitarian thrust, invoking the folk past to create a "community of memory" (in Royce's terms), to revitalize a community of expression and a "community of hope" (Royce again) for a continentally scattered *urban* middle-class readership—just as the old "colored aristocracy" of Philadelphia, Washington, and elsewhere was being eclipsed by "New Negro" elites, especially in New York.

The Spirit and the Folk

Articles on "Negro folk song" exemplify the American cultural nationalist/cultural pluralist and socially conscious nature of *Opportunity*'s advocacy of a black aesthetic. In a feature essay of 1923, for example, John W. Work emphasized the social and historical context of the creation of folk songs, building on Dvořak's oft-cited opinion that "if America ever had a national music, it must be based upon the songs found among the southern Negroes."[34] Devoting himself to the argument that "this music is original with the Negro, and that it is genuinely American," Work proceeds to demonstrate that "the evolution of the pentatonic (African) into the sexatonic (American) scale was contemporaneous with the evolution of the African into the American."[35] The black slaves had created an entirely new scale and new forms of rhythmic syncopation in the process of responding lyrically to their experiences on the North American continent. The result was America's only folk song. Hence, "conditions point to the plain truth that, since the Negro Folk Song is the only American Folk Music that meets the scientific definition of Folk Song, since it is so rich in theme and in the beauty of its melody, since it is so comprehensive, so strikingly original and so strong in its appeal, it is the only natural basis and inspiration for American National Music."[36]

The point was made over and over again—in Newell Niles Puckett's "Race-Pride and Folk-Lore," for example, which tried to liberate the black bourgeoisie from its shame about its connections with the rural "folk"—and notably in Laurence Buermeyer's "The Negro Spirituals and American Art." Buermeyer, associate director of education at the Barnes Foundation and a pragmatist aesthetician, cites the frequent complaint that Americans have no "deeply felt religious experience," that American life suffers from "emotional poverty." As a result, "American art . . . has been in the main a rather feeble and savorless echo of European art, not growing out of the soil of national life, but transplanted from abroad and kept alive in a hot-house."[37] The sole exception is "Negro art," the only American tradition upon which future self-expression can productively build, for such tradition requires "roots that go down into the deeper soil of experience, of common activities inter-related at many points." It must have "primitive" elements in the sense that it is not grafted onto an older stock but rather has an origin *here* (as only Whitman's work, among that of white artists, did), in response to the humble experiences of everyday living.[38] The aesthetics of black experience, rich with emotional response and "deepened" by the need to give meaning to suffering in the encounter with radical evil, had produced an unmatched tradition of native spirituality and artistic expression.

The interest in black folklore, then, was not restricted to its assimilation to the romantic and pastoral, let alone the exotic. In "Self-Portraiture and Social Criticism in Negro Folk-Song," for example, B. A. Botkin featured the ways in which secular folk forms such as the blues responded to historical oppression and the conditions of industrial work. "An inseparable part of the self-portraiture of Negro workaday songs," he writes in his *Opportunity* essay, "is their social criticism. Out of the Negro's sense of self-pity develops an inevitable conviction of social injustice and an indictment of the existing order."[39] Botkin draws attention to the powerful irony directed toward white supervisors (and stereotypes of black workers) in such lines as "White man in starched shirt settin' in shade, / Laziest man that God ever made"—and the development of the trickster motif:

> I steal dat corn
> From de white man's barn,
> Den I slips aroun',

Tells a yarn,
An' sells it back again.[40]

Botkin notes not only the different personae and character types (for example, trickster and bad man) but also the formal virtuosity of the songs, which employ parallelism and compression, narrative by elliptical suggestion.

Moreover, these techniques match the modern social context of the songs' creation: "The child-like faith of slave-days is giving way to the worldly cynicism, the disillusionment of freedom, the product of industrial exploitation, migration, and concentration in cities."[41] While a continuity with the spirituals can be found in the note of homelessness, Botkin wants to distinguish the secular songs on the basis of their social reference and contemporaneity. Similarly, in the 1920s Botkin was ahead of his time in stressing the importance of urban folklore, objecting to the antiquarian and pastoral emphases of most "collectors" and their neglect of the contemporary, the modern.[42] This counterweight to nostalgic pastoralism is also evident in *Opportunity*'s appreciation of jazz, which one editorial identified as the preeminent expression of "modern American life," with broad appeal to the "masses" and "artists" alike: "The amusing and yet profoundly significant paradox of the whole situation is that it is the Negroes, who not only can best express the spirit of American life, but who have created the very forms of expression." Through jazz, Negroes have "forged the key to the interpretation of the American spirit."[43]

African Classicism and American Art

Opportunity criticism drew a distinction between respecting black folklore as a basis of American art and extolling the exotically "primitive." This distinction corresponded to the distinction between Franz Boas' interests in classical African civilizations, on the one hand, and the ecstatic, Bergson- and Freud-inspired fantasies of de Zayas and other "high modernists." Here, in fact, is one of the most significant homologies of the Harlem Renaissance; for the interest in a particularized and historicized yet respectful revaluation of African cultures went along with an attitude toward the African American "folk" that resisted their enshrinement as exotic "others," drawing attention to historical experience in America as determinant of a specially "native" American/Negro cultural matrix. In tension with the exotic primitivism that conflated African American with African identity was a more carefully contextualized, historical understanding of both the "folk" and of African peoples. Those who approached the relationship between African and African American cultures from this standpoint argued for study of the African past and engagement with current African struggles as part of a program for the modernist reconstitution of sundered identity and for political solidarity against racist oppression. It was also from this standpoint, specifically through the researches of Boas' students, that the actual historical connections between African and African American cultures began to be appreciated in the 1930s on nonracialist grounds.

The perceived correspondence between the "new" approach to the folk and the historical understanding of Africa is exemplified by the fact that, in the same essay in which he praised the work of Peterkin, Fisher, and McKay, Locke concluded with what he regarded as "the most significant of all recent developments; the new interest in Negro origins. If there is anything that points to a permanent revaluation of the Negro, it is the thorough-going change of attitude which is getting established about Africa and things African" in such books as Blaise Cendrars' anthology of African folklore, *The African Saga;* Captain Canot's *Adventures of an African Slaver;* Mrs. Gollock's *Lives of Eminent Africans* and *Sons of Africa;* Donald Fraser's *The New Africa;* Milton Staffer's symposium, *Thinking With Africa;* and "very notably, I think, J. W. Vandercook's *Black Majesty* [on Le Roi Christophe of Haiti]."[44]

Understanding of African cultures would provide a foundation for the wholesale revaluation of Negro achievement and potential globally, while it would also supply ideas to young artists who wanted to affirm a nonessentialized Negro identity as a psychosocial fact—indeed, a necessity, given the inescapable racialization of identities spread by Western imperialism. "Because of our Europeanized conventions, the key to the proper understanding and appreciation of [African art] will in all probability first come from an appreciation of its influence upon contemporary French art, but we must believe that there still slumbers in the blood something which once stirred will react with peculiar emotional intensity toward it. *If by nothing more mystical than the sense of being ethnically related, some of us will feel its influence at least as keenly as those who have already made it recognized and famous. Nothing is more galvanizing than the sense of a cultural past.*"[45]

Closer knowledge of African art forms—as the Barnes Foundation was advancing—would give incentives for "fresher and bolder forms of artistic expression and a lessening of that timid imitativeness which at present hampers all but our very best artists."[46] Locke cites Alexander Goldenweiser's point that "primitive art has in it both the decorative and the realistic motives, and often as not it is the abstract principles of design and aesthetic form which are the determinants of its stylistic technique and conventions."[47] Locke then takes direct aim at the identi-fication of all things African with the "primitive" and "exotic":

> Perhaps the most important effect of interpretations like these is to break down the invidious distinction between art with a capital A for European forms of expression and 'exotic' and 'primitive' art for the art expressions of other peoples. Technically speaking an art is primi-tive in any phase before it has mastered its idiom of expression, and classic when it has arrived at maturity and before it has begun to decline. Similarly art is exotic with relation only to its relative incom-mensurability with other cultures; in influencing them at all vitally it ceases to be exotic. From this we can see what misnomers these terms really are when applied to all phases of African art.[48]

Locke would continue to call African American folk forms "primitive" on *this* basis, as would, for example V. F. Calverton, while calling African sculpture "classical."

African American folklore, then, was not "organically" continuous with classical African cultures (a claim Locke would have identified with "scientific" racism) but rather an indigenously American "mixed" cul-tural tradition still at a relatively early period of development. Mod-ernist African American art would draw from both sources in the pro-cess of its own "impure" and "cosmopolitan" development of "cultural racialism." The desire to "recapture" the African heritage and promote pan-African consciousness coexists with pride in African American cul-ture as both "mixed" and uniquely "American"—in fact, with a commit-ment to American cultural nationalism. Hence, Nathan Huggins' influential formulation is curiously ironic:

> The Negro intellectual's fascination with primitivism was filled with ironies. Contrary to assertions of the soul-community of black folks, the American Negroes had to learn to appreciate the value of African art and culture. Too often they were taught by Europeans for whom Africa had a powerful, but limited, significance. . . . It was liberating

for these men who stood squarely on a tradition and who would never wholly abandon it. But when the black American intellectual got the news, he wanted to be able to identify completely with Africa, to find his tradition there. Now that was quite fanciful.[49]

The criticism is ironic because the treatment of Africa in *Opportunity* suggests not so much the "finding" as the self-conscious construction of a tradition borrowing from Africa while holding fast to American ground.

The point I am suggesting here is that the dominant view of the approach of the New Negroes—and their white friends—to African identity and its relationship to African American identity simply does not square with the documentary evidence. It recognizes only one side of a complex dialectical relation and ignores the real significance of Boasian anthropology, pragmatism, literary realism, and historicism to the New Negro movement—all of which exerted a powerful and salutary counterpressure to the exploitation of "primitive and exotic" projections of the white racial psyche.

The distinction I am drawing was not absolute, of course. Langston Hughes, Eugene O'Neill, Paul Green, Countee Cullen, and others were capable of "exotic primitive" tableaus as well as more disciplined and durable performances, whether of African or African American social reality. Alain Locke's selected authorities on African art—Paul Guillaume and Albert Barnes—produced a discourse mixing arguments for the self-consciousness of African art forms with belief in the sense of rhythm as racially innate; Guillaume even fell for De Gobineau's statement that "the source from which the arts have sprung is concealed in the blood of the blacks."[50] (This idea had greater force in Europe—especially surrealist-inspired Paris—than in the United States in part because of the different anthropological schools on either side of the Atlantic.) The same text could gesture in both directions simultaneously, and supposed "realists" could spout ecstatic attestations to the Negro's "natural" acting ability, sense of rhythm, and so forth. But the primitive and exotic was a focus for neither the white nor the black critics who wrote for *Opportunity* and the other chief journals of the movement—these critics were, in fact, early in recognizing the more neurotic and exploitative offshoots of the "vogue."[51] After the second *Opportunity* awards dinner, for example, Columbia professor Leon Whipple attacked the "profiteers and parasites" in his report for *The*

Survey: "This sorry crew are not important in themselves. Next year they will be flittering round the candle of some new fad. But they may misguide the Negro for a time unless he can steel himself in anger or wrap himself in his own guffaws against their flattery, false witness, and bribes. It would be the final tragedy if after exploiting the Negro's body for two centuries we ended by exploiting his heart and soul."[52]

Modern Measures, Native Sounds

The recognition of the "indigenous" spirituality of black folklore and its significance for "native" American art carried over into the criticism of black poetry in *Opportunity*. Reviews of the work of four quite different poets reveal an emphasis on poetic strategies that witness the indivisibility of spiritual from social experience, and that, for this very reason, make African American poetry crucial to "native" modernism. Thus Joseph Auslander, reviewing James Weldon Johnson's *God's Trombones,* wrote that the volume was "native, necessary, valid. It is novel without being peculiar and beautiful without being orthodox. It belongs to the literature of the spirit. Racial at the root though it is and must be, it coincides, none the less, with our common humanity, towering like poetry, like prayer beyond its origin."[53]

Auslander's comments are important for a number of reasons. It is clear that he is striving self-consciously for terms that appreciate "racial" difference without exoticizing, terms that recognize spirituality without reference to racialist primitivism. In fact, Auslander (who also served as a judge in the *Opportunity* literary contest) locates the source of spirituality in the aesthetics of existence and resistance: "Never servile, though enslaved, the Negro is speaking out in accents that condemn with as keen a bitterness and celebrate with as jubilant a measure as any poets alive."[54] He appreciates the sermons not on pastoral or antiquarian grounds but for the way they show the "Afro-American imagination making new applications of old ecstasies," in such lines as "Put his eye to the telescope of eternity, / And let him look upon the paper walls of time."[55] In short, he views Johnson's use of the "sermon sagas" of his people as expressly modernist: "The Renaissance of American poetry that seemed a feeble and sorry affair at Amy Lowell's death, rests more than ever with the turbulence and candour of our Negro contemporaries."[56] But Auslander disagrees with Johnson's "contention touching dialect." Recognizing the limitations fixed upon the medium by "popular superstition which confines its use to the stage burlesque or sob variety of Negro humour and pathos," he nonetheless argues that "it is better to explode a superstition than to abandon a gold mine."[57]

To some extent, the enthusiasm of poets like Auslander for New Negro poetry was an effect of their reaction against the expatriate modernism of Pound and Eliot, whose high status came at the expense of the "native" cultural nationalists. Thus, in her featured review of Langston Hughes's *Fine Clothes to the Jew*, Margaret Larkin holds up Hughes's work as "a valuable example for all poets of what can be done with simple technique and 'every day' subjects"—in contrast to "the neurotic fantasies of more sophisticated poets."[58] Capturing the "dialect, speech cadence, and character of the people," Hughes writes an accessible, socially engaged poetry that expresses the philosophy of the black working class. Poets looking for "native American rhythms" can learn something from his deft use of the blues. Hughes's work exerts an important counterforce to the elitist philosophy "that art is the precious possession of the few initiate." Larkin, who did publicity work for New York labor organizations in addition to writing poetry, regards Hughes not as an exotic primitive (she ignores his poems along those lines) but as a poet and prophet of social consciousness.[59]

Indeed, contrary to Du Bois's suspicions, *Opportunity* was certainly no forum of "art for art's sake." In striving to extricate black artists from enclosure in propaganda, it did not counsel the evisceration of the artist's social conscience. Nor did it play to white interest in the primitive. Robert T. Kerlin, in a review of *Cane, The Weary Blues,* and *Color,* wrote: "It is easy enough to conceive of the American Negro outstripping every competitor in every art and in every spiritual quality or achievement"— not because of some natural endowment but because of the wisdom born of suffering in the struggle for freedom. "And wisdom is more precious, according to very good authority, than the choicest residential sections of cities, and Pullman privileges, and theatre seats, and equal educational opportunities. *Though it is only by demanding these that those experiences come whose fruit is wisdom.* And such wisdom always finds embodiment in poetry. It is now doing so."[60] A teacher of Langston Hughes at Lincoln University, Kerlin was not one to rationalize the sublimation through poetry of activism against injustice; he had lost two faculty positions in a row for his public stance against racism and black peonage; and his first book was *The Voice of the Negro, 1919,* a survey of editorials from the black press in the year of the Red Summer, illustrating the new black militancy of the postwar period. His next book would be an important anthology for the rise of the renaissance, *Negro Poets and Their Poems* (1923), published by the African American press Associated Publishers.[61]

The attitude toward the folk heritage as sole reservoir of native "spirituality" also carries over into appreciations of Countee Cullen's poetry. Thus E. Merrill Root praised Cullen's "sensuous rhythms" and "translation of heart's blood into words." Cullen offers tones of revolt, grief, "pantheistic mysticism," and, like A. E. Housman, "the ache and ecstasy of love." What Root most likes is Cullen's hard-won affirmation of life and acceptance of death, both attributes connected with the "sensual mysticism" that suggests he could be the "spiritual leader of a new day" and the greatest of American poets. Cullen is the poet Keats might be, had Keats been born in "this Labrador of the soul which we call America."[62] Again the praise of Cullen carries an implicit (and sometimes explicit) critique of the despairing "wasteland" visions, as Root would have it, that characterize the most prestigious modernist poetry, a poetry that had carried the day against more accessible "native" art.

Joining the staff of *Opportunity* after receiving his master's degree from Harvard, Countee Cullen himself published seventeen columns entitled "The Dark Tower" from December 1926 through 1928, discussing both black and white writers and frequently taking exception to those, like Locke and Hughes, who stressed the importance of race for "Negro poets" and the need for an exploration of new literary forms. The tone was set in his review of *The Weary Blues*. Here Cullen took deliberate aim at Hughes's "jazz" poems, which he regarded as "interlopers in the company of the truly beautiful poems in other sections of the book." To Cullen, these poems create a superficial and transporting excitement, like a religious revival meeting, "but when the storm is over, I wonder if the quiet way of communing is not more spiritual for the God-seeking heart; and in the light of reflection I wonder if jazz poems really belong to that dignified company, that select and austere circle of high literary expression which we call poetry."[63] With views like these (echoing those of William Stanley Braithwaite, whom Cullen had come to know well in Cambridge),[64] it is little wonder that Cullen felt Hughes and others were being misled by white critics encouraging a vernacular approach (to Cullen, stereotypical treatments of black life).

In his "Dark Tower" columns, as Gerald Early and Alan R. Shucard have shown, Cullen consistently resisted "racial" poetics and stressed a "respectable," "representative" middle-class approach, showing how concerned he was about displaying the "embarrassing" aspects of the race to white people: "Negroes should be concerned with making good impressions. . . . Every phase of Negro life should not be the white man's concern. The parlor should be large enough for his entertainment and instruction."[65] However, Cullen was never the "dominant" presence in *Opportunity*, let alone in the Harlem Renaissance.[66] In *Opportunity* he represented the "loyal opposition"—a respected minority view, brought on to the staff perhaps because Charles Johnson wanted to give a forum to all perspectives in the period of Du Bois's crescendo of attacks on the "sewer-dwellers."

"If There Is to Be One, It Will Be Yours": American Drama

Like *The Crisis, Opportunity* expected drama to be a particularly important genre for African American artists, and it continually exhorted black writers to turn their hands to writing plays. "Negro plays" by white writers were frequently held out as inspiration and challenge. In one of its first issues (April 1923), *Opportunity* ran Esther Fulks Scott's "Negroes as Actors in Serious Plays," which focused particularly on Chicago's All-American Theatre Association, which, as we have seen, became known as the Ethiopian Art Theatre under Raymond O'Neil's direction, with Tennessee Anderson as producer. Initially, Fulks Scott relates, the repertory included a mixture of works, mainly by whites, based on "Negro life" as well as classical subjects. The choice of *Salome*—the first play the group produced—was particularly interesting, since it could be regarded as neither "Negro" nor "all-American," but it gave an opportunity to the black actress Evelyn Preer to reinterpret the notorious title character—to the reviewer's delight—as a virtuous religious fanatic who wanted neither to attract nor to dance for Herod, being in love with a man of her own ethnicity. The infamous dance of Salome was therefore made chaste though intense—a subtle retort to theatrical exploitation of black female sexuality. Hinting at the parallelism between biblical and black American historical experiences, the play also enacted a traditional strategy of African American cultural politics.[67]

Opportunity's reviewer drew special attention to the fact that prior to this production Evelyn Preer had been confined to comic parts with the Chicago Ladies Amateur Minstrels, Oscar Micheaux Film Productions, and the Lafayette Players—all black production companies. Members of the *Salome* cast attested to their own changed views of the possibility of "serious" black drama as a result of their experience with O'Neil and blithely thought such drama could be "an ideal means of fostering racial co-operation"; "the so-called race problem could well be solved thru artistic and cultural avenues, giving each group a common interest," as one actress attested.[68] Strangely, the *Opportunity* critic gives barely a mention of Willis Richardson's *The Chipwoman's Fortune,* which served as curtain-raiser for the *Salome* performance.

The ambiguity in "Negro theatre" is prevalent throughout *Opportunity*'s drama criticism. Was it a theater composed of Negro actors? Producing plays on Negro themes? By Negro playwrights? There is no question but that the ideal would be to have black-run companies performing plays written by black artists and performed by black actors—but *Opportunity* never accepted the definition of "Negro drama" as drama written by and for Negroes. Part of the problem is that the sort of theater the *Opportunity* critics (or the *Crisis* critics, or the *Messenger* critics) wanted to see developed—so-called legitimate theater—had little support within the black community. Furthermore, they complained that few talented black writers were turning their attention to drama. No wonder, when the most promising "serious" dramatic treatments of "Negro life" were met by hostility or simple disinterest. Montgomery Gregory, himself a playwright and founder of the Howard University Players, approvingly summarized Max Reinhardt's statement that "the chief contribution of America to the drama of tomorrow would be its development of Negro folk-drama. But what has been the attitude of the Negro himself? Unqualified opposition to the utilization of his mass life in fiction, in music, or in drama."[69] Warming to his theme, Gregory went on: "What has this attitude meant? It has robbed the race of its birthright for a mess of pottage. It has damned the possibilities of true artistic expression at its very source," and left the entire field of "Negro" literature in the control of white artists.[70]

Invoking the authority of Max Reinhardt to make his point was a significant move on Gregory's part, for Reinhardt was the rage of New York at the time. (He was also, incidentally, the man under whom Robert Edmond Jones had studied in Berlin before helping form the Provincetown Players and importing Reinhardt's concept of "total theatre" to the United States;[71] Jones made his debut with Ridgely Torrence's *Three Plays for a Negro Theatre* in 1917.) In another article based on an interview with Reinhardt, Alain Locke, co-founder with Gregory of the Howard University Players, quoted the director as saying that if he ever tried to do "anything American" he would build it on the musical comedies of the American Negro. This was not exactly what Locke or Charles S. Johnson (who was also present) wanted to hear, but Reinhardt went on to clarify that what he admired was the black genius for "pantomime," the primitive and crucial element of all drama. Though currently "prostituted to farce" and "trite comedy," the distinctively African American technical mastery of the body was the treasure of American drama.

How, Locke and Johnson inquired, could this technical gift be utilized rather than exploited? How avoid its perversion in the face of the American demand for caricature? "Only you can do it, you yourselves," Reinhardt responded. "You must not even try to link up to the drama of the past, to the European drama. That is why there is no American drama as yet. And if there is to be one, it will be yours."[72] Reinhardt's chief interest was in folk drama, so it is not surprising that this is the direction he thought black American drama should take. It was also, of course, the direction Locke, Johnson, and Montgomery Gregory thought it should take, as opposed to stark "propaganda" and "race pride." Their position on this point, as we have seen from an article Locke wrote for *The Crisis* the year before *Opportunity* came into existence, was the occasion for the founding of the Howard University Players when Locke and Gregory split from the NAACP drama committee.[73] Not surprisingly, *Opportunity* generally criticized the "pitfalls of propaganda and moralizing on the one hand and the snares of a false and hollow race pride on the other hand," in the words of Gregory—clearly taking a swipe at several of the cultural arbiters of the NAACP.[74]

As the months went on, *Opportunity* continued to look in vain for the movement it wanted; the plays it most praised were almost exclusively those written by white playwrights. Charles Johnson even dedicated an editorial to the topic in 1927, lamenting that Negro drama had not kept pace with advances in the other literary arts. This disappointment could not be blamed entirely on a lack of audience; the submissions for the magazine's drama prize were mediocre, showing a lack of attention to effective techniques of play construction—a problem *The Crisis* had also noted. In fact, despite the differences between the aesthetic emphases of the magazines, *Opportunity*'s remarks on drama often echo those of *The Crisis*. "The recent plays of Negro life, which include Ridgely Torrence's *Three Plays for a Negro Theatre, The Emperor Jones, All God's Chillun, The No 'Count Boy, The Chip Woman's Fortune,* have all with the exception of the last been written by white playwrights," Johnson lamented.[75] Although Willis Richardson, Eloise Bibb Thompson, Frank Wilson, and Eulalie Spence had shown some promise, on the whole Negro writers had not "sensed the possibilities of Negro drama. . . . They have been too ashamed of the material of their own lives to give it artistic portrayal. The new writers [mostly white] are beginning to see these situations and are clothing them in a new beauty. Herein lies the great future of the Negro in drama."[76]

Johnson, Locke, and Gregory were joined by Edwin D. Johnson a year later. The drama by black playwrights, Edwin Johnson charged in 1928, remained mediocre: "The concrete efforts have little if anything to recommend them." Again, the old problem of racial self-defensiveness appeared as the culprit: "The most serious obstacle that the Negro theatre has is that race-conscious specimen of the literati of color that styles itself dramatic critic."[77] Although a few magazines have well-trained editors, Johnson charged, "the most baldly incompetents show themselves in the Negro weeklies"; their "so-called criticism" is "the sheerest sort of twaddle."[78] While noting that *Porgy* had justly been well received by most black critics, he protested the simplistic condemnation of *Lulu Belle* (a play written by Edward Sheldon); none other than James Weldon Johnson had been roundly denounced merely for coming to the play's defense as "a work of art."[79] The *Opportunity* critic accused the black public of cultural antimodernism, arguing that "Negro drama" did not focus more often on "high" society because modern drama in general had broken from Victorian conventions. Johnson's final judgment on the situation for African American drama was bleak indeed: "With self-conscious critics, weak playwrights, and no clientele seriously interested in the theatre, it seems that our excellent actors of color must feed from the hands of the white play-makers for a long time to come."[80]

Edwin Johnson's complaints were seconded by the playwright Eulalie Spence. Like all the writers for *Opportunity,* Spence (though black herself) held that "Negro drama does not of necessity include the work of the Negro dramatist"; rather, it is drama that strives to portray the life of the Negro. Sadly, Negro dramatists capable of accomplishing such portrayal scarcely existed, wrote Spence. The vehicles for the talents of Gilpin, Robeson, Rose McClendon, and Julius Bledsoe were plays by whites. "Some there are who have shuddered distastefully at these plays;

been affronted by Paul Green, degraded by DuBose Heyward, and mis-understood by Eugene O'Neill. But ask the Negro artist if he is grateful to these writers. He will tell you. And ask the Negro dramatist what he feels about it. If he is forward-thinking, he will admit that these writers have been a great inspiration; that they have pointed the way and her-alded a new dawn."[81] Like Edwin Johnson, Spence lamented that Negro dramatists had failed to appreciate the need for study and hard work to gain the technical mastery of playwriting; and, like all the *Opportunity* critics, she warned against the conventional protest play, both because of its tendency to fall into outworn patterns and because it was unpalat-able to both white and black audiences. Propaganda plays on Negro subjects were not likely to meet with success when even the propaganda plays of John Galsworthy were failing at the box office.

Opportunity repeatedly defended "Negro plays" by white artists that would be interrogated today for their complicity with racist ideology. It defended them not merely because they were an improvement upon the blatant racism of earlier drama, nor because any "positive" attention to black life was better than none, but also because the *Opportunity* critics considered the plays of Ridgely Torrence, Eugene O'Neill, DuBose Heyward, and Paul Green to be models for black playwrights to learn from. When David Levering Lewis suggests that "among them-selves Harlem's intellectuals had serious doubts about this new wave of white discovery" and argues that "Harlem intellectuals *pretended* they were enthusiastic about the new dramatic and literary themes," he ignores a wealth of evidence and makes two related mistakes.[82] One is to amalgamate distinctly different responses on the part of different black intellectuals to "Negro writing" by whites; the other is to amal-gamate different works by white authors—works distinctly differenti-ated by black intellectuals of the period—into one category. Perhaps Harlem intellectuals were blind to the more subtle shadings of racist ideology; but certainly several of them were not merely pretending to admire, for example, O'Neill's plays. African Americanists today might want to believe that New Negroes were only feigning admiration for *The Emperor Jones, Porgy,* and *In Abraham's Bosom,* but the evidence suggests otherwise—they were either unabashedly attacking these plays or unabashedly praising them. Specifically, contributors for *Opportunity* were not only glorifying them but incisively attacking their critics—a tactic completely unnecessary to a program of pretended enthusiasm meant to win white patronage.

Paul Robeson's "Reflections on O'Neill's Plays," for example, appeared in the December 1924 issue of the magazine, calling *The Emperor Jones* "undoubtedly one of '*the* great plays'—a true classic of the drama, American or otherwise."[83] Robeson regarded *All God's Chillun* as another great play, despite the "ridiculous critical reaction" accorded it by both white and black critics. When asked whether in the future he would play more "dignified" roles than those he had played in these productions, he responded: "I honestly believe that perhaps never will I portray a nobler type than 'Jim Harris' or a more heroically tragic figure than 'Brutus Jones, Emperor,' not excepting 'Othello.'"[84] Finally, Robeson came to the point so often made in the pages of *Opportunity*, one even made by Du Bois apropos the reception of O'Neill's plays: "The reactions to these two plays among Negroes but point out one of the most serious drawbacks to the development of a true Negro dramatic literature. We are too self-conscious, too afraid of showing all phases of our life,—especially those phases which are of greatest dramatic value. The great mass of our group discourage any member who has the courage to fight these petty prejudices."[85] In addition to Robeson's essay, *Opportunity* reprinted E. A. Carter's review of *All God's Chillun* from *The American Mercury*, printed James Light's "On Producing O'Neill's Play"—obviously as a lesson in stage production—and assigned Eric Walrond to review the play, which he did in a curiously schizophrenic piece, calling it both "another instance of the supreme triumph of art" and "a dull, morbid play."[86] Other *Opportunity* contributors who came to O'Neill's defense, sooner or later, included Sterling Brown and Rudolph Fisher—two authors famously sensitive to white exploitation.[87]

One could go on. Eulalie Spence regretted a poor production of Torrence's *The Rider of Dreams* and contrasted it with the original presentation by the Hapgood Players in 1917, saying the play "will always take its place in every noteworthy collection of Negro plays."[88] Gwendolyn Bennett found Paul Green's *In Abraham's Bosom* worthy of regard as a "powerful tragedy," while an editorial in the June 1927 issue of the magazine expressed enthusiasm for Green's speech at the recent *Opportunity* dinner and gushed, apropos the play that had won him a Pulitzer Prize, "He was the artist who comprehended his materials; who felt the force of tragedy in the lives he portrayed." No wonder that in his remarks at the *Opportunity* gathering, "he found himself, without a single appeal beyond his own sincerity, strangely akin to his audience.

Before them was the new South itself, speaking, but strangest of all, seeming to comprehend and to be understood."[89] Here was a model of Johnson's hope for interracial understanding that would nourish a composite national community.

This is not to say that reviewers in *Opportunity* failed to attack literary exploitation and white thirst for the primitive and exotic; but the works they attacked along these lines were not the works of Torrence, O'Neill, and Green in drama, or of Waldo Frank, Julia Peterkin, and DuBose Heyward in fiction. The works they attacked along these lines were ones we never even hear of today, works of a different order, such as Roark Bradford's *This Side of Jordan,* T. Bower Campbell's *Black Sadie,* Lily Young Cohen's *Lost Spirituals,* Hugh Wiley's *Lily,* Vera Caspary's *The White Girl,* William Seabrook's *Magic Island,* and the stories of Octavus Roy Cohen. Moreover, they did not single out white exploiters; they also lamented inappropriate and "degrading" uses of the spirituals by "Negro revues," black-directed and -produced shows deriving from the black blackface minstrel show tradition.

These were the shows, ironically, that a fairly large black public *would* support. Obviously, something was happening in these shows to which the *Opportunity* critics, in their search for "art theatre," were deaf and blind. At the same time, in proposing "Negro plays" for the "legitimate stage," directors ran into a kind of black resistance *Opportunity* tried to combat. Indeed, when Rowena Woodham Jelliffe first became associated with a "Negro Little Theatre group" in 1920, according to her article of 1928, "both actors and audience were emphatically opposed to Negro plays and thought them highly degrading to their race."[90] The actors all wanted to play heroic leading roles, and none would play a character of "lowly state." They would play a villain only if he was well dressed and not black.[91] The audience demanded comedies, whereas the actors wanted to present serious drama. Gradually they warmed to the idea of presenting a play based on "Negro life," but the majority would only accede to a theater of propaganda. Hence the group—the Gilpin Players of Cleveland—stuck chiefly to European drama in their early years. Finally, in 1924, after an inspirational visit from Charles Gilpin (who was performing *The Emperor Jones* in Cleveland), they tried two "Negro plays"—Ridgely Torrence's *Granny Maumee,* followed by Willis Richardson's *Compromise.* Subsequently, they were happiest doing "Negro plays," and when they moved into their own building they gave it the Swahili name Karamu House and decorated it with African designs. Rowena Jelliffe, the white director, thus saw her aims accomplished: "It has been my fundamental purpose . . . to capture, preserve and develop the dramatic qualities peculiar to the Negro race. I have tried always to avoid the use of the proverbial trick bag of the white theatrical world. We strive to develop a sound dramatic technique which shall strengthen us without subduing us; which shall give us freer mediums through which to make our contributions to the Nation's drama."[92]

Jelliffe's personal history deserves a further gloss here.[93] Recent graduate students at the University of Chicago, Rowena and Russell Jelliffe had had ambitions of founding a cultural center on the order of Hull House when they moved to Cleveland in the early teens, and in 1915 they befriended Langston Hughes. He found solace at their home during a particularly lonely period of his adolescence, when he was living alone in a rooming house. He spent countless hours reading at the Jelliffes' during his high school years, and shared his first poems with them at a time when his mother scorned his poetic ambitions. Rowena Jelliffe was probably the first person with whom he shared "When Sue Wears Red," his first "racial" poem. He also became one of the first teachers at the Jelliffes' settlement house and later returned to work with the Gilpin Players. Rowena Jelliffe, as Arnold Rampersad writes, "staged most of [Hughes's] plays in the thirties"—over the objections of middle-class African Americans, who considered them "Awful."[94] The resemblance between his and Rowena Jelliffe's ideas about black drama is, then, more than coincidental.

Jelliffe's reasons for believing in "Negro drama" fit the overall *Opportunity* line, recalling Reinhardt's observations. The chief talent the Negro actor brings to the stage is "his peculiar quality of motorness, his extraordinary body expressiveness," followed by his "sense of rhythm" as evidenced in both movement and diction, and his "vitality." But aside from the actor's distinctive attributes are the dramatic qualities inherent in black vernacular expression. "The picture building quality of Negro dialect, its rhythmic rise and fall, the earthy quality of Negro folk life," are the prime advantages of black drama. Jelliffe concludes that the greatest Negro drama will be written and produced by Negroes themselves, and that its possibilities have yet to be fully explored.[95] And yet by the end of 1928, the majority of "Negro plays" the Gilpin Players had presented were white-authored.[96]

What the gamut of *Opportunity* drama criticism shows us is that interest in "folk drama" was anything but a decisive attempt on the part of black artists to make a clean break from white American modernism. "Native" white modernists, in alliance with those black intellectuals who were followers of the European-American modernist transformation, tried their damnedest, as they saw it, to awaken African Americans to the riches of their folk heritage. Nor were their attempts motivated mainly by the vogue of Freud (who is not mentioned once) or a fascination with the primitive and exotic. Rather, they were motivated by a decisive reinterpretation and reevaluation of the inherent theatrical qualities of black vernacular speech and distinctively black traditions of mime—inverting the values attached to these qualities in the minstrel show to make them vehicles of "classical" tragedy—and by a Herderian romanticization of the folk inspired chiefly by the successes of the Abbey Theatre and the Moscow Art Players in the years immediately preceding the "Negro renaissance." These are the same theater groups that had inspired Edward Sheldon, Ridgely Torrence, George Cram Cook, Susan Glaspell, Floyd Dell, Robert Edmond Jones, and others to fulfill the need for an American "native stage for native plays," to prove that "the finest culture is a possibility of democracy."[97]

Fictions of Race

I do not mean to suggest that *Opportunity* critics were blind to the stereotypes that could be found in much white "Negro" literature, particularly fiction, and in much European-American criticism of African American writing. Charles S. Johnson felt that even the most "sympathetic" white authors worked at a great disadvantage in treating "Negro themes," as they had "never yet been wholly admitted to the privacy of Negro thots."[98] Yet Johnson clearly felt that African American authors must learn aspects of technical mastery from the examples of white authors, and the works he thought exemplary were those of the native realists; hence the short story judges for the first *Opportunity* literary contest, for example, were Blanche Colton Williams, Carl Van Doren, Zona Gale, Fannie Hurst, Robert Hobart Davis, Dorothy Canfield Fisher, Edna Worthley Underwood, Alain Locke, and Dorothy Scarborough. There was never much question that the great literature about the Negro would be written by African Americans themselves according to aesthetic criteria they would develop, but these criteria could only be formulated gradually; in the meantime, *Opportunity* criticism would define certain parameters of success, more often than not through the criticism of fiction by white authors. *Opportunity* reviewers could be scathing in their denunciation of exploitation by the Irvin Cobbs and Octavus Roy Cohens; and they could provide just critiques of such "well-meaning" efforts as Clement Wood's novel *Nigger.* The criticism of fiction reveals a particularly nuanced reading of contemporary racial writing. Eric Walrond, for example, liked to thumb his nose at the "philistines" and polemicists, in the context of recommending such novels as Ronald Firbank's *Prancing Nigger,* "a work of haunting, compelling beauty."[99] A native of Panama, Walrond finds the novel remarkable for its evocation of the lush beauty of the Caribbean islands, defending the book against the anticipated criticism of those who will find "its content, like its title, . . . a gesture of opprobrium." Apparently to its credit, in the reviewer's eyes, the book makes no overt statement against the British colonial system. Its characters, to Walrond, are absolutely authentic. Most remarkably, the novelist has for once captured the quality of West Indian humor while avoiding minstrel show stereotypes—"It is a delicate, subtle, sophisticated, almost Rabelaisian touch with which 'Prancing Nigger' is consistently shot through. Sometimes it is almost breathtaking."[100] Walrond, an admirer of Van Vechten's preciosity and near-decadence, liked to strike the pose of the apolitical, bohemian aesthete.

Charles S. Johnson, on the other hand, was more sober and politically judgmental. He could appreciate the attempt in Clement Wood's *Nigger* to avoid the "pit falls of over sentimentality one way or the other" while critiquing its attempt to include every form of degrading misfortune in the life of one black family, and its suggestion that the main activity of the African American fraternal lodge was the hatching of rebellions. Lightened by occasional attempts at humor that only rehash old jokes about the Negro, *Nigger* in Johnson's estimation suffers from its author's lack of true intimacy with black life: "His sympathies have carried him a long way, but he could not make his characters live, feel, think and act"—except in frequently stereotypical ways. And yet Johnson ultimately judges the novel "serious, honest, and tremendously impressive—a real tragedy."[101] Apparently he was willing to discount the novel's sins in the interest of promoting it as a "step forward," addressing controversial racial issues in a way that was helping to discredit earlier and even contemporary types of exploitative racist fiction. He even published work by Wood in *Opportunity* and chose him to chair the poetry selection committee for the *Opportunity* awards in literature.

Further evidence of Johnson's taste can be found in his review of Walter White's *The Fire in the Flint*, which he characterizes as the sort of book only an African American could write: "Even the magnificent effort of Clement Wood, despite its earnestness, failed to capture the essense [*sic*] so familiar to Negroes, so incomprehensible to others."[102] Johnson stresses fidelity to the experiences of educated blacks in the South and realistic characterization; in this respect *The Fire in the Flint* is a "trailblazer" like Upton Sinclair's *The Jungle*, "an epoch marker of sociologic interest." When the novel stumbles, it does so through heavy-handed treatment of character types the author cannot allow himself to treat understandingly: "The white mind could be made more intelligible. They are mad men, most of them. Certainly this conduct has some justification in their own minds even if irrational and unsound."[103] Yet as a tragedy breaking the tradition of Southern apologetics, the work marks a new standard—to be followed, Johnson hopes, by realistic fiction of the "lower classes": "There is yet even more poignant tragedy in the lives of the droning millions who are ground down and broken and who are not permitted even the escape of death."[104]

In stark contrast to Johnson's method, but similarly indulgent to white racial fiction, is Eunice Roberta Hunton's rhapsodic review of Waldo Frank's *Holiday*, written in the same overwrought style as the novel itself: "It isn't poetic prose. It is sheer poetry—poetry running riot, an epic too rich in beauty, hate, and tears to be held in the bonds of meter and form; now singing, now wailing itself to its tragic close thru chapters painted clear by an author who has indeed probed America's open sore and dipped his pen in its blood, cleansed somewhat of its putridness by kind understanding."[105] Hunton, a frequent contributor to *Opportunity*, finds *Holiday* brilliant both as art and as social analysis, coming up short only in its hopelessness, its inability to see beyond the division between the races to their violent and passionate interrelationship: "Yes, there is black and white but between there is red, the red of rivers of blood, of red hot iron, of glowing coals and barbarous fires, and too, oh God, the red of flaming passion!"[106] This orgiastic closing exclamation seems oddly blind to the fact that Frank's whole novel focuses upon precisely this suppressed interracial blood-kinship, a focus that seems even to have inspired Hunton's own red vision. Perhaps she wanted a more "positive" denouement.

Waldo Frank's own review of Eric Walrond's *Tropic Death*, beautifully featured on one page of *Opportunity* under the title "In Our American Language," deserves some comment here. Walrond was one of those writers most given to what might be called exoticism, a feature white intellectuals, it has been assumed, always demanded in black fiction. Yet the "exoticism" in *Tropic Death* is exactly what Waldo Frank does not like: "I find here taints of what I might call the *Vanity Fair* school: cleverisms, forcedness, devotions to brash effects for their own sake, which bungling American writers have tried to naturalize from the sophisticated schools of France and England."[107] The "chief feature of interest and importance" in the work, for Frank, is its language—for Walrond is recognizably a modern New World writer, developing a new language like other authors of the Americas, whatever their ethnic ancestry may be: "How can I make clear that the basis of this book—the very substance of its language—relates it to Poe, Melville, Thoreau even—and to their contemporary successors: excludes it radically, moreover, from the noble and long lineage of English literary prose?"[108]

He does not suggest that Walrond should adopt the language of white American writers, only that, like them, he should develop his art as one would labor in native ground with the tools at hand: "Perhaps one of your ancestors was a Caribbean peasant. When he wielded the hoe or the knife, did he not grasp it loose in his brown hand? Do you likewise with your language. . . . I prophecy that forthway a miracle will happen. Your story will open, too. It will achieve overtones, undertones, vistas, dimensions—which in this book it lacks."[109] The review is redolent of Frank's usual mistiness, presumptuousness, and prophetic condescension, but it is virtually the opposite of a counsel to exotic primitivism. And it is quite in line with the overall emphasis in *Opportunity* upon vernacular experimentation with literary language, connected with the drive to realize "native" American life in fiction.

Critics for *Opportunity* repeatedly hailed a decisive change in "Negro portraiture" even while acknowledging the great disadvantages of white writers in this area. The general argument was that mastery of the techniques and social analysis required by fiction would grow slowly; white novelists would provide models initially, and gradually black authors would learn from and finally surpass them in fiction about black life. Sterling Brown's "The New Secession—A Review" makes explicit the hopes raised among New Negro authors by the realist fiction of the New South, and suggests that this fiction provided models of technical experimentation for black writers themselves. Ostensibly a review of Julia Peterkin's *Black April,* Brown's piece ends up being a more general commentary on the "new" Southern white writers' secession from their "Bourbon" predecessors: "Ambrose Gonzales helped start it, DuBose Heyward continued it. And now Julia Peterkin shows herself of their ilk. . . . It is one of the paradoxes of history that this should be so; that North Carolina, with Odum, Johnson, and Paul Green; and that South Carolina with these capable writers; should at last be recognizing in the Negro what Synge has seen in Aran Islanders, Gorki in Russian peasants, and Masefield and Gibson in the lowly folk of England."[110] One of the most influential critics of black stereotypes in the white American literary tradition, Brown finds apparently no primitivism and exoticism in this new realism; what stands out for Brown is the turn to the vernacular and "indigenous."

In this respect Brown claims Peterkin as a model for African American authors. She has shown the truth of Wordsworth's belief in going back to the "soil," as black writers ought to do, "digging our roots deeply therein. . . . If we do decide to try this, there could be few better mentors than Julia Peterkin."[111] Brown differentiates Peterkin's fiction from that of Sherwood Anderson, Carl Van Vechten (whose *Nigger Heaven* he detested), and Walter White, likening it to Toomer's *Cane.* Her limning of the folk is nearly flawless: "Where does she get this uncanny insight into the ways of our folk; their superstitions, their speech, the 'rhythm' of their lives; she of such entirely different beliefs, speech, rhythm."[112] Those elements that Brown does find unlikely are interesting in view of recent fiction by black women integrating folk spirituality and superstition into the lives of college-educated urban heroines: "Joy, who has been away to college comes back and her first words swing into the old Gullah dialect, and her later acts show an ineradicable faith in folklore. To the reviewer it would seem more likely to flaunt some of her newly acquired words as well as her red satin." Moreover, "the coincidence of Zeda's curse and April's gangrene is a bit too fortuitous"—suggesting that the curse really *worked.* After Toni Morrison's *Beloved,* Alice Walker's *The Temple of My Familiar,* and especially Gloria Naylor's *Mama Day,* the grounds of Brown's criticism seem curiously ironic. Again, however, Brown feels the need to defend *Black April* against the objections of black middle-class "philistines" who will accuse Peterkin (as Du Bois was doing) of exploiting old stereotypes: "Those who read into it what is not there, namely propaganda against the Negro, because the characters are not all 'successes'; will alas, have to be of that opinion still. But that Julia Peterkin would consider illegitimacy to be Negroid; betrays scant reading—and insults a writer as sane as she is brilliant."[113] In his "Dark Tower" column for the same issue of *Opportunity*, Countee Cullen likewise praised the volume and upbraided those who had criticized it. But Cullen and Brown may have overestimated black resistance to the book; a report in *Opportunity* two years later noted that Peterkin's next novel, *Scarlet Sister Mary*, was one of the two most popular books at the 135th Street branch of the New York Public Library, the hub of "literary" Harlem.

The criticism in *Opportunity* shows unmistakably that texts interpreted by university professors today as continuous with plantation tradition read as major disruptions of that tradition to New Negro writers of the 1920s, *particularly* to those intent on developing a "Negro aesthetic" from vernacular resources. The new understanding on the part of white writers confirmed Charles Johnson's faith in fiction's potential to undermine the walls of "mutual ignorance and prejudice, hatred and fear" which came between the races in America. Again, it was "native modernism" developing in the wake of the work of black reformers such as Booker T. Washington and W. E. B. Du Bois that Johnson perceived as the impetus behind the new understanding. But this "understanding" should also, according to *Opportunity* critics, be an inspiration to *self*-understanding on the part of African American authors and audiences.

In "Our Literary Audience," for example, Sterling Brown offers no apology for the works of O'Neill, Peterkin, Green, and Heyward on the basis that they had done pretty well for "crackers"; he argues instead that Peterkin's and Heyward's particular uses of dialect in fiction, for example, were expanding the possibilities of black fictional form and technique, breaking out of the conventional limitation to humor and pathos.[114] These writers were helping show the way to a revitalization of the African American cultural tradition by inspiring a new regard for the culture of the "lowly": "But there is more to lowliness than 'lowness.' If we have eyes to see, and willingness to see, we might be able to find in Mamba, an astute heroism, in Hagar a heartbreaking courage, in Porgy, a nobility, and in E. C. L. Adams' Scrip and Tad, a shrewd, philosophical irony. And all of these qualities we need, just now, to see in our group."[115] Readers who object to these fictional characters, Brown suggests, are "ashamed of being Negroes" and lack "mental bravery"—

like many Irish readers of Bernard Shaw—and their shame and timidity threatens to nip in the bud the black literary renaissance as exemplified by Langston Hughes, Jean Toomer, and George Schuyler (not to mention Sterling Brown, whose *Southern Road* would appear two years later). Criticism of these New Negroes' work, in Brown's view, was of a piece with the criticism of Heyward and Peterkin.

Alain Locke thought *Scarlet Sister Mary* destined to become a classic, surpassing "surface realism" to go down "deep to the bone and marrow of life" and to strike "living truth and vital spirituality. It is a tragedy to record that only one or two Negro writers of prose have found the depth of analysis or the penetration of spirit which characterized DuBose Heyward's 'Porgy,' or which characterizes Mrs. Peterkin's 'Scarlet Sister Mary.'"[116] His retrospective review of the literature of 1928 ranked the novel's publication with that of McKay's *Home to Harlem* and Rudolph Fisher's *Walls of Jericho* as one of the "three really important events" of the year. "An appraisal of the outstanding creative achievement in fiction a year ago would not have given us a majority on the Negro side. That in itself reflects a solid gain, . . . for no movement can be a fad from the inside."[117] While he does not base his discriminations on the racial identities of authors, Locke thus recognizes the absolute necessity of a self-determining movement with its own aesthetic and high standards of judgment. The same issue in which Locke lauded *Scarlet Sister Mary* as a classic carried his scathing review of William Seabrook's *Magic Island,* "the product of the intersection of two rapid streams of contemporary interest and taste,—the fad for things Negro and the cult of the primitive."[118]

Opportunity critics, while often adhering to the concept of a New Negro aesthetic, lamented that black writers, by the late 1920s, were not being held to the same standards of excellence as white authors; much mediocre work was being unduly praised and too easily accepted for publication.[119] As a result, writers on "Negro themes" were not being forced to do their best and were acceding to facile exploitation of temporary (white folks') fascinations. Eunice Hunton Carter wrote in 1929, "The more quickly the novelty of the Negro theme wears off and publishers and critics begin to exact from Negro writers that same high standard which they do from others, the more quickly may we expect something better from writers like Wallace Thurman who are capable of things infinitely better than they give."[120] To "win a hearing," Alain Locke acknowledged, the "true" Negro artists had had to tolerate exploitation and endure some "forcing" of meager talent—"There is as much spiritual bondage in these things as there ever was material bondage in slavery"—but the time of true critical appraisal was near: "Certainly the Negro artist must point the way when this significant moment comes, and establish the values by which Negro literature and art are to be permanently gauged after the fluctuating experimentalism of the last few years."[121] Locke lamented that the "Negrophile movement" had swelled to a fad by 1929, and looked forward to the inevitable devaluing of "inflated stock" that would make it possible to discriminate between the "fair-weather friends and true supporters, the stock-brokers and the real productive talents"[122]—prophetic metaphors for that fateful year!

Locke (like Theophilus Lewis in *The Messenger* and H. L. Mencken in *American Mercury*) noted that black fiction was developing more slowly than black poetry, "for creative fiction involves one additional factor of cultural maturity,—the art of social analysis and criticism."[123] The statement exemplifies the approach to fiction taken in *Opportunity* generally, an approach largely shaped by early twentieth-century American realism and naturalism in the wake of Dreiser—whose *An American Tragedy,* by the way, was the most popular book at the Harlem branch of the New York Public Library in November 1926, according to an *Opportunity* report.[124] In *Home to Harlem,* Locke found "the peculiar and persistent quality of Negro peasant life transposed to the city and the modern mode, but still vibrant with a clean folkiness of the soil instead of the decadent muck of the city-gutter." Rudolph Fisher's *Walls of Jericho,* on the other hand, would stand "as the answer to the charge that the Negro artist is not yet ripe for social criticism or balanced in social perspective" (a charge Locke implicitly accepted with regard to earlier black fiction generally!).[125] In fact, in the same article Locke criticizes Du Bois's *Dark Princess* for falling "an artistic victim to its own propagandist ambushes."

In contrast, Nella Larsen's *Quicksand* "is truly a social document of importance." While Locke shares Du Bois's admiration for this novel, his interpretation markedly differs from the *Crisis* editor's. Larsen, in Locke's astute reading, departs from typical renditions of the "tragic mulatto" theme by focusing on "the problem of divided social loyalties and the issues of the conflict of cultures" rather than the "grim tragedy of blood and fateful heredity." In other words, while subverting racial essentialism Larsen explores the force of social constructions of racial identity and the conflicts deriving from the fact that not everyone "belongs" to just one "race."[126] *Quicksand* reveals the contradictions inherent in the binarism of American racial discourse.

Expectations similar to Locke's inform Gwendolyn Bennett's review of *Plum Bun* by Jessie Fauset. Bennett emphasizes the working through of social issues surrounding constructions of personal identity in this novel of passing. The critical way in which these issues affect "mixed-bloods" helps foreground the operation of "race" in American culture generally. And if the thematic importance of the novel derives from its social analysis, its specific texture derives from the author's fidelity to her personal experience of life in particular places. Fauset's strength lies in the precision of her scenes depicting middle-class African American home life in Philadelphia; her weaknesses show in her attempts to produce more "cosmopolitan" scenes in New York.[127] Bennett's evaluation thus reveals again a major division in New Negro fiction, based not on whether one should treat "high" or "low" class life but on attitude and perspective, particularly concerning cross-cultural relationships.

In her review of a decidedly different novel—Claude McKay's *Banjo*—Bennett again stresses the author's intimacy with the experiences and styles of life he successfully depicts. Rather than playing his novel off against those of Jessie Fauset, the reviewer praises it—as she did *Plum Bun*—for its "priceless observations" about aspects of black life in a particular, little-known context. "I wondered as I read the book how the people who will criticize it from a moral standpoint would have written a novel around Marseilles. But I suppose the answer to that is that one should not choose Marseilles for a subject under any circumstances."[128] Bennett does not feel that McKay panders to primitivist delectations: "To him this tale was life as he saw it about him in Marseilles. There is no snigger of wrong emphasis in his discussion of the most taboo subject."[129]

The criticism of critics of "bourgeois" black fiction was undertaken on the same grounds of social "realism" as Bennett's critique of McKay's fiction. Hence, in a review of *Passing* immediately following Bennett's of *Banjo*, Mary Fleming Labaree (a white critic and contributor to the *Saturday Review*) writes: "There is no layer or segment of humanity that is *verboten* to the maker of novels, if he be an honest workman. And the honest reader need not flinch from honest fact or honest interpretation of any phase of life. Yet certain literary somebodies and other literary nobodies would have us believe that only life in the raw or bloody-rare is life at all and worth writing up. The pity of it!—if 'Walls of Jericho' and 'Home to Harlem' perched upon our bookshelves with 'Plum Bun' and 'Passing' nowhere to be seen."[130] Labaree—a good friend of Langston Hughes, who studied the social sciences under her husband at Lincoln[131]—praises Larsen's ability to avoid melodrama while exploding "the stupid Nordic complex and its unlovely sequelae" through subtle, precise development of character and social interaction. Regretting that the novel falls short of "greatness," Labaree hopes Larsen will take her time in her next effort and "give the world its needed epic of racial interaction between thinking members of the American social order belonging to both African and European stocks."[132] Labaree dismisses interest in primitivism and exoticism, looking instead for fidelity to "native" life. This aesthetic preference is connected with a kind of social philosophy. The exploration of otherness in novels of social analysis trains self-understanding and expands the range of human solidarity: "Doctors, lawyers, men of affairs, their wives and daughters are neither less valuable nor less richly human members of society than jazz boys and girls, roustabouts and drunks—though it takes a more gifted, understanding and highly experienced artist to make them breathe and move and speak so that we know them for what they really are, so that we ourselves breathing, moving and speaking with them, come to perceive more clearly what we ourselves really are—of one blood with them and all humanity."[133] The statement epitomizes the criteria for black fiction *Opportunity* generally stressed, whether promoting literature of the "folk" or of the "bourgeoisie." It is of a piece with Charles S. Johnson's personal philosophy.

Of a piece with that philosophy, too (though appearing after Johnson's departure), is Sterling Brown's laudatory review of Langston Hughes's first novel, *Not Without Laughter*: "Tolerant, humane, and wise in the ways of mortals, he has revealed beauty where too many of us, dazzled by false lights, are unable to see it."[134] Brown admires the "simplicity" and accessibility of the story along with its fidelity to social relations and sensitive characterizations, products of Hughes's ability to identify sympathetically with different personalities. The book falters, in fact, only through Hughes's failure to sympathize with the "bourgeois" worshiper of white folks' ways, Tempy; the result is unconvincing caricature in the portrait of this too easily dismissed "type." Lack of sympathy effects the erasure of otherness through caricature as surely as does the *premature*, socially naïve leap to human "universals." It is interesting to

note Brown's association of realistic characterization and social awareness with "universality," for here universality signifies not the erasure of
difference but a counterforce to its exploitation as the exotic:

> Excepting Tempy, who to the reviewer seems slightly caricatured, all
> of the characters are completely convincing. There is a universality
> about them. They have, of course peculiar problems as Negroes. Har-
> riet, for instance, hates all whites, with reason. But they have even
> more the problems that are universally human. Our author does not
> exploit either local color, or race. He has selected an interesting family
> and has told us candidly, unembitteredly, poetically of their joy light-
> ened and sorrow laden life.[135]

By "universality" I take it that Brown is attempting to define human
mutuality as against racial essentialism, rather than a category effacing
historical particularity. The same "universality" typifies the "laughing to
keep from crying" motif of the blues that imbues the entire work with
authenticity in its quiet blending of tragedy and comedy—that is, a distinctive aspect of African American expression that is accessible to all
who read in "sympathy." Through such fiction, and such reading, is
the realm of solidarity expanded, enriched, articulated with ever-
increasing precision.

Charles S. Johnson's rationale for the *Opportunity* literary contests
reveals the purpose behind his impressive labors in service of a "New
Negro aesthetic." In a deliberate statement of that rationale, he
stressed the

> extreme usefulness for the cause of inter-racial good-will as well as
> racial culture and American literature in interpreting the life and
> longings and emotional experiences of the Negro people to their
> shrinking and spiritually alien neighbors; of flushing old festers of
> hate and disgruntlement by becoming triumphantly articulate; of
> forcing the interest and kindred feeling of the rest of the world by
> sheer force of the humanness and beauty of one's own story. . . . There
> is an opportunity now for Negroes themselves to replace their out-
> worn representations in fiction faithfully and incidentally to make
> themselves better understood.[136]

Johnson added that he particularly wanted the contests "to stimulate
and foster a type of writing by Negroes which shakes itself free of delib-

erate propaganda and protest."[137] What is remarkable about Johnson's work is not only the coherence of his aesthetic, sociological, and philosophical positions, but also his success in bringing diverse artists and critics together into a community of discourse that expressed his vision across a broad array of genres and racial as well as class positions. While he fostered the growth of a "Negro aesthetic" in literature, he did so with the understanding that it was an aspect of the development of an American literature—central, indeed, to the development of such a literature. The Negro aesthetic, moreover, was neither an extension of a *hermetic* tradition nor a growth out of some organic racial truth. African American literature would not tear aside distorting veils to the Real reality but would make a cultural reality out of the beauty of familiar things.

In 1928 Johnson resigned from the Urban League to head the department of social sciences at Fisk—in part, apparently, because of financial difficulties that were forcing the Urban League to reconsider *Opportunity*'s role. After his departure, *Opportunity*'s connection with cultural affairs declined considerably, although Alain Locke would continue to express the critical orientation of *Opportunity* throughout the 1930s and Sterling Brown made some crucial contributions. Together with Du Bois's disaffection with the Harlem Renaissance artists, Johnson's departure from the magazine was a severe loss; yet in the few years of his editorship, *Opportunity* had an impact out of all proportion to its circulation. To put it another way, it achieved a critical mass the force of which can be detected throughout important sectors of the American literary field of the 1920s and 1930s, creating new spaces and shaping new vectors of power for the development of African American culture, for the "Americanization" of the United States.

7

Reading These United States:
The Nation and *The New Republic*

Of the "white" magazines, the two most important forums for black literature from the beginning of the Harlem Renaissance into the thirties were two weeklies with similar political bearings: *The Nation* and *The New Republic*. The two magazines had a number of other characteristics in common. Both published articles by such Harlem Renaissance luminaries as W. E. B. Du Bois, James Weldon Johnson, Walter White, Eric Walrond, Langston Hughes, and George Schuyler. Both reported regularly on incidents of lynching and on race riots. Both opposed American imperialism, particularly in Haiti (on which James Weldon Johnson did an important series of articles for *The Nation*).[1] Both had intimate links with philosophical pragmatism, going back to the years in which Charles Sanders Peirce had published articles in *The Nation*. Here, too, in 1913, Horace Kallen first published his views on cultural pluralism. On the other hand, John Dewey had a singularly powerful influence upon *The New Republic* and its editors. Both magazines relied on the Boas school for commentary and reviews concerning anthropology and racial theory (Edward Sapir even published poetry in these magazines). The letter that had gotten Boas censured and kicked off the board of the American Anthropological Association had been published in *The Nation*.

Both *The Nation* and *The New Republic* tended to push the "American tradition" as exemplified in the works of what we call today the American Renaissance, along with Dickinson and Mark Twain. In fact, their editors were instrumental in rescuing Herman Melville from obscurity and establishing him as one of the world's great novelists. Both magazines promoted American cultural nationalism in terms of cultural pluralism. Both lacked the sophisticated cosmopolitanism exhibited by *The Dial* in the twenties as well as the experimentalism of the more self-consciously avant-garde "little magazines" that were promoting what we know today as high modernism. By contrast, Carl Sandburg published virtually all of his poetry in 1923 and 1924 in *The Nation* and *The New Republic*. Their focus was far more upon fostering a native cultural resurgence and liberal or socialist politics than upon European and expatriate American artistic movements—although *The New Republic* was notably more receptive to those movements (and, perhaps not incidentally, more prone to "primitivism and exoticism" in its approach to black America) than *The Nation*. Support for the New Negro fit into these broad commitments.

If a magazine reveals its cultural orientation in great part by the books it chooses to review and how it reviews them, *The Nation* and *The New Republic* distinguished themselves in both their attention to books on racial subjects and the points of view generally brought to bear on those subjects. Considering the massive quantity of books released in the publishing boom of the 1920s and the minute percentage of these books that had any relation to the Harlem Renaissance, the two magazines were remarkable for their promotion of the "Negro awakening" and related intellectual movements. Relatively few works by black authors in the fields of belles-lettres and social criticism escaped them. More to the point, they frequently asked black writers to review these works—including particularly Du Bois, Walrond, and White. Like *The Crisis* and *Opportunity*, in anthropology and racial theory they consistently drew upon Franz Boas or his students—usually Melville Herskovits, Alexander Goldenweiser, Ruth Benedict, or Edward Sapir. Moreover, it was fairly common for an editor or contributing editor of *The Nation* or *The New Republic* to review a Harlem Renaissance book in the other periodical, or in the *Herald Tribune* book section, or in another related periodical—even in *Opportunity*.

What Susan J. Turner has said of *The Freeman* could be said equally of *The Nation* and *The New Republic*: their interests were in writing that "lay close to the changing moral and social structure of America—in the literature of the small town, in the culture figures of the past, and in critiques of American life."[2] A *New Republic* editorial of 1921 stated: "The new pioneer in this country is the man or woman who . . . brings provincial experience into aesthetic and spiritual and above all critical consciousness. . . . [America's] present critical acceptance of its own existence is its greatest triumph of social imagination. It is the beginning of one kind of national fullness and integrity, and this is the work of the novelists who have Main Street in hand."[3] Pragmatism, Boasian anthropology, cultural pluralism, and the vogue of the "new regionalism" and critical realism had far more to do with the support the New Negro met with in these magazines than did Freudianism. On such grounds Zona Gale—the then-famous Wisconsin writer—encouraged and promoted Georgia Douglas Johnson and Jessie Fauset, while Sinclair Lewis aided Walter White and Claude McKay. Sherwood Anderson and Tennessee Anderson, Clement Wood, Julia Peterkin, Paul Green, Du Bose Heyward, and a score of others who wrote and reviewed for *The Nation, The New Republic, The Crisis,* and *Opportunity,* all connected the new critical regionalism with interest in Harlem Renaissance writing. Freudianism and primitivism were subordinate to these connections and for the most part came later, as a result of the revolt against the Anglo-Saxon genteel tradition—but even then most often in connection with social and political critique. Although the magazines often provided valuable criticism of African American writing and served as important venues for black intellectual work, one must add that they did not recognize the larger claims made by *The Crisis* and *Opportunity* about the centrality of African American experience and culture to U.S. culture and society. Black culture and history remained minor add-ons to a cultural vision centered in white (and mostly middle-class) experience and discourse.

The Nation

Founded in 1865 with the express purpose of promoting the interests of the Southern freedmen and diffusing "democratic principles,"[4] from its beginning *The Nation* identified the "nationalization" of the United States with the destruction of caste. Its name expressed its founders' sense that out of the Civil War the United States had been reborn as a *nation* rather than merely a *union* of federated states, and they identified this nationhood with the fate of black Americans newly freed. Of the seven major objectives listed for the magazine, three concerned the condition of the black freedmen. However, by the late 1880s, the paper had backed off from championing black empowerment. From these years until 1918, *The Nation* was also a voice of cultural conservatism and Anglo-Saxon hegemony; but in January of 1918 Oswald Garrison Villard took over the editorship, sold the *Evening Post* (to which it had become attached), and returned the magazine to its former crusading self, with the example of William Lloyd Garrison's *Liberator* clearly in mind.

In the three decades before 1918, *The Nation* was not a likely supporter of either African American culture or the new critical American cultural nationalism. Paul Elmer More, Anglophile high priest of the New Humanism and literary editor from 1910 to 1914, was one of the men whose criticism could provoke H. L. Mencken, Van Wyck Brooks, and company to their most impassioned denunciations of the genteel tradition. Carl Van Doren would remember that "before the war the Nation had been as conservative as it could find reasons for being. By the end of 1921 it was offering an annual prize for poetry, in the new manner, and a pick and shovel man could say to it: 'You are dedicated to defend the immense cause of the oppressed.' Pre-war had given way to post-war."[5]

Villard, who had taught American history at Harvard from 1894 to 1896 before helping start the NAACP, not only took on the causes of black civil rights and women's suffrage; he also turned the magazine from support for the war to pacifism and then attacked the Treaty of Versailles and the League of Nations as secretive attempts by the five victors to carve up the world for their own imperial advantage. Villard was in the habit of hiring people who had been fired from academic or editorial jobs for adherence to progressive causes, such as Ernest Gruening and Freda Kirchwey. Gruening had been managing editor of the *New York Tribune* in the teens until he published, in 1918, "a picture juxtaposing a Southern lynching with a parade of black troops returning from combat in France"; for this, he and everyone he had hired (including Kirchwey) were terminated—just as Villard began remaking *The Nation*. Gruening became managing editor in 1920, and Kirchwey, originally hired in 1918, became managing editor some years later; she would buy the magazine in 1937.[6] *The Nation*, then, became a progressive, not an old-fashioned liberal, organ; it tended toward socialism but felt that Americans would not support a party of that name. Indeed, it shared the more radical *Liberator*'s sense that socialism must be translated into native terms, its roots found in traditions and institutions of the nation's own past. Villard himself wanted *The Nation* to be radical in politics but conservative in literature, caring for literature only as propaganda for virtue and justice, but he gave Van Doren a free hand when the latter came on board in 1919. Immediately the old subscribers began crying out that *The Nation* had become "unAmerican."[7]

The fact that Villard made the attack on racism a major issue did not go unnoticed by black readers. In August 1919, in an editorial entitled "Oswald Garrison Villard," *The Messenger* lauded him and his magazine. Likewise, Claude McKay, before he had published anything in the United States, "especially admired *The Nation* and held Villard in high esteem."[8] Villard was one of the first supporters of Du Bois's proposal to start a magazine for the NAACP.[9] (Significantly, despite the tension between Du Bois and Villard that led to the latter's resignation from the NAACP chairmanship, Du Bois attested at the time that no members of the organization were "in closer intellectual agreement on the Negro problem.")[10] At first the NAACP operated out of an office in the *New York Evening Post* building, under arrangements made by Villard. His magazine published important articles on racism and lynching by such people as Villard himself, Walter White, William Pickens (field secretary of the NAACP), and Herbert J. Seligmann (publicity director for the NAACP). Villard ran frequent editorials on racist crimes and on peonage in the South; and he wrote stinging rebukes of other papers, such as the *New York Times* and the *Washington Post*, for aiding and abetting white mobs.[11] He reprinted for his readers the statement "To the World" of the 1921 Pan-African Congress in London. And he strongly supported Indian nationalism and Gandhi's movement for liberation through nonviolent direct action.

Villard's crusading zeal no doubt had something to do with the attention Van Doren paid to black writing as literary editor. Yet Van Doren came with an already pluralistic view of literary value, and particularly a commitment to ethnic and regional diversity in American literature: "There are many kinds of literature," he wrote, "because there are many kinds of life. . . . There are no universal poets, not even Homer and Shakespeare."[12] Van Doren specifically encouraged the younger black writers because he thought they had much to contribute to a pluralistic, native American culture.[13] V. F. Calverton later remembered that in this period *The Nation* was one of the strongest voices expressing the need for a genuinely "American" art. Others associated with the magazine included Albert J. Nock (associate editor), H. L. Mencken (contributing editor), Ludwig Lewisohn (drama critic), and John Macy, who succeeded Carl Van Doren as literary editor. Macy was followed by Irita Van Doren, Carl's wife, who subsequently moved on to the *Herald-Tribune* books section; through her influence, that review then became an important supporter of African American modernism. Meanwhile, Mark Van Doren, Carl's brother, became literary editor at *The Nation*, carrying on the family tradition through the rest of the decade. Mark's wife, Dorothy, in turn became an associate editor in the late 1920s. As a group, then, the Van Dorens had a lot of clout in determining *The Nation*'s cultural agenda; and the initial outline of that agenda was set by Carl in 1919–1922.[14]

Many of the new American writers of the 1920s (particularly those who stayed "at home") turned to *The Nation* because it spoke up for them through Van Doren's and Ludwig Lewisohn's literary criticism. In a series of articles on "contemporary American novelists" in 1921 Van Doren coined the phrase "the revolt from the village" to characterize such works as Clarence Darrow's *Farmington* and Edgar Lee Masters' *Spoon River Anthology*—considering the latter the beginning of "the newest style in American fiction"—along with works by Sherwood Anderson, Sinclair Lewis, Floyd Dell, and Zona Gale.[15] Several of these Midwestern-born authors would also contribute criticism and reviews to the magazine, consistently emphasizing that, despite handicaps, a native literature was on the rise; expatriation was not the answer for the committed artist.

Zona Gale's "The United States and the Artist" provides a significant example, and is of particular interest because Gale played an important role in the careers of Georgia Douglas Johnson and Jessie Fauset. She addresses the alleged hazards of being an artist in America, noting that "if the artist is a Negro, his difficulties are needlessly greater in this country than in any other land of the civilized world." Nonetheless, Gale writes, the writer should remain at home—as she herself stayed in Wisconsin to base her fiction and drama upon the life around her.[16] As Harold Simonson points out, Gale's Portage, Wisconsin, "takes its place with Lewis' Zenith and Gopher Prairie, Anderson's Winesburg, and Carl Van Vechten's Maple Valley" in the regionalist cross-sections of provincial America. Her novel *Miss Lulu Bett,* contemporaneous with *Main Street,* "was hardly less influential in establishing the new direction in provincial realism," as it was adapted to the stage and won a Pulitzer

Prize in 1921.[17] Her regionalism expressed the chastened yet durable Roycean hope for "wholesome provincialism" in the United States. Indeed, Gale published extensively on political and social action as well as literature in such magazines as *The Nation, The New Republic*, and *The World Tomorrow*. She was, by the way, a neighbor and mentor of another Wisconsin author, Margery Latimer—Jean Toomer's first wife—and was very close to Ridgely Torrence.[18] She was also a judge for *Opportunity* literary contests. Georgia Douglas Johnson dedicated her third book of poems to Gale, and shared the manuscript of her play *Blue Blood* with her.[19] Gale also convinced Frederick A. Stokes to publish Jessie Fauset's *The Chinaberry Tree* (at Fauset's request, after they had turned the book down) and wrote the introduction to that novel.[20] Gale's web of relationships is just one of many examples of the extensive connections between the interest in regional realism, American cultural nationalism, and New Negro writing.

Ludwig Lewisohn, drama critic at *The Nation* in the early 1920s and one of its most powerful critics, characterized the new "native" literature as "naturalistic" and rebutted charges that it was alien to "the traditions of our American life" (a position the new humanists often took) by arguing that its spirit flowed from Whitman and the democratic ethos: "To it there are no outcasts; none are disinherited, none wholly guilty, none stale or discarded."[21] Lewisohn, furthermore, advocated a stringent cultural pluralism. "There is . . . no such thing in nature as an abstract human being. Man is embodied concretely in cultural species. . . . [T]hat which becomes a universal possession was first born of an ethnic and historical womb. . . . [W]e must accept each other as brothers with those differences of outlook, instinct, aptitude, which have been forged in the smithies of historic time."[22]

It should be clear that, overall, the critics of *The Nation* who set the tone of its cultural criticism in the early twenties were not of the sort who would be looking in African American literature for proof of the Negro's humanity *or* for unselfconscious primitivism. They read it instead with the belief that it should embody forms of consciousness integral to a historic and ethnic tradition of long-running American provenance. In contrast, a *Nation* editorial of 1922 took the trouble to notice Thomas Nelson Page's death in order to attack his sentimental fiction of the South as "false to history and to human character."[23]

Well before Negro writing was in style, *The Nation* thus facilitated an opening for it. An editorial in 1921 addressed the rumor that the

Drama League had intended to bar Charles Gilpin from its annual dinner, which had called forth an immediate and emphatic protest from other invited guests; *The Nation* reported that seven immediately announced they would boycott the dinner, including Robert Edmond Jones, Eugene O'Neill, and Lee Simonson. "The episode is the more significant in view of the controversy here and there stirring over the true color and quality of the national genius," the author of the editorial pointed out, before launching an attack on nativist Anglo-Saxonism as well as the dismissal of American culture by the "contemptuously cosmopolitan." The United States is a pluralistic nation—"Our hope lies in our fusion of many cultures."[24]

The general orientation of the literary editors toward American literature largely determined the nature of their response to the new black writing. In his speech for the Civic Club dinner—the coming-out party of the New Negro movement—Carl Van Doren expressed his belief that "the Negroes of the country are in a remarkable strategic position with reference to the new literary age which seems to be impending. . . . [T]hey will bring a fresh and fierce sense of reality to their vision of human life on this continent, a vision seen from a novel angle by a part of the population which cannot be duped by the bland optimism of the majority." Van Doren addressed the art-versus-propaganda issue with realism and sensitivity: "That Negro writers must long continue to be propagandists, I do not deny. The wrongs of their people are too close to them to be overlooked. But it happens that in this case the vulgar forms of propaganda are all unnecessary. The facts about Negroes in the United States are themselves propaganda—devastating and unanswerable. A Negro novelist who tells the simple story of any aspiring colored man or woman will call as with a bugle the minds of all just persons, white or black, to listen to him."[25] There is not a trace of interest in the "primitive and exotic" here; if anything, Van Doren was suggesting a realistic fiction of middle-class black life, consistent with his earlier attention to the critical, regional realism of the midwestern renaissance. Van Doren concluded his comments in a vein many black authors were glad to hear: "If the reality of Negro life is itself dramatic, there are of course still other elements, particularly the emotional power with which Negroes live—or at least to me seem to live. What American literature decidedly needs at the moment [as a supplement to the drab *Main Street* style?] is color, music, gusto, the free expression of gay or desperate moods. If the Negroes are not in a position to contribute these items, I do not know what Americans are."[26] The speech was published in the next issue of *Opportunity*, and in the following year Van Doren would be chosen as short story judge for its first literary contest.

In 1920 Van Doren's view had been somewhat different. Noting the "indigenous" quality of Native American and African American folk-lore, he had written: "Indian and Negro materials, however, are in our poetry still hardly better than aspects of the exotic. No one who matters actually thinks that a national literature can be founded on such alien bases."[27] (Mary Austin was arguing at this time for an essential "American rhythm" in poetry derived from Native American oral poetry, which she claimed had influenced Whitman.) Van Doren's prejudices were clearly *against* the "primitive and exotic." He connected an interest in multiethnic literatures with a "melting-pot" expectation that at some future date a mixed Americanism would emerge: "Our hope lies in diversity, in variety, in colours yet untried, in forms yet unsuspected. And back of all this search lie the many cultures, converging like immigrant ships toward the narrows, with aspirations all to become American and yet with those things in their different constitutions which will enrich the ultimate substance."[28] "Experimentation and exploration and excavation must be kept up," even if at some far-off date, as ancient history would lead us to expect, the United States reached a "fusion" of its disparate elements. William Stanley Braithwaite reprinted this editorial anonymously as "Tap-Root or Melting-Pot" to introduce his *Anthology of Magazine Verse for 1920*, saying the piece "comprehensively expresses the character and quality of the art in America today."[29]

When Van Doren moved to *The Century* as part of a major shakeup at that old bastion of gentility, black writers began publishing *there*.[30] However, *The Nation* remained an important outlet for the New Negro writers and a voice of American cultural nationalism. And as a contributing editor to *The Nation*, with which he kept in close contact even as he served as literary editor to *The Century*, Van Doren solicited poems from Langston Hughes in 1925.[31]

If anything, the magazine's interest in black literature grew after Carl Van Doren's move, first under the literary editorship of John Macy (October 1922 to October 1923), whose *Spirit of American Literature* (1913) had fired some of the opening salvos of the American cultural nationalist "rebellion"; Macy also served as a regular reviewer of literature for *The Freeman* from 1921 to 1922.[32] Taking a page from Josiah

Royce's book, Macy had recommended a "wholesome provincialism" for American literature, complaining that it had "too little savor of the soil" and tended to the idealistic, the delicate, the nicely finished—with the exception of works by Thoreau, Whitman, Stowe, and Mark Twain.[33] At the second *Opportunity* awards meeting, which he chaired, Macy charged, "All artists in the world must express intensely their race, nation, time, family, personality." A New England Yankee cannot write like a Russian novelist or a French poet: "every man to his own racial and individual nature and belief and mother tongue." Countee Cullen, he objected, was wrong to marvel that God would "'make a poet black and bid him sing.'"[34] Macy's attitudes, well in tune with Carl Van Doren's, would be carried on after his departure; one finds many articles in *The Nation* criticizing chauvinism and "vulgar" nationalism while nonetheless stressing the need for a "native literature" developing out of local experience and the vernacular.[35] Indeed, at the same time that *The Nation* promoted New Negro writing, it helped establish Herman Melville's reputation.

Upon the publication of the *Survey Graphic's* special Harlem issue, *The Nation*—in an unusual step for a mostly political magazine—devoted a front-page editorial to an appreciation of the New Negro movement. While recognizing the African background and the long history of African American culture, the writer considered the special issue "a notable contribution to the fact and philosophy of a democratic America. . . . For the first time it brings together an interpretation of this new Negro from the standpoint of his poetry, his music, his gifts of temperament and philosophy and character toward the making of an American democracy."[36] *The Nation* was receptive to both the "best-foot-forward" school and the "bohemian" wing of the Harlem Renaissance. Its usual reviewer of black fiction was Walter White, hardly a celebrant of the primitive and exotic.

The magazine published articles, reviews, and poetry by Du Bois, White, E. Franklin Frazier, Cullen, McKay, Hughes, Schuyler, Locke, and Mordecai Johnson (the first black president of Howard University). In his article Johnson appealed to the ideology of American exceptionalism while placing the condition of the Negro at the center of that ideology:

Can the Christian religion bind this multi-colored world in bonds of brotherhood? We of all nations are best prepared to answer that question, and to be their moral inspiration and their friend. For we have the world's problem of race relationships here in crucible, and by strength of our American faith we have made some encouraging progress in its solution. If the fires of this faith are kept burning around that crucible, what comes out of it is able to place these United States in the spiritual leadership of all humanity. When the Negro cries with pain from his deep hurt and lays his petition for elemental justice before the nation, he is calling upon the American people to kindle anew about the crucible of race relationships the fires of American faith.[37]

Of McKay's work, *The Nation* published the lovely poem of nostalgia for lost youth, "Home Song," which has been virtually forgotten, perhaps because it fails to fit the various functions black literature is expected to serve in college classrooms:

> Oh black boys holding on the cricket ground
> A penny race!
> What other black boy frisking round and round
> Plays in my place?
>
> When picnic days come with their yearly thrills,
> In warm December,
> The boy in me romps with you in the hills—
> Remember![38]

Other poetry *The Nation* published in these years included Countee Cullen's "The Wise" and "The Loss of Love," Scudder Middleton's tribute "To W. E. Burghardt Du Bois" ("Beyond the creaking tree, the faggot's flame, / Your eyes have caught the vision of a race / Rising by greater truths than pity yields. / And you have made it dream, speak out its name—/ Proud of that ancient ebon of its face!"), and James Rorty's "The Walls of Jericho," which envisions the walls of white oppression tumbling down as white Americans are converted to singing the Negroes' song and adopting the humanistic principles of the African American tradition.[39] Not one of these poems fits the "primitive and exotic" designation.

The Nation was thus a crucial forum for competing visions of African American literature. In back-to-back issues it published George Schuyler's satirical "The Negro-Art Hokum," which ridiculed the idea that black American culture was in any respect different from white

American culture, and Hughes's "The Negro Artist and the Racial Mountain," which Freda Kirchwey had solicited.[40] The interchange is, of course, important because of the reverberations of Hughes's essay down through subsequent African American literary history; but it also exemplifies the way opposing sides of the New Negro movement defined themselves in relation to the overarching problematic of American cultural nationalism. That the exchange took place between the covers of *The Nation* is therefore only fitting. Schuyler, on the one hand, argues that there is no "Negro" culture in the United States, only "American" culture:

> Aside from his color, which ranges from very dark brown to pink, your American Negro is just plain American. . . . The Aframerican is subject to the same economic and social forces that mold the actions and thoughts of the white Americans. . . . When the jangling of his Connecticut alarm clock gets him out of his Grand Rapids bed to a breakfast similar to that eaten by his white brother across the street; when he toils at the same or similar work in mills, mines, factories, and commerce alongside the descendants of Spartacus, Robin Hood, and Erik the Red; when he wears similar clothing and speaks the same language with the same degree of perfection; when he reads the same Bible and belongs to the Baptist, Methodist, Episcopal, or Catholic church; . . . when he smokes the same brands of tobacco and avidly peruses the same puerile periodicals; in short, when he responds to the same political, social, moral, and economic stimuli in precisely the same manner as his white neighbor, it is sheer nonsense to talk about "racial differences" as between the American black man and the American white man.[41]

The foundations of Schuyler's reasoning (however flawed that reasoning may be) are both pragmatist notions of the relation between experience and culture and Boasian notions of the fiction of "race," combined with a Marxist tendency to ignore the power of culture and the cultural effects of racialization in order to emphasize economic determinism.

However, Schuyler actually gives primary status to *national* identity rather than class, and specifically uses literature as evidence: "Consider Coleridge-Taylor, Edward Wilmot Blyden, and Claude McKay, the Englishmen; Pushkin, the Russian; Bridgewater, the Pole; Antar, the Arabian; Latino, the Spaniard; Dumas, *père* and *fils*, the Frenchmen; and Paul Laurence Dunbar, Charles W. Chestnut [sic], and James Weldon

Johnson, the Americans. All Negroes; yet their work shows the impress
of nationality rather than race. . . . Why should Negro artists of America
vary from the national artistic norm when Negro artists in other countries have not done so?" The only explanation for the popularity of the
"Negro-art hokum," Schuyler concludes, is its appeal to a rehashed version of the racialist belief in "'fundamental, eternal, and inescapable
differences' between white and black Americans." Schuyler implies that
racial chauvinism and the desire to cash in on a fad explain the willingness of some black artists themselves to "lend this myth a helping
hand."[42] But here is a great contradiction in Schuyler's thinking: if
racism is a powerful factor in American society (as Schuyler acknowledges) and if racialist thinking is an ingrained aspect of the American
character, then does not the very "Americanism" of whites and blacks
in the United States (to a far greater extent than the "Frenchness" of
whites and blacks in France) effect cultural differentiation along
"racial" lines?

Freda Kirchwey sent Langston Hughes the proofs of Schuyler's essay
to provoke him, as Arnold Rampersad has shown: "She wanted not so
much a rebuttal of Schuyler as 'rather an independent positive statement for the case of a true Negro racial art.'"[43] The result was Hughes's
classic expression of the case for black artistic autonomy, which established the cultural, social, and political legitimacy of African American
art *within* the framework of American nationality. What was at stake in
the conversation between Hughes and Schuyler was not only the nature
of African American literature but at the same time, and integral to that
issue, the nature of Americanism.

In Hughes's view, just *because* of the significance of the fiction of
"race" in the United States, the undeniable power of this fiction in
determining daily experience over a period of some three hundred
years, the Negro who attends to the specific qualities of his or her experience cannot help but produce a "racial" art. Hughes, then, works out
from the same set of primary assumptions as Schuyler—an essentially
pragmatist notion of the relationship between aesthetics and experience, a Boasian understanding of race and culture, and a recognition
of the fundamental importance of *national* identity in the modern
world. "The mountain standing in the way of any true Negro art in
America" is the "urge within the race toward whiteness, the desire to
pour racial individuality into the mold of American standardization,
and to be as little Negro and as much American as possible."[44]

We should not be misled here by Hughes's conventional use of the term "American" as synonymous with "Nordic." For he goes on to show how the very worship of "Nordic" features by American Negroes is at odds with democratic individuality; and the contradiction between the "urge to whiteness" and such democratic individuality requires "the American Negro artist" to relinquish the former: "We younger Negro artists who create now intend to express our individual dark-skinned selves without fear or shame. If white people are pleased we are glad. If they are not, it doesn't matter. We know we are beautiful. And ugly too. The tom-tom cries and the tom-tom laughs. If colored people are pleased we are glad. If they are not, their displeasure doesn't matter either. We build our temples for tomorrow, strong as we know how, and we stand on top of the mountain, free within ourselves."[45] This ringing conclusion is, from one point of view, an example of the power and suppleness of the American ideology of democratic individuality; it has as much in common with Hughes's ancestor Walt Whitman as with Frederick Douglass.

The interchange between Hughes and Schuyler provoked interesting letters to the editor.[46] Schuyler responded to Hughes by arguing that "if there is anything 'racial' about the spirituals and the blues, then there should be immediate ability to catch the intricate rhythm on the part of Negroes from Jamaica, Zanzibar, and Sierra Leone"—an argument that completely misunderstood Hughes's reasoning. The emphasis of some black artists on black difference (which Schuyler took to equate *automatically* with "primitivism") Schuyler interpreted as a misplaced "protest against a feeling of inferiority."[47] Michael Gold backed up Schuyler's point from another angle with the claim that "the only real division is that of economic classes," and he blamed the mirage of "racial culture" on white decadents: "Mr. Hughes believes with the white dilettantes that jazz and the cabaret are the ultimate flower of his people. . . . If the Negro intellectuals really care for their race they will forget the cabarets and colleges for a while, and go down into the life of their own people."[48] This, of course, is a type of critique that has been echoed in many quarters ever since. Hughes came back with the response that "as long as the Negro remains a segregated group in this country he must reflect certain racial and environmental differences which are his own. The very fact that Negroes do straighten their hair and try to forget their racial background makes them different from white people." As for black folksongs, "the spirituals and blues are American, certainly, but they are also very much American Negro."

Finally, "until segregation and racial self-consciousness have entirely disappeared, the true work of art from the Negro artist is bound, if it have any color and distinctiveness at all, to reflect his racial background and his racial environment."[49]

Hughes's argument undoubtedly carried more weight than Schuyler's or Gold's with *The Nation*'s editors, but they did not close their pages to the iconoclastic view, *particularly* if it served to criticize "exotic" trends in the development of African American literature. Thus Schuyler's "Blessed Are the Sons of Ham" appeared in 1927.[50] In 1929, the magazine published Schuyler's attack on the cult of primitivism in black literature, "Negro Authors Must Eat" (written under the pen name George W. Jacobs), which held up Nella Larsen and Jessie Fauset as models, arguing that "today, granted the same environmental conditions, the Harlem black and the Broadway white fit not dissimilarly into the mold of our mechanized American culture."[51] Schuyler argued that the popularity of "Africanisms" in Negro literature was leading black artists astray.

On the whole, *The Nation* took a stance somewhere between that of *The Crisis* and that of *Opportunity* relative to the "literature of the Negro." It avoided and even strongly criticized primitive and exotic tendencies (with a few notable exceptions) and emphasized the Negro's Americanism rather than Africanism;[52] yet at the same time most contributors felt black Americans must cultivate their own unique cultural attributes. In a review of Hughes's *Fine Clothes to the Jew*, Harry Alan Potamkin—a regular *New Masses* contributor and founder of the John Reed clubs, as well as a poet published in *Opportunity*[53]—praises Hughes's recognition of the need "for a separate expression of a racial material," although he has not yet achieved aesthetic mastery of it. Potamkin uses the occasion of this review to stress that "Whatever hope there is for an American art lies with the minor races. To urge cultural assimilation of the Negro is to urge the Negro to lose his singular identity and to enter into something only nominal. . . . For what shall he exchange his native systemic heritage; for contradictions unfused?"[54] To Potamkin, American culture will come into being only as a convergence of diversely cultivated vernacular traditions—shaped *especially* by the "minor races." Similarly, in a review of *Negro Workaday Songs* an anonymous critic would call for some gifted writer to use the life of traveling blues musicians as the basis of a classic picaresque narrative.[55] The United States had no better heroes for such fiction.

Alain Locke's important essay "Beauty Instead of Ashes" (1928) clearly fit *The Nation*'s general orientation. "Like a fresh boring through the rock and sand of racial misunderstanding and controversy," he wrote, "modern American art has tapped a living well-spring of beauty, and the gush of it opens up an immediate question as to the possible contribution of the soil and substance of Negro life and experience to American culture and the native materials of art." Welcoming the interest of white as well as black writers in "Negro" materials, Locke credited the "source" (black folk culture) for the aesthetic achievement. Countering black reformers and intellectuals who had criticized the works of Eugene O'Neill, DuBose Heyward, Paul Green, Clement Wood, and T. S. Stribling, Locke believed such critics mistook "for color prejudice the contemporary love for strong local color, and for condescension the current interest in folk life." Citing Toomer, Walrond, Fisher, McKay, and the *Fire!!* circle, he stated, "The younger Negro artists as modernists have the same slant and interest." The treatment of more urbane subjects would follow the mastery of techniques developed through the "objective" treatment of folk material; the current focus would help black artists develop idiomatic styles based upon vernacular speech (rather than traditional "dialect" or "academic" diction), realism (rather than "didactic sentiment"), and "folk temperament." Ultimately the racial temperament, through its "group expression," would enrich all of American literature, whether remaining "a separate body" or pouring itself "into the mainstream."[56]

The general position one culls from *The Nation* in the 1920s and early 1930s, then, is that the development of a distinct black American aesthetic and the growing appreciation of black culture can do much to help the United States achieve a civilization both adequate to its particular *place* and history and worthy of its high ideals. Notably, in his perceptive review of *The Chinaberry Tree,* Gerald Sykes finds that the very way in which Jessie Fauset's mulatto heroine strives for "respectability" and the language which conveys that striving reveal a special sort of black psychology and style: "The sympathetic white reader, once he appreciates the difficult position of this refined colored girl, by transferring an allied psychology to the book itself will perceive the drama beneath even such a line as 'The food was wholesome, well cooked, and attractively garnished.' It is a world in which such little things mean much: a touching world, its humility displayed through its pride." Sykes faults the novel only for attempting "to idealize this polite colored world in terms of the white standards that it has adopted." While treating the special difficulties as well as the strengths and ambitions of her characters, Fauset strives to justify their world according to a white standard, and thus writes out of the same scarred consciousness, the same "pride of a genuine aristocrat," that she so masterfully depicts. "To be one of Miss Fauset's amber-tinted, well-to-do, refined Negroes—not having to deal much with whites, but surrounded on all sides by the white standard—posits a delicate psychological situation. It is for this reason that few white novels have anything like the shades of feeling to be found in 'The Chinaberry Tree.' Every moment speaks of yearning. That is why, once it is seen as a whole, even its faults are charming, for the story they tell is poignant and beautiful, too."[57] Fauset's biographer has called Sykes's review the most discerning contemporary appreciation of any of Fauset's novels.[58] While it opposes Alain Locke's view of Fauset's work, it actually shares Locke's interest in the development of a black literary tradition, illuminating Fauset's contribution to it as well as her chief (class-related) shortcoming.

By 1931 and 1932 *The Nation* would repeatedly stress that only black authors could do justice to black subjects; it was even more emphatic on this point than, say, *Opportunity*. The aim, however, was not to ghettoize black culture—in fact, *The Nation* published essays attacking the restriction of black authors to racial subject matter, and published work by African Americans having nothing to do with race or black culture. In a celebrated series later imitated by *The Messenger,* "These United States," the editors called upon Du Bois to write the contribution on Georgia.[59] They had both black *and* white writers do reviews of books concerning black subjects (although blacks did not review books without some racial significance), and they drew contributors from most camps of the renaissance, with the notable exception of women— few black women contributed to *The Nation*. Moreover, the magazine did not abandon black subjects when the "vogue" of the Negro ended; the issues of the 1930s show no diminution in *The Nation*'s attention to racial issues or black literature. An interesting side-note is that one regular contributor to the magazine was Henry G. Alsberg, who later ran the Federal Writers' Project and, according to Sterling Brown, did all he could both to help black writers and to see that the lives and culture of blacks were fairly represented in federal programs.[60] Thus, the legacy of *The Nation* in addressing issues of race in American culture continued into the 1930s; its 1920s-era, leftist liberalism (as opposed to Marxism) connected with its support for the cultural racialism of the Harlem Renaissance, which, much like *Opportunity* magazine, it regarded in Boasian, nonessentialist terms and associated with a general movement to make American letters responsive to local conditions of life.

The New Republic

Shortly before Oswald Garrison Villard had taken over *The Nation* and detached it from the *New York Evening Post,* Willard Straight and Herbert Croly had founded *The New Republic* "as a means of applying to current issues 'the political and social ideas'" sketched in Croly's book *The Promise of American Life.*[61] According to Arthur Frank Wertheim, Herbert Croly had been the first to articulate the new cultural nationalism, initially in articles for the *Architectural Record,* which he edited from 1900 to 1906.[62] Van Wyck Brooks, who declined an offer to help edit the new magazine, later remembered the sense of expectancy with which it was greeted: "*The New Republic,* as one first heard of it, seemed already the symbol of a great coming epoch."[63] The journal's purpose, as Brooks saw it, was "to infuse American emotions with American thought," to put philosophy into action. It was socialistic in direction but not in explicit allegiance or terminology. (The New Deal later incorporated a conservative version of much of its philosophy, but not to the satisfaction of the editors, who wanted the social system more thoroughly transformed.) Indeed, the spirit of John Dewey pervaded the magazine and shaped its cultural nationalist emphases. In line with this interest, *The New Republic's* "cultural" side was carried mainly by Francis Hackett and (briefly) Randolph Bourne in the early years, when the magazine's cultural tone was set.[64]

An Irish immigrant, Hackett had been a leader of the Chicago Renaissance from very early on, even before the founding of *Poetry* or the arrival of Floyd Dell. He had, in fact, lived at Hull House from 1906 to 1907, regarding it as his "first real home" and his "real introduction to the meaning of America." "Hull House," he would later write, "was American because it was international and because it perceived that the nationalism of each immigrant was a treasure, a talent, which gave him a special value for the United States."[65] Americanism, Hackett came to feel, was a kind of internationalism that reconfigured one's ethnic identity for life in the "American rainbow." The existence of blacks in the United States strongly affected Hackett's sense of the national identity and the meaning of his own Americanization. In the opening scene of his autobiography he would emphasize his notion of the difference between American and Irish nationality in terms of America's racial diversity. His first memory of seeing an American on American soil was of a black man on a dock waiting to catch the hawser from Hackett's incoming ship—"giving a hand to us to land in his country. . . . America was his fate. It was going to be mine, so we would be having the country in common."[66] This sense of sharing a new nationality with Negroes—a people previously almost unknown to Hackett—was so new it somehow represented the newness of his life altogether. "Ireland was forsaken. It was ten years to the day since Parnell died. Now I was entering into fraternity with another people, the white man and the black man."[67] The memory represented for Hackett both the multiracial quality of American society and the special centrality of black/white racial experience to it—as if, for example, the Irishman in Ireland is not "white." The relationship between "white" and "black" Americans is in part constitutive of American identity.

Hackett was already editor of the literary supplement to the Chicago *Evening Post* when Floyd Dell arrived in Chicago and became his assistant. From early on, he promoted the work of poets like Sandburg, Masters, and Lindsay and the fiction of Sherwood Anderson, Sinclair Lewis, and Willa Cather. He was also involved in the little theater movement, having staged plays at Hull House (shortly before the Jelliffes, Langston Hughes's friends and organizers of the Karamu House theater in Cleveland, would have been there). In 1910 he wrote a rave review of Herbert Croly's *The Promise of American Life,* at a time when Croly was virtually unknown. But in 1911 Hackett left the *Evening Post* supplement in Dell's hands and returned to Ireland to nurse his dying father. The connection with Dell is revealing, because while the two shared many of the same views and both essentially began their careers at Hull House, they differed politically in the same way that *The Masses* and *The New Republic* differed. Although considering himself a socialist, Hackett rejected "revolutionary Socialism" and Marxism. Indeed, he regarded the importation of Marxist theory as a kind of intellectual snobbery. The premises of Marxism did not apply to a democratic republic with a large middle class; the idea of the dictatorship of the proletariat seemed ridiculous in the North American context: "I welcomed Floyd Dell's contrariety, but I kept waiting for the music in American terms." Dell had too much "intolerant theory," Hackett felt, but his criticism was "living."[68]

Ironically, Dell would be attacked by a later generation for not showing *enough* allegiance to Marxist theory; he, too, thought socialism had to be "Americanized."

Remembering Hackett's review of *The Promise of American Life,* Croly thought of him while planning *The New Republic* in 1913 and asked him to be literary editor, a position he filled from 1914 to 1922—the period when Jean Toomer and Langston Hughes, among others, were reading it and forming their literary ideals. Randolph Bourne, on the other hand, was brought on as contributing editor, following Croly's advice of promoting national literature through book reviews.[69] In 1914 and 1915 Bourne contributed to *The New Republic* his own transnationalist and cultural nationalist views, envisioning a society of diverse national cultures living in sympathy with one another.[70] Like Hackett, he supported the social realists, admiring Theodore Dreiser in particular. However, *The New Republic*'s preoccupation with politics initially curtailed attention to cultural developments, and the magazine supported American entry into World War I as a way of weakening the supports of reactionary conservatism (a position equally advanced by Joel Spingarn, Du Bois, and *The Crisis*).[71] Outspokenly opposed to this self-deception, Bourne moved on to *The Seven Arts*. Hackett, also on the left wing of the editorial board, steered the books and art section in the anti-Anglophile, cultural pluralist direction, a natural tendency for one who had been raised in the atmosphere of the Celtic Revival.

A sense of Hackett's point of view can be gleaned from "Our Literary Poverty," an editorial of 1914 in which he complains that the United States is still a cultural vassal to England. One hindrance to national "individualization" is the fact that we lack a language that is uniquely our own; a differentiated language helps a nation preserve and develop its own distinctive culture. "Even if the ruling classes employ a formal medium, the other language is fostered and mellowed, and in course of time becomes the natural medium for story-teller, poet and seer. It registers the characteristics and intimacies of the people, and as nature inflects their lives, so their speech becomes expressive and idiomatic. When the artist arrives to give form to what has been enjoyed and endured, he employs a language creatively evolved."[72] Although the United States lacks a distinct language, it should nonetheless stop thinking of its cultural heritage as *English*.

Any black reader would have been struck by the Irish Padraic Colum's 1915 appreciation of Robert Burns: "Burns's mind moved amongst communal creations; around him were the folk-melodies that, as one might almost say, are the only begetters of lyric poetry; the popular verse forms that anonymous poets had evolved. . . . Whoever touches Burns's book touches even more than a man—he touches a community and a territory."[73] The advantage Burns had over Whitman was an authentic folk heritage of song and story. What the Scotsman lacked, however, was a "militant political feeling," whereas "in Ireland political propaganda has helped to perpetuate a national culture."[74] Hence the connection between political activism and "vernacular poetics" that Hackett had known in Ireland was welcome from the beginning in *The New Republic;* and the example of the Irish writers would be often in the minds of black American writers of the "folk" persuasion, for obvious reasons.

It should be no surprise that Langston Hughes turned early to *The New Republic* as an outlet for his poetry. By that time Hackett had brought on Ridgely Torrence as poetry editor, a move that prompted Carl Sandburg, Hughes's favorite living poet, to begin sending most of his poetry there.[75] Hughes would later write to Olivia Torrence, after learning of his friend's death: "It was he, I think, who accepted my very first poems to appear in other than a Negro magazine—those taken by the New Republic."[76] Actually, Hughes was misremembering; the first of his poems printed in a white journal appeared in a special issue of *The World Tomorrow* (May 1923) on African American culture, edited by Ridgely Torrence.[77] Torrence followed Hughes's career closely ever after, soliciting him for poems, recommending him for a grant to do a series of one-act plays, and recommending him for the American Academy of Arts and Letters' "Award of Merit" in 1946. In the same year, Hughes sent Torrence the manuscript of *Fields of Wonder* for criticism.[78] And he included Torrence's "The Bird and the Tree" (1915) in *The Poetry of the Negro*.[79]

Torrence was best known for his *Three Plays for a Negro Theatre* of 1917—*Granny Maumee, The Rider of Dreams,* and *Simon the Cyrenian.* As we have seen, these works were literally an attempt to establish a "national Negro theatre," which Torrence believed could be the jewel of the American cultural nationalist movement. With his friends Edwin Arlington Robinson, Henry Vaughan Moody, and Percy MacKaye, Torrence sought to advance native "poetic drama" along the lines of the Abbey Theatre in Dublin. He turned to African American materials as the most promising basis for such a drama, and in September 1917 was named "man of the month" by *Crisis* magazine, which attributed to him "the very fact of [the] existence" of "The Negro Theatre."[80] In the original staging of *Granny Maumee* in 1914, to which he had invited James Weldon Johnson and which Carl Van Vechten reviewed, Torrence had failed to get the Stage Society to allow him to use black actors; thus the 1917 production proved to be an important revelation to white theatergoers of black acting ability, even though the United States' entry into the war forced the show to close after only a few nights.[81] Francis Hackett raved over it in a review for *The New Republic*, contrasting it with previous literary treatments of black American subjects: "It is, all things considered, as fine an enterprise as the American theatre has seen for years. It is the emergence of an artistic Cinderella into the palace where she belongs."[82] Robert Benchley gave it advance notice for the *New York Tribune* in an article entitled "Can This Be the Native American Drama?"[83] James Weldon Johnson, looking at the play from a different perspective thirteen years later, would write: "April 5, 1917 is the date of the most important single event in the history of the Negro in the American theatre; for it marks the beginning of a new era." In Torrence's three plays, Johnson asserted, "the stereotyped traditions regarding the Negro's histrionic limitations were smashed."[84]

The motive behind Torrence's interest in Hughes's work is clear. He had a longstanding desire to see American folk material used as a basis of poetry, fiction, and drama; and his concern for the situation of black people in the United States is ultimately rooted in his childhood in Xenia, Ohio, a town with a rich abolitionist history and the site of Wilberforce University. Torrence never suggested that his own work concerning black life could substitute for the work of black artists themselves. He believed that only black dramatists could really establish a black theater, and he intended for his work merely to serve that effort. Neither did he abandon it after the 1920s. In fact, in 1939 he prepared a study of Negro theater in America for the Rockefeller Foundation, with the aims of establishing a complete bibliography of plays by African Americans and of encouraging black playwrights, and in 1948 he published a laudatory biography of a great black educator, *The Story of John Hope*. His interest in black subjects was one with his interest in the development of a native, pluralistic national culture; he was no mere exploiter of a Negro "vogue."

When Francis Hackett left *The New Republic* in 1922 to write a history of Ireland, the books section was turned over to Robert Morss Lovett and Robert Littell. W. E. B. Du Bois considered Lovett "perhaps the closest white student friend I had at Harvard" (which is not to say they were very close, but to suggest a background to later developments).[85] A disciple of John Dewey, Lovett taught English at the University of Chicago, lived at Hull House in the 1920s, and helped edit *The Dial* in its early, Chicago Renaissance phase, when it propagated the views of Dewey and Bourne. He was also active in the Chicago Civil Liberties organization and the NAACP, chaired the Sacco-Vanzetti National League, and became president of the League for Industrial Democracy after it succeeded the Intercollegiate Socialist Society in 1921.[86] A close friend of Norman Hapgood, Vachel Lindsay, and Carl Van Vechten, he met James Weldon Johnson, Langston Hughes, and other "New Negroes" at Van Vechten's, and he would serve as a judge in *Crisis* literary contests.

Lovett's fight for civil rights and against American racism continued long after the 1920s and ultimately cost him a career in the government. During the late 1930s he became government secretary of the Virgin Islands, proceeding to combat the most blatantly racist and exploitative U.S. policies there, until the House Committee on Un-American Activities interrogated him for association with socialists and communists, for protesting United States imperialism in Latin America, and more pointedly for his 1933 investigation of police brutality toward striking Negro women at a Chicago apron factory (which was interpreted as evidence of his contempt for the American system of justice). Harold Ickes, a former student who had been much impressed by Lovett at Chicago, was finally forced to move him to a technically different post, where Lovett continued his work without salary; but even this did not satisfy HUAC. At last Ickes had to dismiss him or jeopardize appropriations for the entire Department of the Interior. Lovett was then invited to join the faculty of the University of Puerto Rico, which led several Congressmen to introduce a bill calling for the removal of the governor of Puerto Rico![87] Lingering bitterness in the Islands over Lovett's ouster may have had something to do with Harry Truman's decision, when he became president, to name the first black governor to the Virgin Islands, William Hastie.[88]

We can see that for Hackett, Torrence, and Lovett the "problem of the Negro" was not a passing interest; it fatefully affected their careers. Crucial issues of civil rights and social reconstruction helped determine their interests in African American culture. Moreover, for them the

Negro Renaissance was not a fad but rather an integral aspect of both American national self-realization and international decolonization.

From the time of its founding *The New Republic* had taken up the cause of black civil rights, assailing Woodrow Wilson in 1914 for not living up to the promises he had made to black leaders before his election.[89] In January 1915 it attacked the feature of a new immigration bill that prohibited "all future immigrants of African blood," as "a new insult flung at ten million Americans, who because of their color are for the most part voteless and deprived of fundamental civil and political rights."[90] Herbert J. Seligmann of the NAACP contributed articles on the race riots of the "Red Summer" and on African Americans' determination to fight back against Jim Crow.[91] *The New Republic* also published one of the most stinging sections of Du Bois's *Darkwater* (1920) before that book appeared—an excerpt condemning not only racism but European civilization in general, arguing that whatever of value Europe had produced she had built upon foundations established by others.[92] When the book did come out, Hackett's review of it challenged critics who charged Du Bois with "bitterness," pointing out that the facts were their own argument; Du Bois had fairly condemned white civilization on the basis of its own tenets of morality.[93] Hackett, in fact, called on Du Bois as a reviewer and contributor to the magazine.

Just as Du Bois and other black leaders had learned that racial inequality could not be rooted out by rational discussion alone but required *cultural* transformation, *The New Republic* was learning a related lesson. With the election of Harding in 1920, the progressivism espoused by *The New Republic* seemed to have come to a halt, leaving the editors in a quandary. The failure of progressivism as a political program suggested that social and political means alone could not achieve peace and justice. Even Wilson, after all, had turned his back on the good cause—nowhere more clearly than in his suppression of civil liberties, his racism, and his acquiescence to the terms of the peace after World War I. At this point an editor, Alvin Johnson, suggested that the magazine should start concentrating on cultural matters, and Croly took his advice; hence the strong interest in belles-lettres in the 1920s, the decade of the Harlem Renaissance.[94] (Conversely, in the 1930s, like *The Crisis* and *Opportunity*, the magazine turned away from cultural issues to focus on hard-hitting economic and political analyses).[95] Croly and his staff came to feel that beneath social relations and political forms, democracy depended on free transcultural communication and a pluralistic aesthetics of experience. It required a new existential stance to the world, dependent upon a new kind of "culture." Democracy as a strictly *political* conception seemed insufficient to cure the ills of modern civilization. (Croly himself, like Jean Toomer, even became a follower of G. I. Gurdjieff in the late 1920s).[96] *The New Republic* looked toward the arts and culture for clues to understanding and transforming the "national life."

In *The New Republic*, pragmatist philosophy had important implications for the form of modern American culture and the functions of literature. Contributors as diverse as Dewey, Bourne, Lewis Mumford, Lovett, E. C. Lindeman, Edmund Wilson, Abbe Niles, and Harry Alan Potamkin objected to ideologies of aesthetic purity based on the separation of existence and essence, which they connected with positivist notions of scientific knowledge and, ultimately, political reaction. These were issues fundamental to the nature of modernism in their view, and had direct implications for their approach to African American literature. Dewey's insistence, for example, upon dismantling the division between objects of thought and those of nature led him to the conclusion that "thought and its characteristic objects are, like bare action or practice, but a means for a transformation of raw nature into products of art—into forms of existence which are directly significant and enjoyed."[97] This approach places stress upon art as the realization of meaning in natural existence—produced by the very form of human experience. Insofar as the form of experience is always affected by the environment of the individual, with social categories and negotiations of power shaping that environment, art will be a form of historical action realizing the specific qualities of experience in the world and in turn effecting transformations (however small) in that world.

Hence, when Lewis Mumford in 1929 criticizes Joseph Wood Krutch's *The Modern Temper* as a "lyric of despair" in tune with *The Waste Land,* he does so on the basis of Krutch's assumption that modern science reveals patterns of nature to be completely unrelated to human needs and desires. This point of view results in an unbridgeable separation between "animal nature" and "spiritual values," and ultimately in romantic conceptions of the artist-hero as one who resents the claims of social duty and practical activity. Krutch's views of modern art and the position of the artist, then, derive from positivist premises concerning science. In contrast, Mumford argues that our most ideal aims and values are continuous with our animal and social functions; reciprocally, even the most abstract scientific representations of nature depend upon scientists' "physical and temporal relations," their "faiths and fantasies": "Through the glasses of our ideologies, we see and discover Nature, giving it the 'style' of our own lives; so the very conception of an 'impersonal Universe' hostile to man's inner strivings" is an ideological construction, the outcome of a particular historical moment.[98] Since Krutch cannot settle for the idea that the universe is neither all for us nor all against us, he ends up with the idea that the human spirit in the modern age finds a home in art alone. The recognition that nature does not correspond to human desire and thus that art does not spring naturally from and express such harmony should not be cause for despair, Mumford argues; Krutch (and by extension other modernists of his sort) is concerned with a false problem. Mumford substitutes pragmatism and meliorism—"a universe that partly responds to man, an ideology that is partly successful in finding expression, a home for man that is clean and comely, but still subject to the invasion of insects or bacteria"—for alienation and despair provoked by positivist conceptions of reality and supporting a hermeticized conception of art.[99]

From a related perspective, Edmund Wilson uses the occasion of a review of T. S. Eliot's *For Lancelot Andrewes* to attack the general "escapism" of contemporary American writers, who, he charges, do not want to come to terms with their actual world. Eliot escapes to classicism, monarchism, and Anglo-Catholicism, Dos Passos to idealized visions of American workers as "proletarians" just dying to overthrow the bourgeoisie; Mencken envisions an intellectual community resembling a German university town before the Great War, where people read books, drink beer, and respect the local nobility; Southern (white) writers reminisce about antebellum plantation life; and Pound fantasizes a medieval Provence. But, Wilson writes, everywhere one looks, the actual world, including Europe, is becoming more and more like the prosaic America to which all of these writers turn their backs. "It is up to the young American writers to make some sense of their world," a world of many religions and cultures, a world in which the restoration of monarchy is a pipe dream. "We shall, I fear, not be able to lean upon the authority of either Church or King, but shall have to depend for our new social and moral ideals on a resolute study of contemporary reality, and upon our own imaginations."[100]

Clearly, this position issues in a preference for realism and a literature of social engagement—not propaganda that abstracts experience into a morality play, but something closer to the work of the ethnic and regional realists, their almost ethnographic attention to cultural processes combined with a self-conscious reflection upon the artist's own engagement with those processes even as he or she writes. This processual and engaged notion of a possible modernism seemed, to *New Republic* editors, distinctly American and new. Hence, in an editorial entitled "European vs. American Culture" and responding to Andre Siegfried's condemnation of the United States in *America Comes of Age,* they attack the European's (and traditional Euro-American's) segregation of "spirituality" from materiality as a reflection of a conservative, formalist, and metaphysical denaturing of culture:

> The traditional European culture . . . tends to conceive the realities of human life as performances which should obey rules or dance attendance on intellectually formulated values. The experimental American culture accepts the realities of human as well as natural life as processes, rather than as conclusions or laws. In order to understand them, and, by understanding, to control them in the interest of human fulfillment, human beings can try to combine participation in the event with the utmost effort to be aware of every phase of its and their behavior. They will, in that case, act as if they can find out what they are capable of becoming only by the most inveterate, alert and methodical consciousness of their actual performances.[101]

I quote this passage at length because of its central importance for a theory of "indigenous" modernist aesthetics. Here "participation in the event" is part of the process of understanding and representing it; the "event" is inseparable from performance; the performance is an art of experience that attempts to shape the "realities" of life toward human fulfillment.

It was only too easy for artists to dodge the disciplines of experience in fascination for the exotic and complaints about the conditions supposedly needed for "great art." E. C. Lindeman charged that a "new kind of softness" was appearing in American literature in the late twenties. Artists were beginning to feel they must be apart from or above society, their art abstracted from "actual life"; many expressed the feeling that the artist must live in some special environment with appropriate "conditions of creativity": "Ordinary communities where life is lived on the level of necessity are consequently uncongenial to the artist; he must be surrounded by a social atmosphere of sympathy; he requires a degree of freedom which is not essential to the ordinary worker; in short, he needs in some way to be abstracted from the homely scene of the world's work before his creativeness can blossom. Art, according to this view, is exotic, not indigenous."[102] In pursuit of conducive conditions, artists sought picturesque locales, attached themselves to cliques in metropolitan centers, founded artists' colonies, and avoided coming to terms with industrialized America. "Is the esthetic function in man something separable from his total functions?"[103]

The pragmatist view of the modern situation obviously supported *The New Republic*'s cultural pluralist ideals, combated romanticization of the "folk" or the "primitive," and tended to blur distinctions between aesthetic and social criticism. An editorial meditation on the meaning of the Sacco and Vanzetti executions thus became the occasion for reflections upon contemporary multiethnic literatures and their meaning for the national identity. Noting how often the term "Americanism" came up in the trial to represent Anglo-Saxonism and business interests, a Ku Klux–style weapon to wield against Jews, Negroes, Catholics, and now Italians, the writer contrasted this usage with "true" American ideals. America must be regarded, he charged, as "an experiment, not only democratic, but also international." The United States is less a "nation" than an "international institution," and nowhere is this more evident than in American literature:

> It is through our literature . . . that the real spirit of the country finds expression; and that literature is perhaps the most polyglot and the most heterogeneous that the world has ever seen. For the literary critic, it constitutes a veritable Tower of Babel and offers many disturbing problems; but its social significance is plain: it is the first incoherent attempt to arrive at a common understanding on the part of a society at once denationalized and representative of all nations—a society as different as possible from that which, in the last century, in New England, produced a literature written almost entirely in the English tradition and by men of the English stock.[104]

The people of the United States must formulate a new set of ideals to "harmonize" their different cultures and evolve a new civilization, to shape a new language—surely "a drama sufficiently absorbing for the most curious and active mind, and sufficiently exacting to call into play the most distinguished abilities." With this challenge facing them, one of the great and "representative" challenges of the twentieth century, what were the "high modernists" doing in Europe? One thing they were certainly in no position to do was to address issues of African Americans' relationship to American culture.

A striking contribution to the conversation about African American arts was Robert E. Park's "The Negro Problem," a 1927 review of E. B. Reuter's *The American Race Problem* that puts the issues of American nationhood and African American acculturation in a transnational context. The social and cultural transformation of the Negro in the United States, writes Park, throws "a vivid light on the whole cultural process as it is taking place under modern conditions of communication in other parts of the world." What Park seems most interested in is whether the world is witnessing the extinction of non-Western cultures or their transformation and continued viability; for Park, the case of the American Negro seems to promise the latter.

Reuter, he notes, regrets the growth of Negro "race consciousness" (particularly in literature) because it emphasizes the current racial and cultural isolation: "the effect has been to the disadvantage of both peoples," in Reuter's view.[105] This, Park points out, "is the very crux of the problem." As long as the Negro remains isolated and segregated by "racial marks" that distinguish "him" from the rest of the society, he will be the object of "sentiments" that isolate him, creating greater racial consciousness on his own part that, in turn, reinforces the segregation imposed by whites, and so on. However, Park disagrees with Reuter concerning how the racism of American society must be confronted by black culture-workers: "The question is whether the Negro, through the medium of a peculiar racial culture, and particularly through a literature which gives full and free expression to his racial experience, is not, after all, creating the most effective means of breaking through and breaking down the prejudices which must shut him out from the common life and understanding of the people of whom he has already become an integral part."[106] This question, Park avers, is relevant not just to the issue of American cultural identity but has world-historical implications in the context of Western hegemony and then the reconfiguration of national cultures when imperialism gives way to a postcolonial situation.

Support for the new emphasis upon black cultural distinctiveness did not mean an embrace of black exoticism for *New Republic* contributors, generally speaking—although they had greater tendencies in this direction than *Nation* critics, just as they were more open to the "high modernism" of the expatriates. Even the treatment of African art avoided primitivist ecstasies over the "prelogical" mentality that, for example, the French anthropologist Lévy-Bruhl was propounding at the time (and that Boasians attacked in the pages of *The New Republic* and *The Nation*). Stark Young's "Primitive Negro Sculpture," for example, made no claims about the primitive "spirit" of the African but merely held that for the time being, given Western ignorance about African cultures, the significance of African sculpture to the Western artist must be sheerly formal.[107] Lewis Mumford, reviewing Paul Guillaume and Thomas Munro's *Primitive Negro Sculpture,* on the other hand, noted that this art was significant as an example of the current extension of aesthetic sensibilities made possible by worldwide communication. Its function for Western artists was to push them outside "the dead convention of literalism and superficial representation." Yet its greatest significance would be realized by African American artists, who could use it as a more integral aspect of their cultural revitalization. Mumford's terms here are a revealing amalgam of stereotypical jungle motifs, on the one hand, and a more naturalistic understanding of the social construction of "racial" tradition. African art will speak most deeply to New Negroes, he writes, "with the very beat of the stark, humid, vegetal life of the Gold Coast or the Congo; for these happy persons Negro art will not merely be a contribution to aesthetic form, but an extension of consciousness." The book would not fully satisfy New Negro readers, but the authors could justly say that "such matters do not lie within their province or competence."[108]

From the early 1920s, Eric Walrond often reviewed fiction by and about African Americans for *The New Republic,* although Hubert Harrison contributed "Caliban in the Slums," a stinging critique of Howard Culbertson's play *Goat Alley.* (Culbertson knew nothing about the subject of the play, Harrison charged, despite what Mencken and *The Nation*'s Ludwig Lewisohn might think.)[109] Other notable reviews were by Robert Littell, including his perceptive piece on Jean Toomer's *Cane* (lauding the work but lamenting its echoes of Waldo Frank's vaporous mysticism) and his attack on the plays of the Ethiopian Art Theatre at the Frazee Theatre:

> In at least four ways the Ethiopian Art Theatre is far from being Ethiopian. It is directed by a white man . . .; it offered plays by white men

(Wilde, Shakespeare); its members are far from being what Granny Maumee called Royal Black; and they had behind them not the South which is the Negroes' true background, but the dancing and vaudeville background of Chicago. . . . We must look for the real thing in other directions, and wait for the time when Negroes will build a theatre based not on envy or imitation of things written by white men which even white men cannot play very well, but upon a bitter scorn of what we can do, and a bitter pride in what they have within themselves.[110]

This does not sound like an attempt to co-opt black creativity for white people's amusement. However, it does hint at a prescriptive criticism in which black aesthetics is tied to folk origins and to a blackness purified of white influence. *The New Republic,* far more than *The Nation,* stuck resolutely to a line that evaluated black literature on cultural pluralist grounds, calling for a literature in which black vernacular tradition would remake "English" conventions at least, and at best create new forms of expression adequate to modern African American "experience"—taking experience to include the enculturation of what "happens." *The New Republic*'s privileging of realism was *not* based on an idea of grounded truth and thus faith in an "objective" perspective, but understood perspective and the forms of discourse as effective in all knowledge and representation. But the greater prescriptive approach of *The New Republic,* its call for a black cultural nationalism, went together with greater weaknesses for the primitive and exotic as well as impatience with writing by African Americans that was insufficiently "Negro."

Emphasizing the need for a distinctive African American aesthetic tradition, *New Republic* reviewers criticized authors such as Countee Cullen and Jessie Fauset for failing to recognize the value of the vernacular, in this respect differing from *The Nation* and *The Crisis.* Harry Alan Potamkin's "Race and a Poet," a review of Cullen's *Copper Sun,* charges that Cullen's "interpretations and manner, his attitude of mind, are drawn, not from the evidences of his personal and intimate life, but from a tradition entirely literary, and, by now, anemic. That his own poems do not lack corpuscle is due to the impact of his nativity."[111] Rather than simply capitalizing thematically upon his racial identity, Cullen ought to let it thoroughly inform his poems. He has enviable advantages over white American poets, who would "give half their lives for the chance to identify themselves with a racehood. . . . Mr. Cullen has everything in his favor save the literary associations which have fastened themselves upon him. He has the initial talent and a nativity which is powerful in his environment. Are his experiences not worth more than elementary craft, lines that have no flow one into the other, and epithets that find no *milieu*? The Negro folk has had its poet in Dunbar; will the Negro race produce a Synge?"[112] Cullen should work more along the lines pioneered by James Weldon Johnson in *God's Trombones.*

Potamkin provided a similar critique of the anthology *Caroling Dusk,* edited by Cullen. Once again the critic found too many of the poems attempting to put Negro experience in forms derived from British tradition—and with little attempt to stretch or transform that tradition. The complaint was not with the use of English poetics as such but rather with what Potamkin regarded as a timidity about truly *appropriating,* challenging, and remaking the English tradition: "In the utilization of a tradition, transformations must occur." Though the Negro's intellect may have been shaped insistently by English tradition, "it must still be submissive to the more qualitative experience of folk or race. This submission is the necessary fusion of form and content."[113] Only Toomer's poems exemplified the kind of fusion Potamkin admired. And only Toomer, not coincidentally, could be ranked, in Potamkin's view, with the best English and American poets of the day. Cullen's volume, Potamkin further complained, suppressed the vernacular tradition indicated by Dunbar's work, explored tentatively by James Weldon Johnson but wanting more bold development of its "poetic values." Over all, *Caroling Dusk* exemplified not racial self-revelation but "the Negro's wish to avoid himself." If the Negro has two selves, one for the white man and one for himself, then the volume in question suggested that the poetry of the Negro so far revealed the self shown to the white man.[114]

The kind of poet Potamkin was looking for might have been Langston Hughes, whose *Fine Clothes to the Jew* he had praised the previous year in *The Nation.* Similarly, a couple of years earlier, Elizabeth Shepley Sergeant had reviewed *The New Negro* and *The Weary Blues* with enthusiasm, cheering what she interpreted as signs of black cultural self-determination.[115] And Hughes continued to receive the most unqualified praise of all the African American poets mentioned in *The New Republic.* A review of "Real and Artificial Folk-Song" by Abbe Niles (co-editor with W. C. Handy of *Blues: An Anthology*) admiringly ranged Hughes's poems alongside collections of performed blues and other black folksongs to conclude that Hughes was not simply imitating his models but rather appropriating their thought and technique for his own poetic purposes. Hughes's understanding of the blues far exceeded that of anyone who had so far written on them, capturing the complexity and range of emotion they expressed. His thorough absorption of the form allowed an effective transmutation to the page as he developed extended blues sequences, going beyond mere pastiche. Hughes could follow the thought and technique of the blues artists at will, Niles wrote, but "it is still his thought, not theirs, so that he expresses the feelings of the porters, elevator boys, Harlem prostitutes and Memphis bad men into whose shoes he momentarily steps, with an explicitness and coherence which would be beyond most of them."[116] His broad range and growing power of expression, Niles concluded, could not be adequately suggested in one review, but Hughes was bound to attract increasing critical attention.

The most extensive critical essay to appear in *The New Republic* on New Negro writing further advanced Hughes's reputation as it placed him at the forefront of his generation. Wallace Thurman's "Negro Artists and the Negro," which appeared in August 1927, deserves rereading on a number of counts. Although written virtually at the height of what was later regarded as the vogue of the New Negro, it talks about the fad in past tense and welcomes the new period of sober reflection in which the "wheat" could be sorted from the "chaff" of renaissance writing. Furthermore, in analyzing the resistance of the black bourgeoisie to the new racial writing, it compares the black author's problem of a divided audience with that of the white American, seeing both in the context of the process of decolonization.

For Thurman, too much mediocre writing had been celebrated simply on the basis of the black author's race. "Sentimental" white liberals and black race propagandists indiscriminately praised any creative effusion as evidence of black artistic genius. To make matters worse, they particularly celebrated the more mediocre manifestations of racial art—the novels of Jessie Fauset, the poetry of Countee Cullen, the propagandist fiction of Walter White and W. E. B. Du Bois. All were written to prove that Negroes were not inferior to whites; in particular, "Miss Fauset's work was an ill-starred attempt to popularize the pleasing news that there were cultured Negroes, deserving of attention from artists, and of whose existence white folk should be apprised."[117] Cullen's *Color* was equally conventional, yet he was the darling of the black bourgeoisie and sentimental whites, especially for poems like "Yet Do I Marvel" and "Incident," examples of "correct" attitudes conveyed in proper forms. The unhealthy condition of black cultural criticism derived ultimately, Thurman lamented, from the unenviable position of the "bourgeois Negro"—American society rewards "him" for "being what he ain't," and he reproduces this strategy of domination in his own judgments on African American art.

The poets who caused the greatest discomfort to race propagandists and their white friends, conversely, had the most to offer the world, the United States, and black America precisely because of their dissociation from the "colonial" mentality. Hughes's work carried the "major disturbing note in the 'renaissance' chorus. . . . He went for inspiration and rhythms to those people who had been the least absorbed by the quagmire of American Kultur, and from them he undertook to select and preserve such autonomous racial values as were being rapidly eradicated in order to speed the Negro's assimilation." Although few people publicly commented against him, privately many deplored his "jazz predilections, his unconventional poetic forms, and his preoccupation with the proletariat." After the publicaton of *Nigger Heaven,* the philistines could no longer hold back; against that book and *Fine Clothes to the Jew,* the black bourgeoisie vented all its pent-up resentment. Hughes and Van Vechten were joined by the contributors to *Fire!!,* Eric Walrond, Richard Bruce, and the artist Aaron Douglas as the targets of black middle-class wrath. (Thurman probably has in mind the recent *Crisis* article by Allison Davis, discussed above in Chapter 5.) Thurman puts this critical vituperation in the context of a theory of the process of cultural decolonization.

The process underway resembled how spirituals had become acceptable. Blacks at first objected to the singing of spirituals for general audiences, but when white critics said these were deep and moving songs, "Negroes joined in the hallelujah chorus."[118] Such a process of acceptance was not unusual, however. The same class of Negroes who were protesting against Hughes's evidently nonjudgmental poems of black prostitutes "have their counterpart in those American whites who protest against the literary upheavals of a Dreiser, an Anderson, or a Sandburg. And those American Negroes who would not appreciate the spirituals until white critics sang their praises have their counterpart in the

American whites who would not appreciate Poe and Whitman until European critics classed them as immortals."[119] The decolonization of American literature vis-à-vis Europe, then, parallels the decolonization of African American literature vis-à-vis white culture. In each case the "inferiority complex" of the cultural subordinate inhibits self-recognition. Moreover, the process of cultural dissociation and self-determination is initiated, ironically, by a transcultural violation of boundaries that remakes the cultural field. For Thurman, tellingly, *Cane* was the first work to exemplify the new tendencies, but it was really pre-renaissance, for "it was published too soon to be lifted into the best-seller class merely because its author was a Negro"; furthermore, it went over the heads of both "sentimental whites" and "Negroes with an inferiority complex to camouflage."[120]

A fairly consistent standard of criticism emerges from the reviews and essays in *The New Republic* concerning literary treatment of "Negro life." The work should be true to black experience in the sense of being expressed through the "vernacular" forms of African American culture and realizing the complexity of human motivation, perception, and action within specific "realistic" settings. Writers who, in the judgment of the reviewer, depended for the interest of their work upon the exoticism of black life to whites, upon moral melodrama, or upon the sado-masochistic appeal of "voodoo" scenes and lynchings, could not usually expect an enthusiastic reception. Hence the review of Fauset's *Plum Bun* called that work "a novel of a very ordinary sort about a subject of extraordinary interest." Aside from the fascinating subject of "passing" and of the life of the mulatto elite, the novel is hardly worth discussing. Most of it is "inconsistent and trivial," the story "melodramatic, unreal." Moreover, "not only has Miss Fauset disdained all use of dialect, but she has discarded as well the full rich idiom of the colored race. Instead of being satisfied with the presentation of one important idea, Miss Fauset has crammed into this novel all her reactions to life in general."[121] Similarly, in *Flight*, according to another reviewer, Walter White "seems to feel that he can handle his people from the same angle that one would use in treating a group of whites, and yet create a special interest by assuring us from time to time that they are colored, and by introducing the dramatic episode of Negro persecution. He fails, inevitably. The main outline of this story is not essentially the problem and struggle of the Negro." It could just as easily be about whites, except in a few details such as the "wholly unconvincing denouement." On the other hand, "that part of the book which fits the Daquin family into its Louisiana background of radiant sunlight, vivid gardens and Creole indolence is full of charming bits."[122] There is more than a hint of exotic interest expressed in that sentence, and a shrinking from the social implications of White's novel, but again the dominant concern is for "realism"; the problem is not that the novel deals with uncomfortable truths—far from it—but that these truths do not emerge from a convincing interplay of setting, characterization, and plot. Rather than bringing an experience to aesthetic fruition, White has written a treatise, intellectually abstracted from processes of meaningful action. Furthermore, White has not adequately adapted the forms of the genre to his subject matter; he thinks of his "topic" as a mental substance to be dispensed into a traditional vessel.

A similar objection informs Edmund Wilson's response to the play *Deep River* by Laurence Stallings and Frank Harling. "It is . . . merely an American imitation of the Italian opera of yesterday. By laying the scene in the Louisiana of a hundred years ago, the authors were able, while still remaining on American soil, to get as far away from the reality of modern America and as close to the fictitious realm of opera as possible." Despite the subtitle, "A Native Opera with Jazz," the work was not distinctively American. It depended for its interest entirely upon appeals to exoticism, and failed even in this area: "The scene of voodoo incantation, which is intended to be sinister and violent, gives an impression of jollity moderated by good taste."[123] Stark Young's 1927 essay, "Negro Material in the Theatre," takes a similar approach to the current white exploitation of "Negro" subject matter. Negro plays, he argues, are overpraised because they are exotic and because some white people want to posture as courageous critics with progressive opinions. Yet the acting really is not, overall, any better than most acting by whites with equivalent training and experience—a point Theophilus Lewis was making in *The Messenger* at the time. The interest in plays about black life can be explained chiefly by the general white audience's conflicting desires for the realistic and the exotic. American audiences expect drama to be "true-to-life," yet they go to the theater for the escape it offers from quotidian existence. They like the Negro drama, therefore, because the material is more exotic and "dramatic" than they normally get to see in an American play, and yet they can convince themselves that it is about "real life."[124]

Abbe Niles's unenthusiastic review of *Nigger Heaven* likewise attributes its success entirely to the novelty of the subject matter to most readers. Unlike some contemporary reviewers, however, he does not accuse Van Vechten of indulging in primitivism. On the contrary, Van Vechten is all too self-conscious about doing "justice" to the black bourgeoisie and indicting white racism. (Alain Locke had a similar but more flattering view. He wrote to Hughes: "My! What propaganda! But it's a big step toward objectivity even at that. I think it's a bit too kindly."[125]) The novel, Niles continues, is "a study of a race laboring under the relentless pressure of prejudice." Unfortunately, Van Vechten's propagandistic purposes and concern to avoid comic stereotypes distort the narrative form of the work: "The dialogue, the soliloquies sag beneath too heavy a weight of information. The author, for the first time as a writer of fiction, adopts a tone of seriousness which for a while he himself seems to find strange; good taste has suppressed humor at the expense of his characters, a type of humor in which he excels." Moreover, he falls into the trap of melodrama; of the white characters, only two "avoid idiocy"; they are almost uniformly unconvincingly evil or stupid. Thus the interest of the novel resides entirely in its informational, touristic appeal: "This is the guide to Harlem par excellence . . . ; an introduction to Negro literature; a photograph-album of cabarets, drawing-rooms, garrets and dives; another reminder, finally, of the way in which its song is woven into the life of the race."[126] Niles shows as fine a judgment in his objections to Van Vechten's work as he does in his praise of Hughes's, and reveals in the process the burden under which an unusually sensitive *white* novelist works in relation to the double audience when he or she turns to "black" subjects. The more insensitive white exploiters could face a stiffer reception in *The New Republic,* as did T. Bower Campbell for *Black Sadie:* "It ends by just singing another song of types and fads and where is Mr. Van Vechten leading us after all. It will sell so well, it will dramatize so well, it is so deftly, though in spots so cheaply written, it starts out with so soaring an exuberance—too bad its author couldn't quite get over being brought up in the land of Unc's and Massa's."[127]

Two reviews of Julia Peterkin's novels reveal other fissures in the white "realist's" attempt to limn African American life, and contrast with the ecstatic greetings her novels received in *Opportunity.* A review of *Black April* by "J.R." (probably James Rorty, a onetime *Masses* author and co-founder of *New Masses*) praises Peterkin's avoidance of the "easy popularity" to be gained by "playing off the white race against the black," but takes her to task on the grounds of exoticizing her subjects, "tabulating quaint or gruesome folk-ways for the sake of their picturesqueness, reporting conversation for the sake of amusing, idiomatic tricks of Negro speech."[128] Apparently Robert Herrick disagreed with this view of *Black April* while adopting the same critical approach in his own review of *Scarlet Sister Mary*. To Herrick, in *Black April*, "that sense of strangeness of the looker-on, which the most sympathetic treatment of the Negro by the white has always betrayed, as if the 'superior' were trying to comprehend the 'inferior' across the racial barrier, was never once present." *Scarlet Sister Mary*, by contrast, gives the impression of a narrative told by an alien observer. Yet Herrick's equation of blackness, particularly black femininity, with nature betrays his romantic racism as he praises the rich atmosphere of the plantation Peterkin conveys, "all that background of fecund nature of which the black race seems intimately a part." Herrick especially admires the characterization of Sister Mary: "In her fecundity, kindness, health and happiness, as well as in her indifference to social stigma, she embodies many essential qualities of all strong women, more frankly because more primitively than would be possible for her sophisticated white sisters. How many of the latter would admit even in secret that 'men are all alike,' good only for 'pleasuring,' while work and children are women's realities?"[129]

Herrick, in fact, had a tendency to fall for the folk-romantic despite his objections to the more obvious examples of this mode. His review of William Seabrook's *Magic Island*, which Alain Locke had attacked in *Opportunity*, calls the book a worthy attempt to understand Haiti, and particularly voodoo, on its own terms, not as a "ghoulish rite" but a form of syncretic religion. While attacking white racism and American imperialism, Herrick also applies terms such as "primitive" and "backward" to the Haitians as he admits that "we" must protect "them" from alien exploiters.[130] The point of view also surfaces more subtly in Herrick's admiring review of Eric Walrond's *Tropic Death*, which praises Walrond's ability to handle his material "from the inside" as no white author could. "The African temperament, modes of thought, have never been more exactly interpreted in language. He has no propaganda, raises no race question, nor is there in the writer's mind a mutinous background of controversy or resentment. He writes of this colored world as if practically it was the only world—as he should and as no other Negro so far as I remember has written." One might argue that to write of the colored world as if no white world existed, and as if an "African temperament" and "modes of thought" were shared by all black people in the twentieth century, was to evade important social determinations and inescapable political issues. But Herrick also liked the fact that Walrond developed a "manner" suited to his particular "material" rather than working "in subservience to the accepted literary traditions of an alien race."[131] Herrick's insistence on racial integrity shades into essentialist premises and racist stereotypes as well as an evasion of politics. Thus the drive to develop a purely "aesthetic" presentation of black culture and a purely "black" aesthetics could lead to unexpected problems, as one finds in Walrond's criticism itself.

The *New Republic* review most fully abandoning itself to effusions of the primitive and exotic is, in fact, Eric Walrond's piece on Paul Green's *Lonesome Road.* "There is in [this play] the budding of half a dozen alluring virginities. From the lungs of ebony bucks, lush with the sweat of the turpentine swamps, issue songs nowhere to be encountered in our collections of blues or spirituals. Legends compounded of the fates of goateed sires and dusk-blown Venuses from leaf-shredded huts are stripped of their romantic fantasticality. All is dark, hot, gem-like, among the Negroes of this region, and Mr. Green's plays are executed with beauty, economy, austerity."[132] Even more baldly primitivist than Green's work, Walrond's description appeals to the white gaze with a barely subliminal imagery of dusky young virgins—"dark, hot, gem-like"—and their "sires" in a sort of peepshow, complete with jungle setting, "stripped" even of the mediating veils of "romantic fantasticality" to convey nothing less and especially nothing *more* than "the real thing."

It would seem that the stress upon root "purity" rather than complexity, in aesthetics as in racial "experience," and the search for a hermetic "blackness" rather than articulation of the shifting boundaries of racial sameness and difference in an ideologically racialized and rapidly modernizing society, tends toward various types of exoticism and escapism. This conclusion emerges with even greater clarity when one reads T. S. Matthews' "What Gods! What Gongs!," a review of Roark Bradford's *Ol' Man Adam an' His Children,* Nella Larsen's *Quicksand,* Claude McKay's *Home to Harlem,* and John W. Vandercook's *Black Majesty.* Matthews pans Bradford's book as a reversion to the "Plantation school," full of childlike and genial "niggers" worshiping a "Lawd" who resembles an easygoing Southern colonel. *Quicksand* "is compact of 'fine writing,' but it is not funny: it makes you uncomfortable. You have met the Negro." Nonetheless, Matthews concludes, the book treats its

subject "as falsely as its characters ape the envied and hated whites"—
one gathers because it too closely resembles a "white" novel; it is not
"black" enough. On the other hand, *Home to Harlem* presents us with
neither a black-faced minstrel nor the "stilted creature of a white man's
culture" but a working man of the city streets who lives in "a world of
pure sensation." Unbothered by "ideas," he is a genuine urban "nigger"
living with "a free and animal rhythm," in contrast with the one character who is bothered by "ideas." This "educated Negro" is "morose,
ineffectual and priggish. And he makes us uncomfortable: he reminds
us of the Problem."

While Matthews sees value in such discomfort, he nonetheless prefers
the character who is more purely "black," as his comments on *Quicksand*
would suggest. Thus it is not surprising that of all the novels he most
likes *Black Majesty*, an epic of King Christophe of Haiti. Although *Home
to Harlem* has greater "documentary interest" for its simple portrait "of
the crude and violent life of the jungle nigger in the jungle city," *Black
Majesty* "captures our imagination, for it shows the Negro, not as we
know him, but as he might have been, perhaps might be—it is the tale
of a black man who tried to be, not a white man, but a giant."[133]
Throughout his review Matthews presents a relentless example of white
"liberal" racism, however well-intended to stress black autonomy. The
privileging of black "purity"—ironic, in view of the importance of
French enlightenment inspirations to the Haitian revolution—at the
expense of the complicated "educated Negro" whose relation to white
culture is disturbing and complex, works equally in the critic's
responses to novels focusing on a black political hero, a black work-
ingman imagined as a "jungle nigger," and a biracial woman confined
by the dominant ideologies of race and gender. What Matthews' review
reveals, then, is the ideological continuity between the more obvious
forms of primitivism and exoticism and the far less recognized (because
ostensibly "radical") romanticizations of the black political warrior-
hero, a kind of exoticism that still emerges with depressing regularity
among ostensibly left-wing white intellectuals today.

The shift from the carefully contextualized criticism of a Niles or a
Potamkin to the racialism of Matthews and, to a lesser extent, Herrick,
indicates the slippage from the understanding of a black aesthetic as a
creative response to specific conditions of life, the making of meaning
as a form of participation in a community and a confrontation with
radical evil, to the reification of racial boundaries and the view of

"blackness" as a spiritual essence or fact of nature. Matthews wants his Negro protagonists "pure" and "African"—without a trace of "whiteness"—which is why he finds Larsen's treatment of her subject as "false" as its so-called mixed-race protagonists. It is also why specific cultural contexts and attributes of North American, Haitian, and African peoples disappear behind terms such as "jungle nigger" and "African temperament." Although Matthews has caught the drift of an antiracist cultural movement, his aesthetic judgment remains wedded to concepts of race and culture that subvert and pervert his liberal desires. But while this scenario was only too common, particularly in the popular culture and, no doubt, among the white tourists slumming in Harlem,[134] it was not the whole story—not, in any case, in the journals the African American writers were reading and writing for.

8

The Native Arts of Radicalism and/or Race

Perhaps the most flamboyant, and certainly the most radical, of the new magazines of the "rebellion" was *The Masses,* which died in the war years, to be reborn as *The Liberator. The Liberator,* in particular, had an important impact on the Harlem Renaissance both because Claude McKay helped edit and constantly contributed to it, and because many young black writers read it and aspired to publish in it in the years before the movement really took off. Although, from today's perspective, it paid scant attention to racial issues,[1] it was far ahead of most white magazines in recognizing the importance of the challenge African American history posed to the myths of white America—myths that, among other things, were used to justify entry into World War I. Opposition to the war cost *The Masses* its existence. *The Liberator,* moreover, saw black Americans as a potential vanguard of the international struggle of "colored" peoples against white domination.[2] *The Masses* and *The Liberator,* often citing John Brown, consistently argued for the necessity of racial self-defense, by violence if necessary, and repeatedly published works emphasizing the irony of (white) American freedom being bought with black lives.[3] This struggle, in turn, they regarded as an important aspect of a worldwide class struggle. I do not mean to suggest that the white editors of the magazines were racially "innocent"; but to categorize their interest in the New Negro under such broad clichés as "exotic primitivism," while failing to examine carefully their cultural

250

politics and aesthetic positions or the actual *effects* of their work in African American cultural history, is to abandon historical consciousness for a pseudo-politics of timeless identity and ideological transcendence.[4]

Native Radicalism: Early Years of *The Masses* and *The Liberator*

Piet Vlag, a Czech immigrant who ran a cooperative restaurant in the basement of the Rand School, had founded *The Masses* as a cooperative magazine in 1911 and abandoned it after an unsuccessful year when the remaining contributors wrote Max Eastman that he had been elected editor, without pay. Although it remained a cooperative venture, Eastman quickly put his stamp on it, making it, as Daniel Aaron has written, "unabashedly 'red' and pagan."[5] Subsequently, after *The Masses* had been banned from the mails, essentially for its antiwar stance, Eastman resurrected it as *The Liberator*—this time with himself and his sister, Crystal Eastman, in control of 51 percent of the stock. *The Liberator* was distinctly Eastman's magazine until 1921, when he turned it over to Claude McKay and Michael Gold.

Eastman was just finishing a stint as a philosophy instructor at Columbia University, where he had been hired by none other than John Dewey, when the *Masses* group "elected" him. To say that he was influenced by Dewey is an understatement; Eastman claimed he "swallowed down Dewey's total mind and attitude in great gulps." Dewey seemed to Eastman "to embody in his social attitude, as Walt Whitman did in his poetry, the very essence of democracy."[6] Every Sunday for two years Eastman had dinner at the Deweys' home. "After the dishes were cleared away, Dewey and I would sit and talk together, or when talk ran out, just sit and think—sometimes for a whole afternoon or evening. We must have talked or thought about pretty nearly every subject that ever engaged the attention of a philosopher."[7] During these years he also met William James, —for whom he felt a "reverential love," and at Columbia he heard the famous lectures on pragmatism, "a new word for some old ways of thinking."[8] In his examination for the Ph.D. in 1910, Eastman named aesthetics as his specialty within psychology/philosophy, and subsequently lectured on poetics as a branch of psychology at the university.

Undoubtedly Eastman's distaste for dogmatism, particularly in the arts, had much to do with his philosophical orientation as a pragmatist. He went "in fear of abstraction," albeit differently from Pound, and just as he rejected ideas of intellectuals as a class responsible to a Platonic "Mind" "above the battle,"[9] he rejected notions of universalism in values: "I see such variety of persons and predicaments in this world that I believe no rule to be ultimate but the rule imposed by the given man in the given situation."[10] Nonetheless, denying the availability of absolute Truth or a transcendental basis for ethics was no inhibition to using specific and relative truths for worthy ends. Clearly, Eastman's (and his associate Floyd Dell's) pragmatism made for an unorthodox approach to Marxism and socialism, just as his commitment to radical democracy made him one of the first American socialists to denounce Stalin, at great personal cost.

As Daniel Aaron and Peter Conn have pointed out, the socialism of *The Masses* and *The Liberator* harked back to Thoreau and Wendell Phillips more than to Marx; it was a Whitmanesque "Debsian socialism," largely homegrown and as individualistic as collectivistic, rejecting theoretical dogma.[11] Dell recalled, for example, a stirring May Day demonstration by conscientious objectors imprisoned at Fort Leavenworth (where Debs was serving time). Tearing a Boardman Robinson portrait of Lincoln out of a socialist magazine, they fastened it to a broomstick and marched behind it singing the Internationale.[12] Floyd Dell believed that Marxism, as an "evolutionist theory" based in scientific determinism, threatened free will and the impetus to action; it had bad "spiritual effects," undermining the sense of personal responsibility. Like a good student of William James, he argued that "at the moment of action we must conceive ourselves free to act."[13] Resistance to the loss of free will, Dell believed, is what caused the Anarchist movement, under Bakunin, to oppose Marx. Despite its defeat, its spirit had been carried on by such individualists as Thoreau, Emerson, and Whitman.[14] In Dell's view, the examples of these men, with Lincoln and the abolitionists, could provide spiritual leadership in the years immediately following World War I, and his thoughts on his trial for sedition came straight out of Thoreau's "Resistance to Civil Government."[15]

Another important contributor to *The Masses* was William English Walling. Walling, as we have seen already, felt that Marxism had to be drastically modified to suit American society; he also was closely associated with Whitman's Boswell, Horace Traubel, who often hung out at The *Masses* offices when in New York before his death. Thus Walling's book *Whitman and Traubel* (1916), one of the first A. & C. Boni titles, attempted to show how Whitman's poetic prophecy anticipated modern socialism.[16] And yet Walling's role at *The Masses* was to keep readers abreast of the news about *international* socialism![17] Walling also belonged to the Walt Whitman Fellowship, a group determined to spread what its members took to be Whitman's prophetic message about human liberation and radical democracy. (The black educator Kelly Miller, who contributed to *The New Negro,* also served on the board of the Fellowship from 1904 to 1917.)[18] In fact, many *Masses*-affiliated radicals (including Eugene Debs, Helen Keller, Emma Goldman, and Clarence Darrow) belonged to the Whitman Fellowship or attended its annual banquets. Whitman was the patron saint of the *Masses-Liberator* operation.

Not surprisingly, the view that those connected with *The Masses* initially took of the Russian Revolution was deeply affected by their prior cultural bearings. It is difficult yet crucial for us today to recover a sense of the close relationship between American cultural nationalist impulses and the native left-wing response to the Russian Revolution. These writers found in postrevolutionary Russia a realization of "updated" Whitmanesque ideals—an optimistic, if ethnocentric, tendency only fostered by Whitman's immense prestige in the new Russia. (McKay himself would later spend time with Whitman's Russian translator.) Similarly, much as Traubel had enjoyed comparing Tolstoy to Whitman in the poet's last years, they frequently compared the new "realistic" fiction of the United States with Russian fiction of Turgenev, Tolstoy, Dostoevsky, Gorky, and Chekhov.[19] This connection had important ramifications for the Harlem Renaissance, because a significant number of writers, both white and black, came to believe that rural African Americans of the South were the American equivalent of Russian peasants and that "Negro culture" was the truest "workers' culture" in the United States.[20]

Claude McKay was immediately attracted to *The Masses* when he came to New York in 1914. He particularly liked the slogans, the cartoons, and the "sympathetic and iconoclastic items about the Negro"—some of which would strike us today as stereotypical and racist.[21] McKay considered the drawings of black people by Stuart Davis "the most superbly sympathetic drawings of Negroes done by an American. And to me they have never been surpassed."[22] Indeed, the artists of *The Masses* and *The Liberator* were a remarkable group, several of them now celebrated for their "realistic" depictions of American life, including its racial and ethnic diversity—particularly Robert Henri (whose "Negro" sketches Locke initially considered including in the Harlem issue of the *Survey Graphic*), John Sloan, and George Bellows. In their rebellion against commercial journalism, they also introduced a new style of cartoon— the evocative illustration with a one-line quip—that was picked up by other magazines, including *The Crisis* and *Opportunity*. These artists of the "Ash Can School" were American cultural nationalists as well as socialists (Sloan ran for the New York Assembly on the Socialist ticket in 1908), grounding their endeavors in an American tradition of dissent, with its "uniquely American idealization of the rabble. Their appeal was to folk Americanism. Quite reasonably, the 'Apostles of Ugliness' in their 1910 exhibition chose the pine tree to be their emblem, thereby connecting their cause with that of the American Revolution."[23] Disciples of Whitman, the painters of the Ash Can School counted Horace Traubel a member of their intellectual circle. Vachel Lindsay studied painting under Robert Henri, while Luks, Glackens, and Sloan (all close friends of Albert Barnes) frequented Petitpas' restaurant with Van Wyck Brooks and John Butler Yeats. The Armory Show of 1913 spelled the end of their brief eminence on the American art scene, although some of them had been instrumental in instigating the show.[24] Yet they did not disappear in the 1920s; furthermore, their work continued to influence the American scene in many areas, including magazine design; and some of their tendencies would be revived by the muralists of the 1930s.

Claude McKay expressed in Whitmanesque terms his differences with the expatriates, differences that help explain his seemingly paradoxical kinship with the cultural nationalists and his important role on the staff of *The Liberator*:

I was in love with the large rough unclassical rhythms of American life. If I were sometimes awed by its brutal bigness, I was nevertheless fascinated by its titanic strength. I rejoiced in the lavishness of the engineering exploits and the architectural splendors of New York.

I never could agree that literature and art could not flourish in America. That idea was altogether contrary to my historical outlook. I believed that there would be an American art and culture mainly derived from Europe and augmented by the arts and cultures of other countries precisely as there had been a distinct Roman art and culture mainly derived from Greece, but augmented by the arts and cultures of the countries that Rome had conquered.[25]

Neither could McKay sympathize with the expatriates' desire for the sort of adulation that artists in France traditionally enjoyed: "I am partial to the idea of an artist being of and among the people, even if incognito." He was also partial to the aesthetic orientation of Max Eastman.

Aesthetics

Eastman's pragmatism and iconoclasm partly accounted for his general openness to artistic experimentation, with the proviso that the aim of art is the communication and intensification of experience; Eastman rejected the obscurantism and allusive density of the "high modernists" and believed that traditional poetry had the advantage over free verse of entrancing its audience with metrical regularity, appealing to the bodily enjoyment of rhythm and repetition. It is not surprising that Eastman would consider Claude McKay one of the best modern American poets, nor that McKay considered Eastman one of the best modern critics; McKay was precisely Eastman's type of poet. He was also, without question, *the* featured poet of *The Liberator.* Yet rather than exploring Eastman's aesthetic theory as a way of understanding his attraction to McKay's poetry (and of interpreting McKay's poetics), scholars of the Harlem Renaissance are prone to quoting statements that portray Eastman as a condescending racist, and leaving it at that.[26]

Eastman's theory is indicated in part by "American Ideals of Poetry," the preface to *Colors of Life* (1918), in which Eastman outlines his views by reference to Whitman and Poe, "the fountains of the two strongest influences in all modern poetry of the occident."[27] Eastman feels that there is "modern validity" in the qualities of both poets, but a science of aesthetics must adjudicate between their rival claims. Whitman's most original gift was "that large grace of freedom from the pose and elegance of words in a book," combined with the possession of a "mood that is truly primitive, and social, and intelligible to the hearts of simple people—the mood that loves with a curious wonder the poised and perfect existence of a thing." Whitman should have developed this strength more, "towards an increasing objective perfection which should still cling to the new and breathless thing, the presence of one who lives and speaks his heart naturally."[28] These are qualities, incidentally, that both Eastman and Dewey found precisely in Claude McKay's poetry.

What Whitman needed, in Eastman's view, was Poe's greater understanding of the imperative of form. Although Whitman may have been the greater democrat in belief, Poe was the more democratic in poetic execution. Poe took a more objective stance to the construction of a poem and thus achieved closer "social communion with humanity." Eastman feels one should make a poem an "object" that "can be experienced in the same form at different times by different persons."[29] Such a poetics is more truly social than the "subjectivist" poetics of a Whitman. Furthermore, Whitman's free verse lacked both the musical subtlety allowed by a careful formalism and the inherently popular basis of its appeal. Meter and rhyme "are the heart of rhythmical speech expressed and exposed with a perfectly childlike and candid grandeur"; they appeal to powerful sources of aesthetic delight, like the monotonous, heartbeat rhythms that act as aids to ecstasy in every culture.[30] This primitive appeal derives, for Eastman, from the relationship between nature and human experience, for Nature urges playfulness and the enjoyment of living. Eastman's politics, in turn, urges social revolution to make such play and enjoyment available to all people.

Clearly, McKay offered an amazingly close approximation to the sort of poet Eastman envisioned. Infused with both the democratic inclusiveness of Whitman and the formal mastery of Poe, both "the mood that loves with a curious wonder the poised and perfect existence of a thing" and the popular, social appeal of rhythm and rhyme, McKay's poems balanced the strengths of the fathers of poetic modernism. Moreover, they did so while urging social revolution that would make the "enjoyment of living" a possibility for all people. McKay was able to express and provoke heightened political consciousness without sacrificing the playfulness of poetry on the butcher-block of ideological correctness. Some of his most effective poems are precisely those that reveal the plight of the sensitive lover of life who must work at demeaning and low-wage jobs simply to survive under the industrial-capitalist regime. The political point is made not by abstract argument but by sensuous appeal, the "primitive" and musical appeal of great poetry.

Thus such statements as Leslie Fishbein's that "blacks were exploited for their exotic value by white radicals" completely obscure the *most significant* reasons for Eastman's admiration of McKay as a poet—rea-

sons transparently evident in Eastman's writing on poetry.[31] One can
certainly attack *Masses* artists for failings in racial sensitivity—the very
artists whom McKay so admired were capable of offensive stereotyping—but along with such attacks one ought to note the more pragmatic effects their overall editorial direction and aesthetic tendencies
had for African American modernism, *regardless* of their feelings about
black people. This requires at least some attention to their aesthetic
theories and the African American writing they published and
reviewed.

Furthermore, rather than positing ahistorical models of black literary
transformation, one ought to give a modicum of attention to the institutional contexts in which various black poets worked. This would prevent
such travesties as Houston Baker's assertion that McKay was *forced* to use
standard forms in order to get a hearing, according to the belief that
white culture-brokers would not take black poetry seriously until black
poets showed they could handle Western forms as well as whites. Baker
thus argues that McKay mastered the traditional sonnet form in order
to subvert or "denigrate" it by turning it to political use—yet Baker
makes no attempt to find out whether other, nonblack poets were doing
the same thing, at the same time, in the same journals.[32] In the teens
and twenties, it was hardly uncommon for left-wing poets to use traditional forms for nontraditional, political purposes—as, for example,
Ridgely Torrence did in his 1915 lynching poem, "The Bird and the
Tree," and as Max Eastman himself occasionally did.[33] The more
important point is that all evidence suggests that McKay chose to write
in traditional verse forms not because he had to—he published in journals that were hardly bastions of English literary tradition—but because
he felt, like Eastman *and for the same reasons,* that these forms were effective for his purposes. (In fact, *The Seven Arts,* whose poetry editor wrote
in Whitmanesque strophes, initially rejected McKay's poems *because*
they were in traditional forms and were not sufficiently "racial.")[34] That
The Liberator's editors liked McKay's sonnets did not prejudice them
against other forms for African American poetry, however; witness
Floyd Dell's response to James Weldon Johnson and the later publication of works by Toomer, Fenton Johnson, and others.

Floyd Dell, newly arrived from Chicago (where he had worked under
and then succeeded Francis Hackett at the *Evening Post,* as we have
seen), came to *The Masses* as associate editor in 1913 and stayed on to
be a part of the *Liberator* staff. He was a confirmed cultural nationalist

of the Midwestern stamp, whose departure from Chicago accelerated a series of defections of Midwesterners (including Hackett and Carl Van Vechten some years earlier) to New York and Greenwich Village and contributed to the Debsian, anti–New England strain of the "Little Renaissance." Dell claimed partial credit for turning Vachel Lindsay (one of Hughes's early models) toward an oral and musical emphasis in his poetry, borrowing ideas from the Irish Renaissance. "We need to know that the nature of poetry is akin to the nature of dancing—the manifestation of a natural human impulse to create rhythmical beauty, and to create it with some part of our physical being," he wrote, in the hope of guiding poets toward a recovery of the *actual* voice. The performative aspects of Lindsay's spectacular poetry "readings" particularly impressed Dell and suggested an important lack in the post-renaissance Western tradition. His comments on Lindsay would have hit Langston Hughes with great force, for Dell claimed that poetry "begins to become again under his influence a social and not a solitary enjoyment—a communal ritual of beauty, akin in its spiritual effects to mass-singing and to common (or communal) prayer."[35] Dell's poetic ideas bore a clear connection to his social philosophy; they also anticipate several tenets of the Black Arts Movement of the 1960s.

Ultimately, the aspects of Lindsay's aesthetic that Dell encouraged are more important to American (especially African American) literary history than Lindsay's well-meant but ludicrous stereotypes of black people, African American culture, and Africa in his (in)famous poem "The Congo." Sterling Brown, for one, considered Lindsay a very important poet for his rhythmic innovations.[36] Yet another point worth considering is the extent to which Lindsay's own poetic practice—and thus Dell's poetic theorizing—was influenced by his (mis)interpretations of "Negro" aesthetics (as well as Christian revival preaching). But to this factor would have to be added both men's (mis)interpretations of the pose and the poetry of W. B. Yeats and the Celtic Revival, which affected their response to African American expression. The Celtic Revival, in turn, drew on Whitman, and so forth. The interplay and counterplay of racial traditions here escapes schematization.

A related area in which Dell apparently had a direct effect was in that of black poetic language. Reviewing James Weldon Johnson's *Fifty Years and Other Poems*, Dell criticized Johnson's use of "literary English" and standard poetic techniques, stating that the most important task of the Negro poet—the task no white poet could perform—was to create poetry true to the temperament, sensibility, and tongue of the racial tradition. This meant breaking out of the tradition established by renaissance Englishmen, which was suitable for *them* only because it developed from within their own customs and ways of speaking and gave voice to perceptions of actual experience. Sir Walter Raleigh did not make up phrases out of "memories of things he had read in books written two hundred years ago by people with different customs, traditions, and ideas. When he spoke he revealed his race, colour, and previous condition of servitude pretty unmistakably."[37] Unlike Johnson.

Dell insisted that he was not calling for "darky" poems or even the formula to which Dunbar was often forced to adhere; in fact he felt that *both* the dialect section and the "standard English" section of *Fifty Years* came up short. The problem with the dialect poems was that they did not capture the quality of black vernacular lyricism but rather assimilated it to mainstream rhythmic conventions: "What is here in question is an instinctive arrangement of vowel and consonant sounds, of word-joinings that permit a free passage for a rhythm, and of a sure feeling for the progress of the rhythm itself."[38] This sort of lyrical gift could be found in even the less "smashing" lines of the spirituals but not in conventional dialect poems. Verses such as

> Seems lak to me de stars don't shine so bright,
> Seems lak to me der's nothin' goin' right,
> Seems lak to me de sun done loss his light,
> Sence you went away,

exhibited "the rhythmic banality characteristic of all but the very best . . . of the contemporary American white man's songs."[39] Ironically, Dell found there was nothing truly "Negro" about such poetry. The criticism was acutely perceptive, though joined with romantic racialist notions:

The Negro—again I fall back upon dogmatic assertion—is an instinctive poet. His words do have a natural rhythmic grace and order of a peculiar kind. It is the business of the Negro poet to attune his ear to that peculiar grace, to study it just as Synge studied it in the speech of the fishermen and tinkers and peasants of the Aran Islands, and to find ways perhaps of heightening, or at all events of making clear and unmistakable, that which he has heard. He is, as Synge found it his glory to be, the mouthpiece of his race, speaking their speech so that all men may hear. And that which he utters is to be theirs no less. In their words, in their cadences, he is to tell their thoughts, express their feelings, reveal their hearts and souls.[40]

Nor did Dell believe those feelings and thoughts were limited to humor and pathos. He hoped for poems of love, tragedy, bitterness, natural beauty, "the terribleness of life," and "the secret of the butterfly's perpetual and lovely holiday."[41] Dell was indeed given to the notion that African Americans experience life with a greater intensity and natural passion than whites; his comments slid into stereotypical notions to which Johnson would be sensitive. Thus, in a letter of response, Johnson initially objected that dialect was too limited as a medium to express the "higher" and "deeper" notes of modern Negro life; he felt Dell was attempting to restrict black expression, a point Fishbein adopts to fault Dell for forcing black poets into a racial box.[42] Yet Johnson ended up following Dell's advice and producing some of his most important poems as a result.

In *The Book of American Negro Poetry* and the preface to *God's Trombones*, Johnson would alter only slightly Dell's prescription in setting out the task of the black poet:

> What the colored poet in the United States needs to do is something like what Synge did for the Irish; he needs to find a form that will express the racial spirit by symbols from within rather than by symbols from without—such as the mere mutilation of English spelling and pronunciation. He needs a form that is freer and larger than dialect, but which will still hold the racial flavor; a form expressing the imagery, the idioms, the peculiar turns of thought and the distinctive humor and pathos, too, of the Negro, but which will also be capable of voicing the deepest and highest emotions and aspirations and allow of the widest range of subjects and the widest scope of treatment.[43]

Sterling Brown would later attest to the importance of Johnson's experiment, noting how the limitations of the dialect poems in *Fifty Years* had been overcome when Johnson "turned to the model of Synge dealing with the Aran Islanders." Poems such as "Go Down, Death" and "Listen, Lord" belonged, Brown believed—just one year before the publication of his own *Southern Road*—with the "most moving poems of American literature."[44]

Both Dell and Eastman—like Claude McKay—tended to think of art as something to be pursued without ideological prescriptions, but this did not mean that a poem could not be frankly political or propagandistic. (The great Whitman, after all, had written many propaganda poems.) If there was a kind of writing that the aesthetic preferences and cultural orientation of the *Masses-Liberator* group worked directly against, it was the new expatriate modernism—Eastman never did have any use for *The Waste Land,* for example, and he considered *The Great Gatsby* overrated. In "The Cult of Unintelligibility" (1929) and "Poets Talking to Themselves" (1930) he directly attacked high modernism.[45] "Of course I lost the war," he would muse in 1964. "A gap in my memory indicates that I was carried unconscious from the field of battle. . . . I disappeared under a cloud of awfully overwhelming language called the New Criticism, and as a critic of poetry I have not been heard of since"—to McKay's misfortune as well as his own.[46] To Eastman, the so-called modernists—whom he called "neo-classics"—and the humanists were fundamentally alike in seeking to defend a caste-bound idea of "humane letters" against the encroachment of science and experimental knowledge. They were, in short, antimodern. Essentially wedded to the social status quo, and therefore fearing any challenge to their cultural capital (Eastman borrows here from Thorstein Veblen), both groups attacked realism because realism might prompt social action that would dethrone gentlemen-professors and elite "neo-classics" alike. Gesturing their presumptuous superiority to industrial civilization, they were homesick for feudalism, which they were prone to fantasize in the budding fascism of Mussolini.[47] Regarding art as essentially an act of communication and intensification of experience, helping to make others *aware* of experience, Eastman could not make sense of modernist obscurantism except as an arrogant retreat from actuality and from human need. Like Van Wyck Brooks, Dell and Eastman condemned the rising "aestheticism" of *The Dial* in the twenties, and viewed "the postwar writer's preoccupation with form, his cultish conception of literature as an 'esoteric mystery of the elect,' and his 'celebration of the ugliness and chaos of life' as a symptom of infantile regression."[48]

Yet their editorial policy made their magazines attractive to aspiring black writers. McKay's first attempt to publish in America would be with *The Masses;* the work was rejected, but he did not give up, and ultimately his first poems published in the United States after those printed in *The Seven Arts* would appear in *The Liberator.*[49] He particularly wanted to publish there because it was a "group magazine." Moreover, "the list of contributing editors was almost as exciting to read as the contributions themselves. There was a freeness and a bright new beauty in those contributions, pictorial and literary, that thrilled. And altogether, in their entirety, they were implicit of a penetrating social criticism which did not in the least overshadow their novel and sheer artistry. I rejoiced in the thought of the honor of appearing among that group."[50] The "group" would be equally attractive to Langston Hughes, not least because McKay became closely identified with it.

And/or Race: Black Writers in *The Liberator*

Even before McKay's arrival, *The Liberator* was encouraging certain directions McKay had taken. Mary Burrill's *Aftermath,* appearing a month after Stuart Davis' drawing "The Return of the Soldier" (which portrayed a disillusioned black veteran jaggedly fingering a piano), was a featured contribution to *The Liberator* in April 1919, bringing together a number of the magazine's leitmotifs while dramatizing a militant New Negro political consciousness. It is, at the same time, a sort of Negro folk play, though with a sharper edge than most. Set in South Carolina at the end of the war, *Aftermath* concerns the conflict between traditional black Christian faith and the "modern" consciousness of a black soldier returning from France, where he has learned that survival depends on qualities other than religious belief. The loss of faith in old nostrums, however, is no tragedy for John, the protagonist; instead, it liberates him into conscious "manhood" and belief in his own powers. While he has been abroad fighting for white people's freedom, his father, a devout Christian, has been lynched for striking a white man in self-defense. Burrill delays the revelation of this fact to John, thus allowing for ironic tension to build between the family's pride in him as a soldier and their traditional non-militant survival strategies of "masking," Christian humility, and pacifism (represented in the father's beloved Bible and the mother's fearful faith). When John comes home, these ironies are brought to a head symbolically as he places two service pistols on the mantel where his father's Bible is normally kept and makes it clear that he knows how and when to use them. To make it appear that the father has just stepped out, John's sister has placed the Bible on a table, open to a page with the text "But I say unto you, love your enemies, bless them that curse you, and do good to them that hate you." By the time John learns of his father's fate, we know the denouement. The God of militant Christianity embodied in the hymns Mam Sue, the mother, has been singing earlier—

> O, Yes, yonder comes mah Lawd, . . .
>   Wid his sword in his han'—
> He's gwine ter hew dem sinners down
>   Right lebbal to de ground'

—is transformed into the figure of the son going off armed into the night after the men who lynched his father.[51]

This is not a play *The Nation*—opposed, like *The Masses* and *The Liberator,* to American participation in the Great War but, unlike them, resolutely pacifist—would have approved; nor does it fit the *Crisis* line that typically portrayed black soldiers as Christlike saviors risking their lives in Europe for a worthy cause; or *Opportunity*'s favored type of folk (as opposed to propaganda) play. It also embarrasses the pro-war line *The New Republic* had taken. But it perfectly matches the editorial bent of *The Liberator* as it combines vernacular drama with class consciousness, a view of the Great War as an elaborate confidence game played on the oppressed peoples who fought in it for their overlords, and a stimulus to open rebellion against American racial oppression. As if to emphasize this last point, the editors filled out the final page on which the play was printed with Claude McKay's "The Dominant White," his first publication in the magazine:

> You have betrayed the black, maligned the yellow;
>   But what else could we hope of you who set
> The hand even of your own against his fellow;
>   To stem the dire tide that threatens yet?
> You called upon the name of your false god
>   To lash our wounded flesh with knotted cords
> And trample us into the blood-stained sod,
>   And justified your deeds with specious words:
> Oh! you have proved unworthy of your trust,
>   And God shall humble you down to the dust.[52]

After this poem's appearance, McKay's real debut was a two-page spread of poems, including "If We Must Die," along with an editorial introduction by Eastman. As Wayne Cooper points out, this appearance "signalled the beginning of his life as a professional writer." Between April

1919 and August 1923 McKay would publish no less than forty-two poems and eleven articles and book reviews in the magazine.[53]

McKay quickly became an important member of the *Liberator* staff— as well as Eastman's best friend there—and his presence, in turn, made the magazine even more attractive to black readers.[54] In fact, Eastman agreed to return as editor after a brief hiatus in 1921 only if McKay were given editorial duties formerly assigned to Floyd Dell, who had taken leave to write a book.[55] Ultimately the magazine published creative work by James Weldon Johnson, Fenton Johnson, Mary Burrill (all before McKay's arrival), Georgia Douglas Johnson, and Jean Toomer ("Carma," "Georgia Dusk," and "Becky"), in addition to McKay. It also published protest poems by white authors attacking racism.

Jewish friends of Langston Hughes, when he was still in high school, lent him *The Liberator* and *The Call*, a socialist publication. According to Arnold Rampersad, "As Hughes would recall it, his introduction to *The Liberator* was crucial" in his intellectual development.[56] "I read every copy of that magazine I could get my hands on during my high school days. I learned from it the revolutionary attitude toward Negroes. Was there not a Negro on its staff—and what other 'white' American magazine would have a colored editorial member?"[57] Subsequently Hughes would send his "own earliest poems (young and very bad) to the LIBER- ATOR. Of course, they were returned to me." But he was persistent, and when *The Liberator* was transformed into the *Workers Monthly* (a more strictly "communist" journal, sans McKay, Eastman, and Dell), he did have poetry accepted there.[58]

McKay's defiance of the color line and criticism of high-class black society were among the very qualities Hughes liked about him; he repre- sented a freedom from the stifling atmosphere of both the dominant white mainstream culture and the black bourgeoisie. "He wore a red shirt and mingled with the white radicals and writers of the town—a thing that shocked both Negroes and whites who were not used to seeing a big black boy breaking away from the color line. . . . The 'best' Negroes and the 'best' white folks shook their heads doubtfully" because he had broken racial taboos, danced with white women, and even gone to Russia.[59] The point, of course, is not that McKay had found his way into the coveted company of whites but that he had defied time-honored conventions in going where he had to for intellectual nourishment and personal plea- sure. McKay encouraged Hughes to do the same while warning him of the possible consequences: "I see by your letter you are determined not to get spoiled in that silly monkey-society atmosphere. But on the other hand my dear old top the folks may consider your refusal to attend their functions intellectual snobbishness on your part!"[60]

Another important writer who kept somewhat aloof from what McKay considered bourgeois black society, Jean Toomer was also an avid reader of *The Liberator* and sent his first submissions for publication there. The day before he left Sparta, Georgia, he mailed "Georgia Night" to the magazine, where it was rejected by Claude McKay,[61] who nonetheless thought highly of later work Toomer submitted and carried on a brief correspondence with him. ("Georgia Dusk" would be published in the September 1922 issue, along with "Carma.") Joseph Freeman—the magazine's literary editor at the time—remembered receiving "Carma" and "Becky" in the mail, along with "a twenty-page letter in vibrant and lucid prose" detailing Toomer's mixed racial inheritance along with the feeling of solidarity with Negroes he had felt for the first time in Georgia. Freeman accepted the prose sketches and began a regular correspondence with Toomer, but tore up the letters and manuscripts during a later police scare.[62] Toomer may have been drawn to *The Liberator* in part because Waldo Frank was by then connected with the magazine. Certainly its American cultural nationalist thrust and openness to unconventional writing by and about blacks attracted him, although by this time he was disaffected with socialism and was moving in the direction of the aesthetic avant-garde. *The Liberator,* meanwhile, was moving precisely in the opposite direction, against what came to be regarded as the "bohemian" and politically "irresponsible" preferences of McKay, Eastman, and Dell.

Later, Hughes would serve as a contributing editor of *The New Masses,* criticizing McKay, Eastman, and Dell as revolutionary "backsliders." His criticism showed his association with Michael Gold, who would write the introduction to Hughes's *A New Song,* and whose fight with McKay had led to the latter's resignation from *The Liberator.* After Max Eastman had turned the editing of the magazine over to these two, Gold wanted to devote the literary pages of *The Liberator* to "proletarian" writing, while McKay objected that little of this writing had any artistic value—fine work in poetry or prose required discipline, practice, hard labor with the media under hand. His own background had taught him to respect the difficulty of artistic achievement. Gold, McKay believed, must have known this, too; he had also had to work his way "up" from a proletarian background, "and like myself he was getting hard criticism and kind

encouragement from Max Eastman. But Michael Gold preferred sentimentality above intellectuality in estimating proletarian writing and
writers."[63] Ultimately the two men flatly admitted their incompatibility,
forcing the editorial board to choose between them. The board chose
Gold and the proletarian direction.

Yet another factor credited by Tyrone Tillery for McKay's leaving *The
Liberator* was its failure to devote sufficient attention to the "race question." Indeed, well before his departure McKay deliberately took white
comrades to task in his article "Birthright" over their blindness to the
nature of racism: "Some friendly critics think that my attitude towards
the social status of the Negro should be more broadly socialistic and
less chauvinistically racial as it seems to them. These persons seem to
believe that the pretty parlor talk of international brotherhood or the
radical shibboleth of 'class struggle' is sufficient to cure the Negro
cancer along with all the other social ills of modern civilization."[64] By
failing to recognize *racism* as a psychological and social force independent of class consciousness, the white radical "not only aids the bourgeoisie, but also the ultra-nationalist negro leaders who, in their insistent appeal to the race prejudice of blacks against whites, declare that
no class of white people will ever understand the black race."[65] The
result is a crucial weakening of the proletarian movement, threatening
to make black workers unwitting allies of white capitalists in containing
the possibility of working-class revolution—*especially* in the United
States. McKay connected Negro race consciousness specifically to the
American environment in his book *The Negroes in America* (originally
published in Russian), which expands upon the weakness of white
American socialism; to those (like Gold) who object to McKay's "excessive" race consciousness, he replies: "For the Negro in America it is very
useful to be imbued with race consciousness. . . . The Negro in America
is not permitted for one minute to forget his color, his skin, or his race.
The American Negro who is not imbued with race consciousness would
constitute a strange phenomenon."[66]

The Liberator's stance on racial issues was the subject of a series of
revealing letters between McKay and Max Eastman in the Spring of
1923. Eastman felt that a presentation of "materials on the race question" proportional to the population of Negroes in the United States
would cost the magazine—whose audience was almost entirely white—
its existence, thus destroying the very organ that could most effectively
address racial issues relative to the class struggle.[67] Eastman felt the

white readership had to be trained gradually out of its inherited racial prejudices and ignorances, that too great an emphasis on the Negro all at once would merely cause them to stop reading the magazine. This response, of course, did not satisfy McKay, who concluded that *The Liberator*'s white editors could not appreciate the *central* importance of race to the class struggle in the United States. Michael Gold was particularly adamant that race consciousness be subordinated to class consciousness. However, Tyrone Tillery's argument that McKay split with *The Liberator* over the race issue is contradicted in McKay's own letter to Eastman, which clearly states that he had other reasons for leaving and did not mean to imply that he left because of a conflict over *The Liberator*'s treatment of racial issues.[68] In fact, he took offense at Eastman's interpreting his work in this way.

These letters are chiefly puzzling because, coming as they do after McKay's disagreements with Gold's insistence on proletarian, explicitly propagandistic literature for *The Liberator*, they contradict McKay's own statements to Langston Hughes that he preferred the "Bohemian dilletanti" to the very "political" types at *The Liberator*. In his letters to Eastman, he charges that not only the race question but also "national" questions regarding Ireland and India and even "the labour movement" were never discussed seriously at *The Liberator*. "I don't know why, my dear Max, but the atmosphere of the Liberator did not make for serious discussions on any of the real problems of Capitalist society much less the Negro."[69] There is a good chance that McKay's rather haughty charges at this time were colored by, on the one hand, his bitter parting with *The Liberator* and, on the other, his enthusiastic reception in Moscow, where, he said, he was feted as a "black ikon in the flesh."[70] It was easy for him to think of himself as more politically serious than his benighted comrades who were so far from the center of true communist consciousness. His sudden political intensity, however, is decidedly at odds with statements not only in his autobiography but also in letters to Hughes of 1925. They are also at odds with Eastman's recollection: "When you joined the Liberator you were like some of the rest of us a poet. You wanted more than anything else free time to write your poetry. You had not yet discovered in yourself—at least so it seems to me—this very solemnly consecrated political soul that now appears, and looks down upon the Liberator, discovering what I never knew, that it had a cult of 'Playful Work.'"[71] McKay would very soon be the target of attacks for just such bohemianism.

Despite his own radical politics, McKay did not like "politicians," and he particularly objected to making the arts fit specific political requirements. He told Hughes to scotch the "propagandistic" line he used in contributions to *Workers Monthly* and *The Crisis:* "I love when you say you write to amuse yourself. I hate when you deliberately write 'propaganda stuff for the Crisis or cheap stuff to buy a meal'" (apparently quoting from a letter sent by Hughes).[72] Another letter to Hughes, of April 24, 1926, indicates McKay's allegiances on the *Liberator* staff: "While I was on the Liberator I was never in with the very political set. I always preferred the Bohemian dilletanti and the more decadent they were the better I liked them."[73] The word "decadent," in current usage, could not describe Eastman and Dell. McKay was adopting the late-1920s Marxist usage typical of *The Workers Monthly* and *The New Masses.* Dell himself objected to the decadence, self-consciousness, and theatricality that afflicted Greenwich Village after the war, blaming it on newcomers from uptown catching on to a fad—a complaint that would also arise in Harlem by the late 1920s.

Hughes, on the other hand, eventually chided his onetime hero in an article that was generally laudatory of McKay: "What happened to Claude McKay? Don't ask me. I don't know. But then what happened to most of the old LIBERATOR crowd—Floyd Dell and Max Eastman and Arturo Giovanitti? Well, they're old and fairly well-off and as revolutionary as kittens now. And the latest news from North Africa is that McKay is thinking seriously of taking up the Mohammedan faith!"[74] What had happened, in part, was that the growing insistence on strict political prescriptions for art had turned them off. This division between "politicians" and "artists" was merely the intensification of a split that had characterized *The Liberator* since 1916 and finally led to its being turned over (at Eastman's suggestion) to the Workers' Party in 1922, finally to join with the *Labor Herald* to become *The Workers Monthly.*[75]

The New Masses: Caste or Class

By late 1924 and early 1925, members of the old *Masses* and *Liberator* group began talking about starting another *Masses*-type publication, one that would develop revolutionary artists without being a party organ. Joseph Freeman, a former student of Carl Van Doren's at Columbia, made the proposal to the Garland Fund for support.[76] His prospectus, as Daniel Aaron has pointed out, "revived the spirit of cultural nationalism.... Echoing the manifestoes of Emerson and Whitman, of Bourne and Van Wyck Brooks, it called upon American artists and writers to face up to America's 'potential riches' and its problems."[77] When the first issue of *The New Masses* came out, its list of editors included familiar names: Egmont Arens, Michael Gold, Joseph Freeman, Hugo Gellert, James Rorty, and John Sloan. Its contributing editors were Sherwood Anderson, Van Wyck Brooks, Miguel Covarrubias, Floyd Dell, Max Eastman, Waldo Frank, John Howard Lawson, Claude McKay, Lewis Mumford, Eugene O'Neill, Elmer Rice, Lola Ridge, Carl Sandburg, Jean Toomer, Louis Untermeyer, Mary Heaton Vorse, Eric Walrond, Walter White, Edmund Wilson, and Art Young—a combination of *The Masses, The Liberator, The New Negro, The New Republic,* and *The Seven Arts.* Waldo Frank was originally elected editor-in-chief—an indication of the strength of the cultural nationalist and "spiritual" thrust—but he resigned before the publication got started, so Gold and Freeman became the executive editors.[78] Some years later Langston Hughes became a contributing editor, and eventually Richard Wright and Ralph Ellison would join the magazine very early in their careers. The *Masses-Liberator-New Masses* legacy is one significant institutional link between three generations of path-breaking African American writers. It is also a significant institutional link between three generations of American cultural nationalists of the political left. According to Joseph Freeman, *The New Masses* was out to "discover America"; on this even the "liberals" and "revolutionaries" could agree. And, at least at the beginning, they would try to convey a socialist political vision free of "imported" Marxist terminology, which provoked angry denunciations from the party-line *Daily Worker.*

Initially *The New Masses* opened its pages to a wide variety of writers, though with a general emphasis on "realistic" art true to ordinary experience, particularly of the lower class. It generally attacked high modernism and the worship of esoteric formal experimentation, calling instead for an art of social engagement, but its political requirements were vague enough to allow for the participation of a diverse collection of authors. In these early years, work by Claude McKay as well as Walter White appeared, and *Opportunity* advertised in the magazine, featuring the Negro as a "victim of the economic class struggle" and "an art-mite destined to color the whole range of the American aesthetical experience."[79]

Langston Hughes's *The Weary Blues* elicited a provocative criticism of the "New Negro" movement in general from James Rorty (father of today's neo-pragmatist philosopher Richard Rorty). Too much of the Negro renaissance, Rorty charged, was concerned with the amusement of white folks: "I want the Negroes to stop entertaining the whites and begin to speak for themselves. I am waiting for a Negro poet to stand up and say 'I—I am *not* amused.'" Rorty found Hughes saying nothing like this in his first book—"nothing as bitter, nothing as masterful, nothing as savage. Why not?" The black writers "look, talk and write like sophisticated, tamed, adapted, behavioristic white men, and if that is what they want to be, it is nothing in the way of an aspiration." In some of his comments Rorty hit the mark. He admired the poem "When Sue Wears Red" but not

> All the tom-toms of the jungle beat in my blood.
> And all the wild hot moons of the jungles shine in my soul.
> I am afraid of this civilization—
>   So hard,
>   So strong,
>   So cold.

"I hope and trust Hughes doesn't mean this," wrote Rorty. "If he does, I'd rather have Garvey, who may not be intelligent, but who at least seems more angry than afraid."[80] Undoubtedly the criticism hit home: one does not find another poem of this sort in Hughes's corpus after *The Weary Blues.* One finds instead a growing political radicalism and satire of exotic primitivism as Hughes moves more decisively into the *New Masses* fold (despite the patronage of the primitivist Charlotte Osgood Mason). Two months later, four Hughes poems—"Brass Spittoons," "Saturday Night," "Argument," and "The New Girl" showed up in the magazine; none was of the "exotic primitive" type. Indeed, generally speaking, Hughes would never return to the manner of his early stereotypical African "tom-tom" songs of wistful escape. Also in a December 1926 issue, George Schuyler published "Some Southern Snapshots" and Calverton critiqued Van Vechten's *Nigger Heaven* as exemplary of the new "progressive attitude" toward Negroes but "superficial."[81] Soon *The New Masses* would be scapegoating Van Vechten for co-opting Negro writers into entertaining the white bourgeoisie, helping set a pattern of criticism that converged with Du Bois's (though developing from a different hermeneutic base) and that has remained in place ever since.

As these examples would suggest, on the whole *The New Masses* encouraged black writers to avoid romantic appeals to racial essences or what it would term the "decadent" interests mainstream whites wanted to indulge in Harlem. By the late twenties, there was a danger that the revolutionary potential of the New Negro movement (like the vitality of Greenwich Village over a decade earlier) would be lost in the glitter of the age of fads, spoiled by fawning "sentimental" criticism, diverted from the serious task of enlightening and leading the masses. In "Awake, Negro Poets!" William C. Patterson lamented, "Our Negro poets voice the aspirations of a rising petty bourgeoisie. Occasionally they express the viciousness of black decadents. And that is all. They are sensationalists, flirting with popularity and huge royalties. They are cowards. Instead of leading heroically in the march of the world's workers, they are whimpering in the parlors of black and white idlers and decadents."[82]

The year 1927 was a high point of *The New Masses*' interest in black culture. After that, a more "vulgar Marxist" line would gain the upper hand and emphasize class consciousness at the expense of caste consciousness. Additionally, the sort of exploration of the racial self and the stylization of cultural identity that characterized the "bourgeois" black writing of the Harlem Renaissance would become anathema, in part because the journal was reorganized in early 1928 and shifted direction. The July 1928 issue asked for confessions, diaries, documents, letters from hoboes and peddlers, "revelations by rebel chambermaids and night club waiters," "the poetry of steelworkers," and so forth.[83] Its emphasis turned increasingly to proletarian writing when younger, more sectarian authors such as those associated with the John Reed clubs became impatient with the equivocal political commitments of the older "radicals" and artists who balked at subordinating their work to the party line.[84] For example, beginning in 1926, Floyd Dell became the target of increasingly bitter attacks, finally resigning from the editorial group in 1929. Michael Gold then lashed out harder than ever against "individualists" and "bohemians."[85]

Gold did not spare the New Negroes, but he blunted his critique of them by blaming their weaknesses on a white man. Hence in 1930 he would write:

We believe Carl Van Vechten the worst friend the Negro has ever had. This night-club rounder and white literary sophisticate was one of the first to take an interest in Negro writers in this country. He has thus influenced many of them. He has been the most evil influence.

Gin, jazz and sex—this is all that stirs him in our world, and he has imparted his tastes to the young Negro literatuers [sic]. He is a white literary bum, who has created a brood of Negro literary bums. So many of them are now wasting their splendid talents on the gutter-life side of Harlem. . . .

I believe that Negro art and literature are only beginning. This cabaret obsession is but an infantile disease, a passing phase. There will be Negro Tolstoys, Gorkys and Walt Whitmans. . . . Negroes are plowing into the revolutionary movement. It is the Negroes [sic] only remaining hope. And among these masses the Negro will at last find his true voice. It will be a voice of storm, beauty and pain, no saxophone clowning, but Beethoven's majesty and Wagner's might, sombre as night with the vast Negro suffering, but with red stars burning bright for revolt.[86]

I have quoted Gold's manifesto at length because it is such a fascinating study in cultural contradiction and attempted co-optation. The critique of the Harlem Renaissance here is integral with a vision of African American culture being in no essentials different from proletarian culture anywhere, a vision in which even jazz (as opposed to Wagner!) is perceived as little more than a product of the white capitalist culture industry, a minstrel-show travesty of black expressivity.

Despite such problems, and despite Gold's attack on Van Vechten, Langston Hughes lined up basically in the same camp as Gold, apparently never joining the Communist Party but criticizing Eastman and McKay (who were now "revolutionary as kittens") and promoting proletarian writing. Once Gold won control of *The New Masses*, according to V. F. Calverton, it "became an exclusively proletarian magazine" trying to appeal directly to workers rather than the intelligentsia.[87] This happened at about the same time Langston Hughes began expressing dissatisfaction with the failure of New Negro writers to address a predominantly black and working-class audience. In fact, his 1930s-vintage views of the Harlem Renaissance match the *New Masses* line in every respect except his continued loyalty to Carl Van Vechten. Yet by 1932 even Gold and Joseph Freeman were under attack from the left for being insufficiently critical of "bourgeois" critics and artists, including Max Eastman and V. F. Calverton.[88]

A kind of critique of the Harlem Renaissance begins to show up in *The New Masses* in the middle 1920s (evident in Rorty's 1926 review of *The Weary Blues*) and gains steam by 1930, subsequently manifesting itself throughout the rest of the history of commentary on the movement. This critique contrasts work songs of secular protest with the spirituals, scapegoats Carl Van Vechten for corrupting naïve young artists, takes the NAACP and Urban League to task as timid and bourgeois, and dismisses the Harlem Renaissance generally as irresponsible and "inauthentic," a show put on for decadent whites. By 1930 all the elements of critique are solidly in place in *The New Masses,* when Langston Hughes was a regular contributor (and practically the *only* black one), two to three years before Richard Wright would join the John Reed Club in Chicago. The shift toward a more insistent party-line stance in the early thirties, ironically, coincided with a relative falling-off in representation of black writers as well as a muffling of the American cultural nationalist bent that had typified the magazine initially (partly in response to commands from the International Union of Revolutionary Writers, based in Moscow). This is not because the editors had stopped being interested in the writing of black authors so much as because the black authors, with a few exceptions, were not interested in producing what the editors wanted. (About the same time, authors like James Rorty, who had been insightful critics and supporters of black writers, renounced communism and disaffiliated with *The New Masses.*)

As it identified more closely with Soviet communism, the magazine emphasized class solidarity at the expense of recognizing the specific features of "racial" culture in the United States. Walt Carmon's 1930 review of Langston Hughes's first novel can serve as an example. Entitled "Away from Harlem," it attempts to wrest Hughes away from his own cultural coordinates to ensconce him more securely in the "nonracial" (but white-dominated) international proletarian-intellectual community. Carmon, one of the chief book reviewers of *The New Masses,* terms *Not Without Laughter* "the first definite break with the vicious Harlem tradition of Negro literature sponsored by Van Vechten and illustrated by Covarrubias." Even McKay's *Home to Harlem* and *Banjo,* charges Carmon, were "products of this travesty on Negro life."[89] Expressing a view later to become dominant in Harlem Renaissance scholarship, Carmon lays the blame on the fact that only decadent bohemian work could find an outlet: "For years, this perverted literature has been practically the only opening in the literary field for the Negro writer. He has been allowed only to porter and clown at the literary bawdy-house."[90] Nor had Hughes escaped its baneful influence. In *The Weary Blues* and *Fine Clothes to the Jew*, "the scent of the vicious Van Vechten patronage which Hughes still acknowledges" tainted a budding proletarian talent. *Not Without Laughter*, while not yet completely breaking with the "Harlem tradition," marks a major advance by providing a realistic treatment of working-class black family life in the Midwest. Significantly, Carmon finds the book most akin to Agnes Smedley's *Daughter of Earth*, which proves "proletarian class kinship; the life is one that both black and white share in common." However, in Hughes's novel, "class issues are beclouded by race feeling" as the Negro's bitterness is misdirected toward the white race as a whole rather than focusing on the ruling class.

Carmon submerges issues of cultural difference and identity, as well as specific forms of social domination by race, beneath the "universals" of Marxist theory. In the process he attempts to appropriate Hughes's talent for a putatively nonracial, "universal" community of international workers. "*Not Without Laughter* is a race novel. It concludes in a misty pointless fashion. There is no clear class consciousness nor revolutionary spirit which distinguished some of Hughes' early poems. But under its black skin, there is red proletarian blood running through it. With all its faults, *Not Without Laughter* goes far beyond Harlem. It is *our* novel."[91] The falsely "universal" point of view of scientific socialism inherently glosses over local cultural forces and identities from its transcendent vantage, a fact that Richard Wright would finally come to recognize and that *Native Son* brilliantly dramatizes. It is also a point, of course, that the recent history of Eastern Europe has written in blood.

Black authors tended to get more opportunities to pursue and publish their work according to their own understanding of African American experience when the left-wing cultural nationalists were in control rather than the Marxist theorists and party hacks looking for Proletcult.[92] This was not for lack of trying, on the editors' part, to attract black contributors and a black audience. For example, a 1931 editorial admits the magazine's failure to connect "organically" with workers' struggles and pleads for more African American contributions, noting the magazine's publication of Hughes's work and articles on protest songs.[93] The magazine also regularly published cartoons attacking lynching. At the same time, however, it tended to ignore the extent to which white working-class culture in the United States was saturated with racism and spoke all too hopefully about how white workers were waking up to black America's dignity and heroism.

Legacies

Despite the magazine's attempts to differentiate the "Harlem" movement of the 1920s from the "workers" movement of the 1930s, one must note significant continuities between the cultural politics of *The New Masses* and that of *The Masses* and *The Liberator.* Even Michael Gold continued to extol the "realists" of the twenties such as Dreiser, Sandburg, Anderson, and Lewis, pitting them against the "New Humanists" and "Modernists": "The men of the 1920's, as they are now labelled, established the first organic contact between American art and American life. . . . They were massive pioneers in a new realism. Their tasks were so new and strange that minor artistic crudities are irrelevant. They had a new continent to explore: America of the machine age. They did their work with courage and power. They blazed clear trails for the proletarian writers of tomorrow to follow."[94] What was needed was a further development of consciousness toward scientific socialism (as opposed to pragmatism) and proletarianism (as opposed to bourgeois reformism and bohemianism). And, in fact, Theodore Dreiser became precisely the symbol of this development. Thus, in "The Titan," of 1931, *The New Masses* celebrated him as the intellectual leader of the United States, a heroic model to younger authors.

It is worthwhile, in this context, to review briefly Richard Wright's emergence as an author. As he wrote in his autobiography, he was reading a Memphis newspaper in 1927 that attacked H. L. Mencken in such terms as to inspire him to read Mencken's work. Slyly working out a method to check Mencken's *A Book of Prefaces* and *Prejudices* out of the public library, he found himself captivated by Mencken's masterful use of prose as a weapon. The impact on his imagination, as Keneth Kinnamon has pointed out, was "overwhelming." He had been "simmering, and H. L. Mencken brought him to a boil."[95] Wright then began reading voraciously the authors mentioned by Mencken: Sinclair Lewis, Edgar Lee Masters, Joseph Conrad, Sherwood Anderson, and especially Dreiser. "All my life had shaped me for the realism, the naturalism of the modern novel, and I could not read enough of them," he would attest in *Black Boy*.[96] Particularly, his reading gave him hope, a budding faith in "life's possibilities": "But what enabled me to overcome my chronic distrust was that these books—written by men like Dreiser, Masters, Mencken, Anderson, and Lewis—seemed defensively critical of the straitened American environment. These writers seemed to feel that America could be shaped nearer to the hearts of those who lived in it."[97] Such for Wright was the meaning of literary modernism.

Appropriately, he moved to Chicago in late 1927, the same year he had come across the realist prose and poetry of the Midwestern renaissance. Falling in with the John Reed Club in 1933, he served his apprenticeship as a writer at the time when *The New Masses*, with Langston Hughes contributing, was implementing the party directives "to clarify and elaborate the point of view of proletarian as opposed to bourgeois culture" and to "create and publish art and literature of a proletarian character."[98] *The New Masses'* reductive reading of the Harlem Renaissance answered to such imperatives, and Richard Wright accepted it completely, just as he began publishing crude agitprop poetry in *The New Masses* and other communist organs. Hence, Wright's "Blueprint for Negro Writing" (1937) rejects Harlem Renaissance writers because they allegedly pandered to a white audience instead of directing themselves to the needs of black people. They "ignored the collective consciousness embodied in black folklore" and abdicated their social responsibility while clowning and posturing for the amusement of the white bourgeoisie.[99] His critique follows exactly the line *The New Masses* had been taking since about 1926.

Wright's first big "success" as an author, however, came with the publication of "Big Boy Leaves Home" in *The New Caravan*, which was published by none other than those stalwart cultural nationalists of the teens and twenties, Alfred Kreymborg, Lewis Mumford, and Paul Rosenfeld. Moreover, as director of the Chicago Negro Division of the Federal Theatre Project in 1936, Wright would try to produce Paul Green's *Hymn to the Rising Sun*—only to be rebuffed by the black cast (apparently at the direction of Communist Party members who were growing suspicious of Wright). Angry that Wright had brought in a white director, the actors also considered the play indecent. The whole episode, ironically enough, finds Wright cast in the role of the "New Negro" he would use as the straw man in his blueprint for the next generation of African American modernists.

When Wright moved on to the Federal Writers' Project in New York, he became the central figure in a new constellation of young writers including Robert Hayden and others, when the League of American Writers had displaced the John Reed clubs to become more welcoming to writers on the left who were not communists—writers like Van Wyck Brooks. Once again, the stress upon American cultural nationalism coincided with a move away from a hard-core Marxist approach, and African American modernism grew, nourished by federal agencies that were led by people whose cultural orientation had been formed in the literary culture of the 1920s. (Floyd Dell himself, initially the top prospect to head the Writers' Project, actually served as advisory editor for the Federal Arts Project and wrote the summary report on the WPA as a whole.)[100]

It would appear, then, that the stress on specifically "American" cultural traditions of dissent, criticism, and social activism was the most consistent form of cultural politics opening a space for African American expression throughout the existences of *The Masses, The Liberator,* and *The New Masses.* What this implies is that more institutional, aesthetic, and ideological continuities exist than have so far been recognized between the Harlem Renaissance and later African American social realism, between Langston Hughes's "I, too, sing America" and Richard Wright's *Native Son.* To recognize these continuities is, at the same time, to recognize both the intimate relationship between American cultural nationalism and African American modernism, and the way that African American modernism demanded that the white left keep its vision closely in contact with "native" ground.

9

V. F. Calverton, *The Modern Quarterly,* and an Anthology

Closely related to *The Masses* and *The Liberator,* and perhaps initiated because the demise of *The Liberator* in 1922 left room in the market, V. F. Calverton's magazine, *The Modern Quarterly* (1923–40), also showed significant interest in the "Negro renaissance." According to Sidney Hook, *The Modern Quarterly* was one of the major expressions of "an independent American revolutionary Marxism," thus provoking virulent attacks in the 1930s from the Communist Party and its front organizations, when it was also one of the few journals in which Max Eastman could get published.[1] Until 1930 Calverton (born George Goetz in 1900) contributed regularly to *The New Masses,* and he also wrote for *The Nation.* In his own magazine, as a matter of policy, Calverton featured at least one piece by a black author in each issue, in a journal that usually included only eight or nine articles.

An admirer of people like Max Eastman, Floyd Dell, Van Wyck Brooks, Waldo Frank, Langston Hughes, and Claude McKay, Calverton ran the magazine roughly along the lines of Eastman's magazines; it took a more insistently ideological line in its literary criticism but was undoctrinaire enough to call down the wrath of the same people (Joseph Freeman and Michael Gold, for example) who began attacking Eastman in the late twenties and the thirties. Buckling under to pressure from the hard-line International Union of Revolutionary Writers, *The New Masses* went to the trouble of devoting almost an entire issue to attacking Calverton and his magazine.[2] Because of his focus on American conditions, Calverton was attuned to the relevance of Marxism to African Americans and vice versa; but, as Harold Cruse argues, Communist Party attacks on him prevented black Marxists from giving him the attention he deserved. Black writers, however, found a welcoming atmosphere in his pages; he allowed "more uncensored comment" than communist publications and a greater range of topics.[3]

In the opening number *The Modern Quarterly* set itself off against *The Nation* and *The New Republic,* calling those "liberal" rather than "radical" magazines; but *The Modern Quarterly* adhered to the same cultural nationalist and anti-"high" modernist line that characterized them.[4] The white contributors also are often familiar: Eastman, Dell, Dewey, and Herskovits, for example. Among black writers, between 1925 and 1929 the magazine published Abram L. Harris, Jr., Charles S. Johnson ("The Negro Migration" and "The New Negro"), W. E. B. Du Bois ("The Social Origins of American Negro Art"), Langston Hughes ("Listen Here Blues"), Alain Locke ("American Literary Tradition and the Negro"), Hubert Harrison, Clarence Cameron White ("Labor Motif in Negro Music"), Thomas Dabney, E. Franklin Frazier ("La Bourgeoisie Noire"), and George Schuyler. Nothing in any of these pieces exploited the white fixation on traditional black stereotypes, as the list of contributors alone would suggest—which is not to say that the editor himself was immune to unrecognized stereotypes in his own mind, as we will see.

Calverton placed advertisements in *The Messenger, Opportunity,* and *The Crisis,* in hopes of attracting a black readership; and both *Opportunity* and *The Crisis* advertised in *The Modern Quarterly* under the impression that its readership would be interested in the magazines that were promoting, as one *Opportunity* advertisement put it, "A New Negro Aesthetic." Using a practice typical of the period, the editors of *Opportunity, The Crisis,* and *The Modern Quarterly* also offered combined subscriptions at a reduced price, hoping to attract one another's audiences.

Calverton's interest in black writing (like the interest of Carl and Irita Van Doren, Ridgely Torrence, Robert Morss Lovett, Max Eastman, and so on) predated the Civic Club dinner of 1924 that is often credited with introducing white editors to black arts. In January 1924—almost immediately after the founding of his magazine—he contacted Charles S. Johnson, and solicited articles on Negro subjects for *The Modern Quarterly.* What he was looking for was a "frank and unapologetic discussion of subjects long tabooed."[5] While getting his own magazine off the ground Calverton also tried to strengthen his ties to black publications. At the end of September 1925 he asked to review *The New Negro* for *Opportunity,* and Johnson wrote to Locke for advice: "I had thought to ask some person like Zona Gale or Carl Van Doren [to review the book] or—someone who had already had a hand in the fostering of this school represented in the book, and at the same time commands attention."[6] Locke suggested letting Calverton do the review, and Johnson decided to get Van Doren to do one for a different publication.

As it turned out, Calverton also published his review of *The New Negro* in *The Nation,* where he stated: "This book marks an epoch in the hectic career of the Negro. . . . In undermining and annihilating the Negro myth it functions as a clarifying and signal contribution to contemporary thought."[7] He worked hard to draw attention to the book, inviting Locke to give a lecture entitled "The New Negro" at his home in Baltimore, which would be attended by twenty to thirty selected people.[8] Five days earlier Calverton had solicited an article from Locke on "the new literature growing up about and by the Negro," treating both white- and black-authored works.[9] Ultimately Locke contributed "American Literary Tradition and the Negro," a "survey" of American attitudes to the Negro as expressed in works of literature.[10] Meanwhile, Calverton kept stumping for *The New Negro:* "You see I am doing everything I can to boost this book of yours, and I do hope it will sell in no mean way."[11] He had both Charles S. Johnson and Howard Odum do reviews of the book for *The Modern Quarterly* (knowing pretty well what they would have to say about it) and suggested that Locke send a review copy to Odum for the *Journal of Social Forces.* He even told Locke to send copies to Havelock Ellis and Bertrand Russell—two of the intellectual celebrities of the age—"and write to me immediately, special delivery, so that I can know they have been dispatched. I shall take care of the rest" (Ellis was a friend of Calverton's, as well as an author whose work Locke had followed for some years).[12] Still Calverton was not done pushing the book; he wrote yet another article on it for *Current History.*[13] Locke liked the article but suspected it would get Calverton in trouble with the *Crisis* crowd. Calverton planned to "wear extra armour" for a lecture he was to give at the Sun Rise Club in Harlem on April 19, 1926.[14] Having made the "New Negro" cause his own, Calverton went on to lecture on the subject at Syracuse University in February 1926 and to spark the organization of a "racial cooperative group" there. He even asked Locke about the advisability and possibility of his getting a job teaching sociology or literature at Howard University.[15]

It is clear from his solicitations to Locke and Charles S. Johnson, as well as from the nature of the work carried in the magazine generally, that Calverton asked his contributors for "social" approaches to literature. *Modern Quarterly* essays by W. E. B. Du Bois and Alain Locke are worth a close look for the ways they fit Calverton's critical approach and his interests in black American literary tradition.

Du Bois's contribution, "The Social Origins of American Negro Art," explains the "social compulsion" behind the development of a distinct African American tradition in literature, which he predictably locates not in *formal* characteristics but rather in content. To Du Bois, a new American Negro "school" of art is inevitable, as he explains with a thoroughly pragmatistic rationale: "They may not bring anything particularly new in method, but the content of such an art contribution must always be new because as every individual differs from another so every group and set of group experiences differs, and the truth about them has something fundamentally new and different from anything else in the world."[16] Just as the social oppression of the Negro has to a large extent determined the nature of Negro arts to the present, concludes Du Bois, social conditions "are going to determine its future very largely." Either social oppression will continue, shutting out the light from the black writer-prophets, or the wall of oppression may be broken, "so that the very blaze of coming light may illuminate the former darkness and make the intricate path over which this group has come all the more thrilling for its shadows, turns and twists. The American who wants to serve the world has unusual opportunity here."[17] Du Bois's aesthetics do not match Calverton's, insofar as Du Bois does not recognize a transformation in aesthetic form as a necessary aspect of the development of a new literary tradition. Neither does Du Bois come anywhere near suggesting the development of a proletarian art; on the contrary, he thinks of artists as Old Testament or Romantic prophets. On the other hand, his emphasis on the close link between social conditions and the production of art, along with the corollary of the "Americanness" of black American art, fall very easily into the general critical orientation of *The Modern Quarterly*.

Alain Locke's "American Literary Tradition and the Negro" examines "the literary treatment of Negro life and character" as a record of the social history of the Negro in America.[18] Such an investigation, Locke believes, reveals "fundamental attitudes of the American mind," changing in seven major phases determined by social history: "a Colonial period attitude (1760–1820), a pre-Abolition period (1820–45), the Abolitionist period (1845–65), the Early Reconstruction period (1870–85), the Late Reconstruction Period (1885–95), the Industrial period (1895–1920), and the Contemporary period since 1920."[19] In each period, the figure of the Negro in American literature has dramatized two aspects of white psychology: "first, the white man's wish for self-justification, whether he be at any given time anti-Negro or pro-Negro, and, second, more subtly registered, an avoidance of the particular type that would raise an embarrassing question for the social conscience of the period."[20] Locke finds the image of the Negro in literature all the more revealing insofar as it is not deliberately propagandistic but is actually considered "accurate" by the white authors and audiences of any given period; it thus expresses an "unconscious social wish" responding to socioeconomic conditions.

Locke's explanation for the sudden "liberation" of Negro literary portraiture in the twenties must have pleased Calverton. The growth of literary realism played its role, as did the interest in "local color" and the "exotic tendencies of conscious aestheticism."[21] However, "the really basic factor in the sharp and astonishing break in the literary tradition and attitude toward the Negro came in the revolt against Puritanism. . . . The release which almost everyone had thought must come about through a change in moral evaluation, a reform of opinion, has actually and suddenly come about merely as a shift of interest, a revolution of taste. From it there looms the imminent possibility not only of a true literature of the Negro but of a Negro Literature as such."[22]

The contrasts between Locke's thinking and Du Bois's are revealing. Whereas Du Bois, the prophet-propagandist and moralist, looks for a moral conversion that will liberate black literature from its hidden and oppressed circumstances, Locke (also an ethicist as well as aesthetician and, not coincidentally, a homosexual) finds such liberation resulting instead from a revolution in aesthetic taste—that is, a transformation in structures of "feeling" encouraged by the revolt against "Puritan" repression of the sensual body. While recognizing that this development has led to a fascination for "the primitive and pagan and emotional aspects of Negro life and character," Locke remains hopeful that an independent literature of greater authenticity will emerge; for, in contrast to the sensationalistic fictions of paganism, "the work of Waldo Frank, Jean Toomer, Walter White, Rudolph Fisher, and DuBose Heyward promises greatly."[23]

Locke's list of authors is interesting today in that he differentiates between the white exploiters of exotic primitivism and such white authors as Frank and Heyward, whom more recent critics usually lump in with the white fans of the primitive Negro. Locke was not merely making concessions to his white audience; in black periodicals and letters to black friends, he regularly mentioned selected white novelists as important pioneers of and participants in the black literary movement. What differentiates Frank from other white novelists, presumably, is the greater social consciousness that informs his novel—it is, if nothing else, a direct attack upon the contradictions of Southern white racial mythology, which the novel links to economic oppression, the sexual unconscious, and white evangelical Christianity. Heyward, on the other hand, was an important precursor of the "folk school" of black fiction. Overall, Locke's critical methodology—though less hospitable to economic determinism—fits more closely with Calverton's critical and ideological orientation than does Du Bois's, as Locke's review in *Opportunity* of Calverton's book, *Sex Expression in Literature* (1927), would later show.[24]

Calverton's support of the "Negro renaissance" did not stop with his editorial decisions at *The Modern Quarterly* and his lecturing. He helped found the short-lived American Inter-Racial Association, intending to launch a more radical economic attack on American racial oppression than the NAACP or the Urban League.[25] Perhaps even more important, he compiled and edited one of the most significant anthologies of black literature ever published, in Henry Louis Gates's estimation: "Calverton's was the first attempt at black canon-formation to provide for the influence and presence of black vernacular literature in a major way."[26]

In compiling *An Anthology of American Negro Literature* (1929), Calverton expressed his own vision of the history and possibilities of African American literature, but he also solicited the advice and criticism of black authors such as Alain Locke and Walter White.[27] Calverton based his selections on his sense of the history of black literary forms, believing that this history constituted a distinctive African American expressive tradition.[28] At the same time, he thought this tradition constituted the most original contribution to a truly "American" literature:

The white man in America has continued, and in an inferior manner, a culture of European origin. He has not developed a culture that is definitely and unequivocally American. In respect of originality, then, the Negro is more important in the growth of American culture than the white man. . . . While the white man has gone to Europe for his models, and is seeking still a European approval of his artistic endeavors, the Negro in his art forms has never gone beyond America for his background and has never sought the acclaim of any culture other than his own. This is particularly true of those forms of Negro art that come directly from the people.[29]

Gates notes that "Calverton couched his argument in just that rhetoric of nationalism, of American exceptionalism, that had long been used to exclude, or anyway occlude, the contribution of the Negro. In an audacious reversal, it turns out that *only* the Negro is really American, the white man being a pale imitation of his European forebears."[30] By 1929, however, as we have seen, this reversal was no longer "audacious"; it informed much of the criticism of the American cultural nationalists when they concerned themselves with black arts.

Calverton did not regard what he called the "primitivism" of black folk forms as expressive of a racial essence or even an African cultural background. Rather, the folk forms were "a singular evolution of our American environment. In describing them as primitive, we do not mean that they are savage in origin, or that the instincts of savagery linger in them, but that they are untutored in form and unsophisticated in content."[31] Calverton was hardly a perceptive student of black folk arts, but neither can his views on black art be slotted neatly into the usual categories of white racism. In fact, he was quick to point out the long history of black culture and literature, noting the extensive if neglected history of African civilizations such as Songhay and Mali and great universities such as that in Timbuktu. African art is "rigid," less "exuberant," and more classically disciplined than American Negro art—in short, more the product of a traditional culture than of a modernist "New World."[32] On the other hand, free of age-old traditions and conventions, the American Negro created art without thought of what was "Art" and what was not; "he" was thus able to create art from his "soul," art springing from the life of "the people," "an artless art," "the most genuine art of the world." This art stands in stark contrast to white American art as well as to African art. "The exuberance of sentiment, the spirited denial of discipline, and the contempt for the conventional, that are so conspicuous in the art of the American Negro, are direct outgrowths of the nature of his life in this country."[33] A variety of romantic primitivism invests Calverton's comments, combined with his cultural nationalism; but the terms of his praise are virtually identical in these particular respects to the terms he used in characterizing the work of his great poetic hero, Walt Whitman—another New World artist, in the fullest sense, according to Calverton. Whitman, however, was a lonely voice, hardly a true proletarian or folk poet; in vain had he longed to be the voice of "the people." The Negro folk poets enjoyed advantages he never had. By extension, African American poets to come, building on the work of their precursors rather than upon feeble "white" models (as Calverton felt most poets in the literary tradition had so far done), would be the harbingers of a real American literature.

In developing his anthology, Calverton stayed in close touch with Locke, who encouraged the project and agreed to contribute, if Calverton would in turn contribute to a volume Locke was thinking of publishing in Europe about "the movement."[34] It was a suggestion from Locke that led Calverton to include a section in his anthology on "artificial blues" by Langston Hughes and other young poets, in addition to the blues and labor songs he had already planned to include. Calverton also asked for Locke's advice on which plays to use in the volume.[35] Calverton had been a fan of Hughes's blues since early 1926, when he had invited the poet to his home for a reading before the *Modern Quarterly* group; and he published "Listen Here Blues" in the magazine. Hughes was, of course, just the sort of poet Calverton would have been looking for—writing alternately in a Midwestern free-verse style and in folk forms, often advancing a political message (implicit when not explicit), and flouting "bourgeois" and "Puritan" attitudes to sex and social convention. Calverton stayed in touch with Hughes for years, continuing to review his work, soliciting reviews from him, and inviting him to visit. In 1929, newly an editor for the Macauley Company, Calverton even tried to lure Hughes away from Knopf, perhaps suspecting that the Knopfs' distaste for proletarian writing was making Hughes restless.[36]

Representative of the breadth of Calverton's interest in black writing is his relationship with Hughes's chief antagonist, George Schuyler.[37] After soliciting work from the then-socialist satirist, who particularly enjoyed ridiculing notions of radical "racial" or cultural differences between black and white Americans, he published Schuyler's "Emancipated Woman and the Negro" in the fall 1929 *Modern Quarterly.* Schuyler also published a review of the book *Black Genesis* and, in 1934, the article "When Black Weds White."[38] Calverton encouraged Schuyler to write his first book, *Black No More* (1931)—surely the most iconoclastic (not to mention hilarious) product of the Harlem Renaissance—and was instrumental in getting the book published by the Macauley Company.[39] The important point to notice here is that Calverton was actively promoting an author, and a novel, that attacked with devastating satire the stereotypes of African Americans as primitives or as exotic "pagans" in the urban jungles of America, fundamentally different in nature or nurture from white Americans. The revolt against "Puritanism," insofar as the latter is perceived as one aspect of the "colonial complex" (to borrow Calverton's term) that also fosters racism, does not shade seamlessly or inevitably into a racialist vision of Negroes as exotic primitives; and even when it does, it does not necessarily entail a strong resistance to other types of black fiction. No doubt Calverton was largely responsible for Macauley's hiring of Wallace Thurman for an editorial position at the firm.

Calverton's role in Melvin Tolson's career was also noteworthy, and reveals the continuities between Harlem Renaissance networks and the next generation. (The strongest influences on Tolson's early poetry were Hughes and Schuyler, and his M. A. thesis, written in the 1930s, was entitled "The Harlem Group of Negro Writers.") In the 1930s Tolson came across a copy of *The Modern Quarterly* that impressed him and informed him that the editor had published a book of Negro poetry. Tolson sent Calverton some poems, and they soon became friends. In fact, "throughout his life, Tolson referred to Calverton as 'the best friend I ever had.'"[40] When visiting New York, Tolson even had a key to Calverton's home. Calverton published several of Tolson's poems in *Modern Monthly* in 1937, his first appearance except for one poem published in a Dillard University arts magazine.[41] Subsequently, in a column for *Current History* Calverton introduced him to a wider audience as a poet "who in his *Harlem Gallery* is trying to do for the Negro what Edgar Lee Masters did for the middlewest white folk over two decades ago."[42] Indeed, Tolson himself said Masters, Sandburg, Frost, and Robinson had been the inspirations that turned him, in 1932, away from writing Anglo-Saxon sonnets in the form of a "dead classicism."[43]

Calverton's treatment of black literature in his most significant book

of criticism, *The Liberation of American Literature,* reveals even more per-
suasively than his anthology his view of the importance of African American culture to the national identity as a whole. The most important
development in modern American literature, for Calverton, was the
long-needed liberation from a "colonial" mentality; the next needed
development, in his view, was a break from "petty bourgeois individualism" into a revolutionary "proletarian ideology."[44] This final liberation
had been approached by *The Masses,* but Eastman, Dell, and company
had not matched their revolutionary ideology with a suitable validation
of proletarian *art;* moreover, they had failed to reach beyond a bourgeois audience of intellectuals. Calverton's culture-heroes from what we
now call the American canon were Whitman, Mark Twain, and Theodore Dreiser. He applauded the "rediscovery of America" in the first
two decades of the twentieth century, pioneered by writers from outside
the orbit of New England—particularly Midwestern muckrakers, critical realists, and free-versifiers. By the mid-teens, the nation finally had
a poetry in the language of the American people, "rooted in the American soil,"[45] and this "native" thrust of the literature survived into the
twenties undiminished.

Along with the literary movement, Calverton emphasizes, came a
serious study of American folklore; John A. Lomax first hunted up
cowboy songs and ballads (which "belong as definitely and natively to
American literature" as the old English ballads belong to English literature) before turning to other folk traditions, and these works became
the basis for more "self-consciously" artistic treatment. Similarly,
interest in Native American songs and tales grew. "But more important
than either the Indian or the cowboy literature which has been recov-
ered, and added to the native stock of our tradition, is the growth of
Negro literature which has made a far greater contribution to American
culture. The contributions of the Negro to American culture are as
indigenous to our soil as the legendary cowboy or gold-seeking frontiersman. In fact, I think it can be said without exaggeration, that they
constitute a large part of whatever claim America can make to originality in its cultural history."[46] Black folklore presents a rich resource
for the development of an authentic as well as revolutionary American
cultural tradition.

Calverton tended toward an emerging political view of black intellectuals as the vanguard of proletarian revolution—even when he viewed
black people as more spontaneous, joyous, and rhythmic, than the

repressed "Nordics." For Calverton, capitalism and the repression of sexuality were intimately intertwined, and black folk culture had particular significance because of its inherent subversion of these deep structural afflictions of the bourgeois psyche and society. Predictably, however, Calverton found that, like white American cultural nationalists, the "New Negro" writers failed to be sufficiently suffused with class consciousness; their work, with a few exceptions like works of the thirties by Langston Hughes and Eugene Gordon, did not go "beyond" a bourgeois "racial" emphasis. For black as for white writers, then, cultural nationalism—crucial as it was to the "liberation of American literature"—had so far failed to develop into the needed ideology of scientific socialism. Calverton could be crude in his sweeping applications of "vulgar Marxism" to literary history, but his brand of Marxism always served a cultural nationalist vision. That vision informed his promotion of a distinctive African American literary tradition, socialism, and racial equality.

10

Mediating Race and Nation: The Cultural Politics of *The Messenger*

American cultural nationalism took a very different form in the pages of *The Messenger* from the form it took in *The Crisis* and *Opportunity*. As we have seen, the cultural criticism of *The Crisis* revolved around a political and social indictment of white America on the grounds of "American ideals," served by the propaganda of art; and *Opportunity* emphasized cultural self-revelation as such, the aesthetics of experience, and "cultural racialism" (a "harder" form of cultural pluralism than that of *The Crisis*). *The Messenger*, on the other hand, adopted a stridently iconoclastic approach, more often than not ridiculing the notion that African American culture was distinctly different from European American culture and stressing the "mulatto" character of U.S. culture. (Far more than the other two African American monthlies, however, *The Messenger* relied almost exclusively upon black—and male—contributors.) It addressed issues of racial and cultural amalgamation more boldly than any other publication, in provocative and often satirical fashion, with as yet unexamined consequences for understanding the "racial" culture of the United States. One gleans from *The Messenger* the notion that cultural similarities between black and white Americans are hidden by a shared racial discourse, a culturally specific "American" (that is, U.S.) phenomenon sustaining the widely shared faith in essential racial differences. Moreover, at the heart of the rituals of this faith one finds an ironic deconstruction of it, a flirting with the color line that hides while enacting the "miscegenation" continually going on beneath the cover of racial reasoning.

Theodore Kornweibel has argued that *The Messenger* was never fully committed to the Harlem Renaissance and lacked a coherent editorial attitude toward the movement. The magazine's editorial columns "never embraced the cultural movement or attempted to spell out a coherent philosophy for it. What philosophy did appear was incidental, the product of columnists and reviewers, chiefly drama critic Theophilus Lewis."[1] However, while Kornweibel is right in saying that the magazine did not present a coherent philosophy, *The Messenger* did in fact present a more united front on the issue of racial and national identity than Kornweibel suggests. In fact, Lewis' interest in the development of a black aesthetic went counter to the general drift of the magazine's cultural politics, which stressed that the U.S. was or would become a "mulatto" nation. Despite *The Messenger*'s eclecticism, other than Lewis the editors most concerned with cultural history and aesthetics did share similar views about the relationship between "white" and "black" cultural identity in the United States, and these views had definite ramifications for their attitude toward efforts to develop a black aesthetic in literature and the fine arts. Moreover, their views of the shared cultural identity of black and white America fit the magazine's specifically North American socialist political vision.

Beginnings: Socialism, Race, and U.S. Culture

The main force behind the magazine in its earliest years, A. Philip Randolph, had a long-standing interest in literature; according to Arna Bontemps, he provided the "original literary impulse of the magazine."[2] Randolph was no black cultural nationalist. He disapproved of blues and jazz, preferring Western classical music, and his favorite author was the Bard of Avon. Indeed, Randolph (a Southerner by birth) picked up his arresting "Oxford-style" English accent learning to recite Shakespeare with the help of a tutor before World War I, when he performed Shakespearean roles in amateur theater in Harlem. Some of his first acting experience along these lines was with the drama club at the Salem Methodist Church, where Countee Cullen's father was minister and where he met Theophilus Lewis, later the drama critic for *The Messenger*. Subsequently, Randolph and his wife, Lucille, organized a Harlem-based amateur troupe known as Ye Friends of Shakespeare.[3]

Although he often rightly stressed the importance of autonomy for black groups involved in the movement for justice, Randolph conceived of the racial struggle within the context of "an indigenous movement for social and economic change"—which suggests the kinship between *The Messenger* and the other socialist journals I have discussed.[4] Both the "indigenous" and the ultimately antiracialist aspects of Randolph's vision help account for the virulence of *The Messenger*'s attack on Marcus Garvey and led to W. A. Domingo's withdrawal from the editorial staff.[5] Randolph and others at the magazine viewed the programs of such West Indian–led groups as the UNIA and the communist, black nationalist African Blood Brotherhood (Garvey's bitter opponent) as foreign to the realities of black life in the United States.[6] *The Messenger* attributed racial prejudice to capitalism, insisted on the "Americanness" of African Americans, and continually called for interracial worker solidarity, even when it promoted black control of black groups as a tactical necessity. A. Philip Randolph opposed affiliation of American socialists with the Third International in Moscow, believing they should resist direction from outside the United States—in part, it would seem, because of the specific conflict between Marxist ideology and American racial reality. His struggle on this point during the 1920s developed into the virulent anticommunism that typified the rest of his career.[7] But if the United States was to be the site of a new form of "indigenous" socialism, it also, *The Messenger* often suggested, would give birth to a new people and a "mulatto" national culture. Race pride did not conflict with militant integrationism or even assimilationism—it seems, overall, to have been considered essential to the achievement of true integration. Thus J. A. Rogers, a chief contributor and one of the most persevering historians of global black achievement, was at the same time an avowed proponent of American "amalgamation."

Like Randolph, Chandler Owen, co-founder of *The Messenger,* did not consider African American cultural nationalism to have much purchase on the social situation of black America. Owen clearly advocated integration in every sense. He regarded the cabaret, for example, as a useful social institution because, more effectively than any other, it was breaking down the color line: black and white common people could be found together there, lured by the two basic instincts of hunger and sex. It was thus "one of the most democratic institutions in America," though some Negro leaders were joining with white "committees of Fourteen" to segregate the clubs or close them down.[8] A similar point was later made by two other *Messenger* regulars, in George Schuyler's *Black No More* and in J. A. Rogers' contribution to *The New Negro,* "Jazz at Home."[9]

Black America in the Melting Pot

The involvement of *The Messenger* with the literary Harlem Renaissance really began after George Schuyler joined the magazine in 1922. Until then, the magazine criticized *The Crisis* and Du Bois, for example, on the basis of their over-emphasis upon the arts and "culture," and what creative work *The Messenger* published unambiguously served its founders' social and economic message.[10] But by late 1922 Chandler Owen was spending most of his time on the road soliciting advertising from black businesses (which helps account for the dramatic shift in the tone of the magazine's socioeconomic criticism), and Randolph needed someone to help him get the magazine out, so he turned to the young iconoclast who had been attending his and Owen's Friends of Negro Freedom meetings.[11] Soon Schuyler was effectively the managing editor, particularly after Owen moved to Chicago in 1923. When Randolph's involvement in the Brotherhood of Sleeping Car Porters began taking up more and more of his time, Schuyler became the main force in keeping the magazine going.[12] Thus the very period in which the magazine was controlled by an editor most vociferously opposed to black cultural nationalism, and in which the magazine had become most "middle class," was the period when its readership was most black.[13] Also because of Schuyler's role, the magazine during this period bears an interesting if seemingly self-contradictory relationship to *The Modern Quarterly* on the one hand and *American Mercury* on the other— two extremely different magazines in which Schuyler and a number of his favorite contributors (particularly J. A. Rogers and Eugene Gordon) published many essays.

The period of Schuyler's greatest influence was from 1923 to 1926, at which time he took a leave of absence to tour the South, and from early 1927 to July 1928, when the magazine folded. The latter span was the period during which Schuyler published such satires as "The Negro-Art Hokum" and "Blessed Are the Sons of Ham" in *The Nation,* "Southern Snapshots" in *The New Masses,* several pieces in *American Mercury,* and "The Negro's Greatest Gift to America" in *Ebony and Topaz,* the collection edited by Charles S. Johnson. (The gift: "simply that of being present here, which made white people assume a superiority unknown in Europe.")[14] Schuyler adhered to a particularly provoking and rather paradoxical form of American cultural nationalism, closely related to that of *American Mercury*. On the one hand he insisted on the mutual cultural identity of "so-called" (as he always emphasized) Negro and Caucasian Americans. On the other, he stressed the grim significance (and insanity) of that culture's most characteristic if self-destructive discourse: the discourse of "race." Unquestioned faith in this discourse was one of the distinctive cultural attributes all Americans seemed to share, despite pervasive evidence of its stupidity. Yet Schuyler's thinking on this issue has logical consequences he repressed: if the "fiction" of racial difference is so embedded in the way "white" and "black" Americans perceive each other and themselves, is it not productive of cultural difference—cultural difference that is at one and the same time distinctively "American" and, *because it is "American,"* racially marked? This effect, indeed, is nowhere more evident than in Schuyler's own blackly humorous fiction.

In 1923 Schuyler had brought on board his friend J. A. Rogers, who wrote on black history, contemporary events, and international affairs. A favorite topic of both Schuyler and Rogers was the "mixing" of the "races" in America, and this became a recurrent theme for the duration of *The Messenger*'s existence. Rogers, for example, argued that the United States was becoming less "Anglo-Saxon" over time, and that the "Anglo-Saxon-ites" were not true "Americans": "There is another kind of 100 per cent Americanism, whose ideals, it seems, would be to take the composition of this nation (be it good or bad) as an inescapable fact, and after a process of selection of the best qualities in other nations, absorb those qualities, evolving in the course of time an individuality of its own."[15] An advocate for a thoroughgoing melting pot, Rogers, author of such books as *Nature Knows No Color Line*, liked to emphasize the extent of passing and "miscegenation" in the United States.

In a piece entitled "Is Black Ever White?" Rogers completely rejected the racial discourse initiated by white racists for their own profit and now shared by both white and black Americans. A supposedly "black" man like Walter White should be called white, according to his physical appearance: "One of the first things towards 'solving' this so-called race problem is to learn to call things by their right name." Refusing to accept the racial discourse foisted upon all Americans by white racists, he argued that "right here is the fountain-head of the so-called color line."[16] Instead of an artificial "racial" dualism of "whites" and "blacks," wrote Rogers, "I see but one American people, speaking a common language, and at bottom having a common ideal, shading in color by imperceptible degrees from white to black, or black to white, as you will"—the difference is "of little moment."[17]

Similarly, Schuyler vehemently rejected the notion that there were major cultural or racial differences between so-called white and black Americans. His early work for *The Messenger* included most importantly a series of articles on "Hobohemia" and the transracial urban underclass. Among the homeless one found little racial discrimination—even among the well-read and well-educated. Racial differences seemed minimal among the "hobos," who had their own distinctive, nonracial culture and vocabulary that were indigenously "American"—free of much of the hypocrisy that characterized the bourgeoisie and working classes of both black and white Americans. Schuyler constantly notes that two-thirds of "so-called Negroes" are partly white, that white men pursue black women while black men prefer "yellow" women and "Nordic" blondes: it is a fact of nature, in Schuyler's view, that "unlike people attract each other."[18] Schuyler deliberately stressed such mutual attraction, along with the cultural similarities of "black" and "white" Americans, to sharpen his satirical attack upon American racism. This was an essential weapon in his rhetorical repertoire, which he first developed in his monthly column, "Shafts and Darts"—in Langston Hughes's view, the most valuable feature of the magazine.[19]

Like Schuyler and Rogers, Thomas Kirksey argued in a 1926 article that "amalgamation" is inevitable; the "races" are bound to merge—have, in fact, already merged to a great extent—so whites should stop being contemptuous of their brothers and sisters. The New World, in any case, is not a "Nordic" environment, and there are few differences between black and white Americans. Finally, history shows that amalgamation is "natural."[20] Looking back over world history at the emergence of great peoples and nations of the past, many contributors to and readers of *The Messenger* apparently concluded that the United States was at an early stage of development toward a new racial identity such as had never been seen before.

In late 1926 and 1927, about the same time that W. E. B. Du Bois was publishing the results of his survey "The Negro in Art: How Shall He Be Portrayed?," *The Messenger* ran a poll (no doubt drafted by Schuyler) entitled "Group Tactics and Ideals" that questioned whether race consciousness helped or hindered the black struggle for equality. The questionnaire consists of a series of leading questions, in this respect much like Du Bois's in *The Crisis*, though with a very different intent that suggests the differences between the journals' general cultural politics:

1) Is the development of Negro social consciousness (a definite group psychology, stressing and laudation of things Negro) compatible with the ideal of Americanism (Nationalism) as expressed in the struggle of the Aframericans for social and industrial equality with all other citizens?

2) Will this ideal of equal rights and privileges be realized within the next century?

3) If and when this ideal is realized, will it or will it not result in the disappearance of the Negro population through amalgamation?

4) If the struggle for the attainment of full citizenship rights and privileges, including industrial equality, is to result in the disappearance of the Negro through amalgamation, do you consider the present efforts to inculcate and develop a race consciousness to be futile and confusing?

5) Do you consider complete amalgamation of the whites and blacks necessary to a solution of our problem?

6) Do you desire to see the Aframerican group maintain its identity and the trend toward amalgamation cease?

7) Can a minority group like the Aframericans maintain separate identity and group consciousness, obtain industrial and social equality with the citizens of the majority group, and mingle freely with them?

8) Do you or do you not believe in segregation, and if so, in what form?[21]

The range of responses to this questionnaire is fascinating even today. A surprising number questioned the premises of Negro "race consciousness," noting that many "Negroes" were mostly white—certainly much more so than African, and that to accept the "Negro" designation was to accept the racist discourse of whites (a position that would fit the socialist line that racialism was a capitalist invention to foster the exploitation of workers). However, most respondents believed that "group" consciousness and effort were necessary as long as whites oppressed blacks on the basis of "race."[22]

Eugene Gordon, a *Boston Post* staff member who had been recruited by Schuyler to do monthly commentary for *The Messenger* on "the best editorials appearing in the Negro press," replied that he believed "the doctrine of race consciousness to be harmful to the American Negro." "Amalgamation" was both inevitable and desirable. He completely rejected "race consciousness," arguing that complete "Americanization"—realization of the democratic ideals of liberty and justice for all—could come only with the merging of the races. The Negro masses should be taught *national* rather than *racial* consciousness: "They are no longer more to Africa, and will never again be more to Africa, than are their white compatriots to Caucasia."[23] A different position was taken by the next respondent, Floyd J. Calvin, the Eastern district manager of the *Pittsburgh Courier* (for which Schuyler was already writing). He was neither for nor against amalgamation, but he did not see it as likely to happen on a large scale or as realistically necessary for the achievement of equality. Moreover, Calvin wrote, race consciousness was not at odds with "Americanism."[24]

Most respondents believed amalgamation would occur sooner or later, at the very least as a result of growing equality—even if they stressed that race consciousness was a present necessity. Robert Bagnall of the NAACP even argued that "the more pride [one] has in his race, the greater the probability of amalgamation," a position with which J. A. Rogers would probably agree. "As no minority group in history," he continued, "has ever attained a position of equality and remained separate from the majority group, I do not believe that this is possible for the Aframerican." Nonetheless, for the time being race consciousness was important for mass action.[25] J. A. Rogers felt that if "Americanism" ever became the "dignified homogeneous thing" it ought to be, rather than synonymous with "white Americanism," then stress upon racial consciousness would not be compatible with it; but at present "America" was a white man's country. Ultimately, Rogers noted, amalgamation was inevitable and not to be regretted.[26]

Similarly, N. B. Young, responding for the faculty of Lincoln University in Jefferson City, Missouri, wrote that they had come to a consensus that amalgamation was inevitable and necessary to full equality, but racial solidarity and self-segregation were currently needed. Amalgamation should be a blending of *both* races, culturally and biologically, so race consciousness would help ensure that some Negro traits entered into the formation of the new group. Thomas Kirksey, sometime *Mes-*

senger contributor and a Chicago lawyer, believed the solution to social inequality on the basis of race would come about only with amalgamation, which he considered, predictably, both natural and inevitable. "Raceless" (racially "mixed") people, he noted, were sought after by whites and blacks alike, particularly by the blacks who were the loudest agitators for race consciousness. Harold Simmelkjaer, a clerk in the New York Supreme Court, also considered amalgamation inevitable and desirable, but he did not see any contradiction between race consciousness and Americanism. And C. H. Douglas of Macon, Georgia, a bank president, felt race consciousness was needed to defend the rights of African Americans but should not be overstressed, because "we are all Americans"; amalgamation, moreover, was eventually bound to occur and was the quickest way to achieve equality. Only William M. McDonald, president of a Fort Worth bank, came out strongly against amalgamation, holding forth for segregation but equality.[27] However unrepresentative of bourgeois black thinking during the Harlem Renaissance the responses to *The Messenger*'s survey may be, they suggest an important ideological undercurrent during the period that has been largely ignored in subsequent criticism, even in commentary on *The Messenger* itself.

This undercurrent was, however, notably countered by one of *The Messenger*'s own most astute contributors, Theophilus Lewis, in his theater column. After commenting on a production of Willis Richardson's play *Compromise,* Lewis indulged in a brief essay about the advisability of legalizing interracial marriage so that white men could be forced to marry black women who became pregnant by them—a line the NAACP happened to be pushing at the time. Lewis emphatically did not want interracial sexual relations, and particularly interracial marriage, to become as acceptable as intraracial sex and marriage. Free interracial marriage would be disastrous for the Negro people, for "if able Negro women had a fair chance to become the wives of substantial white men instead of only their paramours considerable numbers of them would seek unions across the line, impelled by the cosmic urge . . . to secure well placed fathers for their children." Black men would thus be robbed of the "counsel and inspiration" intelligent black women provide in a marriage. But Lewis went further, anchoring his position in an explicitly eugenicist and racialist rationale that went against the antiracialist reasoning (reliant in part upon Boasian anthropology) that generally informed *The Messenger:*

Furthermore, the loss of able mothers would cause a falling off in the average quality of pure bred Negro children. Nor would the race gain anything from the infusion of Caucasian blood in the colored children intelligent Negro women bore their white husbands; for the white race the world over is losing vitality and petering out while the African peoples, having lain fallow a thousand years, are showing signs of resurgent energy. It follows that the way of wisdom lies in not only preserving the present order which offers straight women no inducement to mate outside the race but to begin now to build up protective sentiment against the day when white people will want to let down the bars. . . . I shall drive a stake in the ground here and watch how many years it takes Dean Pickens, J. A. Rogers and the cohorts of the N.A.A.C.P. to reach this point.[28]

Lewis' black cultural nationalism here is linked to a more overtly patriarchal racial nationalism stressing biological "purity" and racial "ownership" of women and assuming the existence of cycles of racial destiny. It may be significant that this column was published while George Schuyler was on leave. In any case, it patently opposes the usual position of *The Messenger* on the issue of racial separatism. While at odds with the ultimate hopes of writers such as Schuyler and Rogers, Lewis' reasoning assumes the truth of their belief that amalgamation in the United States would be inevitable but for segregationist laws and mores. The very intensity of his fear on this subject indicates how intimate the vision of amalgamation is to racial nationalism, and helps highlight the psychic structure of attraction/repulsion in American racial reasoning.

Another issue brought up in *The Messenger* was that of what term for themselves Americans of (at least partially) African descent should adopt, given the reality of the caste system. In "What Are We?", George S. Grant recommended the term "Black Americans" as filling "a long felt want": "The argument for it begins with the fundamental assertion that we are not Negroes (niggers) or colored people (culled fellahs) but Americans; if it is necessary to distinguish us from the white Americans, then we are BLACK AMERICANS; not all of us are black, not all of white people are white, but 'black' and 'white' are used here to classify rather than to describe." Grant developed his position on strictly strategic grounds, with regard to the rhetoric of national idealism: "As the whole machinery of education and publicity in the United States is designed and operated to build up respect and romantic idealism around the word 'American,' by merely including that term in our

group name, we inevitably appropriate the effect of that propaganda."
On the other hand, by adopting the term "black" as a "logical mark"
distinguishing the group from "white" Americans, "we endow both it
and ourselves with a dignity" that would combat notions of white superiority.[29] Effectively, Grant's logic comports with the idea that race pride
is a necessary tool in the battle against American racism, even though
it must coexist with an ironic understanding that "race" is a social fiction
foisted on the world by white capitalist civilization. This, indeed, is a
position shared by George Schuyler and J. A. Rogers.

For example, in his review of Du Bois's *The Gift of Black Folk*—at the
very time he was ridiculing the notion of major cultural differences
between black and white Americans—Schuyler hailed the book as a
useful weapon against the Negro "inferiority complex": "I have always
felt that a knowledge of the history and achievements of the Negro in
America and elsewhere would do much to dispel [the] illusion of inferiority."[30] As Du Bois's book demonstrated, the Negro had been the most
important factor in the making of the United States; every American
Negro should know this and take pride in it. But such knowledge would
not, in Schuyler's view, lead to any belief in the distinctiveness of black
culture. The notion of the "peculiarity" of African American culture
seems always to have connoted "racial" inferiority for Schuyler, despite
the fact that his own fiction suggested a preference for the "warmth"
and "spontaneity" of black folks. As salutary as his satire was, Schuyler's
chief fault lay in his tendency to attack any suggestion of cultural difference between black and white Americans, and particularly any identification of African with African American cultural identity, as racist exoticism.

Clearly this point of view distinguished Schuyler from most of the
canonical Harlem Renaissance writers, whose efforts to develop a black
aesthetic he regarded as submission to the racialist absurdities of white
supremacy. It is therefore not surprising that, unlike some of the other
authors of his generation, Schuyler was particularly fond of Jessie
Fauset's fiction. In an admiring 1924 review of *There Is Confusion* he
praised the portrayal of the "best" Negroes, people of whom whites
know nothing and who are "the inspiration of the rising generation."
In tune with Fauset's own thematic focus (and that of *The Crisis*) he
stressed the "Americanism" of the black middle classes and the female
point of view: "I believe this is the first novel, not obviously propaganda,
by an American Negro woman about American Negroes (who are more

truly American than the loud mouthed 'Nordics' and Kluxers who must try the patience of the gods with their ignorant gibberish)."[31] Unfortunately, as Schuyler and J. A. Rogers saw it, too few people were writing realistic fiction about the "best" Negroes, for publishers were responding to a white demand for the sensational and exotic.[32] In a review of *Nigger Heaven*, Rogers did not blame Van Vechten or his publishers for coming out with the novel, for they were merely responding to public demand: "If so-called Negroes" want "the more respectable" side of life presented, they must do it themselves or support those who do—"Until this is done, I say, it serves us right." After all, both Gertrude Sanborn's *Veiled Aristocrats* and Fauset's *There Is Confusion* had suffered very poor sales.[33]

In his January 1926 "Shafts and Darts" column (coinciding with Du Bois's attack on Van Vechten and his essay "Criteria of Negro Art"), Schuyler offered facetious counsel to aspiring New Negro writers. Come to New York and join a Young Writers' Guild, he advised, to meet Negro intellectuals who belong to the Civic Club or the Community Church and associate with white writers. "Success depends, however, on the ability of the striving writer to do the Charleston, sing the spirituals, and chatter amiably with the abandon supposed to be characteristic of members of a race with a primitive background."[34] Soon white writers or editors will ask for a manuscript, which must display "true Negro psychology." "Such matter should always without exception be bizarre, fantastical and outlandish, with a suggestion of the jungle, the plantation or the slum. Otherwise it will not be *Negro* literature, and hence not acceptable. The predominant characteristic of the writing offered should be naiveté, as befits simple children just a century or two removed from the so-called uncivilized expanses of the Dark Continent."[35] Yet, contrary to the assertions of his satire, Schuyler was having little trouble, apparently, placing his own work in the chief "white" journals connected to the Negro literary movement, and, as we have seen, he was pressed by V. F. Calverton (who strongly supported the idea of a "Negro aesthetic") to write the novel that became *Black No More*.[36] Regardless of the actual contradictions to his point, Schuyler's sarcasm calls in question not only the alleged insistence upon the primitive and exotic, but the ahistorical notions of Africa that ignore its ancient civilizations; Schuyler also, however, rejected the supposed "Africanism" of the New Negro: "If the mistake is made of presenting the American Negro as a product of machine civilization, just like other people in the same environment, an immediate rejection slip can be expected."[37] Along the same lines, Schuyler's "Ballad of Negro Artists" in the August 1926 issue satirized the foisting of "New Negro Art" upon a gullible public, cashing in on so-called racial differences; and "The Curse of My Aching Heart," a limerick by "Carl Von Vickton," lampooned Van Vechten for boosting New Negro trash.[38]

At least on this subject Theophilus Lewis apparently agreed with Schuyler and Rogers. Emphasis on black primitivism was a white capitalist trick that must be countered by black capital development and the founding of new publishing concerns. In a review of Eric Walrond's *Tropic Death* that panned the book for its exploitation of "paganism" and the exotic, Lewis suggested a strategy for building up an independent publishing industry. Moneyed blacks should start a publishing house to sell cheap "trash" books—mysteries, "sex books," crime novels, and so on, which sold best in the American mass market—to create a large Negro audience for fiction, then branch off into "better literature" so that black authors would not be so dependent on white publishers, who in turn depended on white audiences.[39] The fact that white editors and publishers remained interested in the work of authors such as George Schuyler and Jessie Fauset (whose novels, like Walrond's and Toomer's, were published by Boni & Liveright!) apparently did not register with Lewis. Yet only a few weeks later he would be praising Langston Hughes's much-maligned *Fine Clothes to the Jew* (published by Knopf), which many black critics considered a prime example of Van Vechten's baneful influence: "Instead of the passion, sensuousness and wild music which throbbed from his first poems the later blues exhale the ascetic delicacy one finds in the lyrics of Thomas Hardy and A. E. Housman."[40] *These* blues, the review's title argued, were admirably "refined."

On the complicated issue of the "low" versus the "high" and "white" versus "black" interpretations of African American culture, James Ivy— later an editor of *The Crisis*—tried for a more balanced approach than Lewis or Schuyler. "All able sympathetic novels about the lower class Negro," he suggests in a fawning review of Julia Peterkin's *Black April,* "are written by whites, while those of the middle and upper classes are written by Negroes with a greater talent for sociology than literature."[41] This division of labor will continue for some time, he feels, because whites either do not know anything about "intelligent Negroes" or have ingrained in them the idea that there is no such thing. Black authors, on the other hand, suffer from an inferiority complex and a fear of whites' stereotypes which cause them to write only of the elite. What Ivy would like to see, it seems, is a rapprochement between the two groups, paralleled by a maturation of the interracial audience for fiction about black life. Again, the recognition of racial constraints in contemporary American culture here *coincides* with an assimilationist and even amalgamationist vision of the future. In his review of E. C. L. Adams' *Congaree Sketches,* Ivy calls Paul Green's introduction for the volume "the best preface to any book by or about Negroes" because it argues that whites and blacks have assimilated a mutual tradition and practice: "'Black and white are inextricably mingled in blood and bone and intention.'"[42] The destiny of the Negro, Ivy agrees with Green, is the destiny of the United States. Yet he finds Green overly optimistic in believing that whites are waking up to this fact, the counterevidence being their taste for portrayals of only "lower-class" black characters.

Ivy points out a disturbing aspect of the context in which whites and blacks encounter representations of African Americans. However culturally similar they may be (class and region being more significant cultural influences than race, in *The Messenger*'s general view), one aspect of their common culture is their deep-seated racialist ideology, the chasm across which they fail to see each other for what they truly are— Americans. On the one hand, Ivy argues, black readers can find *only* the stereotypical in white representations of blackness because of their assumptions about white subjectivity and perception. This suspiciousness—however well founded—hampers both self-recognition and interracial dialogue, not to mention the development of black art. On the other hand, a question remains about just what the white audience is seeing in even the most "realistic" representations of lower-class black life if these are the only representations they can recognize. They seem to be taking comfort in the distance these portrayals reinforce between themselves and African Americans as a whole. *Messenger* critics like Ivy and Schuyler would challenge this distance by forcing recognition, for example, of the class- and region-based differences that cut across race. Fiction of middle-class black life is particularly significant because it gets the middle-class white audience "where they live" and undermines their assumptions of racial difference/superiority.

Even when conventional differences between the races were affirmed in *The Messenger*—black "warmth" versus white "coldness," for example—their "American" mutuality and tendency to merge was emphasized, although that very tendency might precipitate the brutal

rituals of racial exorcism as whites sought to repress their own desire
for the merging, a desire psychologically interwoven with fear of racial
"dispossession" and extinction. Thus Robert W. Bagnall's rave review of
Waldo Frank's *Holiday:*

> It paints with stark colors the bitter, barren brutality of the white world
> in a Southern small town, its barren monotony, its sordid hidden fear
> that the colorful, warm life of the Negro may dominate it. Here is
> shown for the first time in a white novel the contempt as well as the
> hatred felt by the Negro for the white, and here you have a white virgin
> with arid passion drawn irresistibly to throw herself into the arms of a
> Negro, and the Negro turning his back upon her and walking away, in
> spite of the fact that he is drawn toward her. Then you have the inevi-
> table self-rebuke, hurt pride, sadistic desire for revenge, the determi-
> nation that he shall not live to tell or to look at her whom he has
> repulsed—and so she has him lynched.[43]

Bagnall finds the novel "daring" and more—"understanding in a
remarkable way." This reading of *Holiday* (which Jean Toomer considered a sort of companion text to *Cane*) comports well with the idea
that the races are *naturally* drawn to each other but that artificial social
constraints and racial oppression cause repression of interracial desire.
The blocking of this desire leads to violence in place of sexual fusion, a
fusion that would be inevitable if those constraints could be dismantled.

    In the pages of *The Messenger,* emphasis on the ways in which the
racialization of identity pervasively shapes both black and white "American" selves unwittingly puts in question the magazine's overt resistance
to ideas of racially identified cultural differences. (After all, if the social
construction of race is so important in the United States, does it not
condition cultural development differentially?) But it also works against
the recognition of continuities between African and African American
cultural phenomena. This point is particularly evident in the magazine's drama criticism, which, despite differences between particular
writers, consistently rejected notions of the Negro's "natural" dramatic
ability and of African survivals in the black American traditions of performance. According to Wallace V. Jackson's 1923 discussion of the subject, slave life left the Negro with "certain leanings in emotional expression, a litheness of movement in the dance, a facility in songs and music
and a peculiar aptness at mimicry—slavery will leave any people with
such tendencies, witness the Russian serf." Hence the "materials" with

which Negroes began their artistic career in North America were not African but the products of slavery. Songs and dances were the principal forms of entertainment because "all peoples pass through a stage in which the song and dance form the principal forms of enjoyment."[44] Jackson, an associate of the publisher William Stanley Braithwaite at B. J. Brimmer, hoped for the development of "serious" drama, which would come after further experience in European drama and the further spread of amateur black dramatic clubs.

Jackson rejected not only the notion of a connection between African and African American cultural performance (which he regarded as a racist notion) but also the idea that white Americans were somehow better suited than black Americans to perform European drama. After all, when the American Negro "entered man's estate he was an occidental and American." He was just as much a Moor, Spaniard, Roman, or Jew as the white American—"he knows and feels as much of Ibsen's Norwegian characters as the next American."[45] Hence the objection that a "Negro Stage" should not perform the plays of Wilde, O'Neill, or Shakespeare smacked of Jim Crow—a point Abram L. Harris (contra *The New Republic*'s reviewer) would reiterate in a defense of the Ethiopian Art Players' performance of *Salome;* furthermore, the performance of these plays would contribute ultimately to the development of the drama by black playwrights about black American life.[46]

Theophilus Lewis and the Black Theater

The greatest hindrance to the development of that drama, according to *The Messenger,* was the dearth of good black playwrights and of an appreciative black audience.[47] To combat this problem was virtually an obsession for *The Messenger*'s regular drama critic beginning in 1924, Theophilus Lewis. Lewis provided the most biting and consistently interesting commentary on the situation of black theater in the Harlem Renaissance—much of the time, ironically, by ridiculing the notion that African Americans had any particular aptitude or interest in "good" theater. This point went directly contrary to the optimistic pronouncements frequently made in *The Crisis, Opportunity, The Nation,* and other magazines heralding the New Negro. Lewis's satirical iconoclasm in this regard, at least, fit in well with *The Messenger*'s general tone on "cultural" matters, despite the fact that he presented more of a black cultural nationalist position than did the other editors.

Much of Lewis' criticism seems intended as overt provocation of racial pride: "Where considerable racial or national theatrical talent exists you quite naturally expect to find an indigenous theatre striving to interpret the group life and character. The alleged excessive fertility of the Aframerican has not produced any such theatre making any such effort." Even the Lafayette Players, "the premier theatrical organization of the race," had failed to reveal any dramatic achievement of note. "In a decade of almost continuous activity it has neither found an embryo Pinero in its own ranks nor inspired a would-be Yeats to write a single sensible play; it has made no appreciable effort to bring the lush and colorful life of the black belts on the stage; it has not attempted to achieve distinction by presenting anything novel or provocative of thought; it has not even kept pace with the white theatre it set out to imitate." And, more surprisingly still, Negro theatergoers were not seriously upset about this state of affairs. Twisting the knife, Lewis charged: "If you know of a single energetic attempt to make the Negro Theatre mature and virile, or, rather, to put it more accurately, if you know of a single serious effort to create a Negro Theatre that was not fostered by white folks you are a wiser bird than I am."[48] Like W. E. B. Du Bois, Lewis wanted a theater of, by, for, and near black folks, but he saw no evidence that many other black folks shared his interest.

Lewis, moreover, differed from Du Bois both in blaming African Americans themselves for failure to develop their own theater and in his approach to the development of a black national drama. Lewis was never very specific about what the "aesthetics" of black theater would be, for he believed its qualities could emerge only over time. The first step toward emergence, however, must be the establishment of actual theatrical troupes and institutions supported from within the black community. Any community that could support myriad churches and musical revues should certainly be capable of sustaining its own theater, regardless of the preferences of "outside" audiences. If African Americans were really adapted to the theater and enjoyed it, most urban "black belts" would have at least a company or two. Yet, in 1921–1922, according to the *Negro Year Book,* there was not a single theater in the United States "devoted to the production of serious drama by or for Aframericans."[49] The three black theaters—the Lafayette (Harlem), the Dunbar (Philadelphia), and the Attucks (Norfolk)—mostly did vaudeville and motion pictures, just like most white theaters.

Furthermore, African American actors on the whole—despite the pronouncements of white liberals and black optimists—had displayed little actual dramatic ability, for the simple reason that they had not trained for the theater. The virulence of Lewis' critique of black actors and the (almost nonexistent, in his view) black drama may be partly attributable to his belief that other critics were not being honest, perhaps having been blinded by what they *wanted* to find in black theater, the theater of the "other," so to speak. In this respect, despite the black cultural nationalist thrust of Lewis' overall project, his criticism fit well with the tone of *The Messenger*'s other cultural criticism, both in its flamboyant iconoclasm (like Schuyler, Lewis greatly admired H. L. Mencken) and in its satire of the romanticization of black difference. According to Lewis, even "mediocre" black actors were rare: "The best informed colored theatrical observer in America once declared to the writer that if a producer wanted to cast a single play requiring ten characters he would find it impossible to fill the parts with competent players from the ranks of colored professionals." Moreover, "there is nothing which can be said in extenuation of this condition. It is simply an evidence of the marked lack of virility of the Negro actor and a rebuttal of his vaunted 'natural' ability to excel on the stage."[50] The statement implicitly notices a connection between contemporary beliefs in the Negro's superior acting ability (to which a number of white directors had attested) and the stereotype of the sensual and "virile" black male. If there was to be a black dramatic tradition, it would not, in Lewis' view, depend upon any racialist notions of organic black difference. Such notions could too easily become excuses for lack of effort. A major hindrance to the black drama, Lewis charged, was sheer lack of commitment on the part of black actors. While recognizing the obstacles of public apathy and the opposition of profit-seeking managers (many of them white), he charged that "a handful of actors of courage and stamina, like Holcroft, the sturdy Englishman, or the robust American, Joseph Jefferson would certainly have swept aside opposition tenfold as formidable in the course of the generation during which the Negro actor has been firmly established in the theatre."[51] Clearly, black Americans had demonstrated neither much interest nor much inherent ability in "serious" drama, as Lewis defined it.

In contrast, they had shown a remarkable passion and aptitude for dancing and "low comedy," and by late 1926 Lewis began to think this fact might indicate the way out of the impasse he still lamented. In January 1925 he had traced the popular black drama to the blackface minstrel show in which white actors "imitated" the supposed imbecilities of blacks; black actors had unfortunately tried to fit into the same tradition: "It was to this vogue that the builders of colored musical comedies and revues went to school."[52] The popularity of the form (among black audiences as well as white) had restricted the development of "serious" black theater. In particular, for example, "serious" black actors, playwrights, and critics (including Du Bois!), in reacting against this popular tradition, equated the "legitimate" stage with the "white" stage, "a presumption the white theatre has never claimed for itself."[53]

Black theater, it seemed, suffered from something like the highbrow/lowbrow split Van Wyck Brooks had noted in white American culture, and the split was having similar effects in stunting the development of an "indigenous" black drama. On the one hand was a lower-class audience with vulgar tastes, "which means [the theater] must devote itself to exaggerated buffoonery, obscene farce and sex-exciting dancing, supplemented with such curiosities as giants, midgets, acrobats, musical seals and mathematical jackasses." On the other hand were the "better class Negroes" who stayed away and criticized. Instead, Lewis felt by July of 1926, they should attend the shows to function as a "leavening factor," causing the theater to adjust itself to tastes of both the higher and the lower elements, and come up with an "Aristotelian" mean.

Like the "highbrow" white American, the "highbrow" black American sought a theater that bore little relation to his or her actual life. Rather than seeking entertainment adjusted to "indigenous ideas of propriety," the "higher Negro" commonly ignored even his own tastes and adhered to "alien standards" of judgment: "He insists on the Negro theatre copying the suave manners and conventions of the contemporary white American theatre [a theatre aping European drama], unaware that the white stage reflects the racial experience of a people whose cultural background has never resembled ours since the beginning of history."[54] Appealing to the genuine, if crude, tastes of the lower class was at least better than trying to please this upper-crust audience.

By the fall of 1926, Lewis had decided that the way to develop an indigenous black drama was precisely to build upon the traditions roughly developed in the "vulgar" comic revues that had emerged from the black appropriation of the "white" blackface minstrel show—the most "indigenous" white American drama, and itself a caricature of black cultural performance. Lewis was the only black critic I know of to take this approach to the possible future of black theater, although it can be compared to suggestions the German director Max Reinhardt had expressed to Charles S. Johnson and Alain Locke in a 1924 interview (discussed in Chapter 6) and bears some resemblance to the position outlined by Jessie Fauset's "The Gift of Laughter" in *The New Negro*.[55] Lewis' reasons for suggesting this approach, however, differed slightly from both Fauset's and Reinhardt's—as well as from Johnson's and Locke's reasons for coming to embrace Reinhardt's ideas. Rather than emphasizing the unique dramatic qualities of black popular performance in relation to modern Western theater as a whole, Lewis stressed the strategic importance of developing a theater based on what black communities would actually enjoy and support. His position, therefore, had a stronger economic as well as cultural black nationalist content. Equally significant, however, is the thinness of the line dividing this ostensibly racial nationalism from the sort of amalgamationism propounded by Schuyler and Rogers. For if the black comic revue, appealing to male sexual interest (usually in "mulatto" women, as Lewis noted) and subversive "masked" humor exploiting racialist stereotypes, is the vulgar origin of indigenous black drama, it is nonetheless a form in complex relationship to a popular "white" drama that, while consciously racist, flirted with racial "cross-dressing" and unconscious transracial identification, as Eric Lott has recently argued.[56] This is not a point that Lewis mentions, but it inhabits his criticism even when he is most insistent about racial identity.

Like Fauset, Locke, and Johnson, however, Lewis regarded popular black entertainment as the *basis* for the development of "serious" drama. Its dancing and ribald comedy could turn out to be augurs of the future if such resources could be brought to serve the "dramatist" and the "real" needs of the African American community. For Lewis, the main motif of both the dancing and the humor of the popular black stage was sex, shading frequently into "indecency" but nonetheless representing the "natural and sane attitude toward the subject characteristic of the Negro race."[57] This emphasis, however, served the needs of white audiences more than those of blacks themselves; according to Lewis (and so many other critics of the time), whites needed "paganism" to revitalize their "spiritual life," whereas blacks did not: "our way of living is naturally fecund and exuberant and we have a frank way of facing life."[58] Each race, in fact, had what the other needed. Hence, while the popular black theater performed a valuable function for American culture as a whole and white culture in particular (a function of which Lewis approved), it was not providing what the black community most needed to achieve cultural "maturity." It resembled the Attic revels that preceded "the advent of Aeschylus."[59] Moreover, while it was not "necessarily fatal to hardy talent," it was "inimical to the development of good acting"—which explained why the really great black actors, in Lewis' view, had had to rely on productions by *white dramatists* to develop and showcase their abilities. The ironies of the development of "racial" cultures through national drama are inescapable; all are interdependent in their very striving for *self*-development and even self-determination.

However, while Lewis occasionally praised "white" plays on "black" subjects, he was generally more circumspect in this regard than the critics of both *The Crisis* and *Opportunity,* particularly concerning "folk plays." His chief objection was to romanticization of black folk life in the South and other forms of idealization. Hence, while Eugene O'Neill's plays had performed the important function of combating discrimination against black actors, they had also "idealized" blacks. O'Neill, David Belasco, DuBose Heyward, Paul Green, and others had unfortunately established, by 1926, "the celestial origin of black folks." Here again, what Lewis was objecting to is rather different from what other black critics tended to single out at the time. For example, the play *Black Boy* by Jim Tulley suffered from the typical faults of the morality play (a seemingly irresistible form for "sympathetic" drama about black life in America)—the black characters were all paragons of virtue and the whites were all devils.[60] Similarly, Em Jo Basshe's *Earth* "offers an elaborately camouflaged Greenwich Village conception of an Uncle Tom's Cabin version of the Book of Job."[61] For the same reasons Lewis, unlike the critics for *The Crisis* and *Opportunity,* had little enthusiasm for Paul Green's plays: "He writes about sordidness in a sentimental way and winds up his stories with a sad ending," then calls the result a "Negro play."[62] (In fairness, however, the critic acknowledged that Green did the same thing with his "poor white" plays, and with only slightly better results.) Lewis feared for the future when he noticed that a "Paul Green cult" was forming among black intellectuals and actors.

The main point of Lewis' criticism was that black drama needed to focus upon the present needs of the African American community; this entailed a skeptical attitude toward the nostalgia for lost origins, a strategic and historically contingent conception of blackness, and discomfort with the inevitable shortcomings of a Negro drama that was not economically as well as creatively controlled by Negroes themselves. Lewis did not usually attack the white culture industry for the state of affairs of black drama; he put the responsibility squarely on the shoulders of black actors, playwrights, and audiences. If it hadn't been for the white theater, Lewis argued, the talents of the few great black actors (Charles Gilpin, Ira Aldrich, Opal Cooper, Paul Robeson) could never have come to light: "Their dramatic vehicles, the opportunity for expression and the appreciation of their ability have been donated by the buckra folks."[63] More than any other black critic of the period, however, Lewis recognized the ways in which the white playwrights' attempts to advance black drama were caught up in the problems of the representation of "otherness," tending even in the best cases toward romantic idealization. White playwrights, obviously, could not be inventors of a modernist black culture, even if they played significant roles in its development. Given this fact, Lewis presented specific ideas about how an indigenous black drama might be developed from entirely within the black community itself.

In his most radical moments Lewis put this hoped-for development in the larger context of the modernist predicament and what we might today call a postcolonial project:

> Now the Negro Problem is this: It is the question whether a youthful people living in the midst of an old and moribund civilization shall die with it or find themselves able to shake loose from its complexities and build their own culture on its ruins. . . . This condition of doubt will find its esthetic expression in dissonances of sound and color, and such explosive comedy and tragedy as results from the struggles of a passionate people to escape the restraints of the Calvinist version of the Ten Commandments.
>
> The task for the Negro artist, then, is to observe the confusion of rusting flivvers, vanishing forests, migratory populations and expiring faiths which confronts him and reveal its meaning in a felicitous manner. He will show us, perhaps, the convulsions of a world breaking down in chaos. Perhaps the nuclei of a new world forming in incandescence.[64]

Ironically, this is a very Toomeresque scenario, but in Toomer's case the vision would be of a new "mixed" race emerging from the chaos; for Lewis this role is filled by a "new" Negro. Here Lewis completely repudiates the idea that the new black culture will be an organic growth out of the folk or African past. American Negroes are a "new" people—in fact, the *newest* people—faced with the challenge of inventing them-selves out of the fragments of collapsing civilizations, migratory popula-tions (not "rooted" ones), dying religions. Surprisingly, this argument ends up buttressing and extending in certain respects the more typical amalgamationist tendencies of *The Messenger*'s cultural politics, though redefining the amalgamated identity as Negro while characterizing white culture as prone to extinction, "old and moribund." Further-more, if the drama Lewis imagines here is that growing out of the pop-ular black musical revue, then a main source of its very vitality is the extent of its conscious hybridity, of its double reversal upon American racial differentiation and its subversion of the color line.

While Lewis occasionally spoke in essentialist terms of a racial "spirit," his main thrust was in the direction of a more historically contingent and pragmatic understanding of African American culture (including its relation to the global situation) and the potential role of drama in its reinvention. The ultimate form of that drama remained open, but it must begin with the popular, the "low," the "vulgar." This meant not some pure racial origin, nor some Herderian folk past such as Alain Locke and Montgomery Gregory stressed, but rather the modern, urban, erotic, both morally and culturally "impure" comic revue, "ille-gitimate" offspring of an illegitimate, patently racist (though subcon-sciously miscegenationist), and pronouncedly indigenous "white" American drama that owed its own existence to African American cul-ture as much as to the peculiar fantasy life of the white American mind. Thus the amalgamationist strain in *The Messenger*'s cultural criticism was not so very far removed from the *black American* cultural nationalism of Theophilus Lewis' criticism as it at first appears. The view of the Amer-ican Negro as a new and specifically American racial type (a view put forth from a "scientific" standpoint in Melville Herskovits' *The American Negro* in 1928) related in shifting ways to the vision of the future of Americans in general—potentially all to become a new amalgamated type, different from any of the Old World. In this way African American cultural nationalism and amalgamationist expectations stood in uncer-tain, inherently ironic, and productively experimental relation to each other, together providing a crucial issue for African American mod-ernist authors—such as Jean Toomer, George Schuyler, Georgia Douglas Johnson, and Nella Larsen—to address in varying ways. That both tendencies were featured within the same magazine illustrates the importance of the tension between them to the Harlem Renaissance—indeed, to U.S. racial ideology generally—and makes *The Messenger* all the more significant for readers today as we confront an even more complicated pattern of racialized and hybridized "American" identities.

11

"Superior Intellectual Vaudeville": *American Mercury*

In his detailed study of H. L. Mencken's relationship to African American writers of the 1920s, Charles Scruggs has provided extensive evidence of the importance of Mencken and *American Mercury* to the Harlem Renaissance, although he exaggerates the singular role of Mencken in shaping the directions of the movement, at the expense of other factors, both "white" and "black."[1] My purpose here will not be to duplicate Scruggs's efforts, nor to trace Mencken's "influence," but to point out the interrelationships between Mencken's ironic cultural nationalism, the inherently "ethnic" and "racial" form of his satire, and his interest in black writing, in the process articulating the connection of *American Mercury* with the network of writers and critics of which the literary "Negro renaissance" was a part.

American Mercury concerned itself intensively with investigations into the total nature of American civilization; it was, in a sense, the first American Studies journal. Its elitist appeal was apparent in its scholarly design, its fine paper, its sedate green cover, and the hand-sewn binding that allowed it to be opened flat like a book. The disciplines of sociology, anthropology, literary criticism, folklore, medicine, political science, and history were all represented, often by significant scholarly contributions. As one reads these contributions, one is struck by how often they address the role of race and racism in American culture, often with implicit if not explicit questions concerning that culture's future: Is the United States becoming a unified, essentially homogeneous, nonracial society; a permanently racialized yet "harmonized" society of different cultures; or a radically divided society headed for race war? The magazine—veritably mercurial in its allegiances—gives no single, consistent answer, in part because its emphasis on satire and criticism rather than prophecy and reconstruction defers any reconciliatory, utopian or consensual vision. The difference between the possible futures corresponded to the different emphases, in *American Mercury*, upon the common identity of black and white Americans (whether by "blood" or "culture") and the distinctiveness of black culture. One is driven to the conclusion that the racial/cultural politics of *American Mercury* (rather like that of *The Messenger*), while pretty consistently antiracist, did not cohere. This lack of coherence matched that of the Harlem Renaissance itself.

Bastard Origins

When Alfred A. Knopf decided to start a magazine in 1923 with his friend H. L. Mencken as editor, he put out a news release announcing his intentions:

> The aim of The American Mercury will be to offer a comprehensive picture, critically presented, of the entire American scene. It will not confine itself to the fine arts; in addition, there will be constant consideration of American politics . . . , American industrial and social relations, and American science. The point of view . . . will be that of the civilized minority.
>
> It will strive at all times to avoid succumbing to the current platitudes, and one of its fundamental purposes will be to develop writers in all fields competent to attack these platitudes in a realistic . . . manner.[2]

Mencken was, of course, the perfect choice as editor of such an endeavor. He was also, Knopf later noted, "all in all . . . my most intimate friend and influenced me more than anyone else." Knopf would even describe himself as "a child . . . of H. L. Mencken"—a rich irony, considering Mencken's recently discovered, apparently intense anti-Semitism.[3]

Having started his company with the aim of publishing new American novels, Knopf had been disappointed with the quality of American fiction, which helps explain the function he hoped *American Mercury* would play in fostering artists and creating a climate of opinion favorable to the sort of work he wanted to print. Earlier, in his publishing plans for 1921, Knopf had stated his belief that American belles-lettres were too deferential to English models and opinion—a point Mencken was famous for making—and had announced his plans to focus attention on American writing (this would include Latin American writing). The creation of *American Mercury* was connected with this determination. In fact, Mencken's magazine was run out of offices on the same floor as Knopf's offices in Manhattan.

The end of the war had something to do with the new feasibility of Mencken's and Knopf's program. The attack on Anglo-Saxon dominance had not played well in the midst of World War I, particularly coming from a critic of German extraction and sympathies. Along with the *Masses* group, the *Seven Arts* critics, and others later associated with the Harlem Renaissance (such as the vocally pacifist Oswald Garrison Villard), the sage of Baltimore had suffered for his opposition to the war and his suspicions about what it was fought for. If World War I was in part a conflict over which European nations would control Africa, in the United States it was paralleled by a kind of ethnic purification campaign to ensure Anglo-Saxon dominance at home, and this affected Mencken personally. However, in the aftermath of what was increasingly recognized (by intellectuals, at least) as an international catastrophe, a growing number of readers were shifting stance. Mencken's *A Book of Prefaces* (with its blistering "Puritanism as a Literary Force" and its championing of Dreiser) had sold poorly in 1917; by 1924, when Knopf reissued it, it enjoyed a wide audience. "Only a few rebels could stomach him during the war . . . ; after the return of the conquering armies, a whole generation accepted the Menckenian theses as gospel."[4] Van Wyck Brooks would later honor Mencken as the most influential of the "anti-colonial" critics—which, in Mencken's case, meant those who cut the "umbilical cord" to England and played up "foreign" strains. The nation, Brooks added, was becoming transnational, and Mencken helped this development along: "He performed an invaluable work in helping to establish the interracial American literature of the future."[5] As early as 1911, Mencken (with Francis Hackett and others) had helped introduce Americans to the works of the Irish Renaissance. But he did not stop there, and the postwar explosion of interest in other literatures owed much to Mencken. Suddenly criticism citing German, Russian, and French sources gained a new authority, played off against Anglo-Saxonism and Puritanism, which became conflated with "Ku Kluxism" in the satirical rhetoric so effectively wielded by Mencken and his cohorts. At issue was a conflict of ideas about the nature of American culture.

Of all the other "white" magazines, *American Mercury* was perhaps ideologically closest to *The Nation*. In fact, Mencken was on very close terms with Oswald Garrison Villard in the early years of *American Mercury*, and he wrote in 1925 that he would "rather be editor of the Nation than . . . any of the other journals."[6] This comment is particularly relevant in that Stuart Sherman's vicious xenophobic attack on him of 1917 had been published in *The Nation* (shortly before Villard had taken over control of the magazine). After the war, as we have seen, with Villard in charge of *The Nation*, the literary editor was Mencken's friend Carl Van Doren—an occasional contributor to *American Mercury*—and then John Macy; Mencken was even named a contributing editor.

Thus the end of World War I was significant for the Harlem Renaissance not only because of its relation to the new militancy among the entire African American national community that it had helped to forge; it was significant because of its effect on literary institutions, among which *American Mercury* was particularly important. Moreover, the black writers and Mencken had common enemies that brought them together. Those who attacked *A Book of Prefaces* in 1917 were called by Ernest Boyd "Ku Klux Kritics," and in the pages of *American Mercury* "Ku Kluxism" (whether of "high" or "low" culture) was a perennial butt of ridicule and devastating critique. When Stuart Sherman, the New Humanist, attacked Mencken's language studies as Anglophobic, calling *The American Language* "over-ambitiously designed as a wedge to split asunder the two great English-speaking peoples,"[7] Mencken responded by accusing Sherman of being a Ku Kluxer in disguise. Unable to defeat the new "multiethnic" writers and critics through fair argument, he hauled out racialist brickbats and 100 percent Americanism: "'Call out the American Legion! Telephone the nearest Imperial Wizard!'" Mencken mocked, in a *Smart Set* review of Sherman's *Americans*.[8] Similarly, in *American Mercury*, the Klan became symbolic of a whole array of American attitudes clustered around a concept of the United States as monocultural, Anglo-Saxon, Protestant.

The Klan was particularly identified, of course, with the racial barbarism of the American South, and it is important to point out that, while most white Southerners recoiled at such devastating Mencken essays as "The Sahara of the Bozart," the effect of his satire was actually to help revitalize Southern fiction. According to Fred Hobson, Mencken "played perhaps *the* central role in the first phase" of the Southern renaissance—"the 1920s phase which stressed a critical examination of southern life," particularly in the fiction of T. S. Stribling and Julia Peterkin, the "folk drama" of Paul Green and the Carolina Playmakers, and the sociological studies of Howard Odum and *Social Forces* magazine at the University of North Carolina. (Mencken, in fact, had advised Peterkin to write about Gullah life, and Green was a Southern "Menck-enite" from his youth.)[9] Many representatives of the pre-Fugitive phase of the Southern revival would publish in *American Mercury*. They were also followed with great interest, as we have seen, in *Opportunity* magazine.

With its almost ethnographic focus on cultural particularity, regional critical realism of the kind Mencken was encouraging privileged the "indigenous" and vernacular. Thus American culture as a whole began to emerge as a quiltlike complex of regional and ethnic cultures. New England lost its dominant position in representations of the national identity, and American literature was decolonized at the same time that it gained local specificity. This tendency was the obverse of Mencken's satire, which tended to lump everything bad about American culture under the heading Puritanism, a category in many respects indistinguishable from "Ku Kluxism." The movement to specify local and ethnic American cultures, then, undermined the "Puritanism" that had previously conveyed a unified and morally whitewashed conception of American civilization, and that had thus impeded the development of a truly distinguished literature and culture.

Power of Babble: In the American Language

It was what he perceived as the homogeneous, naïve yet self-righteous, Anglocentric (and New Englandish) concept of American culture that, to a great extent, Mencken blamed for the poverty of American literature—that is, this concept in conjunction with the lack of a genuine intellectual aristocracy that might have been able to combat it. Perhaps the "civilized minority" to which *American Mercury* addressed itself was intended to be such an aristocracy. The virulence of Mencken's attacks upon "the Americano" can easily obscure the real motive of his criticism, an American cultural nationalism as intense as that of Whitman—whom, in fact, *American Mercury* did much to canonize.

Even as he attacked the imbecilities and outright cruelties that he believed endemic in the culture, Mencken somehow evoked the gaudy, complex spectacle that he always hoped would awaken a distinctively American aesthetic consciousness. Thus Irving Babbitt's charge that the best one could expect from him was "superior intellectual vaudeville" was curiously on target, though Babbitt could never have suspected the honor in the tag, as Joseph Wood Krutch would in likening Mencken to a satirical vaudeville Whitman and naming him the best prose stylist of the twentieth century.[10] Mencken's greatest achievement was a brilliant idiomatic use of the American language in a transnational and transregional sense. His criticism remains readable today less for the salience or even coherence of the ideas than for the amazing range, energy, and inventiveness of the language, including its inimitable rhythm and melodic juxtaposition of syllables, its peculiarly American music. Nonetheless, his "ideas" do demand examination, if only because they provided the tenor to his vehicle.

Mencken insisted that in any great national literature one finds an attention to actual life, the creation of a literary language beholden to the spoken vernacular, and a grappling with "the primary mysteries of existence" as these occur to believable characters. The development of particular attitudes and preoccupations vis-à-vis such "mysteries" (today one thinks preeminently of the blues), to Mencken, "raise a literature above mere poeticizing and tale-telling; they give it dignity and importance; above all, they give it national character. But it is precisely here that the literature of America, and especially the later literature, is most colorless and inconsequential."[11] In the contemporary literature of the first two decades of the twentieth century, he charges, the actualities of American life could scarcely be discerned; moreover, "one never remembers a character in the novels of these aloof and de-Americanized Americans." What foreigner reading the current pap, Mencken asked, could "imagine such phenomena as Roosevelt, Billy Sunday, Bryan, the Becker case, the I.W.W., Newport, Palm Beach, the University of Chicago, Chicago itself—the whole, gross, glittering, excessively dynamic, infinitely grotesque, incredibly stupendous drama of American life?"[12]

Mencken published numerous essay-length burlesques of American "types," such as Gerald W. Johnson's "The Ku Kluxer" in the second issue, and the series by L. M. Hussey entitled "American Portraits," which ran through several early issues (the installment called "The Medicine Doctor" is one example). Along with these sketches were scholarly essays such as Thomas Oliver Mabbott's "Walt Whitman and the *Aristidean*" and Fred Lewis Pattee's "Call for a Literary Historian"; contributions by Boasian anthropologists such as Melville J. Herskovits' "What Is a Race" (attacking theories of racial supremacy on the grounds that race and culture are unrelated and that one can give no plausible definition of "race"); Margaret Sanger's "The War Against Birth Control"; and historical studies such as Morris Fishbein's "The Rise and Fall of Homeopathy." Additionally, Mencken included many pieces—both fictional and nonfictional—about American heroes and folk heroes (always male): Billy the Kid, Paul Bunyan, Sam Houston, Davy Crockett, Kit Carson, Washington, Lincoln, Jefferson, Audubon, cowboys, mountain men. There were frequent essays on "ethnic" theater and literature—Yiddish-, Italian-, Czech-, African-American—and on "regional" literature from Montana, Oklahoma, Chicago, Iowa, and so forth. Concerning earlier American authors, some fourteen essays appeared on Whitman alone in the 1920s (including important ones by Emory Holloway, Mabbott, Louise Pound, Horace Traubel, and others); next most popular was Poe, followed by Melville, Dickinson, Mark Twain, and Stephen Crane. These are also the authors to whom allusions were repeatedly made in general criticism of American literature.

To Mencken—and it was a point not lost on those New Negro artists who chafed under the strictures of the black bourgeoisie—most American artists had sacrificed all notions of beauty to notions of right and wrong. Precisely this sacrifice distinguished the mainstream of American literature from all others: "In none other will you find so wholesale and ecstatic a sacrifice of aesthetic ideas, of all the fine gusto of passion and beauty, to notions of what is meet, proper and nice." Whitman was the most remarkable exception: "On the one hand he offered a courageous challenge to the intolerable prudishness and dirty-mindedness of Puritanism, and on the other hand he boldly sought the themes and even the modes of expression of his poetry in the arduous, contentious and highly melodramatic life that lay all about him."[13] Indeed, Mencken would continually hark back to what later became known as the American Renaissance as an aborted revolt of the kind that he longed to see again, and that he faintly heard coming in the rebels of the teens and early twenties. Mencken's arguments had, one suspects, an enormous impact on the future canonization of Hawthorne, Poe, Emerson, Thoreau, Melville, and Whitman, although that canonization eventually came under very different auspices and with exclusionary effects. His cultural nationalism, while presented in ironic and pessimistic tones, recurrently echoes theirs: "Despite all the current highfalutin about melting pots and national destinies the United States remains almost as much an English colonial possession, intellectually and spiritually, as it was on July 3, 1776."[14] American authors lacked the "unshakable egoism" upon which any self-reliant culture must depend—"It must not only regard itself as the peer of any other culture; it must regard itself as the superior of any other."[15]

Mencken first worked out this cultural nationalist position in relation to the inhibitions on American writing. Later, as Charles Scruggs has emphasized, he would tell black authors they must not regard themselves as the peers of whites; they must regard themselves as *superior;* this was the key to cultural greatness. Indeed, his whole point of view would be bodily translated: "The extraordinary colonist, moved to give utterance to the ideas bubbling within him, is thus vastly handicapped, for he must submit them to the test of a culture that, in the last analysis, is never quite his own culture, despite its dominance. Looking within himself, he finds that he is different, that he diverges from the English standard, that he is authentically American—and to be authentically American is to be officially inferior."[16]

Attacking the alleged American inferiority complex, Mencken worked out a whole cluster of such cultural nationalist positions, which matched what was being developed simultaneously by New Negro aesthetic theorists. One of the great problems of American authors, to take another example, was the lack of a native class of authoritative critics; thus the truly original artist "is forced to go as a suppliant to a quarter in which nothing is his by right, but everything must go by favor—in brief to a quarter where his very application must needs be regarded as an admission of his inferiority."[17] Unlike the more optimistic American prophets, Mencken was not sure an autonomous American literary culture would ever emerge: we might be destined to remain "hewers of wood and drawers of water."[18] The only hopeful sign was the rising undercurrent of revolt, the skepticism and iconoclasm of Harold Stearns, Waldo Frank, Dreiser, Anderson, and others. After all, as Mencken would have it, "a great literature is . . . chiefly the product of doubting and inquiring minds in revolt against the immovable certainties of the nation."[19] Such qualities are precisely the ones that *American Mercury* authors would locate repeatedly in African American culture.

As the author of *The American Language*, Mencken was particularly concerned with the omnivorous and ever-forming *language* of American peoples, and of the effect that language might have on literature. Over time, a series of essays appeared on the "American language," investigated in Louise Pound's "Notes on the Vernacular," Vachel Lindsay's "The Real American Language," Babbette Deutsch's "The Plight of the Poet," and George Philip Krapp's "The English of the Negro."[20] Deutsch's essay, like Pound's and Lindsay's, argues that great poets must get their language from the *vulgus,* and to do this must work from local knowledge. Foreign residence "can only divert the American poet from his real task and his real adventure." After all, poets in America, Deutsch argues, do not really have it any worse than those in other lands; the great artist is always an "outsider." But to succumb to the lure of expatriation is to sacrifice one's true calling and to break one's vows: "The American poet must stick, for better or worse, for richer or poorer, to this country that wants none of him."[21] Only by staying home and cocking one's ear to local voices can one become "learned in the vulgar tongue," the language of poetry.

None of his contemporaries was as learned in that tongue as Mencken. As early as 1921, in an article for *The New Republic*, Edmund Wilson had observed that Mencken's "gloomy catalogues" were "the poetry of modern America": "He makes his poetry of the democratic life which absorbs and infuriates him. He takes the slang of the common man and makes fine prose of it. He has studied the habits and ideas and language of the common run of his countrymen with a close first-hand observation and an unflagging interest. And he has succeeded in doing with the common life what nobody else has done . . . : He has taken it in all its coarseness and angularity and compelled it to dance a ballet."[22] The ballet is a satiric one, granted—one choreographed by an artist who has "never ceased to regard his native country with wounded and outraged eyes."[23]

No doubt it was features like this that prompted the reviewer for T. S. Eliot's *Criterion* to write:

Nowhere does the American nation wear the aspect of a cohering and decisive unity as in the pages of this magazine, and this despite its denunciation of national shams. . . . The mystifying quality about Mr. Mencken's achievement is a certain unity, consistency and character which is maintained month after month. It is this quality which suggests a new type of culture . . . an indigenous culture, and there is no parallel in England . . . no parallel and no possibility of a parallel. To appreciate and understand the *American Mercury* implies an *a priori* interest in the American scene.[24]

One reason for this "unity" was surely the force of Mencken's style, approach, and attitudes, which many tried to imitate. But one also has to stress that Mencken really crafted each issue with amazing artistry.

(Anti-) Genealogies

If Mencken was right in saying that every great literature is "the product of doubting and inquiring minds in revolt against the immovable certainties of the nation," one might add that every cultural revolt requires satire. In the early phases of transformation, the delegitimation of traditional authority depends less upon rational argument than upon withering ridicule. Typically, Mencken's cultural nationalist motives are disguised, particularly in *American Mercury,* by the vigor and comprehensiveness of his satire, which also helps explain the role of racialist rhetoric in his critique of American culture. No other American writer, with the possible exception of Ishmael Reed, has so completely lost himself in the role of satirist—a fact all the more appropriate when one thinks of the devilish satyrs on the cover of *The Smart Set,* the magazine Mencken edited before *American Mercury* (also the first he worked on, through Dreiser's influence). Like the fully developed satirist, Mencken ended up tainted by the very stains on the American conscience he relentlessly exposed. Caught up in the traditional mode of satirical rhetoric that exposes bastardy, degeneracy, the illegitimacy of inherited genealogies, Mencken used racialist—and often racist—weapons against white American culture and ended up, with the recent discovery of his diary, hoisted by his own petard. He thus completed the full cycle of the career of the satyr-trickster who exposes the corruption at the origins of cultural authority, reveals the fallacies and cruelties submerged by heroic cultural narratives, but ends up the victim of his own cleverness, consumed by the decadence of his tales.[25]

Michael Seidel's probing exploration of the nature of satire does much to reveal the significance of *American Mercury* and of Mencken's career. The true satirist, Seidel points out, is not a moral "scourge." He is not interested in reform, only in breaking down, degeneration. Perhaps in his own thorough reading of the great satirists such as Cervantes, Swift, and the Mark Twain of "What Is Man?," "Pudd'nhead Wilson," and "The Man That Corrupted Hadleyburg," Mencken came to conclusions about the nature of satire akin to Seidel's. In any event, in 1922 he protested that he was not interested in the reform of American culture, had no interest in national "uplift": "I am wholly devoid of public spirit, and haven't the least lust to improve American literature; if it ever came to what I regard as perfection my job would be gone."[26] The motive of his satire was sheerly aesthetic pleasure, a reveling before the spectacle of decay. In his influential early essays on Dreiser, he insisted, his motive "was simply and solely to sort out and give coherence to the ideas of Mr. Mencken, and to put them into suave and ingratiating terms, and to discharge them with a flourish, and maybe with a phrase of pretty song, into the dense fog that blanketed the Republic."[27] The final metaphor belies the claim to strictly private motives: his motive is not only public but specifically national. What is equally significant, however, is that just before he moved from *Smart Set* to *American Mercury* Mencken was adjusting his role in a more purely satirical direction, at the same time that he abandoned literary criticism as such. His essay "Footnote on Criticism," published the year before Knopf announced plans for *American Mercury,* advertised Mencken's intention to begin pursuing satire as a form of artistic performance, which helps explain the relative inattention of *American Mercury* to literature as such.[28] To Mencken, the magazine itself was literature.

Mencken's Nietzschean skepticism has much to do with his understanding of satire and its antagonistic relation to the genealogy of morals.[29] If the goal of satire is not to find truth but to reveal the barbarism covered over and legitimized by official narratives, its effect is to draw people into the battle over "culture" and thus—regardless of motive—transform and invigorate it.[30] Such was the overriding aim of his new magazine.

In the role of satirist, however, Mencken pretends that such invigoration is impossible in America. As Seidel shows, fully realized satire reveals the predominance of degeneration and disinheritance. Satire *can* be co-opted, made to fit within a larger narrative of restitution, but in fully sustained satire, "the line of degeneration is permanently marked."[31] It thus subverts genealogies of "legitimacy," heroic cultural narratives intended to show historical continuity. If myths of origin and regeneration attempt to order and justify events of the past to authorize current social arrangements, satire reveals that the origin itself was tainted or illegitimate, and that from that origin only degeneracy has followed. Thus Mencken's satire—and the satire of *American Mercury* generally—takes as its most common subjects both the degeneracy of the "original" Anglo-American stock and the inability of the "pure" Anglo-American heritage (both genetic and cultural) to propagate itself. Indeed, Mencken's most offensive racialist statements, as Arnold Rampersad has pointed out in a different context, attempt to dramatize how the "pure" Anglo-Saxon American is literally of a "degenerate" breed, best typified by the Ku Kluxer.[32] Conversely, the best American writers are all ethnic or racial hybrids at odds with the "Puritan" establishment.

Mencken's caricatures of "Puritans" from the founding of Massachusetts Bay Colony to the twentieth century must thus be seen in part as attempts to profane the myth of American origins. "The land was peopled, not by the hardy adventurers of legend, but simply by incompetents who could not get on at home, and the lavishness of nature that they found here, the vast ease with which they could get livings, confirmed and augmented their native incompetence." Furthermore, the immigrants who followed them were of "even lower grade." "The truth is that the majority of non-Anglo-Saxon immigrants since the Revolution, like the majority of Anglo-Saxon immigrants before the Revolution, have been, not the superior men of their native lands, but the botched and unfit: Irishmen starving to death in Ireland, Germans unable to weather the *Sturm und Drang* of the post-Napoleonic reorganization, Italians weed-grown on exhausted soil, Scandinavians run to all bone and no brain, Jews too incompetent to swindle even the barbarous peasants of Russia, Poland and Roumania."[33] The ethnic stereotyping and implicit eugenicism here (directly and continually contradicted by the numerous essays Mencken published by Boasian anthropologists discrediting the myths of "race") are almost an inherent, formal aspect of the satirical mode. Exploding the idea that Americans are the "youngest of the great peoples," Mencken argues that they are prematurely senescent, born of exhausted stock. Nor has the ease of life in the United States strengthened them; it has only given them a comfortable security in their mediocrity. Americans are "peasants" sinking ever further into the muck of their wallow, erecting taboos around all their delusions to safeguard their mediocrity and ensure its rule.[34]

For the satirist, none of this is cause for despair: "Only the man who was born with a petrified diaphragm can fail to laugh himself to sleep every night, and to awake every morning with all the eager, unflagging expectation of a Sunday-school superintendent touring the Paris peepshows."[35] Mencken thus agrees wholly with the expatriate "young intellectuals" about the stupidity and dishonesty of the American government as well as the cowardice and ignorance of the American people. "Yet I remain on the dock, wrapped in the flag, when the Young Intellectuals set sail. Yet here I stand, unshaken and undespairing, a loyal and devoted Americano."[36] Identifying with the "Americano"—often, indeed, as his most astute contemporaries pointed out, betraying the residue of "puritanism" in his own critiques—Mencken inadvertently reveals his complicity in the degenerate record he writes down.[37]

The approach to American culture Mencken had developed by the early 1920s set the tone for much of the cultural criticism in *American Mercury*. In "The Comic Patriot," for example, Carl Van Doren provides a Menckenesque portrait of the American critic who "feels toward his native land and its inhabitants much as a comic poet or dramatist feels toward the race of men at large."[38] The key to the comic patriot's stance is his skepticism toward all national mythologies. He knows the nation is not a transcendental entity but a temporary organization of human beings, yet he insists on being a good neighbor. He delights in the national memories and "savors the common tongue."

> He responds to the laughter, recognizes the prejudices, participates in the fears, thrills to the songs, looks forward toward the hopes of his fellows. These things are familiar and so are dear to him, because he loves the feel of life when it comes close. To be a lucid critic of the show and to laugh at it as much as he must are, he considers, among his rights as a citizen as clearly as to look to the courts for justice. He fulfills his duties as a citizen none the less because he insists that he owes them to his neighbors and not to a metaphysical state, with a special soul and a particular destiny.[39]

Here Van Doren connects a number of significant themes. He expresses the cultural nationalist realist's emphasis upon both the vernacular language and "the feel of life when it comes close," as well as the critical realist's resistance to grounded knowledge and the national myths of American exceptionalism. His patriotism derives not from metaphysical nationalism but from neighborliness, the ordinary necessities of getting along among people who, thrown together within a national grouping, have developed their particular manners and customs in relation to one another and thus, to greater or lesser extent, become "assimilated."

The comic patriot is immune to the mythologizing of the Revolutionary War as a noble conflict by exceptionally noble men for a noble cause. Similarly, the myth of the frontier he eyes askance: romancers "had to turn it into something epic to make it fit for patriotic digestions." As for the Civil War, "it was as muddled as a street brawl." When their myths were debunked, the deluded patriots violently defended them, while disappointed patriots were terribly let down and ashamed. "But the comic patriot, since he was never taken in, cannot be taken aback."[40]

Van Doren's glib aloofness (like that of Mencken's favorite black contributors) disguises an ethical and political position, however; he refuses to take a "mystic's attitude toward his country" specifically because in that direction lie notions of "souls" of peoples, national exceptionalism, and racial destinies, concepts that justify moral outrages most people would not think of justifying as individuals—concepts that, one might add, had precipitated World War I and the greatest crimes of American civilization. His chief example from American culture is telling and provides the moral centerpiece of his essay: "He may be touched by the unselfish zeal with which the general run of Americans set out to free Cuba from Spanish misrule, but he still remembers that those same Americans were enduring within their own borders a misrule as gross—that of the Negroes by their white landlords and employers and terrorizers. Moreover, this spasm of unselfish zeal ended in as cool a piece of land-grabbing as any nation ever perpetrated."[41] The instance was, in fact, a parable of American history. As this example suggests, the issue of racism played an important role in *American Mercury,* not only in essays directly concerned with black/white racial topics but in general criticism of American culture.

Racism and the Burlesque Anatomy of Race

The importance of racism in American history and the white American character, as Charles Scruggs has shown at length, was not a submerged theme in *American Mercury*'s surgical "anatomies" of the national scene. Yet it is important to see the treatment of this topic within the context of the magazine's other emphases. A feature in each issue, for example, was "Americana," the collection of quotations from various periodicals exemplifying the inanities of American culture in each state.[42] Introduced by brief annotations citing the source, often with a witty gloss, these entries provide a running cultural critique in the form of a documentary collage, many of them concerning the absurdities of American racism and the color line. "Viewed over a span of several years," as M. K. Singleton has aptly pointed out, "Americana" "constituted a vast comic epic of Coolidge's America, a satiric panorama nearly as important to America as Pope's *Dunciad* was to the England of his day."[43] The protagonist, in this case, was the incomparable "boobus Americanus," whose chief characteristics included racism and xenophobia.

One way of attacking racism was to debunk the fiction of "race," a strategy that could easily slide into the erasure of cultural difference, as we have already seen in the case of George Schuyler. George Philip Krapp's condescending "The English of the Negro" (which may have been the source of some of Schuyler's claims in his *Nation* article, "The Negro-Art Hokum") exemplifies the flux of racial attitudes and thoughts concerning the relationship between African, African American, and European American cultures. Krapp's intentions are antiracist in denying any "Africanisms" in Black English and stating that much of what is considered uniquely "Negro" in black speech simply reflects the survival of archaic English pronunciation (as among other culturally segregated groups, such as Appalachian whites). To Krapp, the English of the Negro is indistinguishable from that of a white person of similar class, region, and education. Krapp clearly aims to undermine racial stereotypes in literary and popular culture; literary transcriptions, he emphasizes, exaggerate black difference by seeking phonetic exactness in representing Negro speech while rarely doing so in representing the speech of whites. The radical difference in the sheer appearance of printed words representing white and black speech (the vernacular of whites never being as tortured in its spelling) reinforces pernicious stereotypes about black intelligence and overemphasizes supposed "racial" and cultural differences. Against the stereotypical inarticulateness of a people supposedly incapable of "higher" culture, and thus incapable of moving beyond a childlike, half-barbarous (in Krapp's view) pidgin

English, Krapp believes the Negro has "progressed" in the use of English to the point where now "Negro English" is "merely one of the colloquial forms of our many visaged mother tongue."[44]

For their progress in the mastery of a European language, "the Negroes deserve much credit. . . . Their acquisition of mature English proves that they have been eager to assimilate a higher culture when the way was open." On the other hand, from the standpoint of moral evolution, "the white man likewise deserves credit for the black man's progress," for the white man has also "grown." Relations between the races are becoming, Krapp avers, "more kindly and humane," evidencing the moral progress of the white man and, by extension, the nation. Here hardcore Eurocentric assumptions and patronizing argument support an explicitly antiracist and even antiracialist thesis.[45] Like a Boasian anthropologist, Krapp argues for the lack of inherent connection between race and language or culture; yet unlike a Boasian (or the Deweyan pragmatist), he adheres to nineteenth-century evolutionary assumptions about "civilization" and ethics that were among the supports of racist thought. This is all the more surprising in that *American Mercury* relied exclusively—and extensively—upon Boas and his students for its offerings on current anthropology.

One finds a similar cluster of assumptions in other contributions to *American Mercury* that emphasized the Americanness (as opposed to the Africanness) of the American Negro—antiracist in intent but inevitably Eurocentric and elitist. Thus one scholarly essay argued at length that the spirituals, contrary to the beliefs of white "sentimentalists" and black race promoters, originated chiefly from white gospel hymns in the camp-meeting revivals of the rural South. Little of what was considered distinctive about the songs was purely "Negro" in derivation. The point of the argument was not to libel African Americans as uninventive but rather to emphasize the extent of transracial cultural commonality.[46] Similarly, Mencken himself argued in a review of two books on black Southern folklore that African survivals had been exaggerated and that the vast majority of superstitions, religious practices, healing rituals, and so forth, which were commonly thought of as distinctively "Negro," were actually shared by many rural Southern whites. Indeed, he alleged, Negroes would seek out a white conjurer almost as readily as a black one—and there were plenty of white ones to be found. From a strictly cultural standpoint, the American Negro did not differ significantly from the American Caucasian. This, of course, is a point that

George Schuyler, one of Mencken's favorite black contributors, was fond of pressing.[47]

Mencken's position, however, was not consistently assimilationist in any conventional sense. *American Mercury* fluctuated between critiques of what was perceived as an overemphasis upon racial difference (as opposed to class and regional difference) and insistence upon black self-reliance—made necessary by racism. Racism, after all, used the concept of radical racial difference to justify social inequality, and racial difference was "proven" by evidence of cultural difference. What distinguished black from white Americans was not race or basic culture— both groups fell for the same religious scams from their respective "shamans," for example—but *racism*. *American Mercury* did not, however, present a consistent point of view on the importance of racism to differential cultural formation. On the one hand, essayists demonstrated how racism had fostered the development of a profoundly ironic consciousness, traditions of masterful vernacular "performance" (masking the self), and a sophisticated "cynicism" that distinguished the average black American from the average white. On the other hand, as part of the antiracist and "Americanist" emphases of the magazine, major cultural differences were denied. Such ambivalence, of course, characterized the Harlem Renaissance itself. What the offerings of the magazine on the whole revealed but failed to articulate consciously was the way that the very structure of cultural difference, as shaped by what Alain Locke would term "cultural racialism," was deeply and distinctively American—as the "vulgar" racial epithets of the American language should have revealed to H. L. Mencken, who reveled in them.

Yet Mencken understood racism to be a crucial aspect of American culture. Topics concerning "race" and racism were among those that provided continuity to his magazine, and in issue after issue one can find articles not only by African Americans on "racial" topics but also by Boas or his students exposing the fallacies of racialist thinking, such as Boas' own "The Question of Racial Purity" in October 1924. Such attacks upon the fictions of genetic purity fit the satirical thrusts against 100 percent Americanism and such contributions as Henry J. Ford's "The Anglo-Saxon Myth" (September 1924), which pointed out that the so-called Anglo-Saxon was a genetic and cultural hybrid formed of a welter of ethnic "stocks"—stocks that were, in turn, hybrid themselves. This sort of argument also reinforced the satires on the color line provided by the likes of Walter White and George Schuyler. In "Across the

Color Line," for example, M. S. Lea presented a series of semifictional sketches about people of "mixed race" to point out the absurdity of the idea of race.[48] The essay demonstrates how "black" and "white" identities are determined differently in different societies of the Americas, and how the color line has been drawn inconsistently over time and region even within the United States itself. Many of the aristocratic Southern "white" families, she points out, are probably "mixed"—a point that had been made in earlier American fiction and drama.

This program of relativizing race and exposing it as a social construction, in turn, reinforced Mencken-style satirical attacks upon the racism of the white "Americano." The reader of Walter White's "I Investigate Lynchings," for example, would have seen a series of satires on the KKK and Southern fundamentalism, fictional and nonfictional treatments of lynching, and attacks on the idea of race purity and Negro inferiority. Moreover, in manner White's essay shifts between the Sinclair Lewis–style attack on stifling small-town mores and the Menckenian satirical style. "Nothing contributes so much," he begins, "to the continued life of the investigator of lynchings and his tranquil possession of all his limbs as the obtuseness of the lynchers themselves." White connects the stupidity of small-town Southern lynchers to the general ignorance, "moralism," and hypocrisy he sees in Americans generally:

> In any American village, North or South, East or West, there is no problem which cannot be solved in half an hour by the morons who lounge about the village store. . . . When to their isolation is added an emotional fixation such as the rural South has on the Negro, one can sense the atmosphere from which spring the Heflins, the Ku Kluxers, the two-gun Bible-beaters, the lynchers and the anti-evolutionists. And one can see why no great amount of cleverness or courage is needed to acquire information in such a forlorn place about the latest lynching.[49]

This paragraph should be read in the context of *American Mercury*'s attacks on small-town "moronia," the essays of Clarence Darrow it published, its use of the KKK as symbolic of several aspects of the American national character—not only racism but, perhaps even more frequently, religious intolerance and superstition (qualities that, ironically in this context, blacks and whites shared). Indeed, Mencken had previously called the Klan a natural extension of the Southern fundamentalism that had expressed itself in the "monkey trial" in Dayton, Tennessee.

Attacking racism not as an aberration but as a normative aspect of white American personality does not necessarily do much to illuminate African American culture on its own terms, but *American Mercury* writers also developed arguments about how the necessity of adapting to a social order dominated by such personalities affected African American culture itself, for both good and ill. Thus, in "Homo Africanus," L. M. Hussey writes of how the American Negro has learned to survive by wearing the mask and performing the part of the "good nigger." "What is, in plain words, the aim of this universal histrionicism? Its clear aim is to flatter the white man, to confirm him in a sense of preconceived superiority."[50] A highly effective survival tool that is almost instinctive, this skillful play upon the vanities of the dominant race is practiced not only by black Southerners of the lower classes but by preachers, teachers, editors, and tradesmen South and North—above all in their dealings with white philanthropists. It is thus a *national* characteristic of the American Negro.

But Hussey, who had briefly worked for a white philanthropic foundation in the South, had found that behind the mask lay a profoundly cynical view of even the white "friends of the Negro." "It was a view neither gracious nor flattering. Lumping all the white-inspired uplifts together, the institutes, the schools, the urban leagues, the bi-racial programmes, he whiffed suspiciously of the whole stew. He was not, unhappily, bubbling with gratitude. His soul was not, alas, inundated with a great, tepid wash of good-will. For, betrayed into an unwonted frankness, what he saw and sees back of all the pious labor in his favor was and is the continued efforts of the Caucasian to make of him—a good nigger!" This cynical attitude had to be carefully disguised, for even the white man could not perpetually trust his supposed superiority. Whenever he began to doubt himself he would envision the blacks "ripping off their masks, no longer paying tribute to his accidental eminence."[51] This humiliating and fearful nightmare inspired lynch mobs and race riots.

Increasingly, however, Hussey finds a new restiveness and militancy, disdain for "uplift" efforts as further efforts at co-optation and control, open contempt and cynicism, as in the pages of *The Crisis, Opportunity,* and *The Messenger.* The very uses of irony and the minstrel mask were now being self-consciously revealed: the "ability to laugh, and to laugh ironically and cynically," were being used to illuminate not only the sophistries of Nordics but the aspirations of Negroes themselves. What

Hussey is pointing out is the kind of "mastery of form" Houston Baker, has discussed as a basic vernacular style of African American cultural performance. Moreover, Hussey's argument implies that when the "mask" is re-deployed as an object of cultural recognition and aesthetic appreciation, it is transformed into a "deformation of mastery," taken off and thrown right in the master's face. Hussey's entire essay is, in a sense, a kind of analysis and appreciation of a conscious cultural performance being further developed by the New Negro.

But Hussey also notes a growing desire to simply do away with the mask entirely, in the manner of Du Bois, whose essay "The Dilemma of the Negro" in October 1924 revealed the quandary faced by African Americans in deciding whether to continue seeking integration in a joint American society or to give up on that dream and build a separate society, possibly leading toward race warfare. Du Bois wants integration, but he sees no alternative to self-segregation and autonomy if white America refuses to change. With the development of greater self-reliance and race pride and a growing cadre of "educated" and capable leaders, black people find themselves on the verge of being able to develop separate institutions at least as good as those of whites. Should that happen, contact between the races would decline and contempt would replace the desire for community:

> If black colleges are forced by illiberal and insulting policies to demand complete colored control they will cut the strongest spiritual tie between the white and black races in America. This cultural contact of white and colored teachers with each other and of students with a mixed faculty has undoubtedly been one of the greatest sources of racial peace in the United States. To end it would be not only unfortunate; it would be calamitous. But if social contact can be had only at the cost of such racial degradation as has been described, then the Negro race is almost forced to ask for its own teachers and to support its own colleges and universities—or to demand State aid for Jim Crow higher training.[52]

The growth of separate institutions and the eschewing of hope for integration on equal terms, however, raises a specter of fratricide: "What will be the end? Can we not see it plainly looming? Insult, separation, race pride, hate, war: there is the nasty horrible world-old thing creeping on us."[53] The real struggle of current American culture, Du Bois suggests, must be to erase the color line and build a common national future. But if whites will not join in such an effort, well then . . . The alternative to an American nation (not just an American state) is an American apocalypse.

Journalism like Du Bois's essay was of course an effort to recruit whites to the effort of creating the "nation" and averting the apocalypse, as were other efforts at awakening whites to the American racial crisis by dramatizing the sociocultural crossroads facing the New Negro. This was a moment when national symbols and white heroes like Lincoln and John Brown still appealed to the imagination of many blacks, despite continuing atrocities that sapped hope. Albon L. Holsey's "Learning How to Be Black," an autobiographical piece by R. R. Moton's secretary at Tuskegee, presents the dilemma of the Negro and the growing sense of possible independence. Holsey discusses the moment when every black child in America learns that he or she is black and despised in a white-dominated, racist nation, and reveals, in this generational story, the changing ways of being black. He recalls the tales his parents and their friends had told, when he was becoming aware of race, of their own fistfights and rock battles with white children in the late 1860s and 1870s, "when the bitter memories of the Civil War were fresh and hate flamed between the children of the two races. The jeers and taunting songs which precipitated the clashes bore the impress of these war memories."[54] It was a time of not only pride but hope, and faith that the "winning" traditions of the nation were on the black child's side. Holsey remembers the words of the song his parents would sing as they approached a group of white children:

> Abe Lincun was a gent'man,
>> Jeff Davis was a fool,
> Abe Lincun rode a milk white horse,
>> Jeff Davis rode a mule.

To this taunt, the white children would respond with "They hung John Brown's body to a sour apple tree" and then, in Holsey's words, "the fight was on."[55]

A number of details of the story should interest us here. One is the fact that the different *white* men are identified with the pride of each group; the black children do not find a contradiction to their race pride in this identification—nor even in the valuing of Lincoln's "milk white horse" on the basis of its whiteness. (Even Holsey does not seem to see an irony here, though we will see in a moment how, for *his* generation, the association of whiteness with purity and goodness will be questioned.) One way of interpreting this phenomenon is to say that the children still accept the hegemonic values of the white world. Another is to say that, for them, the very notion of racial identity was being thrown in question—Lincoln and Brown had been incorporated into their notions of self-identity in such a way as to be "blackened," to relativize the color line and throw its viability in doubt. The battle, in any case, is joined over symbols of national identity, over the kind of nation the outcome of the Civil War had (perhaps) promised that the United States would ultimately become. The black children identify with the winning side, with the nation—imaginatively a deracialized nation—and with its martyrs. Within the context of the national symbolic field, moreover, one is struck by the congruence between the children's song and the significance of Lincoln and John Brown some thirty and forty years later to poets and historians, essayists and activists, including the organizers of the Niagara Movement and the NAACP. For this generation—most notably and movingly for Du Bois—Lincoln and Brown were martyrs to a cause that might well be lost.

The remainder of Holsey's essay reveals black adaptations to the sense of that possible defeat. In his own childhood, blacks were put back in their "place" and depended on the protection of "good" whites. Along with this came a resurgence of racial self-hatred. Here Holsey does draw attention to the association of whiteness with purity and holiness, and to the assertion of racial pride by a rejection of that association. A new kind of "learning how to be black" is brought into the picture in the persons of Bishop H. M. Turner of the A.M.E. Church and W. E. B. Du Bois. When the pastor of Holsey's church had instructed the congregation to sing "Wash me and I shall be whiter than snow," Turner—visiting the church that Sunday—shot up and halted the organist to say, "That's the trouble with you colored folks now. You just want to be white. Quit singing that song and quit trying to be white. The time has come when we must be proud that we are black and proud of our race."[56] Turner then launched into a spellbinding hour-long sermon on the subject that galvanized the congregation. For Holsey, this was a moment of racial initiation on his way to becoming a New Negro.

The next episode of this sort in Holsey's life came with a visit by Du Bois, who stayed in Holsey's home for a couple of days when visiting the town (Athens, Georgia) to address a teachers' meeting (Du Bois was then teaching at Atlanta University). At the end of the visit, Holsey escorted the guest to the train station and was struck by his way of dealing with the ticket agent. Without the slightest deference in his manner, Du Bois asked the agent for a ticket at a special rate. When the agent responded that tickets were not offered at that rate, Du Bois matter-of-factly told him he was wrong and demanded he look it up. Struck by this breach of Southern racial custom but cowed by Du Bois's manner, the man did so and discovered his error, then sold the ticket without further incident. Unlike virtually any local black citizen, Du Bois had neither accepted the white man's judgment nor sought out another white man to "straighten things out." Holsey, looking on, was astonished—as he later told his parents, Du Bois had acted "just like a white man." Without any apparent consciousness of the rhetorical irony, Holsey offers this as yet another crucial stage in his "learning how to be black." Once again, the essay evinces the sort of ideological contradictions so common in an era when the nature of racial distinctions, of the lines between "white" and "black," were being destabilized—a destabilization to which *American Mercury* itself was contributing. This instability is related to the uncertainty about whether to fight racialism as such or to accept the necessity of racialist discourse to mount a black nationalist oppositional culture and autonomous social institutions—the conflict Du Bois had pinpointed in "The Dilemma of the Negro." The issue, of course, had profound implications for the nature of American cultural nationalism and the role of race within it. Could there be, in the United States, a "*we*, the people"? What are the challenges to claiming an inclusive "we," and what are the possibilities? How do you go about *making* such a "we"? Well, one way you do it is with satire.

Divided Audiences

Much has been written over the years about the problem of audience in the Harlem Renaissance. Indeed, much black literary theory is based upon recognizing the problematic of the double or "divided" audience, and this theory has been developed particularly in relation to the Harlem Renaissance. Yet the assumptions about the audience of Harlem Renaissance writing need to be scrutinized, if only because the whites who read New Negro books were, in many cases, people who *also* read *American Mercury, The Nation, Opportunity,* and *The Crisis*—magazines in which the problem of the double audience was explicitly addressed, primarily though not exclusively by black authors themselves. The white audience that has read critiques of American racism, racial stereotypes, Ku Kluxism, plantation fiction, and "monoculturalism" at a steady rate may not be purged of racism, but members of that audience are unlikely to approach a work of African American fiction with the assumptions and expectations of the reader who has not read such critiques. Yet most general discussions of the Harlem Renaissance carry on as if the white audience was made up of precisely the latter sort of reader; the "white audience" (not to mention the black audience) is presented in quite monolithic and stereotypical terms, as if there is little essential difference between the reader of *American Mercury* and the typical subscriber to the *Saturday Evening Post.* In fact, the black contributions to *American Mercury,* while taking for granted a majority white readership, often assume an audience that is divided to some extent but moving toward commonality—accepting mutual enemies (Ku Kluxers), mutual terms of derision, mutual forms of irony and cynicism regarding the "American character." Such forms of mutuality, initially evoked through the scapegoating strategies of satire, suggest the beginnings of a new "transracial" yet "national" discursive formation.

In "The Dilemma of the Negro Author," published in December 1928, James Weldon Johnson addresses himself to the problem of the dual audience—the white audience with its stereotypical expectations for "Negro literature," and the African American audience with its sensitivity to perceived "betrayal" by black artists not putting the best foot forward. Johnson concludes that the two audiences must be combined into one: "That, I believe, is the only way out. However, there needs to be more than a combination, there needs to be a fusion. In time, I cannot say how much time, there will come a gradual and natural rapprochement of these two sections of the Negro author's audience."[57] In fact, Johnson's very essay is an effort in this direction—as are the many satires on American racism published in *American Mercury.* Does not satire, after all, bring people together around the common targets of ridicule?

Johnson envisions whites' conceptions of Negroes being broken up and remodeled, and black America's "taboos" being abolished, as a common audience develops—not through artistic means alone, but through political, social, and economic effort as well. Standing on his own "racial foundation" with his best abilities and his most intimately known material, the Negro author "must fashion something that rises above race, and reaches out to the universal in truth and beauty. And so, when a Negro does write so as to fuse white and black America into one interested and approving audience he has performed no slight feat, and has most likely done a sound piece of literary work."[58] To Johnson, such a work would be the crowning achievement of the Negro renaissance—an *American* renaissance indeed. Coincidentally, his essay is followed immediately by Lewis Mumford's "The Writing of 'Moby-Dick,'" which addresses itself to Herman Melville's problem of a divided audience, and how that problem helped shape his greatest (and yet un-"canonized") achievement. The problem of audience is not, however, the same; race makes it different. Johnson's direction is not assimilationist in the conventional sense of de-emphasizing black cultural integrity—his poem "Go Down Death," first published in *American Mercury,* is surely convincing evidence of this. His direction, rather, is assimilationist in the more precise sense of desiring an assimilation of cultures to each other, *at least* to the extent of achieving interracial communion in the experience of the work of art. Using marks of race, as in most dialect poetry, *just* for the sake of marking race and dividing audiences—or dividing speakers and audiences—went against his grain.

The issue of the black author's audience is taken up from another angle in L. M. Hussey's "Aframerican, North and South," which concerns the way Northern white liberals overenthusiastically praise black artists and thus mislead them. Whites of standing go out of their way to get to know the suddenly "discovered" black genius and magnify his accomplishments, gushing over a singer, for example, who is really no better than many white singers to whom they would pay no attention. "Indeed, I find these talented black men in a measure the victims of white sentimentalists. That is to say, they become victims when, no longer simply profiting by the sentimentalities of Northern sympathizers, they begin to sentimentalize themselves."[59] Guilt-induced white flattery and patronage, in short, could be a deadly trap. If frank and careful criticism is sacrificed to gushy, purely race-motivated effusions, how can the black artist know which direction is up? How distinguish between the "authentic Parnassians" and mere "rhymsters"? Fortunately, the wise artist, recognizing that he has yet to find a "genuinely free outlet" and that "great cultures come only from assured peoples, from peoples of abounding self-esteem," accepts white flattery with a concealed grin and retains the saving cynicism of his race: "He knows that the white sentimentalist still regards him, after all, as a kind of *lusus naturae.*"[60]

Hussey feels that the black artist is praised for those qualities in his work that match "white qualities," whereas the real task is to achieve a clearly articulated expression of "black values" and qualities, in which whites (like Hussey) can be of limited help. Hussey reaches toward a consciousness of the opposition between cultural integrity as an extension of the aesthetics of experience, and the idealization of race as such—whether by artist or audience. One cannot help but note with some skepticism, however, what Hussey considers the special "gifts" of the Negro that will infuse his art: "His magnificent gift of laughter, his superbly cynical viewpoint, his regal gestures, his abounding capacity for play, his indifference to industrialism—who lauds these things? and who urges the Negro intellectual to give them cultural expression?"[61] By the time of Hussey's essay, 1926, one would have to say that only too many people were lauding these qualities, and perhaps "sentimentalizing" them. There is a tendency in *American Mercury,* indeed, to project an image of the African American as more transcendently "above" the actual daily pain and humiliation of life in industrial America than can be realistically believed. The haughty attitude of the cynic and satirist shades into apolitical fantasies of omnipotence. For although the person behind the mask of performance may be able to distance herself from the role she performs, as Claude McKay's "The Harlem Dancer" so movingly revealed, she may also be in pain. To bear witness to the pain is no admission of inferiority or spiritual defeat to the one who inflicts it.

The arrogant aloofness of the satirical persona Mencken and *American Mercury* in general promote is not unrelated to the editor's disdain for democracy, and thus it connects with a belief in the aristocracy of intellect that would exacerbate the black artist's distance from the average black audience, ironically, in the name of racial "self-possession." Hence, Mencken, in his review of *The New Negro,* calls the work a representation of "the American Negro's final emancipation from his inferiority complex, his bold decision to go it alone."[62] Like Hussey (whose essay appeared in the same issue), Mencken also argues that "the patronage of sentimental whites" has done more harm to the black artist than good—"It has forced him to be tenderly considerate of Caucasian *amour propre,* of all sorts of white prejudices, and so it has hampered his free functioning as his own man."[63] Mencken admires the fact that finally a group of black artists is overcoming the sense of inferiority behind the Negro's "bellowing . . . for his God-given rights," his self-pitying complaints about the obstacles besetting him, and his squeamishness about frankly acknowledging his people's weaknesses. Finally black artists are proceeding with their work irrespective of what white people—or even black people—will think.

Yet Mencken recognizes the problem of audience; forgoing the white "sentimentalists" and black philistines, who can they hope will support their venture in self-reliance? "The vast majority of the people of their race are but two or three inches removed from gorillas: it will be a sheer impossibility, for a long, long while, to interest them in anything above pork-chops and bootleg gin."[64] He might have added, as Whitman had famously written and as Sterling Brown would write in 1930, that to have great poets you must have great audiences, and no such audiences were yet evident for the New Negro.[65] The audience for the work (as, indeed, for Whitman's, for Melville's and Dickinson's work) had to be created; this was the role, preeminently, of magazines.

Charles Scruggs has shown how, within a year of his review of *The New Negro,* Mencken had begun criticizing African American artists for failing to produce any important achievements. Of course, his sense of what constituted an "important achievement" was formed by the sort of works he most admired, works by white artists, usually male. Thus Mencken claimed in an article for the *New York World* that the greatest jazz was being created by George Gershwin and Paul Whiteman. The best nonfiction on "the [Negro] race's wrongs" was by white, not black, authors. All of the poetry by African Americans put together "is not worth much more than any one of a dozen of the epitaphs in 'The Spoon River Anthology,'" and as for fiction, "no Negro novelist has ever written a novel even remotely comparable to such things as *Babbitt* and *Jurgen.*"[66]

In short, even as he called for black cultural self-reliance, Mencken looked for the same qualities in African American writing that he looked for in all writing: critical realism, vernacular language, exposure of the follies and prejudices of average people as well as their small heroisms, and an exploration of "character in decay" as a result of humanity's tragic yet moving attempt to triumph over circumstances that inevitably block its aspirations. Applied to fiction about African

Americans, these qualities could only awaken howls of protest from the black middle-class audience, to whom they smacked of old stereotypes.

The tendencies Mencken was encouraging in black authors were undoubtedly what prompted the composer Will Marion Cook to respond, "Stop Van Vechten-ing and Mencken-ing my race."[67] Charles Scruggs has discussed this issue at length, and there is no point in repeating his argument here, but it is important to put Mencken in context, once again, of the whole network of writers, critics, editors, and publishers that were transforming the "culture industry," and particularly the institutions of literature, in the 1920s. Their sense of American culture's shortcomings, needs, and resources (including both its best available traditions and the traditions from abroad that had most to offer it) profoundly shaped their sense of what African American culture was and might be. They were not, however, simply projecting their own fantasies onto African American culture. They were listening to black intellectuals and often forming their views in dialogue with them. They critiqued those racist stereotypes they could recognize, and they repeatedly insisted on the importance of African American cultural independence. Yet even the nature of that independence was projected within a particular ideological frame: thus Mencken could insist on black cultural self-reliance even though, in his notion of how such self-reliance could be achieved, he (much like Wallace Thurman, as a matter of fact) anticipated a movement paralleling what he encouraged in American literature by white authors such as Dreiser, Anderson, and Lewis—which he predicated in turn on his interpretation of Nietzschean philosophy and continental European and Russian fiction.

One should be careful about assigning a godlike role to critics like Mencken, however; if white critics and patrons affected black artists' representations and performances of African American culture, the converse was also true. And to the extent that black authors responded to *American Mercury,* it was because their own cultural assumptions and ideas about literature, race, and culture approximated those the magazine presented. How else explain their sheer delight in the magazine? Indeed, one could, I suppose, interpret Mencken as an incarnation of Esu-Elegbara or Anansi if one wished. But this would be to deny the adequacy of the American contexts and the American languages in which he, his fellow actors, and their divided audiences lived.

The social drama they played out was, of course, another form of containment—as is every experiment in cultural formation. But it was also a form of liberation. It was a liberation of black authors from one set of contexts into another, more varied, open, and productive one. Black writing in the Harlem Renaissance, even in its pan-Africanist moments, remained largely within the forms and possibilities suggested by the American cultural nationalist field—but at the same time it altered that field; it reshaped ideas of "America"; it looked beyond. The white allies of the movement were, likewise, "contained" within the field they were simultaneously opening. And one is chastened by the fact that when their positions were institutionalized in academic curricula, anthologies, and other functions of the ideological apparatus of a mainstream thickening toward empire at midcentury, little of the black presence remained. It was not only the New Negro experiment that was co-opted and forgotten or repressed as it was absorbed—so thoroughly, indeed, that even the prophets of the Black Arts Movement could not appreciate its importance. The whole movement toward a new idea of American culture, of which the New Negro was a part, suffered a similar fate—so thoroughly that the new generation of "multiculturalists" is barely even aware of it.

12

Black Writing and Modernist American Publishing

Students of the Harlem Renaissance often speak as if a sudden fascination of whites for the "primitive and exotic" caused profit-seeking white editors at established firms to become interested in black contributors. George Kent, for example, maintains that "the quest of whites for the primitive . . . helped unlock doors of prestigious publishing houses to black writers who had formerly found the doors locked, barred, and bolted"; and more recently Cary Wintz has written that, because of the interest in the primitive and exotic, "publishers and editors who had once routinely dismissed manuscripts by black authors no longer placed racial restrictions on what they published."[1] However, a closer attention to the institutions that fostered and supported the Harlem Renaissance shows that long-established publishers opened their doors to the new black writing to a very minimal extent if at all. In fact, the movement came on the heels of a massive transformation of the publishing industry that was spearheaded by *new* publishers, centered in New York, that began publishing black writing fairly early in their existence.

Moreover, contrary to exaggerated accounts of the "vogue" of the Negro, the overwhelming majority of publishers showed absolutely no interest in publishing the work of black authors. *Publishers' Weekly*'s chief treatment of the New Negro movement was a ten-inch column buried in the middle of a 1926 issue, apparently written at the behest of the

342

NAACP.[2] The publication of black writing was limited to an amazingly small, though historically important, group of interconnected firms. Sterling Brown noted this fact in 1942: "One of our leading critics used to characterize the New Negro Movement as the time when 'every publisher wanted a Negro book.' This was a peeved exaggeration. A few new and liberal publishers were genuinely interested in Negro expression; a few attempted to create and/or cash in on a fad; but when all was said and done comparatively few books on the Negro were published."[3] To go through the magazine book review indexes, publishers' lists, and *Publishers' Weekly* issues of the 1920s is to become massively aware of how infinitesimal the representation of and genuine interest in black writing really was. It also helps one to recognize the differences between the few publishing institutions that were connected to the renaissance and the many that were not.

The booklists of the white publishers of the Harlem Renaissance show that they concentrated initially in critical realism and regionalism, left-wing political theory, modernist anthropology (Boasian and Malinowskian), American cultural nationalist and ethnic writing, modern continental European fiction, and new studies of sexuality and gender. They became publishers of the American high modernists, but their intellectual and institutional centers of gravity—and their closest personal relationships—were with the editors of and contributors to the magazines discussed earlier in this book, not with the expatriates or the avant-garde. They published virtually all the books concerned with the new ideology of cultural pluralism, which—far more than interest in the primitive—helps explain their interest in black authors. Although these institutions were receptive to writing about black people that focused on the primitive and exotic, this was far from the only type of black writing they were interested in.

The new magazines had much to do with the historic changes in the publishing world without which the Harlem Renaissance might not have happened as and when it did. According to Henry May, "New York publishing, with its traditions and taboos, still presented a formidable conservative front in 1912. By 1917 the Rebellion had cracked the front at many points; this may well be the most important evidence of its strength."[4] Some publishers of the "rebellion" actually launched their own magazines to help alter tastes and complement their publishing programs. Thus Mitchell Kennerley—a forerunner of such publishers as Knopf, the Bonis, and Liveright—started *The Forum;* and Knopf founded *American Mercury* with his friend H. L. Mencken at the helm. In any case, the great majority of the authors who edited or regularly contributed to *The Seven Arts, The Masses, The Liberator, The Nation, The New Republic, The Crisis, Opportunity, American Mercury,* and other magazines closely related to the Harlem Renaissance had their books published by Alfred A. Knopf, Harcourt and Brace, Boni & Liveright (or Albert and Charles Boni), and Ben Huebsch (who merged with Viking in the mid-1920s). These men (mostly Jewish, outsiders to the established industry) and their houses were new insurgents in the late teens and early twenties, and they contributed crucially to the dramatic rise of New York as the publishing capital of the nation, without which the Harlem Renaissance as such would have been unthinkable.[5]

One key to the transformation in publishing and the eclipse of Boston by New York was the massive influx of immigrants, including, until 1917, those from southern and eastern Europe and from Germany, who helped make the publication of books from such regions profitable and thus affected the general literary climate in which writers of the "rebellion" tried to detach American literature from its dependence on the English tradition.[6] The new cosmopolitanism actually *contributed* to the new cultural nationalism; publishers interested in fostering the "native" movement started out (like Knopf) publishing Russian fiction, Irish drama, and other previously "exotic" literatures. This strategy had an ideological and ethnic as well as economic motive. The new publishers wanted to disaffiliate American from "Anglo-Saxon" literature (a disaffiliation associated also with the shift from Boston to New York City); they were almost all Jewish and had been excluded from the inside circles of the established, Anglo-dominated industry even in New York. As Bennett Cerf attested, "There had never been a Jew before in American publishing, which was a closed corporation to the rising tide of young people described in *Our Crowd.* Suddenly there had burst forth on the scene some bright young Jews who were upsetting all the old tenets of the publishing business."[7] The most important of these "young Jews" were Liveright, Knopf, and Huebsch.

The old-line publishers, even if located in New York, still operated by late-nineteenth-century methods and adhered to late-nineteenth-century tastes. "In 1917," Walker Gilmer has written, "a house might have its headquarters in New York, but the prevailing influence upon it remained Bostonian."[8] And "Bostonian," in most cases, meant "Anglophile." It is no coincidence that Whittier, Holmes, Lowell, and Longfellow lost ground to Whitman, Poe, and Melville as the center of publishing moved to Manhattan. The books (new editions, biographies, critical studies, anthologies) that contributed to the rising status of the latter three authors were published mainly by the same new publishers in New York that published New Negro books. In addition to matters of taste, however, the actual methods of handling books "looked to England" before the rise of the new houses. Books were chosen and edited by "cultivated Christian gentlemen" and issued for a select audience in conservative Victorian bindings.[9] The vision of American literature and its potentialities fit the Anglocentrism of the publishers, as it did the editorial tastes of the established magazines before World War I. And the vision of who would have a future in the business did not include Jews. Hence, when men like Huebsch, Liveright, and Knopf started their own houses, they "lacked any allegiance to the entrenched Anglo-American literary heritage, that foundation of respectable conservatism which had proved so profitable to their older rivals."[10] Furthermore, they had nothing to lose by taking risks—no influential contacts, no contracts with established writers, no debts to the publishing establishment. And they knew that important new sectors of the book market were not being served. There was a hunger for books from outside England and New England, books not only of new styles and contents but of a new physical appearance and feel.

The contrast with an earlier cultural moment and location is instructive. Alexander McClurg, a Chicago book and stationery seller, went into publishing for several years out of a desire to promote American literature, and particularly to foster the arts in Chicago and the Midwest.[11] His bookstore became the "mecca of literary Chicago" and its rare book section, Saints and Sinners Corner, a gathering-place for writers in the 1880s, incubating the first "movement" in Midwestern literature.[12] McClurg's publishing concern was an extension of the sort of bookselling that interested him. In 1880, with Francis Fisher Browne, he also founded *The Dial*, partly to promote his own books, and proved that a literary review could survive in Chicago. A Civil War veteran who had organized a group called the Crosby Guards and participated in Sherman's March to the Sea, McClurg was particularly interested in fiction dealing with the South, which accounts in part for his suggesting that W. E. B. Du Bois collect a number of essays (including one published in *The Dial*) for publication as a book, now known as *The Souls of Black Folk*.[13] Not long thereafter, however, McClurg lost heart, telling his friend Francis Hackett, "I make ten times as much selling stationery."[14] There was no market for the sort of book McClurg wanted to publish.

Restricted by tariffs and other factors before World War I, the international book trade grew dramatically in the 1920s, even taking into account the general increase in demand for books stimulated by the war.[15] Such changes had several important implications for the Harlem Renaissance. For one thing, they were critical to the rise of the ideology of cultural pluralism as a retort to "100 percent Americanism" and Anglo-Saxonism. For another, the prestige of Russian and Irish literature partially transferred to the "literature of the Negro," as young critics and cultural theorists found in African American culture America's closest analogue to the peasant cultures of those nations. Furthermore, much of the initial success of the new publishing houses derived from the fact that they were responding to a *new* market for continental European literature that the older houses had not picked up on; as they established themselves they branched out and were able, in part because of strong backlists, to pick up titles unlikely to turn a large profit but considered worthy of publication for cultural or ideological reasons. New Negro writing fit predominantly into this category. Contrary to what some more recent cultural historians have insinuated, no publisher was reaping large profits from African American poetry and fiction. Liveright was keeping his firm afloat (briefly) because of the Modern Library, not because of books like *Cane, There Is Confusion*, and *Tropic Death*.

Scholars have often intimated that white publishers would publish only works conforming to mainstream white audience expectations, but evidence for this is slim. The publishers that accepted Harlem Renaissance manuscripts do not seem to have been thinking mainly about the bottom line in doing so. (Of course, neither were they nonprofits.) Many of the early volumes of the movement were collections of poetry, and such books were not expected to make money regardless of the poet's race. They were intended, instead, to give "tone" to a publishing house, as Countee Cullen would later point out to a young James Baldwin.[16] Liveright told the attendees at the 1924 Civic Club dinner (in part celebrating Jessie Fauset's new Boni & Liveright book) that publishers had a responsibility to publish worthy books that probably would not sell well, using *Cane* (which sold five hundred copies) as an example.[17] Indeed, Liveright eventually went out of business largely because he did not pay enough attention to profitability and did not take care of his backlist. Knopf became legendary in the publishing industry because of his commitment to excellence regardless of anticipated early profit, and he stuck with authors like Langston Hughes and Carl Van Vechten through the early years when their books were only costing him money. The "success publishers" of the 1920s (such as Simon and Schuster) were not those that accepted the books of black authors.[18]

Moreover, so far no masterpieces in manuscript have turned up that were rejected by publisher after publisher. The "canon" of the Harlem Renaissance looks today much as it did in the 1920s and 1930s, except that Zora Neale Hurston (whose *Their Eyes Were Watching God* did not appear until 1937) has enjoyed a belated ascendancy. Black writers and critics themselves feared that the publishers, by the late 1920s, were becoming indiscriminate in their consideration of manuscripts by African Americans—that black writers were not being held to rigorous standards, and that this could only hurt the development of black literature.[19] Since certain instances of difficulty in publication have been used to typify the supposed repressive effect of publishers upon the Harlem Renaissance, I would like to address the most important of these and show how they have been used in misleading ways.

Perhaps the best-known instance of the supposedly monolithic "white" industry's turpitude is that of Walter White's difficulty with Charles Doran. In two of the major recent studies of the Harlem Renaissance, this has been used as the primary "typical" instance of white publishers' squeamishness about publishing socially uncompromising, non-stereotypical black fiction.[20] To put this story into perspective, it is worthwhile to know a few things about Doran that earlier scholars have neglected to mention. In his autobiography, Doran includes black-authored books of the 1920s among what he calls the "exotics," which "increase their numbers by a subtle devastating, degenerating system of proselyting," "profiting by the decadence of an overstimulated and blasé social order."[21] The prime example of this degeneracy is the shocking new prevalence of openly homosexual authors; these people, Doran feels, ought to be segregated and put in sanatoriums. Closer to our topic, Doran's favorite author, not to mention one of his closest friends, was Irvin S. Cobb, the champion of Dixie whose immensely popular "darky" stories—staples of such magazines as *The Saturday Evening Post*—were the antithesis of New Negro fiction. Doran approvingly notes that Cobb was a "puritan. Never having danced, the jazz age left him untouched except to earn his withering scorn."[22] Cobb was one of Doran's most profitable authors, a man whose judgment of fiction, Negroes, and Southern life he valued highly.

In 1922, Walter White decided for some reason to send his manuscript of *The Fire in the Flint*—a blistering antiracist novel about the South, written at the urging of H. L. Mencken—to Doran. As Cary Wintz has pointed out, Doran asked for changes in certain characterizations that were not "what readers expect." Since White refused to water the novel down, it was rejected.[23] This almost comical anecdote has been used to demonstrate that "white publishers" were resistant to socially conscious black literature. Aside from the fact that it is hardly the usual case for a first novel to be accepted by the first publisher to receive it, one must recognize that Doran was about as unlikely a choice as could be imagined for White's manuscript. This is not, however, even a consideration to David Levering Lewis, who reads the story of White's encounter with Doran as an allegory of the New Negro's relation to white publishers: "If one of the principal officers of the NAACP failed to find a publisher for a surprisingly competent and accurate first novel about racism in a small southern town, what hope was there for Charles Johnson's program? Moving beyond the cloaked symbolism of *Cane* to a literature of exposure and denunciation, to a use of the arts to promote social change, the Afro-American ran headlong into the politics of publishing."[24] But of course White did *not* fail to find a publisher. Immediately after the rejection, White sent the book to Knopf and it was accepted almost instantly. And the house that published *Cane* was in many respects the very antithesis of Doran.

The publishers that were unreceptive to a book like White's were equally unreceptive to the fiction of Theodore Dreiser, Sherwood Anderson, Waldo Frank, and other authors of the "rebellion"—whose work they considered "sordid" and "sensationalistic," above all not "uplifting." Conversely, the publishers that were receptive to the "new" fiction and poetry were receptive to New Negro writing but were not interested in more "conventional" literature. Hence the experience of Georgia Douglas Johnson, which has also been used to typify white publishers' racism. Johnson had difficulty placing *An Autumn Love Cycle;* Boni & Liveright had rejected it because they did not want to put out poetry volumes solely on "the love theme," as she explained to Walter White; and Knopf had already sent its fall catalogue to press. White weighed in on her behalf at Knopf without success: "The only fault that can be found is that [the poems] follow a much traveled path—so many others have written of the self same experiences and emotions. . . . Publishers and the poetry-buying public have become rather fed up on this particular style of poetry no matter how well it may be done."[25] There is no reason to doubt that the manuscript was turned down at these firms on nonracial grounds, as Johnson herself understood: "I realize," she responded, "it is not modern as things go now."[26] For Knopf or Liveright to have accepted *An Autumn Love Cycle* would have been a fine example of sheer racial patronizing. Johnson ended up placing her manuscript with an African American editor-in-chief (William Stanley Braithwaite) in Boston who typically published poetry in similar forms and on similar topics by white authors.

The view of African American literature held by Braithwaite, first at Cornhill and then at B. J. Brimmer, was resolutely assimilationist, if nonetheless nationalistic. Braithwaite's very weaknesses as a critic (and he is a more important critic than is usually recognized) follow from his social and cultural position in the "polite" Boston literary order and his attempts to achieve a "central" position in that order in part by trying not to antagonize anyone. One does not have to analyze Braithwaite's racial psyche to understand how his efforts to fit into a literary culture that was already, in the late teens, being superseded by happenings in New York, left him in an impossible position. Thus, after helping to make a way for poetic modernism in the United States, he found himself awash in its wake by the 1920s, a figure by then of marginal importance even to New Negro writers who had once admired and learned from him.

The Harlem Renaissance publishers were not just a different group, as Wintz has documented,[27] from those who earlier had published the works of Charles Chesnutt, W. E. B. Du Bois, James Weldon Johnson, and Paul Laurence Dunbar; they were an entirely *new* group, with new attitudes in every phase of the business, from stylistic and ideological preferences, to cultural and geographical range, to marketing techniques, typography, and jacket design. It is not surprising that culturally conservative critics from an earlier generation, such as W. E. B. Du Bois and Benjamin Brawley, would attempt to cast suspicion on these publishers on racial grounds, objecting to the "sordid" and "defeatist" qualities of the new writing—thus echoing the charges of the older white editors and publishers against the critical realists and naturalists. It is equally unsurprising that the authors of the younger generation almost universally rejected their interpretations. As we have seen, the result of Du Bois's poll for *The Crisis* about how the Negro should be portrayed was to show that except for Du Bois and Brawley, and to some extent Jessie Fauset and Countee Cullen, writers and critics found publishers receptive to all sorts of modern black writing—perhaps even *too* receptive![28] After all, Knopf published both Nella Larsen and Langston Hughes; Boni & Liveright published both Jessie Fauset and Jean Toomer; Harcourt, Brace published both W. E. B. Du Bois and Claude McKay.

The similarities between Knopf, Boni & Liveright, Harcourt, Brace, and other publishers of New Negro books should not be overstated, however; the differences between them (or at least perceived to be between them) actually gave black writers a range of options for the marketing of their books. But the fact that these three firms in particular were the chief publishers of the American modernist transformation (not only in literature but in such fields as anthropology, political theory, and economics), that they had strong personal and institutional interconnections, and that they all identified with the American cultural nationalist, cultural pluralist "movement" is crucial to understanding their relationship to the Harlem Renaissance.

From Dusk to Dawn: The Trials of William Stanley Braithwaite

William Stanley Braithwaite is one African American who has not received his due, either as a key figure in the emergence of American modernism or as a publishing connection of the Harlem Renaissance. Information about his publishing operations is hard to come by, and disdain for his "assimilationist" tendencies has probably inhibited reconsideration of his importance to African American writers in the early twentieth century.[29] Actually, Braithwaite not only promoted overtly "racial" poetry by black poets in his anthologies but also helped get such poetry published in book form, despite what were, by the late teens, already rather "old-fashioned" aesthetic preferences. He moved into publishing as an extension of his anthologizing, focusing on poetry (overwhelmingly by white authors) in rather conventional forms and late-romantic tones, motivated by an American cultural nationalist ideology of an especially Anglocentric bent, which is not surprising for his Boston location and his rather elite "mulatto" West Indian descent.

Braithwaite had a burning, almost quixotic, love for poetry; the work of his life was to nourish an American poetic tradition that would rival England's and help America develop a "soul." His publishing efforts, like his better-known annual *Anthology of Magazine Verse and Yearbook of American Poetry,* grew out of this ambition.

When, in 1904, Braithwaite proposed to editors of the *Boston Evening Transcript* that they print a review of the best examples of magazine verse for the year, they laughed in his face.[30] Editors at the time had little use for poetry except as filler. They held "magazine poetry" in contempt. In fact, little poetry was appearing in the United States, either in the magazines or outside of them. Thus, when Braithwaite succeeded in starting his column in 1906, he did not have much to write about, but the column expanded quickly and by 1913 had swelled to a volume, *The Anthology of American Magazine Verse.*[31]

Few aspiring poets between 1906 and 1920 did not read his annual roundup of contemporary poetry, gaining from it a sense of the great variety of new work appearing in contemporary journals. From Braithwaite's correspondence one can see that magazine editors longed for poems they had published to appear in his collections or to be mentioned in his introductions; undoubtedly, then, his work helped stimulate demand. Poets, too, cared deeply not only about whether they were included but about which of their poems were included. Braithwaite probably was not, as Kenny J. Williams has suggested, a "king-maker" (many of the better poets, including Claude McKay, secretly disdained his criticism), but he did wield considerable power in the American literary field, particularly in the early teens, and helped launch poetic careers, including those of Ridgely Torrence, John G. Neihardt, Harry Kemp ("the tramp poet"), Robert Frost, and James Weldon Johnson.[32] He also helped along the careers of Edwin Arlington Robinson, Henry Vaughn Moody, Scudder Middleton, Lizette Woodworth Reese, Louise Imogen Guiney, Bliss Carman, and Richard Hovey. Unfortunately, Braithwaite's warmest interest remained centered in these poets and those he considered their followers. Soon other anthologies of contemporary poetry began appearing, often anthologies that, unlike Braithwaite's, paid contributors. Moreover, his own anthology was always on the verge of discontinuation for lack of funds, which helps explain its journey through five publishing houses in fifteen years.[33] In his valiant struggle to keep the anthology alive, Braithwaite adopted strategies that damaged his reputation.

Furthermore, his catholic embrace of all sorts and qualities of poetry began irritating poets of all stripes, even arousing suspicion by the late teens as Braithwaite tried to accept the new without shaking off the old. One reason his anthology usually included just two or three pieces each by a vast number of poets may have been financial—the hope that this in itself would create a market by stimulating orders from the poets and their friends. Often Braithwaite would ask for donations, loans, or advance orders for the book in the same letters with which he asked poets for permission to reprint their work—a particularly dubious practice in the case of little-known and often very weak poets who were desperate for recognition (and whose work, subsidized by the authors, Braithwaite often published through Cornhill and B. J. Brimmer).[34] Thus, because of Braithwaite's perpetual financial difficulties, the anthology had some of the features of a vanity publication.

In his critical introductions, moreover, Braithwaite would give special attention to poets whose work was coming out from his own presses—unbeknownst to his readers, since the presses did not carry his name. And featured poets would review the anthology in magazines with which they were connected, thus providing free advertising of sorts. This sort of log-rolling no doubt lies behind Carl Sandburg's disillusionment with Braithwaite; in 1917 he wrote Alice Corbin Henderson that if she wanted "to organize to stay out of Braithwaite's anthologies, I'm with you. Two with God are supposed to be a majority. If you know more than two, send me their names. A pathetic personage has been permitted to grow into a fungus mistaken for what it grows on. The popery and kaiserism of it, the snobbery, flunkyism and intrigue, I'm on to it."[35]

Moreover, although the Boni brothers inquired about publishing his anthology in 1915, indicating that it continued to be important to poetic "radicals," by that year his influence was already fading because of the proliferation of new literary journals and anthologies for which his work had helped open the way. Particularly, the appearance of *Poetry* magazine in Chicago (two months before his own short-lived *Poetry Journal* in Boston) began moving American poetry in new directions; indeed, Braithwaite became a butt of ridicule in journals like *The Dial* by 1917, the year before he was awarded the Spingarn medal by the NAACP.[36]

As Braithwaite welcomed, rather lukewarmly until they achieved undisputed prestige, imagism and free verse but failed to cast off the late-romantic "sentimentalists," he developed a not undeserved reputation for indiscriminately praising every sort and quality of poetry. Thus Clement Wood—a would-be Whitman of the "radical" free verse and socialist stripe—advised him in 1916 to be more judgmental: "Praise in full what is meritable, but don't let the wishy-washy 'asphodel and amaranthine' rhymers, or the merely 'odd' vers-librists, have your backing in their false claims to genuine inspiration."[37] A few years later Braithwaite's friend Brookes More, on the other hand, urged him to attack Clement Wood. In talking to many poets More had learned that Braithwaite had "a reputation for *praising everybody*." To rescue himself he should choose a worthy target on whom to unleash his critical fury; did he not share More's opinion about Wood? "I feel that such a man is detrimental to American poetry. I believe that his wild ideas are absolutely harmful."[38] (A letter to Malcolm Cowley of the same period, a copy of which More sent Braithwaite, lambastes Cowley for praising Sandburg—poets like Sandburg and Amy Lowell "are debauching American literature.")[39] Harry Kemp advised him not to let the "Free Verse crowd" get a grip on him—"For you have a virtue most critics lack—generosity toward your contemporaries; Don't let them make a vice of it."[40] Such charges also came from Claude McKay (a New Negro "radical") and, albeit more gently, Benjamin Brawley (a "conservative").[41]

Braithwaite declined to attack the "newer" poets, however—before the 1920s, when they became impossible to ignore, he preferred to pay them no attention or to include them without comment in lists of names—while at the same time betraying his basic preferences. His correspondence suggests that his warmest relationships through the 1920s were with poets entirely forgotten today who detested the critical realists, vernacular poets, and free-versifiers, while he developed thinly veiled antagonisms with competing editors and anthologists such as Harriet Monroe.[42]

In the 1920s Braithwaite came around to listing the likes of Sandburg and Masters among the torchbearers of American poetry, but this was too late to save his reputation. Even Claude McKay, who had sought encouragement and advice from Braithwaite in early 1916, attacked him bitingly in letters to Langston Hughes in the mid-1920s, calling his influence on American literature "both bad and worthless," and adding: "Braithwaite is the Booker T. Washington of American literature—a bred-in-the-bone sycophant—perhaps an unconscious one by necessity and environment."[43] Some of the poets Braithwaite had helped out in their early years deserted and even turned on him. Robert Frost never forgave Braithwaite for introducing Edward Arlington Robinson to him as his better, and Frost ultimately descended to the basest sort of racist attacks in private correspondence with Louis Untermeyer—poor repayment for the real aid Braithwaite had been to his career when he first returned to the States. Adding to Frost's resentment was Braithwaite's (like Untermeyer's) equal admiration for Edgar Lee Masters, and his listing of Frost's name with those of Amy Lowell and Wallace Stevens.[44] Frost's ugly response to Braithwaite was not unique, and the effect of sheer racism in its baldest forms upon Braithwaite's career would be impossible to calculate, particularly because of his own reticence on the issue. Others who benefited from his encouragement and publicity smiled to his face and called him "nigger" behind his back;[45] but Braithwaite's closest associates and most fervent supporters appear to have always been white—and the poets whose reputations he tried hardest to build were also white, such as Richard LeGallienne (about whom he and Benjamin Brawley co-authored a book in 1917) and Thomas S. Jones, Jr.[46]

Although he never called attention to his racial identity, and although many white poets who admired him and published through his agency were initially unaware that he was black, Braithwaite clearly did want to help black poets along, even if he did not regard them as creators of a distinct racial tradition. Moreover, young black poets, learning he was black, approached him for guidance and aid. His own preferences therefore probably had a particular impact upon the early efforts of African Americans such as Countee Cullen, who sought Braithwaite's advice when he was yet eighteen, "imbued with the desire to be one of the grandest of all men, a poet."[47] Years later Cullen would dedicate *Caroling Dusk* (1927) to Braithwaite, whom he regarded as "the real begetter of this anthology."[48]

Braithwaite's literary tastes, as the connection with Cullen would suggest, remained essentially late romantic. Even the modernist poems that he came to admire he tended to assimilate to older criteria of "moral idealism" and "spiritual" mystery—criteria roughly appropriate for many of the poems published in *The Crisis* before the advent of Langston Hughes. Braithwaite consistently read African American poets in terms of the various "schools" he used to categorize American poets generally, and if he paid more attention than most critics to black writing, he rarely ranked it with that of the "masters." In 1927, at the peak of the Harlem Renaissance, his list of the best contemporary American poets was composed of Robinson, Frost, Sandburg, Lindsay, Masters, Lowell, Aiken, and Teasdale—and John G. Neihardt (later of *Black Elk Speaks* fame) was one whose greatness, he felt, had yet to be recognized.

The manner in which Braithwaite conducted his anthology sheds light on the nature of his publishing activities, which dovetailed with it. In his valiant if at times ethically questionable efforts to make a living through letters, Braithwaite often shifted from attempting to act as an agent for little-known poets (whose work he put in his anthology and praised in his *Transcript* columns) to forming presses that would publish subsidized books. Thus, in 1919 he promised to get a book by Arthur Inman published by Dutton and in 1921 approached the same poet with a proposition to bring out his manuscript "Of Castle Terror" at a cost of $750 (and 40 percent of profits) through B. J. Brimmer.[49] The two presses Braithwaite helped create and worked for were vanity presses in the main. Frequently Braithwaite would solicit poems (usually two) for his anthology, or a budding poet would send a sheaf for his criticism, introducing herself as someone who had been learning from his criticism and anthologies. Braithwaite would respond with generous advice and encouragement, then ask, in some cases, if the poet might have enough work to fill out a volume. If the poet expressed interest, Braithwaite would clarify the financial terms and then preparations for publication would begin. He would use his *Transcript* column to bring attention to the author, and after the book came out he would give it generous mention in his anthology. According to Arthur Inman, Braithwaite generally used circulars for advertising, at least while he was with Brimmer;[50] and he depended heavily on his authors to sell their books—by using mailing lists they provided, for example. Occasionally he would bring out a limited edition at a steep price and have the author write to friends for advance subscriptions.

The extended correspondence between James Weldon Johnson and Braithwaite that led to the publication of Johnson's first volume of poems gives an intriguing look into Braithwaite's methods while also providing unique insight into Johnson's maturation as a poet. Johnson first contacted Braithwaite in 1911 to thank him for mentioning his poem "Mother Night" in the *Transcript*'s annual review of magazine verse. Thanks to Braithwaite's comments, Sherman, French had asked

Johnson if he had poems enough to fill a volume. (He did not, but the next year the company would publish his first novel.) In 1914 Sherman, French approached him again, pointing out that a book of poetry might aid the sale of his *Autobiography of an Ex-Colored Man*. In response, Johnson turned to Braithwaite for advice, mailing him a package of poems for criticism. So began a close literary relationship of several years' duration that led to Braithwaite's publication of *Fifty Years and Other Poems,* the composition of which owed much to his critical judgment.[51]

By August 5, 1914, Braithwaite had returned the poems with suggestions for revision; Johnson, taking the suggestions to heart, wrote back for advice about publishers. During that year and the next, the two men corresponded frequently about Johnson's poetry, and Johnson thanked Braithwaite for "nudging" W. E. B. Du Bois about his work, mentioning that Du Bois had decided to publish "The White Witch" in *The Crisis*.[52] At the same time Johnson suggested they collaborate on a textbook, a subject he would bring up repeatedly for several years but in which Braithwaite apparently was not especially interested.[53]

Nothing immediately came of Johnson's projected volume, yet he continued sending poetry to Braithwaite for advice, including free verse experiments that were never published. (Johnson thought *The Masses* might be interested in them, but Braithwaite suggested *Others,* a strictly literary magazine; he was not a fan of the political "radicals.")[54] In the summer of 1917 Braithwaite resurrected the plan of two to three years earlier, that Johnson publish a book of poems, this time through Cornhill, a new press where he was editor-in-chief.[55] In a flurry of correspondence the two men planned the format of the book (following a design suggested by Columbia professor Brander Matthews in 1914–1915),[56] decided which poems to include, and plotted a marketing strategy. From the beginning, Braithwaite expected Johnson to come up in advance with the money for publication. Johnson struggled to raise funds in time for a fall 1917 publication. The timing was critical, because October publication would allow Braithwaite to extol the book in his anthology for the year, boosting sales. Yet the price was steep. Johnson was to come up with $520 in three installments ($400 by the time he received proofs), plus sign up 100 subscribers to a special edition (his own idea) costing $5 per copy—here the NAACP mailing list came in handy.[57] Johnson was to write to potential subscribers himself.[58] On August 17 he did not think he could make it: "To fail in seizing this opportunity to get my poems to the public will be one of the keenest disappointments of my life." By August 23 Johnson had given up hope—he had neither the money nor the time to gather subscriptions; but next morning, the thought of failure steeled his resolve: "I have made up my mind to get the book out, no matter what the cost."[59]

It was Johnson's idea to ask Brander Matthews to write the introduction, as Matthews had "expressed a willingness" to do such an introduction several years earlier.[60] The choice is emblematic, for Matthews by then represented a rather conservative, Anglocentric literary nationalism, allied to Theodore Roosevelt's, that the radicals of *The Liberator* and *The Seven Arts* were attacking—and after the publication of *Fifty Years and Other Poems,* as we have seen, Johnson would move in their direction, instigated in part by Floyd Dell's review of the book. As Johnson became increasingly independent as a writer and moved into new literary circles (becoming close friends with Alfred A. Knopf, Joel Spingarn, and Carl Van Vechten), his correspondence with Braithwaite began to trail off, but he continued jogging his mentor with the idea of a school anthology of Negro literature, which he felt would make money.

He also shared his poem "The Creation" with Braithwaite in draft form.[61] Braithwaite suggested he send the poem to the *Yale Review,* but Johnson was not enthusiastic about this suggestion: "If the Yale Review accepts, when in the world would the verses be published; in the course of a year or two?"[62] Again, the differences between Braithwaite's view of the "place" of poetry and Johnson's find expression in the choice of journals. Whether or not Johnson ever sent the poem to the *Yale Review,* he ended up placing it in *The Freeman,* no doubt with Spingarn's help. Nonetheless, upon publication he had a marked copy sent to Braithwaite, wanting to know how he liked it in print.[63] By this time, however, Johnson was drifting farther out of Braithwaite's orbit. When Walter Reid of Cornhill approached him about bringing out a new, expanded edition of *Fifty Years and Other Poems,* Johnson diplomatically rejected the idea in favor of saving his new poems for a separate volume with a different publisher at some later date.[64] In 1922 he published *The Book of American Negro Poetry* not with Braithwaite's B. J. Brimmer but with Harcourt, Brace.

As an indication of how the sort of dealings that led to *Fifty Years'* publication were viewed among larger houses, one can use Alfred Harcourt's response to Braithwaite's efforts for a young poet named David

O'Neill in 1916. At the time, Harcourt was with Henry Holt, who had rejected O'Neill's manuscript; Braithwaite had then suggested that he could line up people to subsidize publication. Harcourt responded, however, that the house had a hard and fast rule "not to publish any subsidized books in the realm of creative literature." Subsidized books might be warranted in some cases, such as scientific works of genuine value with a limited audience; but "in the case of poetry, we are scrupulously avoiding it."[65] One could argue that the very fact that Cornhill was chiefly a vanity press accounts for its openness to the publication of work by African Americans, particularly work that did not fit the prevailing trends in poetry or that publishers simply did not expect to have a large audience—which describes African American poetry generally between Dunbar's death and the mid-1920s.

In 1918–1919 Cornhill published a number of collections by poets frequently featured in *The Crisis:* Joseph S. Cotter's *The Band of Gideon, and Other Lyrics;* Maud Cuney Hare's *The Message of the Trees;* Charles Bertram Johnson's *Songs of My People;* and Georgia Douglas Johnson's *The Heart of a Woman, and Other Poems,* along with seventeen books of poetry by white American authors long since forgotten. The press also published Angelina Weld Grimké's play *Rachel* (1917), a production of the NAACP drama committee in Washington. In 1919 Claude McKay wrote Max Eastman that if Knopf turned down the collection of poems he had sent out, he would go to Cornhill—"But I won't have Braithwaite's name in it," an indication that at this time Cornhill was considered a likely (if unprestigious) place for black poetry to be accepted.[66] McKay's letter also, of course, suggests that by 1919 a "new poet" and radical would not want his work introduced by Braithwaite. On September 29, 1919, however, while sending poems Braithwaite had solicited for his anthology, McKay postscripted that Knopf had accepted his book of poetry. A year later he sent *Spring in New Hampshire* from London, mentioning that he hoped to arrange for its publication in the United States, "Knopf having failed me at the last moment."[67] McKay was, in fact, turned down by Knopf, as we will see, but he did not follow through on his plan to turn next to Cornhill; chances are that it would have been futile at that point. Concentrating heavily in volumes of poetry by unknown writers, Cornhill was already in bad financial straits when the poet Brookes More, a friend of Braithwaite's, bought into it in 1919. By 1921 he had acquired complete control, firing Reid the next spring and reducing the size of the company.[68] Presumably More had no interest in publishing African American poets; in any case, he published no more of them, and in the same year that More took control of Cornhill, Braithwaite founded B. J. Brimmer, which issued Georgia Douglas Johnson's next book, *Bronze* (1922).

As editor-in-chief at Brimmer, Braithwaite continued to show interest in African American authors.[69] However, it appears that he published only three books of African American poetry or fiction, plus one non-fiction book on the black soldiers of the Great War, and Braithwaite's closest literary relations continued to be with white New Englanders. It is not difficult to see that Braithwaite's efforts as a publisher were continuous with his aims as anthologist and as literary critic for the *Boston Transcript*. He definitely wanted to do what he could for "the race," but always within the context of his vision of American culture as a whole—a pluralistic culture destined to be a melting pot in the long run. As I have pointed out in the discussion of *The Crisis*, Braithwaite did not regard the black artist as binational: "Thus, if it is convenient to speak of Negro literature as a classification of American literature," he would write in a 1934 appreciation of Jessie Fauset's fiction, "it is essential to insist that the standards are one and the same."[70]

The Brimmer spring list of 1924, advertised in *The New Republic,* also included a novel about the "race problem" by one Joshua Henry Jones and a book of poems about New England by Braithwaite's partner and treasurer in the house of Brimmer, Winifred Virginia Jackson, reputedly a *Mayflower* descendant. Other titles, by authors utterly forgotten today, included books of poetry by Mary Esther Cobb, Lucius Beebe, Nelson Antrim Crawford, Zoe Patricia Hobbs, Donald Fay Robinson, Edna Davis Romig, and Bella Flaccus.[71] Unfortunately, these were not the makings of a list that could provide financially for the survival of a publishing company. Even Braithwaite's *Anthology,* for all its reputation, never made any money to speak of, and every firm that published it went bankrupt.[72] Hence, always courting disaster during its short life, Brimmer was not able to do as much for African American writers as Braithwaite might have hoped. But after the demise of Brimmer, both Braithwaite and Georgia Douglas Johnson published their next books through another firm with which Braithwaite had connections. This company was Vinal—owned by the Boston poet Harold Vinal, whose work Braithwaite had featured in his anthologies and whose firm, in fact, published the *Anthology* in 1928 before—in the by-then-well-established tradition—going out of business.

Braithwaite's endless difficulties can be attributed in part to factors over which he had little control: generational changes in American writing that explicitly aimed at liberation from the regional and ideological positions with which he identified, the difficulty of making a living by pushing poetry, and institutional racism. As a largely self-educated black man without the sort of access to financial backing and prestigious journals, writers, or publishers some white editors and critics of his stature (many of them Ivy League graduates) might have been able to attract, Braithwaite struggled against enormous odds and at tremendous personal cost in behalf of American poetry. He performed a crucial service, not least to African American poetry; but in the end he was of minor importance to Harlem Renaissance publishing. His difficulties illustrate the near impossibility of establishing a black-directed publishing enterprise focusing on literature, even if (perhaps *especially* if) that enterprise was not conceived chiefly in relation to African American literature. It may be ironic that of all the publishers of the Harlem Renaissance, it was Braithwaite who adopted the most insistently "assimilationist" (in the sense of "melting-pot") perspective on American cultural reality; even as he recognized the significance of regionalism, he actually downplayed race as a differential factor in literary production. Yet undoubtedly the encompassing importance of race in the United States had much to do with the nature and limits of his own literary production.

American Cosmopolitan: Alfred A. Knopf

Alfred A. Knopf, according to Doran, was one of the first young publishers to sense the new and growing market for books outside the conventional Anglo-American orbit in the second decade of the twentieth century.[73] As a member of the Columbia class of 1912 and frequenter of secondhand Harlem bookstores, he was indirectly guided toward publishing by Joel Spingarn, one of Knopf's closest friends and most admired teachers at Columbia. Each year Spingarn gave a prize for the best essay in his comparative literature class, in which Knopf was enrolled the year before Spingarn was ousted from the comparative literature program by President Butler. Knopf, writing on John Galsworthy, finished second in this competition—the prize went to Randolph Bourne!—but in doing his research he contacted Galsworthy and eventually got into publishing, acting in a sense as Galsworthy's

American agent.[74] Under Spingarn, who would become chairman of
the NAACP the year after Knopf's graduation, Knopf learned about
new debates in cultural and literary theory as well as modern European
literature. Spingarn also first taught him to value the details of publishing, introducing him to differences in typography, the physical
appearance of books, and editions of the classics—thus inspiring an
interest in quality for which Knopf became famous as his business rose
to renown for its book designing.[75] His "Borzoi Credo" expresses his
commitment to quality in all aspects of publication: "*I believe that* a publisher's imprint means something, and that if readers paid more attention to the publisher of books they buy, their chances of being disappointed would be infinitely less. *I believe that* good books should be well
made, and I try to give every book I publish a format that is distinctive
and attractive. *I believe that* I have never knowingly published an
unworthy book."[76] Knopf aimed to become known for publishing only
the best so that discriminating readers would buy his books on the sheer
strength of his firm's reputation. In fact, Knopf would be held in awe
by other publishers and by authors for his adherence to his creed and
his amazing ability to judge outstanding writing. Ben Huebsch, a publisher who in some ways anticipated Knopf as an outlet for the prewar
"rebellion" and later merged with his competitor, Viking, at its
founding, voiced a widely shared opinion of the man: "His catalogue is
not a mask, it is his face."[77]

Knopf started out with Doubleday, Page immediately after graduation
in 1912; but according to Charles Doran, "Knopf chafed under the
restriction and the scarcely emerging puritanism of Doubleday. He
came to me and suggested an alliance, but while less puritan than Doubleday I was not broad enough for Knopf."[78] Knopf quickly moved to
become general assistant for Mitchell Kennerley, who, along with
Huebsch, had been among the first of the New York publishers to
respond to the new intellectual ferment after the turn of the century,
publishing the likes of Edna St. Vincent Millay, Van Wyck Brooks, Witter
Bynner, and Vachel Lindsay.[79] Kennerley was also the editor of *The Smart
Set* in its years before Mencken, and he acquired *The Forum* as a magazine outlet for his authors (a practice Knopf imitated in founding *American Mercury*); this journal became an American conduit of the Celtic
Revival and one sympathetic to African American concerns—its editor's
wife, Mrs. Henry Goddard Leach, served on the board of the National
Urban League and donated the prizes for the first *Opportunity* literary

contests, for which her husband served as an essay judge (joined by Van Wyck Brooks).[80] Knopf deeply admired the beauty of the books Kennerley published, but the man's inability to keep his *financial* books straight and to deal fairly with his authors did him in. In the final analysis, he was "a damn bad publisher."[81] Knopf learned from him both what to do and what not to do; then Kennerley fired him for disloyalty—negotiating with a Kennerley writer (Van Vechten's friend Joseph Hergesheimer) to publish with his own firm when he was ready to make it a go![82]

The first book Knopf published was a translation from the French of four plays by Emile Augier. As Knopf himself would later recall, "It was, on all counts, a pretty tame beginning for a young fellow who really wanted to publish American novels. But in 1915 not many American novels were being written that seemed worth publishing to the like of me (Dreiser had only just gone from Harper's to John Lane)"; so most of the firm's early books were translations of Russian novels and stories. Spingarn's onetime comparative literature disciple felt he would have to expose American writers and audiences to new types of writing to build up a stable of authors and a market for the sort of work he really wanted to print. As an owner of an international bookstore at the time later recalled, "We were going 'Russian' in America and Knopf encouraged the trend."[83] Remembering today the importance of the Russian example to the Harlem Renaissance and the "new" realists such as Dreiser, Knopf's pioneering work in, shall we say, the *intertextual* field of "native" modernism exemplifies the relationship between American cultural nationalism, continental European and Russian modernism, and the New Negro.

Knopf pretty quickly made good on his promise to nourish the second American renaissance by publishing "American" books of what V. F. Calverton would later dub "the newer spirit." In 1916 he published twenty-nine books: twelve by Russians, nine by Americans, six by Britons, and two by Germans. Among the Americans were Max Eastman, Alfred Kreymborg, and Carl Van Vechten (then considered a regionalist)—all later linked closely to New Negro authors.[84] In 1917 Knopf published fourteen American books and fourteen British out of thirty-seven titles. Still he was not satisfied, and in his plans for 1921 he expressed the hope of giving more attention to American authors. According to Adolph Kroch, "He believed that American publishers showed too much deference to work that reached us from England.

This was good news for the native literati."[85] Founding *American Mercury* in 1923 as a journal devoted exclusively to the American scene under the leadership of H. L. Mencken was another way in which Knopf acted on his desire to foster native literature.

One of the reasons Knopf originally got into publishing was that he enjoyed the company of writers; he was friends with many of his authors, and some of them scouted for him. Mencken, though twelve years his senior, was his "most intimate friend" (also a close friend of Blanche Knopf's) and "influenced [him] more than anyone else."[86] Mencken recruited such authors as Thomas Mann, Walter White, Julia Peterkin, and Ruth Suckow to Knopf. Another lifelong friend, of course, was Carl Van Vechten, who brought many first-rate authors to Knopf's attention, including Wallace Stevens and Elinor Wylie as well as Langston Hughes and other New Negroes. But the writers to whom Van Vechten introduced him occasionally became Knopf's good friends as well. One remarkable instance of such friendship was later remembered by Langston Hughes: "For several pleasant years, [Van Vechten] gave an annual birthday party for James Weldon Johnson, Young Alfred A. Knopf, Jr., and himself, for their birthdays fall on the same day. At the last of these parties the year before Mr. Johnson died, on the Van Vechten table were three cakes, one red, one white, and one blue—the colors of our flag. They honored a Gentile, a Negro, and a Jew—friends and fellow-Americans."[87]

Knopf's choice of authors was very selective. He and Blanche Knopf depended on their own tastes and enjoyed helping authors get started. They went not for anticipated "best sellers" but for *writers* they had faith in and books that would sell moderately well over many years; and, as John Tebbel points out, they "stayed with authors [they] believed in as long as there was any possibility of fulfilling the promise [they] saw in them."[88] (Van Vechten, whose early novels sold very poorly, was one of these; Langston Hughes was another.) A strong backlist was thus the bulwark of the firm once it got off the ground, and this is what helped it weather the Great Depression and other vicissitudes.[89] Had this not been the case one must wonder what Langston Hughes's fate would have been in the thirties.

Knopf claimed that he preferred not to have his firm involved in "editing" authors' books.[90] Every now and then the Knopfs might suggest a book idea, but the results, he felt, rarely turned out to be among the author's best efforts. A couple of exceptions to this preference have previously been presented as examples of how the relationships between black authors and white publishers could become strained, so they deserve examination. After republishing *The Autobiography of an Ex-Colored Man*, Blanche Knopf urged James Weldon Johnson to write another novel, even suggesting a topic, the life of the prizefighter Jack Johnson. The author being busy with other projects, she turned to Walter White with the idea; but she still encouraged Johnson to write a novel of some sort, even sending him a contract in August 1930, after he had finished *Black Manhattan* (another Knopf title).[91] What is most clear from this story is that Blanche Knopf had great faith in Johnson as a novelist; while the topic she proposed could be regarded as stereotypical, it is also true that it would lend itself in Johnson's or White's hands to political treatment, since Jack Johnson, as Gerald Early has emphasized, was a symbol of black male power identified with the New Negro attitude.[92] Furthermore, she was not bent on exploiting exotic primitivism; the two authors she approached with the topic would hardly have been obvious choices for primitivist fiction, as both of them tended toward critical realism and social analysis of middle-class black life. The topic, in any case, was clearly not uppermost in the Knopfs' minds; the main point is that Blanche Knopf wanted these two men to write more fiction. She thought a book on Jack Johnson would find a ready market and would fit their talents.

There were, of course, those who accused the Knopfs of exploiting exotic primitivism. Thus Benjamin Brawley returned a copy of Langston Hughes's *Not Without Laughter* with comments Knopf's publicity department passed on to the author. Brawley felt he could not review the book, "at least not without calling attention to its very unpleasant tone, and that I should prefer not to do. . . . I have sometimes had to wonder how such an excellent firm as yours brings out such books as this, but I guess you know best what you want to publish."[93] This wasn't the first time the Knopfs had been accused on such grounds. Countee Cullen had been upset by the title of Langston Hughes's first book of poems. Writing to Alain Locke, he complained: "Van Vechten, in answer to my query, says the book will be called 'The Weary Blues.' That is just the title to suit him (Van Vechten), and many other white people who want us to do only Negro things, and those not necessarily of the finest type."[94] Cullen hoped Locke would convince Hughes to alter the title. The actual appearance of the book when it came out, an example of Knopf's bold experimentation with book design, was a source of further

difficulty for the poet. Gwendolyn Bennett, hardly a bohemian, was
moved to write and console him from Paris: "Never you mind about the
colored people not liking the Covarrubias cover nor the Van Vechten
introduction. . . . You're not writing your book only for colored people.
And if they who chance to have a kinship of race with you dont like
your things . . . well, let them go hang!"[95] Significantly, when Van
Vechten had approached Countee Cullen a year earlier about publishing his first volume with Knopf, Cullen held back; as he wrote Locke,
he was "terribly keen on Harper's"—an older and more conservative
establishment in every respect.[96] The choice of publisher was as much
a choice about how one wanted one's work presented as a commercial
decision.

Despite Cullen's suspicions, it simply is not true that Van Vechten,
and the Knopfs, wanted to *confine* black writers to "Negro things . . . not
necessarily of the finest type," although Van Vechten obviously encouraged such fiction and poetry, with reason. In answer to Du Bois's poll
on how the Negro should be portrayed, Knopf had responded that if
not enough "Negro" novels portrayed Negroes "positively," Negroes
should simply "write books—fiction and non-fiction—to supply the
deficiency." To the question "Can publishers be criticized for refusing
to handle novels that portray Negroes of education and accomplishment, on the ground that these characters are no different from white
folk and therefore not interesting?" he had tersely answered that the
question seemed "senseless." When asked "Does the situation of the
educated Negro in America with its pathos, humiliation and tragedy
call for artistic treatment at least as sincere and sympathetic as 'Porgy'
received?" he replied simply "Yes."[97] Du Bois was angry, of course, about
Knopf's publication of *Nigger Heaven*. But Knopf would also publish
Nella Larsen's novels, which Du Bois loved.

There is just not much evidence that Knopf was guilty of the sort
of exploitative mentality that supposedly typified the white publishers'
approach to black authors' works. Not only had the Knopfs published
Johnson's and White's fiction, but they also encouraged Hughes's work
on a collection of "black and white" stories that, at Blanche Knopf's
suggestion, would be entitled *The Ways of White Folks*.[98] In this collection
Hughes offered devastating satire of liberal whites' views of African
American culture—more precise and effective than anything penned
by W. E. B. Du Bois.[99] And to aid Hughes financially, the Knopfs held
off publication of the volume to allow time for him to sell several of the

stories to magazines.[100] What the Knopfs did *not* like was the kind of "proletarian realism" that became popular in the thirties, which led to tension with Hughes over publication of some of his political poetry written while he was in the Soviet Union. But race was beside the point here—the Knopfs did not publish such poetry by white authors, either. Although Max Eastman was one of their first American authors, his *poetry* was neither "proletarian" nor generally political. The tastes of the Knopfs, if apparently avant-garde, really tended toward the classical. Part of what was considered unique about them was their uncanny sense of which emerging authors would endure and their disdain for the merely topical or faddish—characteristics directly at odds with the stereotype of publishers cashing in on a vogue and borne out notably, as a matter of fact, by the African American writing they published (and which Knopf has continued to publish to the present day). Nonetheless, it was Blanche Knopf who had the foresight to set Langston Hughes up with the agent Maxim Lieber, a child of the Warsaw ghetto and an open socialist (in fact, a Soviet spy, as was later revealed), who represented many of the best socialist and communist writers of the thirties.[101] Hughes then published his "proletarian" poetry through International Publishers, with the Knopfs' full knowledge and, apparently, approval.

The Knopfs' list of books is not obviously that of cultural nationalists. They were perhaps best known for their wide international range, from their earliest years publishing works out of Norway, Sweden, Poland, China, Lebanon, and Russia. This program connects with their cultural nationalism in that they wanted to wean American literature from its dependence on *English* ideas and standards, to make U.S. intellectual life more cosmopolitan. They were the first North American publishers to travel to South America looking for new fiction, and much later among the first to publish African fiction (Peter Abrahams' *Mine Boy*). But the cultivation of American writing was their chief motivation, particularly through the twenties. And their house was important in the development of an American canon centered outside Boston. Knopf published, early on, the first complete edition of Stephen Crane's fiction, Emory Holloway's biography of Whitman (crucial to establishing Whitman's reputation with scholars), and Joseph Wood Krutch's *Edgar Allan Poe*. His interest in publishing African American writing surely was not attributable solely to the influence of Carl Van Vechten, for H. L. Mencken, Joel Spingarn, Max Eastman, and Carl Van Doren—all his friends and authors, as well as key figures in the cultural nationalist movement—were also among the most important white contacts of New Negro authors from early on, as we have seen. Knopf got some of the best black writing of the era—Hughes, Johnson, Larsen, Rudolph Fisher, Walter White. He also published Melville Herskovits' *The American Negro* and the books of Alexander Goldenweiser, important anthropological texts for New Negro cultural theory. The Borzoi imprint is a sort of sign for a web of intertextual relations spun out of the "rebellion" against genteel Anglo-American publishing and "100 percent Americanism," connecting that rebellion—and the Harlem Renaissance—with cultural transformations worldwide.

Impresarios of Greenwich Village: Boni & Liveright, A. & C. Boni

Founded in 1917, Boni & Liveright was another prime publisher of the "new" American literature as well as the New Negro, and in certain respects resembled Knopf. It fostered similar literary developments—in fact, several of its authors were also Knopf authors—and it was similarly important in bringing modern continental literature to the United States. Boni & Liveright's main concern in the beginning was the Modern Library, which reprinted significant contemporary texts, chiefly from Europe, along with a few older works the editors considered to be important for modern writers.[102] The house placed greater emphasis than Knopf upon political and sexual radicalism and "native" authors, and it was overall a more daring firm, more closely identified than Knopf with *The Masses* and *The Liberator* (in which it was a major advertiser) and with Greenwich Village bohemians. Boni & Liveright would fit better than Knopf the image of the publisher caught up in the "vogue" of the New Negro's primitivism, exoticism, and "natural spontaneity." Yet even its list in fact shows an interest in varied forms of black writing rather than a restrictive attempt to censor or control the movement.

In 1913 the brothers Albert and Charles Boni had opened the Washington Square Bookshop at 137 MacDougal Street in the Village and began very limited publishing soon thereafter, backing Alfred Kreymborg's little magazine *The Glebe* (most famous for the number entitled *Des Imagistes: An Anthology*). *The Glebe* died because Kreymborg wanted to publish unknown American poets (he actually did print works by Horace Traubel and William English Walling) while the Bonis wanted him to focus on prose translations of continental writers. In any case, the Washington Square Bookshop, physically connected with the Liberal Club and a basement restaurant, was one of the gathering places for the young intellectuals in the years before World War I, giving birth to the Washington Square Players in 1914 and, by subsequent mitosis, to the Provincetown Players.[103]

In 1917 the Bonis met Horace Liveright as they were planning to publish inexpensive editions of continental European literature that other American publishers would not handle. Liveright joined Albert Boni in starting the Modern Library—an important event for the development of American literary modernism—and the firm Boni & Liveright. Thomas Seltzer, a former editor (before Eastman) of *The Masses* and the Bonis' uncle, bought one-third of the firm, so it is not surprising that they were very receptive to political radicals. Frustrated by the timidity of Doubleday, Theodore Dreiser came to them, and they quickly became the "unofficial publishers for all writers living below Fourteenth Street," according to Gilmer.[104] But by 1918 the firm was split between Liveright's desire to publish new American authors and Boni's desire to stick with "proven successes."[105] That July they tossed a coin to decide who would get the company. Liveright won and bought out Boni, continuing, however, to issue books under the Boni & Liveright imprint, "primarily leftist political analyses."[106] Now able to indulge his own interests more freely, Liveright began publishing even more of the works of Greenwich Village types. In 1918, for example, he published Jack Reed's *Ten Days That Shook the World,* Waldo Frank's *Our America,* and Eugene O'Neill's first book, *The Moon of the Caribbees.* By 1920 he saw the times changing and shifted from overtly political works to racier titles—"sex novels," fictions of contemporary life, and psychoanalysis (he requested, and got, permission to publish Freud for the first time in the United States).

With the profits he made on a sex novel or another predictably profitable venture, Liveright would publish good work that he could not expect to sell. The backlist built up by the Modern Library also helped him in this respect. In fact, after Albert Boni's departure, he began including recent American work in the series—Ludwig Lewisohn's *Modern Book of Criticism,* Sandburg's edition of Whitman, John Macy's *The Spirit of American Literature,* and works by Frank Norris, Gertrude Atherton, and Hart Crane.[107] Other authors that Liveright was publishing on the eve of the Harlem Renaissance were Edgar Lee

Masters, Theodore Dreiser, Sherwood Anderson, Max Eastman, William Faulkner, Lewis Mumford, Eugene O'Neill, Padraic Colum (his anthology of Irish poetry), Michael Gold, Konrad Bercovici (a contributor to the Harlem issue of the *Survey Graphic*), and Horace Kallen. He also published work by the Boasian ethnologists. Several of his authors, including Jean Toomer, were steered to him by his good friend Waldo Frank.

Liveright was known as the flashiest and riskiest of all the New York publishers, his risks being taken for the sake of the cultural ferment that soon included the Harlem Renaissance.[108] "If Liveright did not invent the literary renaissance of the twenties," writes John Tebbel, "he was at least its chief conductor, often acting on what seemed to be no more than hunches or sheer instinct."[109] Deeply resented by the publishing establishment, according to one of his subordinates who later took the Modern Library from him and started Random House, Liveright "didn't care about the old fogies he was competing with. It was Knopf he had his sights set on. By the same token, Knopf disliked and resented Liveright, and didn't want to be considered in that class of 'fresh young Jews.'"[110] Liveright came far closer than Knopf to fitting the image of the Jazz Age impresario. His sex life was legendary, he gambled dangerously in stocks, and his parties never lacked for liquor. Ethel Ray Nance later remembered a party Liveright hosted in his penthouse office to honor the publication of one of Countee Cullen's books. When she started to pull a book from a shelf in the library, the wall suddenly moved to reveal a hidden bar.[111] Apparently, she was not favorably impressed; it was the only "downtown" party Charles Johnson's assistant would ever agree to attend.

Studies of the Harlem Renaissance occasionally imply that white publishers first met black authors as a result of the famous Civic Club dinner of 1924. However, most of the editors and publishers invited to the affair had already had some involvement with black authors. Liveright met Jean Toomer through Waldo Frank in 1922 at the latest, publishing *Cane* in 1923 and then sending him a contract for another book, undescribed, that Toomer never completed.[112] When Locke learned of *Cane*'s acceptance, he congratulated him, noting, "You are particularly happy in the publisher."[113] Toomer later objected to Liveright's desire to identify him as a "Negro" in publicity for the book, to which Liveright responded that he did not see why Toomer should want to deny his "race." This is not to suggest, however, that Liveright wanted to pigeonhole African American authors. In May of 1923 the publisher wrote to Countee Cullen asking if he might have enough poems as good as "To a Brown Boy" and "King Arthur to Guinevere" to make a book. He added, condescendingly, "Your gift is certainly so much above the average of our minor poets that I want to encourage you all I can."[114] At the time, however, Cullen did not feel he had enough poems for a book. All of this happened before the Negro was in vogue.

The Civic Club event itself, of course, grew partly out of a desire to mark the publication of Jessie Fauset's *There Is Confusion* by Boni & Liveright. In his own remarks to the gathering, Liveright told of the difficulties of marketing "books of admitted merit," citing the example of *Cane;* but he exhorted the young authors to further effort while warning against the "inferiority complex" that leads some African American writers to "overbalanced emphasis upon 'impossibly good' fiction types."[115] Good fiction requires a "rounded picture." It was a point *Opportunity* critics themselves were fond of making. Liveright's openness to Fauset's novel is a good example of the fact that resistance to novels about "the better class of Negroes" was not monolithic, although it was to Fauset's advantage to suggest that such was the case. If anyone should have been resistant to *There Is Confusion* because of its class orientation and old-fashioned reticence about sexuality, Liveright should have been. Yet, as one contemporary reporter noted, the ads for this novel "mark[ed] the beginning of a new era in the treatment of colored authors."[116] The ads presented pictures of Fauset and a generous blurb about the Civic Club dinner, "which the intellectual leaders of the metropolis attended. They were celebrating the birthday of a new sort of book about colored people—the birthday of a fine novel about Negroes of the upper classes of New York and Philadelphia—as impressive and vital in their special environment as the upper class whites whom Edith Wharton or Archibald Marshall love to write about."[117] Horace Liveright rejected a second novel manuscript (entitled "Marker") by Fauset, but no evidence exists that he rejected it because of its subject matter; *There Is Confusion* had not been a best seller, but it had sold respectably for a first novel.[118]

A month after the Civic Club dinner at which Liveright had spoken, Walter White was trying to get him interested once again in a volume of Cullen's poetry, despite Carl Van Doren's advice that Cullen wait until he had more topnotch poems and could cull the mediocre ones. Van Doren (who published with both Liveright and Knopf) was concerned for Cullen's budding reputation as a literatus; but Cullen and White hoped a volume of poetry could serve in lieu of athletic prowess to help win a Rhodes Scholarship. After seeing the poems, Liveright advised that Cullen should wait and believed that in another year the poet would be glad he did. Even White agreed with this judgment. As it happened, Cullen's first book, *Color* (which Knopf had also tried to get), would appear on the Harper Brothers' list the following year, but only after they had suggested several deletions.[119] Not long after this, while Locke was putting *The New Negro* together (at the request of the Boni brothers), Liveright paid for a trip by Eric Walrond to his native Panama; the result would be the novel *Tropic Death*.[120] Between Toomer, Cullen, Fauset, and Walrond, Liveright was trying to cover much of the spectrum of New Negro writing in poetry and fiction. As the first American publisher of Freud and one known for his sometimes outré fascinations, he was not averse to the sensational and exotic; but the evidence suggests that he encouraged African American men and women to write about *whatever* they knew, in the forms they chose. His interest in nourishing the Harlem Renaissance was consistent with his longstanding commitment to the American literary renaissance and its break from the genteel tradition that was by now virtually defunct—in part because of Liveright's efforts.

Not long after his parting of the ways with Liveright, Albert Boni started a new venture with his brother Charles. Founded in 1923, the house of A. & C. Boni did not play as wide-ranging a role in the Harlem Renaissance as did Boni & Liveright, but what role it did play was uniquely significant, for the Bonis were the publishers of *The New Negro*. Here again it is important to notice that the publication of African American texts was not a late development in the history of the firm and that their interest in this field connected with their desire to nourish the "new" pluralistic American cultural nationalism. One of the Bonis' most important ventures was the American Library (obviously modeled on the Modern Library), which they initiated with Christopher Columbus' *Journal;* by 1926 the series included twenty volumes, including the *Jesuit Relations* and texts by Crevecoeur, Melville, Bierce, Henry James, and Artemus Ward.[121] The Bonis also became Max Eastman's publishers during their firm's brief existence, and they brought out William Carlos Williams' *In the American Grain*. In addition to *The New Negro*, their brief list of works related to the Harlem Renaissance included W. C. Handy's *Blues—An Anthology,* and R. Emmett Kennedy's

Mellows: Negro Work Songs and Spirituals. In 1926 they offered a $1,000 prize for the year's best novel by an African American—but never awarded it, as the judges' committee found no worthy recipient. Composed of Henry Seidel Canby, W. E. B. Du Bois, Charles S. Johnson, James Weldon Johnson, Edna Kenton, Laurence Stallings, and Irita Van Doren, the committee was hardly dominated by primitivists.[122]

A. & C. Boni went out of business at the onset of the Depression because of distribution setbacks that came just as the brothers had begun a Paper Books Club.[123] The same fate soon overtook Horace Liveright. Gambling on unprofitable books, he neglected the Modern Library and his backlist. When the risky ventures failed, he had to sell partnerships to his subordinates. In 1925 his assistant, Bennett Cerf, left to begin his own firm (eventually Random House), and Liveright had to buy back Cerf's stock; lacking the resources, he was forced to give Cerf the Modern Library as a substitute.[124] Thus he had no foundation to carry the firm when his gambles failed. He could no longer afford to publish expected poor sellers (perhaps a partial explanation for his rejection of Fauset's second novel), although he did start a "Black and Gold Library" in 1927 (which included *The Shorter Novels of Herman Melville,* containing *Benito Cereno* and the first edition of *Billy Budd*).[125] The Crash of 1929 put Liveright, who had invested heavily in Wall Street, on the ropes. To survive, he borrowed money from his office manager (giving him stock in the company as collateral) until one day the office manager owned the business and kicked Liveright out. He died broke and lonely while staying in a cheap hotel on West Fifty-first Street, not far from his former offices.[126] Thus another of the most important and fearless publishers of the Harlem Renaissance met his end. He never had time to lose interest in the "fad" of the Negro, if fad he ever thought it was.

Harcourt, Brace, and Spingarn

While the Bonis, Liveright, and Knopf published the most famous books of the Harlem Renaissance, no firm was more closely and diversely connected with the movement than Harcourt, Brace, which published African American writing from its very beginning in 1919. With fewer links to the avant-garde than Liveright or Knopf, the firm had closest ties with such magazines as *The Nation, The New Republic,* and *The Crisis.* Like Boni & Liveright and Knopf, however, its creation was integral with the "low" modernist revolt that began in Chicago and lower Manhattan prior to the Great War, and its publication of African American writing, from its first year of operation, derived in part from a commitment to the transformation of U.S. culture.

Alfred Harcourt and Donald Brace had served for a number of years on the staff of Henry Holt, whose general publishing, according to Charles Doran, "was distinguished, conservative, almost precious, until the arrival of Alfred Harcourt."[127] One of Harcourt's more important coups for Holt was the acquisition of American rights to Robert Frost's *North of Boston.* Another was getting American rights to the translation of Romain Rolland's *Jean-Christophe.* He also acquired Du Bois's *The Negro,* recognizing the book's importance immediately.[128] But Harcourt grew restless under the restrictions of the firm as he fought for new authors, against the opposition of Holt, his son, and other partners.

While selling Holt books in the Midwest at the peak of the Chicago Renaissance, Harcourt befriended staff members of *Poetry* magazine and expressed to them his admiration for Carl Sandburg's work. A mutual friend then contacted the poet and urged him to send a book-length collection to Harcourt in 1915. Sandburg sent him *Chicago Poems,* and Harcourt, by various stratagems revealed only after Holt's death, pushed them through the editorial channels over opposition to their "rawness."[129] After further strains in his relationship with the Holt family, Harcourt began thinking over his career options: "I saw I was not going to be able to publish books dealing with the new ideas with which the world was seething, and that Henry Holt would never feel safe with me again."[130] Frustrated by the creative restrictions at Holt, he and Donald Brace founded their own company, with the assistance of none other than Joel Spingarn, their former professor at Columbia.[131] Sandburg (like Du Bois) deserted Holt to come with them and remained a good friend of Harcourt's for decades afterward.

About the time Harcourt had begun tiring of Holt, another friend, Sinclair Lewis (later an important Harlem Renaissance contact and advisor to Claude McKay and Walter White), actually provided the shove he needed to start on his own. The two men knew each other from when Lewis was an editor for George H. Doran (the man who would later turn down Walter White's novel after consulting Irvin Cobb) and trying at the same time to succeed as a fiction writer. In fact, they lunched together regularly, discussing the need for a critical, realistic fiction of small-town American life; these talks produced the seed of *Main Street*. In 1916 Lewis gave up his job to work on the novel *Free Air*. In the spring of 1919, Harcourt quit Holt, writing Lewis that he could not decide what to do next but would probably try to find another publishing job. Immediately upon receipt of this news, Lewis set out from Minnesota for New York, traveling all night by rail just to talk Harcourt into starting his own firm, and pledging himself, his books, and all of his savings to the effort.[132]

Donald Brace, a friend of long standing and treasurer at Holt, joined Harcourt; they then recruited Will Howe (an Indiana University English professor) to head a textbook department that would bring the house financial stability.[133] Knowing they needed advisors with wide connections, Harcourt and Brace asked Walter Lippmann (a *New Republic* editor) to advise on economics and international relations, Joel Spingarn on literature generally, and Louis Untermeyer on poetry (because of his intimacy with the native "new poetry" movement represented by Frost, Masters, Sandburg, and others).[134] Later, when Spingarn fell ill, Van Wyck Brooks filled his spot for a couple of years, bringing in Vernon L. Parrington's *Main Currents in American Thought* and naming Sandburg's *The Prairie Years*.

Harcourt believed strongly in cultivating a select list of titles that he or one of his chief staff members found personally compelling. He thus depended on the connections of his top personnel—people such as Spingarn, Brooks, Lippmann, Lewis Mumford, and Untermeyer, all of whom, he said, "had a significant share in whatever standing the imprint of Harcourt, Brace & Company enjoys."[135] These staff members would attract authors, who in turn attracted other authors, allowing the company to develop a strong reputation in its areas of focus. Clearly, writing related to the Harlem Renaissance was one of these areas. Indeed, Harcourt, Brace was connected with *The Crisis* and the NAACP in a way not entirely different from the Bonis and Liveright with the *Masses-Liberator* circle; and Harcourt, Brace would remain an important publisher of work on African American concerns right through the Depression.

The first year's list of books under the Harcourt, Brace imprint included Sandburg's *The Chicago Race Riots, July 1919*, Louis Untermeyer's *Modern American Poetry* (written at Harcourt's request), Lewis' *Free Air*, and W. E. B. Du Bois's *Darkwater*. The first great successes, ensuring the firm's survival, came soon thereafter with John Maynard Keynes's *Economic Consequences of the Peace* (recruited by Lippmann), and

Lewis' *Main Street* (both in 1920).[136] The connection with Keynes would prove fruitful, as Keynes recommended Harcourt to his friend Lytton Strachey and then to the entire Bloomsbury circle.[137]

Spingarn, a partner and vice president of the company after the departure of Howe, started the firm's "European Library" in 1920 (paralleling the similar efforts of Boni & Liveright and Knopf) with the intention of exposing American intellectuals to the most significant new developments in continental European literature. But Spingarn was also a link to the "young intellectuals" and recruiter of work concerning African Americans.[138] He thus played a critical role in setting the firm's course and developing its reputation in key areas. The rewards for him came chiefly from the feeling that he was putting his learning and intellect to the service of the nation's cultural advancement.[139] The development of African American literature was, for Spingarn, an essential element in the larger multiethnic struggle for a national soul.

While Spingarn's "new criticism" differed in important respects from that of his friend Van Wyck Brooks, it was similarly dedicated to the cause of developing American "spiritual values," which he regarded as the unique function of the arts. Believing his thought to have an "American ancestry" in Jefferson, Poe, Emerson, Fuller, and Lowell, he emphasized that the great artist must trust the imagination, not yoke it a priori to a moral or social program.[140] Only in this manner could art best serve the national community. Hence, Spingarn's critical theory is not as divorced from his social concerns as one initially assumes. As Van Deusen has aptly pointed out, "The view of art put forward in *The New Criticism* [just before Spingarn was fired from Columbia] was part of the early beginnings in the first decade of the twentieth century of a critical movement which sought to establish *connections* between American life and literature, to wrench literature and the life of the mind into some meaningful relationship with the national experience."[141] An important reason for his intense attachment to his estate, Troutbeck, was its connection with American spiritual history—here John Burroughs (a former owner) had been introduced to Whitman's *Leaves of Grass;* here Myron Benton (another former owner) had corresponded with Thoreau and hosted Horace Greeley; and here Thomas Lake Harris' Brotherhood of the New Life had flourished before the Civil War.[142] Here Spingarn would host the "younger generation" of American critics as well as two historic Amenia Conferences of the NAACP.

Spingarn believed, however, that "pragmatic, parochial America" could never find herself through a narrow jingoism and intellectual isolation.[143] Spingarn's championing of comparative literature—no less than his championing of Whitman, Melville, Thoreau, and Mark Twain—was an aspect of his cultural (more accurately, perhaps, spiritual) nationalism. He was a "cosmopolitan" cultural nationalist years before his student Randolph Bourne enunciated his transnationalist thesis. Spingarn's own criticism was later featured in *The Seven Arts,* and in *The Freeman* when Van Wyck Brooks was its literary editor (1922–1923).[144]

Not surprisingly, Spingarn's critical theory was attacked by Stuart Sherman in 1923 as un-American, by which Sherman meant it was alien to "Anglo-Saxonia," the work of a "quick Semitic intelligence" working in "super-subtle Italian fashion."[145] Sherman believed that American culture should adhere to a strong "Anglo-Saxon" moral center; his attacks on such authors as Dreiser and Lewis, the new cultural pluralist theory, and the importation of "foreign" ideas from Ireland, Russia, Italy, Germany, and France, were all of a piece. To characterize Spingarn as assimilationist can, then, be misleading.[146] While he wanted to foster America's "spiritual integration" toward a national "religion" of sorts that would destroy the sense of racial difference—as he noted in an address to the NAACP—he rejected the metaphor of the melting pot.[147] Race, he argued, was less an "ethnic entity" than what he called "a spiritual quality of mind made up of imaginative memories and experiences."[148] Spiritual integration of the nation—like spiritual integration of the world, the aim of comparative literature—entailed not prematurely dissolving such spiritual qualities but rather enabling their free development in harmony with the national ideals, combating on both levels ("racial" and "national") the alienation of the soul. Van Deusen argues that his early poetry—particularly "The Alkahest" and "The New Hesperides"—expresses his faith in cultural pluralism as the means to realize the "American spirit."[149]

Despite his idealistic theory of what the "highest" art should aim for, Spingarn actually welcomed literary propaganda. Responding to Du Bois's poll—"The Negro in Art: How Shall He Be Portrayed?"— Spingarn wrote that publishers should publish even those books by African Americans that are not truly "excellent," as a way of assisting cultural emergence and social justice: "From the standpoint of Negro culture it may be important that some writers should get a hearing, even if their books are comparatively poor." Negro authors, he added (accurately, if condescendingly), "should realize that all of the complex problems of literature cannot be magically solved by a childish formula like that of 'art versus propaganda.' They must understand that a book may be of high value to a race's culture without being of high rank in the world's literature, just as a man may be a very useful citizen yet a rather mediocre dentist. The Negro race should not sniff at the *Uncle Tom's Cabins* and the *Jungles* of its own writers, which are instruments of progress as real as the ballot-box, the school-house or a stick of dynamite."[150]

Spingarn—and, chiefly through him, the house of Harcourt, Brace—was demonstrably receptive to a broad range of black writing, "high" and "low," "propagandistic" and "artistic." Through his influence, Du Bois and James Weldon Johnson both came to Harcourt, and in 1922 an expanded edition of McKay's *Spring in New Hampshire* (including militant political poems left out of the earlier English edition) saw print. But Spingarn was not the firm's only white connection to the Harlem Renaissance. In addition to Sinclair Lewis, Dorothy Canfield Fisher (also a close friend of Harcourt's who followed him from Henry Holt) was a Harcourt, Brace author whom Charles S. Johnson called on to judge fiction entries for the *Opportunity* literary contests.

But simply to list the works by African Americans that Harcourt, Brace published is not enough to gain a sense of the firm's commitment and the intertextual context of that commitment. One must consider other, related texts as well: M. T. Pritchard and Mary White Ovington's *Upward Path: A Reader for Colored Children;* Claude McKay's *Spring in New Hampshire* and *Harlem Shadows;* Otelia Cromwell, Lorenzo Turner, and Eva Dykes's *Readings from Negro Authors for Schools and Colleges;* Sandburg's *Chicago Poems, America's Songbag,* and *The People, Yes;* Sterling Brown's *Southern Road;* Albert C. Barnes's *The Art in Painting;* Paul Guillaume and Thomas Munro's *Primitive Negro Sculpture;* Edna Kenton's *The Indians of North America;* Laurence Stallings and Maxwell Anderson's *Three American Plays;* Albert Jay Nock's *Jefferson;* Robert Littell's *Read America First;* Spingarn's *Criticism in America: Its Function and Status;* Vernon L. Parrington's *Main Currents in American Thought;* anthologies of American writing by Carl Van Doren and Louis Untermeyer; James Weldon Johnson's *Book of American Negro Poetry;* Arna Bontemps' *God Sends Sunday;* Lewis Mumford's *Herman Melville;* novels of Dorothy Canfield Fisher; and Harold Stearns's *Civilization in the United States.* More middle-of-the-road overall than Knopf and Boni & Liveright (Doran called it "the happiest possible compromise between the old order and the new"),[151] Harcourt, Brace was nonetheless steady and far-sighted, and its list of publications exemplifies as well as any other firm's the connections between the critical American cultural nationalist movement and the rise of African American modernist writing.

Harper Brothers, Going "Modern"

By the mid-1920s older firms were catching on to the lessons Knopf, Boni & Liveright, and Harcourt, Brace were giving to the American trade-book industry. This was particularly obvious in the case of Harper Brothers, at over a century old perhaps the most venerable house in New York. The fortunes of Harper intertwine tellingly with those of the new firms, for by the 1920s the company was noticeably losing ground. It had lost Joseph Conrad to Doubleday in 1913 because of Knopf's astute work, Sinclair Lewis to Harcourt, Brace in 1919 (just as his career took off), Dreiser to Boni & Liveright because of the author's frustrations with the Harpers' timidity, and James Branch Cabell to McBride. The owners finally knew they had to retool, so they brought in Eugene Saxton as book editor in 1925, hoping to regain their preeminent position in trade-book publishing.[152] Simultaneously they overhauled *Harper's* magazine apparently with the example of Knopf's *American Mercury* specifically in mind—they promoted a new editor with "modern" tastes in art, "morality," and politics to lead the magazine; and they completely transformed its look, hiring W. A. Dwiggins (Knopf's chief designer) to redesign the contents and adopting a modern-looking brick orange cover to compete with *American Mercury*'s green. (Since 1850 the cover had featured bubble-blowing and blossom-strewing cherubs in a classically Victorian style.) The "new" *Harper's* came out in September 1925, and circulation soon doubled.[153] The combined effect of putting Saxton in charge of the trade-books department and overhauling the house-owned magazine (whose editorial independence Saxton himself insisted upon) was to transform America's oldest publishing concern dramatically, to make it approximate the tastes and values established by Knopf, Boni & Liveright, and Harcourt, Brace.

Saxton brought a formidable reputation as an editor and a strong following among authors from his eight-year stint as head of George H. Doran's editorial department, where Walter White had come to know him. He was considered a man of high ideals who depended on his own careful readings of manuscripts for publication decisions. Saxton was the editor who had initially responded enthusiastically to *The Fire in the Flint* and written that the firm would publish it; but Doran himself had then raised questions, and suddenly Doran and Saxton wanted major revisions that White was unwilling to make.[154] Apparently White did not hold Saxton responsible, for he began sending African American authors to him practically as soon as Saxton moved to Harper.[155] Thus the first list to come out under Saxton's leadership included Countee Cullen's first volume of verse, *Color*. After *Color*, Harper remained Cullen's lifelong publisher, in the twenties and thirties producing *Ballad of the Brown Girl* (1927), *Copper Sun* (1927), *Caroling Dusk* (1927), *The Black Christ* (1929), *One Way to Heaven* (1932), and *The Medea and Some Poems* (1935).

Saxton himself, for all his liberalism, could be squeamish in editorial matters. He refused to publish Dos Passos' *1919*, for example, until negative references to J. P. Morgan were omitted; in recent years Morgan had bailed out Harper Brothers financially and the firm still owed his bank money. Claude McKay's initial experience with Saxton was different, however. He had hooked up with Saxton through the efforts of an agent recommended by Louise Bryant in 1926, when McKay wanted to publish a collection of short stories. Saxton responded that Harper would be more interested in a novel, which led McKay to expand the story "Home to Harlem" into what would be his first published novel. McKay was pleased that Saxton made few changes in the manuscript, none of them substantive. However, the more racy vernacular phrasing of his next novel, *Banjo*, was extensively revised by editors at Harper, in McKay's view detracting considerably from its authenticity and artistry. Saxton acceded to his demand to restore the original language, but at the author's expense, as the book was already in proofs.[156] The novel appeared in 1929.

McKay stayed with Harper (and they with him) after *Banjo*, but the market for his works after the stock market crash was not favorable, to say the least. Desperate for income in the early thirties, McKay insisted on publishing a volume of short stories, despite the warnings of his agent and Saxton that short stories would not sell. *Gingertown* came out in 1932 and, as predicted, sank into oblivion. The next year his novel *Banana Bottom* came out, again a financial loss. Harper was losing interest in McKay; the firm had advanced him $1,000 on two failures in the depths of the Depression and did not want further losses, so Saxton conveyed that he was no longer interested in a novel he had earlier encouraged McKay to revise and publish instead of *Gingertown*. Broke and frustrated, McKay tried to get to the bottom of the change in attitude. In a letter of 1934 to Max Eastman he wrote that he thought he had discovered the problem. His agent, Maxim Lieber (also Hughes's agent), had told him that Saxton had confided that the public did not seem interested in Negro authors any more; "the successes of the nineteen twenties were the result of a fad only! Lieber didn't want to tell me but finally did."[157]

This thirdhand account has been recycled recently in the form of a statement that *Saxton* told *McKay* he was part of an "expired fad," which, in turn, has fed the general belief that the Harlem Renaissance—for whites just another vogue of the twenties, as the tale would have it—was "killed" when white patrons and publishers lost interest in African American artists after the Great Crash.[158] However, even after correcting for the inaccurate attribution of a phrase McKay used to characterize what another man said that Saxton had said, and assuming that Saxton said something along these lines to Lieber, one cannot take the account at face value. For one thing, the statement by Lieber, who was a communist, was exactly in line with the reductive Communist Party attack on the Harlem Renaissance, part of its offensive during the early 1930s against the "bourgeois" progressivism and socialism of the 1920s. Furthermore, Lieber was losing faith in McKay as much as Harper Brothers was. McKay's writing was not up to its former quality and there was little reason to believe his next novel would sell. Finally, Lieber—a Soviet spy working for Comintern, as was later revealed—apparently had it in for McKay for political reasons, as McKay (like Max Eastman) had become thoroughly disillusioned with communism after the purging of Trotsky and was persona non grata among the communists.[159]

In any event, whatever his feelings about the Harlem Renaissance, Saxton had not given up on writing by black authors, although he may have temporarily lost faith in McKay. Whatever their personal feelings, Lieber and Saxton probably were both timid about publication of "Savage Loving" (originally "The Jungle and the Bottoms") because of its overt and unapologetic treatment of homosexuality. To be sure, no flood of African American books came out of Harper Brothers in the 1930s, but Cullen's *The Medea and Some Poems* appeared in 1935, McKay's own autobiography, *A Long Way from Home*, was published in 1937, Richard Wright's *Uncle Tom's Children* came out in 1938, and *Harlem*, along with *Native Son*, appeared in 1940.

Although one finds some falling off in the thirties in the quantity of black writing published by Harper, then, there is no indication that the house suddenly abandoned African American authors it had picked up as the result of a "fad." It stood by the two distinguished black writers it had published in the twenties (despite losses), then picked up the next great black novelist just as he emerged at the end of the Depression.

Huebsch *Redivivus:* Viking

Viking Press is another interesting case of the confluence of American cultural nationalism, cultural pluralism, and the Harlem Renaissance. Technically, it was founded in 1925 by Harold K. Guinzburg and George S. Oppenheimer, but B. W. Huebsch had merged his small house with the firm the same year. Guinzburg and Oppenheimer—who had been working for Knopf!—already knew Walter White and were interested in publishing black authors from the beginning.[160] White wrote Rudolph Fisher in March 1925 that he had had a long talk with them, and "it was the feeling of all three of us that the present keen interest in the Negro as an artist had its roots firmly fixed and that instead of being a fad . . . it was a movement that was destined to develop and flower."[161] Huebsch, on the other hand, had been publishing since 1905 and had been instrumental in the earliest rumblings of the Greenwich Village "rebellion." He had cultivated both an important circle of international modernists (including James Joyce, Gorky, Chekhov, Gandhi, Rolland, Hauptmann, and D. H. Lawrence) and the "young intellectuals" Van Wyck Brooks, Randolph Bourne, Waldo Frank, Thorstein Veblen, Sherwood Anderson, and the like. He had also published *The Freeman* from 1920 to 1924, edited by Albert Jay Nock and Van Wyck Brooks, and was later a founder of the American Civil Liberties Union.[162] By acquiring Huebsch, Viking was gaining both an impressive backlist and a visionary editor.

Huebsch can be regarded in many respects as the precursor to both Knopf and Boni & Liveright. His close relationship with the *Masses-Liberator* and *Seven Arts-Freeman* group was important in sustaining the "rebellion" in its early years—he published, for example, *America's Coming-of-Age* and *Letters and Leadership*—and he was the first of the Jewish publishers to break with the Anglo-Saxon bent of the industry. While believing strongly in the need for a "postcolonial" American literature, he was as well known for his publication of texts from what were exotic modern traditions in the first two decades of the century.

According to Christopher Morley, "It used to be waggishly said that any Irish, Hindu, or German artist could find a home in Mr. Huebsch's list when no other publisher would take a chance on him.'"[163] He believed strongly in cultural "cross-fertilization" as a stimulus to great national literatures. Being one of the group that congregated at Petitpas' restaurant with the likes of John Butler Yeats and Padraic and Mary Colum, Huebsch followed the Celtic Revival closely, as well as other anticolonial, cultural nationalist movements, and he was the first American publisher to print books along these lines. "It should be our aim," he later wrote, "to preserve separate languages and separate ways of thinking and to encourage the healthy nationalism that promotes the full expression of a people's genius; to urge students to wrestle with ideas of alien origin by studying languages, by translating and interpreting, so that the concepts and ideals of each group may grind against those of every other. It has happened again and again that the study of one people's literature by scholars of another land has yielded results of value to both."[164] The same was true within a "transnational" nation like the United States; American culture, Huebsch believed, had been continually revitalized by the contributions of immigrant groups and marginalized peoples.

These were the sorts of views that Huebsch, effectively the editor-in-chief at Viking, brought to the new firm, which published James Weldon and Rosamond Johnson's *The Book of American Negro Spirituals* with great fanfare to kick off its first season, followed in 1927 by *God's Trombones* (the very year Braithwaite's B. J. Brimmer went bankrupt). They probably acquired the latter in part by virtue of the fact that "The Creation" had originally appeared in *The Freeman*. Johnson's next volume of poetry, *Saint Peter Relates an Incident,* also came out with Viking, as did his autobiography. Perhaps because most of the other major Harlem Renaissance authors had already found publishers by 1926, Viking did not publish any other important texts of the movement. White had tried to get McKay to submit a book to Viking, but having never heard of the firm and knowing nothing about it, McKay ignored the suggestion.[165]

Traveling Texts and the Contours of the Field

The relations between the various publishers to which African American writers turned are exemplified by Walter White's and Claude

McKay's methods of choosing among them. As Edward Waldron has reconstructed the story, after submitting his revised draft of *The Fire in the Flint* to Doran, White expected rejection.[166] He asked his friend H. L. Mencken what to do. White probably was hoping he would simply recommend the manuscript immediately to Knopf. The request for advice put Mencken in a delicate situation; we do not, in any case, know just what he thought of the manuscript. He first suggested White send it to Liveright, thinking Knopf would not want to "gamble" on it—and, perhaps, that it was not formally "modern" enough for Knopf's tastes. White, however, doubted Liveright, for he had just published Waldo Frank's *Holiday* and was about to come out with Toomer's *Cane* and Fauset's *There Is Confusion*. Furthermore, Liveright had a reputation for publishing risqué and iconoclastic books appealing chiefly to those outside the mainstream, and this was not the kind of venue White was looking for. After the rejection from Doran was final, Mencken suggested Harcourt, "but even Harcourt may feel that he is doing too many Negro books." (Additionally, Spingarn felt the novel suffered from poor prose and characterization and could only hurt White's reputation.) Mencken urged White to send the book to a Negro publisher, who would be unconcerned about appearing to have too many "Negro" books and would welcome White's treatment of his subject. B. J. Brimmer would have been an obvious choice at this point, but White surely knew Brimmer could not promote his book effectively, and he did not want his novel written off as "special pleading."[167] White, moreover, wanted to publish with a "respectable" and "conservative" firm that would reach whites who were ignorant of the "race problem" (hence the initial choice of Doran); he did not want the Bonis or Seltzer because these firms were known to lean toward "the bizarre or the sensational."

Finally Mencken did talk to Knopf, but White had by then already contacted the company, and Blanche Knopf had agreed to have Carl Van Doren give his opinion on the novel. Apparently Van Doren was White's own choice. As a former literary editor of *The Nation*, currently of *The Century*, a well-known critic who had been promoting African American literature for several years, and White's personal friend, Van Doren could hardly be beat as a sympathetic referee for *The Fire in the Flint*. Van Doren recommended the book and acceded to White's request to help edit the prose. The drama was not over yet, however, for White sought advice from Sinclair Lewis by way of Spingarn; Lewis liked the novel and wrote a blurb for Knopf to employ in marketing, but he also recommended that White read *Passage to India* (a Harcourt title) to learn characterization and how to do more justice to villains, the more effectively to attack them. This was advice Alfred Harcourt often gave Lewis himself.

On November 6, 1924, White wrote Claude McKay—then looking for a publisher for his novel—saying Lewis had gone over large chunks of the manuscript of *The Fire in the Flint* page by page and line by line; he then arranged for McKay and Lewis to meet in Paris.[168] By the time they met, McKay had completed a draft of his (never published) novel "Color Scheme." Lewis went through the novel carefully, offering criticism, advice, and money. He subsequently convinced the Garland Fund to extend the grant they had given McKay to work on the novel.[169] About this time White wrote McKay that the newly founded Viking was eager to see "Color Scheme"; but McKay, who had never heard of Viking, had already commissioned Arthur Schomburg to submit it to Knopf, then Harcourt, then Boni & Liveright—judging these firms (like White, one suspects) in order of distinction and marketing clout.

These presses, of course, did publish books that treated the Negro stereotypically, but not in the way that books from other presses did, and one finds an increasing discrimination and sensitivity in their lists. As New Negro books were published, editors at the firms that published them could not help but learn to discriminate between treatments of African American culture—they were reading the reviews of their books, socializing with authors and critics closely associated with the National Urban League and the NAACP, and learning, undoubtedly, more about African American culture than any white publishers had known before. This is not, of course, to say that racist ideology was purged from their systems.

Contrary to popular belief, publishers did not suddenly lose interest in black authors with the onset of the Depression. *None* of the publishers that survived stopped publishing the New Negro writers they had picked up in the 1920s. Indeed, one of the strangest charges against the Harlem Renaissance is that, having been buoyed by white fascination for the primitive, it crashed with the stock market in 1929. Simply consulting the standard bibliographies disproves this notion. Perhaps as much as 40 percent *more* single-authored works of African American poetry, fiction, drama, and autobiography appeared in the 1930s than in the 1920s, despite a major shrinkage in American book publishing (especially fiction) caused by the Depression.[170] Neither is this simply because the Harlem Renaissance got a late start on the decade. More books of black creative writing were published in 1931—and again in 1932, 1935, 1936, 1937, 1938, and 1939—than in any year of the 1920s. Even if we restrict the tally to "major" or "major minor" books coming out of established presses, the 1930s show steady expansion over the 1920s, with slight dips in 1933, 1934, and 1936.[171] In addition, several important anthologies, textbooks, and critical studies of African American literature came out in the 1930s—by the likes of Vernon Loggins, Sterling Brown, Benjamin Brawley, Saunders Redding, and Nick Aaron Ford, among others—giving the field a scholarly institutional base.[172]

The publishers of the 1920s that survived continued to publish books by African Americans and in some cases expanded their lists. They were joined by houses that had not previously attended to black writing, such as Lippincott, Macmillan, Doubleday Doran, Stokes, and Covici-Friede. A new black-directed publishing house also entered the field, Associates in Negro Folk Education—which, according to Locke, its guiding force, took "as its basic viewpoint the analysis of the Negro idiom and the Negro theme in the various art fields as a gradually widening field of collaboration and interaction between the white and the Negro creative artists."[173] Black authors who published their first books in the 1930s included William Attaway, Arna Bontemps, Sterling Brown, Frank Marshall Davis, Angelo Herndon, Zora Neale Hurston, George Schuyler, E. Waters Turpin, and Richard Wright. And this is to leave entirely to the side the work of the new social scientists. Why, then, did certain writers come to imply that 1929 rang the death knell of interest in African American writing? Perhaps because the blossoming of the 1920s had seemed so miraculous, and perhaps because the number of *parties* declined. Being a Negro author—for that matter, being any kind of author—was not as glamorous as it had been in the previous decade.

Even when the amount of black fiction and poetry declined temporarily in the thirties, moreover, it was partly offset by an increase in nonfiction. By and large, this nonfiction came out of the same houses the fiction and poetry had come out of. Meanwhile, black fiction writers, poets, and artists found support and venues for their artwork within New Deal agencies dominated by the network of critics, editors, and artists who had promoted or received favorably the work of the New Negro.

The twenties, nonetheless, was an extraordinary decade in American publishing; the war had stimulated a tremendous demand for books, and the fact that there were far more Americans who had attended or were attending college than a generation earlier allowed for new kinds of ventures to succeed. Furthermore, publishers in the teens and twenties—like Knopf and Harcourt, to take two classic examples—could go into business with relatively little capital. They did not have to do large printings to make money, and they could afford to gamble on their personal tastes. The twenties also saw the rapid development of a mass market for books, reflecting not only an enlarged readership but also, as Tebbel has shown, "the economic necessity of producing ever larger editions to maintain profitability."[174] Whereas publishers like Liveright would gamble on new authors and publish even works they did not expect to make money, they could not afford to do this after the 1920s. With small profit margins, the very structure of the publishing industry was affected by economic changes to which it has always been especially sensitive: "In good times, the business loosened to a relatively large number of small firms, while in hard times it tended to contract into a smaller number of large firms."[175] Between the twenties and the forties, the industry specialized and concentrated in large companies while the costs of publishing substantially increased. There would never be another era quite like the twenties for the American publishing industry, although the sixties did resemble it in important respects— enjoying an expanded market of college-educated readers, diversification and the rise of alternative presses, and a renewed popularity of books in general and books concerned with America's diverse cultures, African American culture in particular. In terms of cultural politics, however, the black writing of the sixties differed notably from that of the twenties and thirties. The New Negro had written African American culture into American culture, as part of a general redefinition of what "American" meant; the black nationalists of the sixties, reacting to the perceived failures of the integration movement, would instead seek to write African American culture out of American culture. In the process, they often wrote the New Negro out of what they saw as "authentic" African American culture as well. How, after all, could a movement so "infiltrated" and "patronized" by whites be authentically black? And how could captive Africans be true to themselves while claiming to be, definitively, American?

III

Producing *The New Negro*

OUT OF THE NETWORK OF RACIAL AND NATIONAL IDEOLOGIES, institutional positions, and intellectual and aesthetic strategies that produced the literary Harlem Renaissance emerged the most comprehensive single text of the movement, *The New Negro*.[1] Produced by a new field of forces gradually taking shape with its own climate of antagonisms, the conflict surrounding and within *The New Negro* testifies to the book's importance in American literary culture, regardless of its partiality and shortcomings. Uneasily coexisting between the book's covers are writers from the entire spectrum of positions I have written about in Part II, although the socialist point of view is distinctly muted, and Locke has chosen and arranged contributions to favor his particular version of cultural racialism. Before interpreting *The New Negro*, however, it will be useful to recount how exactly it came to be, as a striking example of the operation of the forces I have been elaborating.

13

Staging a Renaissance

The real gestation of *The New Negro* occurred in middle-class black intellectual circles, chiefly in Washington and New York, in the early twenties. Many of the themes that would become significant to Harlem Renaissance authors apparently came up during Saturday night discussions at Georgia Douglas Johnson's home in Washington, attended by Johnson, Alain Locke, Jean Toomer, Mary Burrill, Jessie Fauset, Lewis Alexander, Marita Bonner, May Miller, Willis Richardson, Bruce Nugent, William Stanley Braithwaite (on visits from Boston), occasionally Langston Hughes, and others.[1] As Jeffrey C. Stewart has pointed out, the "Saturday Nighters"—originally proposed to Johnson by Toomer—served as an important bridge from the Victorian respectability of the colored aristocracy to the modernism of the new generation.[2] Locke and Johnson "encouraged and supported a distinct strain of Afro-American modernism, a literature of the romantic search for fulfillment by the black self in America"—a strain tending toward spiritual expression as opposed to the more down-to-earth realism of the post-1926 Langston Hughes.[3] Ultimately, literary Washington was unsatisfying to the more adventurous of the young black modernists, however; and most of them, like Locke (and Jessie Fauset, who preceded him by five years), ended up in New York by 1924. Indeed, Locke wrote Langston Hughes before his own move that Washington was a "backwater"; he was obviously anxious to leave before he missed the boat he saw setting off from Manhattan. "We have enough talent now to begin to have a movement—and express a school of thought."[4] Already Locke was expressing the desire to "mentor" this movement, which would set him at loggerheads with Jessie Fauset, not to mention Du Bois.

The awakening was already happening in Harlem. Here the conversations about a New Negro occurred in a broader and more diverse setting than elsewhere. One group, eventually called the Writers Guild, formed the core from which the idea for a "coming- out" dinner developed.[5] On March 4, 1924, Charles S. Johnson wrote Locke: "There have been some very interesting sessions and at the last one it was proposed that something be done to mark the growing self-consciousness of this newer school of writers and as a desirable time the date of the appearance of Jessie Fauset's book was selected."[6] Years later, in a bitter letter prompted by Locke's negative review of one of her novels, Jessie Fauset wrote Locke that "the idea originated with Regina Anderson and Gwendolyn Bennett. . . . How you and one or two others sought to distort the idea and veil its original graciousness I in common with one or two others have known for years."[7] Scholars have increasingly accepted Fauset's (and Du Bois's) view of the dinner's intention, but in fact the idea for the event developed even during the first meeting in early 1924 from a suggestion for a celebration of Boni & Liveright's publication of *There Is Confusion* to a larger event with a more general theme. (The publication of one book would scarcely have merited a banquet for over a hundred, and Johnson would not have organized one for an editor of *The Crisis*.) In his original letter to Locke on the subject, Johnson wrote, "It is the present purpose to include as many of the new school of writers as possible."[8] The inner circle already had Locke in mind "to take a certain role in the movement. . . . You were thought of as a sort of Master of Ceremonies for the 'Movement', and this letter is to draw out your reaction to it."[9]

Almost immediately Locke seized on the opportunity, but he wanted to be sure the event was not to feature Jessie Fauset. Johnson reassured him: "The matter has never rested in my mind as something exclusively for Miss Fauset or anybody else. The real motive for getting this group together is to present this newer school of writers. There seems to be insistence on getting you to assume the leading role for the movement. I regard you as a sort of 'Dean' of this younger group."[10] Since Locke had been an important contact and even a mentor for several of the authors, was a prominent scholar, had published on modernist aesthetics in such prominent journals as the *North American Review*, and was not himself a "creative writer," he was an obvious choice for master of ceremonies; nonetheless, this was a choice with crucial ramifications in terms of cultural politics.

The growing competition between *Crisis* and *Opportunity* for control of the "movement" structured the general frame through which the arts of the New Negro would be dramatized—it determined who would be excluded, who spotlighted, who put in minor roles. Neither NAACP nor Urban League members, much less *Messenger* associates, were likely to make room for Garveyites. Moreover, with the main power struggle taking place between *Crisis* and *Opportunity*, debates over economic radicalism were bound to be shunted aside.

Johnson had an idea of which white literati to invite from the start: Carl Van Doren, H. L. Mencken, Robert Morss Lovett, Clement Wood, Oswald Garrison Villard, Mary Johnston, Ridgely Torrence, Zona Gale, "and about twenty more of this type. Practically all of these are known to some of us, and we can get them."[11] From this core white audience the list expanded to include Horace Liveright, John Dewey, Albert Barnes, Heywood Broun (*Nation* columnist), Freda Kirchwey (*Nation* editor), William H. (III) and Roger Baldwin (son and nephew of a founder of the Urban League, William being secretary of the league and Roger a founder of the ACLU), Konrad Bercovici (author of *Around the World in New York* and a frequent *Nation* contributor), Robert Kerlin, Joel Spingarn, Eugene O'Neill, Raymond O'Neil, Gertrude Sanborn, T. S. Stribling, and others.[12] Thus, contrary to common opinion, many if not most of the white people invited to the meeting had already had some connection with the development of African American modernist writing.[13] Notably, the radical socialists Max Eastman, Floyd Dell, and Michael Gold were not on the list—which helps account for the attacks *The New Masses* soon launched against the New Negroes' weaknesses for bourgeois liberalism.

The meeting itself has been described often in the past;[14] what concerns me here is to point out how it brought together precisely the network of intellectual figures and institutions that had been instrumental in the American cultural nationalist rebellion, and to show that the divisions in the New Negro movement (if it can be called that) were already evident and, indeed, were probably exacerbated by the event before it even took place. Chances are that the white attendees had little awareness of the competition the meeting (and their own presence at it) had set into play. Neither would they have known that, while the dinner was free for them, most of the black invitees were paying to attend. "There are two classes of guests it develops of necessity," Johnson informed Locke, "the 'honorary' and 'supporting'—entirely a mental classification. The point is the group must ask the interested Negroes to pay for their dinners and say nothing of money to the Brouns and Rascoes and Barnes, etc. They are in the habit of doing this here so it won't be as bad as it sounds."[15]

What the dinner accomplished was a concentration of talent great enough to inspire Paul Kellogg of the *Survey Graphic,* who had aided in the founding of the Urban League, to approach Locke about editing a special issue of his magazine. For six years the *Survey Graphic* had been running feature issues on cultural nationalist movements—the "New Ireland," the "New Russia," the "New Mexico"—as well as drawing attention to cultural pluralism in the United States. In fact, the feature artist for the Harlem issue, Winold Reiss, was the same man who had illustrated the Mexican issue the previous year and who would illustrate an Asian American issue in May 1926.[16]

Reiss had recently been painting portraits of Blackfeet Indians and the German working-class actors and actresses of the Oberammergau passion play. His portraits most often were of people in "communities where dramatic social changes were under way," for he wanted to "testify to the persistence of culture under modernization."[17] The artist attempted to capture both the individuality of the subject and the cultural "type"—in Locke's terms, "the folk character back of the individual, the psychology behind the physiognomy"; in his design Reiss looked (like a Boasian ethnographer?) "not only for decorative elements but for the pattern of culture from which it springs."[18] Thus, although Locke would not initially have thought of Reiss for the Harlem issue of the *Survey Graphic,* his approach to cultural diversity, modernism, and the "folk" suited Locke's own tendencies perfectly (and differentiated his work from most modern primitivism).[19]

Du Bois would later imply to readers of *The Crisis* that his business manager, A. G. Dill, deserved partial credit for instigating Kellogg's idea, "at a dinner given to Miss Fauset in honor of the appearance of her novel, 'There is Confusion.'"[20] Whether Dill deserves any credit for nudging Kellogg or not, Kellogg was predisposed to Johnson and Locke's views over those of Du Bois, Fauset, and *The Crisis.* A decade earlier, Du Bois had fallen out with Kellogg over an incident involving an essay Du Bois had written for *The Survey* demanding full social equality, including the right to interracial marriage. Du Bois told *Crisis* readers at the time that Kellogg rejected the essay because he was too timid to publish this demand, prompting Kellogg to charge Du Bois with an outright falsehood and to demand a retraction or else "space to publish the facts as we both know them to be, as a matter of justice to the Survey."[21] Setting aside any lingering grievances between Kellogg and Du Bois, however, Locke's take on the budding artistic movement suited Kellogg's tendencies. Kellogg saw the issue as

> offering a new approach—different from the economic-educational approach of Hampton and Tuskegee on the one hand; and on the other hand, different from the political approach of Negro rights, lynching, discrimination, and so forth. We are interpreting a racial and cultural revival in the new environment of the northern city: interpreting the affirmative genius of writers, thinkers, poets, artists, singers and musicians, which make for a new rapprochement between the races at the same time that they contribute to the common pot of civilization.[22]

The point was to move away from the less "affirmative" direction of "the old protest psychology."[23]

Kellogg was, in other words, of one mind with Charles Johnson's *Opportunity* approach. Even as the issue neared publication, Kellogg had to "stave off" advance criticism from "the philanthropic-economic-education group who thought we were neglecting them" on the one hand, "and on the other a suggestion from an opposite quarter that we go into lynchings."[24] As if to counterbalance Kellogg and Locke's focus, the NAACP took out a two-page advertisement, including a screaming headline asking WHY HAVE LYNCHINGS DECREASED FROM 60 A YEAR TO 16 IN 1924? and listing the organization's legal triumphs.

But if the Harlem issue of the *Survey Graphic* tended to downplay economic radicalism and social complaint, it addressed the issues more directly than would *The New Negro,* which has come in for sharp criticism on this point. As a magazine of "social work," the *Survey Graphic* could hardly have ignored the miseries of Harlem. But more specific and perhaps personal "political" issues interfered along with the timidity and moderation of the chief planners. Locke would complain to Langston Hughes, for example, that he had "wanted an article on 'The Black

Masses' both for the Survey Graphic and for The New Negro. [A. Philip] Randolph refused to write it for me, & then accused me of being a snob and leaving the proletariat out."[25] Moreover, he and Kellogg were under pressure from other quarters—particularly the NAACP—to tone down the critique of living conditions in Harlem.

James Weldon Johnson and others had been worried about the effect of including Winthrop Lane's "Ambushed in the City: The Grim Side of Harlem," which drew attention to gambling, poverty, racism, white-owned "hooch joints," medical quackery by poorly trained white doctors, and particularly rent-gouging fostered by racial segregation. After the magazine appeared, Lane's article was singled out in the *Savannah Morning News* in an editorial stressing the evils of Northern urban life for Negroes, fulfilling Johnson's fears: "The same sort of thing will be done by the majority of the white newspapers in the South. . . . Thousands of Negroes will see these editorials and be affected by them who will never see the Survey or even hear of it."[26] Johnson considered inclusion of the Lane piece "a serious slip." No doubt he was also writing for his father-in-law, the real estate entrepreneur John Nail, who was incensed by Lane's attack on rent practices in Harlem. Paul Kellogg responded quickly: "We would have been extremely vulnerable had we brought out an issue on Harlem which was all made up of 'best feet'. . . . There are evils in Harlem; they do need to be faced"—and they had not been faced "with the vigor and unanimity that the situation calls for."[27] Whatever Locke felt about Lane's article, he would leave it out of *The New Negro*, which therefore gave an even more optimistic view than the *Survey Graphic* of African American urban life.

Many members of the Harlem elite also objected to Reiss's artwork— and to the fact that a white artist's work was featured at all.[28] Elise McDougald, who had recruited subjects to sit for Reiss, wrote Locke that the artwork in the *Survey Graphic* had "created a furore." At a forum at the Harlem branch of the New York Public Library he was roundly attacked. One participant "wondered if the whole art side of the issue were a 'piece of subtle progaganda to prejudice the white reader.'"[29] Jessie Fauset objected especially to Reiss's portrait of two dark-skinned schoolteachers, one of them depicted naturalistically with "nappy" hair, one slightly stylized à la Gauguin or Picasso—both looking, perhaps, just a bit tired after a hard day, but (as Jeffrey C. Stewart has noted)[30] with Phi Beta Kappa keys clearly revealed, and a magazine the size of *The Crisis* or *Opportunity* open before them. A Phi Beta Kappa teacher herself, Fauset did not find this a "representative" image. Even her contribution to *The New Negro* initially included a critical reference to the portrait, a reference Locke excised.[31]

The backstage fight between the NAACP and Locke/Charles Johnson/Paul Kellogg was far from over. Despite Du Bois's positive review of *The New Negro,* NAACP and *Crisis* officers would continue to lob projectiles in Locke's direction—even carrying on an extended battle over the number of typographical and bibliographical errors in *The New Negro.*[32] The important point is that the debates that took place over the creation of the Harlem issue of the *Survey Graphic* affected the shape of the book. In tension with expectations from his core audience—the educated black middle class—Alain Locke would try to orchestrate numerous different voices and points of view into an affirmation of his and Charles S. Johnson's ideal of a national Negro cultural awakening.

14

The New Negro:
An Interpretation

Two months before the Harlem issue of the *Survey Graphic* came out, Albert Boni—whose company placed a full-page ad on the back cover of the issue—contacted Paul Kellogg about republishing materials from the magazine in a book on the New Negro.[1] By the time the issue came out—to brisk sales, thanks in part to mass purchases by Albert Barnes, George Foster Peabody, and Joel Spingarn for free distribution to students and organizations[2]—Boni was planning on a big volume, twice as big as the magazine issue, focusing not just on Harlem but on "the cultural revival as a whole." He was hoping for a book that "practically all the colleges and universities would buy."[3]

Locke has come under heavy fire of late for changes between the *Survey Graphic* issue and *The New Negro*.[4] The changes were not entirely due to Locke's prejudices and elitism, however. Just as important were (black) audience and marketing considerations and the initial plan that the book be more national in scope, as well as Locke's ticklish political situation in relation to the Harlem elite. Locke had to cut down on the Harlem focus, create a greater appeal to colleges, include as many people as possible who would raise hell if they were left out, and in some way deal with the resistance of the black middle class to the cultural program he wanted to push—particularly his interest in Africanism and "the folk." Such factors help account for the addition to *The New Negro* of Kelly Miller's "Howard: The National Negro University" (in place of his attack on Harlem), Robert R. Moton's "Hampton-Tuskegee: Missioners of the Masses," E. Franklin Frazier's "Durham: Capital of the Black Middle Class," and Arthur Schomburg's extensive bibliography at the end of the volume.[5] They also explain the excision of Eunice Hunton's view of Harlem as a ghetto, which directly contradicted the thesis of the imposing James Weldon Johnson essay; and they help explain the elision of some of the Reiss portraits (particularly of working-class women) that had provoked a torrent of abuse, prompting Locke's counterattack on black "philistinism."[6] *The New Negro* would include chiefly the portraits of black "leaders."

Without letting Locke off the hook, then, the criticism of *The New Negro* for elitism and assimilationism must take into account a more complicated institutional context than it has so far. In sly ways, Locke did undermine past elite approaches to African American cultural reality and promoted new types of emphasis on "race values" and the "folk endowment" that would have repercussions throughout the later history of American culture. He tried to further a cultural revitalization based on a racially proud yet cosmopolitan sensibility, drawing confidence from "classical" African and African American folk culture and from a belief that important sectors of white America were prepared for an interracial and cultural pluralist future. Framing all was his, shall we say, Negrocentric vision of American culture.

The New Negro presents varied and in some ways contradictory arguments, which helps explain the diametrically opposed opinions readers have formed of it, usually based on views of the relationship between "blackness" and "whiteness"—as well as "mass" and "class"—that it is presumed to embody. But since the contributors to the book had no agreement on such issues, and Locke's view was different from most of theirs, *The New Negro* is less significant for presenting a particular position than for framing a field of commerce and conflict.

On the one hand, any interpretation of the text as a black nationalist performance is severely challenged by the institutional matrix of the book, by Locke's overt resistance to viewing African America as a "nation within a nation," by the considerable interest several authors show in "mulatto" or multiracial identity, and by the significance of white contributions. On the other hand, the idea that "blacks were almost unavoidably defining themselves according to the terms that whites had constructed about them" because they were adopting a "typical American ethnic nationalism" goes too far in the other direction.[7]

The polarity between these views is, in fact, symptomatic of interpretations of the Harlem Renaissance. Blacks were not to define themselves according to the terms that whites had constructed about them. (We can see this in differences between white and black contributions to *The New Negro* itself.) Blacks would define themselves in "their own" terms, but these terms conflicted, and they were arrived at through a complex, "multiracial," and multilayered exchange, a kind of exchange that was unavoidable in a pluralistic, hierarchically racialized nation of composite cultures. One of the most striking aspects of *The New Negro*—its artwork—exemplifies this point.

An important difference between the Harlem *Survey Graphic* number and *The New Negro* is the appearance in the latter of Aaron Douglas as a featured artist. Charles S. Johnson's secretary, Ethel Ray, who had known Douglas in Kansas City, met Winold Reiss while he was working on the *Survey Graphic* issue; "but he would say often, I should not be doing this . . . these African . . . decorations and pictures should be done by a Negro." When Ray showed him some of Douglas' sketches, Reiss said he should be in New York and kept pressing her to convince him to come.[8] Douglas, with a safe job, hesitated. The *Survey Graphic*'s appearance decided the issue. As Douglas said in a 1973 speech: "The most cogent single factor that eventually turned my face to New York was the publication of the spectacular issue of 'Survey Graphic' magazine (1924) with the splendid portrait of a black man on the front cover drawn by Fritz Winold Reiss."[9] As the *Survey Graphic* number developed into *The New Negro*, Douglas developed into a New Negro artist under Reiss's mentorship, and with a fellowship to his art school that would last two years.

Reiss urged Douglas to think of himself as a black artist: "What kind of picture, what kind of world does a black artist see and transcribe, must be responsible for transcribing. . . . Gradually I commenced to do these little funny things. . . . It looked like nothing to me, the people that saw it in those days looked at it and thought it was something terrific." Douglas still preferred to do landscapes, but "they insisted so vehemently that I finally thought that maybe there is something to this thing. This primitive thing."[10] Over time, Douglas would develop his mature style, which builds upon the beginnings represented in *The New Negro* but moves far from the sort of primitivism many modernists indulged to stress an implicit spirituality and folk background infusing black history, work, and modernity in urban settings.

Reiss's book designs derive strongly, like his portrait style, from *Jugendstil*, which sought to break down the distinction between the fine and applied arts.[11] This tendency in modern decorative arts movements fit well with the European "discovery" of West African art traditions—and with pragmatist aesthetics, as promoted by Albert Barnes and exemplified in the method of display at his foundation, where utilitarian objects with decorative values connected the "art works" to each other and to the space in which they were "experienced." The design of *The New Negro* derives from such developments of its historical moment. On the other hand, it was chiefly in response to the style of Reiss's "fantasies" that Aaron Douglas developed his own style, in the compositions that became the ten featured "drawings and decorative designs" of *The New Negro*.

It would also appear that Douglas was influenced by Jay Hambidge's theory of "dynamic symmetry," then popular in New York art and design schools, and the concept behind the actual scenic art for productions of *The Emperor Jones*—which inspired a series of pieces by Douglas, including one printed in *The New Negro*.[12] Douglas' most striking work for the book, such as "The Spirit of Africa," fits the geometrical principles of dynamic symmetry, based on interlocking root rectangles and prominent diagonals to create illusions of tension and movement within the frame. Hambidge based the theory on his analysis of Greek vases and architecture, though he also believed it was a principle in some ancient Egyptian art, which would have made it that much more attractive to Douglas.

Thus the very image of Africanism so important to *The New Negro* is often mediated through white perceptions and artistic traditions, albeit intentionally shaped by perspectives on race derived from black experience in America—the experience of people of African descent in a country where that descent meant something very different from what it had ever meant in Africa itself. The Africanism of *The New Negro* is unlike any phenomenon preceding it and marks a significant departure from earlier models of American pan-Africanism. Stressing West African cultural connections rather than Egyptianism and Ethiopianism, it displays a more acute historical consciousness as well as a partial disengagement from the sort of exotic primitivism that dominated the Parisian scene and the Stieglitz circle in New York vis-à-vis African art. *The New Negro* is not entirely free of such fantasies; indeed, its weakest moments derive from them. But these are overbalanced by the more careful ethnographic delineation of the African aspects of black American folk culture, the distinctions made between African and African American cultures, the stress on the Americanism of the American Negro, and a pragmatic view of the need for black global solidarity against racist oppression.

The Rhetoric of Americanism

While Locke claims to focus his volume upon "self-portraiture" and the "motives of self-determination," he does not conceive of these tendencies toward the development of a "race-spirit" as separable from the general American literary renaissance. "The New Negro," he stresses in his foreword, "must be seen in the perspective of a New World, and especially of a New America. . . . America seeking a new spiritual expansion and artistic maturity, trying to found an American literature, a national art, and national music implies a Negro-American culture seeking the same satisfactions and objectives. Separate as it may be in color and substance, the culture of the Negro is of a pattern integral with the times and with its cultural setting."[13] Locke's introductory essay, "The New Negro," projecting the Negro's "spiritual Coming of Age," argues that the Negro can provide what white American culture lacks, at the same time taking heart in the belief that white intellectuals are prepared to honor this contribution. It thus sets up a dialectic between black self-pride and a new interracial modernism.

Two fundamental shifts in race relations are taking place, in Locke's view: new "'race radicals' and realists," expressing the rising spirit of self-determination among the masses, grow impatient with any further tutelage to white-sponsored philanthropic institutions; but the New Negro also no longer allows "social discrimination to segregate him mentally, and a counter-attitude to cramp and fetter his own living— and so the 'spite-wall' that the intellectuals built over the 'color-line' has happily been taken down"; black modernists are more open than their elders to interracial intellectual networks (9–10). Such openness to "outside" thinking accompanies a rising self-confidence, pride, and rejection of "special philanthropic allowances." Moreover, if Harlem has served as a site for "race-welding," Manhattan generally has provided the setting for contacts between white and black intellectuals bent on clarifying a "common vision of the social tasks ahead." "Subtly the conditions that are molding a New Negro are molding a new American attitude" (10).

Locke hones an edge, however: "The Negro mind reaches out as yet to nothing but American wants, American ideas. But this forced attempt to build his Americanism on race values is a unique social experiment, and its ultimate success is impossible except through the fullest sharing of American culture and institutions" (11–12). The cultural program is a situated response to a racist society and demands social action; it also complements such action dialectically. The racialism of the New Negro is an effect of America's failure to realize its ideals (the "blackening" of people of African descent in a society that divides white from black to support structures of exploitation); it is a means of concentrating power and energy to force full integration into American culture and institutions. However, the Negro may develop a defiant "counter-hate," a possibility that, to Locke's way of thinking, can only provoke despair. In Deweyan tones, he adds: "Democracy itself is obstructed and stagnated to the extent that any of its channels are closed. . . . So the choice is not between one way for the Negro and another way for the rest, but between American institutions frustrated on the one hand and American ideals progressively fulfilled and realized on the other" (12).

The subsequent essay by Albert Barnes, exemplary of a Deweyan orientation, complements Locke's, stressing that by turning the cruel material conditions of his life into imaginative creations in which the soul, at least, could be free, the Negro has created a tradition that is both his own distinctive expression of being in the world and America's only "indigenous" art. Unlike most white extollers of the primitive, then, Barnes stresses the development of a conscious tradition ranking with that which produced the psalms and "the songs of Zion" (21), a tradition transformed after emancipation, which offered the opportunity "to develop and strengthen the native, indomitable courage and the keen powers of mind which were not suspected [by whom?] during the days of slavery" (21). If the Negro is America's artist and visionary, then "America," as the collective artistic project on which everyone in the United States ought to be working as the realization of a unity of nature, soul, and mind—as "an achievement, not an indulgence"—will center peculiarly around the tradition created by the Negro. That tradition is no primitive effusion, nor an "exotic" (European) transplant to mark class distinctions, but the conscious work of a culture adequate to everyday life. In the work of the New Negro one finds an art developed out of the heart of the folk that bears precisely what "our prosaic civilization needs most." Thus white America must open the doors of opportunity in hopes that the Negro will still accept "our" fellowship: "If at that time, he is the simple, ingenuous, forgiving, good-natured, wise and obliging person that he has been in the past, he may consent to form a working alliance with us for the development of a richer American civilization to which he will contribute his full share" (25).

Barnes's words are a far milder, "safer," more presumptuous version of the ambiguous phrasing of Alain Locke in the preceding essay. In Locke's essay, what holds the Negro "counter-hate" in check, in addition to a "characteristic gentleness of spirit" (13), is a desire to avoid the greater self-destruction that would come with the destruction of the nation, and not a "simple and ingenuous" temperament.

William Stanley Braithwaite's "The Negro in American Literature," parts of which originally appeared in *The Crisis* in 1919, takes up where Barnes's tracing of black artistic traditions leaves off by showing the gradual development of the black presence in American literature from racial caricature through "realism" (like that of Torrence and Stribling) through racially self-conscious black-authored writing to what Braithwaite regards as a new threshold of achievement, independent of racial expectations. His crucial point plays off of the comment of a critic for *The Independent* who had written that "the Negro novelist" must reveal more than the response to white barbarism and injustice: "Such a writer, to succeed in a big sense, would have to forget that there are white readers; he would have to lose self-consciousness and forget that his work would be placed before a white jury. He would have to be careless as to what the white critic might think of it; he would need the self-assurance to be his own critic. He would have to forget for the time being, at least, that any white man ever attempted to dissect the soul of a Negro" (42). To Braithwaite, the years 1923–1924 mark precisely the emergence of such Negro writing, particularly in Jean Toomer's *Cane*. In Jean Toomer, ironically perhaps, Braithwaite finds "the very first artist of the race," a writer so objective that his racial identity could be a "mere accident": "He would write just as well, just as poignantly, just as transmutingly, about the peasants of Russia, or the peasants of Ireland, had experience brought him in touch with their existence" (44). The comment reveals as much about Braithwaite's resentment of the assumption that black writers should write on "racial themes" (perilously close to Locke's assumptions and Reiss's advice to Douglas) as it does about Toomer.

Locke's introduction to the fiction and poetry sections of *The New*

Negro develops Braithwaite's point that the best racial expression breaks away from attempts to be "representative" as well as from Du Boisian "racially rhetorical" styles while nonetheless stressing the new black writers' focus on their own racial background. Emerging from a "group inferiority complex," the new artists speak not "*for* the Negro" but "*as* Negroes" (my emphasis, 48). (It is questionable whether Toomer, Braithwaite, or Cullen would agree with this statement.) While in step with international modernism, they have "declared for a lusty vigorous realism; the same that is molding contemporary American letters," in the process liberating black literature from "cautious moralism," "guarded idealizations," and "Puritanism" (50). "Contrast Ellen Glasgow's *Barren Ground* with Thomas Nelson Page, or Waldo Frank's *Holiday* with anything of Mr. Cable's, and you will get the true clue for this contrast between the younger and the elder generations of Negro literature" (50). The new "realism," he argues, develops new techniques and styles out of vernacular expression and eschews the attempt to be representative. Even in its protest vein, it replaces "wail and appeal" with "challenge and indictment," satire and irony. These qualities express the cultural poise of those who find beauty in themselves.

Fiction and the Folk

Locke then features fiction and poetry that exemplify the qualities his essay privileges. The most notable exclusion is of Jessie Fauset from the fiction section; to Locke, Fauset seemed overly concerned with "guarded idealizations" and representativeness. The fiction Locke includes exemplifies the infusion of modernist form with "Negro temperament" and new methods of using vernacular forms as literary vehicles. Indeed, the fiction has little else in common, yet it anticipates a wide variety of later developments in African American literature. Within this variety one finds the influences of American cultural nationalism, Africanism, cultural pluralism, "amalgamationism," black vernacular expression, exotic primitivism, regionalism, critical realism, impressionism, expressionism, anticolonialism, and other positions aesthetic and political, all straining with and against each other in a collage of widely varying quality.

For example, Rudolph Fisher's "City of Refuge" exploits new forms of impressionistic description and methods of rendering varied forms of black "dialect," folded within what could be called a blues plot. At the

opening of the story, King Solomon Gillis arrives in a Harlem termed a
"land of plenty" and "city of refuge"—twin significations upon the myth
of America that prove to be as deceptive as the American dream. "In
Harlem, black was white," Gillis learns—a discovery that becomes bit-
terly ironic in view of the betrayals and shifts of fortune to follow.

The story incorporates acute social observations and indictment, but
always in convincing relation to the delineation of character. Fisher's
attention to the diversity of Harlem racial consciousness and idiom is
no mere picturesque backdrop to the main story but integral to its
movement. Similarly, the indictment of white supremacy emerges from
the characters' everyday ruminations and activities; it does not come
across as propaganda. Gillis has come north to escape the law for acci-
dentally killing a white man. Hungry for "justice," he aspires to be a
police officer, which proves to be a crucial irony of the story. When he
is fooled into selling drugs and then framed by a hometown friend, two
white police officers move to arrest him; at that moment, he sees a white
man harassing a woman he has been admiring—a scenario that
instantly recalls the interracial sexual heritage of the South and the
emasculation of black men. Gillis, the proverbial rebellious slave, fights
off the white policemen; but in his moment of triumph, a black
policeman—twin of his aspiring self—confronts him in a sudden twist
of "fate": Gillis is stunned, relaxes, and finally stands "erect" as an exul-
tant grin spreads over his face, to the tune of blues in the background.
Thus Fisher brings his story to a brilliant climax that recapitulates the
social indictment of the tale within the form of blues narrative.

"I got the world in a bottle"—but in the final analysis, of course, one
does not have the world in a bottle. The world is full of treachery and
irony. Friends smile in your face and stab you in the back. There's no
refuge. Fisher's is a story saturated in paradigmatic motifs of the African
American folk tradition, translated to modern New York. It looks forward to further development of black urban fiction and explorations of
the formal possibilities offered by jazz and blues motifs.

Other perspectives on Harlem appear in Fisher's "Vestiges"—a gallery of Harlem "types" that may owe something to the *Spoon River
Anthology* style which had spawned myriad sketches of regional American life ("serious" or parodic), including George Schuyler's "Coon
River Anthology," Hurston's "Eatonville Anthology," and later Melvin
Tolson's first version of "A Harlem Gallery."[14] While Fisher attempts to
limn various "types" realistically, the narrative voice remains that of

Standard English—black modernists in fiction had yet to challenge this distinction, although Toomer and Hurston were at least moving in that direction.

John Matheus' "Fog," a rather saccharine winner of the 1925 *Opportunity* prize, is notable chiefly for its foregrounding of American cultural pluralism in the context of a regionalist yet urban and essentially working-class setting on the Ohio River between West Virginia and Ohio. The often crudely stereotyped characters form a microcosm of the United States: Appalachian poor whites (apparently on their way to a Klan meeting), a "Madonna-eyed Italian mother," a pair of "Slovak"-speaking working men, "American" Catholic nuns, a quiet Negro family (religious, polite), a pair of "well dressed and sporty" Negro youths on their way to a dance, and a group of Jews ("enveloped in a racial consciousness, unerringly fixed on control and domination of money, America's most potent factor in respectability") (90).

Employing impressionistic techniques for rendering extreme physical and emotional states (reminiscent of Stephen Crane and Joseph Conrad), the story also tends toward naturalism, both in the depiction of lower-class whites and immigrants, and in the occasion and function of the story's crisis—when a near-wreck on a crumbling railroad bridge in impenetrable fog evokes visceral reactions to impending death. Matheus keys these reactions to the specific cultural/ethnic/religious backgrounds of his characters and then "orchestrates" them toward a resolution—almost literally, as the Negro woman goes into a "shout" and a spiritual at the urging of the white miners, who also ask the Catholic nuns to say a prayer. The white men, ultimately, emerge from the "fog" of their fears and prejudices, and the multiethnic assortment of people achieve emotional solidarity as the tale closes—temporarily, perhaps, but also prophetically for the nation, as the tale would imply.

Whatever its weaknesses, the tale scarcely epitomizes traditional folk pastoralism, black nationalism, assimilationist "best-foot" propaganda, or appeals to black primitivism. (The savages in this story are emphatically "native" white.) Furthermore, it embodies a class-oriented critique in the way it links white working-class bigotry with the position of poor whites in the industrial regime—a central point of the story. Indeed, the story is scarcely a "Negro" one in any expected sense, although its center of consciousness one can identify as Negro through the nature of the ethnic characterizations and the focus of the resolution.

It is a story that focuses conflicts of ethnicity and race through a black American point of view on the possibility of a multiethnic American future.

Matheus' implied resistance to a strict racial dualism in his approach to American culture finds an intriguing and more accomplished echo in the sketch that follows, Jean Toomer's "Carma" (originally published in *The Liberator*). The narrator calls the story of Carma "the crudest melodrama"; but in fact the narrative form, characterization, and style here amount to the very antithesis of melodrama: one finds no moralism, no clear distinctions between light and dark, good and evil, even male and female. The narrative logic of "Carma" precisely inverts the sort of melodramatic plot in which a villain captures a pure woman and threatens to deflower or murder her, only to be thwarted by the hero/lover who takes her home to marry. "Strong as any man," Carma doesn't need a man's salvation, and she freely enjoys her sexuality. When her husband tries to force her into sexual "loyalty" to him she fakes suicide; when he discovers the deception he kills one of his own friends who had helped "rescue" the body. Instead of reuniting with his love, he ends up in the chain gang.

The whole is narrated in a queerly distant, matter-of-fact voice that contrasts with melodrama's violent emotional appeal. This quality carries over to the dramatic "music": in melodrama, orchestral music heightens emotional crisis, with songs interspersed, unambiguously keyed to the Manichaean moralism. Toomer's musical refrain refuses overt emotional appeal while it attempts to capture the spirit of folksong in a "modern" mode. Furthermore, he deploys it expertly at the very center of this lyrical and dramatic tale to establish a credible resonance with the "motherland": "The Dixie Pike has grown from a goat path in Africa," he writes as he leads into the second of three uses of the song. This sudden connection between the rural South of red dust roads and the red lateritic paths, the daily reality, of West Africa, expands in the dramatic sequence immediately following:

Night.

Foxie, the bitch, slicks back her ears and barks at the rising moon.)

> Wind is in the corn. Come along.
> Corn leaves swaying, rusty with talk,
> Scratching choruses above the guinea's squawk,
> Wind is in the corn. Come along.   (97)

Toomer achieves an uncanny evocation of the evening sounds of a West African village at dusk, merged seamlessly with the Georgia country-side—yet without romantic or melodramatic appeals to racial essences and lost African empires. Indeed, he overlays the whole with an aura of subtle ecstasy aided by his fusion of genres and derived from his study of Asian religious practices (implied in the title) and modernist Western versions of "cosmic consciousness." In this respect, the sketch also recalls Emerson's intriguing statement: "My idea of heaven is that there's no melodrama in it at all."[15]

For Toomer, I suspect, melodrama is what George Kateb has called "bad aestheticism," the "aestheticism of duality" that is "averse to nuance, hybrid, and indeterminacy."[16] Toomer's very appearance in *The New Negro* exemplifies the uncertain, contested relationship between "mulatto" and "New Negro" consciousness, for while Toomer's work displays beautifully the effects of cosmopolitan sensibility and fusion of various idioms and genres for an art built on "race values," to borrow Locke's phrasing, the author insisted he was a multiracial "American"; the sketches in *Cane* were swan songs to the violently bifurcated racial past by the prophet of a new people. (He was, in fact, furious at Locke for including his work in *The New Negro*.) This helps explain the ironic deconstruction of melodrama and the genealogically ambiguous religiosity of "Carma"—along with that of the connected sketch Locke included with it, "Fern."

The biracial Fern (Jewish and African American)[17] is an erotic-mystical magnet to black and white alike, but one whom, like a vestal priestess, both black and white men leave alone, sensing something taboo about her: "She was not to be approached by anyone" (100). The narrator, indeed, draws male readers of both races into her spell: "(It makes no difference if you sit in the Pullman or the Jim Crow as the train crosses her road)" (102). The reference to her "weird" mystical eyes as a "common delta," into which both God and the Southern landscape flow, evokes Toomer's consistent trope (from the teens through the thirties) of a river signifying the dissolution of the "old" races into the "New World soul." Moreover, Fern's spiritual "hunger" and frustration as well as her muteness match Toomer's sense of the frustration and inarticulateness of the yet "unawakened" people of his new race.[18] Even as he wrote *Cane* (and certainly by the time *The New Negro* appeared), Toomer had "crossed over" Jordan to a new world for which Fernie May Rosen inarticulately longed—and that Toomer himself could never quite articulate to his own satisfaction. What is interesting is that, despite Toomer's own views of his work ("a spiritual fusion analogous to the fact of racial intermingling," as he wrote to the editors of *The Liberator*),[19] Locke could use it so convincingly to demonstrate the renaissance of "Negro" consciousness.

A very different approach to fiction of the "folk" appears in Zora Neale Hurston's "Spunk," in which whiteness plays no part, and which represents a stage on Hurston's journey to a narrative voice that is itself folklike in its rhetoric, idioms, tones, images, and tropes (what Henry Louis Gates calls the "free indirect discourse" of Hurston's "speakerly text").[20] The tendency appears in the way the formal narrative voice drops out for long stretches as the characters tell stories and converse among themselves, bearing almost the full weight of the narrative. Moreover, the story never impugns or rationalizes the folk belief that is crucial to the climax: that the ghost of Joe Kanty returns from hell and exacts revenge from the man who stole his wife and killed him, Spunk Banks. The tale, at the same time, embodies what Locke meant by objectivity in its unapologetic presentation of a poor black woman who abandons her husband at will to take up with a "badman." The closing sentences of the tale are crucial in respect to issues of representativeness and tone: "The women ate heartily of the funeral baked meats and wondered who would be Lena's next. The men whispered coarse conjectures between guzzles of whiskey" (111). In tone and diction, Hurston works toward her mature style and thumbs her nose at the "best foot."

In stark contrast to the blues-derived structure of "City of Refuge," the nonracialized Africanism and anti-melodrama of "Carma" and the "hybridity" of "Fern," as well as the careful attention to actual folk arts we see in "Spunk," Bruce Nugent's "Sahdji" attempts to present an "African" tale in self-consciously avant-garde forms. Unfortunately, it also embraces the primitive and exotic with a vengeance, along with the sort of bichromatic racial projections typical of European and American Africanism: "That one now . . . that's a sketch of a little African girl . . . delightfully black"; "Numbo was a young buck"; "Sahdji . . . with her beautiful dark body . . . rosy black . . . graceful as the tongues of flame she loved to dance around" (113; Nugent's ellipses). The narrative, too, for what there is of one, would have us believe that the servant of a chief's son murders the chief because of the son's romantic infatuation with the youngest wife; here Western fascination with African polygamy, joined with American concepts of romantic love, provides the entire narrative logic—crowned by the ethnographic fabulation of a chief's youngest wife dancing around his funeral pyre and "giving herself" to him one last time by leaping into the flames. Nugent at least gives us an example of how *not* to go back to Africa, and of how American indeed the New Negro can be.

Eric Walrond's "The Palm Porch" is a far more complicated and intriguing case of the American pan-African reach of *The New Negro*. Despite the ironic title of the story, named for the bordello at its center, there is nothing picturesque about the story's "exotic" tropical city—a city of tenements and of diverse nationalities living cheek by jowl, promiscuously "interbreeding": "native," West Indian, Chinese, "Assyrian," English, "mulatto." Indeed, the central character is racially indeterminate: "Whether the result of a union of white and Negro, French or Spanish, English or Maroon . . . no one knew. And her daughters, sculptural marvels of gold and yellow, were enshrined in a similar mystery. [. . .] To the charming ladies in question, it was a subject of adoring indifference" (119; bracketed ellipses mine). Walrond (raised in British Guiana, Barbados, and the Canal Zone; soon to move to England) consciously flouts the North American obsession with racial definability. But this quality is exploited too often sheerly for its shock effect and exotic appeal, as in the description of Miss Buckner's "flamingo-like brood": "posturing nude, half-nude. [. . .] Purple and orange-colored kimonos fell away from excitably harmless anatomies. Inexhaustible tresses of night-gloss hair, [. . .] hair the color of a golden moon, gave shade and sun glows to rose-red arms and bosoms" (120–121).

The sensibility and technique at times lapse into a glib exploitation of male-oriented exoticism. Yet "The Palm Porch" does have the ironic bite of an anti-imperialist tale playing on contemporary white (and especially English colonial) fascination with the moral, racial, and psychological fraying at the edges of western civilization. Walrond specifically picks up the text from John 3:16 so central to Conrad's symbolism: "And the light shineth in darkness, and the darkness comprehendeth it not" (122, 125). Similarly, the white colonist arrives ostensibly as savior and light-bringer but is trapped and transformed in the languor of the tropics. But the point of view of Walrond's story looks back at that of "Heart of Darkness" from the other side of the "veil," almost exactly inverting Conrad's perspective and blurring his stark white/black duality: for Walrond individual Europeans are shadowy, interchangeable presences drifting somewhat pitifully if barbarously about Miss Buckner's colorful "porch" of the brutally exploited and racially incoherent New World. The story resolutely centers itself and its reading of "the modern condition" in that world, not on the Thames (nor in a purely black world), and shows the white psyche defeated by it. It becomes therefore a worthwhile intimation of a postcolonial and black Atlantic literary sensibility, even as it echoes certain concerns of Jean Toomer's.[21]

Poetry and Paganism

The selection of poetry in *The New Negro*, less diverse than the fiction selection, reveals many of the qualities Locke had previously meditated upon in his earliest critical essays (on Whitman's and Verhaeren's work), as he developed his orientation to modern poetics and American culture between the turn of the century and 1920. His concept of poetic modernism on the verge of the Harlem Renaissance distinctly privileged a sensuous and "pagan" democratic spirituality: "Democracy triumphant, the ethics of fervour, the religion of humanity, the cult of cosmicality, emotional pantheism, Dionysian neo-paganism. . . . For Whitman and Verhaeren it was all one living creed—but their followers have had to cast lots and part their garments."[22] By the 1920s Locke had come to see such qualities in the black folk tradition and envisaged African Americans as providing what Whitman had emphatically called for in *Democratic Vistas*. In fact, if one looks at what Locke (who had lived during high school only two blocks from the house in which Whitman had died) most revered in the "folk temperament" in the 1920s and compares it with the qualities he had found in Whitman's "modern" and "American" temperament in 1911 and 1917, one finds startling correspondences: "a mysticism that is not ascetic and of the cloister, a realism that is not sordid but shot through with homely, appropriate poetry"; an "irresistibly sensuous, spontaneously emotional, affably democratic and naïve spirit."[23] We find these qualities lurking as well in the poems Locke chose for *The New Negro*.

Thus Countee Cullen, for example, in several poems published in *The New Negro*, expresses a longing for Africa and highlights the conflict between his "pagan inclinations" and his "Christian upbringing." Locke (a rather intimate correspondent and mentor in the early to mid-1920s) steered him in this direction, praising his "neo-pagan" and "Dionysian" qualities, his sensuality and spirituality, as evidence of the "emotional endowment" of the race.[24] Similarly, Locke always hoped to convince black poets to connect with Africa—a reflection, perhaps, of his youthful connection to such black nationalists as Alexander Crummell, an old family friend.[25] In "Heritage," "To a Brown Boy," "Harlem Wine," and "Fruit of the Flower," one finds the "paganism" and "pantheism" Locke praised. Yet these are precisely the qualities Cullen would repudiate when Locke broke off with him critically—specifically, over *The Black Christ and Other Poems* (1929).[26]

The split had been in the making since the very year *The New Negro* appeared. In *Four Negro Poets,* Locke had argued that "the present-day Negro poet regards his racial heritage as a more precious endowment than his own personal genius," provoking a quick denial on Cullen's part.[27] As Arthur P. Davis points out, "A Litany of the Dark People" in *Copper Sun* (1927) "is almost a direct repudiation of the earlier pagan stand."[28] And in 1929, rejecting the French poet Claire Goll's claim that among American writers only the Negroes were worth reading, Cullen would ask, "Must we, willy-nilly, be forced into writing of nothing but the old atavistic urges, the more savage and none too beautiful aspects of our lives? May we not chant a hymn to the Sun God if we will, create a bit of phantasy in which not a spiritual or a blues appears, write a tract defending Christianity?"[29] Cullen thought of good poetry as "a lofty thought beautifully expressed" that "awakens a responsive chord in the human heart."[30] He had much in common poetically with the kind of poets William Stanley Braithwaite knew best (he followed Braithwaite's anthologies carefully in high school), and Braithwaite would be a mentor during Cullen's Harvard year (1925–1926).[31]

As Nathan Huggins has pointed out, "Cullen did not serve that function of poetry which molds the language into something new."[32] I would go further: it seems to me that Cullen tenaciously *refused* to alter form and diction, in part for racial reasons. How else could any American poet of his skill and commitment write, in 1925, in a Housmanesque poem entitled "To a Brown Girl":

> Since in the end consort together
> 　　Magdalen and Mary,
> Youth is the time for careless weather;
> 　　Later, lass, be wary.   (129)

Cullen also avoided contemporary directions because—like several of Braithwaite's other acquaintances, who took pride in their ability to compose long sonnet sequences without a single violation of meter, rhyme, or good diction—he found them "bizarre." Likewise, he objected to Langston Hughes's blues and "jazz" poems.[33]

Cullen's racial pride (rather like Braithwaite's) informs his very claim to a free connection with English romantic tradition; he resents the implication that race makes that tradition any less available to him, any less appropriate for him, than for any white American poet—a belief he seems to have passed on to his admiring student James Baldwin in the very years Baldwin began meditating on what it meant to be a writer who was a Negro.[34] As James Weldon Johnson pointed out: "Strangely, it is because Cullen revolts against these 'racial' limitations—technical and spiritual—that the best of his poetry is motivated by race. He is always seeking to free himself and his art from these bonds. He never entirely escapes, but from the very fret and chafe he brings forth poetry that contains the quintessence of race-consciousness."[35] That race consciousness (bred in the heart of Harlem) told him that Hughes had fallen for the white man's game.

Yet Cullen himself could express a militant integrationism in such poems as "Tableau," which reinforces some of Locke's claims that the New Negro moves beyond both "tutelage" and the racial "spite-wall" by glorifying interracial friendship:

> From lowered blinds the dark folk stare
> And here the fair folk talk,
> Indignant that these two should dare
> In unison to walk.
>
> Oblivious to look and word
> They pass, and see no wonder
> That lightning brilliant as a sword
> Should blaze the path of thunder.   (130)

One winces in the moral glare that spotlights this relationship; by the same token, the ballad says something elemental about the strangeness of the society in which it would be sung at all.

Cullen is often discussed in relation to Claude McKay because both men used "traditional" forms, but they are very different poets, as is revealed by their uses of "tropical" themes. Distinguishing Claude McKay's poems of what Arthur P. Davis dubbed the "alien and exile theme"[36] from those of all the other poets of the renaissance is the painfully controlled tension between his nostalgia for a home recalled in sharp, feeling-laden images enriched by lush strings of alliteration, assonance, and consonance—

> Bananas ripe and green, and ginger root,
>   Cocoa in pods and alligator pears,
> And tangerines and mangoes and grape fruit,
>   Fit for the highest prize at parish fairs
> ("The Tropics in New York," 135)

—and a *voluntary* exile that evokes longing not unmixed with guilt: "hungry for the old familiar ways, / I turned aside and bowed my head and wept" (135). These poems contrast starkly with the forced attempts Cullen abandoned. McKay's experience of the United States as a black immigrant was profound, painful, and poetically productive. As Jean Wagner has pointed out, McKay's ways of doing battle with "America" are often difficult to distinguish from his battles with God—"and perhaps in his heart of hearts these two antagonists were but one."[37] The result was a poetry of lasting spiritual force.

McKay's "Baptism" powerfully expresses the poet's struggle with his adopted country, where he *became* Claude McKay, the radical Negro poet. The poem amounts to a form of religious expression, almost Brahmanist, while it demonstrates the speaker's heroic self-control within the chains of the sonnet:

> I will not quiver in the frailest bone,
> You will not note a flicker of defeat;
> My heart shall tremble not its fate to meet,
> Nor mouth give utterance to any moan.   (133)

McKay's choice of an infernal baptism allows him to join the heat of desire with the fire of tempering pain (recalling the English renaissance); the challenge is to resist numbness to experience. Thus passion leads him "naked" into the furnace ("for thus 'tis sweet") and makes possible his transcendence: "Desire destroys, consumes my mortal fears, / Transforming me into a shape of flame." He becomes the fire that consumes him—archetype of immortality—ecstatically earning his identity as "red aspish tongues" "wordlessly" shout his name (133).

The poem stands exquisitely on its own, but one can add moving historical dimensions to the reading when one considers that McKay came to the United States thinking of it as a land of opportunity, to attend Tuskegee, which he regarded as a beacon of hope to all black people. Implacable racism, not great enough to end his voluntary exile, brought out a racial pride and poetic intensity beyond any he had previously expressed.[38] Expatriation did something else to McKay's poetry, as Wayne F. Cooper has pointed out. Whereas his poems set in Jamaica often concerned black urban life there and protested the conditions of the lower classes, after McKay's move to the United States, Jamaica became the rural, even pastoral, "motherland," and all the evils previously found in Kingston were now projected onto the (cold, hard, male) land of "The White House" (published in both the *Survey Graphic* and *The New Negro* under the title "White Houses," to McKay's consternation).[39] That is, the evils were simultaneously racialized and "Americanized." Furthermore, McKay's poems in the United States were never in dialect, whereas his Jamaican poems had been the first to use local island dialect as their "primary poetic medium" and were crucial in the development of West Indian literature.[40] McKay's "Americanization" parallels the development of his mature poetic voice and what John Dewey called his "clean" hatred, "A hate that only kin can feel for kin," according to the poem "Mulatto," which Locke rejected, infuriating the poet.[41] One might add that this poem portrays a mulatto very different from what McKay had known, and resented, in Jamaica.

It is therefore only poetically just that Langston Hughes began composing the forerunner of one of his most famous poems on his Americanism and on the kinship of white and black Americans on the back of a letter he had received from Claude McKay in 1924.[42] This poem became "I Too," which Alain Locke included in *The New Negro*:

> I, too, sing America,
>
> I am the darker brother.
> They send me to eat in the kitchen
> When company comes.   (145)

In the American family home, the "darker brother," disowned by white siblings, prophesies the transforming force of his song's challenge—on the basis of his own aesthetic—to the Americanism of the white kinfolk. At the same time Hughes makes his claim as an heir to Whitman and registers his distinctive poetic identity as both black and American:

"They'll see how beautiful I am / And be ashamed,—/ I, too, am America" (145).[43] The poem was retitled "Epilogue" (from the Greek, meaning "peroration") for his first book a year later; for years he often used it to conclude his poetry readings. James Baldwin would redouble Hughes's defiant stress on the kinship of white and black Americans three decades and more later.

Hughes had come to Whitman by way of such Midwestern rebels as Carl Sandburg prior to the twenties. His was the democratic "transnational," socialist, "comradely" Whitman pushed by Horace Traubel and the *Masses* circle (as opposed to the Whitman of "cosmic consciousness" Toomer responded to). Nonetheless, he early sensed the affinity between the inclusive "I" of Whitman and the "I" of the spirituals,[44] whose fusion shaped one of his first published poems, "The Negro Speaks of Rivers," also in *The New Negro*:

> I've known rivers ancient as the world and older than the flow of
>   human blood in human veins.
> My soul has grown deep like the rivers.
>
> I bathed in the Euphrates when dawns were young,
> I built my hut near the Congo and it lulled me to sleep,
> I looked upon the Nile and raised the pyramids above it.
>
> I heard the singing of the Mississippi when Abe Lincoln went down
>   to New Orleans,
> and I've seen its muddy bosom turn all golden in the
>   sunset.   (141)

Readers rarely notice that if the soul of the Negro in this poem goes back to the Euphrates, it goes back to a pre-"racial" dawn and a geography far from Africa that is identified with neither blackness nor whiteness—a geography at the time of Hughes's writing considered the cradle of all the world's civilizations and possibly the location of the Garden of Eden. Thus, even in this poem about the depth of the Negro's soul Hughes avoids racial essentialism while nonetheless stressing the existential, racialized conditions of black and modern identity.

Returning, however, to the matter of form, I would reiterate the related point that along with the pan-Africanism of Du Bois and the force of the spirituals, the example of Whitman's break with traditional definitions of the "poetic," his attempts to capture the cadence and diction of the voice on the street, in the pulpit, and at the water's edge, provided a partial model for the young black poet looking for a way to sing his own song, which would be at the same time a song of his people. This role of Whitman in Hughes's career is representative of his relationship to folk poetry of the period generally, most dramatically in the case of the author of *America's Songbag*, Carl Sandburg.

Hughes had yet to find himself in the blues and jazz—although he had published "The Weary Blues" already—and few of Locke's selections (except "Jazzonia") suggest his move in that direction. What Locke was interested in at this point, it seems, was the soulfulness of "The Negro Speaks of Rivers" and the kind of "paganism" and "spontaneously emotional, affably democratic and naïve spirit" that he found in the "folk temperament"—not a poetry in actual folk forms, but one exploring the spiritual "endowment" of the race. As Hughes moved closer to Van Vechten, McKay, and others of the left he abandoned "African" primitivism—despite the influence of his patron Charlotte Osgood Mason—and increasingly experimented with the possibilities of jazz and blues.

It did not hurt that he had James Weldon Johnson's "The Creation," also included in *The New Negro*, to mark a direction. (Johnson, too, came back to folk poetry after experimenting with Whitmanesque free verse.) Again and again in recent years critics have taken Johnson to task for abandoning "dialect"; but to abandon "dialect," as Johnson had known it, was not to abandon vernacular. It was Johnson, before any other black poet, who broke the barrier between "dialect" and Standard English—specifically in this poem. Rather than invidiously comparing Johnson's with Hurston's renderings of sermons or Sterling Brown's of ballads (a decade later), we ought to have a look at the kind of literary model Johnson had to work from, such as Dunbar's "An Antebellum Sermon":

> Now ole Pher'oh, down in Egypt,
>   Was de wuss man evah bo'n,
> An' he had de Hebrew chillun
>   Down dah wukin' in his co'n;
> 'T well de Lawd got tiahed o' his foolin',
>   An' sez he: "I'll let him know—
> Look hyeah, Moses, go tell Pher'oh
>   Fu' to let dem chillun go."[45]

What a distance to a stanza like this one from Johnson:

> Then God sat down
> On the side of a hill where He could think;
> By a deep, wide river He sat down;
> With His head in His hands,
> God thought and thought,
> Till He thought, *"I'll make me a man."*   (140)

Such a stanza was virtually unthinkable in "poetry" until Johnson wrote it. It is still ahead of where either Hughes or Hurston was in 1925, as Locke would later point out in a fine review of Sterling Brown's *Southern Road*.[46]

As Hughes, Hurston, and Brown would all recognize, Johnson was after an idiomatic vernacular poetics, recognizing that a break with the "dialect" tradition was prerequisite to a more variously self-expressive poetry. "The Creation" shows, better than anything by Dunbar, the black folk preacher as a superior verbal artist—a virtuoso word-crafter and image-maker; it recuperates precisely the sort of syncretic linguistic feats that had been a butt of humor in the minstrel show:

> And God stepped out on space,
> And He looked around and said,
> *"I'm lonely*
> *I'll make me a world."*   (138)

How can anyone say that such writing "only 'passes for colored'"?[47] This is a stanza that rives the walls of genteel dialect poetry. As Louis D. Rubin has pointed out, most convincingly, Johnson had demonstrated the possibility of moving back and forth between "formal intensity" and "colloquial informality"; just as important, the lessons of free verse are applied to make each line correspond to a breath: "Here was the flowing, pulsating rise and fall of living speech, making its own emphases and intensifications naturally, in terms of the meaning, not as prescribed by an artificial, pre-established pattern of singsong metrics and rhyme."[48] Gayl Jones backs up Rubin's point with the authority of someone who has studied the matter with an eye to getting work done: "Johnson maintains the syntax and expressive language and rhythms of the folk orators and seems to presage more contemporary

ways of transcribing dialect or folk speech as a self-authenticating language."[49]

The problem of "self-authenticating language" takes on a whole other
dimension in Georgia Douglas Johnson's most significant poem in *The
New Negro*. "The Riddle" deals with the "mulatto" theme in a novel
fashion that may owe something to Jean Toomer. In January 1921
Toomer wrote Alain Locke (eight months before his trip to Georgia)
that he had held two meetings at Johnson's home of a group "whose
central purpose is an historical study of slavery and the Negro. . . . The
aim is two fold, first, to arrive at a sound and just criticism of the actual
place and condition of the mixed-blood group in this country, and,
second, to formulate an ideal that will be both workable and inclusive."
Inviting Locke to the meetings, Toomer noted that "as a natural outgrowth" of the meetings "should come the reading of original efforts."[50]
It was about this time that Johnson herself began writing poems of the
"new race." "The Riddle" is one of these:

> White men's children spread over the earth—
> A rainbow suspending the drawn swords of birth,
> Uniting and blending the races in one
> The world man—cosmopolite—everyman's son!   (147)

This poem conveys a very different concept of the "mulatto" than that
of Claude McKay or Langston Hughes—whose "tragic mulatto" would
be not be a cosmopolitan "world man," "everyman's son," but a self-
divided, disinherited, homeless soul, "neither white nor black"—as
opposed to *both* white *and* black.[51]

Indeed, an integral biracial identity rarely appears as a viable possibility in American literature.[52] Even in African American fiction since
the Harlem Renaissance, typically the "mulatto" character either is
destroyed (or spiritually diminished) by inner conflicts caused by his/
her alienated condition in a racially bifurcated society, or becomes
"whole" by becoming wholly "black."[53] Johnson offers a rare retort to
conventional encodings of the "mulatto." She confronts the challenge
of arriving at tropes that combat the negative and "tragic" imagery—
"Behold him! A Triton—the peer of the two" (147). The poem, however, has no truck with notions of "mulatto" superiority to blacks (which
would entail self-division and self-hatred). It expresses a sensibility that
rejects racial hierarchy and deconstructs the binarist discourse under-

girding it; hence the "riddle": "Unriddle this riddle of 'outside in' / White men's children in black men's skin" (147). To answer the riddle requires a new language of identity, as suggested by the term "cosmopolite." Later self-described biracial writers would claim Johnson as a "foremother": "The extent of her influence, of her philosophy of dawn-men born of the fused strength of tributary sources, deserves to be properly recognized. She was the first to give to peoples of mixed origin the pride in themselves that they so badly needed. She was the mother who nourished a whole generation of Eurasians and other 'mixed breeds' like myself," wrote Cedric Dover for *The Crisis* in 1952.[54]

There is nothing, however, in Johnson's writing to suggest that she finds the possibility of multiracial identity to be at odds with African American integrity, which helps explain why "The Riddle" can coexist in *The New Negro* with such a poem as "The Ordeal," in which the black speaker accosts the passing white man:

> Ho! my brother,
> Pass me not by so scornfully
> I'm doing this living of being black,
> Perhaps I bear your own life-pack,

while insisting nonetheless on his difference and self-containment:

> But I have kept a smile for fate,
> I neither cry, nor cringe, nor hate,
> . . .
> I ask—only for destiny,
> Mine, not thine.   (146)

Crisply bitten off, the poem concludes proudly, almost in a veiled threat.

Compared with these poems Lewis Alexander's "Enchantment" reveals the difficulty of leaping into Africa for African American writers of the time, and belies Houston Baker's idea that the writing in *The New Negro* is motivated by the maroon's "firm understanding of African modes of existence."[55] It would be more accurate to say that the writing is occasionally motivated by a *desire to learn* more about African modes of existence. From this standpoint, one can appreciate Alexander's attempt to give a "poetic" rendering of West African–style mask dancing—a considerable feat if he could accomplish it. He does convey something of the method of such dance and the dramatic elements, but he infuses them with popular "voodoo" images and cannot realize the spiritual and emotional complexity of the performance or of the African "audience's" experience of it; the whole emotional complex is flattened to "delight" and "terror":

> The hyena-faced monster jumps
> starts,
> runs,
> chases his own yelps back to the wilderness.
> The black body clothed in moonlight
> Raises up its head,
> Holding a face dancing with delight.
>
> Terror reigns like a new crowned king.   (150)

The page of the text is suitably filled out by one of Winold Reiss's starkly black-and-white designs of a vaguely West African–style mask. From this one cannot help but contemplate why fragments of Toomer's dramatic lyric story "Carma" are the more convincingly African in form, spirit, imagery, feeling.

High Drama of Lowly Life

Locke's placement of Alexander's poem provides a transition to the next section of the book, on drama. Here the spotlight clearly is on folk-derived drama, according to the program laid out in *Opportunity* magazine. With some validity, critics have faulted Montgomery Gregory and Locke for believing that folk expression had to be "developed" into something "higher"; but the criticism lacks historical perspective, as if "vernacular drama" could spring full-blown off of porches, churches, and barber shops onto the stage, or as if the drama of, say, August Wilson had not developed from earlier literary models of how to use vernacular traditions.

Much as James Weldon Johnson had to undermine the boundaries between "dialect" and "literary English," the black dramatist had to bring down the barriers between minstrelsy and "legitimate" theater for a "self-authenticating" drama to emerge beyond farce (which was being explored in the comic revues). It was a problem not unknown to the

Irish playwrights Locke had been reading since his Harvard days, as he
wrote in his inscription on the copy of *The New Negro* that he gave Carl
Van Vechten; and it required confronting the resistance of black theater
audiences to folk plays, as *Opportunity* argued time and again.[56] Thus
Gregory, in "The Drama of Negro Life," writes that "the race must sur-
render that childish self-consciousness that refuses to face the facts of
its own life in the arts but prefers the blandishments of flatterers. . . .
However disagreeable the fact may be in some quarters, the only avenue
of genuine achievement in American drama for the Negro lies in the
development of the rich veins of folk-tradition of the past and in the
portrayal of the authentic life of the Negro masses of to-day" (159).
The comment witnesses to Locke's and Gregory's split with the NAACP
drama committee in Washington and the creation of the Howard
Players. Gregory hopes "little theatre groups" across the nation will
explore the potential Max Reinhardt found in black talents of mime
and the riches of black vernacular indicated by Sheldon, Torrence, and
Raymond O'Neil (misspelled "O'Neill" by Gregory). This vision of
black drama, moreover, derives support from Gregory's embrace of cultural pluralism: "America should not be a 'melting-pot' for the diverse
races gathered on her soil but . . . each race should maintain its essential integrity and contribute its own special and peculiar gift to our composite civilization" (153).

Jessie Fauset's "The Gift of Laughter" complements Gregory's thesis
by tracing the development of a distinctive African American comic theater tradition within the constraints of minstrelsy, finally issuing in such
contemporary musicals as *Shuffle Along:* "A comedy made up of such
ingredients as the music of Sissle and Blake, the quaint, irresistible
humor of Miller and Lyles, the quintessence of jazzdom in the
Charleston, the superlativeness of Miss Mills' happy abandon could
know no equal. It would be the line by which all other comedy would
have to be measured" (166). Moreover, insofar as Negro comedy is a
compensatory response to oppression, it suggests the potential for
tragic drama. If Fauset had anything to do with it, the standards of
American art would be Negro standards—a point one finds central to
There Is Confusion, in the career of Joanna Marshall as actress and singer.

Willis Richardson's *Compromise* responds to both the Du Boisian
desire for drama of social indictment and the Howard Players' stress on
folk drama. Richardson wanted to move away from straight propaganda
without abandoning social militancy and "uplift"; but he also agreed

with Locke and Gregory that the folk heritage was the black playwright's gold mine. *Compromise* thus points the way to a "serious" black drama that relies entirely on vernacular language and folk experience but also shows that poor, rural black Southerners are struggling against great odds for their own "uplift"—the protagonist Jane Lee's main ambition is to see her children educated. The treatment is "realistic" and shows the complexity of white-black personal relationships in the South even as it critiques the imbrications of white dominance throughout such relations. "All them children but Alec's been playin' together like brothers and sisters all their lives," the white neighbor, Ben Carter, points out (180); but he cannot consider the possibility of his son marrying Jane's daughter, now pregnant. The point is particularly focused by the characterization of Carter as a "good" white man. Thus Richardson is able to make evident the operations of racist institutions in the dehumanization of "good" whites and the necessity that, at some point, even the most "understanding" if not obsequious blacks draw a line—by violence if necessary. Jane's inability to take the final step and shoot Carter for betraying her is a result of her own successive "compromises," but the play argues that the time for compromises is over. Richardson himself, however, was not yet ready to show a black man or woman killing a white person on stage. He would start doing this in the 1930s, in plays for schoolchildren that showed, for example, a black Revolutionary War patriot killing a British officer—thus enfolding the threat of violent black rebellion within an American nationalist frame.[57] *Compromise,* though no masterpiece, explores a number of important avenues for later black drama.

Variations on the Theme of Jazz

A section of *The New Negro* that has come in for particular abuse of late is that on music. J. A. Rogers' "Jazz at Home," for example, has been criticized for considering jazz merely a crude resource for "higher" musical forms. The point is fair enough with regard to Rogers' references to the "vulgarities and crudities of the lowly origin" that must be sublimated to produce a "higher" jazz (221). Here is A. Philip Randolph's high-toned *Messenger* essayist concerned about lower-class vulgarity and "overemphasis" on cultural differences between black and white Americans. But Rogers' main interests lie elsewhere—to interpret black popular music in relation to modernism and Americanism.

For Rogers, jazz is a "leveller and makes for democracy" (223), an "assimilator" that creates a liminal environment in which black and white merge. With the power of "reality" and "primitive new vigor," it will drive the "needless artificiality" and "formality" out of American culture, "vulgarizing" in a positive sense (223). Rogers here exploits Leopold Stokowski's statement, quoted early in the essay, that Americans' contribution to Western music will "'have the same revivifying effect as the injection of new, and in the larger sense, vulgar blood into dying aristocracy'" (221)—a metaphor that suits Rogers' (and Schuyler's) amalgamationism. "'Music will then be vulgarized in the best sense of the word, and enter more and more into the daily lives of people'" (222). Jazz is a specifically American music that enhances experiences of everyday life while also disintegrating racial boundaries.

Rogers' essay recapitulates aspects of Toomer's views as expressed in the second section of *Cane*, especially the sketch "Seventh Street":

> Money burns the pocket, pocket hurts,
> Bootleggers in silken shirts,
> Ballooned, zooming Cadillacs,
> Whizzing, whizzing down the street-car tracks.

> Seventh Street is a bastard of Prohibition and the War. A crude, soft-skinned wedge of nigger life breathing its loafer air, jazz songs and love, thrusting unconscious rhythms, black reddish blood in the white and whitewashed wood of Washington.[58]

For Rogers, as for Toomer, jazz is "thoroughly American Negro." While it has certain origins in African music, it is nonetheless unlike anything Africans have created, and it has "absorbed the national spirit, that tremendous spirit of go, the nervousness, lack of conventionality and boisterous good-nature characteristic of the American, white or black, as compared with the more rigid formal natures of the Englishman or German" (220). Rogers regards jazz as a primal American art form inducing "democratization" and racial amalgamation in the context of advanced capitalism—the core meaning, to him, of American modernism.

This view contrasts with that of Gwendolyn Bennett and Claude McKay. In the poem "Song" and the sonnet sequence "Negro Dancers" (included without the author's permission),[59] Bennett and McKay,

respectively, present jazz as a uniquely black, spiritual response to radical evil. They stress not its "high spirits" but a tragic motive at its core:

> Praying slave
> Jazz band after
> Breaking heart
> To the time of laughter. . . .
> Clinking chains and minstrelsy
> Are welded fast with melody.   (Bennett, "Song," 225)

Bennett mixes free verse with attempts at spiritual, jazz, and blues
rhythm, all controlled in the final stanza by couplets in roughly iambic
tetrameter to set off the syncopation of the jazz beat—reminiscent of
methods employed by William Rose Benét, from whose poem "Harlem"
she took the title of her "Ebony Flute" column for *Opportunity*.[60] Her
poem is a high-minded, soulful, and woman-centered interpretation
linking the roots of jazz to its modern emotional coordinates, to stress
the continuity and spiritual authority of African American arts.

Nonetheless, both Bennett and McKay (like Rogers) suggest that the
musicians and dancers are, in McKay's words, "Unconscious even of the
higher worth / Of their great art" as "they serpent-wise glide through /
The syncopated waltz" ("Negro Dancers," 214). Throughout *The New
Negro* one finds this difficulty of thinking of African American art
without reference to European "classical" traditions, and a tendency to
see folk art as spontaneous, not authored. This is a tendency in almost
every nascent movement for a vernacular literature in the West—seemingly a required stage for literary emergence.

Reclaiming the "Classics"

The central section of *The New Negro*, "The Negro Digs Up His Past,"
attempts to overcome this pattern in paradoxical fashion by going back
to Africa through Europe, thus locating a racially identified black "classicism," belatedly rediscovered by African Americans, and through
them of ultimate import to the whole modern world. After reading this
section of *The New Negro*, one finds very strange Cornel West's objection
to the idea that the Harlem Renaissance was in any sense a renaissance.
"A renaissance is a rebirth by means of recovering a classical heritage
heretofore overlooked or ignored," West points out, before charging

that the major authors of the Harlem Renaissance did not "engage in such recovery." "Instead of serious and substantive attempts to recover the culturally hybrid heritage of black folk, we witnessed the cantankerous reportage of a black, middle-class identity crisis."[61] At the center of *The New Negro* (which West accepts as the movement's bible) we find Arthur A. Schomburg opening an essay with the statement that "the American Negro must remake his past in order to make his future" and then presenting a brief for the recovery of buried information about African American history—by a man whose collection would form the center of one of the most comprehensive collections of historical documents on black America, located in the heart of Harlem. This is followed by Arthur Huff Fauset's essay recovering the African American folk heritage from white literary treatments, and Alain Locke's piece on the lessons to be learned from African art.

Fauset's essay also complements Hurston's short story by establishing "scientifically" the existence of distinctive traditions in African American storytelling. Such scientific study of Negro folklore, he demonstrates, can free it of the encrustations imposed by "literary amateurs" intent on interpreting the "Negro character" (243, 240). By this argument Boasian ethnographic and linguistic approaches are prerequisites to a "valid" literary development of the folk heritage, as Fauset suggests in his concluding sentence: "A literary treatment based on a scientific recording will have much fresh material to its hand, and cannot transgress so far from the true ways of the folk spirit and the true lines of our folk art" (244).

Fauset, whose research was supported by Boas and the American Folklore Society, thus provides a path-breaking approach to American Africanism. His empirical and historical method enables him to demonstrate Africanism within the African American folk arts and to suggest that African tales are the "classics" of the European tradition of the fable by way of Aesop. Melville Herskovits, whose essay in *The New Negro* has such different bearings, would later go much further in the direction Fauset explores here.

The foundations of Locke's essay "The Legacy of the Ancestral Arts" similarly correlate with Boasian anthropology, on the one hand, and on the other the views of Albert C. Barnes, who supplied the illustrations for the essay. Garry Wills has recently used this essay to charge Locke with locating black "authenticity" in African culture and eschewing the American "hybridity" of African Americans—using African sculpture "to *rebuke* American blacks."[62] Nothing could be further from the truth, as the contents of *The New Negro* make amply clear. Locke's essay is by no stretch of the imagination a repudiation of African *American* culture; rather, following Boasian tenets, it emphasizes differences between the cultures of the two continents to combat racialist assumptions:

> The characteristic African art expressions are rigid, controlled, disciplined, abstract, heavily conventionalized; those of the Aframerican,— free, exuberant, emotional, sentimental and human. Only by the misinterpretation of the African spirit, can one claim any emotional kinship between them—for the spirit of African expression, by and large, is disciplined, sophisticated, laconic and fatalistic. The emotional temper of the American Negro is exactly opposite. What we have thought primitive in the American Negro—his naïveté, his sentimentalism, his exuberance and his improvizing spontaneity are then neither characteristically African nor to be explained as an ancestral heritage. They are the result of his peculiar experience in America and the emotional upheaval of its trials and ordeals. (254–255)

Certainly Locke thinks African sculptural and decorative traditions provide a rich resource for African American artists to take up on their own. But what Locke "rebukes" is the unthinking conflation of traditional African cultures and African American cultures—linked to exotic primitivist views of jazz and black America. In France particularly, as Laura Rosenstock has pointed out, black American culture was seen as "an extension of African tribal life" (a view that contrasts markedly with most American intellectuals' beliefs that African culture had been "stripped" from American blacks during three hundred brutal years of slavery).[63] While Locke feels black artists should take heart from the European interest in the formal qualities of African sculpture, he is setting himself against certain pervasive assumptions informing that interest. In this, he is in the same camp as Albert Barnes and the Boasian anthropologists. European modernists based many of their views of African art on ideas of "the Negro mentality"—including the idea of "'the physiologically inferior cerebral development of the Africans.'"[64] These are exactly the sort of ideas Boas had discredited in his own work, including *Primitive Art.*

Furthermore, Albert Barnes attacked such views in the United States—specifically, those of De Zayas and the Stieglitz circle, whom he warned Locke and Walter White to ignore.[65] In fact, Paul Guillaume, an early collector of African art (from whom Barnes got his pieces), came from such an orientation himself; but after meeting Barnes he began departing from the surrealists' and others' views of Negro art, insisting that it should be seen as exemplary of "formal perfection," displaying "the highest degree of mastery and civilization," as one of Guillaume's followers wrote in 1930.[66] "What the new generation should ask from the Negroes is a lesson in sculptural knowledge, not clumsiness, . . . a state of universality and not the exotic and savage."[67] It was in dialogue with Guillaume and Barnes that Locke developed his chief orientation to African art. They did not abandon the term "primitive" but stripped it of many of its usual connotations. *Primitive Negro Sculpture* (1926), by Guillaume and Barnes's assistant Thomas Munro (a pragmatist aesthetician), particularly set out to combat the "faddists": "There is apt to be a specious fascination about things that are unfamiliar, exotic and primitive. . . . The lure of strange foreign lands, their manners and products, can be intense but short-lived. Over-civilized and jaded imaginations, especially, tend to worship the rude strength of the primitive, to dream of the noble savage and endow him with mythical virtues. To such minds . . . the African fetish is an excuse for dreaming of deep mysterious forests, tom-toms and weird incantations, of dark warriors and women of the tropics."[68] (One thinks, unfortunately, of Bruce Nugent's "Sahdji" and Lewis Alexander's "Enchantment.") Against such effusions, Guillaume and Munro analyze the art on purely formal grounds, showing what differentiates it from European art while also pointing to the great variation in style according to region and "tribe." Thus the illustrations to Alain Locke's essay include captions that specify location and ethnic origin. (This impetus, by the way, correlates with the Boasian desire to differentiate "culture areas" carefully.) "Abstruse metaphysical theories about the African consciousness" are irrelevant; so are "academic European standards" of aesthetic quality.[69] Guillaume and Munro strive to analyze the artwork according to formal properties alone. They also regard the art as "classical": Barnes and Guillaume actually believed that the masks pictured in Locke's essay dated back as far as the fifth to tenth century—one indication of their zeal for historicism, which also distinguished them from other modernists fascinated by so-called primitive art.[70]

The specific coordinates of Locke's interest in European modernist uses of African art thus make all the difference for the presentation of

African art in *The New Negro,* connected with the cross-influences of Boasian ethnography and pragmatist aesthetics in New York. The New Negro artist must learn from such perspectives, "stimulated by a cultural pride and interest," to master the technical disciplines of what Locke presents as a "classical" tradition; from such training, the modernist Negro renaissance follows. "If after absorbing the new content of American life and experience, and after assimilating new patterns of art, the original artistic endowment can be sufficiently augmented to express itself with equal power in more complex patterns and substance, then the Negro may well become what some have predicted, the artist of American life" (257–258). The Negro renaissance, informed by African classicism, would be the central project of a modernist American renaissance.

The chief inhibition to such development, Locke believes, is "the timid conventionalism which racial disparagement has forced upon the Negro mind in America" (262). Racist caricature has left black Americans at a loss for portraying the beauty of black people. "The Negro physiognomy must be freshly and objectively conceived on its own patterns if it is ever to be seriously and importantly interpreted. Art must discover and reveal the beauty which prejudice and caricature have overlaid" (264). Because it developed free of white denigration, classical African art provides models, such as the bust featured at this stage of the essay (265). Even European artists are ahead of Americans in portraying the Negroes "realistically"—witness Winold Reiss's work, "which . . . has been deliberately conceived and executed as a path-breaking guide and encouragement to this new foray of the younger Negro artists" (266). Here Locke subtly rebukes the "philistines" (in his view) like Jessie Fauset who had objected to Reiss's portraits in the *Survey Graphic.* More important to him than portraiture, however, is the "decorative and purely symbolic material" to be gleaned from African traditions— as in the designs and decorations for *The New Negro* itself. Once the lessons of these traditions have been taken up and developed, then even if the European interest in African arts should pass as an exotic curiosity, "for the Negro artist they ought still to have the import and influence of classics" (267). The notion of a renaissance as a recovery of "a classical heritage heretofore overlooked or ignored" (to quote West's definition again) is precisely what Locke has in mind—and is based on the European "renaissance" concept, though transposed to African American coordinates.

Cities on a Hill

Locke's essay is followed, in the next part of the anthology, "The New Negro in a New World," by its antithesis. Paul Kellogg's "The Negro Pioneers" argues, in effect, that the Negroes moving north for the "democratic chance" are becoming American by entering into the classic experiences of white Americanization—immigration and "pioneering": "In the pioneering of this new epoch, they are getting into stride with that of the old. By way of the typical American experience, they become for the first time a part of its living tradition" (273). This is an argument almost diametrically opposed to the view (in Arthur Huff Fauset's essay, for example) that African American experience has an authority of its own and that its cultural expression is paradigmatic of New World culture. "The great folkway which is America," Kellogg goes on, "need no longer be a thing abstract, apart from them" (273). Did Locke not see how such statements contradicted the spirit of his book? But to give Kellogg his due, his argument springs partly from a desire to combat stereotypes by presenting African Americans as active agents, "builders"—and from a sense of slavery as "social death," to borrow from Orlando Patterson.[71] Thus the migration represents a sort of racial rebirth; Kellogg views the New Negro's development of a distinctive racial culture as a positive aspect of Americanization, "a baptism of the American spirit that slavery cheated him out of, a maturing experience that Reconstruction delayed" (277). African American modernists such as Du Bois, on the other hand, had long been arguing that the folkways of the Southern Negro were the most American folkways, and that African Americans alone expressed the true American spirit.

Kellogg's essay suggests one reason the Harlem Renaissance did not have as lasting an impact upon mainstream American culture as the participants had hoped. For Kellogg shows how white assumptions about Americanism by even a key supporter of the movement keep African American cultural authority in a subordinate position—black people must *become* American because slavery is a fundamentally un-American experience. To recognize slavery in all its dimensions as profoundly productive of what Americanism is would require a transformation of Kellogg's sense of his own Americanism that he simply cannot imagine. Like judgments can be made about John Dewey, Horace Kallen, and Waldo Frank, to name only a few.

Kellogg's essay also exemplifies how the frame of American cultural nationalism shapes the entire field of opposing forces within *The New Negro*. When James Weldon Johnson presents Harlem as a "culture capital" in keeping with Roycean concepts of wholesome provincialism, he simultaneously stresses that it "talks American, reads American, thinks American" (309); in fact, Harlem is a *model* American community. Its very self-sufficiency, as Johnson presents the case, follows the good old American belief in self-reliance. Harlem is, as well, a beacon to the black world. The belief that it will "exert a vital influence upon all Negro peoples" (311), being "the greatest Negro city in the world" (301), falls into a common pattern of American redemptionist thinking.

Such patterns recur throughout Part II of *The New Negro*. Whether Kelly Miller is presenting Howard as the "national Negro University," chartered and funded by the U.S. Congress, directing the "race spirit . . . in harmony with ideals of god, country and truth," and motivated by Emersonian ideals of "The American Scholar" ("The ideal is not a working man, but a man working; not a business man, but a man doing business; not a school man, but a man teaching school" [317]); or whether E. Franklin Frazier is proving the importance of "middle-class respectability" to the black bourgeoisie as it becomes "an integral part of the business life of America" (340); or whether W. A. Domingo is highlighting "the stir and leavening that is uniquely American" and the "democratizing" of consciousness that produces American Negroes out of immigrants from the "black tropics," as well as those immigrants' militant contribution to the fight against "the American brand of race prejudice" (341); or whether Melville Herskovits is pointing out the Americanism of black Harlemites; or whether Elise McDougald is discussing the peculiar burdens, tasks, and heroisms of "Negro Womanhood"—the stress on American identity is not only present but formative.

This fact becomes all the more striking when one turns to the closing essay of the book, Du Bois's "The Negro Mind Reaches Out." Here Du Bois on the one hand cracks the frame of national identity to suggest that identity of "race"—by virtue of global racist imperialism—is more significant than "nation"; but on the other hand, he projects the myths of American providential mission upon Americans of African descent and upon that African nation, founded by black American "colonizationists" and imposed on native Africans, that represents for Du Bois the "promise" of his race and a utopian global future.

Du Bois is concerned to prove that the "labor problem"—considered by most intellectuals of the day the chief problem of the twentieth century—must be seen in relation to "the problem of the color line." The color line, Du Bois demonstrates, maintains imperialism and prevents democracy in the "home" country as well as in the colonies (a point he had earlier worked out in relation to "internal" colonialism in the United States); it also retards economic development, keeps white labor in a powerless relationship to capital, and "puts hard strain on the national soul" of every supposedly "democratic" imperial country (388).

Ultimately, Du Bois argues, labor must recognize that "the denial of democracy in Asia and Africa hinders its complete realization in Europe" (407). Indeed, Du Bois's vision is not exclusively racial, for he regards the coming transformation as one that will release Europeans from spiritual bankruptcy and enslavement to their own machines while it brings to the colored peoples of the world the benefits of Western technology and administrative efficiency. (Here again is the idealistic vision of races complementing each other, evident in *The Souls of Black Folk* vis-à-vis the United States.) Du Bois gradually builds the argument that American Negroes, behind the advance guard of the NAACP, are destined to lead this great, world-historical movement that will redeem all humankind. Thus the very attempt to reach beyond national boundaries, in what is easily the most radical essay in *The New Negro*, is shadowed—no, absolutely formed—by the very structure of American ideology at its most exceptionalist.

"And now we stand before Liberia," he writes in a closing peroration that echoes John Winthrop, "Liberia that is a little thing set upon a Hill;—thirty or forty thousand square miles and two million folk; but it represents to me the world" (414). This at a time when Americo-Liberians had established colonial direct rule over the hinterland and begun, as one historian puts it, "total exploitation of the region." Native Africans had been completely shut out of the political system—an important background to the problems Liberia faces even today.[72] By the middle and late 1920s, Americo-Liberian officials were directing practices scarcely distinguishable from slavery (coerced unpaid labor by "tribal" people captured for this purpose). Moreover, the tightening of that elite's grip on "tribal" groups was a frightened response to two factors: its own shrinking percentage of the total population as it extended its territory, and the rise of nationalist movements in other nearby colonies, especially those controlled by the British. The ruling caste worried about its ability to maintain supremacy (and repeatedly justified its practice on the basis of its being black rather than white).[73] An unintended irony therefore hovers over Du Bois's contention that Liberia, along with Abyssinia and Morocco, is a temptation "to agitation for freedom and autonomy on the part of other black and subject populations," a dire threat to "the whole imperial program" (389). For Du Bois, Liberia foretells African liberation. "Tribal" Africans in Liberia might have told a different story.

One reason Du Bois could not recognize what was happening is that his valiant struggle against American racism and his belief in the redeeming mission of African Americans (a belief that informed Americo-Liberian ideology itself) governed his view of Africa. No doubt his admiration for Alexander Crummell, an old role model who had lived in Liberia, played a part as well.

"The Negro Mind Reaches Out" exemplifies the enclosure of at least one type of 1920s-style pan-Africanism in American racial and national ideology. The contrast with Paul Kellogg's "The Negro Pioneers" is telling: Du Bois does not fit the drama of black modernism within a "white" proscenium; he instead fits the drama of *global* modernism within a black pan-Africanist frame that is, finally, very much in the American grain.

Understanding the institutional background, production history, and collagelike composition of *The New Negro* makes untenable many widely circulating attitudes toward the book and the phenomenon it "interprets." The text is not essentially (although it is occasionally and tangentially) involved in the cult of primitivism as we normally conceive of that cult. It does not hold out a single gauge of black "authenticity";[74] in fact, it implicitly opposes any such gesture. It is not overwhelmingly pastoral in orientation. It does not attack, suppress, or even ignore the cultural hybridity of African America—quite the opposite.[75] It does not reveal that "the only worthwhile expressive project available to *class* is a national, racial expressivity that takes form and draws heart *only* from the 'awakened' Afro-American mass."[76] It does not try to erase the received racist images of black Americans by erasing all differences between them and the white mainstream.[77] It is not "preoccupied with the white normative gaze."[78] It does not reject the Americanness of African Americans in an attempt to present them as lost Africans.[79] It is not a black nationalist or "maroon" performance.[80] It does not present the United States as a nation amenable to the "assimilationist patterns" of Latin America.[81] It does not reveal "a firm grasp of African modes of existence." It does not cast art as "a primary agent for social change or a central medium for protest."[82] It is not the bible of a failed movement that expired in 1929.

No. The most viable general statement that can be made about this amazingly diverse and self-divided text is Robert Hayden's elegantly simple formulation: "It affirms the values of the Negro heritage and expresses hope for the future of the race in this country, stressing the black man's 'Americanism.'"[83] It also announces that a new literary field—not just a "school" or a "movement"—is emerging with its own climate of affinities and antagonisms, though this climate is inseparable from a complex environment of competing forces of national and trans-national range.

Epilogue

If the writing of the 1920s stressed the Americanism of the Negro, the writing of the 1930s would move more emphatically in this direction, to the extent of ridiculing the Harlem Renaissance interest in recuperating African cultural traditions as well as what came to be regarded as the outmoded racialism of the New Negro intellectual leaders. Certainly the New Negro renaissance did not end in 1929, as Sterling Brown has pointed out.[1] Nonetheless, most of the creative writers of the 1920s and the 1930s felt there was a distinct shift roughly coinciding with the turn of the decade, a shift announced by new satirical treatments of the New Negro by such authors as Wallace Thurman, George Schuyler, and Langston Hughes—authors who properly belong to both decades. Alain Locke himself, in 1933, contrasted the "bitter tang and tonic of the Reformation" to "the sweetness and light of a Renaissance."[2] The change in African American writing was part of the general change in American writing that came with the Depression and showed up as well in approaches to social reform.[3]

The thirties witnessed a turn away from stress on race in favor of class and a critique of capitalism—all in the form of a sharper-edged social realism. But it is important to remember that such emphases were a part of the mix in the 1920s. Structural changes in American society favored certain positions over others. As writers shifted direction, they used critiques of the "Harlem movement" to establish their positions, in doing so inevitably characterizing the movement in reductive ways. They thus cast off artistic tendencies that seemed irrelevant or "irresponsible" while using others as a foundation. Sterling Brown disdained what he considered "Van Vechten" influences and eschewed the African revivalism of the 1920s but developed his vernacular form of poetry in conscious response to the models of Jean Toomer, James Weldon Johnson, and Langston Hughes (as well as Robert Frost, Edgar Lee Masters, and Carl Sandburg).[4] Richard Wright developed his fictional approach in response to the models of Sinclair Lewis and Theodore Dreiser, among others; epigraphs for his first novel came from *America's Coming-of-Age* and *Our America*. James Baldwin's first mentor was Countee Cullen. The groundwork for Hurston's fiction of the 1930s was obviously laid in the 1920s. As Arnold Rampersad has claimed, "The Renaissance succeeded in laying the foundations for all subsequent depictions in poetry, fiction, and drama of the modern African-American experience."[5] The movement represented the emergence of a literary sector or field; what becomes important is not individual author-by-author succession but the tension between a variety of possible (and overlapping) positions.

Divisions between "genteel" critics and writers concerned with the folk and the vernacular continued through the 1930s, as James O. Young has shown, while a split widened between even the latter authors and a new crop of critics interested in proletarian literature. This fissure actually opened up, as we have seen, at the peak of the renaissance, in 1926–1927, when aspersions were first cast on the movement for "bourgeois individualism," "race chauvinism," inattention to class issues, primitivism, and stress on African themes. The most fruitful developments of 1930s black writing, then, derived from strains of the Harlem Renaissance and would have been inconceivable without the foundations it laid down, both aesthetically and institutionally.

The Marxist point of view that gained momentum in the 1930s affected the subsequent interpretation of Jazz Age literature. As Edward Abrahams has pointed out, "The Marxists' view that cultural radicalism was essentially a bohemian manifestation of the worst excesses of individualism has had an enduring impact on American thought about culture."[6] In the new era, left-wing intellectuals wanted "objective," hard-boiled modes of expression that contrasted with the "bourgeois" stylization of selfhood common in the black 1920s—whether that stylization expressed "sophisticated" cynicism or lingering romantic idealism. Yet interest in the "native" scene only grew stronger during the Depression, and with it interest in African American culture.

If black writing was in step with the general trends of white American literature, the converse also was true in this period. Contrary to the idea that whites had lost interest in "Negro themes," in 1939 Locke pointed out that "an increasing vogue for Negro themes and materials" was "a characteristic feature" of the 1930s.[7] This "vogue" found particularly fruitful expression in the Federal Writers', Arts, and Theatre Projects, which were instigated and directed by cultural nationalists whose sensibilities had been formed in the culture of the teens and twenties, then further "radicalized" by the literary milieu of the early thirties.[8] The leaders of the Federal Writers' Project developed its goals out of the ideas of the regionalists, cultural pluralists, *Liberator*-style socialists, and cultural nationalists—the ideas of Dell, Bourne, Kallen, Brooks, Mumford, and the like—informed by Boasian ideas of culture, race, and nationality and by pragmatism.[9]

Although the Writers' Project hired only 106 African American writers, it was of no little significance to the development of African American literature. Among those employed were Richard Wright, Robert Hayden, Frank Marshall Davis, Margaret Walker, Katherine Dunham, Frank Yerby, Willard Motley, Ted Poston, Ralph Ellison, Zora Neale Hurston, Arna Bontemps, and Claude McKay. As Sterling Brown would later point out, "Negro writers actually made more money during the Depression than they had made before. Because they got on WPA, they got a regular check. Almost all of the writers were on WPA. . . . There were very few recognized writers when these projects started."[10] Brown himself (recommended to Henry Alsberg by James Weldon Johnson and Alain Locke) led the "Negro" section of the American Guide series and oversaw other, collateral publications on African American culture—some of which, such as the ex-slave narratives, have been priceless resources for subsequent African American fiction and historiography.

The production of the ex-slave narratives reveals the interplay between the Midwestern vernacular literary movement, African American modernism, and cultural nationalism. Initiated by John Lomax, the program of collecting the narratives took a decisive turn when Benjamin A. Botkin took over as FWP folklore editor in 1938. The project's view of folklore grew broader and more contemporary, "and there was a noticeable shift from rural to urban material," as Jerre Mangione has pointed out.[11] Botkin and Brown also pushed hard to have black writers do the collecting of black folklore. The deliberately "American" approach to folklore of Botkin, Brown, and their associates stressed that folklore is always in the making—not the product of an "authentic folk" being destroyed by modernism. It was "a history from the bottom up," as Botkin said of the ex-slave narratives.[12] Rather than rooting folklore in ethnic purity and authenticity, blood and soil, Botkin and Brown stressed syncretism, change, and diversity; "American" folklore, they believed, must never lose sight of the pluralistic, dynamic, and composite character of U.S. cultures.

Botkin's and Brown's ideas about the uses of folk idioms and forms in writing developed from similar sources and had been intertwined since the late 1920s, when both were contributing to *Opportunity*.[13] Both reacted against the pastoralism and "sentimental romanticism" of the dialect school associated with Dunbar and Riley.[14] They attended to the element of social protest in folklore, and they promoted an idiomatic rendering of folk speech that did not depend upon phonetic exactness but rather transmuted its rhythms, structures, images, and tropes into corresponding literary texts.[15]

Of all the American poets of the era, Brown may best exemplify this transracial development of vernacular writing, even as he exemplifies the possibilities of vernacular poetry in African American modernism—which partly explains why he insisted that African American literary tradition was not hermetic but very much a part of American literary tradition generally. Locke agreed with Brown's position: "Tracing an arbitrary strand of Negro authorship and narrowly construed race productivity not only does not do the Negro group cultural justice, but . . . more important, it does not disclose the cultural exchanges and interactions which are vital to the process."[16] Brown's notes on dialect for the FWP black folklore program reflect his literary training and interests. He advised against phonetic spelling and expected "truth to idiom"—models being Peterkin's use of a "modified Gullah" and Howard Odum's transcriptions of black folklore, as well as fiction by Erskine Caldwell, Ruth Suckow, and Zora Neale Hurston.[17]

Ralph Ellison did extensive folklore research for the New York City Living Lore Unit and, as Jerrold Hirsch has suggested, "found a way to create a work of art that in its very structure wrestled with all the issues that had preoccupied the FWP: the nature of the relationship between the individual and the folk group, provincialism and cosmopolitanism, tradition and modernity, the fact of diversity and the need for unity. Ellison found, as Botkin had argued, that folklore was also a part of contemporary urban life."[18] And Botkin had developed his own approach in dialogue with Harlem Renaissance figures such as Locke, Hughes, and Brown.

The changes in literary approaches to black vernacular tradition during the Harlem Renaissance were thus of enduring significance to the culture of the United States. Gayl Jones, one of the most impressive current exponents of this tradition, has attested to the fact that the shift during the Harlem Renaissance from the traditional literary dialect of Dunbar, Chesnutt, and William Wells Brown "made possible a new seriousness and range in subject matter, experiences, and concerns, as well as deeper, more complex characterization."[19] We now have a more specific knowledge of how the transformation came about, and of how thoroughly intertwined were the searches for a vernacular, pluralistic, modern American tradition *generally* and that for an African American tradition.

When black writers developed the vernacular literary approaches Jones identifies as critical to African American literary tradition, they were frequently criticized for acceding to white predilections—a not entirely false charge, since in fact the criticism and example of white artists had played an enormous role in their creative development, as it did also in the work of authors such as Nella Larsen and Walter White. The assumption of a clear bifurcation between "Western" and "African American" approaches to writing—often to support invidious comparisons between black writers—thus creates circular arguments and historical confusion. It ignores history and institutional structures, replacing careful investigation with grand theories of intertextual relations ungrounded in material, emotional, and intellectual relationships—in short, experience. It also requires, inherently, repression of difference and heterogeneity on either side of the boundary. This is not to deny the importance of Africanism in the Americas, or the importance of racial identity in reader response. However, assigning American cultures unilinearly to Old World coordinates prevents an adequate understanding of American cultural phenomena—and frequently has the effect of colonizing and obscuring African culture by reading it primarily in relation to North American racial reasoning and cultural dilemmas.

Ignorance of the intellectual and institutional networks that produced the Harlem Renaissance has affected far more than understandings of the Harlem Renaissance, because the Harlem Renaissance
serves as a linchpin in all sorts of arguments. Here I will simply choose
three recent examples from good books by Charles Scruggs, Cornel
West, and Ann duCille. Charles Scruggs's discussion of "four post-
Harlem Renaissance novels" by Wright, Ellison, Baldwin, and Morrison
is predicated in part on a familiar notion of the Harlem Renaissance as
constrained by white editors', publishers', and critics' fascination for
the primitive and exotic. Locke's alleged presentation of Harlem as a
"heavenly city" responded to this institutional situation and also fit his
own Eurocentrism. But in the 1930s, Scruggs writes, "the Harlem
'vogue' had gone out of fashion," and the American literary institutions
dropped African American culture, bringing a shock of recognition to
black writers of their true relationship to white people, to America, and
to the city.[20]

Subsequent authors such as James Baldwin, claims Scruggs, repudiated the Harlem Renaissance and declared independence from whites'
racial projections. A peculiar reading of "Stranger in the Village"
anchors this interpretation. In this essay, Scruggs believes, Baldwin
rejects Du Bois's and Locke's imaginary identification with Western culture: "Let us not indulge facile illusions, Baldwin implies: slavery and
its aftermath created a division between black and white that cannot be
bridged by imaginative constructs such as Locke's idealized Harlem,
which ignore the constrained reality of black life in America."[21] But it
is precisely the unbridgeability of the division asserted in Scruggs's
interpretation here that Baldwin opposes in his essay about the difference between European and American cultures. "I do not think . . . that
it is too much to suggest that the American vision of the world—which
allows so little reality, generally speaking, for any of the darker forces in
human life, which tends until today to paint moral issues in glaring
black and white—owes a great deal to the battle waged by Americans
to maintain between themselves and black men a human separation
which could not be bridged."[22] Baldwin calls this vision of the world
"dangerously inaccurate."

Yes, slavery has made an inescapable and permanent difference—a
difference constitutive of American identity for both blacks and whites
which they must learn to recognize: "The time has come to realize that
the interracial drama acted out on the American continent has not only

created a new black man, it has created a new white man, too."[23] The contradiction between American democratic ideals and American racism has been formative of American identity, whether black or white. Thus the Negro in America is "not a visitor to the West but a citizen there, an American; as American as the Americans who despise him, the Americans who fear him, the Americans who love him—the Americans who became less than themselves, or rose to be greater than themselves by virtue of the fact that the challenge he represented was inescapable."[24] Baldwin thus shares the primary concerns of diverse contributors to the Harlem Renaissance—particularly those associated with the NAACP ("the nation's conscience"), those more interested in the centrality of racism to Americanism, and thus the prophetic mission of African Americans in the world, than in vernacular aesthetic experimentation.

Another example of how routine assumptions about the Harlem Renaissance function in criticism of American culture more broadly construed is Cornel West's recent essay "Horace Pippin's Challenge to Art Criticism." Here West uses the Harlem Renaissance as a foil for his characterization of Pippin as an artist true to both "black" (as opposed to "white") approaches to black art and Emersonian/Deweyan aesthetics. "The dominant theme of romanticizing the 'primitivism' of poor black folk and showing how such 'primitivism' fundamentally affects the plights and predicaments of refined and educated, black, middle-class individuals . . . looms large in the Harlem Renaissance."[25] This is because black middle-class artists sought to gain attention from the white establishment in order to gain authority for imposing "their conceptions of legitimate forms of black cultural productions on black America."[26] Deeply in hock to white institutions, *The New Negro*, for example, regards popular culture as "raw material for sophisticated artists (with university pedigrees and usually white patrons)"—so speaks the Princeton and Harvard professor who wrote his dissertation under Richard Rorty and has brilliantly connected his vision of African American culture to pragmatism. Is there an echo in this tale?

Professor West is not wrong about Professor Locke thinking of popular culture as "raw material" for "higher" art; but Locke's strategies are not fundamentally different from those of recent African-Americanist critics who argue that the black vernacular tradition embodied deconstructionist, feminist, pragmatist, or otherwise postmodernist forms of critique long before continental philosophers and white American literary scholars developed the concepts—and then proceed to "develop" these vernacular hermeneutic strategies in scholarly terms, at the same time bending scholarly terms toward the vernacular. Here again, qualities whose stock has gone up in the transracial intellectual field are "rediscovered" in the products of the folk and invested in a particular sector of the cultural marketplace, sometimes bringing protests from other scholars who feel the authentic tradition is being betrayed or bowdlerized—in short (to borrow a favored term), "bleached."

West sets Pippin and Sterling Brown against the New Negroes, who "sold out," caught up with trying to prove their sophistication to white people. *They* were "preoccupied with the white normative gaze."[27] In contrast, Pippin's paintings (and Brown's poetry) "are expressions of a rich Emersonian tradition in American art that puts a premium on the grandeur in the commonplace, ordinary and quotidian lives of people. This tradition promotes neither a glib celebration of everyday experiences nor a naive ignorance of the tragic aspects of our condition. Rather, Pippin's Emersonian sensibility affirms what John Dewey dubbed 'experience in its integrity.'"[28]

I hope the irony of such charges is obvious, *The New Negro* being saturated with Emersonian and Deweyan strains. As a matter of fact, Albert Barnes himself "played a pivotal role in the recognition of . . . Horace Pippin. . . . As a result of Barnes' enthusiastic reponse, nearly every important museum and private collector eagerly sought to acquire Pippin's pictures."[29] West feels Pippin fulfills Dewey's principles as expressed in *Art as Experience*—the book Dewey wrote with Barnes's guidance and dedicated to him—but assumes that Deweyan principles had nothing to do with the recognition of Pippin. Instead, Pippin's work was filtered through "exotic primitivist" lenses: "A genuine [Emersonian] artistic concern with the common easily appears as an aspiration for authenticity—especially for an art establishment that puts a premium on the 'primitive' and hungers for the exotic."[30]

Pippin's reception (as well as Sterling Brown's) then serves as paradigmatic of the situation of the black artist—either denigrated, praised for social pleading, or accepted as "exotic." As an admirer of West's work, let me say here that I am very sympathetic to his basic position, and there is plenty of truth to the charge that most "white" institutions (say, universities) reify racial identity even as they "adopt" black artists and intellectuals to serve limiting interests; but his use of the Harlem Renaissance embodies both an unreliable model of that multifarious "movement" and a dualistic rhetorical substructure that must be questioned—one that, in a kind of circular logic, scholars repeatedly use the Harlem Renaissance to reinforce. One could say that West does to the Harlem Renaissance something closely related to what he accuses America of doing to the black artist—calling their work an inferior attempt at white modernist sophistication, on the one hand, and a sop to "primitive and exotic" tastes of whites on the other, *as opposed to* the Emersonian/Deweyan tradition of African American aesthetics. He does this to persuade us of *his* vision of what black art should be and of how it should be received. Is this not what he accuses Locke of having done?

My point is not that there is something wrong with West's desire to persuade; I am concerned with the uses of race in the argument. For, even though West consciously repudiates racial essentialism and embraces Deweyan pragmatism, he falls back on the rhetorical gesture of scapegoating the hypothesized "whiteness" of the black intellectuals he wants to replace, citing their fixation on the "white normative gaze." His notion of the institutional substructure of the Harlem Renaissance—which is simply the universally accepted view—is pivotal to this gesture. Yet almost all of the black intellectuals, as we can see in *The New Negro* itself, thought they were breaking free of the white normative gaze and accused their antagonists of having been caught in its beams: Jean Toomer, Alain Locke, Jessie Fauset, Countee Cullen, Langston Hughes, Claude McKay, W. E. B. Du Bois, and on and on. (Possible exceptions are Nella Larsen and Georgia Douglas Johnson.) That this rhetorical reflex remains so deeply ingrained attests to the immense power of binarist racial discourse to reproduce itself and to structure cultural debate, as it assigns American citizens to their respective roles. It holds a transcendent position.

One need not privilege the vernacular to take this tack, however. Recently, for example, Ann duCille has defended Jessie Fauset and Nella Larsen against charges of being too bourgeois, sexually repressed, and beholden to white norms by pointing out how the implied standard of black womanhood for vernacular critics—the female blues singer— is herself partly a product of white ideology. The idealization of blues lately, duCille charges, falls in with the "primitivism" of the 1920s—and thus gives whites like Van Vechten the last word on black modernism.

(Moreover, Ma Rainey purportedly used skin-lightening creams.)[31] Those critics who have presented views antithetical to duCille's have fallen into traps set by the cultural imperialists and thus missed the ways in which Fauset and Larsen anticipated current postmodern, black feminist concerns.

To enhance Larsen's racial and womanly integrity, duCille then puts Van Vechten and Larsen in direct opposition—casting Van Vechten in the role of the white primitivist valorizing stereotypes about the Harlem "jungle" life, and Larsen in the role of the black artist critiquing him and thus evading his clutches. Yet Larsen, in fact, regarded Van Vechten's novels as absolutely brilliant and counted him one of her very closest friends. She also felt an ethnic connection, apparently, through their mutual Scandinavian heritage.[32]

Continuing along a well-worn path, duCille claims: "By the early 1930s the Harlem moment had largely passed. The economy had failed, and the Van Vechtens, it seemed, had indeed discarded the Negro."[33] But in fact Van Vechten had not discarded "the Negro" by a long shot. He not only initiated the gathering of Harlem Renaissance writers' manuscripts and works but also made significant donations to Fisk University, talked Georgia O'Keeffe into donating much of Alfred Stieglitz's personal art collection to Fisk, and maintained his close friendships with many black intellectuals, including Langston Hughes, James Weldon Johnson, and—*especially*—Nella Larsen, even after she had forever given up on writing. Indeed, Van Vechten was one of the few people (the only one besides her editor, based on evidence so far presented) who defended her publicly against the plagiary charges that ended her literary career, and he remained for years one of her rare loyal friends.[34] Ironically, duCille says that a "central concern" of her own book is "historical specificity." Furthermore, her goal is to reveal how black women's novels have been preoccupied with "the pervasiveness of patriarchal power" and the struggle to reclaim the female body.[35] But consider this—in the final scene of *Quicksand*, Helga Crane remains trapped in a horrifying marriage, unable to escape because of the thought of her children crying for their mother:

> Of the children Helga tried not to think. She wanted not to leave them—if that were possible. The recollection of her own childhood, lonely, unloved, rose too poignantly before her to consider calmly such a solution. Though she forced herself to believe that this was

different. There was not the element of race, of white and black. They were all black together. And they would have their father. But to leave them would be a tearing agony, a rending of deepest fibers. She felt that through all the rest of her lifetime she would be hearing their cry of 'Mummy, Mummy, Mummy,' through sleepless nights. No. She couldn't desert them.[36]

Why is this scene so tragic, so powerful, if not because the voice Helga Crane hears is her own, crying for the Danish mother that "race" in America has stolen from her—indeed, from Larsen herself? To *Larsen* the most unbearable effect of racist patriarchy in the United States was its power to deprive her of her mother. One of the motives of Larsen's friendship with Van Vechten was apparently to maintain connection with her own ethnic background—with her *mother's* ethnic background. Apparently she felt close to Van Vechten also because he accepted her self-definition. To deny this "motherless child" her connection with Van Vechten is, in an important sense, to deny her self, her female self, her deep blues. This is perhaps the most telling irony in duCille's narrative: that Van Vechten should serve as the goat whose expunging asserts the integrity of duCille's subject and approach, enmeshing Larsen as deeply as ever in the patriarchally created racial discourse of the United States, which she resented and resisted to her very death.[37]

I have chosen Scruggs's, West's, and duCille's discussions, almost at random from recent books I much admire, not because they are egregious examples of misuses of the Harlem Renaissance but simply to illustrate how pervasively mythical accounts of the institutional context of the Harlem Renaissance—dating from that movement itself and integral to its "Americanness"—inform not only discussions of that period but also more general ruminations on modernism in the United States, the genealogies of American artistic traditions, and the history of relations between "whiteness" and "blackness" in American culture. All of this has obscured and mystified the complex nature and history of the *racial culture* of the United States, something the Harlem Renaissance itself investigated and acted upon with far greater sophistication and more positive results than have been recognized.

There is nothing more "black" (or less "white") about Wright or Baldwin than about the artists of the Harlem Renaissance, nothing less "white" about Horace Pippin than about Aaron Douglas. And if we can understand this, then perhaps we can understand that Nella Larsen is both "black" and "white," and Danish American—and that her writing is none the worse for it. There is no reason we have to denigrate one of these people on the basis of race; nor do we have to ignore, interpret cynically, or explain away their relationships with "white" people to appreciate their importance. If their art lives, it lives not for racial reasons as such but because, refusing to accept social relations as the locus of ultimacy, the authors challenged the limits of sensibility that their lives presented them. No wonder so many lived along a racial divide: this, too, is a function of their Americanism—of living in a multiracial nation with vaunted democratic-egalitarian ideals, *ideals in which they believed,* daily contradicted by its implacable color line. This contradiction becomes for many a spiritual boundary, a locus of controlled rage and aesthetic intensity. Because of its distinctive features, they called what they wrote "American" and claimed the authority to define what that term meant.

One reason we can see the shortcomings of the Harlem Renaissance is that we take for granted so much of what at the time had to be creatively established and, at an intellectually elite level, institutionalized: new notions of race, nation, and culture; antiracism; anti-essentialist varieties of cultural pluralism; new concepts of the significance of Africa to African America; the aesthetic value of black vernacular expression for "literature" and other art forms; the possibility of reconceiving the United States as something other than a white nation. The imaginative work of the Harlem Renaissance is importantly responsible for the cultural "truths" many of us now work from.

Yet the advances the Harlem Renaissance generations achieved were too easily submerged, particularly in the era of academic expansion and subordination to the Cold War effort. This is partly because by then many important figures were dead, and if alive they were not in universities. But some of the key white figures themselves contributed to this erasure and submersion—such as Max Eastman, whose relationship with Claude McKay plays so small a part in an autobiography largely shaped by his transformation into an arch-conservative anticommunist. Powerful intellectuals like Carl Van Doren and John Dewey likewise never really understood the importance of black history and culture to the United States. Generally speaking, whites did not regard African American history and culture, or the relationship between whites and blacks, as central to the story of the republic. The idea of their own "race" was unexamined; to them, the white immigrant and frontier experiences were central to Americanism. Really internalizing the claims of the Harlem Renaissance would have required a more profound self-revaluation than they were prepared (or forced by circumstances) to undertake. One could say that their Americanization was incomplete. Thus, the Harlem Renaissance achieved only a toehold in mainstream thinking about American national culture and did not make it into the academy—because of racism, and because of the way the institutionalization of the fields of "American literature" and "modernism" took place. That process, followed by the process through which "black American/African American literature" achieved institutional status, is partly responsible for the remarkable ignorance about the interracial modernist networks this book has tried to unearth. The lesson to take away from this is not necessarily that the concept of "American culture" should be abandoned as an outmoded ideological construct. African American modernists were right to make claims on the national identity. It is up to us to reconceive what "American modernism" is, and also to begin thinking of American literature less as a tradition (or set of separate traditions) following noble lines of descent than as the continually reforming product of historical fields of action, power, and experience.

To notice the peculiarities of the conditions that shape the cultural history of the United States is not to embrace exceptionalism—exceptionalism being the belief that our qualities are unique *and* divinely chosen as models for everyone else—but to acknowledge the fact that national borders have played an enormous role (not the only one) in cultural production for the past two hundred years. Premature attempts to deconstruct or "transcend" national boundaries too easily become self-deceptive gestures by which national ideologies take on unacknowledged forms, as current American concepts of "race" become, for example, defining aspects of various forms of "Afrocentrism" that are not, in the final analysis, nearly centered *enough* upon the wisdom, experiences, desires, and expressions of the peoples living in Africa. And so James Baldwin strikes a sympathetic chord (the exceptionalist note of which I would drop) when he explains why we must balance a tragic—indeed, rather grim—understanding of U.S. culture with the knowledge that "black" and "white" on this continent are indissoluble in their hatreds, in their loves, and even in their dreams; that this is so despite—and because of—the many brutal but never entirely successful battles waged to maintain an unbridgeable human separation. "For even when the worst has been said, it must also be added that the perpetual challenge posed by this problem was always, somehow, perpetually met. It is precisely this black-white experience which may prove of indispensable value to us in the world we face today."[38]

Notes

Index

Notes

Introduction

1. See Robert Hayden, "Preface to the Atheneum Edition," in *The New Negro*, ed. Alain Locke (New York: Atheneum, 1968), x–xi.

2. Robert Wuthnow, *Communities of Discourse: Ideology and Social Structure in the Reformation, the Enlightenment, and European Socialism* (Cambridge, Mass.: Harvard University Press, 1989), 5.

3. Ibid., 9.

4. Pierre Bourdieu, "Flaubert's Point of View," trans. Priscilla Parkhurst Ferguson, *Critical Inquiry* 14 (1988): 541, 543.

5. See Hazel V. Carby, "The Canon: Civil War and Reconstruction," *Michigan Quarterly Review* 28 (1989): 41–42.

6. Bourdieu, "Flaubert's Point of View," 544.

7. Ibid., 541.

8. Paul DiMaggio, "Social Structure, Institutions, and Cultural Goods: The Case of the United States," in *Social Theory for a Changing Society*, ed. Pierre Bourdieu and James S. Coleman (New York: Russell Sage Foundation, and Boulder: Westview, 1991), 136.

9. See especially his play *Natalie Mann*, in *The Wayward and the Seeking: A Collection of Writings by Jean Toomer*, ed. Darwin T. Turner (Washington: Howard University Press, 1980), 243–325.

10. Bourdieu, "Flaubert's Point of View," 545.

11. Martin J. Sklar, *The United States as a Developing Country: Studies in U.S. History in the Progressive Era and the 1920s* (Cambridge: Cambridge University Press, 1992), 38.

12. Ibid., 154.

13. See ibid., 170–171.

14. Ibid., 172–173.

15. John W. Tebbel, *A History of Book Publishing in the United States*, vol. 3 (New York: R. R. Bowker, 1972), 4–9, 665.

16. Alan Trachtenberg, *The Incorporation of America: Culture and Society in the Gilded Age* (New York: Hill & Wang, 1982).

451

17. See Sklar, *The United States*, 177–180.

18. Ibid., 39–40.

19. See Judith Stein, "Defining the Race, 1890–1930," in *The Invention of Ethnicity*, ed. Werner Sollors (New York: Oxford University Press, 1989), 77–104; Henry Louis Gates, Jr., "The Trope of a New Negro and the Reconstruction of the Image of the Black," *Representations* 24 (1988): 129–155.

20. Tzvetan Todorov, *On Human Diversity: Nationalism, Racism, and Exoticism in French Thought*, trans. Catherine Porter (Cambridge, Mass.: Harvard University Press, 1993), 386; Werner Sollors, *Beyond Ethnicity: Consent and Descent in American Culture* (New York: Oxford University Press, 1986).

21. See especially Kwame Anthony Appiah's discussion of this point vis-à-vis both Pan-Africanism and Anglo-Saxonism, in *In My Father's House: Africa in the Philosophy of Culture* (New York: Oxford University Press, 1992).

22. Todorov, *On Human Diversity*, 386.

23. Ibid., 386.

24. Benedict Anderson, *Imagined Communities: Reflections on the Origin and Spread of Nationalism* (London: Verso, 1983), 12.

25. Sacvan Bercovitch, "The Problem of Ideology in American Literary History," *Critical Inquiry*, 12 (1986): 635. See also Bercovitch's *The Rites of Assent: Transformations in the Symbolic Construction of America* (New York: Routledge, 1993).

26. Richard Rorty has recently pressed a similar idea, particularly in *Contingency, Irony, and Solidarity* (Cambridge: Cambridge University Press, 1989), xvi, 94.

27. Cary Nelson, recognizing the weakness of binary models, has partly remedied this problem through his more variously attentive, decentered essay on modern American poetry, but his focus upon white far-left, Marxist, and working-class writing in relation to African American and feminist writing skews his sense of how the "Negro renaissance" articulated with white literary institutions. See *Repression and Recovery: Modern American Poetry and the Politics of Cultural Memory, 1910–1945* (Madison: University of Wisconsin Press, 1989).

28. See, for example, Benjamin T. Spencer, *Patterns of Nationality: Twentieth-Century Literary Versions of America* (New York: Burt Franklin, 1981); Arthur Frank Wertheim, *The New York Little Renaissance: Iconoclasm, Modernism, and Nationalism in American Culture, 1908–1917* (New York: New York University Press, 1976); Henry F. May, *The End of American Innocence* (New York: Knopf, 1959); Edward Abrahams, *The Lyrical Left: Randolph Bourne, Alfred Stieglitz, and the Origins of Cultural Radicalism in America* (Charlottesville: University Press of Virginia, 1986); Casey Nelson Blake, *Beloved Community: The Cultural Criticism of Randolph Bourne, Van Wyck Brooks, Waldo Frank, and Lewis Mumford* (Chapel Hill: University of North Carolina Press, 1990); and Charles C. Alexander, *Here the*

Country Lies: Nationalism and the Arts in Twentieth-Century America (Bloomington: Indiana University Press, 1980).

29. Harold Cruse, *The Crisis of the Negro Intellectual* (New York: William Morrow, 1967), 38.

30. Ibid., 52.

31. Nathan Irvin Huggins, *Harlem Renaissance* (New York: Oxford University Press, 1971), 129.

32. A. Philip Randolph, "Comments on the Negro Actor," *Messenger* 7 (1925): 17.

33. George E. Kent, *Blackness and the Adventure of Western Culture* (Chicago: Third World Press, 1972), 17.

34. Chidi Ikonné, *From Du Bois to Van Vechten: The Early New Negro Literature, 1903–1926* (Westport, Conn.: Greenwood Press, 1981), 3.

35. See the epigraph to Hughes's *The Ways of White Folks* (1934; New York: Vintage, 1990).

36. Ikonné, *From Du Bois to Van Vechten*, xii, 39.

37. Wilson J. Moses, "The Lost World of the Negro, 1895–1919: Black Literary and Intellectual Life Before the 'Renaissance,'" *Black American Literature Forum* 21 (1987): 63–75; quotation from 66.

38. Moses, "Lost World," 78.

39. W. E. B. Du Bois, "The Field and Function of the American Negro College" (1933), in *A W. E. B. Du Bois Reader*, ed. Andrew G. Paschal (New York: Macmillan Press, 1971), 63.

40. David Levering Lewis, *When Harlem Was in Vogue* (New York: Knopf, 1981), 24, 305–306.

41. Abby Arthur Johnson and Ronald Maberry Johnson's *Propaganda and Aesthetics: The Literary Politics of Afro-American Magazines in the Twentieth Century* (Amherst: University of Massachusetts Press, 1979), in its worthwhile attempt to cover the literary politics of a broad range of black magazines throughout the twentieth century, is unable to provide an in-depth discussion of even *The Crisis, Opportunity,* and *The Messenger,* let alone to articulate their relationships with "white" magazines of the period. Theodore Kornweibel's *No Crystal Stair: Black Life and the Messenger, 1917–1928* (Westport: Greenwood Press, 1975), usefully analyses *The Messenger*'s approach to the Harlem Renaissance in one chapter but needs to be supplemented. Other studies of the Harlem Renaissance, while ostensibly probing the institutional supports and backgrounds of the movement, provide only fragmentary and sketchy analyses, particularly of the "white" magazines. The notable exception is Charles Scruggs's extremely useful if overstated *The Sage in Harlem: H. L. Mencken and the Black Writers of the 1920s* (Baltimore: Johns Hopkins University Press, 1984). A very useful annotated list of reviews of Harlem Renaissance books is Jon E. Bassett's *Harlem in Review: Critical Reactions to Black American Writers, 1917–1939* (Selinsgrove: Sus-

quehanna University Press, 1992). Cary D. Wintz's *Black Culture and the Harlem Renaissance* (Houston: Rice University Press, 1988) attempts to discuss the institutional matrix of the Harlem Renaissance but does so in a very superficial fashion; and despite presenting some useful information, it is not always trustworthy.

42. Roderick Nash, *The Nervous Generation: American Thought, 1917–1930* (Chicago: Rand McNally, 1970), 30.

43. See, for example, Henry Louis Gates, Jr., *Figures in Black: Words, Signs, and the "Racial" Self* (New York: Oxford University Press, 1987), xxiii.

44. Gates, "The Trope of a New Negro," 148.

45. Barbara E. Johnson, "Response" to Henry Louis Gates, Jr., "Canon-Formation, Literary History, and the Afro-American Tradition: From the Seen to the Told," in *Afro-American Literary Study in the 1990s,* ed. Houston A. Baker, Jr., and Patricia Redmond (Chicago: University of Chicago Press, 1989), 42.

46. Ibid., 43.

47. Houston A. Baker, Jr., *Modernism and the Harlem Renaissance* (Chicago: University of Chicago Press, 1987), 75.

48. Du Bois, by the way, whom Baker characterizes as a "maroon," explicitly rejects this characterization in "The Evolution of Negro Leadership," *Dial* 31 (1901): 54–55, identifying the "maroon"-like leaders with an earlier "stage" of racial development.

49. We do not, for example, get even an inkling of Charles Chesnutt's iconoclastic racial views. And virtually every aspect of *The New Negro* that reveals its strongly interracialist tendencies vanishes in Baker's interpretation. Concerning Chesnutt's Toomeresque views of American racial prospects, see SallyAnn H. Ferguson, "Charles W. Chesnutt's 'Future American,'" *MELUS* 15 (1988): 95–107. Chesnutt specifically advocated "amalgamation" as the solution to American racial problems.

50. Robert Hayden, "Words in the Mourning Time," in *Words in the Mourning Time* (New York: October House, 1970), 49.

51. William E. Connolly, *Identity/Difference: Democratic Negotiations of Political Paradox* (Ithaca: Cornell University Press, 1991), 15.

52. Quoted in Michael Walzer, *The Company of Critics: Social Criticism in the Twentieth Century* (New York: Basic Books, 1988), 232.

I. American Modernism, Race, and National Culture

1. Houston A. Baker, Jr., *Modernism and the Harlem Renaissance* (Chicago: University of Chicago Press, 1987), 4.

2. Cornel West, *The American Evasion of Philosophy: A Genealogy of Pragmatism* (Madison: University of Wisconsin Press, 1989). For a useful characterization

of American modernist culture, see Daniel Joseph Singal, "Towards a Definition of American Modernism," *American Quarterly* 39 (1987): 7–26.

1. Pragmatism and Americanism

1. Daniel Joseph Singal, "Towards a Definition of American Modernism,"
American Quarterly 39 (1987): 16.

2. William James, *Pragmatism* (Cambridge, Mass.: Harvard University Press,
1975), 28.

3. Ibid., 32.

4. Richard Rorty, *Consequences of Pragmatism* (Minneapolis: University of Minnesota Press, 1982), xxxvii. For a more recent, controversial rendition of this
position, see Rorty's *Contingency, Irony, and Solidarity* (Cambridge: Cambridge
University Press, 1989).

5. Notably, T. S. Eliot was an admirer of William James's antagonist, F. H.
Bradley, upon whom he wrote his 1916 Harvard dissertation. As Richard Poirier
has written, Eliot "laments the very conditions of uncertainty which James asks
us to celebrate, even while he recognizes their necessity." *The Renewal of Literature: Emersonian Reflections* (1987; New Haven: Yale University Press, 1988), 107.

6. Singal, "Towards a Definition," 18.

7. Frank Lentricchia, "The Return of William James," in *The Current in Criti-
cism: Essays on the Present and Future of Literary Theory* (West Lafayette: Purdue
University Press, 1987), 188. The phrases Lentricchia quotes are from F. O.
Matthiessen, *The James Family* (New York: Knopf, 1961), 624, 626, 633.

8. Cornel West, *The American Evasion of Philosophy: A Genealogy of Pragmatism*
(Madison: University of Wisconsin Press, 1989), 72.

9. Ibid., 5.

10. See Robert Gooding-Williams, "Evading Narrative Myth, Evading Prophetic Pragmatism: Cornel West's *The American Evasion of Philosophy,*" *Massachusetts Review* 32 (1991–1992): 518–521.

11. Houston A. Baker, Jr., *Modernism and the Harlem Renaissance* (Chicago: University of Chicago Press, 1987), 6.

12. W. E. B. Du Bois, *Dusk of Dawn: An Essay Toward an Autobiography of a Race
Concept* (1940; New York: Schocken, 1968), 33.

13. Du Bois, *Dusk*, 38; and *The Autobiography of W. E. B. Du Bois* (New York:
International Publishers, 1968), 143.

14. Du Bois, *Autobiography*, 133.

15. See the chronology compiled by Bruce Kuklick for his edition of *William
James: Writings 1902–1910* (New York: Library of America, 1987), 1343–1344.

16. *Dusk*, 39.

17. *Autobiography*, 148.

18. Arnold Rampersad, *The Art and Imagination of W. E. B. Du Bois* (1976; New York: Schocken, 1990), 65.

19. W. E. B. Du Bois, *The Souls of Black Folk* (1903; New York: Viking Penguin, 1989), 12.

20. West, *American Evasion of Philosophy,* 146.

21. Frank Lentricchia, "On the Ideologies of Poetic Modernism, 1890–1913: The Example of William James," in *Reconstructing American Literary History,* ed. Sacvan Bercovitch (Cambridge, Mass.: Harvard University Press, 1986), 247.

22. *Pragmatism,* in *William James: Writings, 1902–1910,* 509. Rampersad points out that "Du Bois's career from his college days to his resignation from Atlanta University in 1910 reads like a case study in the acceptance of pragmatism as outlined by James in his Lowell Institute lectures of 1906–1907" (*Art and Imagination,* 65). During this time, Du Bois's "absolute Spencerian faith" in scientific truth gave way to recognition of "the limitations of pure empiricism" (65).

23. Gooding-Williams, "Evading Narrative Myth," 530–531.

24. David Levering Lewis discusses the issue of Du Bois's relationship to pragmatism in some detail in the stunning first volume of his biography, *W. E. B. Du Bois: Biography of a Race, 1868–1919* (New York: Henry Holt, 1993), 86–96. Lewis' study came out after my book was written, but I do not believe his findings conflict with my own. James had a profound impact on Du Bois, and probably vice versa, but in the end Du Bois hung on to a tenuous Idealism, strongly inflected by Hegel and Royce.

25. James, *Pragmatism,* 520; James's emphasis. George Santayana, *Reason in Art* (London: Constable, 1905), 15–16. The important connections between Santayana's aesthetics and the Harlem Renaissance are beyond the scope of this book but deserve careful investigation. A fine discussion of Santayana's pragmatist aesthetics in relation to James and Dewey is Jonathan Levin's "The Esthetics of Pragmatism," *American Literary History* 6 (1994): 658–683. Santayana's broader connections with pragmatism are ably interpreted in Henry Samuel Levinson, *Santayana, Pragmatism, and the Spiritual Life* (Chapel Hill: University of North Carolina Press, 1992).

26. W. E. B. Du Bois, "Criteria of Negro Art," *Crisis* 32 (1926): 296.

27. W. E. B. Du Bois, "Negro Art," *Crisis* 22 (1921): 55–56.

28. Eugene C. Holmes, "Alain L. Locke and the Adult Education Movement," *Journal of Negro Education* 34 (1965): 5. Incidentally, John Dewey sent his own children to such a school in New York City and served in the philosophy department at Columbia with Adler from 1902.

29. Horace L. Friess, *Felix Adler and Ethical Culture,* ed. Fannia Weingartner (New York: Columbia University Press, 1981), 121–137.

30. Quoted in ibid., 194.

31. Ibid., 194. While he supported workers' education and Tuskegee, on pragmatic grounds, Adler's educational philosophy was clearly integrationist.

32. Ibid., 179.

33. Ibid., 195–197.

34. Quoted in Rampersad, *Art and Imagination*, 157.

35. Ibid., 157.

36. Friess, *Felix Adler*, 126.

37. See my "The Whitman Legacy and the Harlem Renaissance," in *Walt Whitman: The Centennial Essays*, ed. Ed Folsom (Iowa City: University of Iowa Press, 1994), 202–207.

38. Jeffrey C. Stewart, "Introduction," in *The Critical Temper of Alain Locke*, ed. Jeffrey C. Stewart (New York: Garland, 1983), 397.

39. Quoted in Ernest D. Mason, "Alain Locke's Philosophy of Value," in *Alain Locke: Reflections on a Modern Renaissance Man*, ed. Russell J. Linneman (Baton Rouge: Louisiana State University Press, 1982), 14.

40. Dewey, quoted in Charles W. Morris, *The Pragmatic Movement in American Philosophy* (New York: G. Braziller, 1970), 108 n.13.

41. John Dewey, *Experience and Nature*, in vol. 1 of *The Later Works: 1925–1953*, ed. Jo Ann Boydston (Carbondale: Southern Illinois University Press, 1981), 269.

42. Mason, "Locke's Philosophy of Value," 15.

43. Rorty, *Contingency*, 189–198.

44. Mason, "Locke's Philosophy of Value," 15–16.

45. For a similar view, and a fine retort to the dominant views of Alain Locke's cultural criticism, see Everett H. Akam, "Community and Cultural Crisis: The 'Transfiguring Imagination' of Alain Locke," *American Literary History* 3 (Summer 1991): 255–276.

46. Richard Rorty, *Philosophy and the Mirror of Nature* (Princeton: Princeton University Press, 1979), 13.

47. Morris, *Pragmatic Movement*, 90. Similarly, Bruce W. Wilshire points out that "the general drift of [William] James's thought is toward a conception of aesthetics so profound that it is part and parcel of an ethics. Perception for James is art-like, and perception as involving action figures in the ground of that developmental continuity which is the good life." "Introduction," in *William James: The Essential Writings*, ed. Bruce W. Wilshire (Albany: State University of New York, 1984), lxix.

48. Morris, *Pragmatic Movement*, 97.

49. Thomas M. Alexander, *John Dewey's Theory of Art, Experience, and Nature: The Horizons of Feeling* (Albany: State University of New York Press, 1987), 186.

50. See ibid., 272.

51. John Dewey, *Reconstruction in Philosophy* (1920), in vol. 12 of *The Middle Works, 1899–1924*, ed. Jo Ann Boydston (Carbondale: Southern Illinois University Press, 1976), 186.

52. See, for example, Dewey, *Experience and Nature*, 293.

53. Du Bois, "Criteria of Negro Art," *Crisis* 32 (1926): 292.

54. John Dewey, "Dedication Address of the Barnes Foundation," in vol. 2 of *The Later Works, 1925–1953,* ed. Jo Ann Boydston (Carbondale: Southern Illinois University Press, 1981), 384.

55. Ibid., 384.

56. Aaron Douglas, oral history interview with Ann Allen Shockley, 17 November 1973, Special Collections, Fisk University Library.

57. William Schack, *Art and Argyrol: The Life and Career of Dr. Albert C. Barnes* (New York: T. Yoseloff, 1960), 76–77.

58. Ibid., 43.

59. Albert Barnes, quoted in Richard J. Wattenmaker, "Dr. Albert C. Barnes and the Barnes Foundation," in *Great French Paintings from the Barnes Foundation: Impressionist, Post-Impressionist, and Early Modern* (New York: Knopf and Lincoln University Press, 1993), 3.

60. Schack, *Art and Argyrol,* 52, 56, 97–98.

61. Ibid., 101–102; Barnes quoted in ibid., 158.

62. Gilbert M. Cantor, *The Barnes Foundation: Reality versus Myth* (1963; 2d ed., Philadelphia: Consolidated/Drake Press, 1974), 81–82.

63. Schack, *Art and Argyrol,* 255–256.

64. "He was a terrific critic. I don't care what they say, he is a terrific critic in his book. These two or three books that he wrote, there is just nothing like it. So he's at the top as far as that is concerned." Aaron Douglas, oral history interview with Ann Allen Shockley.

65. This is not to say that Barnes's and Guillaume's ideas about African art were the same as those adopted or popularized by other modernists. Indeed, Barnes was almost hysterical in his attacks on misinformed "exploitation" and romantic misinterpretation of traditional African art—particularly the views spread by de Zayas, an associate of Alfred Stieglitz at "291."

66. Wattenmaker, "Dr. Albert C. Barnes," 25.

67. John Dewey, *Art as Experience* (1934), in vol. 10 of *The Later Works,* 12, 14, 14–15.

68. Alain Locke, "Art Lessons from the Congo" (1927), in *Critical Temper,* 137–138.

69. Dewey, *Art as Experience,* 15, 15, 16.

70. Ibid., 20–23.

71. Ibid., 63.

72. Alain Locke, "Art or Progaganda?" *Harlem* 1 (1928): 12. Jeffrey C. Stewart also points out Locke's kinship with Dewey on aesthetics, in "A Biography of Alain Locke: Philosopher of the Harlem Renaissance, 1886–1930," Ph.D. dissertation, Yale University, 1975 (Ann Arbor: University Microfilms, 1986), 250–251.

73. Alain Locke, "Negro Youth Speaks," in *The New Negro,* ed. Alain Locke (1925; New York: Atheneum, 1992), 48.

74. Dewey, *Experience and Nature*, 159.

75. Alain Locke, "The Ethics of Culture," in *Critical Temper*, 416.

76. Ibid., 417 ("artificial . . . and exclusive" in italics in the original), 418, 421.

77. Dewey, *Experience and Nature*, 293.

78. Ibid., 290–291.

79. See the following works in the Charles S. Johnson Papers, Special Collections, Fisk University Library: "A Chapel Talk to the Students of Fisk University," 17 October 1928, box 158, folder 23; "Spiritual Autobiography," box 144, folder 1; "Some Notes on a Personal Philosophy of Life," box 174, folder 5; and "Some Suggestions for a New Pragmatic Philosophy," box 174, folder 15.

80. Concerning the legacy of Dewey in the social sciences at the University of Chicago, see Darnell Rucker, *The Chicago Pragmatists* (Minneapolis: University of Minnesota Press, 1969).

81. Charles S. Johnson, "Remarks at the Memorial Service for Robert E. Park, 1944," typescript, box 170, folder 3, Charles S. Johnson Papers.

82. Fred H. Matthews, *Quest for an American Sociology: Robert E. Park and the Chicago School* (Montreal: McGill-Queen's University Press, 1977), 7, 8.

83. Robert E. Park, "Methods of Teaching: Impressions and a Verdict" (1941), in Stanford M. Lyman, *Militarism, Imperialism, and Racial Accomodation: An Analysis and Interpretation of the Early Writings of Robert E. Park* (Fayetteville: University of Arkansas Press, 1992), 311.

84. Robert B. Westbrook, *John Dewey and American Democracy* (Ithaca: Cornell University Press, 1991), 33–34, 52–53, 55, 58.

85. Matthews, *Quest*, 20.

86. Park, "Methods," 310.

87. Charles S. Johnson, "Dr. Robert E. Park: 1864–1944," *Psychiatry* 7 (1944): 107.

88. Park, "Methods," 310.

89. Lyman, *Militarism*, xvii.

90. Ibid., 7.

91. Donald Franklin Joyce, "Reflections on the Changing Publishing Objectives of Secular Black Book Publishers, 1900–1986," in *Reading in America: Literature and Social History*, ed. Cathy N. Davidson (Baltimore: Johns Hopkins University Press, 1989), 230.

92. Park, "Methods," 316.

93. Ibid., 315.

94. Ibid., 315.

95. Ibid., 316.

96. Johnson, "The Social Philosophy of Booker T. Washington," *Opportunity* 6 (1928): 105.

97. Park, "Methods," 317.

98. Lyman, *Militarism*, 94.

99. Ibid., 11.

100. Robert E. Park, review of W. D. Weatherford, *The Negro from Africa to America*, in *American Journal of Sociology* 31 (1925): 260.

101. Quoted from Park's class syllabus, in Martin Bulmer, *The Chicago School of Sociology: Institutionalization, Diversity, and the Rise of Sociological Research* (Chicago: University of Chicago Press, 1984), 69.

102. Ibid., 69, 70.

103. Park, "Methods," 317.

104. Quoted in Bulmer, *Chicago School,* 71.

105. Park, the first president of the Chicago Urban League, had founded the league's Bureau of Investigation and Research and urged the hiring of Johnson to run the bureau—this is how Johnson first came to the Urban League. Park also helped get Johnson named the chief investigator of the Chicago Race Riot report, the project that issued in *The Negro in Chicago* and led to his hiring to lead the Bureau of Investigation and Research at the Manhattan headquarters of the Urban League. See Nancy J. Weiss, *The National Urban League, 1910–1940* (New York: Oxford University Press, 1974), 216–217.

106. Weiss, *Urban League,* 221.

107. Bulmer, *Chicago School,* 91, 96.

108. See Wilson J. Moses, *The Golden Age of Black Nationalism, 1850–1925* (Hamden, Conn.: Archon Books, 1978).

109. Johnson, "Some Notes." Although this speech was not delivered until 1937, it clearly voices a belief that had motivated Johnson in promoting the young black writers of the 1920s.

110. Dewey, *Reconstruction,* 200.

111. Dewey, *Reconstruction,* 200–201. See also Locke's essay of 1917, "Emile Verhaeren," which discusses Whitman as the American democratic prophet and a progenitor of modernism. In *Critical Temper,* 37.

112. Johnson, "Some Notes."

113. Ibid.

114. Dewey, *Reconstruction,* 141–142.

115. Dewey, "The Need for a Recovery of Philosophy" (1917), in vol. 10 of *The Middle Works,* 47.

116. Dewey, *Reconstruction,* 172.

117. Dewey, "The Need for a Recovery of Philosophy," 48.

2. The Americanization of "Race" and "Culture"

1. Quoted in Melville Herskovits, *Franz Boas: The Science of Man in the Making* (New York: Scribner's, 1953), 111.

2. W. E. B. Du Bois, *Black Folk Then and Now* (1939; Milwood, N.Y.: Kraus-Thomson Organization, 1975), vii.

3. Marshall Hyatt, *Franz Boas: Social Activist* (New York: Greenwood Press, 1990), 92.

4. Francesco Loriggio, "Anthropology, Literary Theory, and the Traditions of Modernism," in *Modernist Anthropology: From Fieldwork to Text,* ed. Marc Manganaro (Princeton: Princeton University Press, 1990), 225.

5. "Lake Foresters Pick Up Quills and One Writes a Play 'for Practice,'" clipping from a Lake Forest, Illinois, newspaper, 14 November 1930. Box 48, folder 1010, n. p., Jean Toomer Papers. By this time Sapir was on the faculty of the University of Chicago. In earlier years his poetry and reviews appeared in *The Nation.*

6. See Daniel Joseph Singal, "Towards a Definition of American Modernism," *American Quarterly* 39 (1987): 18–19; and Arnold Krupat, "Irony in Anthropology: The Work of Franz Boas," in *Modernist Anthropology,* ed. Manganaro, 133–145.

7. See, for example, Goldenweiser's *Early Civilization: An Introduction to Anthropology* (New York: Knopf, 1922), 6, a book that influenced Locke's thinking. Not only does Goldenweiser attack inferences of intelligence based on brain size and point out that most blacks and whites have the same brain sizes anyway, but he also disputes assumptions of the cultural superiority of Europeans. Such judgments, he argues, are based on subjective standards. In this Goldenweiser was going further than even Du Bois or Locke had been willing to go.

8. Franz Boas, *Anthropology and Modern Life* (New York: Norton, 1928), 18–61.

9. See George Stocking, "The Critique of Racial Formalism," in *Race, Culture, and Evolution: Essays in the History of Anthropology* (New York: Free Press, 1968), 189, 190. Boas did believe that one might not find as many of "the most intelligent types" among blacks as among whites. He could hardly have argued for absolute racial "equipotentiality," given his empiricist methods; neither would he argue against it.

10. Marvin Harris, *The Rise of Anthropological Theory* (New York: Crowell, 1968), 272.

11. George Stocking, "The Scientific Reaction Against Cultural Anthropology, 1917–1920," in *Race, Culture, and Evolution,* 302–303.

12. See Kwame Anthony Appiah, *In My Father's House: Africa in the Philosophy of Culture* (New York: Oxford University Press, 1992), 28–46.

13. Boas, *Anthropology and Modern Life,* 71.

14. George Stocking, "Franz Boas and the Culture Concept in Historical Perspective," in *Race, Culture, and Evolution,* 203.

15. See Wilson J. Moses, *The Golden Age of Black Nationalism, 1850–1925* (Hamden, Conn.: Archon Books, 1978). Herskovits, *Franz Boas,* 21.

16. Abraham Edel and Elizabeth Flower, "Introduction," in John Dewey, *The*

Later Works, 1925–1953, ed. Jo Ann Boydston (Carbondale: Southern Illinois University Press, 1981), vol. 7, xvn.

17. Herskovits, *Franz Boas,* 96, 97.

18. Boas, quoted in Stocking, "From Physics to Ethnology," in *Race, Culture, and Evolution,* 156; from Boas, "Museums of Ethnology and Their Classification," *Science* 9 (1887): 589.

19. Herskovits, *Franz Boas,* 16.

20. This partly contradicts Hazel Carby's charge, in an influential article, that Boasian anthropology interacted with Zora Neale Hurston's nostalgia for her youth to entrap her in an imperialist "ideology of the folk." "The Politics of Fiction, Anthropology, and the Folk: Zora Neale Hurston," in *New Essays on Their Eyes Were Watching God,* ed. Michael Awkward (Cambridge: Cambridge University Press, 1990), 71–93. Carby bases her contentions on secondary sources discussing chiefly Malinowskian and other anthropological schools, and on some of the work of Benedict and Mead. Boas indeed was not free of "folk" romanticism, but his general thrust was different in stressing historical change and "culture contact," as opposed to organic relations between the "folk" and the "soil." Carby cites George E. Marcus and Michael M. J. Fischer, *Anthropology as Cultural Critique: An Experimental Moment in the Human Sciences* (Chicago: University of Chicago Press, 1986), but Marcus and Fischer's discussion of Boas' approach in this context explicitly contrasts him with Mead (129–130). In fact, Marcus and Fischer call for a "repatriation of anthropology as cultural critique" very like what Thorstein Veblen (whom they cite as a "classic example," 111, 140) did with Boas' work; and what American authors such as Walter White and George Schuyler, especially in *American Mercury,* did using a sort of satirical Boasian ethnographic approach to critique "Homo Americanus."

21. Goldenweiser, *Early Civilization,* 27.

22. Herskovits, *Franz Boas,* 7, 86.

23. Ibid., 79.

24. Stocking, "From Physics to Ethnology," 158–159. The article by Boas is "On Alternating Sounds."

25. Karla F. C. Holloway's slap at Hurston's mentor is therefore particularly ironic. Writes Holloway, concerning the use of black vernacular in *Their Eyes Were Watching God:* "Her reminder to her reading audience was that language is a reliable mechanism to support and develop the cultural consciousness of her characters. What is remarkable about this reminder is that it was offered at a time when anthropological science was bent on indicating the lack of difference between cultures. It was a powerful school of thought to dispute, and any contradiction of this thinking was a reflection on her academic mentor, Franz Boas." *The Character of the Word: The Texts of Zora Neale Hurston* (Westport: Greenwood Press, 1987), 116. In fact, the very quality Holloway values as heroic in Hurston's approach is a basic tenet of Boasian linguistics.

26. Robert E. Hemenway, *Zora Neale Hurston: A Literary Biography* (1977; Urbana: University of Illinois Press, 1980), 128.

27. See Boas, "Introduction to the *International Journal of Linguistics*" (1917), in *The Shaping of American Anthropology, 1883–1911: A Franz Boas Reader* (New York: Basic Books, 1974), 200.

28. Dennis Tedlock, in *The Spoken Word and the Work of Interpretation* (Philadelphia: University of Pennsylvania Press, 1983), 40–46, has criticized the "dryness" of Boas' literal translations, which give no sense of performance. Dell Hymes defends Boas in "Tonkawa Poetics," in *Native American Discourse: Poetics and Rhetoric*, ed. Joel Sherzer and Anthony C. Woodbury (New York: Cambridge University Press, 1987).

29. Herskovits, *Franz Boas*, 93.

30. Quoted in ibid., 89.

31. Hyatt, *Franz Boas*, 33–34; William S. Willis, Jr., "Skeletons in the Anthropological Closet," in *Reinventing Anthropology*, ed. Dell Hymes (New York: Pantheon Books, 1972), 121–152.

32. See Boas, "Living Philosophies, II. An Anthropologist's Credo," *The Nation* 147 (1938): 201–204; and Leonard B. Glick, "Types Distinct from Our Own: Franz Boas on Jewish Identity and Assimilation," *American Anthropologist* 84 (1982): 545–563.

33. Stocking, "Scientific Reaction," 300–301.

34. Claudia Milstead, "Boasian Anthropology: Scientific Underpinning of the Harlem Renaissance," unpublished manuscript.

35. Boas believed that for many types of anthropological research white scholars were at a disadvantage, which may help explain the fact that his white students did not study African Americans more. Melville Herskovits, who taught at Howard for a semester, tried in vain to convince that school to start an anthropology program and encouraged black students there to become anthropologists, even seeking funding for them. Johnetta B. Cole was a student of his at Northwestern; he also gave field training to Ralph J. Bunche and Katherine Dunham. See George Eaton Simpson, *Melville J. Herskovits* (New York: Columbia University Press, 1973), 10. In fact, Dunham claimed that the training she got from Herskovits in the early 1930s, along with his letters of introduction to the Maroon community in Accompong, Haiti, were crucial to her success in studying Haitian dance styles. Subsequently she planned to do graduate work in anthropology under Herskovits, but she decided to attempt a career in dance instead, to his great disappointment. Dunham's use of dance styles from the Caribbean has been of historic importance to the development of African American performing arts. See Terry Harnan, *African Rhythm, American Dance: A Biography of Katherine Dunham* (New York: Knopf, 1974), 57–60, 97–101.

36. See Guido A. Podesta, "An Ethnographic Reproach to the Theory of the Avant-Garde: Modernity and Modernism in Latin America and the Harlem

Renaissance," *MLN* 106 (1991): 397. Podesta's evidence of Hurston's struggle consists entirely of a letter in which she asks Boas to write the introduction to *Mules and Men,* expressing her hope that the "creative" and popular aspects of the book would not inhibit him. Boas, in any case, provided the introduction. See also Karla F. C. Holloway: "It is not unfair to see 'Papa Franz' as the paternal white overseer to this black woman student who called herself Barnard's 'sacred Black cow' in a forthright and unambiguous acknowledgment of her status" (*Character of the Word,* 2). Regardless of Hurston's feeling of her general status at Barnard, her view of Boas was unambiguously positive—a bright student's view of an admired teacher.

37. Herskovits to Locke, 8 May 1924, correspondence files, Alain Locke Papers, Moorland-Spingarn Research Center. King apparently did get the position and worked under Boas. See Herskovits to Locke, 3 July 1926, Alain Locke Papers.

38. See Herbert J. Seligmann, *The Negro Faces America* (New York: Harper & Row, 1920), 306. Seligmann cites comments to this effect by "an anthropologist of international repute" in 1919; the source could only be Boas.

39. Alain Locke, "The Eleventh Hour of Nordicism: Retrospective Review of the Literature of the Negro for 1934" (1935), in *The Critical Temper of Alain Locke,* ed. Jeffrey C. Stewart (New York: Garland, 1983), 232.

40. The strongest statement to this effect is Willis'. One might retain at least some historical perspective, however, in considering charges that Boas was an imperialist, given the tremendous reprisals he suffered for attacking imperialist uses of anthropology. In a letter to *The Nation* of December 20, 1919, Boas had attacked the use of anthropological research for spying in Mexico and Central America. At a moment when American xenophobia was reaching fever pitch, he opened his letter by calling Woodrow Wilson a hypocrite and American democracy a fraud. For this letter, Boas, "who had dominated American anthropology . . . for two decades," was censured by and nearly expelled from the American Anthropological Association, evicted from its governing council, and forced to resign from the National Research Council. Moreover, to deny him the benefit of public self-defense, the association deleted his letter of resignation from its minutes (Stocking, "The Scientific Reaction Against Cultural Anthropology," in *Race, Culture, and Evolution,* 273). At the same time, the administration at Columbia was cutting its support for the anthropology department, trying to "starve" it. By the end of World War I, Boas was the only faculty member left in the department. George Eaton Simpson, *Melville J. Herskovits* (New York: Columbia University Press, 1973), 3; Margaret M. Caffrey, *Ruth Benedict: Stranger in This Land* (Austin: University of Texas Press, 1989), 100.

41. See especially Edward Said, "Representing the Colonized: Anthropology's Interlocutors," *Critical Inquiry* 15 (1989): 205–225; James Clifford and

George Marcus, *Writing Culture: The Poetics and Politics of Ethnography* (Berkeley: University of California Press, 1986); and George W. Stocking, Jr., *Colonial Situations: Essays on the Contextualization of Ethnographic Knowledge* (Madison: University of Wisconsin Press, 1991), especially Talal Asad's "Afterword: From the History of Colonial Anthropology to the Anthropology of Western Hegemony," 314–324.

42. Review of Adolf Bastian, *Die Welt in ihren Spiegelungen, Science* 10 (1887): 284.

43. Cornel West, *The American Evasion of Philosophy: A Genealogy of Pragmatism* (Madison: University of Wisconsin Press, 1989), 67.

44. Krupat, "Irony in Anthropology," 138.

45. Ibid., 144.

46. Franz Boas, quoted by Dewey in "Some Connexions of Science and Philosophy," in *The Later Works,* vol. 17, 404–405. Dewey's essay was not published in his lifetime, but dates from ca. 1911–1912.

47. William James, "On a Certain Blindness in Human Beings," in *The Writings of William James,* ed. John J. McDermott (New York: Random House, 1967), 644–645.

48. Stocking, *Race, Culture, and Evolution,* 149.

49. Boas, from Douglas Cole, "'The Value of a Person Lies in his *Herzensbildung*': Franz Boas' Baffin Island Letter-Diary, 1883–1884," in *Observers Observed: Essays on Ethnographic Fieldwork,* ed. George W. Stocking, Jr. (Madison: University of Wisconsin Press, 1983), 37.

50. Franz Boas, "The Real Race Problem," *Crisis* 1 (1910): 25.

51. Ibid., 24–25. Interestingly, in 1993 Todorov also suggests that the solution to racism such as that in the United States and South Africa is "racial mixing, that is, the disappearance of physical differences." *On Human Diversity: Nationalism, Racism, and Exoticism in French Thought,* trans. Catherine Porter (Cambridge, Mass.: Harvard University Press, 1993), 96.

52. Boas, *Anthropology and Modern Life,* 77–80.

53. Melville Herskovits, *The American Negro: A Study in Racial Crossing* (New York: Knopf, 1928), 57.

54. Ibid., 49.

55. Ibid., 30–32.

56. Ibid., 18.

57. Ibid., 82.

58. John F. Szwed points out that anthropologists in the wake of Boas ended up denying significant cultural as well as biological differences between black and white Americans because of "a deep commitment to the need for social change. Indeed, it was in their very zeal to refute genetic racism for general audiences and to demonstrate a universal capacity for culture that they argued that Afro-Americans shared essentially the same culture as white Americans,

and where they differed, the differences were to be accounted for exclusively as the result of environmental deprivation or cultural 'stripping.'" "An American Anthropological Dilemma: The Politics of Afro-American Culture," in *Reinventing Anthropology,* ed. Dell Hymes, 158.

59. See David Levering Lewis, "Parallels and Divergences: Assimilationist Strategies of Afro-American and Jewish Elites from 1910 to the Early 1930s," *Journal of American History* 71 (1984): 543–564; Glick, "Types Distinct from Our Own," 545–563; and Hyatt, *Franz Boas,* 90–91.

3. Cultural Pluralism and National Identity

1. John Higham, *Send These to Me: Jews and Other Immigrants in Urban America* (New York: Atheneum, 1975), 209; Du Bois quoted in Manning Marable, *W. E. B. Du Bois, Black Radical Democrat* (Boston: Twayne, 1986), 38; from "Strivings of the Negro People," *Atlantic Monthly* 80 (1897): 194–198.

2. W. E. B. Du Bois, *The Souls of Black Folk* (New York: Viking Penguin, 1989), 215.

3. See also Rutledge M. Dennis, "Relativism and Pluralism in the Social Thought of Alain Locke," in *Alain Locke: Reflections on a Modern Renaissance Man,* ed. Russell J. Linneman (Baton Rouge: Louisiana State University Press, 1982), 48. John Higham (*Send These to Me,* 209–211) rightly points out that Du Bois's vision was closer to that of the "melting-pot" than Locke's or Horace Kallen's.

4. William James, *Talks to Teachers on Psychology; and to Students on Some of Life's Ideals* (New York: Henry Holt, 1902), v.

5. John J. McDermott, *Streams of Experience: Reflections on the History and Philosophy of American Culture* (Amherst: University of Massachusetts Press, 1986), 112.

6. Higham, *Send These to Me,* 211.

7. Josiah Royce, "Race Questions," in *Race Questions, Provincialism, and Other American Problems* (New York: Macmillan, 1908), 47–53. White racism at this time was often regarded as an instinctive reaction against other, and particularly "lower," human types, connected with a supposedly natural fear of "amalgamation." These concepts were made to fit Darwinian theory.

8. Royce, "Provincialism" (1908), in *Race Questions,* 66.

9. Ibid., 100–102.

10. For Royce's impact upon another group of modernists, particularly T. S. Eliot, see Frank Lentricchia, "Philosophers of Modernism at Harvard, circa 1900," *South Atlantic Quarterly* 89 (1990): 818–832.

11. W. E. B. Du Bois, "Josiah Royce," *Crisis* 13 (1916): 10.

12. Alain Locke, "Unity Through Diversity: A Baha'i Principle," *The Philosophy of Alain Locke,* ed. Leonard Harris (Philadelphia: Temple University Press, 1989), 137.

13. Royce, "Provincialism," 99.

14. Josiah Royce, *The Problem of Christianity* (1918; Chicago: University of Chicago Press, 1968), 264, 265.

15. Royce, "Provincialism," 102, 103.

16. Horace Kallen, "Alain Locke and Cultural Pluralism," *The Journal of Philosophy* 54 (1957): 119–127.

17. Royce, "Provincialism," 103, 104–105.

18. Alain Locke, "The Negro and the American Stage" (1926), in *The Critical Temper of Alain Locke,* ed. Jeffrey C. Stewart (New York: Garland, 1983), 79–86.

19. Milton R. Konvitz, *The Legacy of Horace M. Kallen* (Rutherford, N.J.: Fairleigh Dickinson University Press, 1987), 17.

20. Horace M. Kallen, "The Promise of the Menorah Idea," *Menorah Journal* (1962): 12. My emphasis.

21. Werner Sollors, "A Critique of Pure Pluralism," in *Reconstructing American Literary History* (Cambridge, Mass.: Harvard University Press, 1986), 269. Quoted from Sarah L. Schmidt, "Horace Kallen and the Americanization of Zionism," Ph.D. dissertation, University of Maryland, 1973, p. 34.

22. Sollors cites letters to Barrett Wendell in which Kallen assented to his teacher's "repugnance" for black people even while trying to counter the racism of Southern white Rhodes scholars who were ostracizing Locke at Oxford. "It seems strange, indeed, that Kallen singled out the early contact with Locke as the stimulus for pluralism when his own letters at the time of the incident make Kallen such an unlikely ancestor for contemporary pluralists." Sollors, "Critique," 270–271, 272.

23. See Alain Locke correspondence with Mary Hawkins Locke, 1904–1905 (boxes 1 and 2), Alain Locke Papers, Moorland-Spingarn Research Center, Howard University. The quotation is from a letter of 2 June 1905, in box 2.

24. The growing cultural nationalism and partial social autonomy of different ethnic groups, argued Kallen, is an "inevitable" consequence of "the democratic principle on which the American theory of government is based." "Democracy *versus* the Melting-Pot," in *Culture and Democracy in the United States: Studies in the Group Psychology of the American Peoples* (New York: Boni & Liveright, 1924), 116. Originally published in *The Nation,* 18 and 25 February 1915.

25. Horace Kallen, "The Ethics of Zionism," *Maccabaean* 11 (1906): 71.

26. Kallen, *Culture and Democracy,* 226.

27. Higham, *Send These to Me,* 208.

28. Kallen's ideas at this point would also have struck Dewey as antidemocratic. As Giles Gunn has pointed out, one of the criteria Dewey developed for judging the democratic quality of a social group was not just the degree to which all members shared in determining its interests and direction, but also "'the fullness and freedom with which it interacts with other groups.'" Giles Gunn, *Thinking Across the American Grain: Ideology, Intellect, and the New Pragmatism* (Chicago: University of Chicago Press, 1992), 77, quoting Dewey, *Democracy and Education* (1916; New York: Macmillan, 1944), 99.

29. See Robert B. Westbrook, *John Dewey and American Democracy* (Ithaca: Cornell University Press, 1991), 213–214.

30. John Dewey, "Nationalizing Education," in vol. 10 of *The Middle Works, 1899–1924,* ed. Jo Ann Boydston, (Carbondale: Southern Illinois University Press, 1976), 205.

31. John Dewey, "The Need for a Recovery of Philosophy," in vol. 10 of *The Middle Works,* 45.

32. Thomas M. Alexander, *John Dewey's Theory of Art, Experience, and Nature: The Horizons of Feeling* (Albany: State University of New York Press, 1987), xvii.

33. See Regna Darnell, *Edward Sapir: Linguist, Anthropologist, Humanist* (Berkeley: University of California Press, 1990), 172; and Margaret M. Caffrey, *Ruth Benedict: Stranger in This Land* (Austin: University of Texas Press, 1989), 152–158. Significantly, Benedict recognized the similarity of William James's categories of the "tough-minded" and the "tender-minded" to her own differentiation (adopted from Nietzsche) between "Apollonian" and "Dionysian" "psychological sets."

34. See Melville Herskovits, *Franz Boas: The Science of Man in the Making* (New York: Scribner's, 1953), 16, 97.

35. See Marvin Harris, *The Rise of Anthropological Theory* (New York: Crowell, 1968), 299. Boas dated his shift to 1910. Dewey came to Columbia in 1904. The influence of Boas on Dewey's work begins to show by 1911–1912, and the two men taught a seminar together in 1914–1915.

36. John Dewey, *Experience and Nature,* vol. 1 of *The Later Works, 1925–1953,* ed. Jo Ann Boydston (Carbondale: Southern Illinois University Press, 1981), 42. He is quoting (with minor liberties) from p. 604 of Alexander Goldenweiser, "History, Psychology and Culture: A Set of Categories for an Introduction to Social Science," *Journal of Philosophy, Psychology and Scientific Methods* 15 (1918): 561–574, 589–607.

37. See George Dykhuizen, *The Life and Mind of John Dewey,* ed. Jo Ann Boydston (Carbondale: Southern Illinois University Press, 1973), 123.

38. Horace Kallen, *Cultural Pluralism and the American Idea* (Philadelphia: University of Pennsylvania Press, 1956), 38.

39. See Matgorzata Irek, "From Berlin to Harlem: Felix von Luschan, Alain Locke, and The New Negro," in *The Black Columbiad,* ed. Werner Sollors and Maria Diedrich (Cambridge, Mass.: Harvard University Press, 1994), 174–184.

40. Kallen, *Cultural Pluralism,* 40, 44.

41. Kallen, *Culture and Democracy,* 43.

42. Ibid., 226n.

43. On Kallen's Eurocentrism, see also Higham, *Send These to Me,* 208; and Sollors, "Critique," 262 n.19.

44. Alain Locke, "The Concept of Race as Applied to Social Culture" (1924), in *Critical Temper,* 423–431.

45. Ibid., 423.

46. Ibid., 428.

47. The point was made in George Devereux and Edwin M. Loeb's classic essay, "Antagonistic Acculturation," *American Sociological Review* 8 (1943): 133–147; extended in Fredrik Barth, ed., *Ethnic Groups and Boundaries: The Social Organization of Cultural Difference* (Boston: Little, Brown, 1969); and adopted by Werner Sollors, most notably in *Beyond Ethnicity: Consent and Descent in American Culture* (New York: Oxford University Press, 1986).

48. Locke, "The Concept of Race," 429.

49. Ibid., 429.

4. Cultural Nationalism and the Lyrical Left

1. John P. Diggins, *The American Left in the Twentieth Century* (New York: Harcourt Brace Jovanovich, 1973), 73–105.

2. For partial exceptions, see Amritjit Singh, *The Novels of the Harlem Renaissance: Twelve Black Writers, 1923–1933* (University Park: Pennsylvania State University Press, 1976), 16–17; and S. P. Fullinwider, *The Mind and Mood of Black America* (Homewood, Ill.: Dorsey Press, 1969), 116–122.

3. Marcus Klein, *Foreigners: The Making of American Literature, 1910–1940* (Chicago: University of Chicago Press, 1981), 44.

4. See Gerald Graff, *Professing Literature: An Institutional History* (Chicago: University of Chicago Press, 1987), 130–131.

5. See, for example, Lajpat Rai, "Young India," *Seven Arts* 2 (1917): 743–758. The spirit of self-determination, which also infuses Claude McKay's sonnet "Invocation" (first published in *The Seven Arts*), attracts similar interest in complementary essays on "Young Japan," "Youngest Ireland," "Young Spain," "The Literary History of Spanish America," and "Young America."

6. Van Wyck Brooks, *Van Wyck Brooks: An Autobiography* (New York: E. P. Dutton, 1965), 649.

7. Stephen Spender, *T. S. Eliot* (Harmondsworth: Viking Penguin, 1976), 10, 11.

8. Spender, 14.

9. Spender, 13.

10. Quoted in "The Looking Glass," *Crisis* 15 (1917): 81.

11. Jonas' poem "Crowded Out" appears in *Shadowed Dreams: Women's Poetry of the Harlem Renaissance,* ed. Maureen Honey (New Brunswick, N.J.: Rutgers University Press, 1989), 72.

12. The work was published as *"The Nigger," An American Play in Three Acts* (New York: Macmillan, 1910). For a fuller discussion of this play in relation to Sheldon's total career and American progressivism, see Loren K. Ruff, *Edward Sheldon* (Boston: Twayne, 1982), 39–48. Initially greeted in the *New York Age* as

a truthful and important effort but panned in *The Nation* as sensationalistic and incredible, the play would later be considered by black critics a significant if fundamentally flawed precursor to the "Negro drama" of the 1920s. The point I would stress, however, is that Sheldon wrote it under the influence of Synge and the Celtic Revival as a pioneering contribution to "indigenous" social realist American drama, exposing racism as a cardinal American sin.

13. Fullinwider, 120, 117–119. See also Nathan Irvin Huggins, *Harlem Renaissance* (New York: Oxford University Press, 1971), 60.

14. Charles C. Alexander, *Here the Country Lies: Nationalism and the Arts in Twentieth-Century America* (Bloomington: Indiana University Press, 1980), 138.

15. Especially significant is Van Vechten's "The Later Work of Herman Melville," *Double Dealer* 3 (1922): 9–20. On *Moby-Dick*, Van Vechten writes, "It is surely Melville's greatest book, surely the greatest book that has yet been written in America, surely one of the great books of the world" (15–16). Van Vechten was one of the first critics to make such vaunted claims for the novel.

16. Alain Locke, "The American Temperament," *North American Review* 194 (1911): 262–270. Rpt. in *The Critical Temper of Alain Locke*, ed. Jeffrey C. Stewart (New York: Garland, 1983), 399–405.

17. Locke's early interest in *The Seven Arts* is implied in a letter from his friend in England, Lionel DeFonseka, of 20 January 1917 responding to one Locke had written: "Where is or are *The Seven Arts?* The title does sound American. . . . Do send me a copy, and if I am not overawed, I shall write something for it." Alain Locke Papers, Moorland-Spingarn Research Center, Howard University.

18. Gorham Munson, *The Awakening Twenties: A Memoir-History of a Literary Period* (Baton Rouge: Louisiana State University Press, 1985), 60.

19. Hiram Moderwell, "A Modest Proposal," *Seven Arts* 2 (1917): 368–376; Carl Van Vechten, "Communication," *Seven Arts* 2 (1917): 669–670. See also Van Vechten's "Music and the Electrical Theater," *Seven Arts* 2 (1917): 97–102.

20. Arna Bontemps, in Frank Durham, *Merrill Studies in Cane* (Columbus: Merrill, 1971), 76. McKay's poems are published under the pen name Eli Edwards—"Invocation" and "The Harlem Dancer," *Seven Arts* 2 (1917): 741–742. Their inclusion is all the more notable for the fact that the magazine generally did not publish poetry in traditional forms. The same issue of *The Seven Arts*, however, carried Bertrand Russell's "Is Nationalism Moribund?" which concludes with this gem of left-wing racism: "Every advance in technical civilization must make war more deadly, and a great war a hundred years hence might well leave the world in the exclusive possession of negroes. If we wish to avert this calamity we must be bold, constructive, and not afraid to be revolutionary" (687). The statement dramatically clashes with the final three lines of McKay's "Invocation," addressed to an ancestral African spirit: "Lift me to thee out of this alien place / So I may be, thine exiled counterpart, / The worthy singer of my world and race" (741). Immediately following "Invocation" and McKay's

"The Harlem Dancer" in this issue is Lajpat Rai's "Young India" (743–758), cited above, which extols awakened Indian nationalism and anti-imperialism, showing connections between the political movement and the "revival of indigenous art and literature," such as Tagore's vernacular poetics.

21. Brooks, *Autobiography*, 176–177.

22. Ibid., 323, 328.

23. Van Wyck Brooks, *Letters and Leadership* (New York: B. W. Huebsch, 1918), 115–116, 19, 100, 111.

24. W. E. B. Du Bois, *The Souls of Black Folk* (1903; New York: Penguin, 1989), 11–12.

25. V. F. Calverton, *The Liberation of American Literature* (New York: Scribner's, 1932), 445.

26. Edward Abrahams, *The Lyrical Left: Randolph Bourne, Alfred Stieglitz, and the Origins of Cultural Radicalism in America* (Charlottesville: University Press of Virginia, 1986), 32, 64–66.

27. Bourne, "Trans-national America" (1916), in *War and the Intellectuals: Essays by Randolph S. Bourne,* ed. Carl Resek (New York: Harper & Row, 1964), 112, 114.

28. Ibid., 114, 119, 114.

29. See Bourne's letter to the editor in the *New York Tribune,* 10 April 1917, p. 10.

30. Randolph Bourne, "The War and the Intellectuals" (1917), in *War and the Intellectuals,* 5. The essay was originally published in *Seven Arts* 2 (1917): 133–146.

31. Ibid., 6.

32. Ibid., 10.

33. See Robert B. Westbrook, *John Dewey and American Democracy* (Ithaca: Cornell University Press, 1991), 195–240.

34. Bourne, "The War and the Intellectuals," 8–9.

35. Quoted in Brooks, *Autobiography*, 281.

36. Brooks, *Autobiography*, 510, 271.

37. Ibid., 275.

38. "The Looking Glass," *Crisis* 26 (1923): 268.

39. Alexander, *Here the Country Lies*, 86.

40. Quoted in ibid., 87.

41. Munson, *Awakening Twenties*, 63–64.

42. Waldo Frank, *Our America* (New York: Boni & Liveright, 1919), 63–67.

43. Ibid., 230.

44. Alain Locke, "The Negro's Contribution to American Art and Literature" (1928), in *Critical Temper,* 448.

45. Du Bois, *Souls,* 11.

46. See Wayne F. Cooper, *Claude McKay: Rebel Sojourner in the Harlem Renais-*

sance (Baton Rouge: Louisiana State University Press, 1987), 30–31; and George B. Hutchinson, "The Whitman Legacy and the Harlem Renaissance," *Walt Whitman: The Centennial Essays,* ed. Ed Folsom (Iowa City: University of Iowa Press, 1994), 203–204.

47. See my "Langston Hughes and the 'Other' Whitman," in *The Continuing Presence of Walt Whitman: The Life After the Life,* ed. Robert K. Martin (Iowa City: University of Iowa Press, 1992), 16–27.

48. See Hazel V. Carby, "It Jus Be's Dat Way Sometime: The Sexual Politics of Women's Blues," in *Gender and Discourse: The Power of Talk,* ed. Alexandra Dundas Todd and Sue Fisher (Norwood, N.J.: Ablex, 1988), 227–242.

49. Langston Hughes to Carl Van Vechten, 17 May 1925, Langston Hughes Papers, James Weldon Johnson Collection, Beinecke Rare Book and Manuscript Library, Yale University.

50. Van Wyck Brooks, *America's Coming-of-Age* (1915), in *Van Wyck Brooks: The Early Years,* ed. Claire Sprague (New York: Harper & Row, 1968), 87.

51. Floyd Dell, "Books: *Fifty Years and Other Poems,* by James Weldon Johnson," *Liberator* 1 (1918): 32–33.

52. See, for example, Locke, "The Drama of Negro Life," *Theatre Arts* 10 (1926): 704; and Willis Richardson, "The Hope of a Negro Drama," *Crisis* 19 (1919): 338–339. Sterling Brown wrote to James Weldon Johnson on 22 March 1932, "I'm working on the *Irish* folk-drama for a course in modern drama—I think the parallels it suggests to our own movement are fruitful" (Sterling Brown Correspondence, James Weldon Johnson Collection, Beinecke Rare Book and Manuscript Library). Similarly, when Hughes turned to drama in the early 1930s, he wrote to Johnson, "I want to talk to you about the possibilities of a Negro Theatre like the *Abbey* in Dublin. I'm writing some plays" (Langston Hughes to James Weldon Johnson, 20 August 1931, series 1, folder 219, James Weldon Johnson MSS, James Weldon Johnson Collection, Beinecke Rare Book and Manuscript Library).

53. See Locke's inscription on the dedication page of the copy of *The New Negro* he presented to Carl Van Vechten, in the Carl Van Vechten Collection, Beinecke Rare Book and Manuscript Library, Yale University.

54. Alain Locke, "The Negro Poets of the United States" (1926), in *Critical Temper,* 45.

55. See Shelley Fisher Fishkin, *Was Huck Black? Mark Twain and African American Voices* (New York: Oxford University Press, 1993).

56. Henry F. May, *The End of American Innocence: A Study of the First Years of Our Own Time, 1912–1917* (New York: Knopf, 1959), 98.

57. See Thomas Bender, *New York Intellect* (New York: Knopf, 1987), 219.

58. Despite my admiration for his reading of "An Antebellum Sermon," I depart here from some of the conclusions of Marcellus Blount's "The Preacherly Text: African American Poetry and Vernacular Performance," *PMLA* 107 (1992): 582–593.

59. See my "Whitman and the Black Poet: Kelly Miller's Speech to the Walt Whitman Fellowship," *American Literature* 61 (1989): 57–58; "Langston Hughes and the 'Other' Whitman," 16–27; and "The Whitman Legacy and the Harlem Renaissance," 201–216. Henry Louis Gates's praise for Jean Toomer, Langston Hughes, and Sterling Brown as models for the use of black poetic diction unwittingly undercuts his own argument for the "hermetic" nature of that tradition. See Gates, *Figures in Black: Words, Signs, and the "Racial" Self* (New York: Oxford University Press, 1987), xxiii; and "Canon-Formation, Literary History, and the Afro-American Tradition: From the Seen to the Told," in *Afro-American Literary Study in the 1990s,* ed. Houston A. Baker, Jr., and Patricia Redmond (Chicago: University of Chicago Press, 1989), 14–39. The same problem afflicts Houston Baker's assertion of the autonomy of African American modernism in connection with his belief that "the blending . . . of class and mass—*poetic* mastery discovered as a function of deformative *folk* sound—constitutes the essence of black discursive modernism" (*Modernism and the Harlem Renaissance* [Chicago: University of Chicago Press, 1986], 93). Such blending was hardly unique to African American authors. Sterling Brown explicitly attacked attempts to distinguish absolutely between black and white traditions on formal grounds. See his introduction to *The Negro Caravan: Writings by American Negroes,* ed. Sterling Brown, Arthur P. Davis, and Ulysses Lee (New York: Dryden, 1941), 6–7.

60. Susan J. Turner, *The History of "The Freeman": Literary Landmark of the Early Twenties* (New York: Columbia University Press, 1963), 1–33.

61. Van Wyck Brooks, "Ezra Pound's Instigations," *Freeman* 1 (1920): 334–335; rpt. in *Van Wyck Brooks: The Early Years,* 230–31.

62. G. A. M. Janssens, *The American Literary Review* (The Hague: Mouton, 1968), 39.

63. W. E. B. Du Bois, *Dusk of Dawn: An Essay Toward an Autobiography of a Race Concept* (1940; New York: Schocken Books, 1968), 80.

64. *Dial* 62 (1917): 45.

65. Westbrook, *John Dewey,* 238–239.

66. John Dewey, "The Sequel of the Student Revolt" (1920), in vol. 12 of *The Middle Works, 1899–1924,* ed. Jo Ann Boydston (Carbondale: Southern Illinois University Press, 1982), 22–27.

67. Dewey, "Americanism and Localism," in vol. 12 of *The Middle Works,* 12–13. Originally published in *Dial* 68 (1920): 684–688.

68. Janssens, *American Literary Review,* 41.

69. Brooks, *Autobiography,* 510.

70. Quoted in Janssens, *American Literary Review,* 59.

71. Raymond Williams, "Theatre as a Political Forum," *The Politics of Modernism: Against the New Conformists,* ed. Tony Pinkney (London: Verso, 1989), 83–85.

72. Williams, "Theatre," 84, 85.

73. Fredric Jameson, "The Ideology of the Text," *Salmagundi,* 31–32 (1975–

1976): 233; Eysteinsson, *The Concept of Modernism* (Ithaca: Cornell University Press, 1990), 7.

74. Eysteinsson, *Concept of Modernism*, 184.

75. On the division between social and personal spheres in "high" modernism, see J. P. Stern, "The Theme of Consciousness: Thomas Mann," in *Modernism, 1890–1930*, ed. Malcolm Bradbury and James McFarlane (Harmondsworth: Penguin, 1976), 428.

76. Williams, "Language and the Avant-Garde," in *The Politics of Modernism*, 79.

77. Ibid., 79.

78. Max Henriquez Ureña, quoted in Ned J. Davison, *The Concept of Modernism in Hispanic Criticism* (Boulder: Pruett Press, 1966), 16.

79. Davison, *Concept of Modernism*, 21.

80. David Lodge, *The Modes of Modern Writing: Metaphor, Metonymy, and the Typology of Modern Literature* (London: Edward Arnold, 1977), 25. Entire passage italicized in the original.

81. See, for example, Catherine Rainwater, "Narration as Pragmatism in Ellen Glasgow's *Barren Ground*," *American Literature* 63 (1991): 664–682.

82. Richard Rorty, *Consequences of Pragmatism* (Minneapolis: University of Minnesota Press, 1982), 153.

83. Eastman, *The Literary Mind: Its Place in an Age of Science* (New York: Scribner's, 1931), 6. Although this book dates from the approximate end of the Harlem Renaissance, it merely systematizes the pragmatist aesthetic theory Eastman had assumed from the time of his teaching of aesthetics under Dewey at Columbia in the pre-*Masses* period. Similar arguments appeared in his criticism of the teens, to be discussed in my chapter on *The Liberator*. I include his argument in *The Literary Mind* here, because in it he directly critiques the "high" modernist positions that had, by the 1930s, displaced his and Dewey's approaches. *The Literary Mind* gives us an enhanced perspective upon the battles of the 1920s.

84. Ibid., 15, 36.

85. Ibid., 38–39.

86. Ibid., 44–45.

87. See John Dewey, "Introduction," in Claude McKay, *Selected Poems* (New York: Bookman Associates, 1953), 7–9. The closing "biographical note" to this volume is by Max Eastman.

88. Richard Rorty, *Contingency, Irony, and Solidarity* (Cambridge: Cambridge University Press, 1989), xvi.

89. This point is made by Casey Nelson Blake in relation to the Young Intellectuals; see *Beloved Community: The Cultural Criticism of Randolph Bourne, Van Wyck Brooks, Waldo Frank, and Lewis Mumford* (Chapel Hill: University of North Carolina Press, 1990), 5–8.

90. Hurston, "What White Publishers Won't Print," in *I Love Myself When I Am Laughing . . . and Then Again When I Am Looking Mean and Impressive* (Old Westbury, Conn.: Feminist Press, 1979), 171.

91. For a discussion of this issue in relation to the Young Intellectuals, see Casey Nelson Blake, *Beloved Community.*

II. The Transformation of Literary Institutions

1. V. F. Calverton, *The Liberation of American Literature* (New York: Scribner's, 1932), 360–361.

2. Marcus Klein has differentiated the left wing of the group to which I am referring from the expatriate modernists in accurate terms: "The participants in the Pound Era nominated themselves to be conservators of the grand western European cultural past, and not incidentally they were conservatives in their social and political choices—fascists, some of the best of them, when the crunch came. On the other side were such writers and critics as Van Wyck Brooks, Paul Rosenfeld, Lewis Mumford, Waldo Frank, Sherwood Anderson, Randolph Bourne, Max Eastman, Floyd Dell, John Reed, and others, who created and sustained such journals as *Seven Arts,* the *Freeman, Modern Quarterly,* the *Masses,* the *Liberator,* and then latterly and for a short while *New Masses.* They, too, were engaged in creating a tradition . . . [T]hey had in common first of all a commitment to an American rather than a Western culture, and then not incidentally they all considered themselves to be socialists." Klein, *Foreigners: The Making of American Literature, 1910–1940* (Chicago: University of Chicago Press, 1981), 39.

3. Although *The New Masses* attempted to be a "proletarian" magazine, it evidently was never very successful in reaching a chiefly working-class audience, as it admitted in the early 1930s in response to criticism from the International Congress of Revolutionary Writers and Artists. See "A Statement," *New Masses* 6 (February 1931): 2.

4. See, for example, full-page advertisements in *New Republic* 48 (25 August 1926): v; and *Nation* 110 (31 January 1920): v.

5. See, for example, the *Opportunity* advertisement in *New Masses* 1 (1926): 30, and the full-page ad for *New Masses* on the inside cover of the first and only issue of *Fire!!* (the inside back cover has an ad from *Opportunity*); or *Modern Quarterly*'s advertisement in the *Messenger* 8 (1926): 194, as "the only radical and revolutionary magazine in America that is avowedly inter-racial, prints articles by Negroes in every issue, and sees economic revolution as the only solution to the 'race problem.'"

6. See full-page advertisement, *New Masses* 5 (February 1930): 24.

7. "Editorial," *Harlem* 1 (1928): 21.

8. Claude McKay, *A Long Way from Home* (1937; New York: Arno Press, 1969), 28.

9. Hubert Harrison, review of McKay's *Spring in New Hampshire,* in *Negro World* (1920), quoted in Wayne F. Cooper, *Claude McKay: Rebel Sojourner in the Harlem Renaissance* (Baton Rouge: Louisiana State University Press, 1987), 165.

10. See, for example, McKay's dispute with Alain Locke over his contributions to the *Survey Graphic* and *The New Negro,* discussed in Part III.

11. McKay to Alain Locke, 27 July 1926, correspondence files, Alain Locke Papers, Moorland-Spingarn Research Center, Howard University.

12. Ibid., 18 April 1927.

13. Ibid., 12 April 1927.

14. McKay, *A Long Way from Home,* 322.

15. Jean Toomer to Mae Wright, 4 August 1922, Jean Toomer Papers, box 9, folder 283, American Literature Collection, Beinecke Rare Book and Manuscript Library, Yale University.

16. Ibid.

17. Ibid.

18. Arna Bontemps, "The Negro Renaissance: Jean Toomer and the Harlem Writers of the 1920's," in *Anger, and Beyond: The Negro Writer in the United States,* ed. Herbert Hill (New York: Harper & Row, 1966), 22, 23.

19. Edward E. Waldron, *Walter White and the Harlem Renaissance* (Port Washington, N.Y.: Kennikat, 1978), 141.

20. See Carolyn Wedin Sylvander, *Jessie Redmon Fauset, Black American Writer* (Troy, N.Y.: Whitston, 1981), 113.

21. *Messenger* 2 (July 1919): 13.

22. "The World Tomorrow," *Crisis* 32 (1926): 61. Contributors to *The World Tomorrow* overlapped with those to the other magazines mentioned. It was associated with the Fellowship Press, the treasurer of which was Hollingsworth Wood of the Urban League. See George S. Schuyler, *Black and Conservative: The Autobiography of George S. Schuyler* (New Rochelle, N.Y.: Arlington House, 1966), 96, 132. Wallace Thurman changed jobs from *The Messenger* to *The World Tomorrow* in 1926, when he was also putting *Fire!!* together; and, indeed, *The World Tomorrow* loaned money to publish *Fire!!*—a debt later paid off in the form of literary contributions by the *Fire!!* group, including Zora Neale Hurston's "How It Feels to Be Colored Me." See Robert Hemenway, *Zora Neale Hurston: A Literary Biography* (Urbana: University of Illinois Press, 1977), 114.

23. Toomer, "Book X," unpublished autobiography in the Jean Toomer Papers.

24. Toomer, "Outline of the Story of an Autobiography," 55–56, box 20, folder 515, Jean Toomer Papers.

25. Arnold Rampersad, *The Life of Langston Hughes,* vol. 1 (New York: Oxford University Press, 1986), 30.

26. This point is discussed below in the chapter on *The New Masses*.

27. David Levering Lewis, *When Harlem Was in Vogue* (New York: Knopf, 1981), 98.

5. *The Crisis* and the Nation's Conscience

1. Alex Haley and Malcolm X, *The Autobiography of Malcolm X* (1964; New York: Ballantine Books, 1973), 375–377; *Malcolm X Speaks,* ed. George Breitman (New York: Grove Press, 1966), 221.

2. On Walling's biography, I rely primarily on James Gilbert, "William English Walling: The Pragmatic Critique of Collectivism," in *Designing the Industrial State: The Intellectual Pursuit of Collectivism in America, 1880–1940* (Chicago: Quadrangle Books, 1972), 200–239; Allen F. Davis, *Spearheads for Reform: The Social Settlements and the Progressive Movement, 1890–1914* (New York: Oxford University Press, 1967), 99–102; and Mary White Ovington, "How the National Association for the Advancement of Colored People Began," *Crisis* 8 (1914): 184.

3. See, for example, Walling's *American Labor and American Democracy* (New York: Harper, 1926), 7–23.

4. Robert B. Westbrook, *John Dewey and American Democracy* (Ithaca: Cornell University Press, 1991), 190–192.

5. See Gilbert, "William English Walling," 219–221.

6. William English Walling, *Whitman and Traubel* (New York: Albert and Charles Boni, 1916), 14. Gilbert, "William English Walling," 226.

7. Mary White Ovington, "How the National Association for the Advancement of Colored People Began," *Crisis* 8 (1914): 184; Walling, "The Race War in the North," *Independent* 65 (1908): 529–534.

8. Davis, *Spearheads,* 101–102. The Neighborhood Playhouse, founded by Alice and Irene Lewisohn in 1915 on the model of the Hull House theater, first introduced the plays of Lord Dunsany to the United States and played a very significant role in the development of "native" drama, particularly ethnic drama and drama of social comment. See Constance D'Arcy Mackay, *The Little Theatre in the United States* (New York: Henry Holt, 1917), 54–60.

9. *Proceedings of the National Negro Conference, 1909* (New York: Arno Press, 1969), 14–21, 71–73.

10. W. E. B. Du Bois, *Dusk of Dawn: An Essay Toward an Autobiography of a Race Concept* (1940; New York: Schocken Books, 1968), 90.

11. See Ovington, "How the NAACP Began," 187–188. The poem was "The Present Crisis."

12. Quoted in Rampersad, *The Art and Imagination of W. E. B. Du Bois* (1976; New York: Schocken Books, 1990), 136, from a letter of 28 October 1914.

13. Du Bois, *Dusk of Dawn,* 82–83.

14. For an excellent discussion of Du Bois and the literary orientation of *The Crisis,* see Rampersad, *Art and Imagination,* 184–201.

15. "Resolutions at the Cooper Union on Lincoln's Birthday," *Crisis* 5 (1913): 292.

16. James Weldon Johnson, *Along This Way* (New York: Viking, 1933), 327.

17. Ibid., 326, 327.

18. Mary White Ovington, *The Walls Came Tumbling Down* (New York: Schocken Books, 1970), 108.

19. The show took place at "291" in November 1914. Seligmann discusses it in "291: A Vision Through Photography," *America and Alfred Stieglitz,* ed. Waldo Frank (New York: Doubleday, Doran, 1934), 109.

20. Sue Davidson Lowe, *Stieglitz: A Memoir/Biography* (New York: Farrar, Straus & Giroux, 1983), 244.

21. Seligmann, "291," 111.

22. Jean Toomer, "The Hill," in *America and Alfred Stieglitz,* 296.

23. Herbert J. Seligmann, *The Negro Faces America* (1920; Harper & Row, 1969), 309. Seligmann's views throughout this book suggest the strong influence of James Weldon Johnson, who was at the time the executive secretary of the NAACP. In fact, Seligmann accompanied Johnson to Haiti to investigate the American occupation, on which Johnson reported in a series for *The Nation.* See Johnson, *Along This Way,* 345.

24. "The Crisis and the NAACP," *Crisis* 11 (1915): 27.

25. Du Bois, *Dusk of Dawn,* 294.

26. James Weldon Johnson, *Black Manhattan* (New York: Knopf, 1930), 258.

27. "Editorial," *Crisis* 17 (1919): 166.

28. James Weldon Johnson, "Father, Father Abraham," *Crisis* 5 (1913): 172.

29. Poem reprinted from the *New York Times,* in "Opinion," *Crisis* 5 (1913): 173.

30. See Wayne Francis, "'Lift Every Voice and Sing,'" *Crisis* 32 (1926): 234–236.

31. Nicholas Vachel Lindsay, "The Golden-Faced People: A Story of the Chinese Conquest of America," *Crisis* 9 (1914): 36–42.

32. "A Letter and an Answer," *Crisis* 13 (1917): 114.

33. See Barbara Joyce Ross, *J. E. Spingarn and the Rise of the NAACP, 1911–1939* (New York: Atheneum, 1972), 28–29. Spingarn's main differences with Du Bois later arose as a result of Du Bois's evolving interest in Marxism and in the tactical use of racial separatism to achieve full equality.

34. Quoted by Du Bois, in *The Autobiography of W. E. B. Du Bois* (New York: International Publishers, 1968), 288.

35. Ibid., 287–288.

36. The dedication of *Dusk of Dawn* (1940) reads, "To keep the memory of Joel Spingarn, scholar and knight."

37. W. E. B. Du Bois, "A Pile of Books," *Crisis* 9 (1915): 199.

38. Ibid.

39. William Stanley Braithwaite, "The Year in Poetry," *Bookman* (March 1917); rpt. in *The William Stanley Braithwaite Reader,* ed. Philip Butcher (Ann Arbor: University of Michigan Press, 1972), 37.

40. Ibid.

41. William Stanley Braithwaite, "The House Under Arcturus, IV," *Phylon* 3 (2d Quarter 1942): 42–43; "The House Under Arcturus, V," *Phylon* 3 (3d Quarter 1942): 191.

42. See his comment on Clement Wood's *The Earth Turns South* in *Anthology of Magazine Verse for 1919 and Year Book of American Poetry* (Boston: Small, Maynard, 1919), 297; and his "Introduction" to *Anthology of Magazine Verse for 1914 and Year Book of American Poetry* (Cambridge, Mass.: W. S. Braithwaite, 1914), ix–x. He considered the outstanding event of the poetic year in 1914 to be Kennerley's publication of *Leaves of Grass,* and the best new volume of poetry James Oppenheim's Whitmanesque *Songs for the New Age.*

43. Braithwaite, "The Year in Poetry," 41. Italicized in the original.

44. "Some Contemporary Poets of the Negro Race," *Crisis* (April 1919); rpt. in *The William Stanley Braithwaite Reader,* 49.

45. Braithwaite, "Introduction," 91.

46. See "Some Contemporary Poets," 50.

47. Ibid., 52.

48. Ibid.

49. Ibid., 53.

50. Braithwaite, "Introduction," 94.

51. "Some Contemporary Poets," 50, 54.

52. W. E. B. Du Bois, "Criteria of Negro Art," *Crisis* 32 (1926): 290, 292.

53. Langston Hughes, *The Big Sea* (New York: Hill & Wang, 1963), 218.

54. Rampersad, *Art and Imagination,* 187.

55. Jessie Fauset, "There Was One Time!" *Crisis* 13 (1917): 273, 276.

56. Ibid., 275. Fauset's interest in Whitman is evident in her comparison of the black painter Henry O. Tanner to the good gray poet of Camden, in "Henry Ossawa Tanner," *Crisis* 27 (1924): 255–258.

57. Fauset, "There Was One Time!" 276.

58. Ibid.

59. Ibid.

60. Ibid., 275.

61. Ibid., 276.

62. Fauset, "There Was One Time!" (continued), *Crisis* 14 (1917): 15.

63. Carolyn Wedin Sylvander, *Jessie Redmon Fauset, Black American Writer* (Troy, N.Y.: Whitston, 1981).

64. Fauset to Hughes, n.d., leaf 71 in Fauset-Hughes correspondence, Langston Hughes Papers, James Weldon Johnson Collection, Beinecke Rare Book and Manuscript Library, Yale University.

65. Fauset to Hughes, n.d., leaf 72, Fauset-Hughes correspondence, Lang-

ston Hughes Papers. The letter lacks a dateline, but it is clearly from the period when Hughes was about to come for a visit to New York from Washington and was corresponding with Van Vechten about it.

66. See Fauset to Hughes, 21 January 1926, Fauset-Hughes correspondence, Langston Hughes Papers.

67. Fauset to Hughes, n.d., leaf 72; and 23 October 1925, Fauset-Hughes correspondence, Langston Hughes Papers. Actually, Van Vechten himself thought that if Hughes wanted to go to a black college, he should choose Howard over Lincoln.

68. McKay to Hughes, 24 April 1926, Langston Hughes Papers.

69. McKay to Hughes, 3 April 1928, Langston Hughes Papers.

70. Du Bois, *Dusk of Dawn,* 271.

71. Alice Dunbar-Nelson, "Mine Eyes Have Seen," *Crisis* 15 (1918): 271–275.

72. Joseph Seamon Cotter, Jr., *On the Fields of France, Crisis* 20 (1920): 77.

73. See "The Drama Among Black Folk," *Crisis* 12 (1916): 169–173.

74. "The New Negro Theatre," *Crisis* 14 (1917): 80–81.

75. "Men of the Month," *Crisis* 14 (1917): 256.

76. "Music and Art," *Crisis* 14 (1917): 34.

77. W. E. B. Du Bois, "Negro Art," *Crisis* 22 (1921): 55–56; "The Negro and the American Stage," *Crisis* 28 (1924): 56–57.

78. Du Bois, "Negro Art," 55.

79. Ibid., 55–56.

80. Ibid., 56.

81. Ibid.

82. See, for example, Loften Mitchell, *Black Drama: The Story of the American Negro in the Theatre* (New York: Hawthorn Books, 1967), 75–76, 82, 95; James V. Hatch, "Introduction," *The Roots of African American Drama: An Anthology of Early Plays, 1858–1938,* ed. Leo Hamalian and James V. Hatch (Detroit: Wayne State University Press, 1991), 25; and Kathy A. Perkins, "Introduction," *Black Female Playwrights: An Anthology of Plays Before 1950,* ed. Kathy A. Perkins (Bloomington: Indiana University Press, 1990), 4.

83. DuBose Heyward, in "The Negro in Art: How Shall He Be Portrayed?" *Crisis* 31 (1926): 220.

84. Harold Cruse, *The Crisis of the Negro Intellectual* (New York: William Morrow, 1967), 37–38.

85. Mark Seyboldt, "Play-Writing," *Crisis* 29 (1925): 164–165.

86. A. Philip Randolph, "Comments on the Negro Actor," *Messenger* 7 (1925): 17.

87. Willis Richardson, "The Hope of a Negro Drama," *Crisis* 19 (1919): 338.

88. Ibid.

89. Ibid.

90. Raymond O'Neil, "The Negro in Dramatic Art," *Crisis* 27 (1924): 155–157.

91. The Ethiopian Art Players developed from the All-American Theatre Association, an interracial group dedicated to organizing and supporting "a theatre for Negro artists" on Chicago's South Side. The association aimed to help establish similar theaters in other cities and begin a federation to allow exchange of plays, companies, and actors—along with training in acting and costume design. Sherwood Anderson sat on the board of directors.

92. O'Neil, "Negro in Dramatic Art," 156.

93. Ibid.

94. Ibid., 156–157.

95. Ibid., 157.

96. Ibid.

97. Ibid.

98. Ibid.

99. Alain Locke, "Steps Toward the Negro Theatre," *Crisis* 25 (1922): 66–67.

100. Ibid., 68.

101. Ibid.

102. "Krigwa Players Little Negro Theatre," *Crisis* 32 (1926): 134–136.

103. Kathy A. Perkins, "Eulalie Spence (1894–1981)," in *Black Female Playwrights*, 106.

104. See, for example, "Krigwa Players," 134–136; "Books," *Crisis* 33 (1926): 81–82; and "Green Pastures," *Crisis* 37 (1930): 162, 177–178.

105. "Green Pastures," 162, 177–178.

106. See especially ibid.

107. David Levering Lewis discusses the personal and editorial friction that prompted Fauset's departure in February 1926. See *When Harlem Was in Vogue* (New York: Vintage Books, 1982), 177. Fauset wanted *The Crisis* to follow *Opportunity*'s lead and expand its attention to the arts, whereas Du Bois was more intent on expanding its treatment of economics and politics.

108. See "Books," *Crisis* 33 (1926): 81–82; and "The Negro in Art: How Shall He Be Portrayed?" *Crisis* 31 (1926): 219–220, 278–280, and *Crisis* 32 (1926): 71–73, 193–194.

109. "The Browsing Reader," *Crisis* 34 (1927): 129.

110. James Weldon Johnson, "Romance and Tragedy in Harlem—A Review," *Opportunity* 4 (1926): 316–317, 330.

111. See especially Fauset's letter to Locke of 9 January 1933, correspondence files, Alain Locke Papers, Moorland-Spingarn Research Center, Howard University.

112. Sylvander, *Jessie Redmon Fauset*, 113. Authors complained, for example, that their poems were appearing without their permission. It should be mentioned, however, that this also happened during Fauset's period as literary editor. Countee Cullen wrote to Alain Locke (while Locke was putting together *The New Negro*), for example, that "Langston's *Dream Variations* was printed in *The Crisis* without his or my knowledge. He will have to give you something else"

(29 July 1924, correspondence files, Alain Locke Papers, Moorland-Spingarn Research Center). As authors shared their work with members of the *Crisis* staff, apparently they ran the risk of seeing it appear unexpectedly in the magazine. Sylvander (113) relates how this later happened to Sterling Brown and Claude McKay as well as to Langston Hughes (again).

113. See Du Bois's review of Fisher's *The Walls of Jericho* in "The Browsing Reader," *Crisis* 35 (1928): 374.

114. Wallace Thurman, "High, Low, Past and Present," *Harlem: A Forum of Negro Life* 1 (1928): 31.

115. "The Browsing Reader," *Crisis* 35 (1928): 202.

116. Ibid.

6. Toward a New Negro Aesthetic

1. Nancy J. Weiss, *The National Urban League, 1910–1940* (New York: Oxford University Press, 1974), 10. The following discussion of the origins of the Urban League derives from Weiss's authoritative study. Unfortunately, Weiss does not devote much attention to *Opportunity*.

2. Ibid., 70.

3. Quoted in ibid., 64.

4. Ibid., 66.

5. Ibid., 67–69.

6. Zora Neale Hurston, *Dust Tracks on a Road* (1942; rpt. Philadelphia: Arno Press, 1969), 175–176.

7. Langston Hughes, *The Big Sea* (1940; rpt. New York: Hill & Wang, 1963), 218.

8. Arna Bontemps, *100 Years of Negro Freedom* (New York: Dodd, Mead, 1961), 229.

9. The best discussion of Johnson so far is Patrick J. Gilpin's "Charles S. Johnson: Entrepreneur of the Harlem Renaissance," in *The Harlem Renaissance Remembered,* ed. Arna Bontemps (New York: Dodd, Mead, 1972), 215–246. However, Gilpin focuses on Johnson's organization of dinners and literary contests rather than showing the connection between his philosophy and the aesthetic criticism in the magazine. Another study focusing on the *Crisis* and *Opportunity* contests is Adell P. Austin's "The *Opportunity* and *Crisis* Literary Contests, 1924–27," *CLA Journal* 32 (1988): 235–246. I have been unable to locate scholarship analyzing in any depth or comprehensiveness the *criticism* Johnson published in *Opportunity*, or any careful study of his philosophy and aesthetics.

10. David Levering Lewis, *When Harlem Was in Vogue* (New York: Knopf, 1981), 90.

11. Charles S. Johnson, "Spiritual Autobiography," box 144, folder 1, Charles S. Johnson Papers, Fisk University Library.

12. Martin Bulmer, *The Chicago School of Sociology: Institutionalization, Diversity, and the Rise of Sociological Research* (Chicago: University of Chicago Press, 1984), 93.

13. Robert E. Park, "Education in Its Relation to the Conflict and Fusion of Cultures" (1918), in Park, *Race and Culture* (Glencoe, Ill.: Free Press, 1950), 266.

14. Leslie A. White, quoted in Fred H. Matthews, *Quest for an American Sociology: Robert E. Park and the Chicago School* (Montreal: McGill-Queen's University Press, 1977), 108.

15. *Opportunity* 1 (1923): 355.

16. Robert E. Park, "Negro Race Consciousness as Reflected in Race Literature" (1923), in *Race and Culture*, 284, 300.

17. Charles S. Johnson, "Social Assimilation Defined," typescript, box 173, folder 25, Charles S. Johnson Papers.

18. Charles S. Johnson, "A Chapel Talk to the Students of Fisk University" (17 October 1928), p. 14, box 158, folder 23, Charles S. Johnson Papers.

19. Johnson, "Social Assimilation Defined." Like the early Du Bois, Park hung on to racialist ideas about the differing "geniuses" of the races. The "innate traits" of a people, Park suspected, led to modifications of traditions "transmitted" to them through contact with others. Cultural "assimilation," it follows, is always incomplete, for the "deep structure" of a culture may remain intact despite extensive borrowing. (His thought on this subject is much like Horace Kallen's initial belief in each race's "psychophysical inheritance" and Du Bois's and Locke's ideas about "temperamental" distinctions between races.) While the external trappings of societies may be quickly exchanged, the sentiments, attitudes, aims, and ideals of a group are very slow to be adopted or transmitted.

Park is perhaps best known to students of African American literature for writing in 1918 that although the "racial temperament" of the Negro had changed as a result of encounters with whites and the influence of slavery, it consists of "a few elementary but distinctive characteristics, determined by physical organizations and transmitted biologically. These characteristics manifest themselves in a genial, sunny, and social disposition, in an interest and attachment to external, physical things rather than to subjective states and objects of introspection; in a disposition for expression rather than enterprise and action" ("Education in Its Relation to the Conflict and Fusion of Cultures," 280). Such temperamental characteristics, one gathers, would determine the Negro's chief contributions to American civilization: "The Negro is, by natural disposition, neither an intellectual nor an idealist, like the Jew; nor a brooding introspective, like the East African; nor a pioneer and frontiersman, like the Anglo-Saxon. He is primarily an artist, loving life for its own sake. His *metier* is expression rather than action. He is, so to speak, the lady among the races" (ibid.). Despite its racism and sexism, this hypothesis (which Park later repudiated) implies the Negro's special "temperamental" advantage for playing the most powerful role in American expressive culture—a belief also held by Alain Locke, W. E. B. Du Bois, and Charles S. Johnson.

20. Johnson, typescript, untitled piece on Negro literature. This is a review, clearly of the 1920s, of ten books concerning the Negro, including Howard Odom's *Rainbow 'Round My Shoulder.* Box 167, folder 30, Charles S. Johnson Papers.

21. Johnson, "A Chapel Talk to the Students of Fisk University," p. 11, 17 October 1928, box 158, folder 23, Charles S. Johnson Papers.

22. Ibid., 14.

23. Ibid., 15.

24. Ibid., 13.

25. Ibid., 12.

26. Ibid.

27. Charles S. Johnson, "The Social Philosophy of Booker T. Washington," *Opportunity* 6 (1928): 105.

28. Charles S. Johnson, "Can There Be a Separate Negro Culture?" Address at the Swarthmore Race Relations Institute (1939), box 158, folder 14, Charles S. Johnson Papers.

29. "Social Assimilation Defined," n.p.

30. "The Social Philosophy of Booker T. Washington," 102.

31. Ibid., 115.

32. Ibid.

33. "Welcome the New South—A Review," *Opportunity* 4 (1926): 374–375.

34. John W. Work, "Negro Folk Song," *Opportunity* 1 (1923): 292.

35. Ibid., 293, 293–294.

36. Ibid., 294.

37. Laurence Buermeyer, "The Negro Spirituals and American Art," *Opportunity* 4 (1926): 158–159.

38. Ibid., 159.

39. B. A. Botkin, "Self-Portraiture and Social Criticism in Negro Folk-Song," *Opportunity* 5 (1927): 41.

40. Ibid.

41. Ibid., 42.

42. Botkin, a professor of English at the University of Oklahoma, would later found *Folk-Say,* a journal focusing on regional and multiethnic folk or folk-derived literature (in which some of Sterling Brown's poems first appeared). During the depression he became folklore editor of the Federal Writers' Project and President of the Joint Committee on Folk Arts of the WPA; upon his accession to the editorship at the Writers' Project, he and Sterling Brown (whom he brought on as his assistant) redesigned the interviewers' question-

naires for the collection of ex-slave narratives throughout the South and pushed to have African Americans do the interviewing. See Jerre Mangione, *The Dream and the Deal: The Federal Writers' Project, 1935–1943* (Boston: Little, Brown, 1972), 263–270, 276; and Joanne V. Gabbin, *Sterling A. Brown: Building the Black Aesthetic Tradition* (Westport, Conn.: Greenwood Press, 1985), 75.

43. Unsigned editorial, "Jazz," *Opportunity* 3 (1925): 132–133.

44. Alain Locke, "1928: A Retrospective Review," *Opportunity* 7 (1929): 11.

45. Alain Locke, "A Note on African Art," *Opportunity* 2 (1924): 138. My emphasis.

46. Ibid.

47. Ibid., 136.

48. Ibid.

49. Nathan Irvin Huggins, *Harlem Renaissance* (New York: Oxford University Press, 1971), 187.

50. Paul Guillaume, "African Art at the Barnes Foundation," *Opportunity* 2 (1924): 141. See also the editorial in the same issue of *Opportunity*, "Dr. Barnes," 133.

51. See, for example, the editorial "Some Perils of the 'Renaissance,'" *Opportunity* 5 (1927): 68.

52. Leon Whipple, "Letters and Life," *Survey* 56 (1926): 517.

53. Joseph Auslander, "Sermon Sagas," *Opportunity* 5 (1927): 274.

54. Ibid.

55. Ibid., 275.

56. Ibid., 274.

57. Ibid., 275.

58. Margaret Larkin, "A Poet for the People—A Review," *Opportunity* 5 (1927): 84.

59. Ibid.

60. Robert T. Kerlin, "Singers of New Songs," *Opportunity* 4 (1926): 164. My emphasis.

61. Kerlin was fired in 1921 from Virginia Military Institute for an open letter published in *The Nation* protesting charges brought against Negro "insurrectionists" who had merely sought to defend themselves against armed whites. Hughes took a course called "The Art of Poetry" from Kerlin (a visiting professor) in the fall of 1926; a year later Kerlin was fired from his faculty position at the nearby West Chester (Pennsylvania) State College for supporting "'the social amalgamation of the races'" after entertaining African Americans at his home. Hughes corresponded with Kerlin and shared drafts of poems with him into the early 1930s. See Robert T. Kerlin, "An Open Letter to the Governor of Arkansas," *Nation* 112 (1921): 847–848; items on Kerlin in *Messenger* 3 (1921): 257; "Robert T. Kerlin" (editorial), *Crisis* 23 (1921): 10; Arnold Rampersad, *The*

Life of Langston Hughes, vol. 1 (New York: Oxford University Press, 1986), 135; and Hughes-Kerlin correspondence in the Langston Hughes Papers, James Weldon Johnson Collection, Yale University.

62. E. Merrill Root, "Keats in Labrador," *Opportunity* 5 (1927): 270–271.

63. Countee Cullen, "Poet on Poet," *Opportunity* 4 (1926): 73. A note on the spelling of "Countee": Throughout *The New Negro,* Cullen's first name is spelled with an acute accent over the first "e." In fact, he and his second wife, Ida Mae Cullen, pronounced the name "count-tay." (Ida Mae Cullen, oral history interview by Ann Allen Shockley, 15 July 1970, Fisk University Library.) However, in letters to both Ida and his father, Cullen signs his name without the accent, and the accent does not appear on the title pages of his books. It appears occasionally, but not usually, in his contributions to *Opportunity, American Mercury,* and other magazines. I have followed the usual practice throughout this book by leaving the accent off. Thanks to Rebecca Hankins, acquisitions archivist at Amistad Research Center, for checking Cullen's family correspondence for me.

64. Alan R. Shucard, *Countee Cullen* (Boston: Twayne, 1984), 11. Shucard calls Braithwaite "one of [Cullen's] Harvard mentors" and points out that Cullen even dated one of Braithwaite's daughters. Braithwaite was not, however, on the faculty at Harvard; nor had he been a student at Harvard, contrary to some sources.

65. Countee Cullen, "The Dark Tower," *Opportunity* 6 (1928): 90. For more detailed discussions of Cullen's aesthetics, see Alan R. Shucard, *Countee Cullen;* and Gerald Early, "Introduction," in *My Soul's High Song: The Collected Writings of Countee Cullen* (New York: Anchor Books, 1991), 3–63.

66. Gerald Early's introduction to Cullen's poetry overemphasizes the poet's role in the Harlem Renaissance, although the treatment of Cullen himself is excellent.

67. Esther Fulks Scott, "Negroes as Actors in Serious Plays," *Opportunity* 1 (1923): 20.

68. Ibid., 21.

69. Montgomery Gregory, review of *Cane, Opportunity* 1 (1923): 374–375.

70. Ibid., 374.

71. Adele Heller, "The New Theatre," in *1915: The Cultural Moment,* ed. Adele Heller and Lois Rudnick (New Brunswick, N.J.: Rutgers University Press, 1991), 221.

72. Alain Locke, "Max Rheinhardt Reads the Negro's Dramatic Horoscope," *Opportunity* 2 (1924): 145, 146.

73. See the discussion in Chapter 5 of *The Crisis*'s drama criticism. Apparently the split came specifically over a performance of Angelina Grimké's *Rachel,* which Locke and Gregory considered too propagandistic. More pointedly than Locke in the *Crisis* article of 1922, Gregory alludes to the argument in "A Chro-

nology of the Negro Theatre," in *Plays of Negro Life,* ed. Montgomery Gregory and Alain Locke (New York: Harper and Brothers, 1927), 412.

74. Gregory, review of *Cane,* 374.

75. Unsigned editorial, "On the Need of Better Plays," *Opportunity* 5 (1927): 5–6.

76. Ibid., 6.

77. Edwin D. Johnson, "The Jewel in Ethiope's Ear," *Opportunity* 6 (1928): 166.

78. Ibid.

79. Ibid.

80. Ibid., 167–168.

81. Eulalie Spence, "A Criticism of the Negro Drama as It Relates to the Negro Dramatist and Artist," *Opportunity* 6 (1928): 180.

82. Lewis, *When Harlem Was in Vogue,* 92. My emphasis.

83. Paul Robeson, "Reflections on O'Neill's Plays," *Opportunity* 2 (1924): 368.

84. Ibid., 369.

85. Ibid.

86. E. A. Carter, *"All God's Chillun Got Wings,"* *Opportunity* 2 (1924): 112–113; James Light, "On Producing O'Neill's Play," *Opportunity* 2 (1924): 113; and Eric Walrond, *"All God's Chillun Got Wings,"* *Opportunity* 2 (1924): 220–221.

87. See Rudolph Fisher, review of *The White Girl* by Vera Caspary, *Opportunity* 7 (1929): 255–256; and Sterling Brown, "Our Literary Audience," *Opportunity* 8 (1930): 42–43.

88. Eulalie Spence, "Negro Art Players in Harlem," *Opportunity* 6 (1928): 381.

89. Unsigned editorial, "Paul Green," *Opportunity* 5 (1927): 159.

90. Rowena Woodham Jelliffe, "The Negro in the Field of Drama," *Opportunity* 6 (1928): 214.

91. Jelliffe, "The Negro in the Field of Drama," 214.

92. Jelliffe, "The Gilpin Players," *Opportunity* 6 (1928): 345.

93. For information on the Jelliffes, I have relied on Arnold Rampersad's *The Life of Langston Hughes,* vol. 1 (New York: Oxford University Press, 1986), 26, 36–39 and passim; and vol. 2 (New York: Oxford University Press, 1987), 16 and passim. Rampersad shows the depth and durability of Hughes's friendship with the Jelliffes, by the 1950s the longest of his life.

94. Ibid., vol. 1, pp. 26, 37; and vol. 2, pp. 16, 39.

95. Jelliffe, "The Negro in the Field of Drama," 214.

96. See playlist in Jelliffe, "The Gilpin Players," 344.

97. George Cram Cook, quoted in Adele Heller, "The New Theatre," 229.

98. Charles S. Johnson, "On Writing About Negroes," *Opportunity* 3 (1925): 228.

99. Eric D. Walrond, "'Prancing Nigger' by Roland [sic] Firbank," *Opportunity* 2 (1924): 219.

100. Ibid.

101. Charles S. Johnson, "*Nigger*—A Novel by Clement Wood," *Opportunity* 1 (1923): 30.

102. Charles S. Johnson, review of *The Fire in the Flint, Opportunity* 2 (1924): 344.

103. Ibid., 345.

104. Ibid.

105. Eunice Roberta Hunton, "'Holiday' by Waldo Frank," *Opportunity* 2 (1924): 59.

106. Ibid.

107. Waldo Frank, "In Our American Language," *Opportunity* 4 (1926): 352.

108. Ibid.

109. Ibid.

110. Sterling A. Brown, "The New Secession—A Review," *Opportunity* 5 (1927): 147.

111. Ibid.

112. Ibid.

113. Ibid.

114. Sterling A. Brown, "Our Literary Audience," *Opportunity* 8 (1930): 44–45.

115. Ibid., 46. See also Brown's review of DuBose Heyward's *Mamba's Daughters, Opportunity* 7 (1929): 161–162.

116. Alain Locke, review of *Scarlet Sister Mary, Opportunity* 7 (1929): 190–191.

117. Locke, "1928," 8.

118. Alain Locke, review of *Magic Island* by William Seabrook, *Opportunity* 7 (1929): 190.

119. Editorial, "A Note on the New Literary Movement," *Opportunity* 4 (1926): 80–81; Locke, "1928," 8–11; Eunice Hunton Carter, review of *The Blacker the Berry,* by Wallace Thurman, *Opportunity* 7 (1929): 162–163.

120. Carter, review of *The Blacker the Berry,* 163.

121. Locke, "1928," 8.

122. Ibid.

123. Ibid., 8–9.

124. Countee Cullen, "The Dark Tower," *Opportunity* 4 (1926): 389.

125. Locke, "1928," 9.

126. Ibid.

127. Gwendolyn Bennett, review of *Plum Bun, Opportunity* 7 (1929): 287.

128. Gwendolyn Bennett, review of *Banjo, Opportunity* 7 (1929): 254–255.

129. Ibid., 254.

130. Mary Fleming Labaree, review of *Passing* by Nella Larsen, *Opportunity* 7 (1929): 255.

131. Rampersad, *Life of Langston Hughes,* vol. 1: 126, 130, 166, 169.

132. Labaree, review of *Passing*, 255.

133. Ibid.

134. Sterling A. Brown, review of *Not Without Laughter*, *Opportunity* 8 (1930): 280.

135. Ibid.

136. Charles S. Johnson, "An Opportunity for Negro Writers," *Opportunity* 2 (1924): 258.

137. Ibid.

7. Reading These United States

1. James Weldon Johnson's "Self-Determining Haiti" ran through several issues of *The Nation* in the fall of 1920 as a special feature, with considerable publicity. Shortly before this series, the magazine also published Herbert J. Seligmann's "The Conquest of Haiti." Advertisement, "The Facts About Haiti *Must Be Brought Out*," *Nation* 111 (1920): iii.

2. Susan J. Turner, *A History of the Freeman* (New York: Columbia University Press, 1963), 134.

3. "Main Street in Fiction," *New Republic* 25 (1921): 184.

4. *The Nation* supported Reconstruction, arguing for equality and protection of the Negro, attacking most moderates, but was not "radical." It supported the franchise only for those with economic independence and education (a position Du Bois essentially took early in his adult years as well). The magazine argued that the freedmen needed to be educated and to achieve self-reliance and economic independence. See Alan Pendleton Grimes, *The Political Liberalism of the New York Nation, 1865–1932* (Chapel Hill: University of North Carolina Press, 1953), 5. I have relied on Grimes for the information that follows concerning the political position of *The Nation*. Grimes does not discuss the magazine's cultural philosophy or literary criticism.

5. Carl Van Doren, *Three Worlds* (New York: Harper & Bros., 1936), 134–135.

6. Sara Alpern, *Freda Kirchwey: A Woman of "The Nation"* (Cambridge, Mass.: Harvard University Press, 1987), 29, 36. Kirchwey, by the way, was the daughter of Dean George Kirchwey of the Columbia Law School, who was president for several years of the Civic Club where black and white intellectuals often met.

7. Van Doren, *Three Worlds*, 135–137.

8. Wayne F. Cooper, *Claude McKay: Rebel Sojourner in the Harlem Renaissance* (Baton Rouge: Louisiana State University Press, 1987), 80–81.

9. W. E. B. Du Bois, *Dusk of Dawn: An Essay Toward an Autobiography of a Race Concept* (1940; New York: Schocken Books, 1968), 225.

10. Quoted in Arnold Rampersad, *The Art and Imagination of W. E. B. Du Bois* (1976; New York: Schocken Books, 1990), 136.

11. See, for example, "Editorial," *Nation* 109 (1919): 133; and Walter White, "'Massacring Whites' in Arkansas," *Nation* 109 (1919): 715–716.

12. Van Doren, *Three Worlds*, 143, quoted from a "Roving Critic" column in *The Nation*. Van Doren, incidentally, was also an editor of the historic *Cambridge History of American Literature* (New York: Macmillan, 1917–1921) and significantly responsible for the canonization of Melville and Whitman. He did the first detailed study and the first extended bibliography of Melville's writings, stating that one did not know American literature if one did not know Melville; and Raymond Weaver undertook his seminal biography of Melville at Van Doren's suggestion as his student at Columbia. Later Van Doren suggested a history of African American writing to his student Vernon Loggins, whose *The Negro Author: His Development in America to 1900* (Ph.D. dissertation, Columbia University, 1921), would be a path-breaking book.

13. See, for example, Carl Van Doren, "The Younger Generation of Negro Writers," *Opportunity* 2 (1924): 144–145; and his review of *The New Negro*, "Negro Renaissance," *Century* 111 (1926): 635–637.

14. I base the succession of literary editorships upon the mastheads for issues from 1919 through 1931: Carl Van Doren, January 1919–October 1922; John Macy, October 1922–October 1923; Irita Van Doren, October 1923–August 1924; Mark Van Doren, September 1924 through the end of the decade. The general criticism of *The Nation* remained remarkably consistent throughout this period, which Gorham Munson termed "the Van Doren dynasty" (*The Awakening Twenties: A Memoir-History of a Literary Period* [Baton Rouge: Louisiana State University Press, 1985], 92).

15. "Contemporary American Novelists," *Nation* 113 (1921): 407–412.

16. Zona Gale, "The United States and the Artist," *Nation* 121 (1925): 22–24; the quotation is from p. 23.

17. Harold Peter Simonson, *Zona Gale* (New York: Twayne, 1962), 16.

18. On the relationship with Latimer, see ibid., 56. Latimer eventually came to resent Gale's domination and attacked her in *We Are Invincible* and *Guardian Angel*, to which Gale responded with the character Marfa Manchester in *Borgia* (1929). Gale and Torrence had a two-year romance in 1902–1904; the breaking of their engagement to be married actually was decisive in Zona Gale's career, as it led her to devote herself wholly to being a writer; she and Torrence remained good friends afterward (Simonson, *Zona Gale*, 26–31).

19. See the dedication page of *An Autumn Love Cycle* (New York: Harold Vinal, 1928); Georgia Douglas Johnson to Alain Locke, 11 August 1925, correspondence files, Alain Locke Papers, Moorland-Spingarn Research Center, Howard University. In 1941 Douglas would reflect back upon Gale's effect on her: "Often I am conscious of a feeling of transcendent thanksgiving that I am living—that I have the privilege of contacting, even from afar, certain superb people. Among that number was Zona Gale, a precious woman, whom when

you read lifts your soul into high places, makes you feel conscious of the finest and most beautiful emotions. She has passed on but there are others still among us with hearts of gold—hearts big with understanding, sympathy— love!" Typescript of an unpublished "interracial column," mailed with a letter to Arna Bontemps of 12 November 1941, Arna Bontemps Collection, Box 9, Syracuse University Library.

20. Carolyn Wedin Sylvander, *Jessie Redmon Fauset, Black American Writer* (Troy, N.Y.: Whitston, 1981), 74–75.

21. "The New Literature in America," *Nation* 112 (1921): 429.

22. Lewisohn, *Mid-Channel: An American Chronicle* (New York: Harper & Bros., 1929), 22–23.

23. Untitled editorial, *Nation* 115 (1922): 513.

24. Unsigned editorial, "Our Aliens and Our Arts," *Nation* 112 (1921): 330–331.

25. Carl Van Doren, "The Younger Generation of Negro Writers," *Opportunity* 2 (1924): 144–145.

26. Ibid., 145.

27. Carl Van Doren, "Tap-Root or Melting-Pot," in William Stanley Braithwaite, ed., *Anthology of Magazine Verse for 1920* (Boston: Small, Maynard, 1920), xi. Braithwaite reprinted the piece from a 1920 unsigned editorial in *The Nation;* that Van Doren wrote it is evident from its inclusion in his collection *The Roving Critic* (New York: Knopf, 1923).

28. Van Doren, "Tap-Root or Melting-Pot," xii.

29. Ibid., ix–xii; the final quotation is from p. ix. More recently, Kenny J. Williams, attributing the passage to Braithwaite, has quoted it as a prime example of *Braithwaite's* originality and critical acumen. Williams, "An Invisible Partnership and an Unlikely Relationship: William Stanley Braithwaite and Harriet Monroe," *Callaloo* 10 (1987): 516–550.

30. Countee Cullen, "Saturday's Child," *Century* 108 (1924): 713; and "Yet Do I Marvel," *Century* 109 (1924): 122. James Weldon Johnson, "My City," *Century* 106 (1923): 716; "The Judgment Day (A Negro Sermon)," *Century* 113 (1927): 682–684; and "The Practice of Lynching," *Century* 115 (1927): 65. In this period *The Century* also published an anonymous article, clearly by Walter White, entitled "White but Black," *Century* 109 (1925): 492–499, exposing Southern racism.

31. Langston Hughes to Alain Locke, April 1925, in Alain Locke Papers, Moorland-Spingarn Research Center, Howard University.

32. An 1899 graduate of Harvard, Macy remembered William James as one of the few professors who redeemed the place from "sterility and impotence." Blasting the "unholy marriage of professor, puritan, and capitalist," Macy, who had been a socialist since 1909 and served as secretary to the socialist mayor of Schenectady, was one of the first of the anti-academic champions of authors

now considered canonized members of the American Renaissance. His death came by heart attack in 1932 as he delivered a lecture on "the rebellious aspects of American literature" to an audience of union workers in Stroudsburg, Pennsylvania. Kermit Vanderbilt, *American Literature and the Academy: The Roots, Growth, and Maturity of a Profession* (Philadelphia: University of Pennsylvania Press, 1986), 202, 205.

33. John Macy, *The Spirit of American Literature* (Garden City: Doubleday, Page, 1913), 8–11.

34. John Macy, "The Kingdom of Art," *Opportunity* 4 (1926): 185.

35. See, for example, "Our Literature and Ourselves," *Nation* 121 (1925): 480; "'Native' Literature," *Nation* 121 (1925): 348; Genevieve Taggard, "May Days," *Nation* 121 (1925): 353–56; and the series "The United States and the Artist," which ran through several issues in 1925.

36. "Editorial," *Nation* 120 (1925): 229.

37. Mordecai Johnson, "The Faith of the American Negro," *Nation* 115 (1922): 64–65.

38. *Nation* 122 (1926): 318.

39. Countee Cullen, "The Wise," *Nation* 119 (1924): 522, and "Loss of Love," *Nation* 121 (1925): 32; Scudder Middleton, "To W. E. Burghardt Du Bois," *Nation* 119 (1924): 39; and James Rorty, "The Walls of Jericho," *Nation* 121 (1925): 707.

40. George Schuyler, "The Negro-Art Hokum," *Nation* 122 (1926): 662–663; Langston Hughes, "The Negro Artist and the Racial Mountain," *Nation* 122 (1926): 692–694.

41. Schuyler, "Negro-Art Hokum," 662–663.

42. Ibid., 663.

43. Arnold Rampersad, *The Life of Langston Hughes,* vol. 1 (New York: Oxford University Press, 1986), 130.

44. Hughes, "Negro Artist," 692.

45. Ibid., 694.

46. George Schuyler, "Negroes and Artists," *Nation* 123 (1926): 36; Dorothy Fox, "Escaping Seventh Street," *Nation* 123 (1926): 36–37; Headley E. Bailey, "Brown-Skinned Nordics," *Nation* 123 (1926): 37; Michael Gold, "Where the Battle Is Fought," *Nation* 123 (1926): 37; and Langston Hughes, "American Art or Negro Art?" *Nation* 123 (1926): 151. A further response to this Hughes-Schuyler debate is in Harry Alan Potamkin's interesting review of *Fine Clothes to the Jew, Nation* 124 (1927): 403–404. The debate continued into the early 1930s in *The Nation;* see Dorothy Van Doren's review of Schuyler's first novel, "Black, Alas, No More!" *Nation* 132 (1931): 218–219; and the response by Josephine Schuyler (George's wife), "'Black No More,'" *Nation* 132 (1931): 382.

47. Schuyler, "Negroes and Artists," 36.

48. Gold, "Where the Battle Is Fought," 37.

49. Hughes, "American Art or Negro Art?" 151.

50. George Schuyler, "Blessed Are the Sons of Ham," *Nation* 124 (1927): 313–315.

51. George W. Jacobs, "Negro Authors Must Eat," *Nation* 128 (1929): 710–711.

52. See, for example, Gustavus Adolphus Steward, "Segregation de Luxe," *Nation* 131 (1930): 295–296. Steward attacks not only emphases on African origins, jazz, and lower-class black life but also the limitation of African American authors to racial themes. A notable exception to *The Nation*'s critique of primitivism and racial essentialism is Joseph Wood Krutch's review of the play *Porgy,* in which he wrote that black actors are excellent at the most "primitive" and essential arts of acting—pantomime, emotional expression, dance, and so forth—but not at dialogue or following a "logical" progression of speech. "Conventional drama" and "intellectualized dialogue" are unnatural to the Negro actor; "ecstasy seems . . . to be his natural state." See J. W. Krutch, "Black Ecstasy," *Nation* 125 (1927): 456, 458.

53. See Harry Alan Potamkin, "African Sculptor," *Opportunity* 4 (1926): 278.

54. Harry Alan Potamkin, review of *Fine Clothes to the Jew, Nation* 124 (1927): 403–404.

55. Anonymous, "Ulysses Singing," *Nation* 123 (1926): 117–118.

56. Alain Locke, "Beauty Instead of Ashes," *Nation* 126 (1928): 432–434; rpt. in *The Critical Temper of Alain Locke,* ed. Jeffrey C. Stewart (New York: Garland, 1983), 23–25.

57. Gerald Sykes, "Amber-Tinted Elegance," *Nation* 135 (1932): 88.

58. Sylvander, *Jessie Redmon Fauset,* 76.

59. The series was subsequently published as *These United States: A Symposium,* ed. Ernest Gruening (New York: Boni & Liveright, 1923–1924), 2 vols.

60. Alsberg was hampered in his effort by the racism of regional organizers, who often resisted his authority. As a result, the attention to black America in the American Guide volumes varies considerably.

61. Turner, *History of "The Freeman,"* 1. Turner quotes Herbert Croly from his book *Willard Straight* (New York: Macmillan, 1924).

62. Arthur Frank Wertheim, *The New York Little Renaissance: Iconoclasm, Modernism, and Nationalism in American Culture, 1908–1917* (New York: New York University Press, 1976), 167–169.

63. Van Wyck Brooks, *Van Wyck Brooks: An Autobiography* (New York: E. P. Dutton, 1965), 223.

64. Wertheim, *New York Little Renaissance,* 172.

65. Francis Hackett, *American Rainbow: Early Reminiscences* (New York: Liveright, 1971), 207.

66. Ibid., 3.

67. Ibid., 4.

68. Ibid., 252.

69. Wertheim, *New York Little Renaissance,* 172.

70. See, for example, "Continental Cultures," *New Republic* 1 (16 January 1915): 14–16.

71. Wertheim, *New York Little Renaissance,* 173; Milton Cantor, *Max Eastman* (Boston: Twayne, 1970), 73–74.

72. Francis Hackett, "Our Literary Poverty," *New Republic* 1 (21 November 1914): 10.

73. Padraic Colum, "Robert Burns," *New Republic* 1 (23 January 1915): 20–21.

74. Ibid., 21.

75. John M. Clum, *Ridgely Torrence* (Boston: Twayne, 1972), 129. For the general biographical information on Torrence that follows I rely on Clum, except where otherwise indicated.

76. Langston Hughes to Olivia Torrence, 30 May 1953, Langston Hughes Papers, Beinecke Rare Book and Manuscript Library, Yale University.

77. Rampersad, *Life of Langston Hughes,* vol. 1, 64.

78. See correspondence of Torrence to Hughes, 25 January 1926, 11 July 1930, 7 January 1941, 18 February 1946, 22 December 1946. Langston Hughes Papers.

79. Hughes to Torrence, 11 October 1948, Langston Hughes Papers. "The Bird and the Tree," a lynching poem, originally appeared in *Poetry* 6 (1915): 20–21.

80. "Men of the Month," *Crisis* 14 (1917): 256.

81. Carl Van Vechten review, *New York Press,* 31 March 1914, mentioned in Clum, 106. See also Eugene D. Levy, *James Weldon Johnson: Black Leader, Black Voice* (Chicago: University of Chicago Press, 1973), 302.

82. Francis Hackett, "After the Play," *New Republic* 11 (14 April 1917): 325.

83. Robert Benchley, "Can This Be the Native American Drama?" New York *Tribune,* 1 April 1917, pt. 5, p. 6.

84. James Weldon Johnson, *Black Manhattan* (New York: Knopf, 1930), 175.

85. W. E. B. Du Bois, *The Autobiography of W. E. B. Du Bois: A Soliloquy on Viewing My Life from the Last Decade of Its First Century* (New York: International Publishers, 1968), 288. Du Bois would remember an anecdote of his friendship with Lovett "to illustrate the paradox of my life," concluding the chapter entitled "My Character" with the following poignant sentences: "When not long before his last visit to New York in about 1950 he wanted to see and talk with me, he proposed the Harvard Club of which he was a member. I was not. No Negro graduate of Harvard was ever elected to membership in a Harvard Club. For a while Jews were excluded, but no longer. I swallowed my pride and met Lovett at the Club. A few months later he died" (288). The incident illustrates an ignorance and insensitivity on Lovett's part as well as the regard the two men had for each other—especially in those late days when both had been

victimized by HUAC. But above all Du Bois uses the anecdote to exemplify the poisonous effects of the color line on all relationships that challenge it.

86. For this and the following information on Lovett, except where indicated otherwise I rely on his autobiography, *All Our Years* (New York: Viking, 1948).

87. Lovett, *All Our Years*, 299–310, 360–361.

88. See William W. Boyer, *America's Virgin Islands: A History of Human Rights and Wrongs* (Durham: Carolina Academic Press, 1983), 202–203. According to the leader of the local legislative groups, people throughout the Islands were extremely embittered by Lovett's ouster; 99 percent wanted the governor (a patent racist who sought to exploit the colony for tourism and who tacitly supported Lovett's dismissal) replaced by Lovett.

89. Unsigned editorial, *New Republic* 1 (21 November 1914): 5.

90. Unsigned editorial, *New Republic* 1 (9 January 1915): 5.

91. Herbert J. Seligmann, "Race War?" *New Republic* 20 (13 August 1919): 48–50; and "Democracy and Jim-Crowism," *New Republic* 20 (3 September 1919): 151–152.

92. W. E. B. Du Bois, "On Being Black," *New Republic* 21 (18 February 1920): 338–341.

93. Francis Hackett, "The Negro Speaks," *New Republic* 22 (7 April 1920): 189–190.

94. Other factors that undoubtedly influenced the shift were personnel-related, as the magazine lost some of its strongest political critics by the beginning of the twenties: Walter Lippmann left, Willard Straight had died of flu during the war, and Walter Weyl had died of cancer. Bruce Bliven, *Five Million Words Later* (New York: John Day, 1970), 161–162; and David Seideman, *"The New Republic": A Voice of Modern Liberalism* (N.Y.: Praeger, 1986), 61–62. Bliven was managing editor of *The New Republic* beginning in 1923 and became chief editor in 1930. He later served on the National Advisory Council of the Federal Writers' Project.

95. Bliven, *Five Million Words*, 221.

96. Lovett, *All Our Years*, 192. This development was disastrous for the magazine, as it influenced Croly's decision to serialize Waldo Frank's *The Rediscovery of America*, which took up immense space, disgusted most of the editors, and drove off subscribers (Bliven, *Five Million Words*, 163).

97. John Dewey, "Philosophy As a Fine Art," *New Republic* 53 (15 February 1928): 354.

98. Lewis Mumford, "The Voice of Despair," *New Republic* 59 (22 May 1929): 37.

99. Ibid., 38.

100. Edmund Wilson, "T. S. Eliot and the Church of England," *New Republic* 58 (24 April 1929): 283–284.

101. Unsigned editorial, "European vs. American Culture," *New Republic* 51 (6 July 1927): 163.

102. E.C.L., "Artists as Human Beings," *New Republic* 51 (3 August 1927): 281. "E.C.L." is E. C. Lindeman, a contributing editor to *The New Republic*.

103. Ibid., 282.

104. Unsigned editorial, "A Nation of Foreigners," *New Republic* 52 (5 October 1927): 161–162.

105. Robert E. Park, "The Negro Problem," *New Republic* 51 (13 July 1927): 209–210.

106. Ibid., 210.

107. Stark Young, "Primitive Negro Sculpture," *New Republic* 50 (23 February 1927): 17–18.

108. Lewis Mumford, "Art, Modern and Primitive," *New Republic* 49 (1 December 1926): 49.

109. Hubert Harrison, "Caliban in the Slums," *New Republic* 35 (18 July 1923): 214. Between June 4, 1924, and March 31, 1926, Walrond (often over the initials E.D.W.) reviewed Robert Kerlin's *Negro Poets and Their Poems,* Gertrude Sandborn's *Veiled Aristocrats,* Fauset's *There Is Confusion* (drawing protests from Du Bois and Arthur Spingarn for certain acid comments on her "bourgeois" approach), Newman Ivey White and Clinton Jackson's *Anthology of Verse by American Negroes,* Walter White's *A Fire in the Flint,* and Countee Cullen's *Color.*

110. Robert Littell, "The Negro Players," *New Republic* 35 (30 May 1923): 21. See also Littell's *"Cane," New Republic* 37 (26 December 1923): 126.

111. Harry Alan Potamkin, "Race and a Poet," *New Republic* 52 (12 October 1927): 218.

112. Ibid., 218.

113. Harry Alan Potamkin, "Color," *New Republic* 53 (18 January 1928): 253.

114. Ibid.

115. Elizabeth Shepley Sergeant, "The New Negro," *New Republic* 46 (12 May 1926): 371–372.

116. Abbe Niles, "Real and Artificial Folk-Song," *New Republic* 51 (8 June 1927): 77.

117. Wallace Thurman, "Negro Artists and the Negro," *New Republic* 52 (31 August 1927): 39.

118. Ibid., 37.

119. Ibid., 38.

120. Ibid.

121. B.K., review of *Plum Bun, New Republic* 58 (10 April 1929): 235.

122. E.B.H. (Emma B. Holden), review of *Flight* by Walter White, *New Republic* 48 (1 September 1926): 53.

123. Edmund Wilson, "Deep River and Gentlemen Prefer Blondes," *New Republic* 48 (20 October 1926): 246.

124. Stark Young, "Negro Material in the Theatre," *New Republic* 50 (11 May 1927): 331–332.

125. Alain Locke to Langston Hughes, 2 September 1926, Langston Hughes Papers. Locke continued even more effusively, "Only another flight (of stairs, not Walter's either) and we'll have our real Negro novel."

126. Abbe Niles, "Aunt Hagar's Children," *New Republic* 48 (29 September 1926): 163.

127. E.G., review of *Black Sadie* by T. Bower Campbell, *New Republic* 57 (19 December 1928): 148.

128. J.R., review of *Black April, New Republic* 51 (29 June 1927): 157.

129. Robert Herrick, "A Study in Black," *New Republic* 57 (26 December 1928): 172–173.

130. Robert Herrick, "Magic, Black and White," *New Republic* 57 (30 January 1929): 298–299.

131. Robert Herrick, "Tropic Death," *New Republic* 48 (10 November 1926): 332.

132. Eric Walrond, "The Negro in the New World," *New Republic* 51 (27 July 1927): 260.

133. T. S. Matthews, "What Gods! What Gongs!" *New Republic* 55 (30 May 1928): 50–51.

134. See the advertisement for the movie *Hearts in Dixie, New Republic* 58 (13 March 1929), following p. 106. The text notes that "to reach his current status The New Negro had to fight against racial ignorance, superstition" and so forth; this plantation background, "with its folk music, dancing, primitive love, and 'Voodooism' is reproduced with fidelity in *Hearts in Dixie*," featuring an all-Negro cast of two hundred, starring Stepin Fetchit.

8. The Native Arts of Radicalism and/or Race

1. Max Eastman believed a greater focus on domestic racial issues would cost the magazine its survival. See letters of spring 1923 between Max Eastman and Claude McKay, McKay MSS, Manuscripts Department, Lilly Library, Indiana University, Bloomington.

2. See, for example, Robert Minor, "The Negro Finds His Place—and a Sword," *Liberator* 7 (1924): 20–25.

3. As early as 1913, Eastman was urging African Americans to fight back in self-defense against marauding whites. See Eastman, "Niggers and Night Riders," *Masses* 9 (1913): 6. This line continued throughout the existence of the *Masses-Liberator* group.

4. For other discussions of *The Masses* and *The Liberator* in relation to African American literature, see Leslie Fishbein, *Rebels in Bohemia: The Radicals of "The Masses," 1911–1917* (Chapel Hill: University of North Carolina Press,

1982), 160–167; Tyrone Tillery, *Claude McKay: A Black Poet's Struggle for Identity* (Amherst: University of Massachusetts Press, 1992), 38–75, passim; and Wayne F. Cooper, *Claude McKay: Rebel Sojourner in the Harlem Renaissance* (Baton Rouge: Louisiana State University Press, 1987), 134–170.

5. Daniel Aaron, *Writers on the Left: Episodes in American Literary Communism* (New York: Avon, 1965), 38.

6. Max Eastman, *Enjoyment of Living* (New York: Harper, 1948), 284, 282.

7. Ibid., 284.

8. Ibid., 286.

9. See Max Eastman's "A Letter to Romain Rolland," *Liberator* 2 (1919): 24–25.

10. Eastman, *Enjoyment*, 289. The pragmatist orientation is evident in Eastman's approach to ethics: "Ethics means, I suppose, the classification and evaluation of human motives and conduct in the light of some general standard. I don't believe there is any general standard. . . . Ethics sweeps on in gestures of lofty generality and abstraction while the man himself sits tangled in a mess of concrete particular trouble" (289).

11. Peter J. Conn, *The Divided Mind: Ideology and Imagination in America, 1898–1917* (Cambridge: Cambridge University Press, 1983), 271–278. Aaron points out the centrality of Whitman to the *Masses-Liberator* group (24–25). See also Marcus Klein, *Foreigners: The Making of American Literature, 1900–1948* (Chicago: University of Chicago Press, 1981), 52. The two indispensable books for an understanding of the writers of the American left from the early twentieth century through the thirties are Aaron, *Writers on the Left;* and Eric Homberger, *American Writers and Radical Politics, 1900–1939: Equivocal Commitments* (London: Macmillan, 1986). Debs himself was a follower of Whitman and a dear friend of Horace Traubel who kept up his association with the Walt Whitman Fellowship. Traubel "was a familiar figure in the offices of *The Masses*" and a contributor to *The Liberator* (Aaron, *Writers on the Left*, 25).

12. Floyd Dell, "Dolls and Abraham Lincoln" (1919), in *Looking at Life* (New York: Knopf, 1924), 229.

13. Floyd Dell, "G. K. Chesterton, Revolutionist" (1918), in *Looking at Life,* 134.

14. Dell, "G. K. Chesterton," 130–142.

15. See Dell's account of the trial in "Not Without Dust and Heat" (1918), in *Looking at Life,* 151–168.

16. William English Walling, *Whitman and Traubel* (New York: A. & C. Boni, 1916).

17. Aaron, *Writers on the Left*, 39.

18. See the *Walt Whitman Fellowship Papers* for these years. Miller also addressed the first meeting of the fellowship with his speech "What Walt Whitman Means to the Negro" in 1895.

19. See, for example, Floyd Dell's "Sherwood Anderson, His First Novel" (1916) in *Looking at Life*, 79–84. Traubel's comparisons of Tolstoy to Whitman can be found sprinkled throughout *With Walt Whitman in Camden*, 8 vols. (various publishers, 1905–1992).

20. See, for example, Philip Schatz, "Songs of the Negro Worker," *New Masses* 5 (1930): 6. *New Masses* did a series of articles on African American workers' songs of protest in 1930–1931 that conveyed the sense of an "indigenous" tradition of workers' consciousness. The cohesiveness of black cultural protest against white power was read by white revolutionary Marxists as a form of class consciousness that had merely to be "purified" of its racialist emphasis to become a crucial part of the proletarian movement.

21. Claude McKay, *A Long Way from Home* (1937; New York: Arno Press, 1969), 28, 29.

22. Ibid., 29. Eastman charged the same artist with "viciously anti-Negro" caricatures, interestingly enough. Quoted in Jeffrey C. Stewart, *To Color America: Portraits by Winold Reiss* (Washington: National Portrait Gallery, 1989), 50. In truth, both McKay and Eastman were right.

23. Klein, *Foreigners*, 52.

24. Henry F. May, *The End of American Innocence: A Study of the First Years of Our Own Time, 1912–1917* (New York: Knopf, 1959), 285–286.

25. McKay, *A Long Way from Home*, 244.

26. Leslie Fishbein, in her *Rebels in Bohemia*, does not discuss Eastman's aesthetic theory. Tillery never discusses it either. Cooper provides the most comprehensive, balanced, and reliable discussion of the McKay-Eastman relationship, but even he devotes scarcely a paragraph to Eastman's aesthetics, noting merely that Eastman liked "classical forms" and disdained "modernists" such as Eliot (*Claude McKay*, 95, 153). Milton Cantor's *Max Eastman* (Boston: Twayne, 1970) provides a useful overview of Eastman's life, politics, and aesthetics, but the relationship with McKay is not even mentioned.

27. Max Eastman, *Colors of Life: Poems and Songs and Sonnets* (New York: Knopf, 1918), 17.

28. Ibid., 37, 38.

29. Ibid., 24, 25.

30. Ibid., 33, 34.

31. Fishbein, *Rebels in Bohemia*, 163.

32. Houston A. Baker, Jr., *Modernism and the Harlem Renaissance* (Chicago: University of Chicago Press, 1987), 85–86.

33. Ridgely Torrence, "The Bird and the Tree," *Poetry* 6 (1915): 20–21. An impressive protest sonnet by Max Eastman is "Eleventh Anniversary," *Nation* 127 (1928): 522.

34. Tillery, *Claude McKay*, 29.

35. Floyd Dell, "Vachel Lindsay's Voice" (1918), in *Looking at Life*, 117–124.

36. Charles H. Rowell, "'Let Me Be with Ole Jazzbo': An Interview with Sterling A. Brown," *Callaloo* 14 (1991): 795–815.

37. Floyd Dell, "Negro Poetry," in *Looking at Life*, 115. The piece was originally published as "Books: *Fifty Years and Other Poems*, by James Weldon Johnson," *Liberator* 1 (1918): 32–33.

38. Ibid., 115–116.

39. Ibid.

40. Ibid., 116.

41. Ibid., 113.

42. Fishbein, *Rebels in Bohemia*, 164.

43. Quoted in James Weldon Johnson, "Preface," *God's Trombones* (1927; New York: Viking Penguin, 1990), 8–9.

44. Sterling A. Brown, "James Weldon Johnson," introductory note for Johnson's poems in *The Book of American Negro Poetry*, ed. James Weldon Johnson. I am quoting from a copy of the note that Brown sent to Johnson with a letter of 13 January 1931, one year before the publication of Brown's *Southern Road*. James Weldon Johnson papers, James Weldon Johnson Collection, Beinecke Rare Book and Manuscript Library, Yale University.

45. The essays were later included in Eastman's *The Literary Mind: Its Place in an Age of Science* (New York: Scribner's, 1931), 57–78, 93–122. See also Klein, *Foreigners*, 47–48.

46. Max Eastman, *Love and Revolution: My Journey Through an Epoch* (New York: Random House, 1964), 518.

47. Eastman, *Literary Mind*, 15–52.

48. Aaron, *Writers on the Left*, 124. The quotation refers to Dell, but it is equally applicable to Eastman.

49. McKay, *A Long Way from Home*, 28–29.

50. Ibid., 34.

51. Mary Burrill, *Aftermath, Liberator* 2 (1919): 10–14.

52. Claude McKay, "The Dominant White," *Liberator* 4 (1919): 14.

53. Max Eastman, "Claude McKay," and Claude McKay, "Sonnets and Songs," *Liberator* 2 (1919): 7, 20–21; Cooper, *Claude McKay*, 103, 144.

54. On Eastman's friendship with McKay, see especially Eastman's *Love and Revolution*, 222. McKay stuck by his friend when the latter was ostracized by other communists for reacting against the purging of Trotsky. Conversely, Eastman would remain McKay's most loyal friend and supporter to the end of McKay's life, a poignant fact in view of the distance suggested by Eastman's comment to his wife on learning of McKay's death, as quoted by Tillery: "It is sad to think of McKay, but he really stopped living years ago. Too bad, for he had such good brains and so much charm. Perhaps we should have kept him as a cook or a maid" (*Claude McKay*, 182).

55. Cooper, *Claude McKay*, 135; see also letter from McKay to Max Eastman, 3 April 1923, McKay MSS, Lilly Library.

56. Arnold Rampersad, *The Life of Langston Hughes,* vol. 1 (New York: Oxford University Press, 1986), 30.

57. Langston Hughes, "Claude McKay: The Best," draft of an article for *American Negro Writers,* in Langston Hughes Papers, James Weldon Johnson Collection, Beinecke Rare Book and Manuscript Library, Yale University.

58. "Claude McKay: The Best," Langston Hughes Papers. Hughes saved what may be his first rejection slip, a card from *The Liberator* signed by Floyd Dell with an encouraging personal note: "We like 'Question' the most of these, but none of them moves us deeply. Sorry!" (Langston Hughes Papers). It is one of the few pieces of correspondence Hughes saved from that early period of his career. "Question" appeared in *Crisis* in March 1922—his fourth poem printed in a nationally circulated journal.

59. "Claude McKay: The Best."

60. McKay to Hughes, 9 May 1925, Langston Hughes Papers.

61. Cynthia Earl Kerman and Richard Eldridge, *The Lives of Jean Toomer: A Hunger for Wholeness* (Baton Rouge: Louisiana State University Press, 1987), 85.

62. Joseph Freeman, *An American Testament: A Narrative of Rebels and Romantics* (London: Victor Gollancz, 1938), 259–260.

63. McKay, *A Long Way from Home,* 139.

64. Claude McKay, "Birthright," *Liberator* 5 (1922): 15.

65. Ibid.

66. Claude McKay, *The Negroes in America,* trans. Robert J. Winter, ed. Alan J. McLeod (1923; New York: Kennikat Press, 1979), 4.

67. Eastman to McKay, March 1923 and 12 April 1923, McKay MSS, Lilly Library, Indiana University.

68. Tillery, *Claude McKay,* 56–61. McKay writes, "The race matter was merely incidental to my quitting the executive work," whereas Tillery writes that in his letter McKay insinuated that a book he was writing "would reveal that racial matters more than anything else had prompted his withdrawal from the *Liberator*" (ibid., 59). This insinuation actually comes from *Eastman's* interpretation of a portion of McKay's book. McKay flatly denied that he was insinuating any such thing, and the book in question did not present such an argument, as Tillery himself notes (ibid., 60). The most thorough discussion of the whole affair is in Cooper, *Claude McKay,* 189–191.

69. McKay to Eastman, 3 April 1923, McKay MSS, Lilly Library.

70. McKay quoted in Cooper, *Claude McKay,* 181.

71. Eastman to McKay, 12 April 1923, McKay MSS, Lilly Library.

72. McKay to Hughes, 9 May 1925, Langston Hughes Papers.

73. McKay to Hughes, 24 April 1926, Langston Hughes Papers.

74. "Claude McKay: The Best," Langston Hughes Papers.

75. A good account of the transformation of *The Liberator* into *The Workers Monthly* is in John Edward Hart, *Floyd Dell* (New York: Twayne, 1971), 106–108. See also Aaron, 114.

76. The Garland Fund had been established by a wealthy young Harvard graduate, Charles Garland, to serve radical causes; it was later a sometime funding source for Harlem Renaissance projects.

77. Aaron, *Writers on the Left,* 118.

78. Ibid., 119.

79. *New Masses* 1 (1926): 30.

80. James Rorty, review of *The Weary Blues, New Masses* 1 (26 October 1926): 26.

81. George Schuyler, "Some Southern Snapshots," *New Masses* 2 (December 1926): 15–17; V. F. Calverton, review of *Nigger Heaven* by Carl Van Vechten, *New Masses* 2 (December 1926), 27.

82. Patterson, "Awake, Negro Poets!" *New Masses* 4 (October 1928): 10.

83. "Write For Us!" *New Masses* 4 (July 1928): 2.

84. Homberger, *American Writers,* 165–167.

85. See Hart, *Floyd Dell,* 121–123.

86. Michael Gold, "Notes of the Month," *New Masses* 5 (February 1930): 3.

87. V. F. Calverton, *The Liberation of American Literature* (New York: Scribner's, 1932), 457–458. Yet even Michael Gold and Joseph Freeman—whom Max Eastman and Claude McKay regarded as too doctrinaire and anti-aesthetic—complained about the excesses of the younger authors (Homberger, *American Writers,* 165–167).

88. Ibid., 137–138.

89. Walt Carmon, "Away from Harlem," *New Masses* 6 (October 1930): 17.

90. Ibid., 18.

91. Ibid.

92. A graphic example of the problems with Communist Party interference with the cultural left was its demand that Richard Wright abandon a novel he was working on to organize a cost-of-living study (Homberger, *American Writers,* 137–138).

93. Anonymous editorial, "A Statement," *New Masses* 6 (February 1931): 2.

94. Michael Gold, "Notes of the Month," *New Masses* 5 (April 1930): 3–4.

95. Keneth Kinnamon, *The Emergence of Richard Wright* (Urbana: University of Illinois Press, 1972), 43, 41.

96. Richard Wright, *Black Boy* (1945; New York: Harper & Row, 1966), 274.

97. Ibid., 283.

98. Kinnamon, *Emergence of Richard Wright,* 51.

99. Richard Wright, "Blueprint for Negro Writing," *New Challenge* 2 (Fall 1937): 53–65.

100. See Hart, *Floyd Dell,* 164.

9. V. F. Calverton, *The Modern Quarterly,* and an Anthology

1. Sidney Hook, "Preface" to reprint of *Modern Quarterly.* Eric Homberger, *American Writers and Radical Politics, 1900–1939: Equivocal Commitments* (London:

Macmillan, 1986), 125. For a brief sketch of Calverton's relationship to Eastman, see Daniel Aaron, *Writers on the Left: Episodes in American Literary Communism* (New York: Avon, 1965), 335. Aaron (335–346) also gives a very informative general treatment of Calverton's position on the cultural left in the 1920s and 1930s. For a useful overview of V. F. Calverton's relationships with African American intellectuals, see Haim Genizi's "V. F. Calverton: A Radical Magazinist for Black Intellectuals, 1920–1940," *Journal of Negro History* 57 (1972): 241–253; Harold Cruse discusses Calverton's unappreciated grasp of the black situation in *The Crisis of the Negro Intellectual* (New York: William Morrow, 1967), 152–158. Leonard Wilcox discusses Calverton's distinctively "American" synthesis of political and sexual radicalism, Marxism and Freudianism, in "Sex Boys in a Balloon: V. F. Calverton and the Abortive Sexual Revolution," *Journal of American Studies* 23 (1989): 7–26; and in his *V. F. Calverton: Radical in the American Grain* (Philadelphia: Temple University Press, 1992), with brief remarks on Calverton's relationship to the Harlem Renaissance, 89–91.

2. David Ramsey and Alan Calmer, "The Marxism of V. F. Calverton," *New Masses* 8 (1933): 9–27. For the story of how this came about, on orders from Moscow, see Aaron, *Writers on the Left*, 340.

3. Cruse, *Crisis*, 152–158.

4. Richel North, "The Limitations of American Magazines," *Modern Quarterly* 1 (1923): 2–12.

5. Charles S. Johnson to Alain Locke, 10 January 1924, correspondence files, Alain Locke Papers, Moorland-Spingarn Research Center, Howard University.

6. Charles S. Johnson to Alain Locke, 1 October 1925, Alain Locke Papers.

7. V. F. Calverton, review of *The New Negro*, *Nation* 121 (1925): 761.

8. V. F. Calverton to Alain Locke, 25 October 1925, Alain Locke Papers. Locke did in fact give the lecture; see Calverton to Locke, 5 November 1925, Alain Locke Papers.

9. V. F. Calverton to Alain Locke, 20 October 1925, Alain Locke Papers.

10. Alain Locke, "American Literary Tradition and the Negro," *Modern Quarterly* 3 (1926): 215–222.

11. V. F. Calverton to Alain Locke, 30 November 1925, Alain Locke Papers.

12. V. F. Calverton to Alain Locke, 5 December 1925, Alain Locke Papers.

13. V. F. Calverton to Alain Locke, 30 December 1925, Alain Locke Papers.

14. V. F. Calverton to Alain Locke, 1 February 1926, Alain Locke Papers.

15. V. F. Calverton to Alain Locke, 31 March 1926, Alain Locke Papers.

16. W. E. B. Du Bois, "The Social Origins of American Negro Art," *Modern Quarterly* 3 (1925–26): 54.

17. Ibid., 56.

18. Locke, "American Literary Tradition," 215.

19. Ibid., 216.

20. Ibid.

21. Ibid., 221.

22. Ibid.

23. Ibid., 222.

24. Alain Locke, review of *Sex Expression in Literature, Opportunity* 5 (1927): 57–58. The review is detailed and enthusiastic, though objecting to Calverton's overemphasis upon economic determinism.

25. See V. F. Calverton, "The American Inter-racial Association," *Opportunity* 5 (1927): 23.

26. Henry Louis Gates, Jr., "The Master's Pieces: On Canon Formation and the African-American Tradition," *South Atlantic Quarterly* 89 (1990): 97.

27. On Calverton's relationship with Walter White, see Waldron, *Walter White and the Harlem Renaissance* (Port Washington, N.Y.: Kennikat Press, 1978), 164–165; White read the first few chapters of the anthology at an early stage. Calverton also sent the book to Elmer Carter of *Opportunity*, who enthusiastically praised it.

28. Gates, "Master's Pieces," 35.

29. V. F. Calverton, "Introduction," *An Anthology of American Negro Literature* (New York: Modern Library, 1929), 4–5.

30. Gates, "Master's Pieces," 98.

31. Calverton, "Introduction," 8.

32. Ibid., 8.

33. Ibid., 4, 8–9.

34. Alain Locke to V. F. Calverton, 19 October 1928, Alain Locke Papers.

35. V. F. Calverton to Alain Locke, 24 November 1928 and 20 November 1928, Alain Locke Papers.

36. V. F. Calverton to Langston Hughes, 19 July 1930, 21 January 1929, 16 April 1929, Langston Hughes Papers, James Weldon Johnson Collection, Beinecke Rare Book and Manuscript Library, Yale University.

37. Aaron, *Writers on the Left,* 335–338, emphasizes how Calverton wanted *The Modern Quarterly* to be a forum for diverse views of the radical left, to help unite warring factions. Thus Calverton's embrace of opposite poles of the Harlem Renaissance (Hughes and Schuyler, Locke and Du Bois) fits the general aim of the magazine.

38. George S. Schuyler, *Black and Conservative: The Autobiography of George S. Schuyler* (New Rochelle, N.Y.: Arlington House, 1966), 170.

39. Ibid., 170. See also Schuyler's "Preface" to *Black No More* (1931; Boston: Northeastern University Press, 1989), 14, which thanks Josephine Schuyler and V. F. Calverton for their help and encouragement.

40. Joy Flasch, *Melvin B. Tolson* (Boston: Twayne, 1972), 29.

41. Robert M. Farnsworth, *Melvin B. Tolson, 1898–1966: Plain Talk and Poetic Prophecy* (Columbia: University of Missouri Press, 1984), 57.

42. Quoted in ibid., 58.

43. Ibid., 42.

44. V. F. Calverton, *The Liberation of American Literature* (New York: Scribner's, 1932), 406–450, 479.

45. Ibid., 417.

46. Ibid., 438.

10. Mediating Race and Nation

1. Theodore Kornweibel, Jr., *No Crystal Stair: Black Life and the Messenger, 1917–1928* (Westport: Greenwood Press, 1975), 107.

2. Quoted in ibid., 120.

3. Jervis Anderson, *A. Philip Randolph: A Biographical Portrait* (New York: Harcourt Brace Jovanovich, 1972), 57–59, 71; Paula F. Pfeffer, *A. Philip Randolph, Pioneer of the Civil Rights Movement* (Baton Rouge: Louisiana State University Press, 1990), 8; and Kornweibel, *No Crystal Stair,* 30.

4. Anderson, *A. Philip Randolph,* 344.

5. See Pfeffer, *A. Philip Randolph,* 17–18.

6. See Anderson, *A. Philip Randolph,* 127–137; and George S. Schuyler, *Black and Conservative: The Autobiography of George S. Schuyler* (New Rochelle, N.Y.: Arlington House, 1966), 120–123, 145. Kornweibel, *No Crystal Stair,* discusses the anti-West-Indian prejudices expressed in *The Messenger* (143–154) and Garvey's general lack of interest in domestic American conditions (152–161).

7. Pfeffer, *A. Philip Randolph,* 17–18.

8. Chandler Owen, "The Cabaret—A Useful Social Institution," *Messenger* 4 (1922): 461.

9. See George S. Schuyler, *Black No More: Being an Account of the Strange and Wonderful Workings of Science in the Land of the Free, A. D. 1933–1940* (1931; Boston: Northeastern University Press, 1989), 20; and J. A. Rogers, "Jazz at Home," *The New Negro,* ed. Alain Locke (1925; New York: Atheneum, 1992), 223–224.

10. See Abby Arthur Johnson and Ronald Maberry Johnson, *Propaganda and Aesthetics: The Literary Politics of Afro-American Magazines in the Twentieth Century* (Amherst: University of Massachusetts Press, 1979), 57–58. Johnson and Johnson provide a useful overview of the cultural politics of *The Messenger* in many respects, but they completely ignore the anti-black-cultural-nationalist thrust of the magazine.

11. Schuyler, *Black and Conservative,* 133–134.

12. Kornweibel, *No Crystal Stair,* 57.

13. In 1921 the editors estimated that the magazine's readership was one-third white (Kornweibel, *No Crystal Stair,* 54). In fact, from 1917 to 1921 the magazine's audience was chiefly made up of white and black radical intellectuals. Subsequently the stance and tone shifted as the magazine became more

sympathetic to black business and the American Federation of Labor, featuring society pages, sports, business and industry, and the achievements of black entrepreneurs. In 1925 it became chiefly an organ of the Brotherhood of Sleeping Car Porters. See Kornweibel, 50–51.

14. Schuyler, *Black and Conservative,* 161.

15. J. A. Rogers, "Critical Excursions and Reflections," *Messenger* 6 (1924): 379.

16. J. A. Rogers, "Is Black Ever White?" *Messenger* 8 (1926): 274.

17. Ibid.

18. See, for example, Schuyler's review of *The Negro in American Life* by Jerome Dowd, *Messenger* 9 (1927): 95.

19. Langston Hughes, *The Big Sea* (1940; rpt. New York: Hill and Wang, 1963), 233.

20. Thomas Kirksey, "Reflections upon Race," *Messenger* 8 (1926): 363–364, 381.

21. "Group Tactics and Ideals," *Messenger* 8 (1926): 361.

22. See, for example, "Group Tactics and Ideals," *Messenger* 9 (1927): 308.

23. "Group Tactics and Ideals," *Messenger* 8 (1926): 361.

24. Ibid., 361, 383.

25. "Group Tactics and Ideals," *Messenger* 9 (1927): 12.

26. Ibid., 11.

27. Ibid., 11–14.

28. Theophilus Lewis, "The Theatre," *Messenger* 8 (1926): 182–183.

29. George S. Grant, "What Are We?" *Messenger* 8 (1926): 300.

30. *Messenger* 6 (1924): 384–385.

31. George S. Schuyler, review of *There Is Confusion, Messenger* 6 (1924): 146.

32. See, for example, Schuyler's "At the Coffee House," *Messenger* 7 (1925): 236–237; and J. A. Rogers, "The Critic," *Messenger* 8 (1926): 365, 380.

33. Rogers, "The Critic," 365, 380. Interestingly, Rogers reports that *Veiled Aristocrats* was the favorite recent book among patients at the Tuskegee Veterans' Hospital.

34. George S. Schuyler, "Shafts and Darts," *Messenger* 8 (1926): 9.

35. Ibid.

36. See Schuyler's acknowledgment of Calverton in the "Preface" to *Black No More,* 14; and Schuyler, *Black and Conservative,* 170.

37. "Shafts and Darts," *Messenger* 8 (1926): 9.

38. Ibid., 239.

39. Theophilus Lewis, review of *Tropic Death, Messenger* 9 (1927): 27–28.

40. Theophilus Lewis, "Refined Blues," *Messenger* 9 (1927): 95.

41. James Ivy, "Book Bits," *Messenger* 9 (1927): 168.

42. James Ivy, review of *Congaree Sketches, Messenger* 9 (1927): 287.

43. Robert W. Bagnall, review of *Holiday, Messenger* 6 (1924): 360.

44. Wallace V. Jackson, "The Theatre-Drama," *Messenger* 5 (1923): 746, 747.

45. Ibid., 747.

46. Ibid., 748; Abram L. Harris, "The Ethiopian Art Players and the Nordic Complex," *Messenger* 5 (1923): 774–775, 777.

47. See, for example, Lovett Fort-Whiteman, "Drama," *Messenger* 5 (1923): 671; unsigned editorial, "The Play," *Messenger* 8 (1926): 111; unsigned editorial, "Do Negroes Want High Class Anything?" *Messenger* 7 (1925): 20; George Schuyler, "Interviews with Actors," *Messenger* 7 (1925): 21–23.

48. Theophilus Lewis, "Theatre," *Messenger* 6 (1924): 291.

49. Theophilus Lewis, "Same Old Blues," *Messenger* 7 (1925): 14.

50. Theophilus Lewis, "Survey of the Negro Theatre—III," *Messenger* 8 (1926): 301.

51. Ibid.

52. Lewis, "Same Old Blues," *Messenger* 7 (1925): 15.

53. Ibid., 14.

54. Lewis, "Theatre," *Messenger* 8 (1926): 214, 215.

55. See Alain Locke, "Max Rheinhardt Reads the Negro's Dramatic Horoscope," *Opportunity* 2 (1924): 145–146; and Jessie Fauset, "The Gift of Laughter," *The New Negro*, 161–167. Fauset (166) cites a Carl Van Vechten essay, "Prescription for the Negro Theatre," as making a similar argument. Van Vechten's essay is in *Vanity Fair* 25 (1925): 46, 92, 98.

56. Eric Lott, "'The Seeming Counterfeit': Racial Politics and Early Blackface Minstrelsy," *American Quarterly* 43 (1991): 223–254.

57. Lewis, "Survey of the Negro Theatre—III," *Messenger* 8 (1926): 301.

58. Ibid.

59. Ibid., 302.

60. Lewis, "Theatre," *Messenger* 8 (1926): 333–334.

61. Lewis, "Theatre," *Messenger* 9 (1927): 157.

62. Theophilus Lewis, "My Red Rag," *Messenger* 10 (1928): 18.

63. Lewis, "Theatre," *Messenger* 6 (1924): 291.

64. Lewis, "Theatre," *Messenger* 7 (1925): 230.

11. "Superior Intellectual Vaudeville"

1. Charles Scruggs, *The Sage in Harlem: H. L. Mencken and the Black Writers of the 1920s* (Baltimore: Johns Hopkins University Press, 1984).

2. Quoted in M. K. Singleton, *H. L. Mencken and the "American Mercury" Adventure* (Durham: Duke University Press, 1962), 35; from "Magazine to Cater to 'Civilized Minority,'" *New York Times*, 18 August 1923, p. 2, col. 3.

3. Alfred A. Knopf, "For Henry with Love," in *Portrait of a Publisher*, vol. 1 (New York: The Typophiles, 1965), 150; and Knopf, "A Publisher Opens His Mind," in *Portrait of a Publisher*, vol. 1, 62.

4. William H. Nolte, *H. L. Mencken, Literary Critic* (Middletown, Conn.: Wesleyan University Press, 1966), 133.

5. Van Wyck Brooks, excerpt from *The Confident Years*, rpt. in *Critical Essays on H. L. Mencken*, ed. Douglas C. Stenerson (Boston: G. K. Hall, 1987), 122.

6. Quoted in Singleton, *H. L. Mencken*, 3 n. 44.

7. Quoted in Nolte, *H. L. Mencken*, 154.

8. Ibid., 156.

9. Fred Hobson, "'This Hellawful South': Mencken and the Late Confederacy," in *Critical Essays*, 184, 179, 180.

10. Irving Babbitt, "The Critic and American Life," in *Critical Essays*, 79; rpt. from *Forum* 79 (1928): 161–168. Joseph Wood Krutch, "This Was Mencken: An Appreciation," in *Critical Essays*, 124–126; rpt. from *Nation* 182 (1956): 109–110.

11. H. L. Mencken, "The National Letters," in *Prejudices: Second Series* (New York: Knopf, 1920), 15–16.

12. Ibid., 19, 22–23.

13. H. L. Mencken, "Puritanism as a Literary Force," in *A Book of Prefaces* (1917; New York: Knopf, 1924), 199, 216.

14. *Mencken*, "National Letters," 91.

15. Ibid., 93.

16. Ibid., 94.

17. Ibid., 95.

18. Ibid., 99.

19. Ibid., 101.

20. Louise Pound, "Notes on the Vernacular," *American Mercury* 3 (1924): 233–237; Vachel Lindsay, "The Real American Language," *American Mercury* 13 (1928): 257–265; Babbette Deutsch, "The Plight of the Poet," *American Mercury* 8 (1926): 66–68; George Philip Krapp, "The English of the Negro," *American Mercury* 2 (1924): 190–195.

21. Deutsch, "Plight of the Poet," 68.

22. Edmund Wilson, "H. L. Mencken," in *Critical Essays*, 71, 70; rpt. from *New Republic* 27 (1921): 10–13.

23. Ibid., 69.

24. Quoted in Singleton, *H. L. Mencken*, 190–191.

25. As Michael Seidel has pointed out, "It is one of the more plaguing paradoxes about the satiric mode that the satirist, having taken on a kind of monstrosity as his subject, makes something of a monster of himself. The rhetorical, forensic, and moral justification for satire and for the positioning of the satirist against his subjects tends to ignore the complicity of the satirist in the degenerate record he formally records." *Satiric Inheritance: Rabelais to Sterne* (Princeton: Princeton University Press, 1979), 3.

26. H. L. Mencken, "Footnote on Criticism," in *Prejudices: Third Series* (New York: Knopf, 1922), 85–86.

27. Ibid., 86.

28. "If [the critic] is genuinely first-rate—if what is within him stands the test of type, and wins an audience, and produces the reactions that every artist craves—then he usually ends by abandoning the criticism of specific works of art altogether, and setting up shop as a general merchant in general ideas, *i.e.*, as an artist working in the materials of life itself" (ibid., 88).

29. Mencken claimed his goal was not to discover truth by exposing error— "Nine times out of ten, in the arts as in life, there is actually no truth to be discovered; there is only error to be exposed. . . . What the world turns to, when it has been cured of one error, is usually simply another error, and maybe one worse than the first one. This is the whole history of the intellect in brief" (ibid., 93).

30. Mencken believed the ferocity of the critical battles engaged in by Poe and Whitman was a healthy sign—not surprisingly, those battles coincided with the healthiest period of American literature. He hoped, not vainly, that a similar period was in the offing in the early 1920s. See ibid., 102–104.

31. Seidel, *Satiric Inheritance*, 57.

32. Arnold Rampersad, "Mencken, Race, and America," *Menckeniana* 115 (1990): 1–11.

33. H. L. Mencken, "On Being an American," in *Prejudices: Third Series*, 22, 23–24.

34. "On Being an American," 24–25.

35. "On Being an American," 14.

36. "On Being an American," 11.

37. See Seidel, *Satiric Inheritance*, 3.

38. Carl Van Doren, "The Comic Patriot," *American Mercury* 1 (1924): 234.

39. Ibid., 236.

40. Ibid., 235.

41. Ibid., 236.

42. As Singleton (96) has pointed out, this series was one of Mencken's original contributions to American journalism, later copied by magazines including *New Masses* and *The Saturday Evening Post*.

43. Singleton, *H. L. Mencken*, 243.

44. Krapp, "English of the Negro," 190–195.

45. Ibid.

46. George Pullen Jackson, "The Genesis of the Negro Spiritual," *American Mercury* 26 (1932): 243–248.

47. Without having done an exhaustive accounting, I would hazard that Schuyler published more in *American Mercury* between 1924 and 1934 than anyone except its editors.

48. M. S. Lea, "Across the Color Line," *American Mercury* 16 (1929): 282–286.

49. Walter White, "I Investigate Lynchings," *American Mercury* 16 (1929): 77.

50. L. M. Hussey, "Homo Africanus," *American Mercury* 4 (1925): 86.

51. Ibid., 87, 86.

52. W. E. B. Du Bois, "The Dilemma of the Negro," *American Mercury* 3 (1924): 184.

53. Ibid., 185.

54. Albon L. Holsey, "Learning How to Be Black," *American Mercury* 16 (1929): 422.

55. Ibid.

56. Ibid., 425.

57. James Weldon Johnson, "The Dilemma of the Negro Author," *American Mercury* 15 (1928): 481.

58. Ibid., 481.

59. L. M. Hussey, "Aframerican, North and South," *American Mercury* 7 (1926): 199.

60. Ibid., 199, 200.

61. Ibid., 200.

62. H. L. Mencken, "The Aframerican: New Style," *American Mercury* 7 (1926): 254. Incidentally, Mencken probably picked up the term "Aframerican" from George Schuyler.

63. Ibid., 255.

64. Ibid., 254, 255.

65. Sterling Brown, "Our Literary Audience," *Opportunity* 8 (1930): 42.

66. Quoted in Scruggs, *Sage in Harlem,* 123, 124.

67. Quoted in ibid., 129.

12. Black Writing and Modernist American Publishing

1. George E. Kent, *Blackness and the Adventure of Western Culture* (Chicago: Third World Press, 1972), 22; Cary D. Wintz, *Black Culture and the Harlem Renaissance* (Houston: Rice University Press, 1988), 154–158.

2. Anonymous, "The New Age of the Negro," *Publishers Weekly* 109 (1926): 1842.

3. Sterling Brown, "The Negro Author and His Publisher," *Negro Quarterly* 1 (1942): 16. See also Charles H. Rowell, "'Let Me Be with Ole Jazzbo': An Interview with Sterling A. Brown," *Callaloo* 14 (1991): 810.

4. Henry F. May, *The End of American Innocence: A Study of the First Years of Our Own Time, 1912–1917* (New York: Knopf, 1959), 290.

5. By 1909, New York City had become a strong publishing center, and by 1914 New York State produced 46.8 percent of the total value of books and pamphlets in the United States. However, in 1936, according to a WPA study, approximately 95 percent of the total number of titles published in the United States "'first saw the light of day within the Manhattan area bounded by 23rd Street, Fourth Avenue, Madison Avenue, and 57th Street.'" Quoted in John W.

Tebbel, *A History of Book Publishing in the United States* (New York: R. R. Bowker, 1972), vol. 3, 669.

6. See Tebbel, *History of Book Publishing*, vol. 3, p. 5; Christopher Lehmann-Haupt, *The Book in America: A History of the Making and Selling of Books*, rev. ed. (New York: R. R. Bowker, 1951), 332; Charles Doran, *Chronicles of Barabbas, 1884–1934* (New York: Harcourt, Brace, 1935), 83.

7. Bennett Cerf, *At Random: Reminiscences of Bennett Cerf* (New York: Random House, 1977), 41.

8. Walker Gilmer, *Horace Liveright: Publisher of the Twenties* (New York: David Lewis, 1970), 6.

9. Ibid., 5; Tebbel, *History of Book Publishing*, vol. 3, p. 9.

10. Gilmer, *Horace Liveright*, 8.

11. For the following information on McClurg I rely chiefly upon Kenny J. Williams, *Prairie Voices: A Literary History of Chicago from the Frontier to 1893* (Nashville: Townsend Press, 1980), 235–237, 264–266.

12. Doran, *Chronicles*, 29; Williams, *Prairie Voices*, 237.

13. W. E. B. Du Bois, *Dusk of Dawn: An Essay Toward an Autobiography of a Race Concept* (1940; New York: Schocken Books, 1968), 80.

14. Francis Hackett, *American Rainbow: Early Reminiscences* (New York: Liveright, 1971), 222.

15. Tebbel, *History of Book Publishing*, vol. 3, 30, discusses the war's stimulation of demand for books generally.

16. James Baldwin, "Rendezvous With Life: An Interview With Countee Cullen," in *My Soul's High Song: The Collected Writings of Countee Cullen, Voice of the Harlem Renaissance*, ed. Gerald Early (New York: Anchor Books, 1991), 603.

17. Anonymous, "The Debut of the Younger School of Negro Writers," *Opportunity* 2 (1924): 143.

18. Lehmann-Haupt, *The Book in America*, contrasts publishers like Knopf with the "success" publishers of the 1920s. The same contrast would hold with Boni & Liveright and with Harcourt, Brace.

19. See especially the unsigned editorial "A Note on the New Literary Movement," *Opportunity* 4 (1926): 80–81; Alain Locke, "1928: A Retrospective Review," *Opportunity* 7 (1929): 8–11; and Eunice Hunton Carter, review of Wallace Thurman, *The Blacker the Berry*, *Opportunity* 7 (1929): 162–163.

20. Wintz, *Black Culture*, 160; David Levering Lewis, *When Harlem Was in Vogue* (New York: Knopf, 1981), 135.

21. Doran, *Chronicles*, 267.

22. Ibid., 248.

23. Wintz, *Black Culture*, 160. Edward E. Waldron, in *Walter White and the Harlem Renaissance* (Port Washington, N.Y.: Kennikat Press, 1978), 47–71, gives the most comprehensive account of the entire process of White's attempts at publication and of his rationale.

24. Lewis, *When Harlem Was in Vogue*, 135.

25. Quoted in Waldron, *Walter White*, 157.

26. Ibid.

27. Wintz, *Black Culture*, 155–157.

28. "The Negro in Art: How Shall He Be Portrayed?" *Crisis* 31 (1926): 219–220; 31 (1926): 278–280; 32 (1926): 71–73; 32 (1926): 193–194. See also Arnold Rampersad, *The Art and Imagination of W. E. B. Du Bois* (New York: Schocken Books, 1990), 195–196.

29. Published information on Braithwaite is scarce, but see the fine *Dictionary of Literary Biography* (vol. 50) entry by Kenny J. Williams, "William Stanley Braithwaite," in *Afro-American Writers Before the Harlem Renaissance*, ed. Trudier Harris (Detroit: Gale Research, 1986), 7–18; and her "An Invisible Partnership and an Unlikely Relationship: William Stanley Braithwaite and Harriet Monroe," *Callaloo* 10 (1987): 516–550; *The William Stanley Braithwaite Reader*, ed. Philip Butcher (Ann Arbor: University of Michigan Press, 1972); Philip Butcher, "William Stanley Braithwaite and the College Language Association," *CLA Journal*, 15 (1971): 117–125; Philip Butcher, "William Stanley Braithwaite's Southern Exposure: Rescue and Revelation," *Southern Literary Journal* 3 (1971): 49–61; and Glenn Clairmonte, "The Cup-Bearer: William Stanley Braithwaite of Boston," *CLA Journal* 17 (1973): 101–108. While these sources are useful for understanding Braithwaite's criticism, they give little information about his work as a publisher.

30. B.K., "William Stanley Braithwaite," *Boston Evening Transcript*, 30 November 1915, clipping in folder 106, William Stanley Braithwaite Papers, Houghton Library, Harvard University.

31. B.K., "William Stanley Braithwaite," n.p.

32. Braithwaite praised Torrence highly from his first *Boston Transcript* column of 1906 ("The Magazines and the Poets," *Boston Evening Transcript*, 14 February 1906, clipping in Braithwaite MSS folder, Braithwaite Papers), and Torrence's letters to Braithwaite were always warm and admiring; Neihardt enjoyed very strong reviews from Braithwaite, and lined up with him in opposition to the *Poetry* group: "O the braying of the ass in these times! Modernity! 'New Beauty'! Fiddlesticks, I say! Cawain, Rice, and Sterling have become disgusted with the Ezra Pound mouthpiece, and I have reason to believe a lot of other lovers of poetry feel the same" (Neihardt to Braithwaite, 6 December 1913, Braithwaite Papers). In an undated letter Harry Kemp wrote, "I think you have done more to keep the standard of poetic art in America high than any other man I know of—may I say that I revere you for it? But I *do* hope the Free Verse crowd don't get too much of a grip on your imagination" (Braithwaite Papers). All citations from the Braithwaite Papers are from shelf numbers bMS Am 1444–1444.2, and quotations are by permission of the Houghton Library, Harvard University.

33. The dates of publication and publishers of the anthology are as follows:

1913–1914, William Stanley Braithwaite (Cambridge); 1915, Gomme and Marshall (New York); 1916, L. V. Gomme (New York); 1917–1922, Small, Maynard (Boston); 1923–1927, B. J. Brimmer (Boston); 1928, H. Vinal (New York); 1929, G. Sully & Co. (New York).

34. A striking example is that of Arthur Inman, an out-and-out racist of Southern birth whose work Braithwaite praised and published. In his diary Inman noted a 1921 visit from the editor, in whose judgment and influence, if not reliability, he placed great faith: "Braithwaite called. What did he want? Why, money, as usual. . . . I gave him fifteen dollars as a loan, only first I obtained a solemn promise that in this year's anthology two poems would be printed, and—ah, Machiavelli that I am—a whole chapter of 120 lines from 'The Crimson Conqueror.' I have his promise. Now the hard part begins, to make him stick to it." Arthur Inman, *The Inman Diary,* ed. Daniel Aaron, 2 vols. (Cambridge, Mass.: Harvard University Press, 1985), vol. 1, 183–184.

35. Carl Sandburg to Alice Corbin Henderson, 27 November 1917, quoted in Williams, "Invisible Partnership," 548.

36. See especially Conrad Aiken, "Poetry as Supernaturalism," *Dial* 63 (1917): 202–203; and Aiken, "Yet Once More, O Ye Laurels!" *Dial* 64 (1918): 195–197. Williams, in "Invisible Partnership," discusses similarities between Braithwaite and Harriet Monroe, arguing that the differences between them were chiefly "semantic" and their antagonism rooted in petty jealousy and regional pride.

37. Clement Wood to Braithwaite, 6 May 1916, William Stanley Braithwaite Papers.

38. Brookes More to Braithwaite, 8 February 1921, Braithwaite Papers.

39. Carbon copy of Brookes More letter to Malcolm Cowley, 1 November 1922, in Brookes More folder of Braithwaite Papers.

40. Harry Kemp to Braithwaite, undated, Braithwaite Papers.

41. Waldron, *Walter White,* 141; Benjamin Brawley, *The Negro Genius* (New York: Dodd, Mead, 1946), 206–214.

42. Harriet Monroe to Braithwaite, 25 September 1917 and 12 September 1921, Braithwaite Papers. See also Williams, "Invisible Partnership," 533.

43. Claude McKay to Langston Hughes, 22 September 1924, Langston Hughes Papers, James Weldon Johnson Collection, Beinecke Rare Book and Manuscript Library, Yale University.

44. See Lawrance Thompson, *Robert Frost: The Years of Triumph, 1915–1938* (New York: Holt, Rinehart & Winston, 1970), 44, 57, 62, 64.

45. See, for example, Arthur Inman, who learned only belatedly that Braithwaite was black: "Now Braithwaite is without doubt part nigger. Is it not quite a drop for me, a dyed-in-the-wool Southerner, to deal in a business and semisocial way with such? It is, emphatically. What then serves me as an excuse? This: I would get down on my belly and go through the motions of making obeisance

to a pink-eyed worm if by so doing I were sure I could further my work. In this case I think I can. Therefore I associate with a nigger. Great shades of my forefathers, how you must kick the sideboards of your graves in futile protestation. I ask pardon of you but keep on my way" (entry for 3 April 1921, *The Inman Diary*, vol. 1, 183).

46. Benjamin Brawley to Braithwaite, 27 June 1917 and 25 December 1917, Braithwaite Papers; *The Poetry of Thomas S. Jones, Jr.*, ed. William Stanley Braithwaite, Edward J. O'Brien, and Jessie B. Rittenhouse (proofs in Braithwaite Papers—I have not found a fully published version of the book).

47. Countee Cullen to Braithwaite, 11 February 1921, Braithwaite Papers. In the same letter Cullen intimated, "For the past four years your anthologies have inspired me and my greatest ambition is that some day I shall have a poem worthy of a place there."

48. The book was *Caroling Dusk: An Anthology of Verse by Negro Poets*, ed. Countee Cullen (New York: Harper Brothers, 1927). See Cullen to Braithwaite, 1 June 1927, Braithwaite Papers.

49. *The Inman Diary*, vol. 1, 162, 223.

50. *The Inman Diary*, vol. 1, 223.

51. The correspondence between Braithwaite and Johnson leading to the publication of *Fifty Years* is also briefly discussed in Eugene Levy, *James Weldon Johnson: Black Leader, Black Voice* (Chicago: University of Chicago Press, 1973), 160–162.

52. James Weldon Johnson to Braithwaite, 28 January 1915, Braithwaite Papers.

53. Johnson to Braithwaite, 2 July 1915, Braithwaite Papers.

54. Johnson to Braithwaite, 30 March 1915, Braithwaite Papers.

55. Cornhill was owned by Braithwaite's friend Walter Reid, who apparently handled business and marketing chiefly.

56. Levy, *James Weldon Johnson*, 160–161.

57. Johnson to Braithwaite, 26 July 1917, 17 August 1917, 29 October 1917, Braithwaite Papers.

58. Johnson to Braithwaite, 23 August 1917, Braithwaite Papers.

59. Johnson to Braithwaite, 17 August 1917, 24 August 1917, Braithwaite Papers.

60. Johnson to Braithwaite, 13 September 1917, Braithwaite Papers.

61. Levy, *James Weldon Johnson*, 299.

62. Johnson to Braithwaite, undated, Braithwaite Papers.

63. Johnson to Braithwaite, 2 December 1920, Braithwaite Papers.

64. Johnson to Braithwaite, 6 July 1921, Braithwaite Papers.

65. Alfred Harcourt to Braithwaite, 16 August 1916, Braithwaite Papers.

66. Claude McKay to Max Eastman, 28 July 1919, Claude McKay MSS, Lilly Library, Indiana University.

67. McKay to Braithwaite, 29 September 1919 and 15 December 1920, Braithwaite Papers.

68. Wilson Brewer, *Life and Poems of Brookes More* (Boston: Marshall Jones, 1940), 32. More and Braithwaite remained on good terms despite the restructuring of Cornhill, which one suspects included Braithwaite's departure. See correspondence from More to Braithwaite in the Braithwaite Papers.

69. See, for example, Gwendolyn Bennett's polite but canny responses to his attempts to interest her in making a book of her "Ebony Flute" columns from *Opportunity* and to write a novel. Bennett to Braithwaite, 21 August 1926 and 24 September 1927, Braithwaite Papers. The tone of the letters suggests that she suspected Braithwaite was trying to hook her into publishing through him at her own expense.

70. William Stanley Braithwaite, "The Novels of Jessie Fauset" (1934), rpt. in Butcher, *The William Stanley Braithwaite Reader*, 96.

71. I take this list from the listings in the "yearbook" section of Braithwaite's anthologies and from page proofs in the Braithwaite Papers. The titles of some of the books reflect something of the general flavor: Romig's *Robert E. Lee, and Other Poems*, Crawford's *The Carrying of the Ghost*, Katharine Adams' *Light and Mist*, and Hobbs's *From Rotterdam to Rangoon in Verse*, for example.

72. William Stanley Braithwaite to "Miss Robinson," 3 January 1930, in *The William Stanley Braithwaite Reader* (Ann Arbor: University of Michigan Press, 1972), 279–280.

73. Doran, *Chronicles*, 53.

74. Alfred A. Knopf, "Some Random Recollections," in *Portrait of a Publisher, 1915–1965* (New York: The Typophiles, 1965), vol. 1, pp. 5–6; and "Joseph Conrad: A Footnote to Publishing History," in *Portrait*, vol. 1, 128.

75. Tebbel, *History of Book Publishing*, vol. 3, 130.

76. Quoted in Herbert H. Johnson and Margaret Becket, "Alfred A. Knopf," *Dictionary of Literary Biography 46: American Literary Publishing Houses, 1900–1980: Trade and Paperback*, ed. Peter Dzwonkoski (Detroit: Bruccoli Clark, 1986), 204.

77. Benjamin Huebsch, "Publisher: *Con Spirito, con Gusto*," in *Alfred A. Knopf at Quarter Century* (Norwood, Mass.: Plimpton Press, 1940), 35.

78. Doran, *Chronicles*, 83.

79. Lehmann-Haupt, *The Book in America*, 332–333.

80. See unsigned editorial, "The Donor of the Contest Prizes," *Opportunity* 3 (1925): 3.

81. Matthew J. Bruccoli, *The Fortunes of Mitchell Kennerley, Bookman* (New York: Harcourt Brace Jovanovich, 1986), 76.

82. Ibid., 84–85.

83. Adolph Kroch, "To Alfred A. Knopf from a Bookseller," in *Alfred A. Knopf at Quarter Century*, 41, 43.

84. Eastman's relationship with Claude McKay is well known, as is, of course,

Van Vechten's role in the Harlem Renaissance; but Kreymborg was close to the often-neglected poet Fenton Johnson of Chicago and published a (very bad) poem to him in *The Crisis* in 1918. "Red Chant," *Crisis* 17 (1918): 31.

85. Kroch, "To Alfred A. Knopf," 44.

86. Alfred A. Knopf, "For Henry with Love," in *Portrait of a Publisher,* vol. 1, 150. See also Tebbel, *History of Book Publishing,* vol. 3, 130.

87. Langston Hughes, *The Big Sea* (New York: Hill and Wang, 1963), 254–255.

88. Tebbel, *History of Book Publishing,* vol. 3, 129.

89. Geoffrey T. Hellman, "Publisher" (1948), in *Portrait of a Publisher,* vol. 2, 108–109.

90. Alfred A. Knopf, "Publishing Then and Now," *Portrait of a Publisher,* vol. 1, 44.

91. Wintz, *Black Culture,* 171.

92. Gerald Early stresses Jack Johnson's importance in his introduction to *My Soul's High Song,* 25–31.

93. Alfred A. Knopf, Inc., to Hughes, 29 July 1930, Langston Hughes Papers.

94. Countee Cullen to Alain Locke, 15 May 1925, Alain Locke Correspondence, Moorland-Spingarn Research Center, Howard University.

95. Gwendolyn Bennett to Langston Hughes, 2 December 1925, Langston Hughes Papers.

96. Countee Cullen to Alain Locke, 23 November 1924, Alain Locke Correspondence.

97. "The Negro in Art: How Shall He Be Portrayed?" *Crisis* 31 (1926): 280.

98. Wintz's study of the correspondence revealed that the title was Blanche Knopf's idea (*Black Culture,* 176).

99. See especially Langston Hughes, "Rejuvenation Through Joy," in *The Ways of White Folks* (1933; rpt. New York: Vintage Books/Random House, 1962), 69–98.

100. Wintz, *Black Culture,* 176.

101. Arnold Rampersad, *The Life of Langston Hughes* (New York: Oxford University Press, 1986), vol. 1, 281.

102. Lehmann-Haupt, *The Book in America,* 339.

103. Gilmer, *Horace Liveright,* 2–3.

104. Ibid., 11, 12, 10.

105. William MacAdams, *Ben Hecht: The Man Behind the Legend* (New York: Scribner, 1990), 79–80.

106. Ibid., 80.

107. Gilmer, *Horace Liveright,* 27.

108. MacAdams, *Ben Hecht,* 80–81; Cerf, *At Random,* 41.

109. Tebbel, *History of Book Publishing,* vol. 3, 138.

110. Cerf, *At Random,* 41.

111. Ann Allen Shockley, taped interview with Ethel Ray Nance (1970), Fisk University Library.

112. Cynthia Earl Kerman and Richard Eldridge, *The Lives of Jean Toomer: A Hunger for Wholeness* (Baton Rouge: Louisiana State University Press, 1987), 100; and George Hutchinson, "Jean Toomer and American Racial Discourse," *Texas Studies in Literature and Language* 35 (1993): 250n.

113. Alain Locke to Jean Toomer, 4 January 1922, box 5, folder 151, Jean Toomer Papers, American Literature Collection, Beinecke Rare Book and Manuscript Library, Yale University.

114. Quoted by Countee Cullen in a letter to Alain Locke, 31 May 1923, Alain Locke Correspondence.

115. Anonymous, "The Debut of the Younger School of Negro Writers," *Opportunity* 2 (1924): 143.

116. Floyd Calvin, "The Digest," *Pittsburgh Courier,* 19 April 1924, p. 20. Quoted in Carolyn Wedin Sylvander, *Jessie Redmon Fauset, Black American Writer* (Troy, N.Y.: Whitston, 1981), 71.

117. Boni & Liveright advertisement, *Pittsburgh Courier,* 19 April 1924. Quoted in Sylvander, *Jessie Redmon Fauset,* 71.

118. Ibid., 73.

119. Waldron, *Walter White,* 149–151.

120. Alain Locke to Langston Hughes, undated, Langston Hughes Papers. Other information in the letter indicates Locke was working on *The New Negro,* for it discusses the order of Hughes's poems in the proofs for the anthology.

121. Tebbel, *History of Book Publishing,* vol. 3, 145.

122. The judges are listed in "$1,000 for Best Novel by Negro," *Publishers Weekly* 109 (1926): 664. See also "Novel Prizes," *Publishers Weekly* 109 (1926): 918.

123. Tebbel, *History of Book Publishing,* vol. 3, 145–146.

124. Lehmann-Haupt, *The Book in America,* 341; James L. W. West III, *American Authors and the Literary Marketplace Since 1900* (Philadelphia: University of Pennsylvania Press, 1988), 23–24.

125. Gilmer, *Horace Liveright,* 103, 187.

126. MacAdams, *Ben Hecht,* 156.

127. Doran, *Chronicles,* 80.

128. David Levering Lewis, *W. E. B. Du Bois: Biography of a Race,* vol. 1 (New York: Henry Holt, 1993), 461.

129. Alfred Harcourt, *Some Experiences* (Riverside, Conn.: privately printed, 1951), 25–26; and Harcourt, "Forty Years of Friendship," *Journal of the Illinois State Historical Society* 45 (1952): 395–399. To get the collection past Holt's chief literary advisor, William P. Trent of Columbia, Harcourt left a half-dozen of the more "radical" poems out of the manuscript he gave Holt and Trent, then silently added them in the collection he sent to the printer. See *Some Experiences,* 26.

130. Ibid., 29–30. Specifically, Harcourt had bought American rights to a Bertrand Russell book that the Holts found shocking for its treatment of Bolshevism.

131. Doran, *Chronicles*, 80.

132. Harcourt, *Some Experiences*, 35.

133. Ibid., 36–37; Harrison Smith, "Introduction" in *From Main Street to Stockholm: Letters of Sinclair Lewis, 1919–1930,* ed. Harrison Smith (New York: Harcourt, Brace, 1952), x–xi; Lehmann-Haupt, *The Book in America,* 342; Tebbel, *History of Book Publishing,* vol. 3, pp. 17, 132; Marshall Van Deusen, *J. E. Spingarn* (Boston: Twayne, 1971), 67.

134. Harcourt, *Some Experiences*, 41.

135. Alfred Harcourt, "Publishing Since 1900" (1957), in *Publishers on Publishing,* ed. Gerald Gross (New York: R. R. Bowker and Grosset & Dunlap, 1961), 259.

136. Lehmann-Haupt, *The Book in America,* 342.

137. Harcourt, *Some Experiences*, 75.

138. Van Deusen, *J. E. Spingarn,* 67.

139. Ibid., 67. Spingarn also had his own small press and published a series of "Troutbeck Leaflets" from 1924 to 1926 that in some ways typifies the point I am making about the connections between Spingarn's various involvements. In addition to poems by himself and Amy Spingarn, they were: (1) Whitman's previously unpublished essay "Criticism"; (2) Lewis Mumford's *Aesthetics: A Dialogue;* (3) Spingarn's *The Younger Generation: A New Manifesto;* (4) *Thoreau's Last Letter, With a Note on His Correspondent, Myron B. Benton, by E. A. Robinson;* (5) Charles E. Benton's *Four Days on the Webutuck River* (with an introduction by Sinclair Lewis); (6) W. E. B. Du Bois's *The Amenia Conference: An Historic Negro Gathering;* (7) *A Troutbeck Letter-Book, 1861–1867: Being Unpublished Letters to Myron B. Benton from Emerson, Sophia Thoreau, Moncure Conway, and Others;* and (8) *John Burroughs at Troutbeck: Being Extracts from His Writings, Published and Unpublished* (with an introduction by Vachel Lindsay).

140. See Joel Spingarn, "The American Critic," in *Criticism in America, Its Function and Status,* ed. J. E. Spingarn (New York: Harcourt, Brace, 1924), 124.

141. Van Deusen, *J. E. Spingarn,* 57.

142. Van Wyck Brooks, *An Autobiography* (New York: E. P. Dutton, 1965), 393.

143. Van Deusen, *J. E. Spingarn,* 33–37.

144. See Joel Spingarn, "The Seven Arts and the Seven Confusions," *Seven Arts* 1 (1917): 507–514; "The Younger Generation: A New Manifesto," *Freeman* 5 (1922): 296–298; and "The Growth of a Literary Myth," *Freeman* 7 (1923): 181–183.

145. Stuart P. Sherman, "The Genius of America," in *The Genius of America: Essays in Behalf of the Younger Generation* (New York: Charles Scribner's Sons, 1923), 9, 17.

146. David Levering Lewis, "Parallels and Divergences: Assimilationist Strategies of Afro-American and Jewish Elites from 1910 to the Early 1930s," *Journal of American History* 71 (1984): 543–564.

147. Van Deusen, *J. E. Spingarn*, 72.

148. Quoted in ibid., 61, from Spingarn's *Dictionary of American Biography* entry on Woodberry.

149. Van Deusen, *J. E. Spingarn*, 69, 164n. For a further example of Spingarn's cultural pluralism, see his *Racial Equality* (New York: NAACP, 1932).

150. Spingarn, in *Crisis* 31 (1926): 278, 279.

151. Doran, *Chronicles*, 80.

152. Eugene Exman, *The House of Harper: One Hundred and Fifty Years of Publishing* (New York: Harper & Row, 1967), 222.

153. Ibid., 252–253.

154. See Waldron, *Walter White*, 47–55.

155. Ibid., 151–152.

156. Wayne F. Cooper, *Claude McKay: Rebel Sojourner in the Harlem Renaissance* (Baton Rouge: Louisiana State University Press, 1987), 232, 236, 253–254.

157. Cooper, *Claude McKay*, 298, quoting McKay's letter to Max Eastman.

158. Wintz, *Black Culture*, 174.

159. Cooper, *Claude McKay*, 298.

160. See ibid., 217.

161. Walter White to Rudolph Fisher, 12 March 1925, quoted in Waldron, *Walter White*, 129.

162. Tebbel, *History of Book Publishing*, vol. 3, 116; Lehmann-Haupt, *The Book in America*, 345.

163. Morley quoted in Tebbel, *History of Book Publishing*, vol. 3, 117.

164. Benjamin Huebsch, "Cross-Fertilization in Letters" (1942), in *Publishers on Publishing*, ed. Gerald Gross (New York: R. R. Bowker and Grosset & Dunlap, 1961), 301.

165. Waldron, *Walter White*, 141–142.

166. The following narrative concerning White and McKay is based on Waldron, *Walter White*, 57–63, with occasional glosses of my own interpolated.

167. Ibid., 57.

168. Ibid., 139–140.

169. Cooper, *Claude McKay*, 217.

170. While it is difficult to do an exhaustive count, after consulting several standard bibliographies I find 76 single-authored books of black fiction, poetry, autobiography, and drama in the 1920s, 127 in the 1930s. Even eliminating what appear to be vanity publications and other works of peripheral interest, sticking for the most part to established presses (but including Cornhill and Brimmer, which boost the totals for the twenties), I find 31 in the 1920s and 47 in the 1930s. One can quibble, of course, with exact inclusions and exclusions,

but the overall evidence shows clearly that publication of black-authored creative writing expanded in the 1930s even as literary publishing in general shrank. Publishers were hit hard by the economic depression. Earnings dropped 50 percent between 1929 and 1933; the number of books published shrank 20 percent between 1931 and 1933. Monty Noam Penkower, *The Federal Writers' Project: A Study in Government Patronage of the Arts* (Urbana: University of Illinois Press, 1977), 4. My sources on African American–authored books of the 1920s and 1930s are Geraldine O. Mathews et al., comp., *Black American Writers, 1773–1949: A Bibliography and Union List* (Boston: G. K. Hall, 1975); Darwin T. Turner, comp., *Afro-American Writers* (New York: Appleton-Century-Crofts, 1970); Dorothy B. Porter, comp., *The Negro in the United States: A Selected Bibliography* (Washington, D.C.: Library of Congress, 1970); Margaret Perry, *The Harlem Renaissance: An Annotated Bibliography and Commentary* (New York: Garland, 1982); Abraham Chapman, *The Negro in American Literature and a Bibliography of Literature by and about Negro Americans* (Stevens Point, Wis.: Wisconsin State University Press, 1966); and Maxwell Whiteman, *A Century of Fiction by American Negroes: A Descriptive Bibliography* (Philadelphia: Saifer, 1968).

171. Based on the lists in Matthews, Turner, Porter, Perry, Chapman, and Whiteman, the peak year for the 1920s was 1928, with twelve books of black-authored "creative writing"; in 1931 fifteen appeared, in 1932 fourteen, in 1935 thirteen, in 1936 seventeen, in 1937 thirteen, in 1938 sixteen, in 1939 fifteen. Eliminating the lesser works, mainly from what appear to be vanity presses, I count five in 1928, six in 1929 (the peak for the 1920s); six in 1931, eight in 1932; and five in each of 1935, 1937, 1938, and 1939.

172. Significantly, the books of Loggins (which had started out as a 1921 dissertation suggested and directed by Carl Van Doren) and Redding came out from major university presses: Vernon Loggins, *The Negro Author, His Development in America to 1900* (New York: Columbia University Press, 1931); and Saunders Redding, *To Make a Poet Black* (Chapel Hill: University of North Carolina Press, 1939).

173. Locke, "The Negro's Contribution to American Culture" (1939), *Critical Temper,* 454.

174. Tebbel, *History of Book Publishing,* vol. 3, 689.

175. Ibid.

III. Producing *The New Negro*

1. This is not to deny the partiality of the book. As Arnold Rampersad has pointed out, one should not read it as *the* authoritative representation of the Harlem Renaissance; nor should one regard its editor, Alain Locke, as the central figure of a "school" for which Charles S. Johnson designated him the "dean." (See Arnold Rampersad, "Introduction," in *The New Negro,* ed. Alain

Locke [New York: Atheneum, 1992], ix–xii, xxii.) The volume reveals the hand and eye of Alain Locke in design and execution; yet it is far more than *his* book. It is a collaborative work, surely one of the most unusual and significant anthologies of a movement in American literary history.

13. Staging a Renaissance

1. For important discussions of these meetings, see Ronald M. Johnson, "Those Who Stayed: Washington Black Writers of the 1920s," *Records of the Columbia Historical Society,* 50 (1980): 484–499; Jeffrey C. Stewart, "Alain Locke and Georgia Douglas Johnson, Washington Patrons of Afro-American Modernism," *Washington Studies* 12 (1986): 37–44; and Gloria T. Hull, *Color, Sex, and Poetry: Three Women Writers of the Harlem Renaissance* (Bloomington: Indiana University Press, 1987), 165. I have also discussed the Washington group briefly in "Jean Toomer and the 'New Negroes' of Washington," *American Literature* 63 (1991): 683–692.

2. Stewart, "Alain Locke," 37–38. On the origins of the meetings, see Hutchinson, "Jean Toomer," 684–687; and Hull, *Color, Sex, and Poetry,* 165.

3. Stewart, "Alain Locke," 38.

4. Locke to Hughes, n.d., Langston Hughes Papers, James Weldon Johnson Collection, Beinecke Rare Book and Manuscript Library, Yale University. The letter is probably from fall 1923 or early 1924; in it Locke says he likes two poems Hughes has sent him—"Gods" and "This Land of Ours"—but adds, "I don't think you are very successful in getting the exact touch which sometimes transmutes the colloquial into the poetic—Toomer has that gift." Hughes wrote the two poems in 1922–1923 as part of a Harlem "triptych," which he also sent Cullen in February 1923. See Arnold Rampersad, *The Life of Langston Hughes,* vol. 1 (New York: Oxford University Press, 1986), 61, 404n. Toomer had been sharing his work with Locke since at least 1921, and it began appearing in journals in 1922.

5. Its chief members, according to Charles S. Johnson at the time, were Jessie Fauset, Eric Walrond, Countee Cullen, Langston Hughes, Gwendolyn Bennett, Eloise Bibb Thompson, Regina Anderson, Harold Jackman, and Johnson himself. Charles S. Johnson to Alain Locke, 4 March 1924, Alain Locke Papers, Moorland-Spingarn Research Center, Howard University.

6. Johnson to Locke, 4 March 1924, Alain Locke Papers.

7. Fauset to Locke, 9 January 1933, Alain Locke Papers.

8. Johnson to Locke, 4 March 1924, Alain Locke Papers.

9. Johnson to Locke, 4 March 1924, Alain Locke Papers.

10. Johnson to Locke, 7 March 1924, Alain Locke Papers.

11. Johnson to Locke, 4 March 1924, Alain Locke Papers.

12. Johnson to Locke, "2nd letter" (undated), Alain Locke Papers.

13. In recent scholarship on the Civic Club dinner, reliance on the testimony of William H. Baldwin III has fostered a belief that Frederick Lewis Allen of *Harper's* (whom Baldwin contacted) determined the "white" attendees and Johnson the "black" ones, as if prior to the dinner the black writers lacked connections in the white publishing world. This was clearly not the case. Undoubtedly, however, *Opportunity*'s report on the dinner, entitled "The Debut of the Younger School of Negro Writers," fostered a misleading impression (*Opportunity* 2 [1924]: 143–144), which would be picked up and even expanded on in later accounts of the affair, such as Patrick J. Gilpin's "Charles S. Johnson: Entrepreneur of the Harlem Renaissance" (in *The Harlem Renaissance Remembered,* ed. Arna Bontemps [New York: Dodd, Mead, 1972], 224–250); and David Levering Lewis' *When Harlem Was in Vogue* (New York: Vintage Books, 1982), 93, which cites Gilpin.

14. See especially "The Debut of the Younger School of Negro Writers," *Opportunity* 2 (1924): 143–144; Ethel Ray Nance, "The New York Arts Renaissance, 1924–1926," *Negro History Bulletin* 31, no. 4 (April 1968): 15–19; Gilpin, "Charles S. Johnson," 224–225; and Lewis, *When Harlem Was in Vogue,* 93–95.

15. Johnson to Locke, "2nd letter," Alain Locke Papers. In the same letter, Johnson asked Locke to suggest two speakers from the whites invited, so it seems likely that it was Locke's idea to have Carl Van Doren and Albert Barnes give what would be two of the keynote presentations of the evening, Liveright being a prior choice as publisher of *There Is Confusion.*

16. Jeffrey C. Stewart, *To Color America: Portraits by Winold Reiss* (Washington, D.C.: Smithsonian Institution Press, 1989), 63–64. The National Origins Act, prohibiting further immigration from Japan and China, prompted the Asian American issue.

17. Stewart, *To Color America,* 18.

18. Alain Locke, "Notes to the Illustrations," *The New Negro,* ed. Alain Locke (New York: Atheneum, 1992), 419–420. Further citations of *The New Negro* will be included parenthetically in the text.

19. Stewart outlines the impact Reiss had on Aaron Douglas and other young black artists of the 1920s (*To Color America,* 56–62).

20. W. E. B. Du Bois, review of *The New Negro, Crisis* 31 (1926): 141.

21. Kellogg to Du Bois, 23 January 1914, copy in *Survey Graphic* files along with letter from Kellogg to Locke, undated, Alain Locke Papers. Du Bois would drag this argument back into the light in his review of *The New Negro,* where he attacked the *Survey* before praising the book.

22. Kellogg to Locke, 5 February 1925, *Survey Graphic* correspondence files, Alain Locke Papers.

23. Ibid.

24. Kellogg to Locke, 17 February 1925, *Survey Graphic* correspondence files, Alain Locke Papers.

25. Locke to Hughes, 5 February 1929, Alain Locke Papers. This is an important point, because the absence of Randolph from *The New Negro* has drawn sharp criticism from Harlem Renaissance scholars, including Rampersad in his excellent introduction to the latest edition of the book (1992), xxi.

26. Johnson to Locke, 9 March 1925, Alain Locke Papers.

27. Copy of letter from Kellogg to Johnson, 11 March 1925, Kellogg folder, correspondence files, Alain Locke Papers.

28. Stewart gives the most complete account of the uproar in *To Color America*, 50–54.

29. McDougald to Alain Locke, undated, *Survey Graphic* correspondence files, Alain Locke Papers.

30. Stewart, *To Color America*, 54.

31. Alain Locke to Charles S. Johnson, n.d., Alain Locke Papers: "Did you see the snide remarks of Miss Fauset on the Reiss drawing. She has had the additional bad taste to go out of her way to insert a similar tirade in her article for the book. I am going to delete it if it deletes me from her list."

32. Walter White wrote Locke in a critical letter that Arthur Spingarn had found "170 mistakes in the bibliography alone. . . . There was hardly a page that did not have from five to ten errors in it." White to Locke, 23 February 1926, Alain Locke Papers. Locke and Herbert Seligmann also exchanged insults over this issue.

14. *The New Negro:* An Interpretation

1. Paul Kellogg to Alain Locke, 15 January 1925, *Survey Graphic* correspondence files, Alain Locke Papers. See also Richard A. Long, "The Genesis of Locke's *The New Negro*," *Black World* 25, no. 4 (1976): 14–20.

2. Long, "Genesis," 16.

3. Kellogg to Locke, 15 January 1925, Alain Locke Papers.

4. Charles Scruggs, *Sweet Home: Invisible Cities in the Afro-American Novel* (Baltimore: Johns Hopkins University Press, 1993), 56–57.

5. Paul Kellogg to Alain Locke, 20 March 1925, *Survey Graphic* correspondence files, Alain Locke Papers. The change in Miller's contribution also has to do with the fact that he was a powerful dean at Howard and a D. C. patriot, part of the Washington black elite going back to the turn of the century—and losing prestige to New York. The difference between his unflattering view of Harlem and his glowing view of Howard, in the nation's capital, is not surprising.

6. Alain Locke, "To Certain of Our Philistines," *Opportunity* 3 (1925): 155–156. The essay is reprinted in *The Critical Temper of Alain Locke*, ed. Jeffrey C. Stewart (New York: Garland, 1983), 161–162.

7. Gerald Early, "Introduction," in *My Soul's High Song: The Collected Writings*

of Countee Cullen, ed. Gerald Early (New York: Anchor Books, 1991), 37.

8. Ethel Ray Nance, oral history interview (transcript) by Ann Allen Shockley, 18 November and 23 December 1970, Fisk University Library.

9. Aaron Douglas, "The Harlem Renaissance," address of 18 March 1973, box 3, folder 2, Aaron Douglas Papers, Fisk University. Quoted by permission of Valena M. Williams (Waits) and Fisk University Library.

10. Aaron Douglas, oral history interview (transcription) by Ann Allen Shockley, 19 November 1973, Fisk University Library. Quoted by permission of Valena M. Williams (Waits), Ann Allen Shockley, and the Fisk University Library.

11. Stewart, *To Color America,* 22.

12. See anonymous, untitled illustrations and captions in *Theatre Arts* 8 (1924): 377–379; and Alain Locke, "The Negro and the American Stage," *Theatre Arts* 10 (1926): 117–118. On "dynamic symmetry," see Jay Hambidge, *Dynamic Symmetry: The Greek Vase* (New Haven: Yale University Press, 1920). Its influence is discussed in Harold J. McWhinnie, "A Review of the Use of Symmetry, the Golden Section, and Dynamic Symmetry in Contemporary Art," *Leonardo* 19 (1986): 241–245.

13. Alain Locke, "Foreword," *The New Negro,* ed. Alain Locke (New York: Atheneum, 1992), xxv–xxvi. Further citations of *The New Negro* will be included parenthetically in the text.

14. On Tolson's use of Masters, see Robert M. Farnsworth, *Melvin B. Tolson, 1898–1966: Plain Talk and Poetic Prophecy* (Columbia: University of Missouri Press, 1984), 42.

15. Emerson quoted in the entry for "melodrama" in *The Compact Edition of the Oxford English Dictionary* (Oxford: Oxford University Press, 1971), 1765. When he was teaching in Georgia and writing the "Southern" sketches of *Cane,* Toomer introduced his young students to "polytheism and deity evolution," as he wrote Alain Locke at the time. Toomer to Locke, 8 November 1921, Alain Locke Papers.

16. George Kateb, *The Inner Ocean: Individualism and Democratic Culture* (Ithaca: Cornell University Press, 1992), 238.

17. Fern has a "semitic" nose, a common Jewish surname, and "cream-colored" skin. On first seeing her, the narrator is reminded of a Jewish cantor's singing. See also Hargis Westerfield, "Jean Toomer's 'Fern': A Mythical Dimension," *CLA Journal* 14 (1971): 274–276, which makes much of Fern's German Jewish surname.

18. I discuss all of these issues in greater detail in "Jean Toomer and American Racial Discourse," *Texas Studies in Literature and Language* 35 (1993): 226–250.

19. Jean Toomer to *The Liberator,* 9 August 1922, Jean Toomer Papers, Amer-

ican Literature Collection, Beinecke Rare Book and Manuscript Library, Yale University.

20. Henry Louis Gates, Jr., *The Signifying Monkey: A Theory of African-American Literary Criticism* (New York: Oxford University Press, 1988), 180–216.

21. For a framework within which Walrond might be fruitfully considered, see Paul Gilroy's *The Black Atlantic* (Cambridge: Harvard University Press, 1993).

22. Locke, "Emile Verhaeren" (1917), *Critical Temper*, 37.

23. Locke, "Beauty Instead of Ashes" (1928), in *Critical Temper*, 25. Compare with Locke, "The American Temperament" (1911), *Critical Temper*, 401–404; and "Emile Verhaeren," *Critical Temper*, 37.

24. See my "The Whitman Legacy and the Harlem Renaissance," in *Walt Whitman: The Centennial Essays*, ed. Ed Folsom (Iowa City: University of Iowa Press, 1994), 207; Locke's review of *Color* praises Cullen's blend of "pagan with Christian, the sensual with the Puritanically religious, the pariah with the prodigal" and finds in the poetry "the seeds of a new stock, richly parented by two cultures." Locke, "*Color*—A Review" (1926), *Critical Temper*, 39–40.

25. See Alexander Crummell to Mary Hawkins Locke correspondence, Alain Locke Family Papers, Moorland-Spingarn Research Center, Howard University. Sterling Brown mentions Locke's determination to find "Africanisms" in black America (in Brown's view jumping over the Southern black tradition) in an interview with Charles H. Rowell, "'Let Me Be with Ole Jazzbo': An Interview with Sterling A. Brown," *Callaloo* 14 (1991): 804.

26. Locke to Claude McKay, 13 March 1930 (carbon), Alain Locke Papers.

27. Countee Cullen, "The Dark Tower," *Opportunity* 5 (1927): 210.

28. Arthur P. Davis, *From the Dark Tower* (Washington: Howard University Press, 1981), 78.

29. "Countee Cullen on Miscegenation," *Crisis* 36 (1929): 373; rpt. in *My Soul's High Song*, 568.

30. Quoted by Alan R. Shucard from a 1928 interview in *Countee Cullen* (Boston: Twayne, 1984), 93.

31. Cullen to Braithwaite, 11 February 1921, William Stanley Braithwaite Papers, Houghton Library, Harvard University. At the time of this letter, Cullen was associate editor of his high school literary magazine (Early, "Introduction," 19). Shucard, *Countee Cullen*, 11.

32. Nathan Irvin Huggins, *Harlem Renaissance* (New York: Oxford University Press, 1971), 213. Gerald Early's judgment that "it must always be kept in mind that Cullen was a great poet" ("Introduction," 23) is, I confess, a bit beyond me. Despite such attempts to inflate Cullen's importance, Early's piece is the best thing available on the poet.

33. Countee Cullen, "Poet on Poet," *Opportunity* 4 (1926): 74.

34. See David Leeming, *James Baldwin: A Biography* (New York: Knopf, 1994), 21–22.

35. James Weldon Johnson, "Countee Cullen," in *The Book of American Negro Poetry*, ed. James Weldon Johnson (New York: Harcourt, Brace, and World, 1958), 220.

36. Davis, *Dark Tower*, 37, 77.

37. Jean Wagner, *Black Poets of the United States: From Paul Laurence Dunbar to Langston Hughes*, trans. Kenneth Douglas (Urbana: University of Illinois Press, 1973), 253.

38. Ibid., 222–224; see also Wayne F. Cooper, *Claude McKay: Rebel Sojourner in the Harlem Renaissance* (Baton Rouge: Louisiana University Press, 1987), 36–62.

39. McKay had even corrected Locke after the appearance of the poem in the *Survey Graphic;* yet Locke repeated his "error" in the book. McKay to Locke, 1 August 1926, Alain Locke Papers: "When you change it to 'White Houses' the poem immediately becomes cheap, flat Afro-American propaganda. What does a man of sensitivity, a poet, care about entering a lot of uninteresting white houses?" McKay came back to the point in another angry letter of 18 April 1927. On the shift in McKay's poetry between Jamaica and the United States, see Cooper, *Claude McKay*, 62.

40. Cooper, *Claude McKay*, 35–36.

41. Dewey, "Introduction," in Claude McKay, *Selected Poems of Claude McKay* (New York: Bookman Associates, 1953), 9. "Mulatto" quoted by Wagner, *Black Poets*, 226. McKay angrily attacked Locke for rejecting the poem: "It isn't the 'Survey' that hasn't guts enough. It is you. The Survey editors would not mind. There are many white people that are longing and hoping for Negroes to show they have *'guts.'"* McKay to Locke, 7 October 1924, Alain Locke Papers. McKay threatened that he would not allow any of his work to appear in the *Survey Graphic* if Locke rejected the poem, prompting the editor to confer with Paul Kellogg, who did not object to its inclusion (Locke to McKay, n.d., Alain Locke Papers). Nonetheless, it was left out.

42. Langston Hughes, "Me and America," MS in pencil, on the back of letter from McKay of 22 September 1924, Langston Hughes Papers.

43. For a similar reading of this poem, see Onwuchekwa Jemie, *Langston Hughes: An Introduction to the Poetry* (New York: Columbia University Press, 1976), 101–102.

44. I have discussed this in "Whitman and the Black Poet: Kelly Miller's Speech to the Walt Whitman Fellowship," *American Literature* 61 (1989): 46–58; and in "Langston Hughes and the 'Other' Whitman," *The Continuing Presence of Walt Whitman: The Life After the Life*, ed. Robert K. Martin (Iowa City: University of Iowa Press, 1992), 21–22. See also Donald B. Gibson, "The Good Black Poet and the Good Gray Poet: The Poetry of Hughes and Whitman," in *Langston*

Hughes, Black Genius, ed. Therman B. O'Daniel (New York: Morrow, 1971), 65–80.

45. Dunbar, "An Ante-Bellum Sermon," in *The Complete Poems of Paul Laurence Dunbar* (New York: Dodd, Mead, 1913), 13.

46. See Locke, "Sterling Brown: The New Negro Folk-Poet," *Critical Temper,* 52. Saunders Redding also reads Johnson's sermons as crucial in black literary history, opening up new possibilities for vernacular writing that would be developed further by Sterling Brown and Zora Neale Hurston. See *To Make a Poet Black* (1939; College Park, Md.: McGrath, 1968), 120–122.

47. Eric J. Sundquist, *The Hammers of Creation: Folk Culture in Modern African American Fiction* (Athens: University of Georgia Press, 1992), 64.

48. Blyden Jackson and Louis D. Rubin, *Black Poetry in America: Two Essays in Historical Interpretation* (Baton Rouge: Louisiana State University Press, 1974), 23. A host of more recent critics have of course disagreed with this affirmation of Johnson's importance, notably Henry Louis Gates, Jr. ("Dis and Dat: Dialect and the Descent," in *Figures in Black* [New York: Oxford University Press, 1986], 167–195), and Sundquist, *Hammers of Creation,* 54–64.

49. Gayl Jones, *Liberating Voices: Oral Tradition in African American Literature* (Cambridge: Harvard University Press, 1991), 24.

50. Toomer to Locke, 26 January 1921, Alain Locke Papers.

51. See especially Hughes's poems "Cross," in *The Weary Blues* (New York: Knopf, 1926), 52; and "Mulatto," in *Fine Clothes to the Jew* (New York: Knopf, 1927), 71–72.

52. Judith Berzon, *Neither White nor Black* (New York: New York University Press, 1978), 14.

53. For a provocative discussion of this issue, see especially Werner Sollors, "'Never Was Born': The Mulatto, an American Tragedy?" *Massachusetts Review* 27 (1986): 293–316.

54. Cedric Dover, "The Importance of Georgia Douglas Johnson," *Crisis* 59 (1952): 635.

55. Houston A. Baker, Jr., *Modernism and the Harlem Renaissance* (Chicago: University of Chicago Press, 1987), 76.

56. See the dedication page of the copy of *The New Negro* that Locke gave Van Vechten, in the Carl Van Vechten Collection, Beinecke Rare Book and Manuscript Library, Yale University.

57. I'm indebted here to Graley Herren's unpublished essay "Willis Richardson's Hope for a Negro Drama."

58. Jean Toomer, *Cane,* ed. Darwin T. Turner (New York: Norton, 1988), 41.

59. McKay, considering this poem a poor one, was furious that Locke had used it. McKay to Locke, 1 August 1926, Alain Locke Papers.

60. Gwendolyn Bennett, "The Ebony Flute," *Opportunity* 4 (1926): 260. Ben-

nett's poem in fact uses similar metrical and rhyming techniques to Benét's "Harlem," which she quotes in the column: "Want a black / Like midnight mire; / Want a gold / Like golden wire; / Want a silver / Like Heaven entire / And God a-playing at his own front door / On a slide trombone with a conical bore!"

61. Cornel West, "Horace Pippin's Challenge to Art Criticism," in *Keeping Faith: Philosophy and Race in America* (New York: Routledge, 1993), 62.

62. Garry Wills, "The Real Thing," *New York Review of Books,* 41, no. 14 (11 August 1994): 9.

63. Laura Rosenstock, "Leger: 'The Creation of the World,'" in *"Primitivism" in Twentieth Century Art: Affinity of the Tribal and the Modern,* ed. William Rubin (New York: Museum of Modern Art, 1984), vol. 2, 478–480. I should add that distinctions should be made among European appropriations of African art. Matgorzata Irek points out the German backgrounds of Locke's and Boas' positions in "From Berlin to Harlem: Felix von Luschan, Alain Locke, and the New Negro," in *The Black Columbiad,* ed. Werner Sollors and Maria Diedrich (Cambridge, Mass.: Harvard University Press, 1994), 174–184. However, Locke's acknowledgment of Luschan's work does not appear by the time of *The New Negro.* Luschan and the Berlin collection were probably of more direct significance to Winold Reiss's work than Locke's in the mid-1920s.

64. Jean-Louis Paudrat, "From Africa," in *Primitivism,* vol. 1, 125–175.

65. Barnes to Alain Locke, 26 March 1924; and Barnes to Walter White (copy sent to Locke), 25 March 1924, Alain Locke Papers.

66. Paudrat, "From Africa," 160.

67. Waldemar George, "Le Crepuscule des Idoles," *Les Arts a Paris,* May 1930; trans. and quoted in Paudrat, "From Africa," 162.

68. Paul Guillaume and Thomas Munro, *Primitive Negro Sculpture* (1926; rpt. New York: Hacker Art Books, 1968), 2–3. The book's dedication acknowledges the authors' indebtedness to Albert Barnes "for the initial impetus toward writing this book, for the method of plastic analysis it employs, for invaluable material and help along the way."

69. Ibid., 5.

70. Paudrat, "From Africa," 160.

71. Orlando Patterson, *Slavery and Social Death: A Comparative Study* (Cambridge, Mass.: Harvard University Press, 1982).

72. Yekutiel Gershoni, *Black Colonialism: The Americo-Liberian Scramble for the Hinterland* (Boulder: Westview Press, 1985), 66.

73. J. Gus Liebenow, *Liberia: The Quest for Democracy* (Bloomington: Indiana University Press, 1987), 56; Gershoni, *Black Colonialism,* 59.

74. As suggested by Garry Wills in "The Real Thing," 4–9.

75. As charged in West, "Horace Pippin's Challenge," 62.

76. Baker, *Modernism,* 81.

77. As charged by Henry Louis Gates, Jr., in "The Trope of a New Negro and the Reconstruction of the Image of the Black," *Representations* 24 (1988): 148.

78. West, "Horace Pippin's Challenge," 66.

79. As per Huggins, *Harlem Renaissance.*

80. As per Baker, *Modernism,* 75–80.

81. David Levering Lewis, *When Harlem Was in Vogue* (New York: Vintage, 1982), 305–306.

82. Baker, *Modernism,* 76; West, "Horace Pippin's Challenge," 66.

83. Robert Hayden, "Preface to the Atheneum Edition," *The New Negro,* ed. Alain Locke (New York: Atheneum, 1968), xiii.

Epilogue

1. See Charles H. Rowell, "'Let Me Be with Ole Jazzbo': An Interview with Sterling Brown," *Callaloo* 14 (1991): 807.

2. Alain Locke, "Black Truth and Beauty" (1933), in *The Critical Temper of Alain Locke,* ed. Jeffrey C. Stewart (New York: Garland, 1983), 215.

3. For a fine treatment of the connections between black writing of the 1930s and the generational shift coinciding with the Depression, see James O. Young, *Black Writers of the Thirties* (Baton Rouge: Louisiana State University Press, 1973).

4. See Rowell, "'Let Me Be with Ole Jazzbo,'" 804, 812.

5. Arnold Rampersad, "Introduction," *The New Negro,* ed. Alain Locke (New York: Atheneum, 1992), xxii–xxiii.

6. Edward Abrahams, *The Lyrical Left: Randolph Bourne, Alfred Stieglitz, and the Origins of Cultural Radicalism in America* (Charlottesville: University Press of Virginia, 1986), 206. See also Frederick J. Hoffman's discussion of this issue in *The Twenties: American Writing in the Postwar Decade* (rev. ed.; New York: Collier Books, 1962), 416–426.

7. Alain Locke, "The Negro's Contribution to American Culture," in *Critical Temper,* 457.

8. See, for example, Monty Noam Penkower, *The Federal Writers' Project: A Study in Government Patronage of the Arts* (Urbana: University of Illinois Press, 1977), 13–22; and Jerrold Hirsch, "Cultural Pluralism and Applied Folklore: The New Deal Precedent," in *The Conservation of Culture: Folklorists and the Public Sector,* ed. Burt Feintuch (Lexington: University Press of Kentucky, 1988), 54–55.

9. Originally Floyd Dell was the top prospect to head the Writers' Project, but his radical reputation undermined his chances, and Henry G. Alsberg got the job. Alsberg had been an editorial writer for Villard's *New York Evening Post* from 1913 to 1918, then became a foreign correspondent for *The Nation* in Russia. Returning to the United States in 1923 disillusioned with Bolshevism,

he became a director of the Provincetown Theatre, helping produce Paul Green's *In Abraham's Bosom*. (Jerre Mangione, *The Dream and the Deal: The Federal Writers' Project, 1935–1943* [Boston: Little, Brown, 1972], 54–57.) He wanted to reconcile cultural pluralism with modernism and American cultural nationalism, at the same time overcoming the split between "high art" and the creativity of common people in their daily lives. He surrounded himself with people of similar views. The original idea for the American Guides developed from suggestions by Marianne Moore and Ridgely Torrence, as well as Katherine Kellock, a Henry Street Settlement worker. (Hirsch, "Cultural Pluralism," 54; Penkower, *Federal Writers' Project*, 13–22.)

10. Quoted in Rowell, "'Let Me Be with Ole Jazzbo,'" 807.

11. Mangione, *The Dream and the Deal*, 269.

12. Quoted in Hirsch, "Cultural Pluralism," 55.

13. Botkin contributed three pieces, including a poem, to *Opportunity* in 1927 and 1928: "Spectacle," *Opportunity* 5 (1927): 22; "Self Portraiture and Social Criticism in Negro Folk Song," *Opportunity* 5 (1927): 38–42; and "The Lighter Touch in Harlem" (review of Rudolph Fisher, *The Walls of Jericho*), *Opportunity* 6 (1928): 346. Botkin also published some of Sterling Brown's first vernacular poems, as well as essays by Brown, Locke and Brown, and Guy B. Johnson in early issues of his journal *Folk-Say* in 1930 and 1931. An entire series of Brown's poetry appeared in the 1931 volume.

14. Brown did not feel Dunbar had really succeeded in capturing the quality and range of black vernacular; nor had he expressed the anger and bitter experience of the black folk. See Joanne V. Gabbin, *Sterling A. Brown: Building the Black Aesthetic Tradition* (Westport, Conn.: Greenwood, 1985), 38–40. Similarly, Botkin explicitly differentiated between the "New Regionalism" and the local color of Riley, which was "provincial without being indigenous," "pastoral," and sentimentally romantic. Botkin, "The Folk in Literature," *Folk-Say* 1 (1929): 12–15. Brown cites Botkin in making a related point in "Negro Character as Seen by White Authors," *Journal of Negro Education* 2 (January 1933): 180–201.

15. Letters from Brown to James Weldon Johnson commenting on Johnson's draft of an introduction to *Southern Road* exemplify Brown's approach in the early 1930s. Folksongs themselves, he writes, "have hardly been my *sources*. Folk experience *has* been. And dealing with the *folk*—I have attempted to use, where suitable, congruous forms. . . . But I have never hesitated to use any poetic form—or to make a variation of the folk form—widely so in *Memphis Blues*, etc. All of this technical discussion is of course obvious to you." Brown repeats the point over and over again in a letter of 17 February 1932, James Weldon Johnson Papers, James Weldon Johnson Collection, Beinecke Rare Book and Manuscript Library, Yale University.

16. Locke, "The Negro's Contribution," 454.

17. Sterling Brown, "On Dialect Usage," in *The Slave's Narrative*, ed. Charles

T. Davis and Hernry Louis Gates, Jr. (New York: Oxford University Press, 1985), 37–39. This was a memorandum circulated to all collectors of Negro folklore in the FWP.

18. Hirsch, "Cultural Pluralism," 61.

19. Gayl Jones, *Liberating Voices: Oral Tradition in African American Literature* (Cambridge, Mass.: Harvard University Press, 1991), 9.

20. Charles Scruggs, *Sweet Home: Invisible Cities in the Afro-American Novel* (Baltimore: Johns Hopkins University Press, 1993), 6.

21. Ibid., 62.

22. James Baldwin, "Stranger in the Village," in *Notes of a Native Son* (New York: Dial, 1963), 157.

23. Ibid., 157–158.

24. Ibid., 156.

25. Cornel West, "Horace Pippin's Challenge to Art Criticism," in *Keeping Faith: Philosophy and Race in America* (New York: Routledge, 1993), 62–63.

26. Ibid., 62–63.

27. Ibid., 66.

28. Ibid., 56.

29. Richard J. Wattenmaker, "Dr. Albert C. Barnes and the Barnes Foundation," in *Great French Paintings from the Barnes Foundation: Impressionist, Post-Impressionist, and Early Modern* (New York: Knopf and Lincoln University Press, 1993), 24.

30. West, "Horace Pippin's Challenge," 57.

31. Ann duCille, *The Coupling Convention: Sex, Text, and Tradition in Black Women's Fiction* (New York: Oxford University Press, 1993), 66–74.

32. See the extensive evidence of Van Vechten's and Larsen's friendship, in Thadious M. Davis, *Nella Larsen, Novelist of the Harlem Renaissance: A Woman's Life Unveiled* (Baton Rouge: Louisiana State University Press, 1994). On Larsen's admiration for *Nigger Heaven*, see 210–213.

33. DuCille, *Coupling Convention*, 79.

34. Davis, *Nella Larsen*, 349.

35. DuCille, *Coupling Convention*, 4, 5.

36. Nella Larsen, *Quicksand*, in *Quicksand and Passing*, ed. Deborah E. McDowell (New Brunswick, N.J.: Rutgers University Press, 1986), 135.

37. Larsen went searching unsuccessfully for her half-sister in California near the end of her life, after she had cut off contact with all her old friends, and her belongings went to that half-sister, who claimed not to know of her existence. Davis, *Nella Larsen*, 448, 545.

38. Baldwin, "Stranger in the Village," 158.

Index